Studies in the History of Law and Justice

Volume 5

More information about this series at http://www.springer.com/series/11794

Maria Gigliola di Renzo Villata
Editor

Family Law and Society in Europe from the Middle Ages to the Contemporary Era

Springer

Editor
Maria Gigliola di Renzo Villata
Department of Private Law and Legal
History
University of Milan
Milan
Italy

ISSN 2198-9842 ISSN 2198-9850 (electronic)
Studies in the History of Law and Justice
ISBN 978-3-319-42287-9 ISBN 978-3-319-42289-3 (eBook)
DOI 10.1007/978-3-319-42289-3

Library of Congress Control Number: 2016944416

Printed on acid-free paper

This Springer imprint is published by Springer Nature
The registered company is Springer International Publishing AG Switzerland

To Antonio Padoa Schioppa
A Great European Legal Historian

Acknowledgments

This book is the product of a collective effort about family law, society and history in Europe, that is still now of great topical interest. It concerns each of us and every change needs our good will to become effective. Family law in Europe over the centuries shows periods of general stability and others of almost frantic evolution up to current times: the family unit is continuously transforming as well as our society. All the papers here published are evidence of a small or a big fragment of this evolution: family changes its function and its structure, its relations within itself but it continues to be a place of reference, a refuge in which to revert back to when the difficulties of the outside world seem impossible to overcome…What I have written corresponds to my profound conviction.

My idea could take shape with the help of many.

First of all, I want to thank Springer for giving me the opportunity to realize a project I cultivated for many years, as well as Diana Nijenhuijzen and Abirami Purushothaman for their work on the project.

I wish to thank the series editors, Prof. Dr. Georges Martyn of Ghent University and Prof. Dr Mortimer Sellers of the University of Baltimore, both of them who are my esteemed colleagues, as well as Neil Olivier for accepting my proposal.

I also wish to thank all the contributors of the volume, young scholars and those not so young, who have done their utmost to achieve the result.

I would like to thank, in particular, Stefania Salvi, senior researcher, and Filippo Rossi research fellow, my dear pupils at Milan University, for their excellent and speedy work: they helped and supported me with commitment, efficiency and diligence in preparing the texts to be submitted to the Editor.

Maria Gigliola di Renzo Villata

Contents

Introduction

Familia id est substantia
(Bartolo, *Comm.* ad D. 28,2,11)
Is it still so?

Bartolus, one of the greatest medieval jurists in Europe, writes in his *Commentaria*: "Familia id est substantia"; Albericus de Rosate, he too is a great contemporary jurist, in turn, underlines, in his *Dictionarium iuris*, *paterfamilias*' powers: "paterfamilias… sicut tenetur educatione corporali filiis et familie providere: sic et in morum disciplina; et qui hoc non servat, etiam fidelitatem naturalem deserit; lastly in the *Additio* to the entry we read: "Familia id est substantia".

Through the centuries a lot of attention has been paid to the patrimony and heritage of the family but, as time went on, the functions of family grew and the *paterfamilias* has not only powers but also duties; the structure of family changes as well as the internal relationships: subjects previously excluded enter fully and divorces become easier and more commonplace. Before the *paterfamilias* was a sort of owner, then he sees his powers fade and his duties grow. The relationships tend to put everyone on an equal footing, but only very lately, above all in the last century. Patrimony apparently decreases in importance but it's always a crucial factor in the lives of families, source of quarrels, while feelings become more and more relevant in the choice of a spouse. The increasing secularization of society involves families.

Family is a private group but the law is interested in it from time to time, especially in many of its aspects, and introduces many new measures suitable to adapt the regime of the family to progress developments in society.

Family law refers to a preeminent social group in all periods of history: it is linked to many other fields of law, such as private law and also public law according to a modern conception; it is strongly linked, in some ages and in some territories of Europe, to religion and theology or to politics.

The following papers are devoted to analyzing some of these transformations in Europe from the medieval to the contemporary ages from a legal and social point of view. The aim is to investigate some aspects of the family's legal history not always conventionally studied in depth by legal historians in order to offer a new and slightly different key interpretation of family law development in Europe.

The focus therefore is on family and Christian influences on its conception, family and patrimony concerning some specific topics related to marriage (matrimonial property law), impediments to marriage, marriage and witnesses, family and criminal law, family and civil liability, children and the law (legitimate, natural and adopted children), family and children labour law, family law connected to society and European juridical science as regards to what university students can learn in a class from their teacher (beginning of the twentieth century).

I will mention them one by one to offer a first sketch of the variety and complexity of the issues addressed.

Mathias Schmoeckel, in "Christian Influence on Modern Family Law", focuses on Christian influences from antiquity to modern times in family law with special reference to marriage law showing how Christian faith shaped European family law and its legal assumptions. Theological ideas helped to shape a very particular approach to family matters, such as the patristic conception of marriage as the monogamous, principally unbreakable union of man and woman, which caused the distinction between legitimate and illegitimate children. He shows how even the concept of "family law" itself was coined around 1800 due to the influences in Germany of Neo-Lutheran protestants who established their political program as a protest against the French Revolution and the French Civil Code with its "droit des personnes". In contrast to the new principles of equality and liberty for everyone regardless of their position within the family, the German 'house-fathers' should maintain authority and rule over their family members and fortunes. Even in the 1970s, the Protestant Church of Germany (EKD) could influence the liberalization of divorce. For this reason and in spite of much harmonization of European legislation in family matters, we can still detect major influences of Christian theology in family law today. He concludes that Churches still have some influence on modern societies. Moreover, we have to recognize different theological traditions and convictions concerning family law in Europe up to the twenty-first century.

Tünde Mikes and Tomàs de Montagut, in "The Catalan *Sagrada Família*: Law and Family in Medieval and Modern Catalonia", look at the history of the 'basic' institution of traditional Catalan society, the family (household); its division with the farmstead (*mas*) and farmhouse (*masia*) as well as with the patrimony (the family estate) and the legal matrimonial and inheritance system. They underline its link to the legal point of view, to the legal European culture since the Middle Ages. The patrimonial archives, the vast majority of which correspond to families of peasant origin who were landholders (the landed peasantry) are clear proof of the strength of the family institution on all levels. The primordial legal documents of these households are marriage contracts: veritable family charters are examples of Catalan contractual law and the basis of the family and patrimonial system, drawn up on a meaningful event for the household. The fact that such contracts were abundant demonstrates the growing strength of the stem family, which revolved around patrimony and a society of households. Even now at the turn of the twentieth century, to ensure the continuity of Catalonia as a population with a political and cultural identity of their own, with a historic private law alive and flourishing, the myth of the ancestral family home (*casa pairal*) emerged showing the strength of the traditional Catalan family—precisely when the construction of the Sagrada Família Temple was moving forward with the greatest strength and vitality.

I (in "Adoption between *Ancien Régime* and Codification: is it in Remission in a Changing World?") follow the evolution of juridical "adoption", in particular with regard to Italian area, from the Early Middle Ages to the nineteenth–twentieth centuries, the age of Codification, and its use over time according to the society's needs. Some scholarship works and documents dating back to the early Middle Ages show adoption sparsely dealt with—in part consistently with Roman law and in part following the trail of the Franc and Longobard law—in which the aim was to ensure the possibility to have a son to whomever lacked one (*imitatio naturae*) or to choose a specific heir. In the lower Middle Ages, the interest for the matter is sparse. Nonetheless, many contributions helped changing the outline of a juridical figure that, over a long time, has hardly been applied. In the Modern Era, a similar development continues, even bigger than the prior beliefs suggested. In fact, at the time, the life of adoption as a juridical figure (although not really widespread) went silently on, prior to its evident resurgence (in different guises) during the French Revolution, in a new conception of family and society, based on more egalitarian principles and, with less success, in the Napoleonic Era (as well as in the *Code civil*). The following centuries attested the necessity of the recourse to adoption, which nowadays finds its reason of being in "natural" grounds. I conclude referring to the law on stepchild adoption now under discussion in the Italian Parliament and to the debate taking place on the legality of surrogacy, while the heterologous fertilization practices are increasingly common and permitted. Is adoption in remission today? The future will have the last say.

Julius Kirshner, in "A *consilium* of Torello di Niccolò Torelli of Prato on *Dos Aestimata*", studies one of Torello's many unpublished *consilia*. Torello was a jurist who migrated from Prato to Florence, a member of the Arte dei Giudici e Notai, professor at the Studio, communal lawyer and diplomat". The *consilium* on dowry law (numerous *consilia* were written on this complex topic), an 'autograph' (original manuscript written by Torello) edited below, concerns a dispute over the restitution of a modest dowry. It suggests that Torello submitted his opinion in the wife's defense, but it's not inconceivable that his opinion may have been requested by the presiding judge in the court of the *podestà*. Torello examines all the main *dubia*, the remaining contentions and resolves all of them: the resolution of the case is so clear-cut that he does not feel compelled to support his arguments with heaps of authorities, as is the practice mainly of the following times. The *consilium*' s edition allows the reader to look directly into an example of legal consulting on a very difficult topic; even a single *consilium* proves to be a large window opened into the world of the legal arguments suitable to defend women's rights.

Thomas Kuehn, in "Property of Spouses in Law in Renaissance Florence", focuses, too, his paper on the Florentine family patrimony, but not only as a single entity under the control of the male head of the household, but also includes the dowry and other property his wife brought to him: however, in law there were, in fact, several types of property a wife could bring to a marriage, and she had rights to manage some of those herself. A dowry was a charge on the patrimony that husbands swore to uphold. They could not easily alienate a dowry, and certainly not without the consent of their wives. An examination of cases by means of *consilia* illustrates how jurists interpreted spousal legal property rights and wives' and widows' disposal of their holdings.

Richard Helmholz, in "The English Law of Marriage and the Family (1500–1640)", provides a survey of English matrimonial law and practice between 1500 and 1640. Throughout this period, the English church retained its hold on this aspect of human life. The Reformation did not lead to eclipse of the canon law or the end of the ecclesiastical jurisdiction over marriage and divorce, as so happened in Scotland and in parts of Germany. That jurisdiction included a criminal side—prosecution of lay men and women who had offended against principles of Christian morality, as well as a civil side—disputes over the validity of marriage contracts and impediments to existing marriages. The surviving records of the ecclesiastical courts show how practice was touched by both stability and change during this period. The former predominated. Most importantly, the Church of England rejected the Council of Trent's decree *Tametsi*. Private exchanges of words of present consent continued to be specifically enforceable as valid marriages. Some tightening of the requirements necessary to prove their legal existence did occur, but no change in the substantive law occurred. The church also continued to exercise its *ex officio* jurisdiction; in fact the courts slightly expanded its scope, punishing some offenses that had been left to the penitential forum during the Middle Ages. Whether this continuity was the result of lawyerly inertia or instead a product of increasing moral seriousness among English people during these years remains an open question.

Stefania Salvi, in "Towards a New Era of Modernity? Late Scholastic Speculation on Bigamy and Polygamy", provides an initial account of how exponents of the *siglo de oro* examined the complex issue of bigamy (more correctly, polygamy), which was of enormous practical impact in an era that was characterized by a high number of secret marriages. By the sixteenth century, canon law had long established a regulatory structure for the institution of marriage. Likewise, jurisprudence had developed a solid doctrinal system to deal with the numerous legal issues that marriage presented. Thus, it should come as no surprise that late Scholasticism offered very little in terms of totally new solutions to the most relevant problem areas. Nonetheless, the late Scholastic contribution to the specific area of family law was anything but trivial, not only because of its influence on the practice of law during that time, but also because of its importance in the history of legal thought. From this point of view, the jurists/theologians of the *siglo de oro* left a fundamental legacy to the subsequent doctrines of natural law and the Enlightenment through the methodology they employed. As innovators of Thomistic thought during the Counter-Reformation, they reflected on the problematic contrast between *pluralitas uxorum* and the natural ends of marriage. While they primarily relied on biblical texts and the word of Saint Thomas Aquinas, to a lesser extent they also considered the *auctoritates* of the *ius commune*.

Though there were some differences of opinion to be found among the various authors, late Scholastic speculation on this issue generally came to defend the traditional stances of the church. As such, it was not the formulation of particularly original solutions that characterized this period, but rather the skill and insight that thinkers exhibited in philosophizing on what was rationally justifiable and in discussing the pros and cons of the issue.

Andrea Massironi's paper ("The Father's Right to Kill His Adulterous Daughter in the Late Ius Commune") focuses on the father's right to kill his adulterous daughter with impunity in case of flagrant adultery (as well as her lover), that had been introduced by Roman law and aroused some interesting discussions among law scholars even in modern age. This right could be deemed as connected to paternal authority. It was a relic of the ancient *ius vitae ac necis*, which meanwhile had developed into a milder right to chastise a disobedient child. Even in modern ages some law scholars dealing with father's powers between sixteenth and seventeenth century dedicated entire chapters of their works to this interesting topic. The father would be granted impunity only if he had killed his adulterous daughter on certain conditions required by Roman law; the law scholars of the late *ius commune* had to update those conditions and to clarify them; furthermore, they discussed some undisputed aspects that had not received a definitive solution yet, such as the father's possibility to ask somebody for help or to kill his daughter even if she was pregnant. The father's right to kill his adulterous daughter also caused moral problems because, although it was lawful, it did not prevent the father to commit a mortal sin: this way, the relationship between internal forum and external forum was often dealt with as a pivotal topic.

Yves Mausen, in "*Duæ animæ in una carne*. The Disqualification of the Spouses in *Common Law*" deals with spouses' witnesses in common law. In modern common law the disqualification of witnesses for family reasons is more or less restricted to the spouse. The first two treatises on evidence law, *The Law of Evidence* by William Nelson (1717) and *The Law of Evidence* by Jeffrey Gilbert (1754), offer a twofold explanation of the prohibition: the identity of interests between spouses and the interest of marriage as such. Coherently the principle does not apply if the wife's testimony is brought forth for the good of the couple or for her own sake as opposed to the wish of her husband. These reasons are not based on any specific English social context but on ancient conceptions of the nature of the union between two human people and on timeless considerations of human psychology. Similarly the absence of the other Roman-canonical relative motives for refusing witnesses (affinity, dependence) cannot be reduced to social or intellectual choices but must be seen as the consequence of the freedom left to the jurors to appreciate the quality of the evidence.

Chiara Valsecchi, in "Fathers by Law, Fathers by Choice. Paternity and Illegitimacy Between *Ancien Régime* and Codification in the Western Countries", focuses on paternity as a legal institute historically marked by an intrinsic ambiguity: its aim is to acknowledge and provide judicial remedies for a natural phenomenon, which however cannot be ascertained and verified through the usual legal procedures. Legislators, therefore, never fail to evoke nature, but then they set off on a path of their own in order to regulate its different legal forms and cases.

Moreover, civil law in Italy, in Europe and elsewhere, during the transition from the law system of the *ancien régime* to modern codifications, is marked by the troubled coexistence of two different and diverse elements: on one hand the tradition of the Roman and canon law, on the other the model provided by the French revolution and the Napoleonic code.

Paternity is thus caged inside the ancient Roman presumption, while bastardy is abandoned to the free will and choice of the parent: given the prohibition to investigate paternity out of wedlock, introduced in the nineteenth century codes, he cannot be compelled to take responsibility. The disparity of the status between legitimate offspring and bastards would shape family law for a long time.

Loredana Garlati deals with infanticide in "Honour and Guilt. A Comparative Study on Regulations on Infanticide Between the Nineteenth and Twentieth Century". Infanticide has been judged by people in so many different ways: such differing concepts are reflected in Italian legislation. From medieval times up to the eighteenth century infanticide represented the betrayal of the 'vocation of motherhood and of maternal instinct', punished with extreme measures such as capital punishment in its most cruel and aggravated form. A new understanding of infanticide emerged with the Enlightenment principles: infanticide was considered not only to deserve a milder conviction compared to that of murder, but could also be liable to being recognized as a self-standing offence. After a cursory analysis of the legislation in force in Italian territories during Napoleonic, Austrian and Restoration regime the paper focuses on the 'Italian' codes. The 1889 code (art. 369) defined infanticide as a lesser form of murder. The apparent straightforwardness of this article did not prevent the proliferation of theories and interpretations, above all as regards to qualifying infanticide as a specific crime, or, instead, as a mitigated form of a crime, in view of an honour killing; the *Corte di Cassazione* gave the crime of infanticide a special qualification; the prevailing doctrine interpreted it as a hypothesis of murder characterized by mitigating and circumstantial evidence. The 1930 code modified the regulation on infanticide: the *causahonoris* explicitly became a constitutive element of the crime and was no longer merely a lessening circumstance of the *species homicidii.*

Filippo Rossi focuses on "The Children Of a Lesser God, The Legalized Exploitation of Child Labour as Revealed by the Liberal Era Judicial Record (Late 19th-Early 20th Century)".

Before the twentieth century, Italian children were routinely exploited in a variety of settings, working in hazardous jobs with little or no wages. When labour laws were still not in existence, ordinary courts played a rule of considerable significance. From the civil codification of 1865 onwards, civil courts went on to deal increasingly, bridging the gaps of a legal order.

Annamaria Monti, in "What Can We Learn from a Family Law Course? The Teachings of an Early 20th Century Italian Professor", aims to explore the concept of the family in Italian legal thought from the end of the nineteenth century up to the first 15 years of the twentieth century. She places the focus on a source which has been largely untapped by historiographers, namely the lecture notes from law courses taught at Universities, and examines the lecture notes which recorded the teachings of Alfredo Ascoli, an eminent civil law expert (also a co-founder of the *Rivista di diritto civile* (Civil Law Journal, 1909), who held professorships at the University of Pavia and Bocconi University in Milan during the period under examination.

The Italian Civil Code of 1865 struggled in many ways to meet the needs of a society that had already embarked upon the path of industrialization. At the same time, many Italian jurists were seeking new solutions in order to reform the study of law. By examining the teaching of law, it is possible to evaluate not only the state of teaching methodologies at the time, but also the extent to which the era's profound social and economic changes were being dealt with in university lecture halls, where the country's future ruling class received their education.

Giovanni Chiodi, in "Torts of Minor Children and Parental Civil Liability: Cases in Nineteenth and Early Twentieth Century Italy" addresses above all the parental civil liability in Italy between nineteenth (since 1865) and twentieth century. According to the Italian 1865 civil code, the father (or the mother) would be liable for the torts of minor children living with them, unless they proved that they could not prevent the wrongful act. Like in France, in this system, liability was based on a presumption of fault, which could be rebutted by evidence to the contrary. This paper analyses the way in which exculpatory proof was interpreted by the Italian courts during the time the 1865 civil code was in force. The tradition starting in the period following the Unification of Italy laid the foundations of longstanding arguments thanks to some interpretative choices whose repercussions lasted well beyond the first Italian civil code. However, to this day there is still no historical analysis of the decisions taken by the courts. The most typical situations of parental civil liability are examined, together with the lines of defense allowed by the judges. Following a widespread line of orientation in case law, the courts considered the parents liable for negligence both in supervising and in educating the child. From the analysis of the cases it emerges that the courts judged the parents according to a series of parameters, such as the nature of the tort, the child's character and temperament, the existence of specific reasons for suspicion, and age. The cases show that the post-Unification experience in Italy was more varied and better developed than was commonly thought. Tendencies denoting extreme strictness in claiming the parents were negligent, for instance, when children committed intentional crimes and were generally ill-natured, or when they rode bicycles or motor vehicles, co-existed with more liberal perspectives, which allowed for the parents' exemption from liabilities by concretely assessing negligence in a more flexible and balanced way, especially when the children were close to the age of majority.

The book is dedicated to Antonio Padoa Schioppa, a great European legal historian.

Milan
January 2016

Maria Gigliola di Renzo Villata

Christian Influence on Modern Family Law

Mathias Schmoeckel

Abstract The Christian faith shaped European family law and its legal assumptions. Throughout history, we find theological ideas that helped to form a very particular approach to family matters, such as the patristic conception of marriage as the monogamous, principally indissoluble union of man and woman, which caused the distinction between legitimate and illegitimate children. Even the concept of "family law" itself was coined around 1800 due to the influence of Neo-Lutheran protestants. They established their political program as a protest against the French Revolution and the French *Code Civil* with its "droit des personnes". In contrast to the new principles of equality and liberty for everybody regardless of their position within the family, the German house-fathers were to maintain authority and rule over their family members and fortunes. In the 1970s, the Protestant Church of Germany (EKD) was able to influence the liberalization of divorce. This example suggests that in spite of much harmonization of the European legislation in family matters, we can still detect the major influence of Christian theology on family law today. The Churches still exert some influence on modern societies. Moreover, we have to recognize different theological traditions and convictions concerning family law in Europe to this day.

1 Introduction

In the German *Bürgerliches Gesetzbuch*, "Book 4" contains the outline of a story, which is entitled "Family law": Starting with engagement, it then explains the rules of marriage, the rights of the married couple, the rules of mutual maintenance, and the rules of divorce. It then explains the rules of affinity, the rights of the parents to both the person and the belongings of their children, the laws of child support, and the laws of adoption. "Book 4" finishes with tutelage and curatorship. We discover

M. Schmoeckel (✉)
Legal History and Civil Law, Universität Bonn, Institut für Deutsche und Rheinische Rechtsgeschichte, Adenauerallee 24-42, 53113 Bonn, Germany
e-mail: rgesch@uni-bonn.de

M.G. di Renzo Villata (ed.), *Family Law and Society in Europe from the Middle Ages to the Contemporary Era*, Studies in the History of Law and Justice 5,
DOI 10.1007/978-3-319-42289-3_1

the outline of a biographical story, beginning with the formation of a marriage, out of which children are born, who eventually grow up. Eventually, the couple becomes senile and infirm, and needs legal support. What appears to be the ideal course of a successful life as perceived by a 19th century novel is actually a rather bold, new approach of the German BGB-legislator in the final decades of the 19th century. It clearly opposes the order of the French *Code Civil*, which wanted to protect the equality of men and therefore only stated the law *des personnes*[1] in its first book. Why did the German legislator choose a different approach?

I will try to explain the ideas underlying these modern codifications and the differences between the German and French codifications. The two codifications represent two different positions that can also be found elsewhere in Europe. My focus is on the Christian faith that formed Europe and its legal assumptions. This simultaneously serves to provide points of unity between the French and German codifications, as well as explaining the notable differences. In order to prove my thesis, we will have to go back to Roman Antiquity. But it is apparent that something happened in the German legal development of the 19th century that provoked the split of the tradition.

It is not without hesitation, however, that we can assume a Roman "Family law". The term already carries undertones of a "German" perspective, although it certainly had a great influence on Romanists in the past century. With regard to Ancient Rome, we have to be particularly careful with regard to the question of what was regulated by law, and what was regulated by religion. The focus on the Christian influence is not meant to deny the existence of the possible influence of other religions in Europe, especially of Hebraic concepts, for example. Moreover, the focus on Christianity is not intended to be seen as proof of monocausal developments.

2 Classical Roman Law

The Roman *pater familias* had an extensive, general competence in family matters, 'family' meaning the people living together.[2] His power included the right to decide whether a new born infant was entitled to survive or not: the *ius vitae necisque*. In the same way, he was the only judge over his wife if she deserted him.[3] He would also decide over the property of his wife, if he had married her in the form of the

[1]Martin, Xavier. 2002. *Mythologie du Code Napoléon. Aux soubassements de la France moderne*. Paris: Editions Dominique Martin Morin, 430s.

[2]Schwab, Dieter. 1975. Familie. In *Geschichtliche Grundbegriffe* 2, eds. O. Koselleck, W. Conzen and R. Koselleck. Stuttgart: Klett-Cotta, 253–301.

[3]Kaser, Max. 1971. *Das römische Privatrecht. Erster Abschnitt: Das altrömische, das vorklassische und klassische Recht* (Rechtsgeschichte des Altertums 2.3.1). München: C. H. Beck, § 82, 341ss.

manus-marriage.[4] With the symbols of a contract of purchase the wife became a member of her husband's family and the husband in turn gave her a gold ring as a handsel.[5] Even though some legal forms were used, most of the marriage consisted of religious ceremony, and we might doubt the extent to which marriage was really considered to be a legal issue at all.[6] Of course, there were legal rules concerning the interdiction of bigamy, of incest, or Augustus' *Lex Iulia de adulteriis coercendis* (18 b.C.), who wanted to oblige all adults to marry in order to ensure the birth of many children, and so future recruits for his army.[7]

However, marriage was basically a private matter. For Modestin, marriage was the lifelong union of man and woman based on divine and human laws.[8] Marriage was concluded by consent[9], but only in special cases did consent lead to a legal contract. Only later did marriage acquire a legal sense, although this may already have been due to Christian influence,[10] since St. Ambrose, in around 392, had already regarded marriage as a *pactio*.[11]

3 The Church Fathers

For the church fathers, marriage was a matter neither of family politics, nor of social aspirations, nor of subjection to the *pater familias*. They cared instead for the individual capacity to comply with the rules of a Christian life. After a short period, in which marriage was only conceived as a stratagem for procreation, St. Paul saw in it a union that helped both to fight Satan and to avoid concupiscence (1Cor 7.9). The early Christian concept of marriage therefore respected the institution as a

[4]Cf. Thomas, Yan. 1993. Die Teilung der Geschlechter im Römischen Recht. In *Geschichte der Frauen* 1: *Antike*, eds. Schmitt Pantel, Pauline,. Frankfurt a.M.: Zweitausendeins, 105–171.

[5]Gaudemet, Jean. 1987. *Le mariage en Occident*. Paris: Editions du Cerf, 25; Kleinheyer, Bruno. 1984. Ordinationen und Beauftragung. In *Sakramentliche Feiern*, eds. B. Kleinheyer, E. von Severus and R. Kaczynski, 2 (Gottesdienst der Kirche. Handbuch der Liturgiewissenschaft 8). Regensburg: Verlag Friedrich Pustet, 7–80, 66.

[6]Very cautious in this respect already is Marquardt, Joachim. 1886. *Das Privatleben der Römer*, 1st part, Leipzig: S. Hirzel, reimpr. 1990, Darmstadt: WBG, 33, 48 and 51.

[7]Mette-Dittmann, Angelika. 1991. *Die Ehegesetze des Augustus: Eine Untersuchung im Rahmen der Gesellschaftspolitik des princeps*, Stuttgart: Verlag Franz Steiner, 39.

[8]Modestinus, D. 23.2.1: "Nuptiae sunt coniunctio maris et feminae, consortium omnis vitae, divini et humani iuris communicatio".

[9]Ulpian, D. 50.17.30 "consensus facit nuptias"; equally Decretum Gratiani, C.27 qu.1 before 1, following Isidor of Sevilla, *Ethymologiarum* 9.7.

[10]Kaser, Max. 1975. *Das römische Privatrecht. Zweiter Abschnitt: Die nachklassischen Entwicklungen* (Rechtsgeschichte des Altertums 3.3.2). München: C. H. Beck, 169.

[11]Ambrosius. *De institutione uirginis et sanctae Mariae uirginitate perpetua ad Eusebium*, ed. F. Gori, 1989 (Biblioteca Ambrosiana 14.2). Roma: Città Nuova, 110–194, here c.6.41, Z.3ss: "Non enim defloratio virginatitis coniugium facit, sed pactio coniugalis".

device to encourage compliance with the Christian standards of morality.[12] Marriage seemed to be a road to salvation.[13]

The episcopal jurisdiction was not only a reason to develop Christian ideas on family life; it also provided the means to introduce the new rules in practice. More and more the Church understood such rules as a way to establish Christian morality and a Christian society with regard to everybody's private life. For this reason, family matters increasingly acquired a central role in the legislation of the Church.

With the comparison of marriage to the unity of Christ and his Church (Eph 5:22), the emphasis was set on the lasting and permanent union of the flesh. This increasingly led marriage to be treated in legal terms, and St. Paul himself even granted, with his famous *privilegium paulinum* (1Cor 7:15), a clear-cut legal rule. The comparison later induced the Church to invent the doctrine of the indissoluble marriage. The episcopal jurisdiction proved to be the best way to develop new Christian standards and to introduce them to the public.[14]

However, it was mostly in the East of the empire that a new law of marriage started to be introduced. Marriage was still considered to be based on marital consensus,[15] but they discussed the possibility of a second marriage (CTh 3.8), which evidences a Christian influence. The imperial constitutions slowly shaped a first Christian law of marriage, although there were many uncertainties and discrepancies.[16] In the West, however, the Germanic kingdoms did not follow suit. They prohibited the robbery of women and stated the invalidity of such a marriage.[17] The Franks cared very little for marriage rules. Charlemagne entertained several women with different titles at the same time. Even marriages by robbery were considered to be valid.[18]

[12]Gaudemet, Jean. 1978. L'interprétation du principe d'indissolubilité du mariage chrétien au cours du premier millénaire. *Bullettino dell'Istituto di diritto romano* 81: 11–69, 11.

[13]Origenes. 1908. Fragmenta in I cor 37. *Journal of Theological Studies* 9: 507; cf. Crouzel, Henri. 1982. Ehe/Eherecht/Ehescheidung V: Alte Kirche, *TRE*, 9, Berlin-New York: de gruyter, 325–330, 325s.

[14]Thus argues Evans Grubbs, Judith. 2008. Christianization of Marriage? Christianity, Marriage, and Law in Late Antiquity. In *Ehe—Familie—Verwandtschaft. Vergesellschaftung in Religion und sozialer Lebenswelt*, ed. A. Holzem and I. Weber. Paderborn: Schöningh, 105–124.

[15]CTh.3.7.1.1 = Brev.3.7.1.1, Valentinianus/Valens/Gratian a.371.

[16]Noonan, John T. 1968. Novel 22. In *The Bond of Marriage*, ed. W. W. Bassett. Washington: Notre Dame Press, 41–90.

[17]*Leges Visigothorum.* ed. K. Zeumer, 1902, (MGH. Legum Nationum Germanicarum, 1). Hannover and Leipzig: Hahnsche Buchhandlung 2.3.2. Recc. Ev, Antiqua, 140.

[18]Saar, Stephan Chr. 2002. *Ehe, Scheidung, Wiederheirat. Studien zur Geschichte der Ehe und des Ehescheidungsrechts im Frühmittelalter (6.–10. Jahrhundert).* Münster: Lit Verlag, 263ss; Marculfi. *Formularum libri duo*, ed. Alf Uddholm, 1962. Uppsala: Eranos, 272 n. 30; Wemple, Suzanne Fonay. 1985. *Women in Frankish Society. Marriage and the Cloister 500–900.* Philadelphia: University of Pennsylvania Press, 38ss.

Only with the famous case of king Lothar II did a new age begin.[19] Here, the Church did not permit the king to divorce his queen and to return to his previous wife, the mother of his only son. Furthermore, the Pope insisted that his queen was his only lawful wife. The Church developed the idea that only marriages concluded according to the new formalities were valid, and only their offspring were "legitimate". For the first time, a king, who could not behave corporally as it was fit for a Christian, was regarded as unfit for the leading position of a monarch.[20] So Lothar was prevented from returning to his previous wife. The son of Lothar II, who was certainly the child of a legitimate marriage according to the old Frankish tradition, was therefore regarded as illegitimate and could not succeed his father. Admittedly, it was a rather special political case, in which the two brothers of king Lothar, the kings of West and East Francia, shared their prize and eliminated a third Frankish kingdom in their middle. In the long run, however, this matter of Carolingian politics helped the Church to establish new rules for marriage and families according to the Church Fathers' teaching. The decretals concerning his case were repeated and eventually incorporated in the *Decretum Gratiani.*

4 From the Irish Penitentials to the Canon Law of Marriage

The Irish Penitentials, manuals for confessors since the 6th century, took the Church Fathers more seriously and treated them, like the Old Testament, as legal authorities. Marriage was the only remedy for sexual misconduct (*remedium concupiscentiae*),[21] but concupiscence was required even in matrimony.[22] The Irish monks often had to deal with these questions in their confessional practices, and the penitentials therefore provided many rules. Misconduct was to be severely punished.

[19]Cf. Schmoeckel, Mathias. 2007. Der lotharische Ehestreit: Seine Protagonisten und ihre Perspektiven. In *Fälle aus der Rechtsgeschichte,* eds. U. Falk, M. Luminati and M. Schmoeckel. München: C. H. Beck, 77–95; cf. more detailed idem. 2008. Ansätze eines neuen Rechtssystems im 9. Jahrhundert. Bemerkungen zum Ehestreit Lothars II. In *Aspecten van het middeleeuwse Romeinse Recht, Iuris Scripta Historica,* ed. L. Waelkens. Bruxelles: Koninklijke Vlaamse Academie van België voor Wetenschappen en Kunsten, Comité Rechtsgeschiedenis 22, 109–132, with further references.

[20]Airlie, Stuart. 1998. Private Bodies and the Body Politic in the Divorce Case of Lothar II. *Past & Present* 161: 3–38, 15.

[21]Manns, Peter. 1995. Die Unauflösbarkeit der Ehe im Verständnis der frühmittelalterlichen Bußbücher. In *Geschieden. Wiederverheiratet. Abgewiesen? Antworten der Theologie*, ed. Th. Schneider. Freiburg i.B.: Herder, 84–111, 93s.

[22]Poenitentiale Vinniai. In *Die Bußordnungen der abendländischen Kirche,* ed. F.W.H. Wasserschleben, 1851. Halle, reimpr. 1958, Graz: Akademische Verlagsanstalt, § 46, 118.

The idea of the indissoluble marriage spread thanks to the Iro-Scottish missionaries of the 7th to 9th centuries. They provided a new stimulus to create a new Christian law of marriage.[23] The official Church as well as the unofficial churches sought ways to establish firmer bonds between spouses. Many ideas were developed that became practice only much later or even in Modern Times. In particular, it was in the 9th century, and through authors writing near to the time of king Lothar's case, that new solutions were offered.

A manual for the Christian people (818–828), written by Jonas of Orléans, called it a sin when a man left his wife. This could only be legal in case of her adultery.[24] Pope John VIII (872–882) condemned a man who left his wife in order to marry another wife.[25] With reference to Mc 10:9 he argued that a man should not separate what God had united. Even the fact that the applicant was a Hungarian prince did not change his mind, because he considered divorce to be a particularly bad comportment of heathens, in which nobody else was "magister et auctor" but the devil himself.

A more pragmatic way was the establishment of necessary forms for the marriage. As the Church increasingly saw the inner will as a sufficient basis for legal obligations, marriage gradually came to be treated like a contract.[26] The idea of the necessary presence of a priest or his benediction of the marriage could not be established. However, the Church successfully imposed the duty of a doted marriage.[27] Any marriage without the provision of the dowry was considered void and illegitimate. Their offspring were illegitimate as well and had no right of succession. This principle was postulated in the case of king Lothar, and slowly the European nobility and rich families began to obey this law in order to ascertain the transfer of their property to the next generation. And so this principle spread in Europe. Even Henri de Bracton still wrote in the 13th century:[28] "Ubi nullum matrimonium, ibi nulla dos".

---

[23]In this sense already Duby, Georges. 1977. Le mariage dans la société du Haut Moyen Âge. In *Il Matrimonio nella società altomedievale* 1. Spoleto: Settimane di Studio del Centro Italiano di Studi sull'Alto medioevo, 24, 15–39.

[24]Orléans, Jonas of. De institutione laicali 2.13. In *Patrologia Latina* 106, 191: "Quod qui uxorem suam, excepta causa fornicationis, dimiserit, et aliam duxerit, moechus sit".

[25]John VIII. ed. Erich Caspar and Gerhard Laehr, 1912. Berlin: Hahnsche Buchhandlung. reimpr. 1993, Munich, ep.17, 282 l.10ss.

[26]Explicitly e.g. in *Summa Sti. Raymundi de Penyafort de poenitentia et matrimonio.* 1603. Rome. reimpr. 1967, Meisenheim-Glan: Gregg, 3.1 De Bigamijs, 259b.

[27]Mikat, Paul. 1978. *Dotierte Ehe—rechte Ehe. Zur Entwicklung des Eheschließungsrechts in fränkischer Zeit.* Opladen (Rheinisch-Westfälische Akademie der Wissenschaften, Vorträge G 227); Reynolds, Philip L. 2007. Dotal Charters in the Frankish Tradition. Into *Have and to Hold. Marrying and Its Documentation in Western Christendom, 400–1600*, eds. Reynolds, Philip and J. Witte Jr. Cambridge: Cambridge University Press, 114–164; Lemaire, André. 1929. La *dotatio* de l'épouse de l'époque mérovingienne au XIIIe siècle. *Revue historique de droit français et étranger* 4.8: 569–580.

[28]Henricus de Bracton. 1640. *De legibus et Consuetudinibus Angliae*. London, reimpr. 2009, New York: Clark, 4.1.9, fol. 169v; cf. also Saar 2002 (as n. 18) 180s.

Already at the time of Paschasius Radbertus, abbot of Corbie (ca.785–ca. 865), a new tradition started that compared marriage with the union of Christ and his Church and therefore detected a "sacramentum" in matrimony.[29] Just as the Church could not be separated from Christ, so the spouses could never be separated either. This was a holy "mystery", and the scholastic theologians Hugo of St. Victor (ca. 1097–1141) and Petrus Lombardus (ca. 1095/1100–1160) developed a new theory of sacraments that became the common, Catholic dogma.[30]

Canon law slowly attempted to amalgamate the different traditions.[31] Even at the time of Gratian, however, there had been no common theory, and the different traditions were the cause of contradictions even in the *Decretum Gratiani*.[32] Furthermore, the ideas of theologians and canonists were still not accepted in most parts of Europe. Only after a very long delay were the Christian conceptions of marriage accepted in European societies.[33]

It was only during the final years of the Council of Trent, after 1562, that the Catholic rules of marriage were established.[34] Marriage maintained its sacramental nature, and the formal necessity of a priest to give his benediction over the marriage and to notify it in the records of the parish was introduced. Based on these new principles, Thomas Sanchez (1550–1610) wrote his famous *Disputationes de sancti matrimonii sacramento* in 1602–5 and thus established the law of marriage from the Roman-Catholic point of view.[35]

---

[29]Paschasius Radbertus, Expositio in Evangelium Mattaei. In *Patrologia Latina* 120, 652.

[30]Cf. Weigand, Rudolf. 1967. *Die Lehre der Kanonisten des 12. und 13. Jahrhunderts von den Ehewecken*. Bologna: Studia Gratiana 12 (=Collectanea Stephan Kuttner 2) 443–478.

[31]Weigand, Rudolf. 1971. Kanonistische Ehetraktate aus dem 12. Jahrhundert. In *Proceedings of the Third International Congress of Medieval Canon Law*, Monumenta iuris canonici, ed. St. Kuttner. Città del Vaticano: Biblioteca Apostolica Romana, C.4, 60–79; cf. also Brooke, Christopher N.L. 1980. Marriage Law in the XIth and XIIth Centuries. In *Proceedings of the Fifth International Congress of Medieval Canon Law*, Monumenta iuris canonici, eds. St. Kuttner and K. Pennington. Città del Vaticano: Biblioteca Apostolica Romana, C.6, 333–344.

[32]Weigand, Rudolf. 1993. *Liebe und Ehe im Mittelalter* (Bibliotheca eruditorum 7), Goldbach: Keip.

[33]Otis-Cour, Leah. 2000. *Lust und Liebe: Geschichte der Paarbeziehungen im Mittelalter*. Frankfurt a.M.: Fischer, 78s.

[34]Concilium Tridentinum, sessio 24 of 11.11.1563: Doctrina de sacramento matrimonii, a.A. In *Conciliorum Oecumenicorum Decreta*, ed. J. Alberigo. 1962. Basel: Herder, 729ss; cf. Wenz, Gunther. 1998. Art. Sakramente 1, *TRE* 29: 663–703, 729.

[35]Cf. Carrodeguas, Celestino. 2003. *La sacramentalidad del matrimonio. Doctrina de Tomás Sánchez S.J.* Madrid: Univ. Pontificia Comillas.

5 The Protestant Reformation

Martin Luther developed a new, rather pragmatic perspective on the law of marriage. He did not deny its legal character, but rather regarded it as a "weltlich ding" (worldly matter).[36] Of course, matrimony was holy[37] as it could help to comply with the rules of Christian morality. In a family, the father and mother should act as "apostle, bishop and vicar" in order to spread the Gospel and the rules of a Christian life.[38] The family was moreover a form of cohabitation of different people. The establishment of the rules for marriage was left to the authorities. The form of the marriage was regarded as a secular question, like clothing and nourishment. The state should declare the conditions of valid matrimony. Without delay, different systems were introduced in the German territories that had converted to the Reformation. They invented, for example, the register for marriages and the matrimonial property regime.[39] Marriage established the family as the smallest entity of human society. Therefore, the new theology actually introduced the secularization of marriage.[40] Only occasionally Luther and his followers treated marriage matters in a rather pragmatic way.[41]

This led to a new definition of society. The *pater familias* ruled his small family group, which formed the smallest entity of society. At the same time, this social unit was seen as the source and origin of each society.[42] For this reason, it had to be recognized and protected. Johannes Althusius even spoke of "iura sanguinis".[43] The traditional *pater familias* acquired a new, theologically conceived role as the head of his family, who taught and controlled Christian morality in the smallest unit of

---

[36]Luther, Martin. Von Ehesachen [1530] (1910), Weimarer Ausgabe 30 III. Weimar: Hermann Böhlaus Nachfolger, 20, 12.

[37]See Kaufmann, Thomas. 2008. Ehetheologie im Kontext der frühen Wittenberger Reformation. In *Ehe—Familie—Verwandtschaft. Vergesellschaftung in Religion und sozialer Lebenswelt*, eds. A. Holzem and I. Weber. Paderborn etc.: Schöningh, 285–299, 290.

[38]Luther, Martin. Vom ehelichen Leben [1522] (1907), Weimarer Ausgabe 10.2. Weimar: Hermann Böhlaus Nachfolger, 275–304.

[39]E.g. Preußische Landesordnung of 1577, Art. 6ss. In *Quellen zur Neueren Privatrechtsgeschichte Deutschlands* 2, part 1 *Polizei- und Landesordnungen*, ed. G. K. Schmelzeisen. 1968. Weimar: Böhlau, 375.

[40]Witte, John jr. 2002. *Law and Protestantism*. Cambridge: Cambridge University Press, 199ss.

[41]Witte, John jr. 2015. *The Western Case for Monogamy Over Polygamy*. Cambridge: Cambridge University Press, 209ss.

[42]Bodin, Jean. 1583. *Les six Livres de la République*. Paris. reimpr. 1961, Aalen: scientia 1.2, 10; Althusius, Johannes. 1614. *Politica methodice digesta*. Herborn, reimpr. 1981, Aalen: Scientia 2.2 and c.3, 12ss, and n.40, 24.

[43]Althusius 1614 (as n. 42) 2. n. 3, 29 and n.18, 33.

society. This should in turn ascertain social control and the orthodoxy of the society.[44] A whole new series of literature was written known as *Hausväter*, the purpose of which was to teach the *pater familias* how to behave correctly in various situations of daily life with regard to the treatment of the people in his household as well as property issues.[45]

6 The Idea of Human Rights for Families

From this Protestant perspective, family became a pillar of society. It was seen as responsible for the maintenance of justice and virtue in the social order. God's vengeance was a permanent threat for any trespassing of these duties. Thus, the protection of families and the position of fathers and mothers with respect to their children became indispensable. Even Philipp Melanchthon therefore declared in his time that princes were bound to respect the law, especially in the interests of the lives of their citizens, their bodies, fortunes and marriages (*connubia*).[46]

It was not only in their private interests to keep the law, but also in the public interest of the nation to be spared of God's wrath. It was God's unmistakable will that children were to be educated by their parents. This is how he created the world and nobody had the right to interfere.

This helped to form the idea of inviolable rights. Medieval scholars had already introduced the idea of natural rights that nobody could deny.[47] Jean Calvin spoke of inviolable rights with reference to God's will and natural law. Reading Calvin, therefore, inspires the idea that he already knew of a large range of human rights.[48] But he spoke rather as a theologian when he explained the Old Testament and the Gospel. He stressed the necessity of respecting the rights of parents, with respect to the new covenant between God and his people, for example, which no man could

---

[44]Frassek, Ralf. 2005. *Eherecht und Ehegerichtsbarkeit in der Reformationszeit* (Jus Ecclesiasticum 78). Tübingen: Mohr Siebeck, 269.

[45]Cf. van Haag, Maike-Franziska. 2014. *Recht in der Hausväterliteratur. Der "Oeconomus Prudens et Legalis" von Franz Philipp Florin im Kontext seiner Zeit* (Juristische Schriftenreihe 276). Berlin: Lit.

[46]Melanchthon, Philipp. 1542. *De aequitate et iure stricto.* Corpus Reformatorum 11, 550–555, 554. German Edition: Billigkeit und strenges Recht (trans. Michael Beyer). In *Melanchthon Deutsch* 1. 1997, Leipzig: Evang. Verlags-Anstalt 170–177, 175: "Deus enim vult et ipsos gubernatores teneri legibus, non vult caecas eorum cupiditates dominari, vult legibus civium vitam, corpora, fortunas, connubia munita esse".

[47]Padovani, Andrea. 1997. *Perché chiedi il mio nome?* Torino: Giappichelli; for the conception of undeniable rights cf. Schmoeckel, Mathias. 2016. Zur Bedeutung der Reformation für die Welt, *ZRG KA*, sub 3, not yet published.

[48]Witte, John jr. 2007. *The Reformation of Rights. Law, Religion, and Human Rights in Early Modern Calvinism.* Cambridge: Cambridge University Press, 58.

alter. For this reason, a new discussion on unalienable rights was started by the early Calvinists like Althusius and his "iura sanguinis".[49]

This discussion was received immediately in England, where it immediately acquired a political significance thanks to the tension between the monarchy and the people. The "leveler" Gerrard Winstanley regarded the family as the foundation of both the economy and society. Only erudite parents could pass on their knowledge and ensure that the next generation was equally well educated. In his "The law of freedom in a platform" of 1652, education in the family therefore became a prerequisite for a well-functioning society.[50]

John Locke proceeded to explain these family rights more closely. In his *Two treatises of government* of 1689, he explained the position of the parents as having the right to exclude state intervention in these private matters. *Fatherhood & property* were the foundation of sovereignty in family and society for Locke.[51] Whereas all men were equal by natural law, children were dependent on their parents, because they were not yet able to use their reason.[52] They had to be taught, therefore, and this was not only a subjective right, but also a duty[53] imposed by God and natural law.[54] Parents would serve as protectors for their children as long as was necessary.

The subjective right that later became a human right is nothing but the secular aspect of a religious idea. Such rights are inviolable, because any intervention would constitute a breach of the new covenant with God. The modern libertarian terminology is the necessary flip side of religious duties towards God.

7 The Neo-Lutheran Formation of "Family Law" in Germany

The Protestant Reformation was not just a short moment in the course of world history; rather, it initiated another strain of theology and a new scientific tradition. Ever since the Reformation's beginning, authors were inspired by the movement and developed new ideas in order to further Luther's or Calvin's initiatives. Particularly at the beginning of the 19th century, we find a movement called "New Lutheranism" in Germany. These authors writing around the time of the theologian

[49]Althusius 1614 (as n. 42), 3.37, 41.

[50]Winstanley, Gerrard. *The Law of Freedom in a Platform*. reimpr. 1973, London: Pelican Books, c.5, 361ss. Cf. also Harrington, James. 1992. A system of Politics. In "*The Commonwealth of Oceana*" and "*A system of Politics*", ed. J.-G.A. Pocock. Cambridge: Cambridge University Press, c.2, 270. Stressing the importance of property as the basis of paternal power in family and society.

[51]Locke, John. 1690. *Two treatises of government*, ed. M. Goldie. 1993. London-Vermont: J.M. Dent, 20, c.7 n. 73, 52ss.

[52]Locke 1690 (as n. 51) 2, c.6 n. 60, 144.

[53]Locke 1690 (as n. 51) 20, c.6 n. 58, 142s.

[54]Locke 1690 (as n. 51) 2, c.6 n. 63, 145 and n. 65, 146.

Schleiermacher tried to understand Luther's writings as legal commandments with immediate repercussions for the state and its law.[55] During the period of Romanticism, they tried to establish a protestant legal order returning to Luther and the first authors of the Protestant Reformation. The establishment of a new "family law" can perhaps be understood within this tradition.

We know that the term "family law" originated from the time around the turn of the 19th century.[56] It is a "collective singular", which Reinhard Koselleck found to be typical of the time.[57] However, the new term also represented a profound change in the concept of the family: it no longer denoted, as in antique Roman law, the people living together in one household, including the servants, but was instead used for the parents and their children alone, thus restricting the term to the cognates.[58] Due to the emancipation of the grown-up children and concerns for the equality of the wife, the rule of the *pater familias* was at stake and family ceased to function as the smallest scale unit of government.[59]

The Prussian *Allgemeines Landrecht* of 1794, however, did not contain a "family law". Influenced by the *iura sanguinis*–tradition, it was concerned with "family laws" instead, which comprised the individual rights granted to a particular family so that each noble or merchant family could have their own choice of "family laws" (ALR 2.3). This was meant to secure the status of the family in the traditional class society.

In France, it is clear that the authors of the *Code Civil* did not want to ignore the revolutionary principle of equality. Thus, they did not want to provide a law of families, legislating instead only a *droit des personnes*. Everybody was treated equally without regard to the position held in his family, or indeed the rank of his family. Consequently, until today France does not have a family law.[60]

German authors were inspired by the French approach and converted to the use of *Personenrecht*.[61] Here we can already see the tendency to use the term in the singular. At the same time, the controversy about whether or not this subject should contain the law of guardians was continued. Furthermore, it was questioned

---

[55]Hornig, Gottfried. 1894. Lehre und Bekenntnis im Protestantismus. In *Handbuch der Dogmen- und Theologiegeschichte* 3, reimpr. ed. C. Andresen. 1989. Göttingen: Vandenhoeck und Ruprecht, 2, chap. 7, 174s.

[56]Cf. Koch, Elisabeth. 2008. Art. Familie, Familienrecht, *HRG* 2nd edition. Berlin: Erich Schmidt Verlag, 1497–1502, 1501s; Müller-Freienfels, Wolfram. 2003. The Emergence of Droit de Famille and Familienrecht in Continental Europe and the Introduction of Family Law in England. *Journal of Family History* 28.1: 31–51.

[57]Koselleck, Reinhart. 2006. *Begriffsgeschichten. Studien zur Semantik und Pragmatik der politischen und sozialen Sprache*, Frankfurt a.M: Suhrkamp, 67.

[58]Schwab 1975 (as n. 2) 278. The household personnel was still part of the family in Krug, Wilhelm Traugott. 1817. *System der theoretischen Philosophie. Erster Theil: Rechtslehre*, Königsberg: Goebbels und Unzer, § 115, 486s.

[59]Schwab 1975 (as n. 2) 283; Krug 1817 (as n. 58).

[60]On the importance of equality in the *constituante* and legislation cf. Lefebvre-Teillard, Anne. 1996. *Introduction historique au droit des personnes et de la famille*, Paris: Puf, 325 § 249.

[61]Hugo, Gustav. 1799. *Lehrbuch eines civilistischen Cursus, 2, ganz von neuem ausgearb. Versuch*, 1, Berlin: August Mylius, § 57, 50.

whether the focus should be on personal matters alone or whether property issues should be included as well.[62] In order to incorporate rights on property, some authors used the notion of the "real-personal right" (*dinglich-persönliche Rechte*).[63]

The first use of the term "Familienrecht" can be found by the theologian and law professor Theodor Schmalz (1760–1831), who in 1795 presented a short overview on the law of marriage and children. He called his text "natural family law" (*Das natürliche Familienrecht*), thus wanting to exclude guardians from his subject. The focus on relatives was a sound reason to exclude guardians and wardens. However, he still wanted to include foster parents in his treatise.[64] In 1817, Wilhelm Traugott Krug (1770–1842) wrote his *System der theoretischen Philosophie*, where one of the chapters was entitled "Familienrecht".[65] He included therein the law on household servants, which could be seen as a continuation of the tradition of the *Hausväter*, and thus revealed his Protestant background.[66] However, he chose not to explain his term. Only with Carl Anton Mittermaier in 1821 and Karl Friedrich Eichhorn in 1824 did the term become popular.[67]

It is necessary here to distinguish between a philosophical discourse and the theological implications. When Fichte used the term in 1796,[68] he wanted to emphasise the moral obligations between the family members. The state, he argued, had to accept these responsibilities, so that "family law" became the first annex to his "natural law". As natural and moral entities, individuals learn to respect each other and to collaborate.

We find a very similar approach from 1796 onwards in the writings of the great protestant theologian Friedrich Schleiermacher. He clearly had no intention of defending the classical patterns of Christian marriage law.[69] Instead, he understood the family as a device to overcome the boundaries of every individual and to understand, for example, how the opposite sex would think. He did not refer here to reason alone, but talked of *Anschauung* instead, because this "perception" referred to intuitive understanding as well.

---

[62]Bergmann, Friedrich Christian. 1810. *Lehrbuch des Privatrechts des Code Napoleon*, Göttingen: Vandenhoeck und Ruprecht, § 63, 91.

[63]Arnold Heise. 1819. *Grundriss eines Systems eines gemeinen Civilrechts*, 3rd ed., 4. Heidelberg: Mohr and Zimmer, 129, although he already knew "family law" (17 n. 5); Björne, Lars. 1984. *Deutsche Rechtssysteme im 18. und 19. Jahrhundert*. Ebelsbach: Gremer, 142, considers "dinglich-persönlichen Rechte" as a model of family law.

[64]von Schmalz, Theodor. 1795. *Das natürliche Familienrecht*. Königsberg: Nicolovius, 27s.

[65]Krug 1817 (as n. 58), § 104ss, 441ss.

[66]Krug 1817 (as n. 58), § 115, 486s; § 117, 501.

[67]Mittermaier, Carl Anton. 1821. *Lehrbuch des deutschen Privatrechts*. Landshut: Krüll, book 5: *Familienrecht*, 321 with § 430; Eichhorn, Karl Friedrich. 1823. *Einleitung in das deutsche Privatrecht mit Einschluß des Lehensrechts*. Göttingen: Vandenhoeck und Ruprecht § 290, 699ss.

[68]Fichte, Johann Gottlieb. 1797. Grundlage des Naturrechts, reimpr. ed. M. Zahn, 1979. Hamburg: Verlag F. Meiner, part 2, *Grundriß des Familienrechts* (as first annex of natural law), 298.

[69]Schleiermacher, Friedrich Daniel Ernst. Gedanken 1. In *Schriften aus der Berliner Zeit 1796–1799*. reimpr. ed. G. Meckenstock, (Critical Edition, 2) 1984. Berlin-New York: De gruyter, 5.

With Georg Friedrich Hegel, family became a natural order of life giving rise to legal duties.[70] Within the family, members did not act as individuals, but rather learnt to care for each other. Property could not belong to one member alone, but had to be related to the family as a group. The state should be obliged to respect this unity and to protect their collective property and interests.

The Romantic philosopher Adam Müller (1779–1829) regarded the protection of the family as a central obligation of the state even more so than Hegel.[71] The youth would tend to call for innovations in society, and the conservatism of the elderly people would be hooted down. For this reason, the state had to ensure that the forces upholding the tradition, including the nobility, were protected in order to prevent another French Revolution.

In his *System of the contemporary Roman law*, Friedrich Carl von Savigny adopted "Family law" as the title of his fourth book of civil law. Only here did he explain his concept of "family law".[72] He defended his choice of title by referring to Hegel and Müller. Within the family everybody would learn to fulfil his moral duties towards his group. The family would therefore rise above the individual in every respect. Once again, the *Anschauung* in the family would help each individual to understand their moral obligations. A look into Savigny's lectures reveals that he had decided on his concept of "family law" much earlier than 1840—at least by 1824.[73] In fact, Friedrich Carl von Savigny had used the term in his courses since 1801.[74] Savigny made it clear that he did not envisage a society of equals. He resorted to Luther's concept of the *Hausvater* as the central authority in domestic matters. Instead of the equality of all men, Savigny envisaged a society dominated by chiefs of family and by the nobility. The old *Hausväter*-concept combined personal and property questions and was used to increase the role of the bourgeois *pater familias*. This neo-Lutheran approach was a device to oppose the tendencies of the French Revolution.

---

[70]Hegel, Georg Wilhelm Friedrich. *Grundlinien der Philosophie des Rechts, (Hauptwerke in 6 Bänden, 5)*. 1999, Darmstadt: Meiner, § 160, 150; Hegel, Georg Wilhelm Friedrich. *Philosophie des Rechts. Die Mitschriften Wannemann (Heidelberg 1817/8) und Homeyer (Berlin 1818/19)*, ed. K.-H. Ilting. 1983, Stuttgart: Klett-Cotta, § 82, 102; Hegel, Georg Wilhelm Friedrich. *Philosophie des Rechts, die Vorlesung von 1819/20 in einer Nachschrift*, ed. D. Henrich. 1983. Frankfurt a.M.: Suhrkamp, 143.

[71]Müller, Adam. 1936. *Die Elemente der Staatskunst*. Berlin: Hendel, 1.5, 67.

[72]Savigny, Friedrich Carl von. 1840. *System des heutigen römischen Rechts I*. Berlin: Veit & Comp, § 54, 345. For the evolution of the German system of civil law cf. Schmoeckel, Mathias. 2003. Der Allgemeine Teil in der Ordnung des BGB. In *Historisch-Kritischer Kommentar zum BGB*, 1, eds. M. Schmoeckel, R. Zimmermann and J. Rückert.Tübingen: Mohr Siebeck, 123–165.

[73]Savigny, Friedrich Carl von. 1824. *Landrechtsvorlesung, Drei Nachschriften*, ed. Ch. Wollschläger et al. 1998. Frankfurt a.M: Klostermann, XVIII and 762; Savigny, Friedrich Carl von. 1824–25. *Pandektenvorlesung*, ed. H. Hammen. 1993. Frankfurt a.M.: Klostermann, XVI, XXIX and 401.

[74]Joachim Rückert kindly informed me of this using his preparatory material for the forthcoming publication on Savigny's classes; cf. Rückert and Schäfer. *Repertorium zu Savigny-Vorlesungsquellen*.

This explains why even the Catholic Mittermaier adopted the term *family law* in 1821, which he had first learned as a student of Savigny in Landshut. Due to their joint influence and fame, the new term spread very quickly both in textbooks[75] as well as in codifications such as the Saxon civil law of 1863. This served as the model for the new German *Bürgerliches Gesetzbuch*.[76] Once again, the fathers of this codification discussed the necessity of including guardians in the book.[77] With a view to combining personal and property matters of the family, this was approved. Once again, this followed the Lutheran model of the *Hausväter*. Consequently, states like France should be more aware of the problems of taking over the "family law" concept. It is for good reason, therefore, that the textbook of Anne Lefebvre-Teillard is not an introduction to the history of family law only, but rather to the law of persons and families.[78]

The strengthening of the bourgeois patriarch appealed to members of all confessions. But the term *Hausvater* was derived from Luther, and the father was still regarded as central for the moral and religious instruction of the family members. Hence, it is clear that, once again, Luther's concept of the family as the germ cell of the state shines through. This moral education in the family was regarded as a way of strengthening the individual and his or her individuality, rather than shaping the youth according to a common standard or teaching liberty as the adoption of moral necessities, as explained by the Church.[79] Particularly with regard to the *Anschauung* of moral duties in a family, the influence of Schleiermacher can be detected. For this reason, it was not only because of the terminology, but also because of confessional reasoning, that Lutheran theology once again played a central role in the development of the law. It is part of a general phenomenon called "Neo-Lutheranism".[80]

As a concept, "family law" was coined against the political agenda of the French Revolution, and is clearly a political reactionary term. However, the term could be seen as problematic, since questions of rule and power should not be the leading concept in family matters any more, and the time has clearly come to acknowledge the equality and liberty of the family members even on the conceptual level. We

[75]von Kamptz, Karl Christoph Albert Heinrich. 1824. *Handbuch des Mecklenburgischen Civil-Rechts*. Schwerin: Stiller, 4. Titel: Familienrecht; Mittermaier, Carl Joseph Anton. 1824. *Grundsätze des gemeinen deutschen Privatrechts*. Landshut: Joseph Manz, 290; Mackeldey, Ferdinand. 1827. *Lehrbuch des heutigen römischen Rechts*. 7th ed., 2, Giessen: Geyer 3. Buch Familienrecht, 312, § 503—differently still in the 5th ed. Gießen 1823, 2, § 221: Personenrecht.

[76]For the evolution of the civil law system that shaped the German codification cf. Mathias Schmoeckel 2003 (as n. 72).

[77]Planck, Gottlieb. 1906. *Bürgerliches Gesetzbuch nebst Einführungsgesetz*, 3rd ed., Berlin: Guttentag, 3.

[78]Lefebvre-Teillard 1996 (as n. 60).

[79]Bonald, Louis-Gabriel-Ambroise Vicomte de. 1880. *Théorie du pouvoir politique et religieux*, Paris: Librairie d'Adrien le clere. Here: Théorie de l'éducation sociale, ch. 10, 355; Bonald, 1880 (as n. 79) l. 6, 235.

[80]Hornig 1894 (as n. 55), 174s.

have to accept that for good reason, many European states never introduced a "family law" into their legislation, just as France still retains its *droit des personnes* until now.

8 Development in the 20th Century

It has become commonplace to deny a leading role to the churches in modern Europe. The replacement of marriage by simple cohabitation or the increasing Muslim population in European States serve as first-hand evidence. Sociologists, however, have had problems in ascertaining that these pre-judices are true. Still, at the same time, the concept of "family law" has lost its theological affiliations and was even used by fascist or national-socialist dictators, as well as by Communist regimes. They certainly tried to adapt this subject to fit their purposes. But the question remains whether or not such a Christian concept retains its Christian core even in an agnostic state. There is perhaps no other subject closer related to Christianity than "family law". It is not necessarily a perpetual term, as it contains values that cannot be explained without their particular Christian background.

Furthermore, a closer look into the Church—State relations of the past few decades reveals a more enduring influence of the Churches on state affairs. In the case of Germany, the Roman Catholic and the representation of the Protestant Churches (EKD) both tried to influence fundamental decisions on modern family law issues. The last major success for the Protestant side was the introduction of the modern law of divorce in 1976.[81]

Any attempt to ignore the lasting influence of the Christian tradition risks misunderstanding these concepts. It might be simpler just to ignore the different traditions in Europe in order to establish a common family law,[82] but this would be to adopt a strategy with blinkers that try to hide what might be difficult. It did not even work for the colonial empires of the 19th century, which failed to introduce their legal systems in other continents in the long run. Evidently, the law is only accepted when it is in accordance with the domestic cultural tradition.

---

[81]Schubert, Werner. 2003. Abkehr vom Verschuldensprinzip im Ehescheidungsrecht, *ZRG GA* 120: 280–346.

[82]Without any respect for cultural or religious traditions Boele-Woelki, Katharina and Martiny Dieter. 2006. Prinzipien zum Europäischen Familienrecht betreffend Ehescheidung und nachehelicher Unterhalt. *Zeitschrift für Europäisches Privatrecht* 14: 6–20.

References

Sources

Alberigo, J. (Ed.). (1962). Concilium Tridentinum, session 24 of 11.11.1563: Doctrina de sacramento matrimonii, a.A. In *Conciliorum Oecumenicorum Decreta*. Basel: Herder.

Althusius, J. (1614). *Politica methodice digesta.* Herborn. reimpr. 1981. Aalen: Scientia Verlag.

Ambrosius. (1989). De institutione uirginis et sanctae Mariae uirginitate perpetua ad Eusebium. (Biblioteca Ambrosiana 14.2). In F. Gori (Ed.). Roma: Città Nuova.

Bergmann, F. C. (1810). *Lehrbuch des Privatrechts des Code Napoleon.* Göttingen: Vandenhoeck und Ruprecht.

Bodin, J. (1583). *Les six Livres de la République.* Paris, reimpr. 1961, Aalen: Scientia Verlag.

Bonald, Louis-Gabriel-Ambroise Vicomte de. (1880). *Théorie du pouvoir politique et religieux.* Paris: Librairie d'Adrien Le Clere.

Bracton, H. de. (1640). *De legibus et Consuetudinibus Angliae.* London, reimpr. 2009. New York: Clark.

Eichhorn, C. F. (1823). *Einleitung in das deutsche Privatrecht mit Einschluß des Lehensrechts.* Göttingen: Vandenhoeck und Ruprecht.

Fichte, J. G. (1797). Grundlage des Naturrechts. In M. Zahn (Ed.), (1979). Hamburg: Verlag F. Meiner.

Hegel, G. W. F. (1983). Die Philosophie des Rechts. Die Mitschriften Wannemann (Heidelberg 1817/8) und Homeyer (Berlin 1818/19). In K.-H. Ilting (Ed.), Stuttgart: Klett-Cotta.

Hegel, G. W. F. (1983). Die Philosophie des Rechts, die Vorlesung von 1819/20 in einer Nachschrift. In D. Henrich (Ed.), Frankfurt a.M: Suhrkamp.

Hegel, G. W. F. (1999). *Grundlinien der Philosophie des Rechts, Hauptwerke in 6 Bänden, 5.* Darmstadt: Verlag F. Meiner.

Heise, A., (1819). *Grundriss eines Systems eines gemeinen Civilrechts.* 3rd edn. Heidelberg: Mohr und Zimmer.

Hugo, G. (1799). *Lehrbuch eines civilistischen Cursus 2. ganz von neuem ausgearb. Versuch, 1.* Berlin: August Mylius.

John VIII. ed. E. C., & Laehr, G. (1912). Berlin. reimpr. 1993. München: Hahnsche Buchhandlung.

Jonas of Orléans. *De institutione laicali.* In *Patrologia Latina* 106, 122–278.

Kamptz, Karl Christoph Albert Heinrich von. (1824). *Handbuch des Mecklenburgischen Civil-Rechts.* Schwerin: Stiller.

Krug, W. T. (1817). *System der theoretischen Philosophie. Erster Theil: Rechtslehre.* Königsberg: Goebbels und Unzer.

Locke, J. (1993). Two treatises on government. In M. Goldie (Ed.), London-Vermont: J.M. Dent.

Luther, M., 1522. (1907), *Weimarer Ausgabe 10.2* (pp. 275–304). Weimar: Hermann Böhlaus Nachfolger.

Luther, M., 1530 (1910). *Von Ehesachen.* Weimarer Ausgabe 30.III (pp. 205–248). Weimar: Hermann Böhlaus Nachfolger.

Mackeldey, F. (1827). *Lehrbuch des heutigen römischen Rechts.* 7th edn. Giessen: Geyer.

Marculfi. Formularum libri duo. In A. Uddholm (Ed.), (1962). Uppsala: Eranos.

Melanchthon, P. (1542). *De aequitate et iure stricto.* Corpus Reformatorum 11, 550–555. (=trans. Beyer, Michael. 1997. *Billigkeit und strenges Recht,* in: Melanchthon Deutsch 1. Leipzig: Evangelische Verlags-Anstalt.

Mittermaier, C. J. A. (1821). *Lehrbuch des deutschen Privatrechts.* Landshut: Krüll.

Mittermaier, C. J. A. (1824). *Grundsätze des gemeinen deutschen Privatrechts.* Landshut: Joseph Manz.

Origenes. (1908). Fragmenta in I cor. 37. *Journal of Theological Studies, 9*, 500–514.
Planck, G. (1906). *Bürgerliches Gesetzbuch nebst Einführungsgesetz* (3rd ed.). Berlin: Guttentag.
Radbertus, P. (1852). Expositio in Evangelium Mattaei. *Patrologia Latina, 120*, 31–994.
Raymond of Penyafort. (1603). *Summa de poenitentia et matrimonio*. Rome. reimpr. 1967, Meisenheim-Glan: Gregg.
Savigny, F. C. von. (1840). *System des heutigen römischen Rechts* 1. Berlin: Veit und Comp.
Savigny, F. C. von. Landrechtsvorlesung 1824, Drei Nachschriften. In C. Wollschläger et al. (Eds.), (1998). (Ius Commune, Sonderhefte 104-Savignyana 3.2). Frankfurt a.M: Klostermann.
Savigny, F. C. von. *Pandektenvorlesung 1824/25*. In H. Hammen (Ed.), (1993) (Ius Commune 62-Savignyana 1). Frankfurt a.M: Klostermann.
Schleiermacher, F. D. E. (1984). *Gedanken 1*. In G. Meckenstock (Ed.), Schriften aus der Berliner Zeit 1796–1799 (Critical Edition 2). Berlin-New York: de Gruyter.
Schmelzeisen, G. K. (Ed.). (1968). *Preußische Landesordnung von 1577*. In Quellen zur Neueren Privatrechtsgeschichte Deutschlands 2. Polizei- und Landesordnungen 1. Weimar: Böhlau.
Winstanley, G. (1973). *The law of freedom in a platform*. London: Pelican.
Zeumer, K. (Ed.). (1902). *Leges Visigothorum*. In MGH. Legum Nationum Germanicarum 1. Hannover/Leipzig.

Bibliography

Airlie, Stuart. (1998). Private bodies and the body politic in the divorce case of lothar II. *Past & Present, 161*, 3–38.
Björne, L. (1984). *Deutsche Rechtssysteme im 18. und 19. Jahrhundert*. Ebelsbach: Gremer.
Boele-Woelki, K., & Martiny, D. (2006). Prinzipien zum Europäischen Familienrecht betreffend Ehescheidung und nachehelicher Unterhalt. *Zeitschrift für Europäisches Privatrecht, 14*, 6–20.
Brooke, C. N. L. (1980). Marriage Law in the XIth and XIIth Centuries. In St. Kuttner, & K. Pennington (Eds.), *Proceedings of the Fifth International Congress of Medieval Canon Law*, Monumenta iuris canonici. Città del Vaticano: Biblioteca Apostolica Romana, C.6, 333–344.
Carrodeguas, C. (2003). *La sacramentalidad del matrimonio. Doctrina de Tomás Sánchez* S.J., Madrid: Univ. Pontificia Comillas.
Crouzel, H. (1982). Ehe/Eherecht/Ehescheidung V: Alte Kirche, *TRE* (Vol. 9, pp. 325–330). Berlin-New York: de gruyter.
Duby, G. (1977). Le mariage dans la société du Haut Moyen Âge. In *Il Matrimonio nella società altomedievale* Settimane di Studio del Centro Italiano di Studi sull'Alto medioevo 24, 1 (pp. 15–39). Spoleto: Centro Italiano di Studi sull'Alto Medioevo.
Evans-Grubbs, J. (2008). Christianization of marriage? Christianity, marriage, and law in late antiquity. In A. Holzem & I. Weber (Eds.), *Ehe—Familie—Verwandtschaft. Vergesellschaftung in Religion und sozialer Lebenswelt* (pp. 105–124). Paderborn: Schöningh.
Frassek, R. (2005). *Eherecht und Ehegerichtsbarkeit in der Reformationszeit (Jus Ecclesiasticum 78)*. Tübingen: Mohr Siebeck.
Gaudemet, J. (1978). L'interprétation du principe d'indissolubilité du mariage chrétien au cours du premier millénaire. *Bullettino dell'Istituto di diritto romano, 81*, 11–69.
Gaudemet, J. (1987). *Le mariage en Occident*. Paris: Editions Du Cerf.
Harrington, J. (1992). A system of politics. In J.-G. A. Pocock (Ed.), *The commonwealth of oceana" and "A system of politics*. Cambridge: Cambridge University Press.
Hornig, G. (1894). Lehre und Bekenntnis im Protestantismus. In C. Andresen (1989) (Ed.), *Handbuch der Dogmen-und Theologiegeschichte* 3, reimpr. Göttingen: Vandenhoeck und Ruprecht.
Kaser, M. (1971). *Das römische Privatrecht. Erster Abschnitt: Das altrömische, das vorklassische und klassische Recht* (Rechtsgeschichte des Altertums, 2.3.1). München: C.H. Beck.
Kaser, M. (1975). *Das römische Privatrecht. Zweiter Abschnitt: Die nachklassischen Entwicklungen* (Rechtsgeschichte des Altertums 3.3.2). München: C.H. Beck.

Kleinheyer, B. (1984). Ordinationen und Beauftragung. In B. Kleinheyer, E. von Severus & R. Kaczynski (Eds.), *Sakramentliche Feiern II*, (Gottesdienst der Kirche. Handbuch der Liturgiewissenschaft 8). Regensburg: Verlag Friedrich Pustet.

Koch, E. (2008). Art. Familie, Familienrecht, *HRG* (2nd Edn., pp. 1497–1502). Berlin: Erich Schmidt Verlag.

Koselleck, R. (2006). Begriffsgeschichte. Studien zur Semantik und Pragmatik der politischen und sozialen Sprache. Frankfurt a.M: Suhrkamp.

Lefebvre-Teillard, A. (1996). Introduction historique au droit des personnes et de la famille. Paris: Puf.

Lemaire, A. (1929). La *dotatio* de l'épouse de l'époque mérovingienne au XIIIe siècle. *Revue historique de droit français et étranger, 4*(8), 569–580.

Martin, X. (2002). *Mythologie du Code Napoléon. Aux soubassements de la France moderne*. Paris: Editions Dominique Martin Morin.

Manns, P. (1995). Die Unauflösbarkeit der Ehe im Verständnis der frühmittelalterlichen Bußbücher. In T. Schneider (Ed.), *Geschieden. Wiederverheiratet. Abgewiesen? Antworten der Theologie* (pp. 84–111). Freiburg i.B.: Herder.

Marquardt, J. (1886). *Das Privatleben der Römer*, 1st part. Leipzig, reimpr. 1990, Darmstadt: Wissenschaftliche Buchgesellschaft.

Mette-Dittmann, A. (1991). *Die Ehegesetze des Augustus: Eine Untersuchung im Rahmen der Gesellschaftspolitik des princeps*. Stuttgart: Verlag Franz Steiner.

Mikat, P. (1978). *Dotierte Ehe—rechte Ehe. Zur Entwicklung des Eheschließungsrechts in fränkischer Zeit*, (Rheinisch-Westfälische Akademie der Wissenschaften, Vorträge G 227). Opladen: Rheinische-Westfälische Akademie der Wissenschaften. Geisteswissenschaften..

Müller, A. (1936). *Die Elemente der Staatskunst*. Berlin: Hendel.

Müller-Freienfels, W. (2003). The emergence of Droit de famille and Familienrecht in continental Europe and the introduction of family law in England. *Journal of Family History, 28*(1), 31–51.

Noonan, J. T. (1968). Novel 22. In W. W. Bassett (Ed.), *The bond of marriage*. Washington: Notre Dame Press.

Otis-Cour, L. (2000). *Lust und Liebe: Geschichte der Paarbeziehungen im Mittelalter*. Frankfurt a. M.: Fischer.

Padovani, A. (1997). *Perché chiedi il mio nome?*. Torino: Giappichelli.

Reynolds, P. L. (2007). Dotal Charters in the Frankish Tradition. In P. Reynolds, & J. Witte Jr. (Eds.), *To have and to hold. marrying and its documentation in western christendom 400–1600* (pp. 114–164). Cambridge: Cambridge University Press.

Saar, S. (2002). Ehe, *Scheidung, Wiederheirat. Studien zur Geschichte der Ehe und des Ehescheidungsrechts im Frühmittelalter (6.–10. Jahrhundert)*. Münster: Lit.

Schmoeckel, M. (2003). Der Allgemeine Teil in der Ordnung des BGB. In M. Schmoeckel, R. Zimmermann, & J. Rückert (Eds.), *Historisch-Kritischer Kommentar zum BGB, 1*. Mohr Siebeck: Tübingen.

Schmoeckel, M. (2007). Der lotharische Ehestreit: Seine Protagonisten und ihre Perspektiven. In U. Falk, M. Luminati, & M. Schmoeckel (Eds.), *Fälle aus der Rechtsgeschichte* (pp. 77–95). München: C.H. Beck.

Schmoeckel, M. (2008). Ansätze eines neuen Rechtssystems im 9. Jahrhundert. Bemerkungen zum Ehestreit Lothars II. In L. Waelkens (Ed.), *Aspecten van het middeleeuwse Romeinse Recht, Iuris Scripta Historica* (pp. 109–132). Bruxelles: Koninklijke Vlaamse Academie van België voor Wetenschappen en Kunsten, Comité Rechtsgeschiedenis 22.

Schmoeckel, M. (2016). Zur Bedeutung der Reformation für die Welt, *Zeitschrift der Savigny Stiftung. Kanonistische Abteilung KA* 101 (in press).

Schubert, W. (2003). Abkehr vom Verschuldensprinzip im Ehescheidungsrecht, *Zeitschrift der Savigny Stiftung. Germanistische Abteilung GA, 120*, 280–346.

Schwab, D. (1975). Art. Familie. In O. Koselleck, W. Conzen & R. Koselleck (Eds.), *Geschichtliche Grundbegriffe* 2 (pp. 253–301). Stuttgart: Klett-Cotta.

Thomas, K. (2008). Ehetheologie im Kontext der frühen Wittenberger Reformation. In A. Holzem, & I. Weber (Eds.), *Ehe—Familie—Verwandtschaft. Vergesellschaftung in Religion und sozialer Lebenswelt* (pp. 285–299). Paderborn: Schöningh.
Thomas, Y. (1993). Die Teilung der Geschlechter im Römischen Recht. In Pauline Schmitt Pantel (Ed.), *Geschichte der Frauen I: Antike* (pp. 105–171). Frankfurt a.M.: Zweitausendeins, 105–171.
van Haag, M. -F. (2014). *Recht in der Hausväterliteratur. Der "Oeconomus Prudens et Legalis" von Franz Philipp Florin im Kontext seiner Zeit.* Berlin: Lit.
Wasserschleben, F. W. H. (1851). *Poenitentiale Vinniani, Die Bußordnungen der abendländischen Kirche*, Halle. reimpr. 1958. Graz: Akademische Verlagsanstalt.
Weigand, R. (1967). Die Lehre der Kanonisten des 12. und 13. Jahrhunderts von den Ehewecken, *Studia Gratiana* 12 (=Collectanea Stephan Kuttner 2), 443–478.
Weigand, R. (1971). Kanonistische Ehetraktate aus dem 12. Jahrhundert. In St. Kuttner (Ed.), *Proceedings of the Third International Congress of Medieval Canon Law*, Monumenta iuris canonici (pp. 60–79). Città del Vaticano: Biblioteca Apostolica Romana, C.4.
Weigand, R. (1993). *Liebe und Ehe im Mittelalter*. Goldbach: Keip.
Wemple, S. F. (1985). *Women in Frankish Society. Marriage and the Cloister 500–900*. Philadelphia: University of Pennsylvania Press.
Wenz, G. (1998). *Art. Sakramente I, TRE 29* (pp. 663–703). Berlin-New York.
Witte, J. jr. (2002). *Law and Protestantism*. Cambridge: Cambridge University Press.
Witte, J. jr. (2007). *The Reformation of Rights. Law, Religion, and Human Rights in Early Modern Calvinism*. Cambridge: Cambridge University Press.
Witte, J. jr. (2015). *The Western Case for Monogamy over Polygamy*. Cambridge: Cambridge University Press.

The Catalan *Sagrada Família*: Law and Family in Medieval and Modern Catalonia

Tünde Mikes and Tomàs de Montagut

Abstract Catalonia is a land of Europe that has been participating in European legal culture since the Middle Ages. The basic institution of traditional Catalan society was the family (household); its articulation with the farmstead (*mas*) and farmhouse (*masia*), as well as with the patrimony (the family estate) and the legal matrimonial and inheritance system, was structural. Clear proof of the strength of the family institution on all levels is the duration over time of thousands of family or patrimonial archives, the vast majority of which correspond to families of peasant origin. The primordial legal documents of these households were marriage contracts: veritable family charters, examples of Catalan contractual law and the basis of the family and patrimonial system. They were drawn up at one of the most significant moments for the household: that of the heir's marriage. The fact that such contracts were abundant demonstrates the growing strength of the stem family, which revolved around patrimony and a society of households. At the turn of the 20th century, to ensure the continuity of Catalonia as a people with a political and cultural identity of their own, a people that had kept their historic private law alive and flourishing, the myth of the ancestral family home (*casa pairal*) emerged and focus was again placed on the strength of the traditional Catalan family—precisely when the construction of the Sagrada Família Temple was moving forward with the greatest strength and vitality.

T. Mikes (✉)
University of Girona, Campus Montilivi, 17003 Girona, Spain
e-mail: tunde.mikes@udg.edu

T. de Montagut
University Pompeu Fabra of Barcelona, Plaça de la Mercè 10-12, 08002 Barcelona, Spain
e-mail: tomas.montagut@upf.edu

M.G. di Renzo Villata (ed.), *Family Law and Society in Europe from the Middle Ages to the Contemporary Era*, Studies in the History of Law and Justice 5,
DOI 10.1007/978-3-319-42289-3_2

1 Introduction:[1] The Catalan Legal System and the Family in History

The Sagrada Família (Holy Family) is a Catholic temple designed by the architect Antoni Gaudí (1852–1926). It is the most emblematic building of Barcelona and, to a certain degree, of Catalan society, given that Barcelona is considered the 'head and home' (*cap i casal*) of Catalonia.

The Catalans wished to build this monument to the model family of Joseph, Mary and Jesus, thereby honouring, and to a large degree sacralizing, the Catalan family as it had historically been expressed through the power of households and family lineages, which were the bedrock of Catalan society and its political and legal institutions.

The Catalan legal system, via customs (customary or consuetudinary law), legislation and jurisprudence, had gradually built the legal framework comprising the Catalan familial, inheritance and patrimonial systems, the foundations of Catalonia's political composition.

This corporatist family model would enter into decline in the second half of the 19th century, due to the Industrial Revolution and the new liberal doctrines that fostered secularization of individual rights and liberties to the detriment of the family and the ties and duties binding individuals to the household of their forebears.

It was at this time of crisis and mystification of the traditional Catalan family that construction began on the Sagrada Família church. This temple was a clear expression of the 'ancestral home' ideology that, in a Romantic and Christian manner, sought to idealize the past—and in this case, the traditional Catalan family as well—in order to legitimize the rebirth of Catalonia and of a new patriotic Catalan social movement that was at once innovative and conservative.

How did Catalan society and the Catalan legal code form insofar as its socio-cultural reproduction over the course of medieval and modern times? What is the history of Catalan familial culture in this context?

In this article, we will discuss the historic dynamics of Catalonia's legal-political framework and, within it, the institutional family processes that allowed the existence of households and their family patrimony, as well as their sociocultural and biological reproduction and perpetuation.

---

[1]Tünde Mikes is the author of the third and fourth parts of this article. Her work forms part of the research done within the ARXIUS FAMILIARS I PATRIMONIALS DE BANDA A BANDA DELS PIRINEUS—2013 CTP 00017 thematic network, in turn part of the programme 'ARCHIFAM—Los archivos de familia en la Península Ibérica (finales del siglo XIII—principios del siglo XVII)', of the École des Hautes Études Hispaniques et Ibériques (EHEHI)/Casa de Velázquez, Madrid. Tomàs de Montagut is the author of the first and second parts of this article. His work forms part of the research project, *Juristas hispánicos: entre el imperio del derecho y la gestión del poder (s.XII–XXI)*, funded by Spanish Ministry of the Economy and Competitiveness (MINECO DER-2013-43431-P), with the support of the Catalan Government (Generalitat de Catalunya 2014 SGR295-SFR.V).

2 The Origins and Historical Evolution of Catalonia and Its Legal System

2.1 The Origins

As is known, the historical antecedents of the birth of Catalonia as a political community with full public power and endowed with its own legal system must be sought in the process of independence from the Carolingian Empire, which the Catalan counts, led by the Count of Barcelona, carried out over a lengthy period of time.[2]

The Moorish invasion of the Iberian Peninsula (711) spelled the downfall of the Visigothic monarchy. Most of its dominions became part of the Caliphate of Damascus and its successor, the independent Caliphate of Cordoba. By 718, the Moors had reached Narbonne, and it was not until 732/733 that Charles Martell defeated them at Poitiers, a victory that initiated the recovery of the Christian lands that had been lost to the South.

With the conquest of Barcelona by Louis the Pious in 801, a number of territories were incorporated into the Carolingian Empire, forming its Spanish March or line of defence. These would eventually become the area of Old Catalonia, organised politically as administrative divisions of the Empire and called counties because they were controlled by counts appointed freely by the Emperor as officials of the Empire.

In practice, however, these county officials rapidly turned into hereditary counts. Among them Wilfred the Hairy of the House of Barcelona became dominant and succeeded in grouping the counties of Barcelona, Girona, Ausona, Besalú, Cerdanya, Berga and Urgell under his command. He too applied private succession rules, sharing out the inheritance of the office of count and the counties among his children. With this affirmation of the right of transferring counties *mortis causa*, the march towards the independence of the counties from the Empire began.

The Moorish punitive attack on Barcelona, led by the troops of the Caliphate of Cordoba under al-Mansur in 985, meant that the relationship of Count Borrell II of Barcelona with the Carolingian Empire was redefined. The initial lack of Carolingian support and the subsequent refusal to accept imperial protection are interpreted by historians as the de facto achievement of Catalan independence. Independence *de iure* came later, and was not recognised by the Frankish monarchy until the 13th century, when King Louis IX of France did so formally through the Treaty of Corbeil, signed in 1258 by King James I, the Conqueror.

The public law in force in the Catalan counties of the Spanish March generally consisted of Carolingian capitularies, which established the legal system, either for the Empire as a whole or specifically for certain territories, individuals or

[2]D'Abadal, Ramon. 1958. *Els primers comtes catalans*. Barcelona: Editorial Teide. This section is partially based on the English version of: Montagut Estragués, Tomàs de. 2015. *Una mirada a la història jurídica de Catalunya i als seus drets històrics*. Barcelona: IEC, 173–176.

communities. It stipulated the personal conditions of the *hispani*—the inhabitants of these counties—, the immunities of certain monasteries and the fiscal contributions of goods and lands by private individuals and communities, among other matters.

Private law in this period was characterised by the survival of the legal regime established by the Visigoths through their book compiling the royal Visigothic laws, known as the *Liber Iudiciorum* or *Liber Iudicum*, which was originally written in the mid-7th century. The *hispani* maintained the Visigothic juridical tradition, in terms of the contents of the *Liber Iudiciorum*, in part because the Franks' legal system was flexible, such that their juridical relations with the peoples subject to their dominion were highly personalized. In this sense, the Catalan counties took part in a type of Roman legal culture derived from the legal tradition of the Western Roman Empire, which had been previously schematised in the Theodosian Code (438) and the Breviary of Alaric (506).

2.2 *The Feudal Monarchy*

The *Liber iudicum popularis* was drawn up on the initiative of Judge Bonsom in a Barcelona scriptorium in 1011. It was a summary of the *Liber Iudicum* created to assist Judges in the administration of the Law. This code bears eloquent witness to the ongoing existence of a link in Barcelona between the Count's public authority and the Visigothic tradition and its law-book, the *Liber Iudiciorum* (the standard code). The adjective 'popular' in this law-book alludes to its character as an instrument of public authority with which the rights of the people were protected, as a whole and regardless of the privileges of the Estates.

Moreover, in the same code we find the complete *Simbolum*, along with a wide variety of formulas of this same symbol of faith, extracted in order to formulate the exorcisms complementing the standard code. They are an example of a type of juridical thought that was different but already coexistent with the thought intrinsic to the laws of the Visigothic monarchs. Remember that this symbol of the apostles was the liturgical prayer that we know today by the name of the *Credo*, the baptismal profession of faith of the Catholic Church. Remember too that with the sacrament of baptism one entered the Christian community at a time when this was the only recognised political community. There was confusion between Religion and Law, which involved the identification of Christian natural law with positive law. '*Credo in unum Deum... visibilium et invisibilium omnium conditorem...*' (p. 622); '*Deus iudex iustus, fortis et patiens qui est auctor et creator*' (p. 796); '*per quem facta sunt omnia*' (p. 794).[3] God is all-powerful and the creator of all things, such that it is He who has established Law in Society. Humans cannot create or

[3]Alturo, Jesús; Bellès, Joan; Font, Josep M.; García, Yolanda; and Mundó, Anscari (eds.). 2003. *El Liber Iudicum Popularis*. Barcelona: Generalitat de Catalunya, Departament de Justícia i Interior.

establish Law, but can discover or choose it directly by affirming it or indicating it by their will, their words and their individual and arbitrary behaviour or conduct.

This *Liber iudicorum* code bears witness to the fact that in early 11th-century Catalonia, two ideas coexisted: an objective concept of law, enshrined in the code containing the tradition of Visigothic Law, and a new and emerging subjective concept of law, appearing in legal thought linked to religion and exorcism through trial by ordeal. It heralded the formation of a new society, in which public power was in decline and mechanisms of self-tutelage linked to feudal and lordly practices were on the rise.

In consequence, 11th-century Catalonia underwent a crisis in the monarchy and a rise in polyarchy, as demonstrated by the prolific construction of castles and establishment of fiefs, phenomena which went hand in hand with the military and repopulating drive southwards from Old Catalonia, at the expense of the Moorish land that would soon be known as New Catalonia. Private individuals sought to achieve important social positions and defended these directly by affirming that their situation, habits, practices and customs comprised their law, inasmuch as God had wished it so. It is the manifestation in Catalonia of that famous European aphorism or motto, "*Dieu et mon droit*" (God and my right). It opened the road to the establishment of the feudal society of the three Estates. The clergy, the nobility and the commoners obtained specific legal status based on the principles of inequality and lordly privilege, but also of communal liberties.

The conflicts occurring within this polyarchic society of Estates in Catalonia were resolved either by coercion or consensus. In the first case, the conflicting parties could legitimately use force to impose their respective subjective law. In this sense, private war, feuding, personal vengeance or extra-judicial pledges were institutions in force in Catalonia. In the second case (i.e. covenants or negotiations), an agreement between persons could be reached. This agreement took the juridical form of the '*communiae*' or the '*convenientiae*'—one of the oldest examples of what is known as Catalan *pactisme* ('pactism'). Conflicts could also be resolved by the intervention of the judicial community and assembly, in which the Count presided over the meeting of '*maiores et meliores*' of corporate society, which had to ascertain which of the litigating parties had the 'good and better' law. In these judicial sessions, called '*placita*' or '*iudicatum*', in which there was no verdict because there was no recognised objective law applicable, it was possible to resort to trial by ordeal in default of other ordinary proofs. The latter was a 'trial of God', given that it was He who declared which was the better law and not man or the public power of the Count, which had entered into crisis.

The excessive violence of this high-medieval Catalan society caused the Church to intervene. It struggled decidedly to restrict violence by calling Assemblies of Peace and Truce, convening the '*maiores*' and '*meliores*', the clergy and nobility, who forbade iniquitous violence under penalty of canonical sanction and gradually limited the cases in which individuals were permitted to exercise legitimate violence in defence of their rights. Under these peace precepts, violence in public or communal places—roads, markets, churches, cemeteries, sanctuaries and the like—was prohibited. Violence against the defenceless, such as widows, orphans, members of religious orders or the poor, who due to their personal position could not directly defend their rights, as they had no arms with which to do so, was also prohibited. With the precepts of the Truce of God (*Treva de Déu*), the imposition of private law by force was forbidden in specific periods and on certain days of the year because of their religious significance, according to the liturgical calendar. Initially religious and ecclesiastic in nature, the Assemblies of Peace and Truce also became a political instrument to strengthen the power of the Counts when they intervened in them. They strengthened their authority by threatening those who broke the observance of the precepts of Peace and Truce with civil penalties. Thus, in Catalonia the rebirth of public power is essentially originally linked to the mission of protecting people's rights.

As of the second half of the 11th century, one can see how the Count of Barcelona was building a feudal monarchy by affirming his political hegemony over the other Catalan counts and lords. Among the means he used to strengthen his power were three particularly relevant ones: leading the war of expansion towards the south against the Moors of Hispania; signing many *convenientiae* with the *maiores* and *meliore*s of Catalonia; and organizing and holding the Judicial Assemblies and Assemblies of Peace and Truce.

Through their military leadership in the wars against the Moors, the Counts of Barcelona won prestige, authority and the financial resources of the *paries* or tributes paid by the Moors in exchange for peace. Through the *convenientiae*, the Count of Barcelona became, *de iure* and through the channel of private contract, the vertex of the feudal pyramid of Catalonia. There was a written record of the oath of loyalty and homage rendered him by the other contracting parties, who received the protection of the Count in return. The judicial Assemblies presided over by the Counts of Barcelona tackled the most difficult issues arising in Catalonia, mostly of a feudal or lordly nature. The normal criteria used to resolve these cases, i.e. the most common at the Assemblies, became, over time and once they were written down, the famous 'Usages of Barcelona' (*Usatges de Barcelona*), the text containing the legal regulations to be used throughout Catalonia, wherever there was belief and trust in the Count of Barcelona's word. The Usages of Barcelona became the leading document in the general law of Catalonia, and at the same time, the Count of Barcelona came to be considered the Prince, i.e. the first among Catalan counts. This is why Catalonia, though a European Christian monarchy, was established as a Principality and not as a Kingdom.

Thus, over time, the Count of Barcelona became the Prince of Catalonia under the authority of the *Usatges de Barcelona*, the first code that contained the general laws of Catalonia, which began to be put into writing in the 12th century.[4] The prince's power, however, ran more deeply, specifically in feudal processes of private power represented by the legal institutions of oaths of fealty and homage, as

[4]Bastardas, Joan. 1984. *Usatges de Barcelona. El Codi a mitjan segle XII.* Barcelona: Fundació Noguera, 7–38.

well as in the earlier tradition of private law, represented by the survival of Visigothic Law contained in the epitomes of the *Liber Iudiciorum* of former Visigoth monarchs.[5]

2.3 *The Monarchy of Estates*

The 12th century also witnessed how the notion of *iurisdictio* (jurisdiction) was used in Europe in the construction of valid processes of public power (Empire and Church). Soon this concept was transferred effectively to different emerging Christian monarchies and became a useful legal-political instrument for the monarchs leading these national communities, which were part of the Christian empire *de jure* but not de facto.[6] Over the course of the Middle Ages, lower-tier political entities that were more personal in nature or smaller in geographical scope, such as municipalities, baronies, guilds and other kinds of *universitates* or corporations, also gained the power of jurisdiction, albeit of a special nature, at a lower rank than the monarch and only in certain matters, since the monarchy reserved some spheres for itself as royalty.

In the 13th century, the *Commemoracions de Pere Albert*, which complemented and updated the *Usatges de Barcelona*, granted the Count of Barcelona—now also the King of Aragon—overall jurisdiction over the entire Principality of Catalonia.[7]

However, this jurisdiction was doubly conditioned, first by the configuration of the Crown of Aragon as a territorial Union made up of the different kingdoms and lands of the monarch, one of whose founding members was the Principality of Catalonia.

This Union meant that the monarch had a certain universal jurisdiction which extended over all the territories in the Crown in certain matters like war, justice and foreign relations, while it respected and protected the general jurisdiction of each of them and the independence of their respective legal systems.[8]

Likewise, the general jurisdiction of the Count of Barcelona—and Prince of Catalonia—was soon conditioned by some of Catalonia's *constitucions* ('laws') and by *pactisme* ('pactism' or making legal pacts), the contractual doctrine according to

[5]Alturo, Bellès, Font, García, and Mundó (as in Note 3).

[6]Costa, Pietro. 2002. *Iurisdictio: Semantica del potere politico en la pubblicistica medievale (1100–1433)*. Milan: Giuffrè, 63–91.

[7]Ferran, Elisabet. 2006. *El jurista Pere Albert i les Commemoracions*. Barcelona: Institut d'Estudis Catalans, 233–256.

[8]Montagut, Tomàs de. 1999. La Justicia en la Corona de Aragón. In *La administración de justicia en la historia de España. Actas de las III Jornadas de Castilla-La Mancha sobre investigación en archivos (noviembre 1997)*. Guadalajara: Junta de Comunidades de Castilla-La Mancha, 650–655; Montagut, Tomás de. 2013. La Constitució política de la Corona d'Aragó. In Isabel Falcón (ed.). *El Compromiso de Caspe (1412). Cambios dinásticos y Constitucionalismo en la Corona de Aragón*. Saragossa: XIX Congreso de Historia de la Corona de Aragón, 104–116.

which some jurists established a range of constitutional principles that affected the nature of the supreme political power of Catalonia and the production, application and interpretation of Catalan laws.[9] Thus, the necessary intervention of the leading social Estates in Catalonia was established through the operation of its supreme governance at the hands of the prince, and the monarch was required to swear his observance of Catalan law if he wished to earn general jurisdiction over Catalonia. In this sense, Catalan law, which is called historical Catalan law today, was made up of the *Usatges de Barcelona*, the *constitucions* and *capítols* (capitularies) approved by the Catalan Courts (parliamentary body), and the other laws of Catalonia, meaning the privileges, freedoms and customs of the universities (municipalities and different corporations) and its people (as individuals or in aggregation as a plurality). Historical Catalan law also included European common law (Roman-canonical) and equality and sound reason, which were determined by jurists (judges, lawyers, consultants, etc.) in the practical exercise of their professions and when resolving the specific cases they were familiar with and weighed or decided.[10]

Therefore, historical Catalan law was a pluralistic legal system due to the number of sources comprising it: laws and customs from Catalonia, judicial and doctrinal jurisprudence from Catalonia and Europe, and civil and canonical norms common to Christian Europe. Another unique feature of historical Catalan law was the fact that it was an open legal system because its application to each specific case depended on the cultural context of the moment, and the job of the jurists and notaries involved was to interpret it. Catalan law was not closed or fully predetermined in a single code or book of laws!

During the historic process that validated 'pactism' (13th–18th centuries), different political and administrative institutions were founded, grew and were formalised, including the *Cort General de Catalunya* (General Court of Catalonia, a parliamentary body) and the *Deputació del General de Catalunya* (General Deputation of Catalonia, another political body). The General Court of Catalonia, whose origins are not yet clear,[11] was the institutional framework that, through a parliamentary procedure,[12] established the pact between the Estates of the People

[9]Ferro, Victor. 1987. *El Dret Públic Català. Les Institucions a Catalunya fins al Decret de Nova Planta.* Vic: Eumo, 295–310.

[10]Montagut, Tomàs de. 2003. Els juristes de Catalunya i la seva organització collegial a l'època medieval. *Ius Fugit* 12, 269–302.

[11]Fernández Viladrich, Jesús. Fernández Viladrich 1982. Notas en torno a las asambleas condales en la Cataluña de la Alta Edad Media. *Estudis Històrics i documents dels arxius de protocols* 10, 7–88; Gonzalvo, Gener. Gonzalvo 1991. Les assemblees de Pau i Treva i l'origen de la Cort General de Catalunya. In *Les Corts a Catalunya. Actes del Congrés d'Història Institucional.* Barcelona: Generalitat de Catalunya, Departament de Cultura, 71–78.

[12]Montagut, Tomàs de. de Montagut 1998. Estudi introductori. In Peguera, Lluis de, (Facsimile, Barcelona: Rafel Figueró, 1701), *Practica, forma, y estil de celebrar Corts Generals en Cathalunya, y materias incidents en aquellas,* VII–LVII. Madrid: Centro de Estudios Constitucionales.

and the King—the branches and head, respectively—of the Principality of Catalonia in the guise of a corporation of corporations.

In effect, the Estates that were represented in the Courts (barons and knights; prelates and men of the cloth; citizens and honorary citizens) took turns to temporarily represent the *Universitas Cathaloniae*, that is the *Populus* of Catalonia, since a fictitious political person required that a permanent body be created which would continuously express its will. This was the origin of the General Deputation of Catalonia, the body that permanently represented the Parliament (*General*), which was soon also known by the name of the *Generalitat*. Royal Decree Law 41/1977, dated 29 September 1977, which created the provisional *Generalitat* of Catalonia, was referring to this historical and political institution when it stated that "*la Generalidad de Cataluña es una institución secular en la que el pueblo catalán ha visto el símbolo y el reconocimiento de su personalidad histórica, dentro de la unidad de España*"[13] (i.e. "the Generalitat of Catalonia is an age-old institution in which the Catalan people see the symbol and recognition of its historical identity, within the unity of Spain).

In consequence, Catalonia as a Principality, that is, as a general community, was politically and institutionally represented by both the Prince and the '*General del Principat de Catalunya*' or government comprised of the three Estates of Catalonia. The latter was represented by the Deputation (*Deputació del General*) or *Generalitat*, a permanent body. The prince also represented all of the Crown of Aragón and each of the other kingdoms and territories comprising it. In contrast, the *Generalitat* exclusively represented the Principality of Catalonia and its political community, the historical, direct forerunner of today's Catalan people.

In the 15th century, the personal union of the Catholic Monarchs led to the personal union of the Crown of Aragon with Castile, as well as the chronic absenteeism of the monarchs, who from then on lived almost permanently outside of Catalonia.

In this context, the *Generalitat* became the only higher institution with supreme representation for Catalonia that actually resided in the Principality itself.

Today we know more about the process of the formation of the Generalitat,[14] the era when it was at its institutional peak,[15] its reform or rearrangement by Ferdinand the Catholic, its adaptation to the universal empire of the Habsburgs,[16] its rupture

---

[13]Benet, Josep. Benet 1990. "Precedentes Históricos del Estatuto", *Comentarios sobre el Estatuto de Autonomía de Cataluña*, 3 vols. Barcelona: Institut d'Estudis Autonòmics 1, 62.

[14]Estrada-Rius, Albert. Estrada-Rius 2001. Els orígens de la Generalitat de Catalunya (La Deputació del General de Catalunya: dels precedents a la reforma de 1413). Barcelona: unpublished doctoral thesis, Universitat Pompeu Fabra.

[15]Sánchez de Movellán, Isabel. Sánchez de Movellán 2004. *La Diputació del General de Catalunya (1413–1479)*. Barcelona: Generalitat de Catalunya—Institut d'Estudis Catalans.

[16]Pérez Latre, Miquel. Pérez Latre 2004. *Entre el rei i la terra. El poder polític a Catalunya al segle XVI.* Vic: Eumo.

with Philip IV and the return to obedience,[17] and its subsequent evolution within the active, modern framework of the dualistic constitution or body politic of Catalonia.[18]

2.4 *Catalonia Under Absolutism and Liberalism*

Also familiar is Catalonia's defeat in the War of Spanish Succession[19] and the abolition of Catalan institutions and public law with the Bourbons' *Nueva Planta* Decree (1716),[20] which mutilated what we today call historical Catalan law, leaving only private, criminal and procedural law barely subsistent and in force—mere fragments of its former legal system.

However, the vindicatory memory of the institutions of self-governance which were eliminated by the Bourbons and the process of rebirth and partial recovery of the autonomy lost in the 18th–20th centuries took shape at critical moments of political rupture or reformist transition during this historical period, especially upon the introduction of the first Constitutional State of Spain with the approval of the 1812 Constitution of Cádiz; and 100 years later with the fall of the monarchy and the proclamation of the Catalan Republic in Barcelona on 14 April 1931, just a few hours before the Spanish Republic was also proclaimed in Madrid.

3 The Family and Family Law in Catalonia in the Middle Ages and the Modern Era

3.1 *The Catalan Legal System, Its Civil Law and Patrimonial Archives*

The role of civil law in 19th-century Catalonia was considered of capital importance, in a manner similar to other northern territories of the Spanish monarchy (the territories of '*dret foral*', i.e. charter or *fuero* civil law).

[17]Capdeferro, Josep. Capdeferro 2004. La Deputació del General al segle XVII. In *L'autogovern de Catalunya.* Barcelona: Fundació Lluís Carulla, 51–56.

[18]Capdeferro, Josep, and Serra, Eva. Capdeferro and Serra 2015. El Tribunal de Contrafaccions de Catalunya i la seva activitat (1702–1713). *Textos Jurídics Catalans* 34, Barcelona.

[19]Albareda, Joaquim. Albareda 2000. *La guerra de Successió i l'Onze de Setembre.* Barcelona: Editorial Empúries.

[20]Gay, Josep Maria. 1982. La génesi del Decret de Nova Planta de Catalunya. Edició de la consulta original del 'Consejo de Castilla' de 13 de juny de 1715. *Revista Jurídica de Catalunya* 81.1: 7–42; Gay, Josep Maria. 1982. La gènesi del Decret de Nova Planta de Catalunya. Edició de la consulta original del 'Consejo de Castilla' de 13 de juny de 1715 (Second Part). *Revista Jurídica de Catalunya* 81.2, 263–348; Gay, Josep Maria. 1997. *El corregidor a Catalunya.* Madrid: Marcial Pons, 90–127.

The relevance of historic civil law—above all family and inheritance law—becomes particularly evident at the time of the 19th-century liberal revolution, when this law and its defence—included in the reports and annexes drawn up in preparation for the Spanish Civil Code of 1889[21]—became one of the symbols of identity in the emergence of Catalan national sentiment; a period in which jurists created a *pairalista* or ancestral home discourse[22] mythologizing the Catalan legal order and its institutions.[23]

Patrimonial archives,[24] one of the most important and abundant places where the most significant private legal documents were kept since medieval times, generally belonged to noble families. In Catalonia, above all in Old Catalonia (*Catalunya Vella*),[25] we also find an exceptional wealth of patrimonial documents among peasant households. The existence of such archives among this social group is an exceptional or highly unusual phenomenon for the Middle Ages or Modern Era in other European regions. They were peasant families with farmsteads of a certain size,[26] which began keeping accounts of the farmstead economy and eventually accumulated more or less plentiful archives. By the 17th and 18th centuries, they would sometimes draw up 'master books' (*llibres mestres*)[27] of their archives and at times also 'family books' (*llibres de família*) drafted by the heads of household for their heirs. These books coincided with a period of economic boom in Catalonia, as

---

[21]Tomas y Valiente, Francisco. 1979. *Manual de Historia del Derecho español*. Madrid: Ed. TECNOS, 571–591.

[22]By the term '*pairalism*' we are referring to an ideological construct of Occitan roots but born in turn-of-the-century Catalonia, with a strong influence from works by Fréderic le Play, which referenced and idealized the world of wealthy farmers and their *masies* (farmsteads) at the historic point when they and agricultural society in general were entering into crisis. Cf: Congost Colomer, Rosa. 1998. El pairalisme. Reflexions sobre una paraula, un concepte i dues conjuntures. *Estudis d'Història Agrària* 12: 7–16.

[23]Terradas Saborit, Ignasi. 2001. La casa mítica i la casa jurídica: reflexions sobre un contrast entre el País Basc i Catalunya. In Ferrer i Mallol, Teresa; Mitgé i Vives, Josefina; Riu i Riu, Manuel (eds.). *El mas català durant l'Edat Mitjana i la Moderna (segles IX-XVIII). Aspectes arqueològics, històrics, geogràfics, arquitectònics i antropològics.* Barcelona: CSIC, Institució Milà i Fontanals, 51–56.

[24]The term 'patrimonial archives' (*arxius patrimonials*) used in Catalan bibliography refers to family collections of archival documentation that bear witness to the formation and transmission of their agriculture-based patrimony.

[25]Old Catalonia (*Catalunya Vella*) was a legal concept created by the jurist Pere Albert in the second quarter of the 13th century. The term was also used by historians of the Modern Age during the 16th and 17th centuries and is understood as the Mediterranean territories of north-eastern Catalonia.

[26]Approximately 100 hectares or more. Cf. Ferrer Alòs, Llorenç. Ferrer Alòs 1998. Sistema hereditario y reproducción social en Cataluña. In *Nécessités économiques et pratiques juridiques: problèmes de la transmission des exploitations agricoles (XVIIIe–XXe siècles)*. Rome: Mélanges de l'École Française de Rome. Italie et Méditerranée, 53–57, 55.

[27]These books, like chartularies, contained all notarized or private deeds relating to the patrimony considered of interest to retain; Bosch, Mònica and Gifre, Pere. Bosch and Gifre 1998. Els llibres mestres dels arxius patrimonials. Una font per a l'estudi de les estratègies patrimonials. *Estudis d'Història Agrària* 12: 155–182.

well as consolidation of the farmstead system and the Catalan *masia*, or farmhouse, typology.[28]

The earliest documents in the patrimonial archives of wealthy peasants can easily go back to the 11th or 12th centuries, although they could be generated at any time. They demonstrate a latent evolution in parallel to the socioeconomic progress of the peasantry or farming class, which gained greater status in the 16th century, strengthened by the medieval crisis and peasant wars of the previous century and entering a period of prosperity. In the second half of the 17th century these peasants experienced a major social rise, eventually becoming the *hisendats*[29] of the 19th century. Their archives grew in parallel to their patrimony. They contained documents regarding the establishment of the patrimony and its administration, as well as papers of personal or family interest relating to the private relations of those who were the subjects of this process of creation. They could also contain some extraneous documentation.

The core of these patrimonial archives are documents referring to the establishment of the patrimony, as for instance, contracts of constitution and negotiation of legal ownership or fee simple, *establiments* (a form of emphyteusis), contracts of purchase or transfer, etc. There are also documents of privilege accrediting a certain social status, legal documents, materials from lawsuits and the like. All of these documents could form part of the archives of families with a great deal of assets, such as peasants or noble families. In any case, said documents identified and justified their rights or served as tools for controlling their patrimony.[30]

The deeds kept in these archives were legal instruments primarily created during the 13th–18th centuries, the Monarchy of Estates period, and were faithful representatives of the Catalan legal system of the time. In the Early Middle Ages, this system was based on consuetudinary or customary law, and to a lesser extent on law arising from royal (comital) legislation, and focussing on the principles of public law. It contained few institutions of civil or private law—which in any case were associated with the tradition of the *Líber Iudiciorum* of the Visigoth monarchs. It was beginning in the 13th century, as part of the Crown of Aragon, that the legal system was enriched through a new form of legislation, negotiated or 'pacted' between the king and the parliamentary body or Courts (the above-stated

[28]Torres Sans, Xavier. Torres Sans 2000. *Els llibres de família de pagès; memòries de pagès, memòries de mas (segles XVI-XVIII)*. Biblioteca d'Història Rural, Col·lecció Fonts 1. Girona: CCCG Edicions; Associació d'Història Rural de les Comarques Gironines; Institut de Llengua i Cultura Catalanes de la Universitat de Girona, 15–63.

[29]The *hisendats*, similar to the landed gentry of England, were members of an urban ruling social class resulting from an economic and social rise of rural origin. They were landowners who moved to cities, often Barcelona, whence they controlled and directed their farmsteads.

[30]Gifre, Pere; Matas, Josep; and Soler, Santi. Gifre et al. 2002. *Els arxius patrimonials*. Biblioteca d'Història Rural, Collecció Fonts 2. Girona: CCCG Edicions; Associació d'Història Rural de les Comarques Gironines; Institut de Llengua i Cultura Catalanes de la Universitat de Girona, 9–25.

'pactism'). Up to the late 16th century—the most productive one—the most typical Catalan civil institutions would be created via such copious legislative work.[31]

Legal creation activity decreased after the General Courts session presided by Philip III of Castile (Philip II of Catalonia) in Barcelona in the year 1599. Legislation was less abundant because the Courts were not called into session: the Estates only met with the king twice during the Minor Habsburg[32] period. Up until the early 18th century, only one *constitució* referred to the principles of civil law.[33] Since the law was not being modernized through legislation created in the Courts, the greatest relevance would go to the work of the Catalan jurisconsults of the time, namely doctors in law and judges. Their work was productive in precepts of civil law arising from practice and the fair resolution of cases, as demonstrated by the works of Joan Pere Fontanella, the Catalan jurist of greatest fame in Europe, known for his books throughout the continent.[34]

This legislation came from the institutions of power, was agreed or 'pacted' in the Courts and reflected the consolidation interests of a new ruling class moving towards nobility. The modern Catalan nobility of mixed origin, which was formed through a reorganization of the traditional nobility, the ranks of honoured citizens[35] and the social rise of legal and medical professionals,[36] was both the creator and beneficiary of this legislation, primarily in the 15th and 16th centuries.[37] Such legislation also accompanied the social rise of the well-off peasantry keeping patrimonial archives and protecting the interests of their families, who ruled from their increasingly magnificent *masies.*[38]

[31]Sobrequés i Vidal, Santiago. 1978. *Història de la producció del dret català fins al Decret de Nova Planta.* Girona: Universitat Autònoma de Barcelona—Collegi Universitari de Girona, 25–64.

[32]The 'Minor Habsburg' Kings (*àustries menors*) were the kings of the House of Habsburg in Spain in their period of decline: Philip III of Castille (II of Catalonia, 1598–1621), Philip IV of Castille (III of Catalonia, 1621–1665) and Charles II (1665–1700).

[33]Regarding contracts and *violaris* (i.e. *violaria* or lifetime pensions), cf. Brocà, Guillem M. Brocà 1918 (1985). *Historia del derecho de Cataluña, especialmente del Civil y Exposición de las instituciones del derecho civil del mismo territorio, en relación con el Código Civil de España y la jurisprudencia.* Barcelona: Generalitat de Catalunya, Department of Justice, 411.

[34]Capdeferro, Josep. Capdeferro 2012. *Ciència i experiència. El jurista Fontanella (1575–1649) i les seves cartes.* Barcelona: Fundació Noguera.

[35]The social stratum of *honoured citizens* was made up of urban petty nobility and certain peasants who became consolidated after the 15th century War of the Serfs (*Guerra dels Remences*), when they appropriated a significant number of farmsteads and between the 16th and the 18th centuries, attained this title of nobility.

[36]Bosch, Andreu. Bosch 1628 [1974 facsimile edition]. *Sumari, índex o epítome dels admirables i nobilíssims títols d'honor de Catalunya, Rosselló i Cerdanya.* Perpignan, 413–414.

[37]Fargas Peñarrocha, M. Adela. Fargas Peñarrocha 2001. Legislación familiar-patrimonial y ordenación del poder institucional en la Cataluña del siglo XVI. In *Cuadernos de Historia Moderna.* Madrid: Departamento de Historia Moderna, Servicio de Publicaciones, Universidad Complutense de Madrid, 93–100.

[38]The *mas* was a type of farmstead developed as of the Middle Ages. The term mas, which is "the house, farmland and forest", should be distinguished from the term *masia*, the farmhouse

As of the issuance of the 1716 Nueva Planta Decree, the absolutist monarch of the Spanish Empire (*Hispaniarum et Indiarum Rex*) granted himself exclusive legislative authority. Catalonia's public law was suppressed and the surviving private, criminal and procedural rights and laws lost their historic source of legislative renewal in the form of decisions made by the Courts.[39] This absence lent greater significance to legal and doctrinal jurisprudence and concrete legal experience, such that notary practice—creating much of the documentation to be found in the patrimonial archives—would become an important channel for renewal.[40]

The study and casuistic analysis of the most relevant legal documents from patrimonial archives—those that justify rights, titles and the possession of various assets of the households—gives us the opportunity to ascertain the basic principles of Catalan civil law in the Medieval and Modern Eras. Among these deeds, the *establiments* and purchase contracts, the *capítols matrimonials* (marriage charters), testaments or wills and 'post-mortem inventories' enabled the perpetuation of the houses, which were a personification of the stem families in Catalonia, and through this perpetuation ensured that they would be remembered. For noble households this meant honour, pride and rights, and for the peasant families, it certified their rights, possession of their assets and the status held by their households in local communities.

3.2 The Inheritance Systems of the Hispanic Monarchy

Inheritance systems in the Modern Era were somewhat varied. In the majority of the northern strip of the Iberian Peninsula, the unipersonal succession system prevailed, consisting predominantly of inheritance going to a single heir, while in the remainder of the territory of the monarchy governed by Castilian legislation, distribution into equal parts supposedly prevailed. Nonetheless, the legal framework could not and cannot explain how there were areas using another system within these two extensive regions.[41]

(Footnote 38 continued)

itself. Etymologically, the word comes from '*mansus*', the participle of *manere*, which means to *remain* or *reside*. Cfr. *The Catalan Mas: Origins, transformations and the end of an agrarian system*; Congost Colomer, Rosa (ed) 2015; Girona; Associació d'Història rural: Centre de Recerca d'Història Rural (Institut de Recerca Històrica) de la Universitat de Girona, Documenta Universitaria.

[39]Sobrequés i Vidal Sobrequés i Vidal 1978 (as in Note 31) 85–95; and *supra* Note 20.

[40]Serrano Daura, Josep. Serrano Daura 2001. Història del dret privat català. In Montagut Estragués, Tomàs (ed.), *Història del dret català*. Barcelona: Edicions de la Universitat Oberta de Catalunya, 183–323, 186.

[41]Ferrer Alòs, Llorenç. 2007. Systèmes successoraux et transmission héréditaires dans l'Espagne du XVIIIe siècle. *Histoire et sociétés rurales* 27, 37–70, and 38–39.

In Castilian regions until the early 16th century, the Visigothic traditions prevailed, consisting of transfer of goods based on the *Fuero Real* or Royal Charter[42] and the legal traditions arising from *ius commune* as reflected in the *Siete Partidas* (Seven Sections).[43] As of the laws and regulations accepted in 1505 by the Court session convened by the Catholic Monarchs in the city of Toro, the Castilian system was definitively established. Inheritances would be divided into five parts, one of which would be reserved for paying off debts and other expenses, and the remaining four parts would be joined again and divided into three parts. Of these, two thirds would go to an obligatory portion comprising the *legítima* (the 'legitimate') and the last third—the '*mejora de tercio*'—would serve to improve the situation of one or several of the married couple's children. In practice, this legislation allowed a great variety of family strategies in which the laws or legal framework were not the determining factors.[44]

The laws of 1505 offered a different solution, not only helping to prevent the dispersal of family lands, but also the deterioration of their income—they introduced the *mayorazgo* or majorat. According to this principle, an individual could do what they wished with the fifth that was available for their use, and they could also create a majorat from which the property attached to it could not be separated. As of this time in the regions of the Hispanic Monarchy under Castilian influence, wealthy social sectors and the peasant elite would use this legal instrument, which would allow the family patrimony to be transferred to a single person. At times, when the need arose to establish or reproduce relations of power or social status, the family history, easily created or recreated through the *mayorazgo*, would lead the system to the use of primogeniture.[45]

3.3 *Inheritance Models in Catalonia*

In Catalonia, the inheritance model developed over the course of history since the Middle Ages was that of the single heir, a product of the seigniorial regime and the socioeconomic changes occurring around the 11th century,[46] which would be

[42]Vallejo, Jesús. 1997. Relectura del Fuero Real. In Andrea Romano (ed.), *"Colendo iustitiam et iura Ferrer Alòs 2007". Federico II, legislatore del Regno di Sicilia nell'Europa del Duecento. Per una storia comparata delle codificazioni europee.* Roma: Edizioni De Luca, 485–514.

[43]The *Siete Partides* was a regulatory text draw up in the Kingdom of Castile during the reign of Alfonso X (1252–1284), with the aim of lending the kingdom a certain legal homogeneity. Its original name was the Book of Laws (*Libro de las Leyes*), but began to be called the "Seven Sections" in the 14th century or so for the number of sections into which it was divided.

[44]Ferrer Alòs Ferrer Alòs 2007 (as in Note 41) 47–49.

[45]Clavero, Bartolomé. Clavero 1989. *Mayorazgo: propiedad feudal en Castilla 1369–1836*. Madrid: Siglo XXI, 211–287.

[46]Terradas Saborit, Ignasi. Terradas Saborit 1980. Els orígens de la institució d'hereu a Catalunya: vers una interpretació contextual. In *Quaderns de l'Institut Català d'Antropologia*, 66–97, 70–77;

socially accepted then ratified by royal legislation in the 14th century.[47] Familial-patrimonial legislation in the 16th century would modify and elaborate on certain clauses and aspects of the code, which remained engraved in the country's legal memory. This legal regime would contribute to the social consolidation of a sector of the nobility or those on the nobility track, and particularly in Old Catalonia, also the upward social movement of a sector of the well-to-do peasantry. By the end of the century, thanks to the last truly productive Courts session of the Modern Era, held in 1599, familial-patrimonial regulations were perfectly configured in Catalonia.[48]

The most common or generalized matrimonial economic system in Catalonia was that of the dowry, with some exceptions in the centre of New Catalonia,[49] where the system of association was preferred, while in the proximity of the most populous cities such as Barcelona as of the beginning of the Industrial Era, the predominant system was that of separation of property.[50]

The society resulting from this matrimonial system and unilateral inheritance practices was a *society of households* defined in terms of their residence,[51] where patrimony lent entity and identity to a household,[52] which thus functioned as the most important support for a policy of continuity. It is above all in the area of the Pyrenees mountains that we can best observe these legal characteristics, for here they display the same attributes but an intensity unequalled in other areas of Catalonia. The head of household passed on his social role, exercised within the family and in the community, to his successor, the heir/heiress, who had to await the time when they would enter into their inheritance in a situation of subordination, the origin of frequent tension within a family. Nonetheless, the household became the main factor of social cohesion and the will for its perpetuity determined the destinies of the individuals comprising it.[53] This was also why the territories along

(Footnote 46 continued)

To Figueras, Lluís. To Figueras 1997. *Familia i hereu a la Catalunya Nord-oriental (segles X–XII)*, Publicacions de l'Abadia de Montserrat, 279–318.

[47]Brocà Brocà 1918 (1985²) (as in Note 33), 363–375.

[48]Fargas Peñarrocha Fargas Peñarrocha 2001 (as in Note 37) 96.

[49]The term *Catalunya Nova* or New Catalonia refers to the territory to the west and south of the Llobregat River Basin, consisting of the former Taifas of Lleida and Tortosa.

[50]Maspons i Anglasell. Francesc. Maspons i Anglasell 1935. *La llei de la família catalana*. Barcelona: Editorial Barcino, 19.

[51]Augustins, Georges. Augustins 1989. *Comment se perpétuer? Devenir des lignées et destins des patrimoines dans les paysanneries européennes*. Nanterre: Société d'ethnologie 11, 315–332.

[52]The *casa* (house or household), the basic unit of society, as an organizing principle of the latter, has a legal personality and real patrimony attached, as well as movable and intangible assets. The transmission of its property demonstrates an organic bond between its regimes of property, matrimony and hereditary rules. Its perpetuation over time occurs through the single heir system. Cf. Lamaison, Pierre. Lamaison 1987. La notion de la maison. Entretien avec Claude Lévi-Strauss. *Terrain* 9: 34–39.

[53]Barrera González, Andrés. Barrera González 1990. *Casa, herencia y familia en la Cataluña rural. Lógica de la razón doméstica*. Madrid, Editorial Alianza, 273–287.

the northern reaches of the Principality had highly dynamic local regulations. The latter consisted of a communal legal regime where a whole series of family strategies could be employed with the aim, among others, of mitigating the social decline of those who were not the main players in the family books or the patrimonial archives.[54]

3.4 Catalan Marriage Charters: The Founding Document for Households and Families

The primordial legal documents of a household, and thus of its patrimonial archives, were marriage contracts:[55] true family charters,[56] examples of Catalan contractual law and the basis of the familial and patrimonial system. They were drawn up at one of the most significant moments for the household: that of the heir's marriage. These documents, at times quite extensive, which in the Middle Ages were originally separate contracts that were signed on the same day, represent the households' spirit of perpetuity and demonstrate the triumph of the single-heir and stem family system as early as the 14th century.[57] They would eventually be incorporated into Catalan legal practice at the turn of the 16th–17th centuries.[58] They reveal the successive chain of people inheriting the patrimony and holding the position of heads of household. The marriage charters—which were considered the external expression of Catalan family law—[59]were not highly regulated by Catalan legislators. In fact, there was no legal obligation to draw them up or sign them; Peter III, at the Perpignan Courts session of 1351, legalized their irrevocability.

[54]Mikes, Tünde. Mikes 2003. Comunitats i 'cases' a la Vall de Ribes en els segles XVII–XVIII. *Pedralbes. Revista d'història moderna* 23.1: 567–578.

[55]Jesús Lalinde Abadia, in his papers on the subject, uses printed document collections. Cf. Lalinde Abadia, Jesús, Lalinde Abadia 1963. Los pactos matrimoniales catalanes. *Anuario de historia del derecho* 33: 133–266.

[56]Derouet, Bernard. Derouet 1997. Dot et héritage: les enjeux de la chronologie de la transmission. In Goy, Joseph, Tits-Dieuaide, Marie-Jeanne, and Burguière, André (eds.), *L'histoire grande ouverte: hommages à Emmanuel Le Roy Ladurie*, 284-292, 288. Paris: Fayard; and Brocà Brocà 1918 (as n. 33) 682–687.

[57]Donat Pérez, Lídia, Marcó Masferrer, Xavier, and Ortí Gost, Pere. Els contractes matrimonials a la Catalunya medieval. In *Els capítols matrimonials, una font per a la història social*. Biblioteca d'Història Rural, Col·lecció Fonts 6. Girona: CCCG Edicions; Associació d'Història Rural de les Comarques Gironines; Institut de Llengua i Cultura Catalanes de la Universitat de Girona, 19–46.

[58]Gifre, Pere. 2010. El procés final d'implantació dels capítols matrimonials (finals de segle XVI–començament de segle XVII). In *Els capítols matrimonials, una font per a la història social*. Biblioteca d'Història Rural, Collecció Fonts 6. Girona: CCCG Edicions; Associació d'Història Rural de les Comarques Gironines; Institut de Llengua i Cultura Catalanes de la Universitat de Girona, 55–69.

[59]Maspons i Anglasell 1935 (as in Note 50) 21.

Compared with these documents, testaments or wills played a marginal role of confirmation or reminder in this marriage system.[60]

The most important prerequisite for a wedding was that everyone be in agreement. The *consent* of the engaged couple and, of course, of their parents, was required. The first legal provisions of this type, designed to foster the family, appeared during the reign of James I,[61] establishing the requirement of parental consent for marrying—in fact, related to the power of the *senyories* or seigniories—in order to inherit the patrimony and the house.

Let us study some of the most significant institutions of this law. The most important institution is *legacy:* the present and/or future donation of property by the parents to their heir (*hereu*) or heiress (*pubilla*).[62] Legacy constitutes Catalonia's most typical legal institution,[63] which is consuetudinary and feudal in nature and historically entrenched. It is a gift of a universal nature on the occasion of matrimony, and is generally expressed in marriage charters. It is irrevocable,[64] yet does not enter full effectiveness until the death of the head of household, usually the heir's father. No law obliged anyone to designate a single heir, but the immense majority of households did so.[65] The consecutive succession of such instances of legacy formed the backbone of the household: they could be established or 'pacted' to the benefit of the wedding couple, or using the formula of the trust (*fideïcomís* or fideicommissum).[66]

This Catalan legacy practice was born of practical experience and not theoretic or legal principles from the Early Middle Ages. The roots of this institution can already be observed in the *Usatges de Barcelona*.[67] The '*hereditamentum*' arose from litigation regarding Early Middle Age feudal covenants (*convinences*) and is closely related to the transformation of the temporary, non-transferable fiefs into lifelong, transferable ones. The *Usatge* or *Usage* No. 76 (*Auctoritate et rogatu*)

---

[60]Derouet 1997 (as in Note 56) 288.

[61]Pragmatic sanction by James I (Pragmática de Jaume I) from 1244: *Constitucions y altres drets de Cathalunya. Compilacions de 1495, 1588–1589 i 1704*. CYADC-1704/2004, 2, 9, 3, 1.

[62]In the absence of a male heir, the head of household can choose a daughter as heiress to his assets.

[63]Brocà 1918 (as in Note 33) 238.

[64]Catalan *constitució* arising from the Perpignan Court session of 1351, Peter III; CYADC-1704/2004, 1,5,2,1.

[65]Ferrer i Alòs, Llorenç. 2010. Les clàusules dels capítols matrimonials. In *Els capítols matrimonials, una font per a la història social*. Biblioteca d'Història Rural, Collecció Fonts 6. Girona: CCCG Edicions; Associació d'Història Rural de les Comarques Gironines; Institut de Llengua i Cultura Catalanes de la Universitat de Girona, 71–88.

[66]Faus i Condomines, Josep. (1907) 2002^2. Els capítols matrimonials a la comarca de Guissona. In *Centenari naixement de l'il·lustre notari Ramon Faus Esteve: 1902–2002,* Guissona, 61–178, and 74–78.

[67]Collection of customs and usages or practices, applied in the *Curia* or Comital Court of Justice of Barcelona as of the mid-11th century, which began to be compiled beginning in the mid-12th century; These *Usatges de Barcelona* would later become the basis for the Law of the entire Principality. Cf. Note 4.

emphasized the irrevocable nature of the pact, which would later be ratified in Usage No. 79 (*Possunt etiam*), linking it to submission with oath of allegiance.[68] Other documents of the same period contain examples of absolute legacies preferentially bestowed upon a future son. By the mid-14th century, these universal legacies were generalized in Catalonia, and the 1351 General Courts of Perpignan under Peter III declared nul *ipso iure* any instrument issued to the detriment of legacies and donations granted on the occasion of matrimony, clearly defending the institution of the heir and future head of household.[69]

The second most relevant institution was the dowry, the patrimony that the bride would contribute to the matrimony. Until the 13th century, there was also a 'Gothic bride price' *(dot goda marital)*, of Visigoth origin—the *decima* (equivalent to a tenth of the groom's assets)—that the groom gave to his future wife. It was a practice generalized throughout Catalonia and not just in Barcelona. In the 13th century, the Roman dowry offered by the bride began spreading.

There was no written norm on the quantity of this donation; the parties would establish it at their convenience or according to the demands of the marriage alliance. Generally, it amounted to the bride's *llegítima*[70] or slightly more, 'according to the household's capabilities.' However, dowry inflation was a constant in notarial documentation and would reach its apogee in the late 17th and the 18th centuries.[71] It was an arbitrary, political decision and, in the dowry system, represented an effective instrument for family and social exclusion of the essential portion of the patrimony of non-heir children. It was designed to establish familial and economic relations between households: the dowry contributed by the bride served to pay the dowries for those excluded from inheritance in the household she was joining. As of its formulation in marriage charters, the differential treatment of the children of the head of household began:[72] the selection of the heir or heiress's future husband or wife was a primordial legal instrument in matrimonial alliance strategies.

In parallel to the growth of legislation on matrimony in general, a tendency can be observed to boost women's rights. 'Pragmatic sanctions' (*pragmàtiques reials*)

---

[68]To Figueras, Lluís. 1998. Droit et succession dans la noblesse féodale à propos des Usages de Barcelone (XIè–XIIè siècle). In Beauchamp, Joëlle and Dagron, Gilbert (eds.), *La transmission du patrimoine. Byzance et l'aire méditerranéenne*, 261–262. Paris: Éditions de Boccard.

[69]Cf. Note 36.

[70]The Catalan 'legitimate' (*llegítima*) represented a limitation of the freedom to bequeath that the law imposed on the testator according to which the latter had the duty to allot his/her relatives a patrimonial amount to be taken from the inheritance. The percentage of the inheritance they were due differed according to the period, and the amount depended on the capabilities of the household.

[71]Congost Colomer, Rosa. 1992. *Notes de societat: La Selva, 1768–1862*. Santa Coloma de Farners: Consell Comarcal de La Selva, Centre d'Estudis Selvatans, 38.

[72]Mikes, Tünde. 2009. Una societat de muntanya a l'època moderna: poblament, població i la seva reproducció (el cas de la Vall de Ribes al segle XVII). In Barraqué, Jean-Pierre, and Sénac, Philippe (eds.), *Habitats et peuplement dans les Pyrénées au Moyen Âge et à l'époque moderne*. CNRS—Université de Toulouse-Le Mirail, Collection "Méridiennes", 291–309, 303–309.

issued by James I, James II, Peter III and Alphonse IV established and strengthened their rights insofar as the dowry:[73] first the dowry was limited to a certain amount, then the wife's obligation to supply certifications to collect her dowry and bride price or dower (*escreix* or *esponsalici*) if her husband died was established. Finally, these 'pragmatic sanctions' or decrees ensured that the wife's right to collect these two items could not be undermined if she had not given her consent when her husband had contracted debts.[74]

The future wife, after receiving her dowry assets from her family, while relinquishing other possible rights she had at her childhood home, formalized the dowry and presented the trousseau she would bring to her new home. The groom certified receipt of the assets through a dowry letter and at the same time, offered her a dower or bride price. This institution, likewise of earlier origin, began spreading and becoming generalized in the 12th century: it was a voluntary donation that the husband gave to his wife to provide a certain compensation for the dowry she contributed.[75] The amount (percentage) of the dower varied according to the period, ranging from 30 to 50 %—except in the Bishopric of Girona, where the '*tantundem*' or amount to be returned was 100 % of the dowry.

The legal institutions regarding the *widow* of the head of household became increasingly important. *Usatge* No. 147 ("Widow"), attributed to James I but eminently consuetudinary, granted the woman who became a widow the possession of her husband's assets as long as she remained a widow and duly fed her children. The Royal Privilege (*privilegi reial*), *Recognoverunt proceres*, issued by Peter II at the 1248 Barcelona Courts Session, held in Barcelona, limited the widow's usufruct to her first year of widowhood—the so-called year of mourning (*any de plor*)—and thereafter until she received her due part of the dowry and bride price.[76]

Peter III, at the Perpignan Courts Session of 1351, would turn this privilege exclusive to Barcelona into a general law throughout Catalonia, as long as an inventory of the husband's assets had been taken in his lifetime. In the 15th century, various laws refer to the widow's dowry option (*opció dotal*), allowing her the right to choose whether to keep her husband's estate in usufruct or sell the latter to recover her dowry and collect her dower as a preferential creditor.

The most significant improvement in the widow's status arose in 1564, when Philip II assigned widows the civil law possession of her deceased husband's estate—*tenuta* or tenancy—[77]and at the same time declared the preferential right of the first wife's ('first bed') children to inherit his household estate. The widow

[73]The 'dowry option' *(opció dotal)* was an institution according to which the wife, should her husband's assets be confiscated, could remove from said assets the amount she considered appropriate or of value proportional to the dowry and the bride price, and she had the right to keep it.

[74]Brocà 1918 (as in Note 33) 232.

[75]Some authors also refer to the *escreix* or bride price as an award for virginity.

[76]Serrano Daura 2001 (as in Note 40) 265–266.

[77]*Tenuta* or tenancy was an institution specific to Catalan family law that granted usufruct of the deceased husband's estate to the widow and her heirs.

usufruct clause was used with increasing frequency and the widow would eventually be called '*senyora, majora poderosa i usufructuària*' (mistress, owner and usufructuary). By the late 16th century, the widow appears in documents as a real substitute to the head of household, protector of the hereditary estate, a link between the father and his heir.

Legal institutions also ensured the role and future of the other children of the head of household, the siblings of the heir—those *excluded* from the system. This exclusion was more radical in certain parts of the northern reaches of the Peninsula and the western Pyrenees. In Catalonia, exclusion was less extreme: socialization of the members of the household allowed the siblings to accept their situation more readily. Just as parents attempt to ensure the wellbeing of all of their children, the same occurred in household systems. Although what the siblings of the heir would be allotted from the family legacy could only offer them a lower economic and social position, the jurisprudence, both through legislation and consuetudinary law, offered various alternatives for them to improve their situation. One of these was the 'legitimate' (*llegítima*), the portion allotted by law to the non-heir children as well. This institution, of Roman origin, would change in the Visigoth period and in Catalonia would vary according to the historic period. In some territories, such as the County of Barcelona and Old Catalonia in general, above all before the 13th century, the 'Gothic' or 'long legitimate' prevailed, which meant that 8/15ths of the inheritance went to the legitimees. In regions of New Catalonia in the same period, the Roman legitimate was in use, which took into account the number of children to establish the amounts of the legitimate allotments: for up to four children, it amounted to a third of the estate, and for more children, the legitimate amounted to half of the father's assets. It was in the 14th century, namely 1333, that the Catalan legal system—evolving in parallel to the formation and territorialization of general Catalan law—unified the percentage used to calculate the legitimate by obligating the entire country to observe the Roman variant while abolishing the Gothic one.[78] Ten years later, a Royal Pragmatic Sanction established the legitimate for the city of Barcelona as a quarter of the inheritance.[79] In Castilian law, *legítimas* were larger, with varied treatment of non-heirs.[80]

It was nearly a century and a half before the enactment of the most important legal provisions of Catalan family and succession law of the Modern Era at the Monzó Courts session of 1585: through the law or *constitució*, "*Zelant per la conservació de les cases principals de Catalunya*" (Ensuring the conservation of the main households of Catalonia), the Courts established the general rule for the entire country. The legitimate became 'short' throughout Catalonia, that is, it would consist of a fourth of the estate, from which the heir had to settle the legitimate of

[78]Alphonse III at the Montblanc Courts, CYADC-1704/2004, 3,6,1,1, Chap. 17.

[79]Serrano Daura 2001 (as in Note 40) 262–264.

[80]Pérez Collados, José Maria. 2005. El derecho catalan de sucesiones en vísperas de la codificación. *Anuario del historia del derecho español* 75, 331–367, 344.

his siblings, either in money or property from the inheritance. It also specified that the legitimate could not be executed during the lifetime of a usufructuary parent.[81]

Succession to the role of head of household as heir and manager of its patrimony was a decisive stage for all matrimonies until contemporary times. This could take place at one of two key points: when the children/heirs got married or when the parents died. These were two radically different situations insofar as their objectives and results. In the general dowry system functioning in Catalonia, as with other household systems, succession came about at the death of the parents, and primarily at the death of the head of household.

The main mechanism of inheritance was through a contract, i.e. the marriage charters, entered into when the heir married: it was a *negotiated* or '*pacted*' inheritance and regulated the future of the essential portion of the patrimony. By will, the parents generally handed down what was left after the appointment of the heir and the payment of any debts accumulated over their lifetimes as well as payment of the legitimates to their non-heir children. This mechanism can be considered effective against the fragmentation of the patrimony, but it did not guarantee the same social status for all members of the family.

The *testated succession* was carried out by drawing up in writing the last will of the testators regarding the distribution of their property and rights after their death. Early Medieval testaments or wills—one type of such documents—were drawn up according to the formal rules of Gothic laws, and these documents did not include the appointment of heirs until the 13th century.

The 'ab intestato' formula at that time was associated with the rights of lords in the case their vassals or peasants should die without having made a will. Hence, certain *Usatges* referred to these rights as bad customs (No. 117: *Rusticus vero*, No. 110: *Similiter de rebus*, No. 138: *De intestatis*), as in the case of the *intestia*, in reference to the Lord's right to compensation for assigning the inheritance to one of the children of the deceased vassal.

Later, certain Pragmatic sanctions by James I and Ferdinand I, which lent greater legal power to the head of household figure, made the inheritance of sons or daughters conditional to having parental consent to marry or take religious vows. In the mid-13th century, stem inheritance was strengthened, as it became limited to the fourth degree of kinship, and legacy was limited to the assets proceeding from ascendants but not to those attained during the parents' lifetime. A century later, the sphere of this succession was expanded to include all property, that is, the goods inherited through stem family relations were expanded.

The Monzó Courts Session of 1585 not only established the regulations for the legitimate, but also strengthened stem family regulations in general: in addition to stepping up the role of the wife, the rights of the maternal household were also boosted through certain clauses on the return of the dowry and other assets stemming from the maternal household.

[81]Brocà 1918 (as in Note 33) 368–369.

During the 16th century, various provisions of the *constitucions* enacted by the different Courts sessions refer to *successió per fideïcomís* (inheritance via trust or *fideicommissum*). The main goal of this institution was to preserve and perpetuate the patrimony in the face of certain adversity that could arise within the family. In inheritance via trust, which was very frequent in Catalonia, three *constitucions* from this century helped to prevent possible fraud between the fiduciary heir or trustee and the definitive heir or fideicommissary, obliging the former to take inventories and later requiring them to be revised by a notary. The severe nature of this preventive measure went as far as threatening first-degree heirs with the loss of their inheritance[82] if the inventory was not prepared within the established period. All in all, here we can observe not only the protection of the fideicommissary and the temporary heir or trustee, who would obtain a fourth of the inheritance, but also the technification of law as a discipline.

All legislation in the first century of the Modern Era demanded improved and expanded legal security—above all in defending households and their patrimony. Relations between the monarchy and the nobility were redefined, but the legal situation of other social strata would also be defined. The organizational space of the head of household was also defined, and households became stronger through the defence of the stem family, whose interests not only the father would look after, but also the usufructuary mother and the maternal stem family.

The 1568 *constitucions* fostered patrimonial exclusion and those of 1585[83] represented the triumph of the logic of accumulation, whereby the heir would be the only one to decide. The children of the first matrimony would take precedence. Not only was the heir's household stabilized, but also the maternal household. Heads of household were given authority not only over children not yet having reached puberty, but also over those over 25 years of age.[84]

This patrimonial integrity was even more reinforced through the constitutions enacted in the last Courts session of the 16th century: even the subtraction of the Trebellianic fourth could be prohibited if expressly indicated in the will.

The period between this legislative effervescence and its decadence and subsequent demise in the 17th and 18th centuries does not allow us to follow the evolution of this phenomenon through the study of the laws, since they were in decline. However, studying doctrinal and judicial jurisprudence would allow it, but we could also follow the changes through an analysis of acts in practice, namely, marriage charters.

Due to lack of space, we will limit ourselves here to discussing the evolution visible through the analysis of the succession clause in three hundred marriage charters from a Pyrenean valley between the early 17th to the mid-18th centuries,

[82]This concerned the Trebellianic fourth and the Falcidian fourth of the estate corresponding to the heir; Cf: CYADC—1704/2004, 1, 6, 8, 3.

[83]Philip at the Monsó Courts of 1585, CYADC-1704/2004, 1, 6, 5, 2, cap. 94.

[84]Fargas Peñarrocha 2001 (as in Note 37) 93, and 97.

insofar as the organizational mechanism of the future of households over three generations.

The concepts we will discuss are nuptiality, gender and primogeniture. It must be kept in mind, of course, that the legal framework had already been established in the 15th and 16th centuries according to the medieval foundations of the system, which were often consuetudinary. Practice could not, however, transform the pre-existing legal framework but rather amend, interpret and adapt it to the needs of the households in the various regions of the Principality.

The succession clause, one of the last items on the marriage charters, stipulated succession for the children of the marrying couple, that is, for a third generation, by way of guideline. In these 'virtual successions', the precedence of children born of the first marriage as a sign of the continuity of the household bloodline grew regularly over these 150 years, with the percentage of charters where this precept was present doubling every 30–40 years. This phenomenon demonstrates the strength of the stem family and by the end of the 18th century, required the restitution of all monetary amounts and all assets to the widow and her heirs.

The gender of the individual who was to inherit the patrimony, i.e. heir or heiress (*hereu* or *pubilla*), would only be explicitly indicated in marriage charters beginning in the 18th century, although there were certain allusions to a preference for male children in previous periods.

The same was true of primogeniture: although the precept was present by the 17th century in marriage charters, it would only become consolidated during the course of the 18th century.

It can be observed that the matters considered most important in the 18th and 19th centuries, which would become basic concepts according to the major 19th-century jurists and the *pairalistes* of the 20th century, were less relevant in preceding centuries. What was important was the process: the increasing importance of the strength of the stem family as an expression of a consanguine community and its integration into a broader political community.[85]

4 Conclusions

Catalunya was and is a European land which, as a general political community—whether independent or with different degrees of autonomy within the Hispanic Monarchy—has been participating in European legal culture since the Middle Ages.

The historic origins of Catalonia meld with those of its legal system. They lie with the process of independence from the Carolingian Empire and the formation of the Principality of Catalonia, under the general jurisdiction or public authority of the Count of Barcelona, who was recognized as Prince in the *Usatges de Barcelona,*

[85]Sanllehy Sabi, Maria Àngels; Bringué Portella, Josep Maria; and Mikes, Tünde. 2011. Evolució Històrica. In *La casa al Pirineu*, 13–41. Figueres: Brau Edicions.

the text that modernized the consuetudinary tradition of the previous Visigothic Law in accordance with the requirements of the new Catalan feudal society of the 11th and subsequent centuries. The political establishment of the Principality of Catalonia would become clearly dualistic, insofar as the powers of the Prince and the Principality (the latter represented by the *Generalitat*, the co-governing body of Catalonia) had to find a balance allowing them to ensure positive public liberties (legal 'pactism' to enact Catalan laws) as well as negative ones (respect for the principle of the Rule of Law by the public authorities) for the Catalans. After the Parliamentary and Estates Monarchy (13th to early 18th centuries), which maintained this status quo, the Absolutist Estates Monarchy and the liberal constitutional monarchy of the 18th and 19th centuries would eliminate Catalan public law with a view to the centralization and uniformization of the lands under the monarchy and the political project of relieving 'the Spains' (*las Españas*) of the kingdoms comprising it to create a single, indivisible Spain based on a Castilian matrix.

Private Catalan law was upheld throughout the period studied, as was the basic institution of civil law and of Catalan society, namely, the family and its association with the farmstead (*mas*), farmhouse (*masia*) and patrimony, together with its matrimonial and inheritance regimes.

Clear evidence of the strength of the Catalan family institution on all levels is its perpetuity and the endurance over time of thousands of family or patrimonial archives that correspond not only to noble or powerful families, but also and in the vast majority, to families of peasant origin.

A comparison between the inheritance systems of other peoples of Spain and those of Catalonia reveals the existence of common elements as well as differences. The *llegítima* system, the matrimonial-economic regime, the documentary protection of patrimonial and familial rights and the conservation of these documents are certainly quite different. But the same or analogous strategies could be planned and executed, as in the case of the conservation of patrimony over time through the heir or heiress in Catalonia, or regulations more hostile to that end had to be avoided or rechannelled in practice, as in the case of the Castilian law of succession.

The primordial legal document of households and thus of patrimonial archives were marriage charters: veritable family charters, examples of Catalan contractual law and the basis of the familial and patrimonial system. They were drawn up at one of the most significant moments for the household: that of the heir's marriage. An analysis of nine hundred marriage charters from a Pyrenean valley showed a growing use of this legal institution of consuetudinary roots over the course of the 16th–18th centuries, such that nearly every 30 years the number of marriage charters signed before a notary doubled. This demonstrates the growing strength of the stem family, which revolved around the *mas* and the *masia*, in a basically agrarian society that began to decline when it could not compete with the new, contemporary society arising from the Industrial Revolution and the emigration to the cities of a large portion of the "secondary" children excluded from the ancestral home of their forebears.

Nonetheless, at the turn of the 20th century, to ensure the continuity of Catalonia as a people with a political and cultural identity of their own, a people that had kept their historic private law alive and flourishing, the myth of the ancestral home (*casa pairal*) emerged and focus was again placed on the strength of the traditional Catalan family—precisely when the construction of the Sagrada Família Temple was moving forward with the greatest strength and vitality.

References

Literature

Albareda, J. (2000). *La guerra de Successió i l'Onze de Setembre*. Barcelona: Editorial Empúries.

Alturo, J., Bellès, J., Font, J. M., García, Y., & Mundó, A. (Eds.). (2003). *El Liber Iudicum Popularis*. Barcelona: Generalitat de Catalunya, Departament de Justícia i Interior.

Augustins, G. (1989). *Comment se perpétuer? Devenir des lignées et destins des patrimoines dans les paysanneries européennes,* Nanterre: Société d'ethnologie, 11.

Barrera González, A. (1990). *Casa, herencia y familia en la Cataluña rural. Lógica de la razón doméstica.* Madrid: Ed. Alianza.

Bastardas, J. (1984). *Usatges de Barcelona. El Codi a mitjan segle XII.* Barcelona: Fundació Noguera.

Benet, J. (1990). Precedentes Históricos del Estatuto. *Comentarios sobre el Estatuto de Autonomía de Cataluña* (3 vols). Barcelona: Institut d'Estudis Autonòmics.

Bosch, A. (1628) [1974 facsimile edition]. *Sumari, índex o epítome dels admirables i nobilíssims títols d'honor de Catalunya, Rosselló i Cerdanya* (pp. 413–414). Perpignan: Pere Lacavalleria; Barcelona-Sueca: Curial.

Bosch, M., & Gifre, P. (1998). Els llibres mestres dels arxius patrimonials. Una font per a l'estudi de les estratègies patrimonials. *Estudis d'Història Agrària, 12*, 155–182.

Brocà, G. M. (1918) (1985). *Historia del derecho de Cataluña especialmente del Civil y Exposición de las instituciones del derecho civil del mismo territorio, en relación con el Código Civil de España y la jurisprudencia.* Barcelona: Generalitat de Catalunya, Departament de Justícia.

Capdeferro, J. (2004). La Deputació del General al segle XVII. In *L'autogovern de Catalunya* (pp. 51–56). Barcelona: Fundació Lluís Carulla.

Capdeferro, J. (2012). *Ciència i experiència. El jurista Fontanella (1575–1649) i les seves cartes.* Barcelona: Fundació Noguera.

Capdeferro, J., & Serra, E. (2015). El Tribunal de Contrafaccions de Catalunya i la seva activitat (1702–1713). In *Textos Jurídics Catalans* (vol. 34). Barcelona: Generalitat de Catalunya, Departament de Justícia.

Clavero, B. (1989). *Mayorazgo: propiedad feudal en Castilla 1369–1836* (pp. 211–287). Madrid: Ed. Siglo XIX.

Congost Colomer, R. (1992). *Notes de societat: La Selva, 1768–1862*, Santa Coloma de Farners: Consell Comarcal de La Selva, Centre d'Estudis Selvatans.

Congost Colomer, R. (1998). El pairalisme. Reflexions sobre una paraula, un concepte i dues conjuntures. *Estudis d'Història Agrària, 12*, 7–16.

Congost Colomer, Rosa (ed). (2015). *The Catalan Mas. Origins, transformations and the end of an agrarian system.* Girona: Associació d'Història Rural: Centre de Recerca d'Història Rural (Institut de Recerca Històrica) de la Universitat de Girona, Documenta Universitaria.

Costa, P. (2002). *Iurisdictio: Semantica del potere politico en la pubblicistica medievale (1100–1433).* Milan: Giuffrè.

D'Abadal, R. (1958). *Els primers comtes catalans.* Barcelona: Editorial Teide.
de Montagut, T. (1998). Estudi introductori. In Peguera, Lluis de (Facsimile, Barcelona: Rafel Figueró, 1701), *Practica, forma, y estil de celebrar Corts Generals en Cathalunya, y materias incidents en aquellas*, VII–LVII. Madrid: Centro de Estudios Constitucionales.
de Montagut, T. (1999). La Justicia en la Corona de Aragón. In *La administración de justicia en la historia de España. Actas de las III Jornadas de Castilla-La Mancha sobre investigación en archivos (noviembre 1997)* (pp. 650–655). Guadalajara: Junta de Comunidades de Castilla-La Mancha.
de Montagut, T. (2003). Els juristes de Catalunya i la seva organització col·legial a l'època medieval. *Ius Fugit, 12*, 269–302.
de Montagut, T. (2013). La Constitució política de la Corona d'Aragó. In F. Isabel (Ed.), *El Compromiso de Caspe (1412). Cambios dinásticos y Constitucionalismo en la Corona de Aragón* (pp. 104–116). Saragossa: XIX Congreso de Historia de la Corona de Aragón.
de Montagut Estragués, T. (2015). *Una mirada a la història jurídica de Catalunya i als seus drets històrics* (pp. 173–176). Barcelona: IEC.
Derouet, B. (1997). Dot et héritage: les enjeux de la chronologie de la transmission. In J. Goy, M. J. Tits-Dieuaide, & A. Burguière, (Eds.), *L'histoire grande ouverte: hommages à Emmanuel Le Roy Ladurie* (pp. 284–292). Paris: Fayard.
Donat Pérez, L., Marcó Masferrer, X., & Ortí Gost, P. (2010). Els contractes matrimonials a la Catalunya medieval. In *Els capítols matrimonials, una font per a la història social.* Girona: Biblioteca d'Història Rural, Col·lecció Fonts 6; CCCG Edicions, Associació d'Història Rural de les Comarques Gironines, and Institut de Llengua i Cultura Catalanes de la Universitat de Girona, 19–46.
Estrada-Rius, A. (2001). *Els orígens de la Generalitat de Catalunya (La Deputació del General de Catalunya: dels precedents a la reforma de 1413).* Barcelona: unpublished doctoral thesis, Universitat Pompeu Fabra.
Fargas Peñarrocha, M. A. (2001). Legislación familiar-patrimonial y ordenación del poder institucional en la Cataluña del siglo XVI. In *Cuadernos de Historia Moderna* (pp. 89–114). Madrid: Departamento de Historia Moderna, Servicio de Publicaciones, Universidad Complutense de Madrid.
Faus i Condomines, J. (1907) (2002). Els capítols matrimonials a la comarca de Guissona. In *Centenari naixement de l'il·lustre notari Ramon Faus Esteve: 1902*–2002. Guissona: 61–178.
Fernández Viladrich, J. (1982). Notas en torno a las asambleas condales en la Cataluña de la Alta Edad Media. In *Estudis Històrics i documents dels arxius de protocols, 10*, 7–88.
Ferran, E. (2006). *El jurista Pere Albert i les Commemoracions.* Barcelona: Institut d'Estudis Catalans.
Ferrer Alòs, L. (1998). Sistema hereditario y reproducción social en Cataluña. In *Nécessités économiques et pratiques juridiques: problèmes de la transmission des exploitations agricoles (XVIIIe–XXe siècles)* (pp. 53–57). Rome: Mélanges de l'École Française de Rome-Italie et Méditerranée.
Ferrer Alòs, L. (2007). Systèmes successoraux et transmission héréditaires dans l'Espagne du XVIIIe siècle. *Histoire et sociétés rurales, 27*, 37–70.
Ferrer i Alòs, L. (2010). Les clàusules dels capítols matrimonials. In *Els capítols matrimonials, una font per a la història social*, Girona: Biblioteca d'Història Rural, Col·lecció Fonts, 6; CCCG Edicions, Associació d'Història Rural de les Comarques Gironines, and Institut de Llengua i Cultura Catalanes de la Universitat de Girona, 71–88.
Ferro, V. (1987). *El Dret Públic Català. Les Institucions a Catalunya fins al Decret de Nova Planta.* Vic: Eumo.
Gay, J. M. (1982). La gènesi del Decret de Nova Planta de Catalunya. Edició de la consulta original del 'Consejo de Castilla' de 13 de juny de 1715. *Revista Jurídica de Catalunya, 81.1*, 3–42.

Gay, J. M. (1982). La gènesi del Decret de Nova Planta de Catalunya. Edició de la consulta original del 'Consejo de Castilla' de 13 de juny de 1715 (Second Part). *Revista Jurídica de Catalunya, 81.2*: 263–348.

Gay, J. M. (1997). *El corregidor a Catalunya.* Madrid: Marcial Pons.

Gifre, P. (2010). El procés final d'implantació dels capítols matrimonials (finals de segle XVI–començament de segle XVII. In *Els capítols matrimonials, una font per a la història social*, Girona: Biblioteca d'Història Rural, Col·lecció Fonts, 6; CCCG Edicions, Associació d'Història Rural de les Comarques Gironines, and Institut de Llengua i Cultura Catalanes de la Universitat de Girona, 55–69.

Gifre, P., Matas, J., & Soler, S. (2002). *Els arxius patrimonials* Girona: Biblioteca d'Història Rural, Col·lecció Fonts, 2; CCCG Edicions, Associació d'Història Rural de les Comarques Gironines, and Institut de Llengua i Cultura Catalanes de la Universitat de Girona.

Gonzalvo, G. (1991). Les assemblees de Pau i Treva i l'origen de la Cort General de Catalunya. In *Les Corts a Catalunya. Actes del Congrés d'Història Institucional* (pp. 71–78). Barcelona: Generalitat de Catalunya, Departament de Cultura.

Lalinde Abadia, J. (1963). Los pactos matrimoniales catalanes. *Anuario de historia del derecho, 33*, 133–266.

Lamaison, P. (1987). La notion de la maison. Entretien avec Claude Lévi-Strauss. *Terrain, 9*: 34–39.

Maspons i Anglasell, F. (1935). *La llei de la família catalana.* Barcelona: Ed. Barcino.

Mikes, T. (2003). Comunitats i 'cases' a la vall de ribes en els segles XVII-XVIII. *Pedralbes: revista d'història moderna, 23.1*, 567–578.

Mikes, T. (2009). Una societat de muntanya a l'època moderna: poblament, població i la seva reproducció (el cas de la Vall de Ribes al segle XVII). In J.-P. Barraqué, & P. Sénac (Eds.), *Habitats et peuplement dans les Pyrénées au Moyen Âge et à l'époque moderne* (pp. 291–309). CNRS-Université de Toulouse-Le Mirail, Collection "Méridiennes".

Pérez Collados, J. M. (2005). El derecho catalan de sucesiones en vísperas de la codificación. *Anuario de historia del derecho español, 75*, 331–367.

Pérez Latre, M. (2004). *Entre el rei i la terra. El poder polític a Catalunya al segle XVI.* Vic: Eumo.

Sánchez de Movellán, I. (2004). *La Diputació del General de Catalunya (1413–1479)*. Barcelona: Generalitat de Catalunya—Institut d'Estudis Catalans.

Sanllehi i Sabi, M. À., Bringué i Portella, J. M., & Mikes, T. (2011). Evolució històrica. In *La casa al Pirineu* (pp. 13–41). Figueres: Brau Edicions.

Serrano Daura, J. (2001). Història del dret privat català. In Montagut Estragués, Tomàs (coord.) *Història del dret català* (pp. 183–323). Barcelona: Edicions de la Universitat Oberta de Catalunya.

Sobrequés i Vidal, S. (1978). *Història de la producció del dret català fins al Decret de Nova Planta*, Girona, Universitat Autònoma de Barcelona - Collegi Universitari de Girona.

Terradas Saborit, I. (1980). Els orígens de la institució d'hereu a Catalunya: vers una interpretació contextual. *Quaderns de l'Institut Català d'Antropologia, 20*, 66–97.

Terradas Saborit, I. (2001). La casa mítica i la casa jurídica: reflexions sobre un contrast entre el país Basc i Catalunya. In Ferrer i Mallol, Teresa; Mitgé i Vives, Josefina; and Riu i Riu, Manuel (eds.), *El mas català durant l'Edat Mitjana i la Moderna (segles IX-XVIII) Aspectes arqueològics, històrics, geogràfics, arquitectònics i antropològics* (pp. 49–64). Barcelona: CSIC, Institució Milà i Fontanals.

To Figueras, L. (1997). *Familia i hereu a la Catalunya Nord-oriental (segles X–XII).* Barcelona: Publicacions de l'Abadia de Montserrat.

To Figueras, L. (1998). Droit et succession dans la noblesse féodale à propos des Usages de Barcelone (XIe–XIIe siècle). In J. Beaucamp & G. Dagran (Eds.), *La transmission du patrimoine. Byzance et l'aire méditerranée* (pp. 247–269). Paris: De Boccard.

Tomas y Valiente, F. (1979). *Manual de Historia del Derecho español* (pp. 571–591). Madrid: Ed. TECNOS.

Torres Sans, X. (2000). *Els llibres de família de pagès; memòries de pagès, memòries de mas (segles XVI-XVIII)*. Girona: Biblioteca d'Història Rural, Col·lecció Fonts, 1; CCCG Edicions, Associació d'Història Rural de les Comarques Gironines, and Institut de Llengua i Cultura Catalanes de la Universitat de Girona.

Vallejo, J. (1997). Relectura del Fuero Real. In Romano, Andrea, *"Colendo iustitiam et iura condendo" Federico II, legislatore del Regno de Sicilia nell'Europa del Duecento. Per una storia comparata delle codificazioni europee* (pp. 485–514). Rome: Edizioni De Luca.

Adoption Between *Ancien Régime* and Codification: Is It in Remission in a Changing World?

Maria Gigliola di Renzo Villata

Abstract The paper follows the evolution of juridical "adoption", in particular with regard to italian area, from the Early Middle Ages to the 19th century, the age of Codification, and its use over time according to the society's needs. Some scholarship works and documents dating back to the high Middle Ages show adoption sparsely dealt with—in part consistently with Roman law and in part following the trail of the Franc and Longobard law—in which the aim was to ensure the possibility to have a son to whomever lacked one (*imitatio naturae*) or to choose a specific heir. In the lower Middle Ages, the interest for the matter is sparse. Nonetheless, many contributions helped changing the outline of a juridical figure that, over a long time, has hardly been applied. In the Modern Era, a similar development continues, even bigger than the prior beliefs suggested. In fact, at the time, the life of adoption as a juridical figure (although not really widespread) went silently on, prior to its evident resurgence (in different guises) during the French Revolution, in a new conception of family and society, based on more egalitarian principles and, with less success, in the Napoleonic Era (as well as in the *Code civil*). The following centuries attested the necessity of the recourse to adoption, that nowadays finds its reason of being in "natural" grounds.

1 Premise

> C'est une idée communément reçue que l'adoption aurait disparu en Occident aux alentours du Xe siècle pour ne réapparaître que sous la Révolution. Reprise aux juristes des derniers siècles de l'Ancien Régime, cette affirmation répétée a tenu lieu de "dogme" jusqu'aux jours où, se tournant vers les actes de la pratique, les historiens du droit ont commencé à la mettre en doute. Trop de témoigner en sens contraire ont été relevés ces dernières décennies pour qu'on puisse y souscrire.

M.G. di Renzo Villata (✉)
University of Milan, Via Festa del Perdono 7, 20122 Milano, Italy
e-mail: gigliola.direnzovillata@unimi.it

M.G. di Renzo Villata (ed.), *Family Law and Society in Europe from the Middle Ages to the Contemporary Era*, Studies in the History of Law and Justice 5,
DOI 10.1007/978-3-319-42289-3_3

The quote is taken from Anne Lefebvre Teillard's thoughtful 1996 *Introduction historique au droit des personnes et de la famille,*[1] a work in which she attempted to trace a more accurate picture of the theoretical and practical aspects of adoption between the Middle Ages and the Modern Era. Though many features of adoptions remain obscure, this fact is not enough to deny its long term existence, in spite of certain unequivocal statements to the contrary found scattered in the works of the late *Ancien Régime* and in the historiography. In France, Olivier Martin, in 1922,[2] and, roughly more than a decade later, the works of Roger Aubenas[3] and Paul Gonnet, (who focused more narrowly on adoption)[4] helped to revise these opinions, which nonetheless have been persistently handed down by many different sources and even today linger on in modern historiographical studies.[5]

In the following pages I make no claim to providing a complete account of how adoption evolved, an institution which, even though it was not widely applied in the Middle Ages and the Modern and Contemporary Era, did continue to be practiced, not only because it met a number of emotional needs, but also (particularly during this period) economic and social needs that were deemed worthy of protection.

Later on, after the end of modern period, society would come to take on a new view of the family relationship, in accordance with nineteenth and twentieth century attitudes that paid more attention to internal interpersonal dynamics (whether in educational, emotional or charitable contexts) than to economic priorities. In this future society, more room would be given to adoption, itself now in need of legal redefinition, and a vision that would no longer be confined to national borders, but would embrace the requirements and "goodwill" of both prospective parents and needy children alike.

In this paper I intend to provide, in particular with regard to the Italian area (but without neglecting here and there laws and practices of other European territories) a historical and legal framework of the institution of adoption whose features were

---

[1]Lefebvre Teillard, Anne. 1996. *Introduction historique au droit des personnes et de la famille.* Paris: Presses Universitaires de France, 286.

[2]Olivier-Martin, François. 1922. *Histoire de la coutume de la prévôté et vicomté de Paris* 1. Paris: Éditions Ernest Leroux, 151, n. 1.

[3]Aubenas, Roger. 1934. L'adoption en Provence au Moyen-Age, *Revue historique du droit français et étranger* 13, 700–726: 700 ff.

[4]Gonnet, Paul. 1935. *L'adoption lyonnaise des orphelins légitimes (1536–1793).* Paris: Librairie Générale de Droit et de Jurisprudence.

[5]Cf. Goody, Jack. 1983. *The Development of the Family and Marriage in Europe.* Cambridge: Cambridge University Press, 71–74 (Italian translation by Maiello, Francesco. 1995. *Famiglia e matrimonio in Europa: origini e sviluppi dei modelli familiari dell'Occidente.* Roma-Bari: Laterza), especially 81–82, where there is also a hiatus from the affatomies to 1892 (*sic*!), date in which affatomies were reinstated. Cf. also Goody, Jack. 1976. *Family and Inheritance. Rural Society in Western Europe, 1300–1800,* ed. Goody, Jack, Thirsk, Joan and Thompson, E.P.. Cambridge-London-New York-Melbourne: Cambridge University Press, 4, 6, 122, 125–126, 128–130, 138, 181, 302–303, where the point is occasionally made that adoption was used to satisfy inheritance needs in the absence of heirs and, in any case, the tendency in many similar situations, to resort to other legal instruments like the recognition of 'bastardi' to serve the same needs.

clearly delineated in ancient law, but later often blurred in the tradition of the Middle Ages, in spite of the efforts of prominent jurists who rose to the challenge of interpreting a set of rules that had been modelled on longstanding practices and what these practices entailed.[6]

I will therefore focus on certain approaches preferred by contemporary scholars, men who were suspended between the past and their own day and who had been trained to recognise how the practice of adoption was evolving and moving away from the traditional schemata, how it was engendering different forms of "adoption" designed to meet the changing needs of daily life.

2 The Early Middle Ages—the Re-Deployment of Adoption According to Society's Needs

The *Summa Perusina* (dating back to the tenth century or even before, between the half of the seventh century and the end of the ninth), just to mention one early medieval juridical source, does not pay a great deal of attention to adoption; in this work adoption appears in its fundamental formalism, so that it may be validly performed only *apud publicum iudicem*, while the *adoptio per chartulam* is deemed as null and void.[7]

[6]Cf., for an initial brief approach, Vismara, Giulio. 1958. Adozione (diritto intermedio). In *Enciclopedia del diritto* 1. Milano: Giuffrè, 581–584 (also Vismara, Giulio. 1988. Scritti di storia giuridica 5. La famiglia. Milano: Giuffrè, 193–199); Marongiu, Antonio. 1958 Affiliazione (diritto intermedio), In *Enciclopedia del diritto* 1. Milano: Giuffrè, 671–673; also Tamassia, Nino. 1886. *L'affratellamento*. Torino: Fratelli Bocca; Tamassia, Nino. 1911–1971. La famiglia italiana nei secoli decimoquinto e decimosesto. Milano: R. Sandron; Roma: Multigrafica), 244 ff.; Pertile, Antonio. 1894. Storia del diritto italiano dalla caduta dell'Impero romano alla codificazione. Torino-Roma-Napoli-Milano: Unione tipografico-editrice, 394–396; Nani, Cesare. 1902. Storia del diritto italiano. Torino: Fratelli Bocca, 219 ff.; Pitzorno, Benvenuto.1914. L'adozione privata. Perugia: Unione tipografica cooperativa (cf. also Pitzorno, Benvenuto. 1904. L'affigliamento della Chiesa. Studio storico giuridico, Sassari: Satta; Roberti, Melchiorre. 1935 Svolgimento storico del diritto privato in Italia. 3. La famiglia (Padova: CEDAM, 329 ff. and Roberti, Melchiorre. 1932. Svolgimento storico della famiglia italiana. Milano: Giuffrè, 280–293; Besta, Enrico. 1933. La famiglia nella storia del diritto italiano. Padova: CEDAM, 46–55; Gualazzini, Ugo. 1957. Adozione (diritto intermedio). In *Novissimo Digesto Italiano* 1. Torino: UTET, 288–290. Now for more details see my papers: di Renzo Villata, Maria Gigliola. 2015a. Adoption between Middle Ages and Modern Era: was it in Decline. In Adoption and Fosterage Practices in the Late Medieval and Modern Age, edited by Maria Clara Rossi and Marina Garbellotti, Roma: Viella, 35–65; di Renzo Villata, Maria Gigliola. 2015b. L'adozione nell'Ottocento: un istituto in irreversibile declino?. In *Studi in onore di Giorgio De Nova*, Milano: Giuffrè, 1067–1098; di Renzo Villata, Maria Gigliola. 2016. Adozione e affido. Uno sguardo alla normativa vigente tra passato e futuro... tra luci e ombre. In Adozione e affido: per un approccio interdisciplinare, edited by Maria Clara Rossi and Marina Garbellotti. Roma: Viella (in press).

[7]*Adnotationes codicum domini Justiniani: Summa Perusina*. 1900/2008. ad C. 8.47 *de adoptionibus*, ed. Patetta, Federico. Romae: sumpt. F. Pasqualucci. Repr. Firenze: M. Pagliai, 286. The text was composed in the tenth century although using primarily seventh-century material; the

The *Lex Romana curiensis* (dating back to the first half of the eight century) briefly outlines the characteristics of adoption and makes the point that it is close to nature (it describes adoption as *naturae similitudo, ut aliquis filium habere possit, quem non generaverit,* which became a commonplace in the following centuries). It deals at length with the effects of *patria potestas* on those to be adopted or arrogated, and on the capacity to adopt or be adopted.[8]

It was, however, this *adoptio per chartulam tabellionis*, considered null and void by the *Summa Perusina,* which was preparing to take over the function of the *adoptio in hereditatem* in order to give an heir to those who had no children of their own, according to the principle of *imitatio naturae,* which is a point I shall return to. Frustrated paternal desires (which would be somehow satisfied by this), as well as Christian and ethical values were behind the push for its promotion and validation, though the adoptee would remain under the parental authority of his natural father. What also counted were the prospects of inheriting the adopter's estate. The documents attest to a widespread use of this instrument, which provided an answer to shared aspirations.[9]

In Lombard Law, the *thinx* or *gairethinx*, ("which Rotari incorrectly defined as 'donation' and was in fact a formal deed used to ensure the succession of an unrelated person *mortis causa* [...]")[10] could be used for the purposes of adoption.[11] If performed publicly, it revealed, through a series of symbolic gestures, the creation of the relationship between the adopter and the adoptee. Within the lombardized territories, the *chartae* contain meaningful formulas—such as that in the

---

(Footnote 7 continued)

manuscript containing the same dates back to the earlier eleventh century or to the tenth: see Cortese, Ennio. 1995.*Il diritto nella storia medievale* 1, *L'alto medioevo.* Roma: Il Cigno Galileo Galilei, 240–241; and Conrat, Max. 1891–1963. *Geschichte der Quellen und Literatur des römischen Rechts im früheren Mittelalter:* 1. Leipzig: J. C. Hinrichs. Repr. Aaalen: Scientia Verlag, 187.

[8]Cf. *Lex Romana curiensis (Sammlung Schweizerischer Rechtsquellen* 15, *Die Rechtsquellen des Kantons Graubünden* 1, *Alträtisches Recht,* I). 1966. ed. Meyer-Marthaler, Elisabeth. Aarau: Sauerländer, L-LIII (on the datation), 428, 594 ss., 614 ss., 657 ss., 675 ss., 722, 736 ss., 742, 753 ss.

[9]See Vismara, Giulio. 1941 Storia dei patti successori. Milano: Giuffrè, 162 ff., 167 ff., 190 ff., 208 ff., 221 ff., 272 ff., 333 ff., 344 ff.: one can read a wonderful reconstruction of the practice presence in the Italian territories during the early Middle Ages.

[10]See Cortese (as n. 7) 159, but also espec. 116n, 119–120, 133, 137–142, 161, 172n, 228, 236; already Id. 1988, *Thinx, gairethinx, thingare in gaida et gisil.* Divagazioni longobardistiche in tema di legislazione, manomissione dei servi, successioni volontarie, *Rivista di storia del diritto italiano* 61: 33–64, also In *Studi in memoria di Mario E. Viora.* 1990 [Biblioteca della Rivista di storia del diritto italiano 30]. Roma: Fondazione Sergio Mochi Onory per la Storia del Diritto Italiano, 279–310.

[11]See Schiaparelli, Luigi. 1929/1960. *Codice diplomatico longobardo.* 1. Roma: Tipografia del Senato. repr. Torino: Bottega d'Erasmo, 323–326: doc. 248; Schiaparelli, Luigi. 1933. *Codice diplomatico longobardo* 2. Roma: Tipografia del Senato, 194–196: doc. 62; Vismara (as n. 9) 272–274; Vismara (as n. 6) 582, also Id. 1988. *Scritti di storia giuridica* 5. Milano: Giuffrè, 193–199. For further details see di Renzo Villata. 2015 (as n. 6).

Audipert *charta donationis*, from 770 CE., and preserved in the *Codice Diplomatico Longobardo* (*in omnibus vos mihi succidatis, tamquam si de semine meo procreati fuissitis, et in omnia, ut dixit, vos mihi heredes legitimi succidatis*),—which contain a reference to the use of the *donatio post obitum* in favor of a brother's two natural children, in order to procure an heir for their adopter. Two conditions were laid down: the adopter's prior death and that no children of his own (either male or female) should suddenly be born; if this occurred then the donated goods were to be reduced by one-half, with the further obligation of donating a gold coin or the equivalent sum in wax, oil or other commodity to the Church of St. Salvatore of the Mount Amiata for the soul of the donor. But according to Vismara, this does not actually confer the *status* of children on the recipients "*and therefore it is not possible to talk about an adoption*",[12] even though the formula equating nephews with sons is, in fact, a form of *imitatio naturae* which is what characterizes adoption.

In another *chartula affiliationis* of 737 CE we find the designation (*Dolcissimis nobis semper et in bonis omnibus nominando [...] viri devote germani fili quondam Rothari optivi filiis meis*) referring to three orphans of a certain Rotari, who were provided with assets and for whom a life annuity was set up, so that they could live *quieti* with their possessions.[13] More generally speaking, we can concur with Vismara's statement that "the *adoptio* or the *adfilatio* are confused with the *donatio,* since the latter ensures the voluntary succession of the adopting person: both terms are even used in the deeds as synonyms".[14]

Under Frankish law affatomy (a complex ceremony unfolding through a sequence of symbolic actions involving numerous participants) served the purposes of an *adoptio in hereditatem*: the *Lex Ribuaria* 50 (623–650 CE) only allowed affatomy to childless persons and also mentions the *adoptio in hereditatem*: Charlemagne allowed affatomies for *qui filium non habuerit et alium quemlibet heredem sibi facere voluerit*; the *Formulae* (e.g. the *Marculfi Formulae*, dating back to the 7th century) that have come down to us show that affatomy was practised for persons who had lost their own children or had never had any and were therefore willing to adopt. While the *Pactus legis Salicae* (c. 510) 46 *de afathamire*, does not specifically refer to the term as an adoption, it was substantially the same thing. A foundational characteristic appears to be the very complex formal rite through which the act took place, a ceremony composed of several actions involving an intermediary who would receive the assets by means of symbolic gestures (like the *festuca* which was thrown to the recipient of the assets) subsequently transferred them to the heir: the patrimonial nature, according to

[12]Schiaparelli. (as n. 11). *Codice diplomatico longobardo*. 2, 323–326: doc. 248. See Vismara (as n. 9). *Storia dei patti successori*, pp. 272–274.

[13]Schiaparelli. (as n. 11). *Codice diplomatico longobardo*. 1, 194–196: doc. 62.

[14]Vismara (as n. 6) 582.

Schupfer, became less important than the willingness to "engender a son" or, what amounts to the same thing, "an heir of one's own".[15]

3 The Late Middle Ages: in the Footsteps of the Past?

While in the early Middle Ages interest in adoption nearly disappeared, this does not mean it re-emerged forcefully in the following centuries, unlike other institutes of family law. The jurists dealing with *ius commune* did not consider adoption in any great detail (one of the results of Franck Roumy's studies)[16]—but neither did they neglect it altogether, since they touched upon briefly it in a number of works dealing with certain essential points in the Justinian code that inspired their interpretative skills.

In the works of many glossators, who provided a detailed interpretation of the abovementioned *Corpus iuris*, various fragments dealing with adoption were scrutinized, in particular, the aspect of *imitatio naturae*; the transfer of the *patria potestas* from the natural father to the adopter; the nature of adoption as an *actus legitimus*, implying that certain formalities had to be complied with, but, above all, the subsequent legal effects deriving from adoption.

One potentially interesting approach involving the revival of Roman law looks at the *Brachyologus iuris civilis*, whose date and place of origin are uncertain but which is widely believed to have been compiled in Southern France at the beginning of the 12th century:[17] Following the Justinian Institutions, the work focuses on

[15]See *Lex Ribuaria* 50. 1969. In MGH. *Leges.Leges Nationum Germanicarum*. 3.2. ed. Beyerle, Franz- Buchner, Rudolf. Hannover: Hahnsche Buchhandlung, 101; *Lex Salica*. 1962. In *MGH. Leges. Sectio* I. 4/1. ed. by Eckardt. Karl August, Hannover: Hahnsche Buchhandlung, 176–181; *Capitularia Regum Francorum*. 1984. In MGH. *Legum Sectio* II/1.*Capitulare legi Ribuariae additum* 803. ed. by Boretius, Alfred. Hannover: Hahnsche Buchhandlung, 116; *Marculfi Formulae*, II.13. 1963. In MGH. *Legum Sectio V. Formulae*. ed. Zeumer, Karl, Hannover: Hahnsche Buchhandlung, 83–84. Cf. Cortese (as n. 10) 116n, 141; furthermore, Schupfer, Federico. 1891 but 1892. Thinx e affatomia. Studi sulle adozioni in eredità dei secoli barbarici, *Atti della R. Accademia dei Lincei, Memorie*, s. IV, 9, 3–44 for an in–depth analysis of the details according to Frankish law. Cf. also Gualazzini, Ugo. 1957. Affatomia. In *Novissimo Digesto Italiano* 1. Torino: UTET, 363–364: containing a brief description of the "*three separate acts*" in which affatomy took place, and with a critique of the mainstream opinion which considered the act as an *adoptio in hereditatem*, while Gualazzini emphasized its "undoubtedly translative" content, without however denying its purpose for inheritance.

[16]Cf. recently Roumy, Franck. 1998. *L'adoption dans le droit savant du XIIe au XVIe siècle*. Paris: Librairie générale de droit et de jurisprudence, in particular 101–103 and also, *passim*, for an effective treatment of adoption in medieval juridical science.

[17]Cf. Cortese, Ennio. 1995. *Il diritto nella storia medievale* 2, *Il basso medioevo*. Roma: Il Cigno Galileo Galilei, espec. 52–53; and also, for a vast bibliography, Weimar, Peter. 1973. Die legistische Literatur der Glossatorenzeit, In *Handbuch der Quellen und Literatur der neuren europäischen Privatrechtsgeschichte*, I. ed. by Helmut Coing, München: C.H. Beck Verlag, 129–260, 207–208.

the two forms of *adrogatio* and *adoptio*, which are distinct with regard to their respective passive subjects (the former is *sui iuris*, the latter *filiusfamiliae*, subject to the authority of another person) and their solemn formalities; with regard to their different effects (mandatory transfer of parental authority to the adrogating party, in the latter case, only in the event of adoption by the grandfather or by the great-grandfather from father's or mother's side); in their capacity requirements (*impotentia generandi* is an exclusion criterion: it also would prove to be an obstacle for later jurists); in the required age difference between parties, at least 17 years between the adopter and adoptee; in the incapacity of women *nisi ad solatium amissorum liberorum*, to adopt *in filium* or *in nepotem*, in the latter case, only with the consent of the son himself.[18]

Azo, the great Bolognese glossator, in his *Summa Codicis*, justifies listing *De Adoptionibus* immediately after *De Patria Potestate*, since adoption is a mechanism which creates paternal authority in the adopting persons who often don't have any children of their own, though this is not strictly necessary, so as to result in a situation *pene naturam imitans*: "Adoptio est legalis actio ad solatium eorum qui liberos non habent pene naturam imitans… Vel sic: adoptio est legitimus actus per quem qui filius non est pro filio habetur. Prima definitio non ita placet quia et liberos habentes adoptare possunt, licet facilius concedatur liberos non habentibus…"; there follows the classification of adoption as an *actus legitimus*, one of whose distinctive features is the legal change that occurs in the adoptee's standing *qui filius non est pro filius habetur*, whereby affiliation is unequivocally considered in relation to the adopting person.[19] A further aspect, affirmed by the *Summa Vindocinensis*, datable between 1164 and 1182 and produced by the school of Placentinus, mature third-generation glossator, is lapidary: *adoptio ius dumtaxat affert succedendi.*[20]

The effects of adoption go beyond inheritance. If the adoptee, notwithstanding and without prejudice for the rights arising out of natural affiliation, is recognized as having the right to inherit *ab intestato* from the adopter, (the 12th century *Summa Vindobonensis* includes among the *sui heredes* not only sons and daughters under the authority of the deceased person, but also his grandchildren—in case of their father's prior death- and adopted children (*Nec distinguo sive sint naturales, sive legitimi, an adoptivi*), and also, of course, adrogated children, then further sets of

[18]*Corpus legum sive Brachylogus iuris civilis*. 1829. lib. I, tit. X *De adoptionibus*, ed. by Eduard Böcking. Berolini: typis Feisterianis et Eisersdorffianis, 16–18, but cf. also lib. I, tit. VIII *de his qui sui iuris vel alieno iuri subiecti sunt*, 11–12.

[19]Azo. 1506/1966. *Summa Codicis*, 8.47 *de adoptionibus*, ed. Papie, repr. Torino: Bottega d'Erasmo, 322–323 of the repr.

[20]Cf. *Summa Vindocinensis*. ed. di Renzo Villata, Gigliola. 1976. Per un'edizione della *Summa Vindocinensis*. *Studia et documenta historiae et iuris* 42: 265–302, 275. The second date has been suggested by Gouron André. 1994. "Placentinus", "Herold" der Vermutungslehre?. In *Festschrift zum 65. Geburtstag und zur Emeritierung von Professor Dr. Hans Hiefner*, Münster: [s.n.], 90–103: 93, also Id. 2000. *Juristes et droits savants: Bologne et la France médiévale* (*Collected Studies Series* 679). Aldershot: Ashgate, 90–103.

rights are also recognized to the adoptees such as the right to receive material support, which Baldus links to the right to inherit *ab intestato*: "... hic dicit quod iste adoptatus ab extraneo habet ius succedendi ab intestato tantum, nisi sit emancipatus adoptante. Ibi, tantummodo, licet hic ponatur dictio taxativa, tamen alimenta debentur: nam si ab intestato succedit, ergo et ali debet...".[21] The same cannot be said about legal inheritance, for which one highly contested text, the l. *si adrogator*, establishes the amount due to the adrogated party as the *quarta*.

Much debated among legal scholars of the day was whether this *quarta* should be the *quarta* of the deceased person's unavailable portion or one-quarter of what the adrogated person would receive in the absence of a last will: otherwise, as scholars noted, the "false" son would inherit from the adrogating person more than the "true" sons, natural or legitimate. Bartolus, who wrote a very detailed commentary on this law, effectively noted that: "*Quarta non debetur totius haereditatis, sed ejus partis, quam quis esse habiturus ab intestato [...]*" and Baldus, just as careful about the fair and equal implications of the fragment, remarked: "dicitur hic quod impubes arrogatus debet habere quartam, ergo plus habebit adoptivus quam naturalis? ... Tamen contrarium deberet esse quia numquam fictio tantum valet ut melior veritate existat. Solutio: intellige sane de ea quarta de qua loquitur lex, scilicet de eius quarta quam habiturus esset ab intestato...".[22]

If there was a last will, the adopter did not have any obligations towards the adoptee but did for his other children, whom he had to bequeath or exclude from inheritance, unless the adoptee was a grandson under his own authority, or had been adrogated.[23]

The scholars tend to consider *adoptio* as a *nomen generale* that also includes *adrogatio*,[24] if the adopted person is *sui iuris*, not subject to another's authority, and *adoptio* of an *alieni iuris*, himself under the authority of a *sui iuris*. The passage in the *Summa aurea* and in the *Lectura* of Henricus Segusiensis, as if meant to

---

[21] *Summa Vindobonensis*. ed. Palmieri, Gian Battista. Wernerii Summa Institutionum cum glossis Martini, Bulgari, Alberici aliorumque. 1913–1962. ad Inst. 3.1. In *Bibliotheca Iuridica Medii Aevi. Scripta anecdota glossatorum* 1, *Additiones*. Bononiae: Società Azzoguidiana, repr. Torino: Bottega d'Erasmo, 93. Among the sources, cf., e.g., Martinus Fanensis. 1953. *Tractatus de alimentis*, 4, ed. Ugo Nicolini. In *Atti del congresso internazionale di diritto romano* (Verona, September 27–29 1948), I. Milano: Giuffrè, 339–371: 341; then Baldus. 1585. *Commentaria in VII. VIII. IX. X. et XI Cod. Lib.* Lugduni: [s.n.], f. 200r: ad C. 8.47 de *adoptionibus* l. *Cum in adoptivis*, no. 4. As to the alimony, cf. Pene Vidari, Gian Savino. 1972. *Ricerche sul diritto agli alimenti*, I. *L'obbligo "ex lege" dei familiari nei giuristi dei sec. XII–XIV*. Torino: Giappichelli, 77 ff., 177 ff.

[22] Bartolus. 1570. *Commentaria in primam ff. Veteris partem*, ad D. 1.7. 22 *de adoptionibus* l. *Si adrogator*, no. 8. Venetiis: apud Iuntas, f. 27r.; Baldus. 1585. *Commentaria in primam Digesti Veteris partem*, ad D. 1.7. 22 *de adoptionibus* l. *Si adrogator*, no. 17 (Lugduni: [s.n.], 52v).

[23] Rolandinus. 1546/1977, "Flos testamentorum", cap. *De legitima liberis tantum*, in Id., *Summa totius artis notariae*. Venetiis: apud Iuntas, 1546, repr. Sala Bolognese: Forni, 248r.

[24] Cf. Accursius. 1551. gl. *similiter* ad D. 1.7.1 *de adoptionibus* l. *Filiofamilias* e gl. *Generalis* ad D. 1.7. 2 *de adoptionibus* l. *generalis*. Lugduni: apud Hugonem a Porta et Antonium Vincentium, 40.

underline the various differences between *adrogatio* and *adoptio*, runs as follows: "*Arrogo qui suus est, et habes meus esse necesse. Patris adopto suum, nec patris desinit esse*"; more or less the same terms were used by the *Summa Coloniensis* (conducted on the *Decretum Gratiani*, of the Franco-Renan school around 1169) and by Rolandinus, in his *Flos testamentorum,*[25] and Johannes Andrea[26] who were following in the footsteps of earlier scholars.

These scholars justify adoption arguing from the principle of *imitatio naturae* which implies likeness but not equal status. Contemporary attitudes saw a profound difference between a natural son, in whose veins there flowed the same blood as his parent's, and an adopted one, linked to the adopter by a relationship that had resulted from his free choice but one that was ultimately artificial and very far from the sort of identification between a natural son and his father whom he resembles "in specie et etiam in effigie, maxime quando virtus in semine patris vincit virtutem in semine matris",[27] a "patriarchal" male-oriented vision perfectly consistent with the period.[28]

It is precisely in this regard that disagreement arose over what requirements adopters and adoptees should have. The glossators wondered whether adoption should only be allowed to those who are childless, especially men, or to women (with exemptions for women who had lost their sons in war and for religious grounds[29]), and whether an *infans*, unable to express his consent, may be adrogated. Accursius recalls the dispute among a number of celebrated scholars of the past

---

[25]Rolandinus (as n. 23) 248r.

[26]Henricus Segusiensis (Hostiensis). 1574–1963 *Summa aurea*, ad X.4.12 *de cognatione legali*, n. 2, Venetiis: apud Iacobum Vitalem, 1574, repr. Torino: Bottega d'Erasmo, 1340: where the variant *adoptio*, has not been corrected compared to what was reported by other sources); Id., *In quartum Decretalium librum Commentaria* (hereinafter, *Lectura*), ad X. 4.12. 1 *de cognatione legali* c. *Si qua*, 25r. But the same sentence is found in almost the same terms in the *Summa* "*Elegantius in iure divino*" *seu Coloniensis [super Decretum Gratiani]*, t. IV, XV.9, ed. by Fransen, Gerard and Kuttner, Stephan. 1990 (*Monumenta iuris canonici*, Series A: *Corpus Glossatorum*, vol. I). Città del Vaticano: Biblioteca Apostolica Vaticana, 102: "Arrogo qui suus est, et habet meus esse necesse. Patris adopto suum nec patris desinit esse". For the dating cf. Nörr, Knut Wolfgang. 1973. *Kanonistische Literatur.* In *Handbuch der Quellen und Literatur*, I (as n. 17), 373. Cf. also Iohannes Andreae. 1581/1963. *In quartum Decretalium librum Novella Commentaria*... Venetiis: apud Franciscum Franciscium Senensem; repr. Torino: Bottega d'Erasmo, 39r: *ad* X. 4.12.1 *de cognatione legali*, super rubr.

[27]Bartolomeus Anglicus. 1609. *De genuinis rerum coelestium, terrestrium et infernarum proprietatibus libri XVIII.* Francofurti: apud Wolfgangum Richterum, sumptibus Nicolai Stenii, 247.

[28]Cf. Roumy (as n. 16) p. 145 ff.; also Krynen, Jacques. 1982. Naturel. Essai sur l'argument de la nature dans la pensée politique française à la fin du Moyen Âge. *Journal des savants*: 169–190. Roumy (as n. 16, 149, mentions Bartolomeus Anglicus).

[29]Cf. *Summa Vindobonensis*. 1914. Ad I.12.3, ed. in *Bibliotheca Iuridica Medii Aevi*, t. I, *Additiones.* Bologna: Società Azzoguidiana, 14.

including (according to Petrus de Anzola, annotator of Rolandinus de Passeggeriis, the great master of *ars notarie*) his own teacher, Azzone[30] whose view he shared: "est autem adoptio secundum Placentinum et Johannem legalis actio ad solatium eorum, qui liberos non habent, pene id est fere naturam imitans. Sed certe et ab iis, qui liberos habent, fit adoptio, ut ff. eodem l. nec ei § praeterea (D. 1.7.17.3), et infra eodem § licet (Inst. 1.11.5); quare sic potest simpliciter definiri. Adoptio est legitimus actus per quem fit quis filius qui non est pene naturam imitans, et haec est veritas ut ff. eodem l. I (D. 1.7.1) et infra eodem § minorem (Inst. 1.11.4)".[31]

The difference, as Accursius recalls (but also Henricus Segusiensis) is grounded on a different way of understanding *imitatio naturae* which the sources say was the purpose of the practice and which, in hindsight and in the light of what we know today, appears not to have been so marked: in the *Lectura Vindobonensis*, a work of the second generation of Glossators, the Author links adoption, *ad solatium eorum inventa qui filiis carentes*,[32] but, shortly thereafter, Placentinus himself (already mentioned above) argued in the *Summa Codicis*, that no distinction should be made between a childless person and a person with children; Placentinus only opposed adoption by a person incapable of generating.[33] Odofredus also did not approve of this distinction.[34] Contemporary canonists, from Henricus Segusiensis to Nicolaus de Tudeschis, agreed that whoever already has children may also adopt, even though adoption more frequently regards those who are childless.[35] On these

[30]Azo (as n. 19). Cod. 8.48 *de adoptionibus*, pr.–no. 1, 322–323: "Adoptio est legalis actio ad solatium eorum, qui liberos non habent, inducta, pene naturam imitans... Vel sic. Adoptio est legitimus actus per quem qui filius non est pro filio habetur. Prima enim definitio non ita placet, quia et liberos habentes adoptare possunt, licet facilius concedatur liberos non habentibus. Sed certe et ab iis, qui liberos habent, fit adoptio".

[31]Cf. Accursius (as n. 24). gl. *adoptio* ad Inst. 1.11.1 *de adoptionibus* § *Adoptio*, 37; Petrus de Anzola, ad *Instrumentum adoptionis*, in Rolandinus, *Summa*... (as n. 23), pars I cap. VII, 174va: see. *infra*.

[32]*Lectura Vindobonensis*, I.12 *De adoptionibus*, ed. in *Bibliotheca Iuridica Medii Aevi*, t. I, *Additiones*, p. 13.

[33]Cf. Placentinus. 1536/1962. *Summa Cod.* 8. 51 *de adoptionibus*: "Adoptare potest qui filium habet, sed et qui habuerit, et non habet; sed et qui non habet, et non habuerit; sed et qui nunquam de iure habere potest, ut sacerdos, qui nec uxorem accipere, sed non is, qui generare non potest". Moguntiae: in officina Ivonis Schoeffer, repr. Torino: Bottega d'Erasmo, 412.

[34]Odofredus. 1522/1968, ad C. 8.47.3 *de adoptionibus* l. *Cum eum*, nrr.1, in Id., *In secundam Codicis partem praelectiones*. Lugduni: Compagnie des libraires de Lyon, excudebat Blasius Guido. Repr. *Lectura super Codice*. II. Bologna: Forni, 174v.

[35]Cf. Henricus Segusiensis. 1581/1965. *Summa aurea*.... (as n. 26) ad X.4.12, 1339; Id. 1574–1963. *In quartum Decretalium librum Comm*.... (as n. 26), ad X. 4.12. 1 *de cognatione legali* c. *Si qua*, super rubr., 25r (in *Summarium*); Nicolaus de Tudeschis (Abbas Panormitanus). 1547. *In quartum et quintum] Decretalium librum interpretationes*... ad X.4.12.1 *de cognatione legali* c. *Si qua*, ed. Lugduni: ad candentis Salamandrae insigne in vico Mercenario apud Senetonios fratres, 36r. ecc.

questions, modern scholars who have looked closely at medieval legal science have reached the same conclusions.[36]

The *imitatio naturae* is a sort of recurring *topos*, repeated almost to a fault[37] (Odofredus, not an "original" jurist, though a competent one, is an example) used to recall the past, but also to justify a future model (natural affiliation) to follow, which it cannot overlap with since it is an *imitatio*: "qui non est filius efficitur filius ei qui non habet liberos pene naturam imitans"; "qui non est filius natura efficitur filius que naturam imitatur"; "qui non est natura filius, efficitur lege filius que naturam veram imitatur".[38] Careful jurists, when considering the characteristics of adoption, immediately flagged its nature of *artificium, fictio, imaginaria paternitas* or *ficta filiatio*, as did Jason de Majno, the Milanese jurist who, near the end of 1400s, very articulately summed up how earlier legal opinion on the *Corpus Iuris* had evolved, describing a father/son relationship which is not natural, but, as it were, artificially reproduced, as far as this is possible.[39] Henricus Segusiensis, in the 1200s, in the *Lectura* correctly referred to a *quaedam propinquitas legaliter facta* (in the same terms used by Antonius da Butrio the following century),[40] and, in the *Summa aurea*, of a *quaedam proximitas ex adoptione proveniens*.[41]

As regards the *infans*, a similar dispute involved Placentinus, Azo and Accursius, who all opposed *adrogatio* in this case[42] while Iohannes Bassianus was open to allowing it if the child's relatives deemed the adrogation useful for it.[43]

---

[36]Roumy (as n. 16) 151 ff. with a broad analysis of the various conditions of *incapacitas generandi.*

[37]Cf. e.g. gl. *adoptio* ("Accursius post Theophilum et Placentinum dicit adoptionem actum esse legitimum, naturam imitantem, ad solatium eorum qui liberos non habent. Pe, e *ut is qui. Et*", to *Corpus legum sive Brachylogus iuris civilis...* (as n. 18) 207).

[38]Odofredus (as n. 34) ad D. 1.7 *de adoptionibus*, in rubr., in Id., *Repetita in Undecim primos Pandectarum libros*, 21r; Id., ad C. 8.47.3..., nrr. 1–2, f. 174v.

[39]Majno, Jason de. 1579. *In Primam Infortiati partem Commentaria*, ad D. 28.2.23 *De liberi et posthumis* l. *Filio quem pater*, no. 13. Venetiis: [Giunta], f. 147v: "Adoptio dicitur imago et sic actus imaginarius et consequenter fictus, non autem verus, et sic adoptio dicitur quaedam immaginaria paternitas"; Id. 1579. *In Primam Digesti Novi partem Commentaria* ad D. 41.3.15 *De usucapionibus* l. *Si is qui pro emptore*, no. 213. Venetiis: [Giunta], 99r: "... adoptio solum habet locum in illis personis, in quibus et natura potest habere locum, ergo adoptio, quae est ficta filiatio, non posset habere locum ubi non posset habere locum veritas et natura, et sic fictio non fingit super impossibili de natura".

[40]Henricus Segusiensis (Hostiensis) (as n. 26), ad X. 4.12 *de cognatione legali*, super rubr., 25r. Cf. also Antonius de Budrio. 1578/1967. *In Librum Quartum Decretalium Commentarii*, ad X. 4.12. *de cognatione legali*, super rubr. Venetiis: apud Iuntas. Repr. Torino: Bottega d'Erasmo, 33r.

[41]Henricus Segusiensis (Hostiensis) (as n. 26) ad X. 4.12, 1339.

[42]Placentinus (as n. 33). ad 8.51 *de adoptionibus*, p. 412; Azo (as n. 19). ad C. 8. 47 *de adoptionibus*, 323 (repr.): the reason was the absence of a *verbum expressum*, that is, the absence of an explicit consent.

[43]Cf. Accursius (as n. 24). gl. *generalis* ad D. 1.7.2 *de adoptionibus* l. *Generalis*, 40; also gl. *adrogatio* ad Inst. 1.11.1 *de adoptionibus* § *adoptio*, 37.

Henricus Segusiensis recalls the practice of "affiliating" a person, noting the term's lack of precision, although it was used *vulgariter*.[44] Johannes Andreae spoke about the practice, with regard to Provence, where unrelated girls were affiliated *sicut vulgariter dicitur in provincia, ipso iudice hoc probante et auctorizante*.[45]

In fact, at the time there was no single terminology in use. *Adfiliatio* was confused with adoption, as we see in Italy in two Cassinean documents of 1271 and 1273: in the earlier, *adoptio* is considered as an *adoptionis species, quae legalem cognationem inducit*, while, in the later, sibi in *filium adoptare sive, ut eorum verbis utamur, affiliare in tota medietate vel tertia parte bonorum suorum*.[46] Historians have investigated the essential meaning of the two terms and have reached different conclusions: Pitzorno saw affiliation as being more autonomous than adoption, Schupfer disagreed, stating that Pitzorno's ideas were the product of a "*dream world*"; in Schupfer's view *adfiliatio* was a generic word that could be used to indicate different kinds of relationships, personal, patrimonial or spiritual.[47]

In the Middle Ages adoption was an act that necessarily had to meet certain requirements of formality and solemnity: this can be inferred from the fact the sources designate it as an *actus legitimus*.

In this regard, Petrus de Ancharano, just to name an example, later distinguished adrogation (but the same arguments apply to adoption) from legitimation, itself an *actus legitimus* characterized by solemn formalities, since the former is *mere civilis*, while the latter is founded *in naturalitate ex consensu amovendo maculam geniturae redigit legitimatum ad statum naturae*.[48]

While the act of adoption's formality is also important because of its effect on the family's composition (which had to be, in a manner of speaking, "registered") how the relationship terminated is equally important. The adoptive relationship terminates, in most cases, when the adopter dies, or if he is stripped of his civil rights—his *damnatio in metallum* or *deportatio in insulam*,[49] in addition to (quite obviously) the death of the adoptee. But apart from these "natural"causes, terminating an adoptive relationship also had to respect certain formalities, just like when

---

[44]Henricus Segusiensis (Hostiensis) (as n. 26). ad X. 4.12.1 *de cognatione legali* c. *Si qua*, in pr., 25r; Id. (as n. 26). *Summa aurea*. ad X.4.12, no. 2, 1339.

[45]Iohannes Andreae (as n. 23), *In quartum Decretalium librum Novella Commentaria....*, *ad* X. 4.12.1 *de cognatione legali* c. *Si qua*, in pr., 39v.

[46]Gattola, Erasmo. 1734. *Ad historiam abbatiae cassinensis accessiones* 1. Venetiis: apud Sebastianum Coleti, 326 e 332.

[47]Cf. Pitzorno.1906 (as n. 6). *L'adozione privata*; also Id. 1906 (as n. 6). *L'affigliamento della Chiesa*; then Schupfer, Federico. 1915. L'adozione privata. Dal mondo dei sogni, *Rivista italiana di scienze giuridiche* 55: 323–355; on the two positions, cf. Marongiu (as n. 6) in particular 672–673.

[48]Cf. Petrus de Ancharano. 1549. *Consilia*. Lugduni: apud haeredes Iacobi Giuntae, 120r: cons. 290.

[49]Cf. Henricus Segusiensis (as n. 26). *Summa aurea...*, ad X.4.12, 1341–1342; Id. (as n. 26). ad X. 4.12.1 *de cognatione legali* c. *Si qua*, no. 10, 25r: both works also in in other cases of extinction attributable to the adoptive father.

the relationship was created: on this point, the most perceptive medieval jurists unanimously agree.[50]

It would be interesting to know what the formalities were in notarial practice for the lawful creation of an adoptive relationship.

One could look at many formulas and almost all might be useful. I have selected just a few examples.

In the *Formularium florentinum artis notariae*, dated by its first publisher between 1220 and 1242, the adoption formula assumes the presence of a childless adopter (*Cum civilis iuris constitutione filium non habentem sibi facere quempiam posse decernitur adoptione, idcirco [...]*), an adoptee who is present and gives his consent, and the latter's adoption *in sua familia et potestate [...] cum omnibus rebus et bonis et iuribus et actionibus suprascriptis, ut sit deinceps plenissime in sua potestate et filiatione, iure, disciplina, ac si propria eiusdem fili agnosceretur natura*: and so (and accompanied by numerous qualifications and conditions so as to render the act as clear and certain as possible) the adoptee is acknowledged completely and fully, made equal to a natural son and promised the adopter's protection *more paterno* who will manage and protect his assets on his behalf, and who, furthermore, promises not to terminate the relationship *sine iusta et probabili ratione*, under a penalty and a security of his own assets (*sub hypotheca rerum suarum, omni merito et launachii*), with an allusion to the Lombard institutions (understandable given the territory the act is destined for), as well as renouncing any other claim.[51]

The *ars notarie* by Rainerius of Perugia (whose content is of no great importance in this field) limits itself, in the *Carta adoptionis et arrogationis* (both alternatives are dealt with), to considering the deed in its aim of creating the relationship (*in filium suum adoptavit et in familia et potestate sua paterno affectu suscepit*) and specifies that the *podestà* must take part in the formal execution of the act along with the *iudiciaria cognitio* of his judge and assessor.[52]

---

[50]Henricus Segusiensis (as n. 49) 25r.

[51]*Formularium florentinum artis notariae (1220–1242)*. 1943. ed. by Gino Masi. Milano: Vita e pensiero, 30–31, rubr. *De adoptionibus filiorum*, also cf. LXIX ff. for the dating; *Un formulario notarile fiorentino della metà del Dugento*. 1997. ed. by Silio P. Scalfati, Firenze: EDIFIR, 75 (cf. also 13–14, concerning Masi's opinion on the origins of the work from a school independent from the Bologna one, contested to the point of being described as groundless by Scalfati.

[52]Rainerius de Perusio.1917. *Ars notarie*, XLVI *Carta adoptionis et arrogationis*, in *Quellen zur Geschichte des römisch–kanonischen Prozesse im Mittelalter*, III/2, ed. by Ludwig Wahrmund, Innsbruck: Wagner, 51. Cf. also, with a simplified formula, Id. 1892. *Ars notarie*, CXII *de adoptionibus*, ed. by Augusto Gaudenzi. In *Scripta anecdota glossatorum*. Bononiae: Società Azzoguidiana, 53: the adoption deed (under the *Liber formularius*, prior to the *Ars notarie*: Wahrmund, *Quellen...*, III/2 already proposed to mention the work this way) is carried out with the due solemnities "auctoritate domini Ranierii de Lacu perusino, domini Ottonis imperatoris iudicis ordinarii". This Emperor had to be Otto IV of Brunswick (1182–1218), tormented and contested Emperor, until he was excommunicated by Innocent III and deprived of the imperial crown he had received in Rome in 1209, following the 1211 election of Frederick to King of the Romans.

The Bencivenne *Ars notarie,* dated around the same period and which appears to have been influenced by Ranierius of Perugia, (mainly his *Liber formularius*) contains a *Carta adoptionis et arrogationis* which also calls for the mandatory presence of the public authority, represented by the Bologna *podestà* Giovanni of Ravenna and his judge and assessor Accursius, in addition to the presence of the adopter, the adoptee, the adoptee's natural father who must give his consent. The act is carried out with the ritual formula (*in filium suum adoptavit*), and is accompanied by the adopter declaring that he will accept the adoptee into his family *paterno affectu*, and includes a protection clause guaranteeing the rights of the natural father (*salvo omni iure sui patris naturalis*).[53]

Martinus Fanensis looks into a series of formulas regarding the *adoptio plena* (the adopter is the adoptee's ancestor implying that the latter will come under his authority) and *minus plena* (the adopter is not related to the adoptee and, usually, there is no passage under his authority), and considers the various possibilities for the adopting-adrogating person, as well as those for the adopted-adrogated person. He supports his examples with a set of principles taken from Roman law. The *adrogatio*, subject to the prior authorization *a Fr(iderico) Romanorum Imperatore* takes the form of a complex procedure performed before the ordinary judge who determines that both the adrogating party and the *sui iuris* adrogated party are participating actively, after which the adrogated party, after being asked, expressly grants his consent to be transferred under the authority of the adrogating party. As regards questions of inheritance, the consequence, clearly indicated, is one of more rights than for an adoptee, *quia in omnibus fere habetur pro filio*, and, in the case of unjustified emancipation or disinheritance, the right to one quarter of the new father's estate upon his death.[54]

Far less exhaustive is Salatiele, author of a by no means mediocre *Ars notarie,* who adds little content to the formula, but focuses on the presence of the public authority. This figure is identified as Giacomo, judge and assessor to the Milanese Rizzardo da Villa, *podestà* in Bologna for the first time in 1250/51[55] (the same person in the Rolandinian formulary) and entrusted with the *iudiciaria cognitio* to attest to the due compliance with the formalities, which in this case were legitimized by the *podestà*; also taking part in the act were the adopter and the adoptee's father who was present and consenting.[56] In another part of the work, the Author clarified the exact legal status of the adopted children, who were only legitimate

[53]Bencivenne 1965. *Ars notarie*, ed. by Bronzino, Giovanni. Bologna: Zanichelli, 72. For the dating, cf. the *Introduzione* of Bronzino, X ff., which leans toward a date between the third and fourth decade of 13th century, not excluding the date of 1235 proposed by Gaudenzi.

[54]Martinus Fanensis. 1907. *Formularium*, rubr. CXLVI *De adoptione*, CXLVII *Libellus*, CXLVIII *Libellus*, CIL *De arrogatione*, CL *Libellus*, ed. by Ludwig Wahrmund, *Quellen zur Geschichte des römisch-kanonischen Processes im Mittelalter*, I.VIII. Innsbruck: Wagner, 61–64.

[55]Rizzardo da Villa was again *podestà* in 1255 and people's captain in 1269.

[56]Salatiele. 1971, *Ars notarie*, vol. II. II, IV, rubr., in *Instrumentum adoptionis*, *La seconda stesura dei codici della Biblioteca Nazionale di Parigi lat. 4593 e lat. 14622*, ed. by Gianfranco Orlandelli (Istituto per la storia dell'Università di Bologna. Opere dei maestri II). Milano: Giuffrè, 300.

because the law declared them as such, and not *legitimi et naturales: quia natura interveniente non procreantur, sed per adoptionem non efficiuntur filii.* A gloss added to the word *filii* distinguishes among the children: *non tamen natura, quia, licet adoptio pene naturam mutet ... tamen adoptive, veritate inspecta, filii non sunt.* The words *pene naturam mutet* convey all the tension in the identification with natural filiation, which, in light of the actual situations, cannot be complete.[57]

Some years later, drawing numerous details from Roman sources, Zaccaria di Martino, the author of a *Summa artis notarie* (dateable to between 1255 and 1273), emphasizes the theoretical premises of the formulas, in line with the principles derived from the Justinian compilation, and considers from among the wide array of schemes suggested to the practitioners, a *carta adoptionis emancipati,* a *carta extranei adoptati,* a *carta non extranei adoptati,* a *carta adoptionis filii naturalis* and a *carta arrogationis impuberis,* to be drawn up by the adrogating party *coram tali domino imperatore et ab eodem interrogatus* in favor of an orphan, *interrogatum et respondentem,* and preceded by a dissertation on the fundamental rules of *arrogatio.*[58]

A firm point in the field is the *Summa artis notariae* by Rolandinus,[59] who situates adoption within the broader context family law. The family whose composition changes over time, since the number of its members change, may remain stable for a longer or shorter period, may shrink or grow by virtue of the birth of legitimate children, adoptions or adrogations. The rarity of the latter practice, is immediately flagged by Rolandinus and Petrus de Anzola, his annotator (like Rolandinus Petrus de Boatteriis would later stress their uselessness),[60] but the former scholar also wished to provide the notaries with a workable scheme they could use, in the wake of earlier experts in *ars notariae.*[61] The latter, also aware of

[57]Salatiele, *Ars notarie, Recensio I, De filiis legitimis et naturalibus et aliorum diversitatibus,* ed. by Orlandelli 1, 37.

[58]Zaccaria di Martino. 1993. *Summa artis notarie,* ed. Ferrara, Roberto. Bologna: s.n. (San Giovanni in Persiceto: F.A.R.A.P.), 357–361. For the chronology ibid., xx, though the work had been in "gestation" for several decades before.

[59]Cf. on this specific point di Renzo, Maria Gigliola. 2002. Il volto della famiglia medievale tra pratica e teoria nella *Summa totius artis notariae.* In *Rolandino e l'ars notaria da Bologna all'Europa* (Studi storici sul notariato italiano). Milano: Giuffrè, 377–458; with an amended title and variants, di Renzo, Maria Gigliola. 2002. Il volto della famiglia medievale tra pratica e teoria nella 'Rolandina'. In *Studi in memoria di Giovanni Cattaneo* 1, Milano: Giuffrè, 615–699.

[60]Cf. Petrus de Boatteriis. 1546. *Expositio…,* VII cap., r. I ("non multum utilibus"), in Rolandinus (as n. 23). *summa totius artis notariae* 2, 45rb.

[61]Cf. *Formularium tabellionum* pseudoirneriano, lib. III, § XIII, 38; Moschetti, Guiscardo. 1990. *Il cartularium veronese del magister Ventura del secolo XIII,* rr. *Quid sit adoptacio, Carta adoptationis.* Napoli: Edizioni scientifiche italiane, 25–27; Rainerius de Perusio, *Ars notarie…,* ed. by Wahrmund, *Quellen…,* XLVI *Carta adoptionis et arrogationis,* 51 (cf. also Rainerius Perusinus, *Liber formularius…,* r. In *Bibliotheca iuridica Medii Aevi,* Bononiae: Società Azzoguidiana, 1892), 53; Martinus Fanensis, *Formularium,* rubr. CXLVI *De adoptione,* ed. by Wahrmund, *Quellen…* CXLVII *Libellus,* CXLVIII *Libellus,* CIL *De arrogatione,* CL *Libellus,* 61–64; *Summa Notariae Aretii composita…,* rubr. CXXVII *carta adoptionis et arrogationis,* 317; see also *supra* for the other *ars notarie* therein mentioned.

how sporadic the practices were, does not miss the opportunity of introducing the topic into a wider array of concepts and giving it a systematic treatment. The author accompanies the categories of adoption and adrogation by describing a hierarchy of legal powers (in line with Roman tradition) while keeping an eye on his own period: from *imperium merum* to the *mixtum*, to the *iurisdictio*, one after another, all the characteristics of the various offices of the day are examined and inserted into a power structure which, though it is new, is also linked to the past, through its reference to ancient laws.[62] Petrus de Boatteriis would later draw distinctions among different kinds of authority. Within the broad category of *potestas* he distinguished: paternal authority, the *dominica potestas* of the master over the slave, the authority of the abbot over the monk, termed *oboedientia*, the authority of the guardian over the child (or the *adultus*) and finally the *dominatio* of the prince over his subjects, all of which he goes on to treat systematically.[63]

[62]Cf. Ficker, Julius. 1869. *Forschungen zur Reichs und Rechtsgeschichte Italiens*, IV. Innsbruck: Wagner, n. 526; Carlyle, Robert Warrand and Carlyle, Alexander James. 1909. *A History of Mediaeval Political Theory* 2. Edinburgh and London: Blackwood, 58 ff., (Italian translation by Luigi Firpo. 1956. *Il pensiero politico medievale*, Bari: Laterza, 371 ff.); Gilmore, Myron Piper. 1941/1967. *Argument from Roman Law in Political Thought 1200–1600* (Harvard Historical Monographs, XV). Cambridge Mass.: Harvard University Press. Repr. New York: Russel & Russel, 17–92; Calasso, Francesco. 1953. "Iurisdictio" nel diritto comune classico. In *Studi in onore di Vincenzo Arangio Ruiz nel XLV anno del suo insegnamento*, IV. Napoli: Jovene, 420–433: 423 ff.; Id. 1957. *I glossatori e la teoria della sovranità* Milano: Giuffrè, in particular 49 ff., 83 ff.; 101; Cortese, Ennio. 1964–1995. *La norma giuridica. Spunti teorici nel diritto comune classico*, II. Milano: Giuffrè, repr. Milano: Giuffrè, 229; 379, in particular n. 29; but also 169 ff.; Costa, Pietro. 1969–2002. *Iurisdictio. Semantica del potere politico nella pubblicistica medievale (1100–1433)*. Milano: Giuffrè. Repr. Milano: Giuffrè, *passim*; relevant allusions also in Quaglioni, Diego. 1983. *Politica e diritto nel Trecento italiano. Il "De tyranno" di Bartolo da Sassoferrato (1314–1357)*. Firenze: Olschki, with the critical edition of "*De Guelphis et Gebellinis*", "*De regimine civitatis*" e "*De tyranno*", in particular 41 ff.; as well as in Martino, Federico. 1983. In tema di "potestas condendi statuta". Indagini sul pensiero di Ranieri Arsendi da Padova, *Quaderni Catanesi*, V, 10, 461–482 (now, with amendments, in Id. 1984. *Dottrine di giuristi e realtà cittadine nell'Italia del Trecento. Ranieri Arsendi a Pisa e a Padova* (Studi e ricerche dei "Quaderni Catanesi", 5). Catania: C. Tringale. Cf. more recently Storti Storchi, Claudia. 1991. Appunti in tema di "potestas condendi statuta". In *Statuti città territori in Italia e Germania tra Medioevo ed Età moderna* (*Annali dell'Istituto Storico italo-germanico in Trento*, Quaderno 30), ed. by Chittolini, Giorgio and Willoweit, Dietmar. Bologna: il Mulino, 319–343, also in the german version. *Betrachtungen zum thema 'Potestas condendi statuta'*. In *Statuten Städte und Territorien zwischen Mittelalter und Neuzeit in Italien und Deutschland*, Berlin: Duncker & Humblot, 251–270), now in Storti Storchi, Claudia. 2007. *Scritti sugli statuti lombardi*. Milano: Giuffrè, 115–138; as well as, on some aspects of the concept, Quaglioni, Diego. 1977. "Quilibet in domo sua dicitur rex" (In margine ad alcune pagine di Francesco Calasso). *Studi senesi* 89: 344–358.

[63]Rolandinus, *Summa*... (as n. 23), pars I cap. VII, 175r; Pietro of Anzola, ad *Praefatio*, in Rolandinus, *Summa*... (as n. 23), pars I cap. VII, 174ra; Petrus de Boatteriis, *Expositio*, VII cap., r. I, In Rolandinus. *Summa* (as n. 23), II, 45rb.

To return to Rolandino, Roman law, in the form Justinian left to the following age,[64] constitutes the essential fabric of the exposition, which is aimed at pratical application, while the more reductive arguments of the Early Middle Ages do not come to the surface.[65]

In the *instrumentum adoptionis*, constructed on the stated premise that it is to be used "*ad solatium eorum qui filios non habent*", the request made by the adopting person to the natural father to adopt the child is followed by the handing over of the latter: the natural father, in the presence of the *domini Sca. Iudicis et assessoris domini Ro. Potestatis Bononiae*, gives the adopted child, who is present and consenting, to the future adoptive father, and places the child under the adopter's paternal *omni naturali iure sibi et in se in integrum reservato.*[66]

The acting judge, "*Scacanellus*" of the abovementioned *podestà* Rizzardo Villa,[67] is constantly referred to in the *Summa artis notariae* (we also saw him in Salatiele's *Ars notarie*) in order to indicate the authorities' intention to intervene decisively in the interest of a minor and act in order to protect the child's position while at the same time affirming their own role of closely overseeing issues that involve the family, which was one of the pillars of the communal organization.

Fully conversant with the institutional situation in Bologna, Rolandinus indicates the "*iudex atque assessor*" of the Bologna *podestà* as the person empowered to

[64]See Branca, Giuseppe. 1958. Adozione (diritto romano). In *Enciclopedia del diritto* 1. Milano: Giuffrè, 579–581.

[65]See Pitzorno (as n. 6). *L'adozione privata*; Vismara (as n. 6) 581–584, but also Roberti (as n. 6) 327 ff., in particular 339.

[66]Cf. Rolandinus, *Summa* (as n. 23), pars I cap. VII, rubr. *Instrumentum adoptionis*, 174r.

[67]Villa is also mentioned as the public official exercising his *auctoritas* in the *Instrumentum adoptionis* by Salatiele (as n. 56), *Ars notarie…*, II, IV, rubr. *Instrumentum adoptionis*, 300 and the fact is pointed out by Orlandelli, in the *Introduzione* of the same *Ars notarie…*, XIX, XXIII; he is mentioned as *podestà* for 1250 in the *Liber sive matricula notariorum Comunis Bononie (1219–1299)*. 1980. ed. by Roberto Ferrara and Vittorio Valentini (Fonti e strumenti per la storia del notariato italiano III). Roma: Giuffrè, 122–123 ("Ego Bonaventura Mafei, notarius imperiali auctoritate et nunc ad dictum potestatis notarius, predictum Petriçolum, visso dicto instrumento Drudoli, mandato domini Iacobi de Luyrago iudicis et assessoris domini Ricardi de Villa potestatis Bononie, die sexto exeunte martio scripsi."); "Anno domini millesimo ducentesimo quinquagesimo, indictione octava, tempore domini Riçardi de Villa potestatis Bononie. Iohannis Danielis, qui fuit de Pançano et nunc moratur ad Chastrum Francum…"; "Et ego Benedictus Guiçardini, nunc comunis Bononie notarius et domini Guidonis Taberne iudicis et assessoris domini Riçardi de Villa potestatis Bononie, ipsius mandato…"; "Millesimo ducentesimo quinquagesimo, indictione octava, die ultimo iunii. Infrascripti notarii fuerunt examinati et approbati per dominum Iacobum de Luyrago iudicem et assessorem domini Ricardi de Villa potestatis Bononie, de conscilio domini Alberici doctoris legum…": there follows the registration of the immatriculation of ten notaries following their exam and approval; Riccardo Villa appears in the *Chartularium Studii Bononiensis* 1. 1909. ed. by Luigi Nardi and Emilio Orioli. Bologna: Istituto per la storia dell'università di Bologna, 129–130.

fully legitimize the process: in this way the governance of the communes under the *podestà* was organized, where the *podestà* surrounded himself with judges called on to perform functions not directly carried out by the person at the top.[68]

In the *instrumentum adrogationis* Antonio adrogates a fatherless child before the judge who, in this case, is not the *podestà*'s delegate, but an *ordinarius* of the Emperor: with all his possessions, assets and rights, he accepts him as a son, and receives him not only *in sua filiatione,* but also *in sua [...] familia potestate paterno affectu [...].* The procedure is carried out by means of questions put to both parties as to their willingness to perform the act and is followed by the judge's confirmation that this is an *actus legitimus*[69] (*Quem quidem legitimum actum idem iudex imperiali authoritate ipsiusque rescripto plenius confirmavit*).

The formula harks back to ancient law, and this may also be seen in the reference to the *actus legitimi*—adoption and adrogation were typical examples—which require the intervention of a magistrate for the purposes of performing a voluntary legal action. Nonetheless, it was Petrus Aldobrandinus, a jurist of the 1500s with a taste for humanistic references who pointed out the formal differences: citing a ceremony described in Aulus Gellius' *Noctes atticae*, Aldobrandus, in his *Nova additio* to the *instrumentarium*, showed the antiquity of the *adrogatio*, and stressed *quam longe distemus a vera contrahendorum negotiorum formula.*[70]

The *Notula doctrinalis* contains a brief outline of the features that distinguish adoption from adrogation: the former pertains to a *filiusfamilias* and may be carried out before any magistrate; the latter pertains to a *sui iuris* party and requires the presence of the Emperor or of an *ordinarius* of his (this was the title for the magistrate who took part in the procedure), acting on behalf of the supreme authority's delegating *rescriptum.* After the most fundamental differences have been identified, a requirement common to both is specified: the eighteen-year age difference between the adopting/adrogating persons, on the one hand, and the adopted/adrogated person, on the other, thereby imitating the natural age difference between father and son. This requirement (the number of years varied) would remain in place until the more recent developments; the direct reference elsewhere in the work to the section *De adoptionibus* of the Institutions shows its strong link with the Roman tradition. Few and essential indications are enough since—as

[68]Cf. Hessel, Alfred. 1910. *Geschichte der Stadt Bologna von 1216 bis 1280* (Berlin: E. Ebering. 1910 (Italian translation by Gina Fasoli: *Storia della città di Bologna 1116–1280*, Bologna: Alfa 1975), 347; as well as, how this was applied in other Italian communal institutions, Salzer, Ernst. 1900/1965. *Über die Anfänge der Signorie in Oberitalien* (Historische Studien. Veröff. von E. Ebering. 14). Berlin: E. Ebering; Valduz: Kraus reprint), 67; also Pertile, Antonio. 1894. *Storia del diritto italiano* 2, 1. Torino-Roma-Napoli-Milano: Unione tipografico-editrice, 99, nt 80.

[69]Cf. D. 50.17.77, where the *adrogatio* was however not explicitly mentioned.

[70]Petrus Aldobrandinus, *Nova additio* in Rolandinus, *Summa* (as n. 23), pars I cap. VII, rubr. *Instrumentum arrogationis*, 174va: the reference is to Gellius, Aulus. 1993. *Noctes atticae*, lib. V, cap. XIX. Pisa: in ædibus Giardini editori e stampatori.

Rolandinus clearly states—*contractus iste non est multe utilitatis, et quia rarissime contingent huiusmodi instrumenta.*[71]

The interpreter of the next generation, who devotes more space to definitions, while also drawing on the prestige of the most prominent glossators, from Placentinus to Iohannes Bassianus, from Azo and Accursius, confirms the master's judgment and, as if to justify its brevity declares that *materia rarissime* de facto *occurrit […]*. That does not prevent him from reconstructing the scholarly debate on certain aspects of the matter which took place among distinguished protagonists of the Bologna school.

4 In the 1300s and 1400s

Adoptio nomen generale comprehendens duas species, adoptionem scilicet et arrogationem: so runs an *additio* by Iohannes Franciscus Decianus to Albericus de Rosate's *Dictionarium iuris*. A few simple words, followed by a reference to the l. I of the title *De adoptionibus* in the Digest.[72] Unlike the more in-depth analysis of the rules governing adoptions and arrogations found in Alberico's other entries and by the authors of the *additiones* to his celebrated text, the clarifications on this point appear to be really minimal. Albericus does, however, reserve a few remarks about adoption under the genus of the *cognatio*, under which, as *cognatio legalis*, adoption itself may be included. The legal and doctrinal sources mentioned by Albericus are those of Canon law: the Gregorian decretals, the relevant sections in writings by Goffredus Tranensis, Henricus Segusiensis and the *Speculum iuris*, in the section *de consanguinitate et affinitate*, which focuses on the impediments to marriage.[73] In another work, the author does not neglect to deal with other controversial issues, like equating the adrogated person to the *legitimi et naturales* children where, appealing to the *iuris fictio*, he concludes that the adrogated person is subject to both civil and natural ties, as that *aequipollet veritati.*[74]

Bartolus deals with adoption following the trail blazed by his predecessors, and highlights the many interpretations given by scholars of 1200s, starting from the gloss, that were still current in his day[75]; he makes a point of repeating (and contradicting the abovementioned opinion by Petrus de Bellapertica, and also

[71]Cf. Rolandinus, *Summa* (as n. 23), pars I cap. VII, 175r.

[72]Albericus de Rosate. 1573/1971. *Dictionarium Iuris tam Civilis quam Canonici.*Venetiis: apud Guerreos fratres et socios, repr. Torino: Bottega d'Erasmo, 26.

[73]Albericus de Rosate (as n. 72) 113; see also 63 under the entry *arrogavero*. "id est arrogare voluero", followed by the *argumentum ex lege* (D. 1.7.3; D. 45.1.133).

[74]Albericus de Rosate. 1585/1974. *In Primam Digesti Veteris partem Commentarii*, ad D. 1.7.22 *De adoptionibus* l. *Si adrogator*, nr. 4. bVenetiis: [Società dell'aquila che si rinnova]. Repr. Sala Bolognese: Forni, 57.

[75]Cf., e.g., Bartolus (as n. 22). ad D. 1.7. *De adoptionibus*, 25r e ff., for the entire title.

Albericus) that, in the case of an adrogated person, the *civilis ratio* and the *naturalis ficte* do not subsist at the same time, so that, according to the French jurist, *quae fictio idem, quod veritas operatur*: would be false, or rather, it assumes something that is false *quia nulla lex fingit arrogatum esse naturalem.*[76]

However, he raises the problem of the legal classification of other relationships, which he was aware of through the education he received from Fratel Pietro, his mentor *in primitivis scientiis*: in Venice a hospital named La Pietà, according to its vulgar Italian name, practiced the custom of placing children with local citizens who treated them no differently from their own children, according to the formalities mentioned in the l. *Quidam cum filium* under the terms of an agreement that specified how these children could (and should) be treated. The great commentator urged caution in agreeing to such terms (which sometimes included a penalty) since they might be the basis for future claims.[77]

At the end of 1300s, Petrus de Ancarano, on the basis of Bartolus' works and drawing on the experience of his mentor Fratel Pietro of Assisi, known in Venice as Pietro della Pietà (since he was the founder of the Pietà foundling hospital) could recall childless Venetians taking into their homes *vel coram vicinis*, little boys or girls *in filiam suam* without complying with any legal formalities as *figli dell'anima* or "children of the soul" (the same epithet was also used in Sicily).[78]

Later, Alexander Tartagni issued a *consilium* dealing with the effects of an agreement dated January 28, 1454 between a certain Geminiano and a certain Baldassarre, whereby they mutually promised to treat each other as father and son; Tartagni did not find any reason that the latter should inherit from the former, as might have been the case had this been an adoption or an adrogation performed under a set of legal formalities resulting (at least for the adrogation, as Tartagni makes clear,) in the transfer of the adrogated party to the adrogater's paternal authority.[79]

Two further *consilia* were issued over the question of whether the beneficiary of a legacy *ad pias causas, pro anima* or aimed to help the poor was required to pay a certain sum to the St. Petronius *fabrica* in Bologna, in compliance with a special law to that effect; the *consilia* discuss whether the legacy recipient, a *famulus* and godchild of thc dcccascd pcrson, as wcll as his adopted son, is legally required to make these payments and they use this as an opportunity to reaffirm the principle

---

[76]Bartolus (as n. 22) 27v.: ad D. 1.7.22 *De adoptionibus* l. *Si adrogator*, no. 10.

[77]Bartolus. 1590. *Comm.* ad D. 45.1.132 *De verborum obligationibus* l. *Quidam cum filium*, nr. 8. Venetiis: [ad signum Aquilae renovantis], 53v–54r.

[78]Petrus de Ancarano. 1535. *Super Quarto et quinto Decretalium Lectura aurea.* ad X.4.12 *De cognatione legali* c. *Si qua*, nr. 4. Lugduni: Joannes Moylin al's de Chambrai, 29r. Cf., as to Sicily, Bresc, Henri. 1986. *Un monde méditerranéen. Économie et société en Sicilie, 1300–1450* (*Bibliothèque des écoles françaises d'Athènes et de Rome*, fasc. 262), Rome: École française de Rome, 692, where between 1385 and 1480 about fifteen cases are mentioned in which the persons involved were called "figlu ou figlia di anima", including one "figla di sancti".

[79]Tartagnus Alexander. 1590. *Consiliorum seu responsorum... liber sextus*. Venetiis: apud Felicem Valgrisium, 80rv: cons. 141, nr. 1.

that adoption does not create blood ties, but has the same consequences as a blood relationship, and even though the legacy recipient here is assumed to be poor (hence beneficiary of a legacy *ad pias causas*), he still must make the compulsory payment.

This was either because simply being named in a last will was not considered to be sufficient to bring about a "real" adoption, since in order for an adoption to be valid, certain formalities had to be complied with, like the *decretum iudicis*, and a will alone could not create a son who wasn't really one. Or again in order to emphasize the specific consequences of an adoption and a blood tie, since the pupillary substitution by a last will in favor of an adopted son does not imply that he will inherit the entire estate of the substituted party, but only the assets that he received in the will.[80]

In another *consilium* Jason de Majno discusses the consequences of an agreement similar to the one discussed by Tartagni and excludes inheritance claims arising from anyone promised to be treated like a son, if the loss of the estate occurred for a sufficient cause; in any other case, the deprived person was owed the penalty indicated in the agreement or, that failing, compensation for damages incurred. In this "generous" *consilum*, de Majno looked back to the foundational characteristics of an adrogation made by a citizen of Genoa, a certain Tommaso de Sanignonis, *authoritate Cesarea*, in favor of the fellow citizen, Agostino de Piacamilio, his nephew *ex sorore*, one of Tommaso's closest relatives, and later designated as his universal heir in his last will; this was followed by an *inter vivos* donation of the assets to a Genoese charitable istitution. De Majno's rigorous argument stresses that the designation of heir has an irrevocable nature compared to a subsequent donation in the last will which lacks the requirements of revocability, and he concludes in favor of the adrogated party against the charity's claims.[81]

5 *Statuta*, Fiefs and Legal Consulting

Many Italian statutes allowed the possibility of adoption: some to ensure the procedure's formalities, like the mid-12th century *Constitutum legis* of Pisa which, considering adoption, adrogation and emancipation as distinct forms, required that the acts should take place *apud iudices Nove curie publice et in publica curia*, and deemed them invalid if this was not done;[82] or the statutes of Novara in the 1300s,

[80]Tartagnus (as n. 79) 104r–105v: conss. 125, 126, in particular nos. 10–11.

[81]Majno de, Jason. 1544. *Consiliorum pars quarta.* Lugduni: apud Stephanum Rufinum, & Ioannem Ausultum, 55r–57r: cons. 141, in particular nr. 14 but also *passim* for the other profiles. Cf. on the great *consiliator* di Renzo Villata, Maria Gigliola. 2012. Giasone del Maino. In *Dizionario Biografico dei Giuristi Italiani (XII–XX secolo)* 1. Bologna: il Mulino, 995–999.

[82]*Constitutum legis pisanae civitatis*. 1870. c. 46 *de adoptionibus et emancipationibus*, in *Statuti inediti della città di Pisa dal XII al XIV secolo*, ed. by Francesco Bonaini. Firenze: G.P. Viesseux, 792.

which granted full effectiveness (*ratas et firmas habebo*) to the *Emancipationes adrogationes et manumissiones et donationum insinuationes aput utranque consulariam et potestates factas legitime in toto meo consulatu.*[83] But other statutes point out negative aspects, like the *Liber Consuetudinum Mediolani*, which expressly excludes adopted children from inheriting fiefs,[84] or the sixteenth century statutes of Vigevano, which, when dealing with the exclusion of females from inheriting when male heirs were present, or with the exclusion of cognatic heirs when heirs in the male line were present, specified that both male heirs and agnatic heirs should in any case be *ex legitimo matrimonio natis, ita quod legitimati per rescriptum vel adoptivi excludantur, et ita de his masculis, et agnatis qui succedere possint, et in effectu succedant.*[85]

Baldus, in considering the *statuta* provision of *exclusio propter dotem* which prevented married daughters who had already received dowries from inheriting from their fathers, in favor of sons and their children, wondered whether adopted sons should also be included among the sons qualified to inherit.

It was a very delicate matter; to which the answer was mainly negative, since according to the commentator, the *statuta*'s wording regarded the true children, not the *filii ficti, et fictio non habet locum in statutis*. However it also seemed to suggest that an adopted child could be designated as heir *tamquam extraneus*, provided that the interest of the children were satisfied through lawful inheritance and a special derogation was given by the prince.[86] Adoption was the subject of another *consilium*, in which the scholar considered as mandatory that both the adopter and adoptee must be present during the act and must give their oral consent.[87] Signorolus de Homodeis had also agreed on it, in two similar cases, when he declared that the act would be invalid if the adoptee was not present, in accordance with the rules on voluntary jurisdiction in force.[88]

---

[83]*Statuta communis Novariae*. 2012. lib. secundus, rubr. *De emancipationibus adoptionibus et manumissionibus firmis tenendis*, in *Statuti di Novara del XIV secolo*, ed. by Gian Marco Cossandi and Marta Luigina Mangini. Varese: Insubria University Press: cf. also the manuscript in Milan, Archivio storico–civico–Biblioteca Trivulziana, ms. Arch. Cod. B1, 96v.

[84]*Liber Consuetudinum Mediolani MCCXVI*. 1949. ed. by Besta Enrico and Barni Gian Luigi. Milano: A. Giuffrè, 129: "Illud autem scire oportet quod tantum filii naturales set legitimi, idest qui legitimo matrimonio sunt procreati, ad successiones feudorum perveniunt. Non ergo adoptivi, nec naturales facti postea legitimi, ad successiones feudorum accedunt".

[85]*Statuta civilia et comunalia civitatis et comitatus Viglevani*. 1532. *Statuta civilia*, rubr. *Quod legitimati et adoptivi excludantur*. Mediolani: typis escussit Gotardus Ponticus, 38r; cf. also *Statuta civilia et comunalia civitatis et comitatus Viglevani*. 1608. *Statuta civilia*, rubr. *Legitimati et adoptivi ut excludantur*. Mediolani: ex Typographia Iacopi Maria Medae, 128.

[86]Baldus. 1575/1970. *Consiliorum sive responsorum liber primus*. Venetiis: [Francesco de' Franceschi & Gaspare Bindoni & Nicolo Bevilacqua & Damiano Zenaro]. Repr. Torino: Bottega d'Erasmo, 16: cons. 24.

[87]Baldus (as n. 86) cons. 349.

[88]Signorolus de Homodeis. 1521. *Consiliorum ac quaestiones*.... Mediolani: per Io. Angelum Scinzenzeler, 92r: cons. 127, nr. 3; 146r–147r: cons. 218, in particular no. 11, also in relation to legitimation, in this case made equal to adoption, being an act of voluntary jurisdiction.

Later, Iohannes de Anania, in another *consilium*, resolved the matter in the same way by performing a thorough analysis of the hermeneutical instruments used for dealing with statutes: the *exorbitans ex iure communi* character of the rules, which required the *exclusio propter dotem* of daughters in favor of sons, implied that adopted and the adrogated sons (who were *legitimi tantum*) could not be included in the same category as sons (who were *legitimi et naturales*) and that the patrimony would go first to the daughters.[89] Ludovicus Bolognini, who took care of the publication of Iohannes de Anania's *consilia*, in his *Additiones* to the work deployed new arguments and *auctoritates* to back up the canonist's opinions.[90]

In the mid of 1500s, Horatius Carpanus, in the renowned commentary on the 1396 Milanese statutes, does not hesitate to include the adopted person (or even the *adrogatus*) in the *parentela*, which included the *familia* and the siblings themselves, who were required to give their consent when transactions or sales of property were made by unmarried women (married ones only needed the consent of their husbands), provided that the adoptee was under the adopter's authority and that his status had not changed.[91]

Carpanus traces the same path taken by the *De contractibus*, a thorough interpretation of chapter 328 of the Milanese statutes *novissima*, by Stefano Lambertenghi. The jurist from Como, besides being of the opinion that both the adopted and the adrogated person were members of the family (as they ceased to be a part of their natural one according to the ancient laws), considers the effects of a *novissima* adoption whether made by an elder male relative or an elder female relative: in the former case, the adoption does not change the agnatic relationship, while in the latter the adoption implies transfer of the adoptee under the adopter's paternal authority. As regards the marriage prohibition between adopted and natural siblings, which was supposed to last as long as the relationship itself continued and ceased in the case of emancipation, the author appears to be contrary to such a union *propter publicae honestatis iustitiam*: the impropriety of the said union and public morality induce him to support the prohibition, (enshrined—as he is quick to point out—in Canon law) and to exclude any other solution.[92]

The *consilia*, mentioned above, were concerned with some of the more "common" instances of inheritance, but *consiliatores* were also often called into deal with the inheritance of fiefs when adopted children were involved.

---

[89]Iohannes de Anania. 1508. *Consilia cum additionibus domini Ludovici Bolognini*. Bononie: per Paganinum de Paganinis brixiensem, 16v–17r: cons. 27.

[90]de Anania (as n. 89) 17r.

[91]Carpanus, Horatius. 1600. *Lucubrationes Novae, innumerae et solidae in omne ius municipale, quod statutum Mediolani appellant*, ad cap. 328, nrr. 504–505. Francofurti: excudebat Romanus Beatus, sumptibus Nicolai Bassae, 1600, 654.

[92]Lambertengus, Iohannes Stephanus. 1576/1574. *Tractatus De contractibus eorum, quibus vel a iure communi, vel a statutis, sine certa solennitate contrahere permissum non est. Opus maxime vtile, in foris versantibus, pro intelligentia diversorum Statutorum Italiae, ac aliarum consuetudinum*, gl. 17 in ver. *De eadem parentela*, nos. 7–8. Mediolani: apud Antonium Antonianum, apud Pacificum Pontium, 384–385.

The rule handed down in the *Libri feudorum* did not permit adopted children to inherit fiefs. While the rule does not appear in the *recensio antiqua* (in the chapter *de feudi successione* only the daughter was excluded, unless she was expressly included in the enfeoffment, and in *De contentione feudi* the heirless vassal was prohibited from bequeathing the fief without the prior consent of the lord[93]), we found it in Ardizzone's revision, and in the *vulgata* of the *Libri feudorum*: *Adoptivus filius in feudis non succedit.*[94] In any case, Accursius's gloss granted the *quarta* to the adopted son.[95]

Franceschinus Curtius, a true expert in feudal questions (he wrote a treatise that ranked him among the highest authorities in the field, and was among the most esteemed scholars to give a qualified opinion[96]), in a *consilium* deals with the succession of a certain *Comes Daniel Raddinus appellatus Todiscus*, who, in his last will dated November 5, 1483 designated his two sons as universal heirs, bequeathing them a portion of his estate. The elder received the castle and the attached rights, with a prohibition that neither he nor his male descendants, *legitimi et naturales, legitimati seu tantum legitimi* should dispose of the property (in whole or in part) in perpetuity. He died without any son *legitimus et naturalis*, but only three grandsons from his daughter, whom he had adopted. The *ius commune* rule on the matter was to exclude the adopted child from the enfeoffment. Although acknowledging the broadness of the rule, which also included the adopted children, Franceschinus raises the suspicion of fraud in the adoption as the act had been carried out in an *extra moenia* church outside Piacenza, *in loco insolito et quodammodo clandestine cum a magis communiter accidentibus adoptiones solent fieri publice coram ius dicentibus in palatiis publicis, ut notissimum est, ex quo generatur fraudis suspitio*; the situation was aggravated by the fact that three children had been adopted simultaneously, a highly unusual event, since according to the Digest it was not possible to adopt more than one child at a time, unless there was a good reason, and even more so because the fact that the adoption had been kept secret until after the death of the testator "*cum facile sit alicui flio adoptare*" shows, in his opinion, the contrary and, therefore, he decides in favor of the sibling.[97]

Another *consilium* by the same author supports the succession to a fief by an adopted child, Filiberto Ferreri, as designated by his adoptive father, Ludovico Fieschi and opposed by Pietro Luca Fieschi, a "natural" family member (the Fieschi

---

[93]Cf. *Consuetudines feudorum*. 1971. ed. by Karl Lehmann (Bibliotheca Rerum Historicarum, Neudrucke 1). Aalen: Scientia Verlag, 13–14 [37–38], 15 [39].

[94]Cf. also *Libri feudorum*, ed. by Karl Lehmann, 151 [229]: II. 26 *Si de feudo controversia fuerit* § 9.

[95]Cf. gl. *succedit* a *Libri feudorum*. Volumen. 1551b (as n. 31) II.26 § 9, 58.

[96]Cf. di Renzo Villata, Maria Gigliola. 1982. Scienza giuridica e legislazione nell'età sforzesca. In *Gli Sforza a Milano e in Lombardia e i loro rapporti con gli Stati italiani ed europei (1450–1530)*. Milano: Cisalpino–Goliardica, especially 111–112; Ead. 2012. Corti Francesco junior. In *Dizionario Biografico dei Giuristi Italiani (XII–XX secolo)* (as n. 81) 584–586.

[97]Corti, Franceschino. 1571. *Consilia*. Venetiis: apud Nicolaum Bevilaquam et socios, 84r–86v: cons. 145, especially nrr. 11–22. Cf. Roumy (as n. 16) 296–297.

Family is mainly known to history for other reasons). Ludovico left the Meserano fief and other castles located in the diocese of Vercelli to his adopted child *antecedente consensu Summi Pontificis ut possit in dicto feudo succedere in praeiudicium dicti domini Petri Lucae et aliorum agnatorum.* Franceschinus deploys a complex and clever line of reasoning that focuses on the derogation to the *ius commune* resulting from the Pope's exemption, and he expresses the view that the act was valid since he considers the adopted child to have been included in the enfeoffment clause to the detriment of the siblings, while insisting on the final words of the formula *seu tantum legitimi*, which would otherwise be without effect if the adopted child were deemed to be excluded. There is a wide array of relevant doctrine at play here: the *auctoritates* Franceschinus cites to oppose his final opinion are of great importance for an author exceptionally steeped in feudalist culture and tradition of Pavia University, but these views do not prevent him from expressing a different opinion, even if this means opposing the rigor of the feudal tradition he evoked.[98] The excluded siblings, in whose favor a substitution was provided in the absence of any designated heir, sought to exclude the adopted person from inheriting, grounding their arguments on the fact that they had not given their consent.[99]

6 In Europe: A Glance at Some Testimonies from the Middle Ages

In France, we have the regional *coutumes* and, especially, notarial documents which show that adoption enjoyed a certain degree of vitality. With regard to the former, adoption cannot be found in the *pays de droit écrit*, where it seems to be absent in urban municipal texts, but it does appear in the Northern *coutumiers*.

Some signs of the sporadic presence of adoption are the samples found by Franck Roumy which for the period of the 1200s were taken from the *Livre de Jostice et de plet*, (a text partly modeled on the Digest *De adoptionibus*) which regulated *avoement*, a term by and large equivalent to adoption; for the 1300s, from the *Somme rural*, by Jean Boutiller, which suggests that adoption was a generalized, but not frequent practice, more common in the *pays de droit écrit* "*qu'en coutume*" or the other instances mentioned by Jean Hilaire practiced by the *gens de champs*, such as the Saintonge, Nivernais and Bourbonnais coutumes.[100]

[98]Corti (as n. 97) 74r–76r: cons. 138.

[99]Corti (as n. 97) 84r–86v: cons. 145, especially nos. 11–22. Cf. Roumy (as n. 16) 296–297.

[100]*Li Livre de Jostice et plet.* 1850. I, 10, ed. by Pierre-Nicolas Rapetti and Polycarpe Chabaille. Paris: Firmin Didot, 1850, 59–63; Boutillier, Jean. 1611. *Somme rural*, ed. by Charondas Le Caron. Paris: Barthelemy Macé, 535; Hilaire, Jean. 1987. Coutumes rédigées et "gens de champs" (Angoumois, Aunis, Santonge). *Revue historique du droit français et étranger*, 65, 545 ff. Cf. Roumy (as n. 16) 188–189.

Because of its very nature, as well as the enormous mass of documents and archives that need to be inspected, the practice cannot be exhaustively studied—but we can learn something. In the 1400s–1500s, the abovementioned Olivier Martin discovered some acts of adoption in the area where the Paris *coutumes* were in force,[101] but over time, others have come to light in Bourgogne, Valais, Poitou, Auvergne and in the Southwest of France, thanks to the researches of Jacques Poumarède.[102] Paul Gonnet, now more than 75 years ago, examined Lyonnais sources and found 42 cases of adoption of orphans or children entrusted to private citizens between 1527 and 1584 by the town's hospitals, while the practice seemed to decline in the 1600s. On the other hand, investigations carried out by Jacqueline Roubert on the same territory for the years 1629–1713 turned up 49 cases of adoption which shows the practice had not ceased.[103]

More recently, Kristin Elizabeth Gager has discovered a series of private adoption deeds, drawn up by Paris notaries between 1545 and 1690, involving artisans and merchants who adopted children from families or hospitals, thereby satisfying, as it were, their personal and emotional needs.[104] Another case that emerged from the documents, describes a sort of quasi-adoption, that is, a contract that allowed a natural uncle, who was also the godfather, to step-in for the father in case the latter refused to, or could not, take care of his son.[105]

This agrees with the account given by Pierre Rebuffe who, in the 1500s, declared that the rarity of adoption was linked to the high fertility of his "people", and that "Adoptiones in Francia raro fiunt, quia singuli generant vel aliquos habent consanguineos. Vidi tamen, in civitate Parisiensi, aliquos mercatores, filiis carentes, accipere pauperes filios ex hospitali Sancti Spiritus, quos alebant et adoptabant". The practice, doubtless, related to the childlessness of the adopting person, seems to be referring to a true adoption (the opinion comes from a jurist), a voluntary act by a

[101]Olivier-Martin (as n. 2) 1, 151 n.1.

[102]Poumarède, Jacques.1972. *Les successions dans le sud–ouest de la France au moyen âge (géographie coutumière et mutations sociales)*; préf. de Pierre Ourliac. Paris: Presses Universitaires de France, 128–129; also Aubenas (as n. 3); Id. 1935. *Documents notariés provençaux du XIIIe siècle*. Aix: E. Fourcine, 82, 86–87 (with reference to a deed of January 18, 1257, where a married couple "reçoivent comme fils" and designate their son–in-law as heir, in the presence of another son); Hilaire (as n. 100) 545 ss.

[103]Cf. Roubert, Jacqueline.1978, L'adoption des enfants par des particuliers à Lyon sous l'Ancien régime, *Bulletin de la Société française d'histoire des hôpitaux*, n. 36–37, 41–67.

[104]Cf. Gager, Kristin Elizabeth. 1996. *Blood Ties and Fictive Ties. Adoption and Family Life in Early Modern France*. Princeton, New Jersey: Princeton University Press, *passim*. See also Gutton, Jean Pierre. 1993. Histoire de l'adoption en France. Paris: Publisud, *passim.*

[105]Cf. Lefebvre Teillard, Anne. 1973. *Les officialités à la veille du concile de Trente*. Paris: Librairie Générale de Droit et de Jurisprudence, 218, n. 271–373: the cases mentioned date back the first years of the 1500s.

merchant who decides to take care of a poor child, to support him and then to adopt him.[106]

There was also another widely practiced form of adoption: *de nom et d'armes*, used by the nobility and the urban bourgeoisie to pass on their name and arms to adoptees if they had no descendants. In the 14th and 15th centuries there are certainly many examples of this in France. The transmission of one's name and arms by a last will or an *inter vivos* donation to a person who was not a male descendant (grandsons *ex filia* and their sons, the son-in-law or an unrelated person) was not strictly defined as adoption, but it was more or less the same thing. Several French authors, like François Connan and Charles Dumoulin, who were interested in the roots of adoption and how it had been applied in the ancient world,[107] did not hesitate to apply the term adoption to this practice.[108]

While the French sources provide many useful indications, in Spain too, there are signs that adoption was alive and well. In the mid-1200s, the *Fuero Real* allowed persons without children to adopt, and adoptees to inherit the estate of their adopter, except when there were surviving natural children.[109] The *Siete Partidas*, compiled under Alfonso X the Wise,[110] also included the possibility for adoption. Treating it in the tradition of the Justinian code, the "*Partidas*" trace adoption's most salient features, and this is attested by Gregorio Lopez's gloss on adoption which is full of references to Roman texts and to the *ius commune* doctrine on the practice, from Bartolus to Jean Fabre, from Bartolus to Angelus de Gambilionibus of Arezzo to Mattheus Mattesilanus.

---

[106]Rebuffe, Pierre. 1589. *Comm.* Ad D. 1.7.2 *de adoptionibus* l. *Generalis enim adoptio. Explicatio ad quatuor primos libros Pandectarum.* Lugduni: apud Gulielmum Rouillium sub scuto Veneto, 43.

[107]Dumoulin, Charles. 1658. *Tractatus analyticus de Dignitatibus, Magistratibus et Civibus Romanis*, in Id., *Opera*, t. IV. Parisiis: apud Carolum de Mesnii, 43, 70, 73–75, with specific regard to Roman law.

[108]Lefebvre Teillard, Anne. 1989. *Le nom. Droit et histoire*. Paris: Librairie Générale de Droit et de Jurisprudence, 45–46, 85, 168; Roumy (as n. 16) 207–210.

[109]*Fuero Real de España diligentemente hecho por el noble Rey don Alonso IX. Glosado por el egregio doctor Alonso Diaz de Montalvo*, 1541. lib. III *De las herencias*, ley VI. Burgos: por Juan de Junta, CXXXIV (containing Alonso Diaz's gloss with references to ius commune law and the sources of the *Siete Partidas*. De Investigaciones Científicas, Delegación de Roma, 1955), p. 120 ff.

[110]*Las Siete Partidas del Sabio Rey Don Alfonso el IX [sic]/ con las variantes de más interés y con la glosa de Gregorio López; vertida al castellano y estensamente adicionada, con nuevas notas y comentarios y unas tablas sinópticas comparativas, sobre la legislación española, antigua y moderna… por Ignacio Sanponts y Barba, Ramón Martí de Eixala y José Ferrer y Subirana*. 2, *Cuarta partida que fabla de los desporios et de los casamientos,* tit. XVI *De los fijos porfijados*. 1843 Barcelona: Imprenta de Antonio Bergnes, 1074–1079. Cf. on these Spanish sources Otero Valera, Alfonso. 1955. *La adopción en la historia del derecho español*, in Id., *Dos estudios historico-juridicos*. Roma: [Consejo Superior de Investigaciones Científicas, Delegación de Roma], 120 ff.

7 In the Modern Age: A Debated Survival

In the anonymous *Vocabularius utriusque iuris* (published in Lyon in 1535 but dating to the mid-1400s, the work would enjoy success for many more years) the different aims of adoption that had emerged over time and which justified it for many different reasons, almost appear to be swept aside: "Adoptio est gratuita quaedam electio qua quis aliquem sibi eligit in filium, et hoc faciunt plerumque hi qui filios habere non possunt ad ipsorum solatium. Et talis qui sic recipitur in filium dicitur adoptivus quasi a patre legitimo sic ei datur et ille qui sic eum adoptat dicitur adoptivus pater… Et imitatur naturam carnalis matrimonii…" in a few brief brush strokes, the essence of a relationship, one that shines light on the generosity of a usually childless father, is portrayed in its "eternal" reality.[111]

It is no coincidence that the *Formularium et solemnitates instrumentorum abbreviatorum et extensorum* of the 1580s defines itself on the cover page as *opus perutile et necessarium profitentibus artem Notarie*. Its author, Iohannes Baptista Caballinus, Milanese notary and causidicus,[112] was a figure who exemplified what, in my view, is a need for certainty, a need he clearly expressed in all his works (with these words in the *Actuarium practicae criminalis … in quo telam iudiciariam fori Criminalis exorditur, additis ipsismet tum statutis, tum Novis Constitutionibus, ad quasque materias asterisco * notatis*, of 1587, or in the *Actuarium practicae civilis*, written, the Author asserts, for the *publica utilitas novitiorum*). In the *Formularium* Caballinus devotes a good deal of space to adrogation, as well as to adoption: in the background, as it were, we can discern the compositional structure of the *Formularium* which weaves together a variety of strands into a design redolent of antiquity, in its evocation of the accumulated doctrine of the *ius commune*, which reverberates throughout the theoretical section and in questions that were debated by the likes of Henricus Segusiensis or the *Speculator*, (expressly mentioned); but at the same time the work is embedded in the contemporary power politics of the Duchy of Milan; in the fact that it considers the legal needs of the Duchy and of its public institutions, especially the Senate, called on to take the place of the *Princeps* in authorizing the Palatine Counts to legitimize the act of adrogation.[113]

---

[111]*Vocabularius utriusque iuris*. 1535. Lugduni, apud Iacobum Wit, Vincentius de Portonariis de Tridino de Monteferrato, entry *Adoptio*, f. 17r. The current attribution refers to Iodocus as the author, a professor of canon law at Erfurt, who might have compiled the work in 1452. The mainly canonistic culture at the basis of the entries emerges in the *Vocabularius*.

[112]On the possibility of practicing the two professions at the same time, cf. now Pagano, Emanuele. 2001. Avvocati ed esercizio della professione legale in Lombardia nel secondo Settecento. I causidici collegiati di Milano, *Rivista di storia del diritto italiano* 74: 355–418, especially 356 ff.

[113]Iohannes Baptista Caballinus. 1605. *Formularium et solemnitates instrumentorum abbreviatorum et extensorum… scriptum et nunc secundo emissum,* Mediolani: apud Hieronymum Bordonum et Petrum Martyrem Locarnum: the dedication by Caballini to the eminent jurist Giovanni Urtado Mendoza, qualified as *quaestor regius*, is of 1580), 97–102.

At the beginning of the 1600s, Cardinal Domenico Toschi, in his *Practicae Conclusiones*, drew on the legal consulting of the 1300s–1400s, to trace a framework for adoption-adrogation in which the consolidated principles were supported by the authority of a tradition of *consilia*: Toschi mentions Signorolus de Omodeis, Baldus, Alexander Tartagnus, Iohannes de Anania, Ludovicus Bologninus and, using these *auctoritates*, he investigates delicate questions regarding aspects of inheritance law.[114]

Iohannes Baptista De Luca tackles the question in a different *discursus* of his *Theatrum veritatis et iustitiae*: in *Discursus* no. 33 *De haerede et haereditate*, he gives his opinion of a Sienese statute on taking possession of and acceptance of an inheritance with benefit of inventory. The *responsum* is issued on a complex case involving a member of the *de Bellantibus* family, who was 9 years old, adrogated in 1625 by Alcibiade Lucarini in compliance with the required formalities, that is to say with the rescript of the Duke of Tuscany, Ferdinand II de' Medici[115]—subsequently executed thanks to a new decree issued by the *Ducissam Mantuae illius status, pro eodem magno Duce regentem, i.e.* Catherine de' Medici, Duchess of Mantua who had just been appointed governor of Siena[116]—along with acts by lower magistrates, authorized ad hoc. It was decided that Francesco, the adrogated party, expressly renounce the inheritance of his natural father. Adrogation—it was repeated—must have certain requirements, such as those found in the case in question, nor could a suspicion of fraud be raised, given the plausible time of the adrogation; furthermore, the transfer of paternal authority from the natural father to the adrogating person and the explicit renunciation of the inheritance were enough to exclude any claim against the adrogated person by the creditors of his natural father's estate. On the other hand, De Luca confirms that adoption does not remove the relationship of natural affiliation, nor original nobility, nor *ignobilitas naturalis*.[117]

---

[114]Toschus, Dominicus. 1634. *Practicarum conclusionum iuris in omni foro frequentiorum… tomus primus*, Concl. 214–216. Romae: ex typographia Stephani Paulini; Lugduni: ex officina Ioannis Pillehotte (the Author's dedication to Pope Paul V is dated 1605), 106–107 (the work was published several times). On the Author, cf. Tiraboschi, Girolamo. 1784/1970. *Biblioteca modenese* 5. Modena: Società Tipografica, anastatic repr. Bologna: Forni, 277–282.

[115]Duke of Mantua from 1616 to 1626.

[116]Ferdinand II was born in 1610 and upon the death of his father Cosimo II de' Medici in 1621, the regency of the Grand Duchy was assumed by Cosimo's wife, Maria Maddalena of Austria together with her mother-in-law Christina of Lorena (who already served as regent in the name of Cosimo), aided by the regency council. In 1628, Ferdinand II assumed power. "Per ducissam Mantuae illius status" refers to Catherine of Ferdinando de' Medici (Florence, May 2, 1593–Siena, April 17, 1629), duchess of Mantua, wife from 1617 of Ferdinando Gonzaga, soon widowed and appointed by Ferdinando II of Tuscany in 1627 governor of Siena: it is in this capacity that she is reported by De Luca as the authority issuing the adrogation decree, in compliance with the legal formalities.

[117]De Luca, Iohannes Baptista. 1678. *Theatrum veritatis et iustitiae*, lib. XVI. *Supplementi pars III*, tit. *De haerede et haereditate*, disc. 33. Romae: ex typographia Reverendae Camerae Apostolicae, 5–8.

Elsewhere, adrogation and adoption serve almost as an excuse for De Luca to make a long historical digression on how these acts evolved in ancient Rome as a safeguard against infertility or lack of heirs; he also refers to more recent times in which frequent aggregations of families were carried out by practicing adrogation or just adoption with a view to increasing their group's power, which is what happened, for instance, "in Republica Ianuensi ac etiam in Florentina, forteque in aliis". In this case, De Luca draws from the highly "informed" *Noctes atticae* by Aulus Gellius, cum quo "non solum Iuriste, sed etiam alij humanarum literarum, seu politioris literaturae, ac eruditionis professores pertranseunt", to reconstruct the details of the ceremonies, but also to recall that in Italy and in the other provinces of Western Europe many previously unkown rules had been introduced, in favor of families and siblings in questions involving fiefs, majorats and the rights of first-born. The rule excluded adrogates, whose rights could not prevail over those of siblings, in particular, in the inheritance ab intestato from persons who were not the adrogant. These legal practices confirmed the *favor agnatorum* and they did not include adrogated persons among the *agnati*.

The particular case under De Luca's lens is an adrogation, carried out in compliance with all the formalities, including a plea made to Innocent X and the intervention of a Roman Senator for the delibation and approval of the act, but whose inheritance effects were contested. De Luca, after examining the matter with his usual competence, rules for the devolution of a limited inheritance, limited to the adrogant person, also in order to avoid a new fraud "in Republica radices emitteret, dum ita infinitae fraudes committi possent, atque status mundi, seu Republicae involverentur, huiusmodi arrogationes praticando cum illis qui creduntur proprii filii adulterini, vel alias ex damnato coitu suscepti, quotiens id in foro sufficienter iustificari non posset, quo nil absurdius, nilve detestabilius": these words by the great jurist amount to a passionate accusation against a practice presumably carried out under his eyes and which he deems intolerable, absurd and hideous.[118]

Again, Marc'Antonio Savelli,[119] at the end of the 17th century, under the entry *Filiatio* of his *Summa diversorum contractuum*, includes adopted and adrogated persons with other *legitimi tantum* children, in keeping with the tradition. On the other hand, he expresses opposition to their being considered equal and on the same footing with children wherever the term is used in acts of transfer or in conditional acts (using the example typical for the period, like the *si sine liberis* clause, the presence of adopted and adrogated children did not prevent the inheritance condition from being applied with regard to the absence of possible heirs); on the other hand, he refers to the *Disceptationes forenses* by Stefano Graziani to affirm the capacity of adopted and adrogated children to inherit fiefs and other assets, enjoying all the prerogatives of a blood relationship "*ac si nati essent de vera et naturali*

---

[118]De Luca (as n. 117) *Supplementi pars III*, tit. *De successionibus ab intestato*, disc. 53, 42–51.

[119]Cf. Edigati, Daniele. 2005. *Una vita nelle istituzioni: Marc'Antonio Savelli giurista e cancelliere tra Stato pontificio e Toscana medicea*. Modigliana: ETS, *passim*.

familia", as long as this was *de mandato testatoris*, that is to say by virtue of an express wish of the testator. That implied the exclusion of the substitute destined to step-in in the absence of the designated children and descendants.[120]

In the *Istituta civile divisa in quattro libri* by Giambattista De Luca "*extended and improved by the scholar Sebastiano Simbeni*" in the middle of the 1700s (the first edition is dated 1733),[121] adoption, as it was known in its essential Roman characters, appears in full decline: "As to this topic (adoptions) the same may be said as above with regard to servants and freedmen that is, that the customs of our day are very different from those of the ancient Romans, on the basis of which their laws were made and to which this passage from the *Instituta* refers; so that we can say that it is a kind of a useless study and a waste of time to dwell on it, and when such a rare case occurs, it is not a topic for Institutists and beginners, but for more experienced and clever scholars, as to what is said on many topics".[122]

In France, Montesquieu considered that adoption as well as substitutions, majorat and *retrait lignager*, should be taken out of the aristocratic Republics.[123]

Towards the end of 1700s the young lawyer Marco Ferro, in the entries *Adottare, Adottivo, Adozione* (the last containing a wealth of information) of the *Dizionario del diritto commune e Veneto*, published in Venice between 1778 and 1781 and addressed to young people wishing to practice law, provides a many sided portrait of adoption, tracing its historical development, from the Greeks to its widespread application by the Romans ("*Adoption was also very common in ancient Rome*"), in its various forms, destined to become even more broadly defined with the practice of adoption by last will "*to designate a person as an heir on the condition that they assume your name, arms,* etc.". With regard to this latter form, Ferro mentions that it continued to be practiced in the Venetian Republic: "we also have this practice, and, so, there are families, most of them noble, with two last names and who bear the arms and the coat of arms of their adoptive parents who did good to them". The list goes on and includes adoption by baptism "*introduced by the Greek Church*", symbolized—he noted (while referring to the Du Cange

[120]Cf. Sabellus, Marcus Antonius. 1717. *Summa diversorum contractuum* 2, § *Filiatio.* Parmae: apud Paulum Montium sub Signo Fidei, 166, referring to Stephanus Gratianus. 1650. *Disceptationum forensium... tomus quintus*, t. V, cap. 930. Venetiis: apud Guerilios, 259–263.

[121]Cf. Birocchi, Italo. 2003. L'*Istituta civile* di Giambattista De Luca, in *Amicitiae pignus. Studi in ricordo di Adriano Cavanna*, I, ed. by Antonio Padoa Schioppa, Gigliola di Renzo Villata and Gian Paolo Massetto, Milano: Giuffrè, 87–119.

[122]De Luca, Giambattista. 1743. *Istituta civile divisa in quattro libri con l'ordine de' titoli di quella di Giustiniano, del cardinale Giambattista De Luca accresciuta, e perfezionata dal dottore Sebastiano Simbeni*...(Pesaro: a spese di Vincenzo Voltolini libraio veneto, 74.

[123]Montesquieu. 1845. *Esprit des loix*, liv. V, cap. VIII *Comment les lois doivent se rapporter au principe du gouvernement dans l'aristocratie*, Paris: Firmin Didot frères, 45–46: "Les lois doivent ôter le droit d'ainesse entre les nobles, afin que, par le partage continuel des successions, les fortunes se remettent toujours dans l'égalité. Il ne faut point de substitutions. De retraits lignagers, de majorats, d'adoptions. Tous les moyens inventés pour perpétuer la grandeur des familles dans les États monarchiques ne sauraient être d'usage dans l'aristocratie".

Glossarium which contains many documented instances of the practice[124]) by the donations offered on this solemn occasion and called *filiolatus filiolagium, "clear evidence of the practice*", in which, "*the godfather was considered to be no different from an adoptive father*"; this is followed by adoption "*by arms ... when a Prince bestowed arms upon a person out of consideration for his merits*"; by adoption "*by hair, which was performed by cutting a person's hair, which was given to the adoptive father*"; by adoption by marriage, when the husband's or wife's children from a previous marriage were accepted "*as legitimate and natural children, not as stepchildren*", and admitted "*to inheritance with the same rights and on the same footing as children from the current marriage*".

Alongside this fragmentary exposition, supported by sources from the remote past and by historical examples of adoptions—such as the adoption of Alfonso of Aragona "*made by Queen Giovanna, as Sovereign*; *through adoptions such as this even Empires and Kingdoms were passed on to the adopted persons*", Marco Ferro also makes some vague allusions to local topics, that confirm his affection for the *ius commune* and maybe a lesser interest in Venetian law.

The Republic continues to be the centre of Ferro's attention in his treatment of a statutory provision that "speaks of filial subjection, and those children usually called *children of the soul*, which shows that in Venice adoption was not always unknown: quite the contrary, in the Zamberti manuscripts housed in the public library, we can find two criminal judgments, one dated August 27, 1452 the other dated June 27, 1475, which sentenced two adoptive fathers to prison and a fine for deflowering their adopted daughters": another historical example provided by an Author well versed in the history of the *Serenissima,* an interpreter of its past but also aware of the practice of adoption.[125]

In spite of being rarely practiced, adoption continued on its way, as attested by the sparse sources which I have cited here and there, only by way of example, since it is impossible to master the enormous quantity of legal texts that have dealt with the practice over the course of centuries and in the various regions, and then attempt to provide an account of them

The fact that adoption was under the radar screen foreshadowed its rebirth, sometimes under a different guise, during the French Revolution, in the context of a new conception of the family and society, founded on more egalitarian principles. Cambacérès, the French lawyer and statesman considered one of the 'fathers' of the

[124]Du Cange, Charles du Fresne. 1883–1887/1954. *Glossarium mediae et infimae latinitatis* 1. Niort: Léopold Favre. Repr. Graz: Akademische Druck–u. Verlagsanstalt, 88: entries *Adoptari per Baptismum,* but also *Adoptare, Adoptare in haereditatem, Adoptare sibi in maritum, Adoptare in militem, Adoptio filiorum, Adoptiva foemina, Adoptarius, Puer ex adoptato natus.*

[125]Ferro, Marco. 1845. *Dizionario del diritto comune e veneto* 1. Venezia: Andrea Santini e figli, 45–48. Marco Ferro (1750–1784), author of only one important work, the *Dizionario,* graduated from Padua and practiced as attorney and tax attorney: cf. Preto, Paolo. 1997. Ferro Marco. In *Dizionario biografico degli Italiani,* 47. Roma: Istituto dell'Enciclopedia Italiana, 198–199; Gasparini, Silvia. 2012. Ferro Marco. In *Dizionario Biografico dei Giuristi Italiani (XII–XX secolo).* Bologna: il Mulino, 857–858.

Napoleonic Code, in his *Rapport* on 1793 9th August, when he introduced the first project of a *Code civil* to the National Convention, in an atmosphere favorable to adoption, gave it credit for contributing to the division of fortunes: "L'adoption est tout à la fois une institution de bienfaisance et la vivante image de la nature. Le respect dû à cette double qualité a déterminé le mode que nous venons de vous soumettre. L'adoption donne plus d'étendue à la paternité, plus d'activité à l'amour filial; elle vivifie la famille par l'emulation; ella la répare par de nouveau choix; et en corrigeant les erreurs de la nature, elle en acquitte la dette en agrandissant son empire. C'est le rameau étranger enté sur un tronc antique; il en ranime la sève; il embellit la tige de nouveau rejetons; et, par cette insertion heureuse, elle couronne l'arbre d'une nouvelle moisson de fleurs et de fruits: admirable institution que vous avez eu la gloire de renouveler, et qui se lie si naturellement à la constitution de la république, puisque elle amène sans crise la division des grandes fortunes".[126] The concept was reiterated in the *Motifs de la méthode que l'on a suivie dans la distribution du code civil*: "L'adoption, cette institution protectrice, cette sage et bienfaisante émule de la nature, n'appartient pas moins à l'état des personnes: elle le confère à l'enfant".[127] In the second draft we find the same favour: "… l'adoption, institution morale, ressource contre la stérilité, nouvelle nature qui supplée au défaut de la première, qui, sans multiplier les êtres, multiplie les familles, augmente les rélations par les sentiments; bienfait de la législation, qui ajoute un lien de plus à la société. L'adoption imite la nature, C'est une raison pour accorder à tous le sexes le droit d'adopter, pour exiger qu'il y ait entre l'adoptant et l'enfant adoptif la distance de la puberté, pour ne pas souffrir qu'un des époux puisse adopter sans le consentement de l'autre…".[128] But already in the third draft in 1796 adoption is not so favored, it's not accessibile to those who already have children. To avoid adoptions being concluded easily, Cambacérès provided for the adoption being irrevocable by the adopter and for the adoptee's freedom to withdraw from the relationship in the first year after the age of majority.[129]

8 Towards the Contemporary Ages: from the *Code Civil* to Italian Civil Code (1865) and … Closer to Our Times

In the 19th century the rules on adoption are unavoidably linked to the needs and ideology of contemporary society, as a sensitive thermometer of its socio-economic and cultural development and of its goals.

[126]Fenet, Pierre Antoine. 1927/1968. *Recueil complet des travaux préparatoires du code civil* 1, Paris: Videcoq, repr. Osnabrück: Otto Zeller, 6–7.

[127]Fenet (as n. 126) 12.

[128]Fenet (as n. 126) 101.

[129]Fenet (as n. 126) 148–149, 208–209.

The difficulties that adoption faces during this century to conserve but above all to keep in action *ancien régime* law, in a more and more complex reality, are the witnesses of its ambiguous aims.

It expresses, on one side, the weight of a tradition hard to die to satisfy egoistic needs, that is e.g. to insure a descendant, and, on the other side, the emersion of a minor's interest.

Thereafter, in the Napoleonic era (as well as in the *Code civil*) adoption went on its way. Wherever the institution took root, the experience that was acquired while it was legally in force would be renewed under different governments.[130]

After the submission of the draft drawn up by the Government Commission appointed by Napoleon in 1800 the approval process was fraught with a series of difficulties. Also if the Emperor sustains with force its opportunity until elevating adoption to "une espèce de nouveau sacrement", enforced by the legislative power, the draft met new obstacles and new variations aimed to overcome objections until March 23rd 1803 when the law was definitely approved: it was enacted in April 2.[131]

The french Civil Code, the future Napoléon Code, destined to become the law of the Kingdom of Italy in 1806, allowed adoption (art. 343–360) but under special conditions: if the adopter was unable to have children, at the age of fifty, and the age difference between the latter and the adoptee had to be at least 15 years, with the adoptee being an adult. It also provides for two other types of adoptions, the testamentary (art. 366) and the 'remunerative'(art. 345), as a reward if the adoptee saved the adopter's life in exceptional circumstances, as in the case of combat, fire or storm.

During the Restoration—it is well known—the french civil code in Italy was the source and 'model' of inspiration but there isn't a slavish imitation: at least some codes provided for different rulings that are expressed local 'sensibilities'. The analysis of the preparatory works in the italian States after the napoleonic era shows the prevalence of different combined trends.

In the Papal States the preparatory work of the code couldn't reach a conclusion, but the texts discussed in the drafts were poised between a dating tradition and new guidelines aimed at favouring the minor's interest (e.g. permitting—it seems—a child's adoption).[132]

In the Duchy of Parma, Plaisance and Guastalla, despite proposing solutions more focused on the care of the adoptee in the course of the preparatory work, the rules of the 1820 Code (Art. 188–209) followed the french legislation, as well as the 1819 code for the Kingdom of the two Sicilies (art. 138 ff.), the 1811 Austrian code

---

[130]Cf. Vismara, Giulio. 1978. *Il diritto in famiglia in Italia dalle riforme ai codici. Appunti*. Milano: Giuffrè, 1978, 30, 44–45; now Id. 1988, *Scritti di storia giuridica*, 5. *La famiglia*. Milano: Giuffrè, 68–69; di Renzo Villata, Maria Gigliola. 1995. Persone e famiglia (diritto medievale e moderno). In *Digesto IV (discipline privatistiche)*. Torino: UTET, 457–527; especially 516, 519; Lefebvre Teillard (as n. 1) 286 ss.

[131]Fenet (as n. 126) 247–402, espec. 288–389, 359 ff., 367–368, 374–378, 403 ff.

[132]For further details see di Renzo Villata. 2015 (as n. 6); di Renzo Villata. 2016 (as n. 6).

(§ 179 ff.) in force since 1816 in the Lombard-Venetian Kingdom, the Albertine Code (1837), the working model for the unified italian codification.

All these codes provided that the adopter gave his surname to the adoptee who added it to his surname, the mutual right to alimony, to succession, but not the right to inheritance from the adopter's family and not in general the right to succeed in nobility and titles except with a concession made by the sovereign as requested by the adopter (Albertine Code: art. 196).[133]

Ludovico Bosellini, professor and judge in Modena, expressing his opinion on the first draft of the Italian civil code, derived from a simple revision of the Albertine Code, considered then adoption a non used legal instrument, disregarding customs, immoral: "Non mi soffermerò sull'adozione, la quale è oggimai lettera morta, avendo contro di sé i costumi…".[134]

In the first steps of the preparatory work of the Italian 1865 Civil Code adoption was absent. In 1863 Giuseppe Pisanelli, the 'father' of the code, in the speech introducing the first book of his draft in the Senate, qualified adoption as opposed to costums, means of fraud, unethical; in the *Relazione* before the Senate he expressed the same concepts.[135]

Between 1863 and 1865, after a parliamentary skirmish, adoption was confirmed and 'accepted' in the new *Civil Code* under strict conditions (absence of legitimate and legitimized children, if the adopter was more than 50 years old and the adoptee was more than 18 years old, if the age difference between the parties was at least 18 years, prohibition on adopting children born out of wedlock, preservation of links with the family of origin to which the adoptee had the same rights and duties etc.).[136]

Also after 1865, adoption was practiced very little and also the doctrine and jurisprudence rarely dealt with adoption. In 1923, after the end of the first world war, when in Italy the idea of reforming the 1865 civil code was developing and the

---

[133]See di Renzo Villata. 2015 (as n. 6); di Renzo Villata. 2016 (as n. 6).

[134]Bosellini, Ludovico. 1860. Intorno al progetto di codice civile. Lettera terza. *Monitore dei Tribunali* 1: 740 (Milano, sabato 6 ottobre: no. 93). The *Lettera terza* (*Monitore dei Tribunali* 1: 737–740) was preceded by a first article 'Intorno al progetto di codice civile' (*Monitore dei Tribunali* 1: 549–551, nos. 69–70); by the following *Lettera seconda (Monitore dei Tribunali* 1: 729–732, no. 92) and by the further *Lettere*.

[135]See Gianzana, Sebastiano. 1887. *Codice civile preceduto dalle Relazioni ministeriale e senatoria, dalle Discussioni Parlamentari, e dai Verbali della Commissione coordinatrice.* 1. *Relazioni.* Torino-Roma-Napoli: Unione tipografico-editrice, 12; *Del Progetto di codice civile pel Regno d'Italia presentato al Senato dal Ministro Guardasigilli (Pisanelli) nelle tornate del 15 luglio e 26 novembre 1863.* 1863. Torino: Stamperia Reale: therein *Progetto di legge per l'approvazione del primo libro del Codice civile pel Regno d'Italia presentato in iniziativa al Senato dal Ministro Guardasigilli (Pisanelli) nella tornata del 15 luglio 1863,* where adoption is absent; see after *Relazione sul Progetto del primo libro del Codice civile presentato in iniziativa al Senato dal Ministro Guardasigilli (Pisanelli) nella tornata del 15 luglio 1863.* In *Del Progetto di codice civile…*, 16–17. See Garlati, Loredana. 2011. La famiglia tra passato e presente. In Patti, Salvatore and Cubeddu, Maria Giovanna. *Diritto della famiglia.* Milano: Giuffrè, 39–40, 43..

[136]See di Renzo Villata. 2015 (as n. 6); di Renzo Villata. 2016 (as n. 6).

preparatory work of a new code started, a complete turnaround came about. The Italian 1942 civil code provides for the traditional type of adoption and also for *affiliazione* (art. 404–413), a sort of fosterage: a link after family law and the special rules on child welfare was introduced. Evolving times highten, also at international level, the sensitivity for the needs of abandoned children. In Italy two new laws (law act 2nd June 1967 no. 431, especially about "special adoption" and law act 4th May 1983 no. 184, introducing also the so-called international adoption) ruled adoption (and also fosterage) focusing more and more on children's interest.[137]

At this time a law on stepchild adoption is under discussion in the Italian Parliament and a debate is taking place on the legality of surrogacy, while the heterologous fertilization practices are increasingly common and permitted.[138]

Is adoption in remission today? The future will have the last say.

References

Accursius. (1551a). *Digestum vetus. Digestorum seu Pandectarum iuris enucleati ex omni iure veteri in libros quinquaginta collecti authoritate sacratissimi principis dn. Iustiniani Augusti tomus primus (Digestum vetus vulgo vocant) primam, secundam, tertiam, ac quartae partis libros quatuor et quinti titulos duos continens: ita in uniuersum ex Pandectis Florentinis recognitus*. Lugduni: apud Hugonem a Porta et Antonium Vincentium.

Accursius. (1551b). *Volumen, complectitur hoc volumen (sic enim peculiari vocabulo vocant) novellas contitutiones Iustiniani principis post repetitam codicis praelectionem editas: Authentica vulgo appellant: Tres item posteriores libros Codicis: Feudorum seu beneficiorum duos: Constitutiones Friderici II Imper. Extravagantes duas Henrici VII Imper. et Tractatum de pace Constantiae. Omnia ad vetustissimorum simul & emendatissimorum exemplarium fidem recognita, emendata. Adiectae sunt plerisque in locis ex doctissimorum hominum commentariis annotationes*. Lugduni: apud Hugonem a Porta et Antonium Vincentium.

Albericus de Rosate (1573/1971). *Dictionarium Iuris tam Civilis quam Canonici*. Venetiis: apud Guerreos fratres et socios. Repr. Torino: Bottega d'Erasmo.

Albericus de Rosate (1575/1974). *In Primam Digesti Veteris partem Commentarii*. Venetiis: [Gaspare Bindoni et Nicolo Bevilacqua et Damiano Zenaro]. Repr. Bologna: Forni.

Antonius de Budrio (1578/1967). *In Librum Quartum Decretalium Commentarii*. Venetiis: apud Iuntas. Repr. Torino: Bottega d'Erasmo.

Aubenas, R. (1934). L'adoption en Provence au Moyen Âge. *Revue historique du droit français et étranger, 13*, 700–726.

Aubenas, R. (1935). *Documents notariés provençaux du XIIIe siècle*. Aix: E. Fourcine.

Azo. (1506/1966). *Summa Codicis*, ed. Papie: per Bernardinum & Ambrosium fratres de Rovellis. Repr. Torino: Bottega d'Erasmo.

Baldus. (1575/1970). *Consiliorum sive responsorum liber primus*. Venetiis: [Francesco de' Franceschi et Gaspare Bindoni et Nicolò Bevilacqua et Damiano Zenaro]. Repr. Torino: Bottega d'Erasmo.

Baldus. (1585). *Commentaria in VII. VIII. IX. X. et XI Cod. Lib.* Lugduni: [s.n.].

[137]See di Renzo Villata. 2015 (as n. 6); di Renzo Villata. 2016 (as n. 6).

[138]I've summarized here only in a few words the intense development in Italy in the 20th century: see di Renzo Villata. 2015 (as n. 6); di Renzo Villata. 2016 (as n. 6).

Bartolomeus Anglicus. (1609). *De genuinis rerum coelestium, terrestrium et infernarum proprietatibus libri XVIII.* Francofurti: apud Wolfgangum Richterum, sumptibus Nicolai Steinii.

Bartolus. (1570). *Commentaria in primam ff. Veteris partem.* Venetiis: apud Iuntas.

Bartolus. (1590). *In primam -secundam ff. Noui partem.* Venetiis: [Societas aquilae se renovantis].

Bencivenne. (1965). *Ars notarie.* ed. Bronzino, Giovanni. Bologna: Zanichelli.

Besta, E. (1933). *La famiglia nella storia del diritto italiano.* Padova: CEDAM.

Birocchi, I. (2003). *L'*Istituta civile *di Giambattista De Luca*, in *Amicitiae pignus. Studi in ricordo di Adriano Cavanna* (pp. 87–119). I. a cura di Padoa Schioppa, Antonio, di Renzo Villata, Gigliola and Massetto, Gian Paolo. Milano: Giuffrè.

Böcking, E. (1829). *Corpus legum sive Brachylogus iuris civilis.* Berolini: typis Feisterianis et Eisersdorffianis.

Bosellini, L. (1860a). Intorno al progetto di codice civile. *Lettera terza. Monitore dei Tribunali, 1*, 740.

Bosellini, L. (1860b). Intorno al progetto di codice civile. *Monitore dei Tribunali, 1*, 549–551.

Bosellini, L. (1860c). Lettera seconda. *Monitore dei Tribunali, 1*, 729–732.

Boutillier, J. (1611). *Somme rural.* éd. Charondas Le Caron. Paris: Barthelemy Macé.

Branca, G. (1958). Adozione (diritto romano). In *Enciclopedia del diritto* 1. Milano: Giuffrè.

Bresc, H. (1986). *Un monde méditerranéen. Économie et société en Sicile, 1300–1450* (*Bibliothèque des Écoles françaises d'Athènes et de Rome*, 262). Roma: École française de Rome.

Caballinus, I. B. (1605). *Formularium et solemnitates instrumentorum abbreviatorum et extensorum... scriptum et nunc secundo emissum*, Mediolani: apud Hieronymum Bordonum et Petrum Martyrem Locarnum. *Consuetudines feudorum.* 1892–1971. *Consuetudines feudorum*, ed. Lehmann, Karl (*Bibliotheca Rerum Historicarum, Neudrucke,* 1). Aalen: Scientia Verlag.

Calasso, F. (1953). "Iurisdictio" nel diritto comune classico. *Studi in onore di Arangio Ruiz nel XLV anno del suo insegnamento 4* (pp. 420–433). Napoli: Jovene.

Calasso, F. (1957). *I glossatori e la teoria della sovranità.* Milano: Giuffrè.

Carlyle, R. W., & Carlyle, A. J. (1909/1956). *A History of Mediaeval Political Theory* 2. Edinburgh and London: Blackwood. trad. it. *Il pensiero politico medievale* a cura di Firpo, Luigi 1. Bari: Laterza.

Carpanus, H. (1600). *Lucubrationes Novae, innumerae et solidae in omne ius municipale, quod statutum Mediolani appellant.* Francofurti: excudebat Romanus Beatus, sumptibus Nicolai Bassaei.

Capitularia Regum Francorum. (1984). In MGH. *Legum Sectio* II/1.*Capitulare legi Ribuariae additum* 803. ed. by Boretius, Alfred. Hannover: Hahnsche Buchhandlung.

Cortese, E. (1964–1995). *La norma giuridica. Spunti teorici nel diritto comune classic* 2, Milano: Giuffrè. Repr. Milano: Giuffrè.

Cortese, E. (1988). Thinx, gairethinx, thingare in gaida et gisilLudovico. Divagazioni longobardistiche in tema di legislazione, manomissione dei servi, successioni volontarie. *Rivista di storia del diritto italiano, 61*, 33–64.

Cortese, E. (1990). Thinx, gairethinx, thingare in gaida et gisil. Divagazioni longobardistiche in tema di legislazione, manomissione dei servi, successioni volontarie. In *Studi in memoria di Mario E. Viora* [*Biblioteca della Rivista di storia del diritto italiano,* 30] (pp. 279–310). Roma: Fondazione Sergio Mochi Onory per la Storia del Diritto Italiano.

Cortese, E. (1995a). *Il diritto nella storia* medievale 1, *L'alto medioevo.* Roma: Il Cigno Galileo Galilei.

Cortese, E. (1995b). *Il diritto nella storia* medievale. II. *Il basso medioevo*, Roma: Il Cigno Galileo Galilei.

Corti, F. (1571). *Consilia.* Venetiis: apud Nicolaum Bevilaquam et socios.

Costa, P. (1969/2002). *Iurisdictio. Semantica del potere politico nella pubblicistica medievale (1100–1433).* Milano, Giuffrè. Repr. Milano: Giuffrè.

De Luca, G. B. (1678). *Theatrum veritatis et iustitiae.* Roma: ex typographia Reverendae Camerae Apostolicae.

De Luca, G. B. (1743). *Istituta civile divisa in quattro libri con l'ordine de' titoli di quella di Giustiniano, del cardinale Giambattista De Luca accresciuta, e perfezionata dal dottore Sebastiano Simbeni....* Pesaro: a spese di Vincenzo Voltolini libraio veneto.

Del Progetto di codice civile pel Regno d'Italia presentato al Senato dal Ministro Guardasigilli (Pisanelli) nelle tornate del 15 luglio e 26 novembre 1863. 1863. Torino: Stamperia Reale.

di Renzo Villata, M. G. (1982). Scienza giuridica e legislazione nell'età sforzesca. In *Gli Sforza a Milano e in Lombardia e i loro rapporti con gli Stati italiani ed europei (1450–1530)* (pp. 65–145). Milano: Cisalpino-Goliardica.

di Renzo Villata, M. G. (1995). Persone e famiglia (diritto medievale e moderno). In *Digesto IV (discipline privatistiche)* (pp. 457–527). Torino: UTET.

di Renzo Villata, M. G. (2002a). Il volto della famiglia medievale tra pratica e teoria *Summa totius artis notariae*. In *Rolandino e l'ars notaria da Bologna all'Europa* (*Studi storici sul notariato italiano*) (pp. 377–458). Milano: Giuffrè.

di Renzo Villata, M. G. (2002b). Il volto della famiglia medievale tra pratica e teoria nella 'Rolandina'. In *Studi in memoria di Giovanni Cattaneo* (pp. 615–699). I. Milano: Giuffrè.

di Renzo Villata, M. G. (2012). Corti Francesco junior. In *Dizionario biografico dei giuristi italiani* 1 (pp. 584–586). Bologna: il Mulino.

di Renzo Villata, M. G. (2015a). Adoption between Middle Ages and Modern Era: was it in Decline. In M. C. Rossi & M. Garbellotti (Eds.), *Adoption and fosterage practices in the late medieval and modern age* (pp. 35–65). Roma: Viella.

di Renzo Villata, M. G. (2015b). L'adozione nell'Ottocento: un istituto in irreversibile declino?. In *Studi in onore di Giorgio De Nova* (pp. 1067–1098). Milano: Giuffrè.

di Renzo Villata, M. G. (2016). Adozione e affido. Uno sguardo alla normativa vigente tra passato e futuro… tra luci e ombre. In M. C. Rossi, & M. Garbellotti (Eds.), *Adozione e affido: per un approccio interdisciplinare*. Roma: Viella (in press).

Du Cange, C. F. (1883–1887/1954). *Glossarium mediae et infimae latinitatis*. I. Niort: Léopold Favre. Repr. Graz: Akademische Druck-u. Verlagsanstalt.

Dumoulin, C. (1658). *Tractatus analyticus de Dignitatibus, Magistratibus et Civibus Romanis*. In Id., *Opera* 4. Parisiis: apud Carolum de Mesnii.

Edigati, D. (2005). *Una vita nelle istituzioni: Marc'Antonio Savelli giurista e cancelliere tra Stato pontificio e Toscana medicea*. Modigliana: ETS.

Fenet, P. A. (1927/1968). *Recueil complet des travaux préparatoires du code civil*, I, Paris: Videcoq. Repr. Osnabrück: Otto Zeller.

Ferro, M. (1845). *Dizionario del diritto comune e veneto* 1. Venezia: presso Andrea Santini e figlio.

Formularium florentinum artis notariae. (1220–1242). (1943). testo ed introduzione storica a c. di Masi, Gino. Milano: Società editrice "vita e pensiero".

Formularium florentinum artis notariae. (1997). Formularium florentinum artis notariae. In S. P. Scalfati (Ed.), *Un formulario notarile fiorentino della metà del Dugento*. Firenze: EDIFIR.

Formularium tabellionum. (1913/1962). Wernerii formularium tabellionum. In *Scripta anecdota glossatorum* 1, ed. curante Palmerio, Iohannes Baptista. Editio altera emendata. Bologna: Società Azzoguidiana. Repr. Torino: Bottega d'Erasmo.

Fuero Real. (1541). *Fuero Real de España diligentemente hecho por el noble Rey don Alonso IX. Glosado por el egregio doctor Alonso Diaz de Montalvo*. Burgos: por Juan de Junta.

Gager, K. E. (1996). *Blood ties and fictive ties. Adoption and family life in early modern France*. Princeton New Jersey: Princeton University Press.

Garlati, L. (2011). La famiglia tra passato e presente. In Patti, S. & Cubeddu, M. G. (Eds.), *Diritto della famiglia* (pp. 39–40). Milano: Giuffrè.

Gattola, E. (1734). *Ad historiam abbatiae cassinensis accessiones* 1. Venetiis: apud Sebastianum Coleti.

Gellius, A. (1993). *Noctes Atticae*. lib. V. Pisa: in aedibus Giardini editori e stampatori.

Gianzana, S. (1887). *Codice civile preceduto dalle Relazioni ministeriale e senatoria, dalle Discussioni Parlamentari, e dai Verbali della Commissione coordinatrice*. 1. *Relazioni*. Torino-Roma-Napoli: Unione tipografico-editrice.

Gilmore, M.-P. (1941/1967). *Argument from Roman Law in Political Thought 1200–1600*. (Harvard Historical Monographs, XV). Cambridge Mass.: Harvard University Press. repr. New York: Russel & Russel.

Gonnet, P. (1935). *L'adoption lyonnaise des orphelins légitimes (1536–1793)*. Paris: Librairie générale de Droit et de Jurisprudence.

Goody, J. (1969). Adoption in cross-cultural perspective. *Comparative Studies in History and Society, 11*, 550–578.

Goody, J. (1976). *Family and inheritance. Rural society in Western Europe, 1300–1800*. Cambridge-Londra-New York-Melbourne: Cambridge University Press.

Goody, J. (1983). *The development of the family and marriage in Europe*. Cambridge: Cambridge University Press.

Goody, J. (1995). *Famiglia e matrimonio in Europa: origini e sviluppi dei modelli familiari dell'Occidente, edizione italiana a cura di Maiello, Francesco*. Roma-Bari: Laterza.

Gouron, A. (1994/2000). Placentinus, "Herold" der Vermutungslehre ?. In *Festschrift zum 65. Geburtstag und zur Emeritierung von Professor Dr. Hans Hiefner*. Münster: [s.n.], 90–103, also In Id.. *Juristes et droits savants : Bologne et la France médiévale(Collected Studies Series,* 679) (pp. 90–103). Aldershot: Ashgate.

Gratianus, S. (1650). *Disceptationum forensium ... tomus quintus*. Venetiis: apud Guerilios.

Gualazzini, U. (1957). Adozione (diritto intermedio). *Novissimo Digesto Italiano 1* (pp. 288–290). Torino: UTET.

Gutton, J. P. (1993). *Histoire de l'adoption en France*. Paris: Publisud.

Henricus Segusiensis. (1574/1963). Henry de Suze, *Summa aurea*. ed. Venetiis: apud Iacobum Vitalem. Repr. Torino: Bottega d'Erasmo.

Henricus Segusiensis. (1581/1965). Henry de Suze, *In quartum Decretalium librum Commentaria*. Venetiis: apud Iuntas. Repr. Torino: Bottega d'Erasmo.

Hessel, A. (1910). *Geschichte der Stadt Bologna von 1216 bis 1280*. Berlin: E. Ebering.

Hessel, A. (1975). *Storia della città di Bologna 1116–1280, a cura di Gina Fasoli*. Alfa: Bologna.

Hilaire, J. (1987). Coutumes rédigées et "gens de champs" (Angoumois, Aunis, Saintonge). *Revue historique du droit français et étranger, 65*, 545–573.

Iohannes Andreae. (1581–1963). *In quartum Decretalium librum Novella Commentaria*. Venetiis: apud Franciscum Franciscium Senensem. Repr. Torino: Bottega d'Erasmo

Krynen, J. (1982). Naturel. Essai sur l'argument de la nature dans la pensée politique française à la fin du Moyen Âge. *Journal des savants,* Avr.-Juin 1982, 169–190.

Lambertenghus, S. (1576/1574). *Tractatus De contractibus eorum, quibus vel a iure communi, vel a statutis, sine certa solennitate contrahere permissum non est. Opus maxime vtile, in foris versantibus, pro intelligentia diuersorum Statutorum Italiae, ac aliarum consuetudinum*. Milano: apud Antonium Antonianum. (Mediolani: apud Pacificum Pontium).

Lefebvre Teillard, A. (1973). *Les officialités à la veille du concile de Trente*, Paris: Librairie Générale de Droit et de Jurisprudence.

Lefebvre Teillard, A. (1996). *Introduction historique au droit des personnes et de la famille*, Paris. Presses Universitaires de France.

Lefebvre Teillard, A. (1989). *Le nom. Droit et histoire*. Paris: Librairie Générale de Droit et de Jurisprudence.

Lectura Vindobonensis. (1914). Lectura Vindobonensis. In Giovan Battista Palmieri (Ed.), *Wernerii Summa Institutionum cum glossis Martini, Bulgari, Alberici aliorumque*. In *Bibliotheca Iuridica Medii Aevi. Scripta anecdota glossatorum* 1, *Additiones*. Bologna: Società Azzoguidiana.

Lex Romana curiensis. (1966). *Lex Romana curiensis*. In E. Meyer-Marthaler (Ed.), (*Sammlung Schweizerischer Rechtsquellen*, XV. *Die Rechtsquellen des Kantons Graubüden*, I *Alträtisches Recht*, I). Aarau: Sauerländer.

Lex Ribuaria. (1969). In MGH. *Leges.Leges Nationum Germanicarum*. 3.2. ed. Beyerle, Franz-Buchner, Rudolf. Hannover: Hahnsche Buchhandlung.

Lex Salica. (1962). In *MGH. Leges. Sectio* I. 4/1. ed. by Eckardt. Karl August, Hannover: Hahnsche Buchhandlung.

Liber sive matricula notariorum Comunis Bononiae. (1980). *Liber sive matricula notariorum Comunis Bononie (1219-1299)* 1980, a cura di Ferrara Roberto and Valentini Vittorio (*Fonti e strumenti per la storia del notariato italiano* III), Roma: Giuffrè.

Libri feudorum. (1896–1971). *Das Langobardische Lehnrecht (Handschriften, Textentwicklung, ältester Text und Vulgattext nebst den capitula extraordinaria)*, a cura di K. Lehmann, Gottinga.

Livre de Jostice et plet. (1850). *Li Livre de Jostice et plet,* éd. Rapetti, Parigi.

Marculfi Formulae. (1963). MGH. In Zeumer, K (Ed.), *Legum Sectio V. Formulae*. Hannover: Hahnsche Buchhandlung.

Martino, F. (1983). In tema di potestas condendi statuta. Indagini sul pensiero di Ranieri Arsendi da Padova. *Quaderni Catanesi*, V, *10*, 461–484.

Martino, F. (1984). *Dottrine di giuristi e realtà cittadine nell'Italia del Trecento. Ranieri Arsendi a Pisa e a Padova,* Catania. Tringale (*Studi e ricerche dei "Quaderni Catanesi*", 5).

Milano Consuetudini. (1216–1949). *Liber Consuetudinum Mediolani MCCXVI* 1949, ed. E. Besta, G. L. Barni, Milano.

Martinus Fanensis. (1907). Formularium, ed. Wahrmund, Ludwig. *Quellen zur Geschichte des römisch-kanonischen Processes im Mittelalter*, I.VIII. Innsbruck: Wagner.

Martinus Fanensis. (1951). Tractatus de alimentis, ed. Nicolini, Ugo. Il trattato "De alimentis » di Martino da Fano. In *Atti del congresso internazionale di diritto romano e storia del diritto* (Verona, 27–28–29 settembre 1948) 1. Milano: Giuffrè, 339–371, also In Nicolini, Ugo. 1983. *Scritti di storia del diritto italiano*. Milano: Giuffrè, 303–335.

Mayno de, J. (1544). Giason del Maino, Consiliorum pars quarta, Lugduni: [apud Hugonem et haeredes Aymoni a Porta], apud Stephanum Rufinum et Ioannem Ausultum.

Mayno de, J. (1579a). *In primam infortiati partem commentaria.* Venetiis: [Giunta].

Mayno de, J. (1579b). *Giason del Maino, In Primam Digesti Novi partem Commentaria.* Venetiis: [Giunta].

Montesquieu (1973). *De l'esprit des lois*. In Montesquieu, *Œuvres complètes* 2. Paris: Garnier.

Moschetti, G. (1990). *Il cartularium veronese del magister Ventura del secolo XIII.* Napoli: Edizioni Scientifiche italiane.

Nardi, L., & Orioli, E. (Eds.). (1909). *Chartularium Studii Bononiensis* (Vol. I). Bologna: Istituto per la storia dell'università di Bologna.

Nani, C. (1902). *Storia del diritto italiano*, Torino: Fratelli Bocca.

Nicolaus de Tudeschis (Abbas Panormitanus). (1547). *In quartum et quintum Decretalium librum interpretationes...*, Lugduni: ad candentis Salamandrae insigne in vico Mercenario apud Senetonios fratres.

Nörr, K. W. (1973). Kanonistische Literatur. In *Handbuch der Quellen und Literatur der neuren europaïschen Privatrechtsgeschichte*, a cura di Coing, Helmut. München: C.H. Beck Verlag.

Novara *Statuti* (2012). *Statuti di Novara del XIV secolo.* ed. crit. a cura di Cossandi, Gianmarco e Mangini, Marta Luigina. Varese: Insubria University Press.

Odofredus (1552–1968). *In secundam Codicis partem praelectiones*, Lione, 1552, rist. anast. *Lectura super Codice* II, Bologna. Forni.

Odofredus. (1550/1967). *Repetita in Undecim primos Pandectarum libros*, ed. Lugduni: Compagnie des libraires de Lyon, excudebat Blasius Guido, repr. *Lectura super Digesto veteri*. Bologna: Forni.

Olivier-Martin, F. (1922). *Histoire de la coutume de la prévôté et vicomté de Paris 1.* Paris: Éditions Ernest Leroux.

Otero Varela, A. (1955). *La adopción en la historia del derecho español*, in Id., *Dos estudios historico*-juridicos. Roma: [Consejo Superior de Investigaciones Científicas, Delegación de Roma], pp. 85–146.

Pagano, E. (2001). Avvocati ed esercizio della professione legale in Lombardia nel secondo Settecento. I causidici collegiati di Milano. *Rivista di storia del diritto italiano, 74*, 355–418.

Pertile, A. (1894). *Storia del diritto italiano dalla caduta dell'Impero romano alla codificazione*. Torino-Roma-Napoli-Milano: Unione tipografico-editrice.

Placentinus. (1536/1962). *Summa Codicis*. Moguntiae, in officina Ivonis Schoeffer. repr. Torino: Bottega d'Erasmo.

Pene Vidari, G. S. (1972). *Ricerche sul diritto agli alimenti* 1. *L'obbligo* "ex lege" *dei familiari nei giuristi dei sec. XII-XIV*, Torino: Giappichelli.

Petrus de Ancharano. (1535). *Super Quarto et quinto Decretalium Lectura aurea*. Lugduni: Joannes Moylin al's de Chambrai.

Petrus de Ancharano. (1549). *Consilia*, Lugduni: apud haeredes Iacobi Iuntae.

Pisa. *Constitutum legis pisanae civitatis (1870)*, ed. F. Bonaini, *Statuti inediti della città di Pisa dal XII al XIV secolo*. Firenze: G.P. Viesseux.

Pitzorno, B. (1904). *L'affigliamento della Chiesa: studio storico giuridico*. Sassari: Satta.

Pitzorno, B. (1914). *L'adozione privata*. Perugia: Unione tipografica cooperativa.

Poumarède, J. (1972). *Les successions dans le sud-ouest de la France au Moyen Âge (géographie coutumière et mutations sociales)*, préf. de Ourliac, Paul. Parigi: Presses Universitaires de France.

Preto, P. (1997). Ferro Marco. *Dizionario biografico degli Italiani 47* (pp. 198–199). Istituto della Enciclopedia Italiana: Roma.

Quaglioni, D. (1977). "Quilibet in domo sua dicitur rex" (In margine ad alcune pagine di Francesco Calasso). *Studi Senesi, 89*(1977), 344–358.

Quaglioni, D. (1983). *Politica e diritto nel Trecento italiano. Il* "De tyranno" *di Bartolo da Sassoferrato (1314–1357). Con l'edizione critica dei trattati* "De Guelphis et Gebellinis", "De regimine civitatis" e "De tyranno", Firenze: Olschki.

Rainerius Perusinus. (1892). *Ars notarie*, ed. Gaudenzi, Augusto. In *Scripta anecdota glossatorum*, Bologna: Società Azzoguidiana.

Rainerius Perusinus. (1917). *Ars notarie*, ed. Wahrmund, Ludwig. *Quellen zur Geschichte des römisch-kanonischen Processes im Mittelalter*, III/2. Ludwig. Innsbruck: Wagner).

Roberti, M. (1932). *Svolgimento storico della famiglia italiana*. Milano: Giuffrè.

Roberti, M. (1935). *Svolgimento storico del diritto privato in Italia 3*. La famiglia, Padova: CEDAM.

Rebuffe, P. (1589). *Explicatio ad quatuor primos libros Pandectarum*, Lugduni: apud Gulielmum Rouillium sub scuto Veneto.

Rolandinus de Passaggeriis. (1546–1977). Rolandino de' Passeggeri, *Summa totius artis notariae*, Venetiis, *apud Iuntas*, 1546. repr. Bologna: Forni.

Roubert, J. (1978). L'adoption des enfants par des particuliers à Lyon sous l'Ancien régime. *Bulletin de la Société française d'histoire des hôpitaux, 36–37*, 3–30.

Salatiele. (1961). *Ars notarie, Recensio I*, a cura di Orlandelli, Gianfranco. vol. I; vol. II *La seconda stesura dei codici della Biblioteca Nazionale di Parigi lat. 4593 e lat. 14622*, Milano: Giuffrè (*Istituto per la storia dell'Università di Bologna. Opere dei maestri,* II).

Salzer, E. (1900/1965). *Uber die Anfänge der Signorie in Oberitalien*. Berlin: E. Ebering. Valduz: Kraus reprint.

Savelli, M. A. (1717). *Summa diversorum contractuum* 2, Parmae: apud Paulum Montium sub Signo Fidei.

Schiaparelli, L. (1929). *Codice diplomatico longobardo* I, Roma: Tipografia del Senato.

Schiaparelli, L. (1933). *Codice diplomatico longobardo* 2, Roma: Tipografia del Senato.

Schupfer, F. (1892). Thinx e affatomia. Studi sulle adozioni in eredità dei secoli barbarici. *Atti della R. Accademia dei Lincei, Memorie*, s. IV, 9 (1891).

Schupfer, F. (1915). L'adozione privata. Dal mondo dei sogni (rec. a B. Pitzorno, *L'adozione privata*, Perugia 1914), *Rivista italiana di scienze giuridiche, 55*, 323–355.

Storti Storchi, C. (1991–1992/2007). Appunti in tema di "potestas condendi statuta". *Annali dell'Istituto Storico italo-germanico in Trento*, Quaderno 30, *Statuti città territori in Italia e Germania tra Medioevo ed Età moderna* a cura di Chittolini, Giorgio and Willoweit, Dietmar. Bologna: il Mulino, pp. 319–343 (Betrachtungen zum thema 'Potestas condendi statuta'. In *Statuten Städte und Territorien zwischen Mittelalter und Neuzeit in Italien und Deutschland*. Berlin: Duncker & Humblot; also In Storti Storchi, Claudia. 2007. *Scritti sugli statuti lombardi* (pp. 115–138). Milano: Giuffrè.

Summa "Elegantius in iure divino" seu Coloniensis [super Decretum Gratiani]. (1990). t. IV, XV.9, ed. Fransen, Gerard and Kuttner, Stephan (*Monumenta iuris canonici*, Series A: *Corpus Glossatorum*, I). Città del Vaticano: Biblioteca Apostolica Vaticana.

Siete Partidas. (1843). *Las Siete Partidas del Sabio Rey Don Alfonso el IX [sic]/con las variantes de más interés y con la glosa de Gregorio López; vertida al castellano y estensamente adicionada, con nuevas notas y comentarios y unas tablas sinópticas comparativas, sobre la legislación española, antigua y moderna... por Ignacio Sanponts y Barba, Ramón Martí de Eixala y José Ferrer y Subirana*. t. II. Barcellona: Imprenta de Antonio Bergnes.

Signorolus de Homodeis. (1521). *Consiliorum ac quaestiones....* Mediolani: per Io. Angelum Scinzenzeler.

Summa Notariae Aretii composita. (1901). *Summa notariae annis MCCXL.-MCCXLIII. Aretii composita*. Prodit curante Cicognario, Carolo (*Bibliotheca iuridica Medii Aevi*, 3). Bologna: Società Azzoguidiana.

Summa Perusina. (1900/2008). *Adnotationes codicum domini* Iustiniani. ed. Patetta, Federico. Roma: sumpt. F. Pasqualucci. Repr. Firenze: M. Pagliai.

Summa Vindobonensis. (1914). ed. Palmieri, Giovan Battista. *Wernerii Summam Institutionum cum glossis Martini, Bulgari, Alberici aliorumque*. In *Bibliotheca Iuridica Medii Aevi. Scripta anecdota glossatorum*. t. I. *Additiones*. Bologna: Società Azzoguidiana.

Summa Vindocinensis. (1976). ed. di Renzo Villata, Gigliola. Per un'edizione della Summa Vindocinensis. *Studia et documenta historiae et iuris, 42*, 265–302.

Tamassia, N. (1886). *L'affratellamento*. Torino: Fratelli Bocca.

Tamassia, N. (1911/1971). *La famiglia italiana nei secoli decimoquinto e decimosesto*. Milano: R. Sandron; Roma: Multigrafica.

Tartagnus, Alexander. (1590a). *Consiliorum seu responsorum ... liber quartus*. Venetiis: apud Felicem Valgrisium.

Tartagnus, Alexander. (1590b). *Consiliorum seu responsorum ... liber sextus*. Venetiis: apud Felicem Valgrisium. Tiraboschi, Girolamo. 1784–1970. *Biblioteca Modenese*. t. V. Modena: Società Tipografica. Repr. Bologna: Forni.

Toschus, D. (1634). *Practicarum conclusionum iuris in omni foro frequentiorum... tomus primus*, Roma: ex typographia Stephani Paulini. Lugduni: ex officina Ioannis Pillehotte.

Vigevano Statuti. (1532). *Statuta civilia et comunalia civitatis et comitatus Viglevani, Statuta civilia*. Mediolani: typis escussit Gotardus Ponticus.

Vigevano. (1608). *Statuta civilia et comunalia civitatis et comitatus Viglevani, Statuta civilia*, Mediolani: ex Typographia Iacopi Maria Medae.

Vismara, G. (1941). *Storia dei patti successori*. Milano: Giuffrè.

Vismara, G. (1958–1988). Adozione (diritto intermedio). In *Enciclopedia del diritto* 1. Milano: Giuffrè; also in Id., *Scritti di storia giuridica* 5, *La famiglia*. Milano: Giuffrè.

Vismara, G. (1978–1988). *Il diritto in famiglia in Italia dalle riforme ai codici. Appunti*. Milano: Giuffrè, also In Id., *Scritti di storia giuridica* 5, *La famiglia*. Milano: Giuffrè.

Vocabularius utriusque iuris. (1535). Lugduni: apud Iacobum Wit, Vincentius de Portonariis de Tridino de Monteferrato.

Weimar, P. (1973). Die legistische Literatur der Glossatorenzeit. In H. Coing (a cura di), *Handbuch der Quellen und Literatur der neuren europaïschen Privatrechtsgeschichte*. I. München: C.H. Beck Verlag.

Zaccaria di Martino. (1993). *Summa artis notarie*, ed. by Ferrara, Roberto. Bologna: s.n. (San Giovanni in Persiceto: F.A.R.A.P.).

A *Consilium* of Torello Di Niccolò Torelli of Prato on *Dos Aestimata*

Julius Kirshner

Abstract The chapter considers one of Torello's many unpublished *consilia*. Torello di Niccolò Torelli of Prato was a jurist who migrated from Prato to Florence, where he became a citizen, member of the Arte dei Giudici e Notai, professor at the Studio, and served the city as a communal lawyer and diplomat. Between the 1390s and 1420s he penned hundreds of *consilia* on local disputes. The consilium on dowry law (numerous *consilia* were written on this complex topic), discussed in the following pages, and edited below, is an autograph; it addresses a dispute over the restitution of a modest dowry and suggests that the litigants belonged to families of middling social rank, that the wife was the commissioning party, and that Torello submitted his opinion in her defense. Alternatively, Torello's rejection of her final claim suggests that his opinion may have been requested by the presiding judge in the court of the *podestà*. After the description of the case (*punctus*, or prefatory summation of the dispute), Torello examines all the main *dubia*, the remaining contentions and resolves all of them: in Torello's eyes the resolution of the case is so clear-cut that he does not feel compelled to support his arguments with heaps of authorities.

This paper, published in Iuris Historia. Liber Amicorum Gero Dolezalek. Berkeley. Robbins Collection. 2008, is now republished in a new version (with abstract, bibliography and other variants) with the permission of the Author, the editors Vincenzo Colli and Emanuele Conte, and Robbins Collection Director Laurent Mayali.

I am grateful to Susanne Lepsius for her comments.

J. Kirshner (✉)
Emeritus of Medieval and Renaissance History, University of Chicago,
227-237 East Delaware Place, Chicago, IL 60611, USA
e-mail: jkir@uchicago.edu

M.G. di Renzo Villata (ed.), *Family Law and Society in Europe from the Middle Ages to the Contemporary Era*, Studies in the History of Law and Justice 5,
DOI 10.1007/978-3-319-42289-3_4

1 Introduction

Torello di Niccolò Torelli of Prato figures among the Tuscan jurists whose works in manuscript are listed in Gero Dolezalek's pioneering *Verzeichnis der Handschriften zum römischen Recht bis 1600.*[1] Torello's legal opinions, or *consilia*, according to Dolezalek's list, survive in manuscript collections of miscellaneous *consilia* found mainly in the Biblioteca Nazionale and Archivio di Stato of Florence and the Biblioteca Apostolica Vaticana.[2] Since the archival materials in Florence documenting Torello's background and career have not yet been systematically explored, our knowledge of his place in Florentine society and jurisprudence is necessarily fragmentary. Like other jurists and consultocrats hailing from Florence's dominion—for example, Francesco Albergotti of Arezzo (d. 1376), Buonaccorso of Montemagno (d. 1429), and Tommaso Salvetti of Pistoia (d. 1472), Torello migrated from Prato to Florence, where he became a citizen, a member of the Arte dei Giudici e Notai and a professor at the Studio, and served the city as a communal lawyer (*sapiens communis*) and diplomat.[3] Between the 1390s and

[1]Four volumes published in Frankfurt am Main, 1972. For the references to Torello's *consilia* in manuscript, see vol. 3, sv. Torellus Nicolai de Torellis.

[2]For Torello's *consilia* and *subscriptiones* and citations of his *consilia* by other jurists, see Archivio di Stato di Firenze, Pareri dei Savi, n. 2, 426r-427v; n. 3, 388r-389v, 421r-428r, 451r-461r; Archivio dei Giudici e Notai, n. 670, 47r (15 Jan. 1392/3), 62r (10 Dec. 1394), 65r (21 July 1395), 71v-72r (7 July 1397), 73r (9 June 1399), 74v (12 June 1399), 81v (3 June 1401), 83r (27 Aug. 1401), 84r (21 May 1402), 96rv (30 June 1402), 102r-103r (13 Feb. 1402/3),110rv (7 June 1406); Archivio del Bene, n. 54, 32r (6 Nov. 1409), 45r-46r (4 Dec. 1409), 78r (8 Apr. 1410), 106r (8 Dec. 1410), 113r (2 Apr. 1411), 114r-116r (26 Apr. 1411); Florence, Biblioteca Nazionale, Fondo Principale, II. III., 370 (third volume of Lorenzo Ridolfi's *consilia*, 1413-1418), 8v, 9v, 11r, 14v, 17r, 27r, 28rv, 51v, 70r, 116v, 130r, 157v, 165v, 179r, 206v, 247r; Magl. XXIX, 117, 88r-89v; XXIX, 161, 139rv, 140r, 161v, 162rv, 231v; XXIX, 172, 161rv, 165r; XXIX, 174, 68v, 105r-106v, 107v-109r, 110v-111r; XXIX, 193, 115r; Landau Finaly, 98, 79r-80r; 97v, 98r-99v; Vatican City, Biblioteca Apostolica Vaticana, Vat. Lat. 8069, 258r, 263r, 368v; Vat. Lat. 10726, 294v, 379v-380r, Vat. Lat. 10962, 83v-85r; (former) Phillips MSS, 8889, 123v-125r, 225rv, 228rv, 234r-236r, 240rv, 297r-300r. This manuscript dates from the early fifteenth century and contains *consilia* of other Florentine jurists in addition to those of Bartolo, Francesco Tigrini, Baldo, and Angelo degli Ubaldi. It was formerly owned by the New York bookseller H.P. Kraus, who sold it to a German bookseller in the early 1980s. See also Campitelli, Ada and Liotta, Filippo. 1961–62. Notizia del MS. Vat. Lat. 8069. *Annali di storia del diritto* 5–6: 387–406, 402; Izbicki, Thomas. 1997. Legal and Polemical Manuscripts, 1150–1500. In *Friars and Jurists. Selected Studies* (*Biblioteca Eruditorum* 20). Goldbach: Keip, 309*-368*, 299*; Kirshner, Julius. 1999. Citizen Cain of Florence. In *La Toscane et les Toscans autour de la Renaissance: Cadres de vie, société, croyances. Mélanges offerts à Charles-M. de La Roncière*. Aix-en-Provence: Publications de l'Université de Provence, 175–189, 186. These references are meant to be indicative rather than complete.

[3]On Torello's career in Florence and other activities, see Martines, Lauro. 1963. *The Social World of the Florentine Humanists, 1390-1460*. Princeton: Princeton University Press, 109, n. 69; and his 1968. *Lawyers and Statecraft in Renaissance Florence*. Princeton: Princeton University Press, sv. Torello di Messer Niccolò; 1991. *Le consulte e "pratiche" della repubblica fiorentina* (1404), ed. Renzo Ninci. Roma: Istituto Storico Italiano per il Medio Evo, 62; Gherardi, Alessandro. 1881.

1420s he penned hundreds of *consilia* on local disputes, some quite fascinating, others run-of-the mill, none of which have ever been gathered into a single manuscript, let alone appeared in a printed edition.

My paper considers just one of Torello's many *consilia*, which I chose because of my long-standing interest in dowry law. This *consilium*, addressing a dispute over the restitution of a dowry, survives in at least two versions: an autograph (edited below) and a copy. Neither version supplies the date and place of the dispute, though there is a hint that it possibly took place in or near Pistoia. The litigants are identified by their Christian names only. The omission of surnames, as well as the modest value of the dowry in question, suggests that the litigants belonged to families of middling social rank.

2 Case

In the *punctus*, or prefatory summation of the dispute, we learn that in his last will a certain Martino instituted his brothers, Andrea and Simone, as his universal heirs. Martino also left his daughter, Agnese, a dowry of 200 florins, plus another 20 for both furnishings (*arredi*) and personal items (*bona paraphernalia*). After Martino's death, Agnese married Antonio, who received from Andrea part of a house that was intended to satisfy his share (110 florins) of Martino's bequest to Agnese. An agreement between the parties fixing the cash value of the property, customarily performed near or at its transfer, for undisclosed reasons was postponed to the future. In an ancillary pact, it was agreed that Andrea—before a deadline to be fixed by a certain Filippo—could substitute for part of the above house a garden located in Pistoia. The value of the garden would be appraised at the time it was transferred to Antonio. If it happened that the appraised value of the garden was more than 110 florins, Antonio was liable to pay the difference to Andrea. If the value of the garden was less, then Andrea had to make up the difference with other goods. In

(Footnote 3 continued)

Statuti della Università e Studio fiorentino dell'anno MCCCLXXXVII seguiti da un'appendice di documenti dal MCCCXX al MCCCCLXXII. Firenze: Tipi di M. Cellini e c., 352, 372, 375, 391–92; Park, Katharine 1980. Readers at the Florentine Studio According to Communal Fiscal Records (1357–1380, 1413–1146). Rinascimento *20: 249–310, 274; Davis, Jonathan. 1998.* Florence and Its University during the Early Renaissance. *Leiden, Boston, Köln: Brill, 30, 34, 41, 56, 58, 169; Cardini, Franco. 1991. La cultura. In* Prato. Storia di una città. *1.* Ascesa e declino del centro medievale (dal mille al 1494). *Prato: Comune di Prato, 841, 864; Kuehn, Thomas. 1991.* Law, Family & Women: Toward a Legal Anthropology of Renaissance Italy. *Chicago: University of Chicago Press, 284, 312; and his 2002.* Illegitimacy in Renaissance Florence. *Ann Arbor: University of Michigan Press, 51, 225, 226. The evidence for his appointment to the office of* sapiens communis *is found in Archivio di Stato, Florence, Tratte 576, 72r (1 Mar. 1416/17), 73r (7 June 1423). For Torello's connection with the wealthy Pratese merchant Marco Francesco Datini, see Mazzei, Lapo. 1880.* Lettere di un notaro a un mercante del secolo XIV, *ed. Cesare Guasti, Firenze: Successori Le Monnier, 1, 370.*

either case, the aforesaid part of house would revert to Andrea without any further contractual arrangement. In satisfaction of the other half of Martino's bequest, Simone gave Antonio a vineyard. Then Antonio, presumably in dotal instruments (*confessiones dotis*) redacted by a notary, promised to restore the dowry to Agnese in those cases legally requiring restitution—namely, if the husband was nearing insolvency (*vergens ad inopiam*) or had become insolvent during marriage (*constante matrimonio*) or upon his predecease.[4]

According to the *punctus*, Agnese neither was present when the agreements between Andrea and Antonio were made nor had direct knowledge of them. In other words, she had given neither passive nor active consent to the agreements. We also learn that Filippo had died without having established the deadline, while Andrea had not substituted the garden for the house. More important, the property conveyed by Andrea to Antonio had not been appraised. Sometime later Antonio died, triggering the dowry restitution process and the ensuing dispute between his widow and his unnamed heir. Four points of contention were outlined.

1. The parties did not really disagree on Agnese's claims as such, but only on whether she should be satisfied by cash or property. Agnese demanded restitution of 220 florins in cash from Antonio's heir. He rejected the demand on the grounds that since neither the house nor the vineyard had been appraised, the heir was legally entitled to restore both properties, which had been conveyed by Martino's heirs to Antonio. The assertion hinged on a technical distinction etched in the *Corpus iuris civilis* between an appraised dowry (*dos aestimata*) and an unappraised dowry (*dos inaestimata*).[5]

An appraised dowry typically consisted of immovables (e.g., buildings, gardens, vineyards, orchards) and movables (e.g., the bride's clothing and accessories, household items and furniture) given a fixed cash value mutually agreeable to the parties. Ordinarily, the agreement was recorded in a *confessio dotis*, the document in which the husband acknowledged the receipt, contents, and value of the dowry, as well as the conditions, as we have seen, under which he and his heirs were obligated to restore the dowry. Fixing the monetary value of the dowry at the beginning of marriage protected wives, by making the husband liable for any depreciation in the value of the dotal properties and goods.[6] During marriage the husband was vested with the administration of appraised immovables and their

---

[4]Kirshner, Julius. 1985. Wives Claims against Insolvent Husbands in Late Medieval Italy. In *Women of the Medieval World. Essays in Honor of John H. Mundy*, eds. Julius Kirshner and Suzanne Wemple. Oxford: Wiley, 256–303.

[5]For what follows, see Corbett, Percy Elwood. 1930. *The Roman Law of Marriage*. Oxford: Clarendon Press, 172–176; Calonge, Alfredo. 1965. Aestimatio dotis. *Anuario de historia del derecho español* 35: 5–57; Streicher, Karl Ludwig. 1973. *"Periculum dotis." Studien zum dotalrechtlichen Haftungssystem im klass. röm. Recht*. Berlin: J. Schweitzer-Verlag; Silveira Marchi, Eduardo Cesar. 2001. Periculum rei venditae e periculum dotis aestimatae. *Labeo* 47: 384–410; Bellomo, Manlio. 1961. *Ricerche sui rapporti patrimoniali tra coniugi. Contributo alla storia della famiglia medievale*. Milano: Giuffrè, 99–118; Pluss, Jacques Anthony 1983. *Baldus de Ubaldis on Dowry Law* (Ph.D. diss., University of Chicago), 116ff.

[6]D. 23. 3. 10 pr, *Plerumque interest*; D. 24. 3. 51, *Aestimatae*.

fruits, but he could not transfer immovables to third parties or use them as security for other transactions without his wife's consent.[7] As a rule, immovables given as dowry (*fundus dotalis*) had to be returned to the wife upon dissolution of marriage. Different rules applied to movables. After the movables were appraised and conveyed to the husband, they were treated as if they had been sold. In effect, the husband became the wife's debtor for the appraised value (*pretii debitor efficitur*),[8] which was treated as the purchase price. In addition, he became the owner of the appraised movables during marriage, and unless he was prohibited by a special pact, he was permitted to transfer the movables to third parties. The husband had the right to choose (*electio*), upon his predecease, to return to his wife the appraised movables he actually received *or* their appraised value in cash.

The husband was vested with legal control of the unappraised dowry, but he could not transfer it without the consent of his wife, who, according to medieval jurists, remained the ultimate owner under natural law of all properties and goods classified as *dos inaestimata*. She bore the risk (*periculum dotis*) should value of the *dos inaestimata* depreciate, and she profited should its value increase. On the whole, the husband's heirs were obligated to return to the wife all unappraised dotal goods.

Agnese rejected the assertion of the husband's heir, arguing that since the house and the vineyard had been appraised, they had to be treated as having been sold (*emptitia*), thereby entitling her to demand restitution of her dowry in cash. How were the properties given a fixed cash valuation? The vineyard had been specifically given as a dowry worth 110 florins, an amount which was understood to be equivalent to a cash valuation. Further, the cash valuation itself had been confirmed by her husband when he had promised to restore the specific amount (*quantitas*) of dowry upon his predecease. Concerning the house, Agnese argued by way of legal fiction that "it appears that the amount of 110 florins given [as dowry] in the said house should be returned and not the house, because, while the house was not appraised, a large part of the house was given which was worth the said amount in the same way as if it were appraised."

2. The husband's heir countered that, assuming that the goods (*bona*) in question had been appraised, the right to return the (*bona*) or their cash valuation belonged to

---

[7]Inst. 2. 8 pr.; C. 5. 13. 1. 15, *Rem in praesenti*, § *Et cum lex Iulia*. For this important issue, on which the jurists were in general agreement, see their commentaries on *lex Si aestimatis* (D. 24. 3. 50): Bartolo. 1528/1996, *Commentaria*, 9 vols (Venetiis: per Baptistam de Tortis. reprint Roma. Il Cigno Galileo Galilei), 3: 32v; Baldo degli Ubaldi. 1586. *In primam et secundam Infortiati partem commentaria*. Venetiis: apud Iuntas, 174r, n. 3; Angelo degli Ubaldi. 1548, *Super prima [-secunda] Infortiati*. Lugduni: per Thomam Bertheau, 13r; Giovanni da Imola.1502, *Pars prima super Infortiato*. Venetiis: per Filippo I Pinzi, 25b; Paolo di Castro.1553, *In primam [-secundam] Infortiati partem commentaria* (Lugduni: [Denis de Harsy], 37r, n. 5; Alessandro Tartagni. 1595, *In primam & II. Infortiati partem commentaria.* Venetiis: [Lucantonio Giunta il giovane], 62r, n. 2; and Bartolomeo da Saliceto. 1515. Lecturae prima [et secunda] pars super Codicis primo et secundo [tertio et quarto] libris. to C. 5. 12. 23, *Si praedium*. Lugduni: per Iacobus Mareschal. al's Roland, 18v.

[8]C. 5. 12. 5, *Quotiens*.

the husband, who in fact had wished to restore the properties. Agnese replied that, as she had already shown, there could be no doubt that the vineyard had been appraised. Further, the decision to return the appraised goods or cash did not belong to the husband's heir but to the husband, and the latter had legally committed himself in the *confessio dotis* to restore to Agnese her 220 florin dowry.

3. In his last will, Antonio left 20 florins to Agnese for personal items (*paraphernalia)*, presumably to satisfy the paraphernal part of the bequest provided by Agnese's father.[9] In view of this bequest, the husband's heir wanted to deduct from the 220 florin dowry 20 florins which, it was stated, Antonio had spent on his wife's personal items at the time they were married. The basis of the heir's contention, although not explained, was this: since the husband continued to be the legal owner of the clothing and accessories that he had purchased for his wife and which she continued to possess, these items now belonged to his heir, who was entitled to just compensation.[10] Conceding that Antonio had left the 20 florins in his last will for *paraphernalia*, Agnese replied that the properties worth 220 florins were given to Antonio in the name of dowry only and that Antonio had promised to restore the dowry only. In other words, Antonio's promise of restitution had made no mention of *paraphernalia.*

4. Agnese asserted that she found unacceptable Andrea's unilateral and arbitrary decision to give part of the house as his share for the payment of her dowry. She wanted Andrea to pay her the 110 florin bequest for which, as the father's heir, he was responsible. Her demand was made in full awareness that weakest part of her claim related to the house, which, she was forced to admit, had never been appraised. Should she lose her claim for the restoration of her dowry in cash, she wanted the option of suing Andrea for the 110 florins.

The events referred to in the *punctus* invite several speculative observations. High death rates owing to successive waves of plague marked the period in which the events occurred. It is conceivable that the death of Agnese's father and husband and Filippo all occurred within short intervals of each other. If that was so, Agnese's marriage to Antonio was short-lived, apparently without surviving children, for mention would have been made if Antonio's heir had been his son or

[9]On paraphema, see Wolff, Hans Julius 1955. Zur Geschichte der Parapherna. *ZRG RA* 72: 335–347; Yiftach-Firanko, Uri. 2003. *Marriage and Marital Arrangements. A History of the Greek Marriage Document in Egypt. 4th Century BCE—4th Century CE.* (*Münchener Beiträge zur Papyrusforschung und antiken Rechtsgeschichte 93*). München: C.H. Beck; Bellomo (as n. 4), 131ff; Kirshner, Julius and Pluss, Jacques. 1979. Two Fourteenth-Century Opinions of Dowries, Paraphernalia and Non-dotal Goods. *Bulletin of Medieval canon Law* (*BMLC*) 9: 65–77; Kirshner, Julius. 1991. Materials for a Gilded Cage: Non-dotal Assets in Florence (1300–1500). In *The Family in Italy from Antiquity to the Present,* eds. David I. Kertzer and Richard Saller. New Haven: Yale University Press, 184–207.

[10]Bestor, Jane Fair. 1997. The Groom's Prestations for the *Ductio* in late Medieval Italy: A Study in the Disciplining Power of *Liberalitas. Rivista Internazionale di Diritto Comune (RIDC)* 8: 129–177; Kirshner, Julius. 2002. Li Emergenti Bisogni Matrimoniali in Renaissance Florence. In *Society and Individual in Renaissance Florence*, ed. William J. Connell, Berkeley-Los Angeles-London: University of California Press, 79–109.

daughter. It seems strange that the part of the house designated as Agnese's dowry was never specifically identified. Contracts prepared by Tuscans and their notaries involving parts of a property typically detailed their magnitude, boundaries, and location.[11] It is likely, however, that Andrea and Simone were living together in the house (*fratres communiter habitantes*), which they inherited from their father and that they had not yet formally divided the inheritance into distinct shares, which would have necessitated an appraisal of the house's value. If this was the case, then Andrea had conveyed to Agnese's husband his unappraised and indistinct share of a house which he owned in common with his brother. The failure of the parties to come to an agreement on the value of the ill-defined part of the house, moreover, hints that its market value was either significantly more or less than 110 florins. In any case, seeming to have anticipated the problems associated with this property, Andrea and Antonio had entered into an agreement to replace it with a readily identifiable property, an entire garden. Their agreement came to naught, not only because the deadline for the substitution was never fixed, on account of Filippo's death, but also because the parties themselves, even after his death, were unable to consummate the deal. Why? Did one or the other party have cold feet? Did Antonio die soon after Filippo?

Motivating all the parties was a lack of liquidity. All things being equal, Antonio, like the large majority of Tuscan husbands, would have preferred, indeed demanded, a cash dowry, but he was constrained to accept the properties, probably because Andrea and Simone did not have the necessary cash to pay him. Likewise, Antonio's heir plausibly did not have the cash on hand to satisfy Agnese's demand. Beyond believing that she was entitled to the cash in view of her father's bequest, and wanting to avoid the expense, worry, and management attending the house and the vineyard, Agnese may have sought the 220 florins in cash to enhance her prospects for remarriage. After all, who could know how much she would receive for the properties if she had to sell them at market prices.

In the *punctus* and *consilium* Agnese was rendered as a speaking subject and full-fledged legal person asserting legitimate claims to her dowry. The representation of female litigants as speaking subjects was a rhetorical conceit. Agnese doubtlessly relied on a jurist, just as male litigants customarily did, to supply the arguments for her claims. It is distinctly possible that the arguments had already been presented in a *consilium pro parte* that she had commissioned and that the dispute had been litigated, with inconclusive results, in court of the podestà. Whatever the case may have been, it was now Torello's turn to present arguments aimed at resolving the dispute.

[11]See, for example, the contracts redacted by Coluccio Salutati in Buggiano. 1963. *Il protocollo notarile di Coluccio Salutati (1372-1373)*, ed. Armando Petrucci, Milano: Giuffrè, 99–105, 111–122.

3 Consilium

Torello began his *consilium* with the model fact case involving a piece of property, the exact amount of which is not ascertainable (*res incerta*), yet which is both appraised and conveyed in the name of dowry to the husband on behalf of the bride. Upon dissolution of marriage, the appraised value of the property must be returned, and it is not in the power of the debtor (husband) or creditor (wife) to choose otherwise, save in special circumstances—for instance, when the husband and the wife have made an agreement that the property should be returned to her in the same condition and at the appraised value. Our case differed from the textbook case, in which the amount of the appraised property was known (*res certa*). Here the husband could elect to return the property itself or its cash valuation. In both cases, the transaction was treated as a sale in which the husband acquired ownership of the appraised dotal property and, in the words of *lex Quotiens* (C. 5. 12. 5), "is constituted, as it were, the debtor for the cash valuation [*velut pretii debitor efficitur*]."

Even granting this premise, it was unclear whether Agnese's dowry had actually been appraised, as she had vigorously claimed. With regard to the vineyard, Torello had no reservations whatsoever. As the entire vineyard had been conveyed to the husband, its size was measurable, ascertainable, and certain. Even though the parties had never entered into a mutual agreement directly fixing the cash value of the vineyard, the husband had indirectly transformed the vineyard into a *dos aestimata* when he had solemnly promised to restore not the vineyard itself, but the 110 florins.

It was less clear whether the part of the house belonging to Andrea that had been conveyed to the husband should be considered appraised. For argument's sake, Torello assumed that the part conveyed to Antonio was worth more than 110 florins. The authority for his assumption was *lex Si quis stipulatus* (D. 46. 3. 57) and its ordinary gloss. The *lex* addressed the paradigmatic case of someone who stipulates for "ten in honey," that is, to be paid a specific amount with a quantity of something else. By way of analogy, the "ten" represented the amount of dowry, the honey the aforesaid part of the house. According to the *Glossa ordinaria* the amount of honey is understood to be greater than the stipulated amount of ten.[12] Although it seemed that Andrea, through the conveyance of the part of the house, with its presumed cash valuation of 110 florins, had satisfied his share of Agnese's dowry, it did not follow that a legally efficacious sale had occurred with respect to the husband, especially since the price of the property, without which there could be no sale, was uncertain or seemed to be uncertain. Nor was size of the part and its proportion to the whole house certain. For these reasons it seemed that the presumption of a sale should be deemed fallacious.

On the contrary, Torello now argued, because it is also true that "one who has and receives property or a specific object for a debt of money is said to have

[12]*Glossa* "fuerit decem" to *l. Si quis stipulatus*: "Quia decem sunt in obligatione, sed mel in solutione tantum.".

performed a contract of sale for property." Concerning the price, Torello maintained, on the authority of *lex Si quis stipulatus*, that the appraised value of the part of the house amounted to 110 florins, though the size of the part remained uncertain. This lingering uncertainty, which was in the nature of the thing itself, however, did not vitiate the sale, which Torello regarded as fully realized and unconditional (*perfecta*), "so that none of the parties could withdraw from the contract." "Who can doubt that this contract is valid? I buy a part of this property which may be worth 100, for the price is certain and the property is also certain, though the property is neither described nor its proportions discerned up to the present time through the faculty of human understanding." Torello's clinching argument was in sync with the observations of other jurists on certain realities that cannot be apprehended on basis of the senses alone. Baldo degli Ubaldi (d. 1400) discussed the real existence of something whose certainty is intrinsic, "although extrinsically, that is, to us it may be uncertain."[13] In the final analysis, what was certain was the cash valuation knowable by the verifiable fact that the property had been given in the name of the 110 florin dowry. Here Torello was relying on a venerable maxim: "that is certain which can be made certain" (*certum est quod certum reddi potest*).

Torello easily resolved the remaining contentions raised in the *punctus*. As he had already shown, the husband was obligated to restore the cash valuation to the wife, and neither party could alter this obligation. On the issue of *paraphernalia*, these goods belonged to the wife during marriage and after the husband's death had to be restored to the wife, just as in the case of the dowry. Torello's answer to the final question—whether Agnese could legally demand 110 florins from her uncles Andrea and Simone together, or Andrea alone, if it was determined that the part of the house conveyed to the husband failed to meet the tests of a *dos aestimata*—was negative. For "the cash valuation is in the dowry, and thus she has 220 florins and she can demand their return. Therefore she should not harass the heirs [with lawsuits]."

Neither the *punctus* nor *consilium* made reference to the party who commissioned Torello's opinion. Given Torello's stout defense of Agnese's position, it appears at first blush that she was the commissioning party and that Torello submitted his opinion in her defense. Yet Torello's rejection of her final claim indicates to me the opposite: that his opinion was requested by a judge in the court of the podestà and numbered among the thousands of impartial *consilia sapientis* requested by judges presiding over problematic cases which demanded the expertise of a jurist. Another aspect of Torello's *consilium* deserves notice. A single reference to Bartolo of Sassoferrato (d. 1357) was the only authority alleged beyond the *Digest*, *Codex*, and *Glossa ordinaria*. The citational economy of his *consilium* is striking, since *consilia* of the early fifteenth century were typically loaded with

---

[13]Baldo. 1586. to l. *Haec Venditio*, § *Huiusmodi* (D. 18. 1. 7. 1), *In primam Digesti Veteris partem commentaria*, Venetiis: apud Iuntas: "Nota id dicitur certum, quod in se est certum, licet extra se, id est, nobis sit incertum, et de hoc rectitudine quantum ad realem existentiam non quantum ad iudicis sententiam."

allegations to earlier jurists. It also seems that in Torello's eyes the resolution of the case was so clear-cut that he did not feel compelled to support his arguments with heaps of authorities.

In the absence of a statistical breakdown of the thousands of legal disputes over dowries, it is impossible to tell whether disputes concerning the *dos aestimata* were common.[14] In the *consilium*, Torello mentioned an analogous case on *dos aestimata* for which he submitted a *consilium*, but so far I have been unable to find it. Based on my own research of published and unpublished *consilia* commissioned to resolve disputes relating to dowries and women's property, my impression is that disputes over the exclusion of daughters with dowries from the paternal inheritance, daughters' demands for larger dowries commensurate with their social rank, husbands' claims to the dowries of their predeceased wives, childrens' claims to maternal dowries, and above all, the restitution of the dowry *constante* and *soluto matrimonio* far outnumbered disputes directly concerned with the *dos aestimata*.

4 Edition

My edition of Torello's *consilium* is based on the text preserved in Florence, Biblioteca Nazionale, Magl. XXIX, 161, 152r–153r (= **A**). The *punctus* penned by a scribe occupies fol. 152r, while the sealed *consilium* penned by Torello occupies fols. 152v–153r. The copy of this text is found in the same manuscript, 26r–27r (= **B**). It is most probable that the copy was based on **A**, which would explain why there are only several minor variants between **A** and **B**. In preparing the edition, I have kept the orthography of **A**, and have not noted in the apparatus minor orthographic variants, such as *promisit/promixit*, *presumpta/presunta*, *resilire/rexilere*, *satisfactione/sactisfactione*, and *sicut/sicud*. The apparatus notes marginal memoranda and corrections. Captilization, punctuation, and paragraph divisions are editorial. Angle brackets (< >) are used to indicate my additions to the text.

4.1 Christus

Quidam Martinus fecit testamentum in quo instituit Andream et Simonem eius fratres heredes universales,[15] et iure institutionis reliquid Agnese eius filie florenos ducentos pro eius dote et florenos viginti pro arredis et rebus parafernalibus. Que

---

[14]Among the few *consilia* I have come across that centered on *dos aestimata* are Lodovico Pontano. 1565. *Consilia*. Lugduni: Servain Claudel, excudebat Claudius Servanius, 81v, cons. 201; Paolo di Castro. 1581. *Consilia*. 1. Venetiis: Società dell'Aquila che si rinnova, fol. 25r, cons. 23; and Alessandro Tartagni. 1549. *Consilia*. 5. Lugduni: per Georgium Regnault, 61v-62r, cons. 79.

[15]instituit eius fratres *in marg. dex.* **A**.

Agnesa nupsit Antonio. Postea Andreas heres pro dimidia dicti Martini, volens sactisfacere quantitatem florenorum centum legati predicti et florenorum decem rerum parafernalium pro sactisfactione dicte quantitatis, tradidit dicto Antonio viro dicte Agnese, ipsa absente et ignorante, pro ipsis florenis centum decem dotis predicte et rerum parafernalium tantam partem unius domus. Que tanta pars, ad iustam extimationem fiendam, capiat ipsos florenos CX., cum pacto quod si ipse Andreas infra terminum declarandum per quendam Filippum, quem ad hoc eligerit, dederit et consignaverit in locum dicte tante partis dicte domus dicto Antonio unum ortum situm Pistorie pro ea extimatione que facta fuerit temporis talis dationis, et quod si plus valeret et extimatus fuerit quantitate dictorum florenorum CX., tunc illud plus ipse Antonius eidem Andree tradere teneatur. Si vero minus, ipse Andreas eidem Antonio tradere teneatur de aliis suis bonis iuxta extimationem in supplementum ipsius quantitatis, qua consignatione facta ut predicta ipsa domus revertatur ad ipsum Andream absque alio contractu. Quam dotem ipse Antonius restituere promisit in omnem casum dotis restituende. Qui Filippus mortuus est, nulla declaratione facta dicti termini et non facta assignatione dicti orti.

Et in alia parte dictus Simon heres pro alia dimidia dicti Martini patris dicte Agnese, volens sactisfacere eidem Agnese de dicto legato et debito pro dimidia, dedit in dotem et dotis nomine ipsius Agnese et in sactisfactionem[16] florenorum CX. predictorum dicto Antonio unam vineam; et ipsam dotem et quantitatem dotis ipse Antonius eidem Agnese restituere promisit in omnem casum dotis restituende. Postea casus dicte dotis restituende evenerit per mortem dicti Antonii.

4.2 Nunc Oriuntur Quamplura Dubia de Predictis

Primum dubium est quia Agnesa repetit ab heredibus sui viri dictas quantitates florenorum CCXX. Dicit heres mariti quod vult restituere domum et vineam, asserens ipsam domum et vineam fuisse inextimatas et pro fundis dotalibus, attentis verbis suprascriptis,[17] et maxime dicit domus est dos inextimata et obstendit sic, quia dicit quod ipsa tanta pars domus fuit data pro extimatione fienda, et sic dicit quod non potest dici extimata. Respondet Agnesa quod ymmo ipsa domus et vinea fuerunt extimata et emptitia funda, et quod ipse debet rehabere quantitates dictorum florenorum et non bona predicta. Allegans ipsa quod vinea clare fuit dat pro extimata, quia data fuit in dotem et in sactisfactionem florenorum CX. et sic colligitur extimatio. Et ultra predicta apparet quod extimatio dicte vinee debet restitui, quia tempore dationis dicte vinee ipse Antonius promisit restituere dotem et quantitatem dotis, ut supra patet. Et dicit etiam ipsa quod apparet quod quantitas florenorum CX. datorum in dicta domo debet restitui et non domus, quia, licet ipsa domus non fuerit

---

[16]sa *post* in *del.* **A**.

[17]Suprascriptis *rep. et del.* **A**.

extimata, tamen data fuit in dotem tanta pars dicte domus, que valeret ipsam quantitatem et perinde est ac si extimatus fuisset.

Secundum dubium est quia heres dicti mariti dicit quod, posito quod essent bona extimata, electio est sua < si > vellit restituere bona vel extimationem, et quod ipse vult restituere bona. Ad hoc respondet ipsa Agnesa quod de extimatione vinee nullum est dubium suo videre, quia apparet vineam fuisse extimatam et quia ipse Antonius promixit restituere dictam dotem et quantitatem dotis, ut superius clare apparet. Ac etiam dicit ipsa quod in bonis extimatis sua est electio et non heredis viri.

Tertium dubium est quia heres dicti viri[18] dicit quod de dictis dotibus extimatis vel non extimatis debet retinere et habere florenos XX., quos dicit Antonium expendisse in rebus parafernalibus tempore quo ipse Antonius[19] duxit ipsam Agnesam, allegans quod in testamento patris dicte Agnese relicti fuerunt ipsi floreni XX. pro rebus parafernalibus. Respondet ipsa quod licet in testamento fuerint sibi relicti dicti floreni XX. pro rebus parafernalibus, tamen ipse quantitates florenorum CCXX. tempore dationum dictarum dotium fuerunt reducte in dotes et ipsas dotes ipse Antonius restituere promixit, ut supra colligitur.

Aliud dubium oritur inter ipsam[20] Agnesam et dictum Andream heredem pro dimidia predicta patris dicte Agnese, quia ipsa dicit quod non vult stare contenta datione[21] dotis facta de dicta domo pro ipsis florenis CX., quia ipsa dictam dationem[22] nescivit et non interfuit, et quod ipsa vult ab ipso Andrea florenos CX.[23] pro dimidia legati sibi facta a patre in dicto testamento. Queritur ergo, ponderatis predictis[24] quatuor dubiis, quid iuris, inspectis verbis suprascriptis que intervenerunt in dationibus dictarum dotium?

In nomine Christi, amen. Pro decisione premessi thematis, premicto quod ubi species vel corpus non consistens in quantitate dotis nomine traditur extimatum, soluto matrimonio ipsum pretium debet restitui,[25] nec hoc[26] potestate debitoris[27] vel creditoris alterari potest, C. de iu. do., l. Quotiens (C.5.12.5), C. de usuf., l. Interest (C.3.33.6), et not. C. de rei uxo. act., l. 1, § Cumque (C.5.13.1.9), nisi appareat extimatam factam alio respectu quam venditio presumatur, ut l. Si inter virum, C. de iu. do. (C.5.12.21), et ff. eo ti., l. Cum post, § Cum[28] res (D.23.3.69.7), ff. sol. ma., l. Si extimatis (D.24.3.50). Est enim debitor pretii qui rem in dotem

---

[18]de dictis *post* viri *del.* **A.**

[19]Restituere promixit *post* Antonius *del.* **B.**

[20]ipsam *rep.* et *del.* **A.**

[21]dationi **AB.**

[22]restiuit *post* dationem *del.* **B.**

[23]quia *post* CX *del.* **B.**

[24]de dictis **B.**

[25]Quando res estimata datur in dotem, quid restitui debet? *in marg. dex.* **B.**

[26]a post hoc *del.* **A.**

[27]debitoris *rep. et del.* **A.**

[28]si **AB** et *post* apertissumus *del.* **A.**

extimatam accepit in dubio, sicud emptor verus et apertissimus[29] in cuius emptoris electione non est pretium soluere aut rem, ut l. Ex empto, in principio, de ac. emp. (D. 19.1.11 pr.), et ita dicit textus in dicta l. Quotiens, ibi velud pretii debitor hinc est quod re evicta que extimata doti est tradita prodita est ex empto actio, ut no. C. de iu. do., l. 1 (C.5.12.1). Videndum est ergo, an hic dos extimata data fuit, et quoad vineam non est hesitandum, quia non steterunt partes in finibus traditionis, sed ultra processum est ad obligationem restitutionis. Cum igitur promissa est restitutio dotis et dicte quantitatis, sumus in aperto, in certis enim non est coniectura habenda,[30] ut ff. de ver. ob., l. Continuus, § Illud (D.45.1.137.4), et not. In l. 1, § Ex actio, de rei uxo. ac. (C.5.13.1.7a). Sed potest probabilius dubitari de domo tradita per Andream, nam dicitur volens satisfacere quantitatem florenorum C. et florenorum X. Pro satisfactione dicte quantitatis tradidit ipsi Antonio pro ipsis florenis CX. tantam partem unius domus, que tanta pars ad iustam extimatam fiendam capiat ipsos florenos CX. Cuius est sensus quod de dicta domo tradita per Andream plus[31] valente habeat CX. florenos, sicud alibi habetur in eo qui[32] stipulatus est X. in melle, ut ff. de solutionibus, l. Si quis stipulatus est X. in melle (D.46.3.57), secundum ultimum intellectum glose.[33] Et isto casu videtur facta traditio domus et eius extimatio, ut a quantitate liberetur qui solvit in domo, non autem ut venditio contrahatur[34] seu emptio per recipientem, et maxime cum pretium non sit certum seu non videatur. Item nec res, scilicet quota vel quanta domus, certa est; ideo non videtur quod possit esse venditio presumpta,[35] l. 1, de contra. emp. (D.18.1.1). In contrarium facit, quia licet hanc domum pro CX. dotis nomine tradat, et per hoc ab obligatione se velit tradens eximere, tamen qui pro pecunia debita rem vel speciem habet et recipit dicitur presumptum contractum emptionis in re, ff. pro emp., l. litis (D.41.4.3), C. de senten. interlo. o. iu., l. Libera (C.7.45.8), et ibi not. et per Bar., ff. de solutionibus, l. Si quis aliam (D.46.3.46).[36] Nam idem vidimus in patre qui pro filia dotem dedit in re pro pecunia, ut maritus videatur emisse, ff. de solutionibus, l. Qui res, in principio (D.46.3.98), secundum verum intellectum. Unde si hic pretium esset certum et res vendita certa, dicerem idem de domo quam de vinea. Sed videamus, an iste effectus inpediatur propter dictam incertitudinem pretii atque rei. Et in hoc dico quod pretium hic esset certum, quia debet esse et est conventum quod sit CX. florenorum, sicut ubi stipulor X. in melle, quia extimatio certa est mella quantum sit non est certum, ut dicta l. Si quis

[29]et *post* apertissumus *del.* **A**.

[30]in certis non est locus coniectura *in marg. sin.* **B**.

[31]plus *corr. ex* pluris **A**.

[32]qui *corr. ex* quod **A**.

[33]Secundum – glosse: *in marg. dex. add.* **A**.

[34]Contrahatur *corr. ex* contrahaatur **A**; trahitur **B**.

[35]presumpta *in marg. dex. add.* **A**.

[36]Bartolus. 1528/1996. ad lex *Si quis aliam* (D.46. 3.46), *Commentaria,* 9 vols. Venetiis: per Baptistam de Tortis. reprint Roma. Il Cigno Galileo Galilei. 6: 100r, n. 3.

stipulatus.[37]Ita[38] hic[39] non est certa quanta pars domus sit illa que venit ratione CX. tradenda. Sed talis incertititudo non vitiat quin emptio sit perfecta, ita quod nulla partium potest ab hoc resilere contractu. Quis enim dubitat quod valet iste contractus? Emo in hac rem partem que sit valoris C., nam pretium certum est et res etiam certa est, licet non demonstrativa nec adhuc per intellectum perceptiva respectu quote. Tamen quia in natura certum est pretium totius domus sufficit, nam ad reddendam rem certam sufficit in natura certum quid esse, licet de presenti humano intellectu sit incertum, ut l. Cum ad presens et l. Respiciendum, ff. si cer. pe. (D. 12.1.37 *et* 38), et l. Cum in secundo, ff. de iniusto testa. (D. 28.3.16). Ita dicimus quodlibet interesse quod debetur certum esse, quia in natura est certum quanti interest, licet homini sit incertum et pro hoc petitur certi condictio, ff. si cer. pe., l. Certi condictio, in principio (D. 12.1.9 pr.); et ibi non quia judex postea illud declarabit et istud probat textus, ff. de contrahen. empt., l. Hec venditio, § 1 (D. 18.1.7.1), ibi "magis enim ignoratur", et cetera.[40]

Concludo igitur quoad domum in dotem extimatam esset, ut in alio casu, et non obstat quod dicit extimata fienda, quia referuntur illa verba ad[41] declarationem partis domus non quod de presenti certa, non sit in natura, quasi dicat: "habeas in domo ista partem valentem C.", que pars extimabitur quanta sit ad hoc ut reddatur certus homini.

Ego Torellus domini Niccolai de Torellis de Prato, civis florentinus, minimus legum doctor, puto iuris esse ut suprascripsi. Ideo subscripsi et sigillum apposui.

Et hec sufficiant de primo et secundo dubio, quia secundum expedivi in principio, quod nullius est electio. Ad tertium breviter respondetur quod bona parafernalia sunt uxoris et ipsi de iure sunt post viri[42] mortem restituenda, ut l. fi., C. de pactis conventis (C.5.14.11). Unde sive dotalia sive parafernalia sint ipsi mulieri debetur soluto matrimonio mortis viri, et pro tanto non est necessarie discutere qualia sint.

Ad ultimum responditur quod si dicte res in dotem date non intelligerentur extimate, quod dicta mulier posset agere ad CCXX. Contra dictum Andream et coheredem vel contra Andream in CX. Sed ex premissis patet contrarium, quia extimatio est in dote et sic CCXX habet et illa potest repetere. Unde heredibus vexare non debet. Et ista breviter dicta sufficiant, salvo maiori[43] intellectu.

[37]stipulatur **B**.

[38]sed *praem.* Ita *del.* **A**.

[39]sicut – hic *in marg. sin. add.* **A**.

[40]Et istud – cetera *in marg. Dex. add.* **A**.

[41]vineam *post* ad *del.* **A**.

[42]bona parafernalia sunt restituenda uxori post mortem viri *in marg. dex.* **B**.

[43]minori **B**.

References

Sources

D. 23. 3. 10 pr, *Plerumque interest.*

D. 24. 3. 51, *Aestimatae.*

Inst. 2. 8 pr.

C. 5. 13. 1. 15, *Rem in praesenti,* § *Et cum lex Iulia.*

C. 5. 12. 5, *Quotiens.*

Glossa "fuerit decem" to *l. Si quis stipulatus*: "Quia decem sunt in obligatione, sed mel in solutione tantum."

Archivio di Stato di Firenze, Tratte 576, 72r (1 Mar. 1416/17), 73r (7 June 1423).

Archivio di Stato di Firenze, Pareri dei Savi, n. 2, 426r-427v; n. 3, 388r-389v, 421r-428r, 451r-461r.

Archivio di Stato di Firenze, Archivio dei Giudici e Notai, n. 670, 47r (15 Jan. 1392/3), 62r (10 Dec. 1394), 65r (21 July 1395), 71v-72r (7 July 1397), 73r (9 June 1399), 74v (12 June 1399), 81v (3 June 1401), 83r (27 Aug. 1401), 84r (21 May 1402), 96rv (30 June 1402), 102r-103r (13 Feb. 1402/3), 110rv (7 June 1406).

Archivio di Stato di Firenze, Archivio del Bene, n. 54, 32r (6 Nov. 1409), 45r-46r (4 Dec. 1409), 78r (8 Apr. 1410), 106r (8 Dec. 1410), 113r (2 Apr. 1411), 114r-116r (26 Apr. 1411).

Florence, Biblioteca Nazionale, Fondo Principale, II. III., 370 (third volume of Lorenzo Ridolfi's *consilia*, 1413-1418), 8v, 9v, 11r, 14v, 17r, 27r, 28rv, 51v, 70r, 116v, 130r, 157v, 165v, 179r, 206v, 247r; Magl. XXIX, 117, 88r- 89v; XXIX, 161, 139rv, 140r, 161v, 162rv, 231v; XXIX, 172, 161rv, 165r; XXIX, 174, 68v, 105r-106v, 107v-109r, 110v-111r; XXIX, 193, 115r; Landau Finaly, 98, 79r-80r; 97v, 98r-99v.

Vatican City, Biblioteca Apostolica Vaticana, Vat. Lat. 8069, 258r, 263r, 368v; Vat. Lat. 10726, 294v, 379v-380r, Vat. Lat. 10962, 83v-85r; Phillips MSS, 8889, 123v-125r, 225rv, 228rv, 234r-236r, 240rv, 297r-300r.

Literature

Bartolo da Sassoferrato. (1528/1996). *Commentaria*, 9 vols (Venetiis: per Baptistam de Tortis. reprint Roma. Il Cigno Galileo Galilei).

Bartolomeo da Saliceto. (1515). Lecturae prima [et secunda] pars super Codicis primo et secundo [tertio et quarto] libris. Lugduni: per Iacobus Mareschal.

Bellomo, M. (1961). *Ricerche sui rapporti patrimoniali tra coniugi. Contributo alla storia della famiglia medievale*. Milano: Giuffrè.

Bestor, J. F. (1997). The Groom's Prestations for the *Ductio* in late Medieval Italy: A Study in the Disciplining Power of *Liberalitas*. *Rivista Internazionale di Diritto Comune* (*RIDC*) *8*, 129–177.

Calonge, A. (1965). Aestimatio dotis. *Anuario de historia del derecho español 35*, 5–57.

Campitelli, A., & Liotta, F. (1961–62). Notizia del MS. Vat. Lat. 8069. *Annali di storia del diritto 5–6,* 387–406.

Cardini, F. (1991). La cultura. In *Prato. Storia di una città*. 1. *Ascesa e declino del centro medievale (dal mille al 1494)*. Prato: Comune di Prato.

Coluccio Salutati in Buggiano. (1963). *Il protocollo notarile di Coluccio Salutati (1372-1373)*, ed. Armando Petrucci, Milano: Giuffrè.

Corbett, P. E. (1930). *The Roman Law of Marriage*. Oxford: Clarendon Press.

Davis, J. (1998). *Florence and Its University during the Early Renaissance*. Leiden, Boston, Köln: Brill.

degli Ubaldi, A. (1548). *Super prima [-secunda] Infortiati*. Lugduni: per Georgium Regnault.
degli Ubaldi, B. (1586). *In primam et secundam Infortiati partem commentaria*. Venetiis: apud Iuntas.
di Castro, P. (1553). *In primam [-secundam] Infortiati partem commentaria*. Lugduni: [Denis de Harsy].
di Castro, P. (1581). *Consilia*. 1. Venetiis: Società dell'Aquila che si rinnova.
Gherardi, A. (1881). *Statuti della Università e Studio fiorentino dell'anno MCCCLXXXVII seguiti da un'appendice di documenti dal MCCCXX al MCCCCLXXII*. Firenze: Tipi di M. Cellini.
Giovanni da Imola. (1502). *Pars prima super Infortiato*. Venetiis: per Filippo I Pinzi.
Izbicki, T. (1997). Legal and Polemical Manuscripts, 1150-1500. In *Friars and Jurists. Selected Studies* (*Biblioteca Eruditorum* 20). Goldbach: Keip, 309–368.
Kirshner, J. & Pluss, J. (1979). Two Fourteenth-Century Opinions of Dowries, Paraphernalia and Non-dotal Goods. *BMLC 9*, 65–77.
Kirshner, J. (1985). Wives Claims against Insolvent Husbands in Late Medieval Italy. In *Women of the Medieval World. Essays in Honor of John H. Mundy*, eds. Julius Kirshner and Suzanne Wemple (pp. 256–303). Oxford: Wiley.
Kirshner, J. (1999). Citizen Cain of Florence. In *La Toscane et les Toscans autour de la Renaissance: Cadres de vie, société, croyances. Mélanges offerts à Charles-M. de La Roncière* (pp. 175–189). Aix-en-Provence: Publications de l'Université de Provence.
Kirshner, J. (1991). Materials for a Gilded Cage: Non-dotal Assets in Florence (1300-1500). In I. K. David & S. Richard (Eds.). *The Family in Italy from Antiquity to the Present* (pp. 184–207). New Haven: Yale University Press.
Kirshner, J. (2002). Li Emergenti Bisogni Matrimoniali in Renaissance Florence. In J. C. William (Ed.). *Society and Individual in Renaissance Florence*. Berkeley-Los Angeles- London: University of California Press, 79–109.
Kuehn, T. (1991). *Law, family & women: toward a legal anthropology of renaissance Italy*. Chicago: University of Chicago Press.
Kuehn, T. (2002). *Illegitimacy in Renaissance Florence*. Ann Arbor: University of Michigan Press.
Lapo Mazzei. (1880). *Lettere di un notaro a un mercante del secolo XIV*, G. Cesare (Ed.). Firenze: Successori Le Monnier.
Martines, L. (1963). *The social world of the florentine humanists, 1390-1460*. Princeton: Princeton University Press.
Martines, L. (1968). *Lawyers and statecraft in renaissance florence*. Princeton: Princeton University Press.
Park, K. (1980). Readers at the florentine studio according to communal fiscal records (1357-1380, 1413-1146). *Rinascimento 20*, 249–310.
Pluss, J. A. (1983). *Baldus de Ubaldis on Dowry Law* (Ph.D. diss., University of Chicago).
Pontano, L. (1565). *Consilia*. Lugduni: Servain Claudel, excudebat Claudius Servanius: cons. 201.
Silveira, M., & Eduardo, C. (2001). Periculum rei venditae e periculum dotis aestimatae. *Labeo 47*, 384–410.
Streicher, K. L. (1973). *"Periculum dotis." Studien zum dotalrechtlichen Haftungssystem im klass. röm. Recht*. Berlin: J. Schweitzer-Verlag.
Tartagni, A. (1549). *Consilia*. 5. Lugduni: per Georgium Regnault: cons. 79.
Tartagni, A. (1595). *In primam & II. Infortiati partem commentaria*. Venetiis: [Lucantonio Giunta il giovane].
Torello di Messer Niccolò. (1991). *Le consulte e "pratiche" della repubblica fiorentina* (1404), ed. Renzo Ninci. Roma: Istituto Storico Italiano per il Medio Evo, 62.
Yiftach-Firanko, U. (2003). *Marriage and Marital Arrangements. A History of the Greek Marriage Document in Egypt. 4th Century BCE—4th Century CE*. (*Münchener Beiträge zur Papyrusforschung und antiken Rechtsgeschichte, 93*). München: C.H. Beck.
Wolff, H. J. (1955). Zur Geschichte der Parapherna. *ZRG RA 72*: 335–347.

Property of Spouses in Law in Renaissance Florence

Thomas Kuehn

Abstract Historians of Florence typically treat the family patrimony as a single entity under the control of the male head of household. That included the dowry and other property his wife brought to him. In so doing these historians follow the cues offered by normative sources. However, in law there were, in fact, several types of property a wife could bring to a marriage, and she had rights to manage some of those herself. And dowry was a charge on the patrimony that husbands swore to uphold. They could not easily alienate dowry, and certainly not without consent of their wives. A closer look at household accounts demonstrates that husbands managed their property with an eye to obligations they had to preserve and return dowry and other spousal property on dissolution of marriage. And examination of cases by means of *consilia* illustrates how jurists interpreted spousal legal property rights and wives' and widows' disposal of their holdings.

1 Florentine Wives: Images and Realities

Piero di Luigi Guicciardini (d. 1441), great grandfather of the well-known Florentine lawyer and statesman, Francesco Guicciardini (1483–1540), found himself in financial straits at several points in his life. At one of those points, determined to meet his obligations and satisfy his creditors, Piero arranged to sell various of his possessions, including his house in Florence. Then things took an unexpected turn, as Francesco noted in his book of family **memorie**:

> and because [the house] was pledged [per sodo] for his wife's dowry, who was a Buondelmonti… he could not sell it without her consent; and having already reached agreement with the purchaser and taken him to his house with a notary to record the

T. Kuehn (✉)
Clemson University, Clemson, SC 29634, USA
e-mail: tjkuehn@clemson.edu

M.G. di Renzo Villata (ed.), *Family Law and Society in Europe from the Middle Ages to the Contemporary Era*, Studies in the History of Law and Justice 5,
DOI 10.1007/978-3-319-42289-3_5

> contract and take down his wife's consent, she did not ever intend to say yes, rather she chased from the house the notary and the one who was set to buy, and seeing the obstinacy of his wife, and perhaps her animosity pleased him, he had patience [with her].[1]

Guicciardini's story ends there, so we do not know how Piero resolved his debts, though Francesco also described Piero's state at his death as one of great civic reputation but relative poverty ("because he did not leave what amounted to 5000 florins"). But Piero's patience seems to have been conclusive about his relationship with Agnola, his third wife and mother of his children.

This story confounds on several levels. Here a head of household—an honorable, powerful, and still rather wealthy household, at that—was unable to execute his strategy to get through a bad patch and hold the family and its property together. And the snag came from within his house and from his wife, of all people. This hardly seems to be what one would expect from a reading of the substantial body of historical work on women and family life in Florence. The many perceptive and careful scholars who have traversed the field have stressed the subordination of Florentine women, especially daughters and wives, even in comparison to those of other cities, like Venice.[2] Nor does this instance of wifely obstinance seem to square with reading the idealized account of married property relations famously recounted by an earlier Florentine, Leon Battista Alberti (1404–1472), a man who was not himself married or head of a household. In his dialogue on family, the character of Giannozzo Alberti discusses household management. On his terms, whether in the small context of "children, wife, and other members of the household, both relatives and servants" or the larger family, separately lodged but still "in the shadow of a single will," there was a sole manager of property.[3] That will was not to be opposed, least of all by a wife.

Giannozzo describes his wife as young, illiterate, humble, and obedient; someone from whom he kept hidden various secrets of his affairs, while revealing to her in confidence what he deemed she needed to know to play her role for the good of the entire household. Much of what he told her was about maintaining a modest and honorable bearing to avoid bringing shame to him and the family, but it also included how to treat the family's possessions:

[1]Guicciardini, Francesco. 1981. *Ricordi, diari, memorie*, ed. Marco Spinella. Roma: Riuniti, 39.

[2]For a sampling, in addition to works cited below by Klapisch-Zuber, Chabot, Kirshner, Kovesi-Killerby, and Kuehn, Heather, Gregory. 1987. Daughters, Dowries and Family in Fifteenth-Century Florence. *Rinascimento* 27: 217–37; Fubini Leuzzi, Maria. 1999. "*Condurre a onore*"*: Famiglia, matrimonio e assistenza a Firenze in età moderna*. Florence: Olschki. On Venice, see Chojnacki, Stanley. 2000. *Women and Men in Renaissance Venice: Twelve Essays on Patrician Society*. Baltimore: Johns Hopkins University Press, but see also Bellavitis, Anna and Chabot, Isabelle. 2005. A proposito di 'Men and Women in Renaissance Venice' di Stanley Chojnacki. *Quaderni storici* 118: 203–29.

[3]Cf. Alberti, Leon Battista. 1969. *The Family in Renaissance Florence* (trans. Renee Neu Watkins). Columbia: University of South Carolina Press, 180 and 186. On Alberti in a civic context, see Boschetto, Luca. 2000. *Leon Battista Alberti e Firenze*. Firenze: Olschki.

> This property, this family, and the children to be born to us will belong to us both, to you as much as to me, to me as much as to you. It behooves us, therefore, not to think how much each of us has brought into our marriage, but how we can best maintain all that belongs to both of us. I shall try to obtain outside what you need inside the house; you must see that none of it is wasted.[4]

These were not sentiments peculiar to Alberti, by any means. One need only cite the Venetian Francesco Barbaro (1390–1454) and his letter on the duties of a wife, addressed to the Florentine Lorenzo de' Medici, brother of Cosimo. A similar image of modest household management was in play there.[5] The point of this paper is that there was no such intermingling of property in law, and thus to some extent not in the realities of family life. There was not a single patrimony, but at least two (we will set aside for now the possible ownership of things by children). And while at times, in some houses, there may have been one effective manager of both, that was not always the case. And the academic "common law" and local statutes did little to simplify matters.

There was no room in Alberti's schema for someone like Piero Guicciardini's wife (for all that one can imagine an argument from her in a fully Albertian spirit to the effect that the family was better served by holding on to the house rather than selling it). A man like Piero might rather have expected behavior like that of Giovanni Morelli's (another Florentine, 1371–1444) sister, who consented to her husband's deals, eventually losing all her dowry in order to meet household debts. Her husband too, like Piero Guicciardini, worked out his deals and then appeared at home with a notary in tow, thus pressuring his wife to give in.[6] But Morelli's sister perhaps did not have the haughty self-assurance of Guicciardini's wife, born to one of the most illustrious and longstanding magnate lineages of the Arno city.

The historically interesting issue, to my mind, is not the differences of temperament among Florentine wives such as these, nor of their husbands, for that matter. Rather the element on which I wish to focus is the fact that uxorial consent had a role to play at all in these incidents.

2 Women's Property in Law

In his now classic evocation of property relations between spouses, Manlio Bellomo detected in the opinions of twelfth- and thirteenth-century glossators a tendency to restrict a wife's capacity to act against an alienation of dotal property

---

[4]Alberti (as n. 3) 211.

[5]Barbaro, Francesco. 1978. On Wifely Duties (trans. Benjamin G. Kohl). In *The Earthly Republic: Italian Humanists on Government and Society*, ed. Benjamin G. Kohl and Ronald G. Witt, Philadelphia: University of Pennsylvania Press, 189–228, especially 215–20.

[6]Morelli, Giovanni. 1956. *Ricordi*, ed. Vittore Branca. Firenze: Le Monnier, 187–88. See also my 1991. *Law, Family, and Women: Toward a Legal Anthropology of Renaissance Italy*. Chicago: University of Chicago Press, 223–24.

by her husband—a tendency, in other words, "aimed at freeing the husband from all links that constrained his powers in the management and governance of the family and the patrimony and leaving the wife on the margins of a position of command." This control over property lay at the heart of "a new type of family," and "broader organism" and "rigidly organized," able to take its place and pursue its interests in the rough and tumble of politics in the late medieval Italian commune.[7] Against this picture we are again faced with moments such as the Guicciardini example that seem to indicate that the situation was perhaps a bit more complex, at least in practice.

It is not that we are unaware of the material contributions of both spouses to their marital life and household. It is not that we cannot see and anticipate the contributions of women to property management. But between the ideological premises of female weakness prevalent in a society like that of Florence and the ideology of patrimonial unity and preservation in the male line, a "well-nigh universal drive," we are not always attuned to the influence of women.[8] And it was not just an influence of informal, moral suasion. Law settled certain rights and powers on women that were real and belied any simple sense of household or patrimonial material unity. Indeed, those rights and powers might make such unity harder to achieve, although they could and did also serve that purpose on occasion. As Renata Ago concluded 20 years ago, women were in fact quite frequently engaged in acts brought before notaries (thus having some legal significance for families), though notaries were able to shape their texts into "a form compatible with the principle of the unity of the family patrimony under the responsibility of the husband, that is to say to cloak them in a 'corporative' logic."[9]

There was an uneasy, ambiguous relationship between the separate pieces of a family's patrimony and the drive or need to see the patrimony as a unit subject to singular, male control. The main element in that uneasy relationship was the dowry the wife brought to the household, but it was not the only piece of the puzzle.

The great fourteenth-century jurist, Baldo degli Ubaldi (1325–1400), active at points in his career in Florence, laid out in a brief *consilium* that there were broadly three types of property that wives might have.[10] There were those things "in dominio mariti" (in fact, an improper use of the legal term for ownership, *dominium*, as dowry was not technically in the husband's *dominium*, though he did

[7]Bellomo, Manlio. 1961. *Ricerche sui rapporti patrimoniali tra coniugi: contributo alla storia della famiglia medievale*. Milano: Giuffrè, 108 and 246–47.

[8]Casey, James. 1989. *The History of the Family*. Oxford and New York: Blackwell, 34.

[9]Ago, Renata. 1995. Ruoli familiari e statuto giuridico. *Quaderni storici* 88: 111–33, at 126.

[10]These issues and Baldo's consilium have been insightfully analyzed in Kirshner, Julius. 1991. Materials for a Gilded Cage: Nondotal Assets in Florence, 1300–1500. In *The Family in Italy from Antiquity to the Present*, ed. David. I. Kertzer and Richard P. Saller. New haven and London: Yale University Press, 184–227, now in his 2015. *Marriage, Dowry, and Citizenship in Late Medieval and Renaissance Italy*. Toronto: University of Toronto Press, 74–93.

not have to seek his wife's consent to invest or convert the dowry).[11] Such property was subject to his control, of which he enjoyed the *fructus*. These were mainly the *res dotales*. They could be used to "sustain the burdens of marriage." The husband was restrained only in that he could not alienate title to dowry (or a portion) without his wife's consent—as with Guicciardini.

Secondly there were items "in dominio uxoris" but subject to the husband's *administratio*, largely because they were brought into the marital home; and these were the *res paraphernales*, for which the husband's property was tacitly obligated, as it was expressly and powerfully obligated for return of dowry. Jurisprudence treated the husband's management of *parapherna* as dependent on his wife's consent, which, as we will see, was not necessarily the way local statutes looked at it. But even learned law took her consent as tacit in the simple act of bringing things into the house with him.[12] The *fructus* of these second sorts of goods were to be consumed for the wife and the "communem familiam" but also served to compensate the husband for the risk he ran in managing them. The wife was due only the *fructus* not consumed for her benefit or that of the family.

Finally, there might be things in the wife's ownership and control. These were *res extra dotem*, generally remaining outside and apart from the marital home. Their *fructus* went to the wife, and any of that used by or for the husband had to be returned to her. Here is where the prevailing ideology behind marriage was most apparent in Baldo's treatment of marital property:

> but truly it seems that either a wife does this [allow her husband to use her property] to assist with the husband's needs, and she does not seek return, for she is held to assist him in cases of need… For they are partners of a divine and human house and one flesh, and one should bear the burdens of the other, but the husband for his wife, because wives always seem to be in need… or she for her husband rarely and contrary to what commonly occurs. But if in fact a husband toils in poverty and his wife is wealthy, she must support him, unless indeed the husband fell into such a state by his own malfeasance… or the wife does this so as to lavish [her property] on her husband, and then the husband must return it, unless the gift be confirmed by the wife's death.[13]

---

[11]Pluss, Jacques Anthony. 1984. Baldus de Ubaldis of Perugia on Dominium over Dotal Property. *Tijdschrift voor Rechtsgeschiedenis* 52: 399–411.

[12]Kirshner 1991 (as n. 10) 77–78.

[13]Baldo, *Consilia* (Venice, 1575), 5 vols. 5 cons. 478, fol. 128va: "sed verius videtur quod aut mulier hoc facit pro subveniendo necessitati viri, et non repetit, nam tenetur ei subvenire posito in necessitate C unde vir et uxor l. i et Authen. preterea et in corpore unde summitur. Sunt enim socii divinae et humanae domus et una caro, et alter alteri onera debet portare sed vir uxoris, quia semper mulieres semper videntur in necessitate ff de donatio. inter virum et uxorem l. quin uxor, autem viri pro raro et contra communiter accidentia. Sed si tamen de facto vir laborat inopia et uxor sit dives virum tenetur alere: nisi forte vir in eadem inciderit propter suum maleficium, ut extra de consuetudi. cap. ex parte vestra aut uxor haec facit largiatur viro, et tunc vir tenetur nisi morte uxoris donatio sit confirmata d. l. si stipulata in princip. in glo. que incipit sive uxor." His text has received a critical edition in Kirshner, Julius and Pluss, Jacques. 1979. Two Fourteenth-Century Opinions on Dowries, Paraphernalia and Non-Dotal Goods. *Bulletin of Medieval Canon Law* 9: 65–77, at 76–77. Also Mayali, Laurent. 2008. Duo erunt in carne una and the Medieval Canonists. In *Iuris Historia: Liber Amicorum Gero Dolezalek*, ed. Vincenzo Colli and Emanuele

From this reasoning Baldo arrived at a decision in his case, which was that a widow's mourning dress should come at the husband's expense.

In fact, Baldo's opinion was offered following an opening *consilium* on the case by Francesco di Bici Albergotti (1304–1376). The suit arose somewhere between 1358 and 1364 at or near Florence. A widow had sought restitution of what her husband had appropriated from her *bona non dotalia*. She claimed she had been both young and respectful as a bride, so there was no extraneous reason to deny her recovery. Albergotti worked with the same tripartite division of property, adding that if the wife had voluntarily conceded the *fructus* to her husband or if the returns on the property were not the result of *natura* but of the labor and effort of the husband, he was entitled to the revenues. There were at least four reasons her consent to his appropriation was not to be presumed, including the particularly avaricious nature posited by law of all women (see below) and the husband's greater obligation to support his wife (than vice versa). Perhaps most telling was the fact that reverence for the husband was expected from the wife, "because of which from her patience results a presumption of dissent or of forced acceptance."[14] Albergotti looked for the meekness Giovanni Morelli's sister had exhibited. But Albergotti also did not address Baldo's concern with situations in which a wife might have to support her husband. He kept the two patrimonies more separate.

Baldo's student, Andrea Alfeo da Corte, utilized the same basic scheme of a wife's *patrimonium* and the husband's varying rights to enjoy *fructus*. A wife, he conceded, could voluntarily give *fructus* to her mate, but such could not be presumed:

> the common nature of both sexes is that no one in doubt is presumed to throw away his money… but to give is to lose… so it should not be presumed it was a gift. Moreover it is proven by the special nature of the female sex, which is that all are most avaricious, so that they are not presumed to give something away.[15]

The ideologized "avarice" of women became a powerful argument for the separateness of their property. Further, the law did not condone gifts between spouses, unless later confirmed on death (as a bequest).

The prohibition on gifts would seem to be the ultimate expression of the separateness of spousal patrimonies, to preclude one gaining at the expense of the other

(Footnote 13 continued)

Conte. Berkeley: Robbins Collection, 161–75; Signori, Gabriela. 2012. Similitude, égalité et réciprocité: l'économie matrimoniale dans les sociétés urbaines de l'Empire à la fin du Moyen Âge. *Annales: Histoires, Sciences Sociales* 67: 657–78.

[14]Kirshner and Pluss 1979 (as n. 13) 70, 75: "propter quam ex paciencia resultat presumptio discensus seu voluntatis coacte."

[15]Kirshner and Pluss 1979 (as n. 13) 70, 75: "communis utriusque sexus natura est ut nemo in dubio presumatur pecunias suas iactare l. cum in debito ff de prob. Sed donare est perdere ut l. contra iuris ff de pac. ergo non est presumendum quod fuerit donatio. Preterea probatur ex speciali foeminei sexus natura, quae est ut omnes sint avarissime, adeo quod donare non praesumantur."

(with some exceptions).[16] Parallel in the Roman law was the fact that spouses fell last in the order of intestate succession, after all other blood relations, agnatic and cognatic.[17] These basic legal points of the relations of husband and wife were in the mind of Baldo's student. He went on to declare gifts from a wife to her husband to be "incongruens et monstruosum." So, lacking clear proof that there was a voluntary gift or any concession of administration of her *res extra dotales* to her husband, the woman, whose case was before him, was due restitution of the *fructus* by her husband's heirs. Much of his opinion here reproduced Albergotti's.[18]

So, whatever the corporate sense of family that figures like Alberti might have embraced and propounded, there was in fact a female patrimony, and the capacity of women to dispose of it by contracts or testaments had to be recognized (if only to try to limit it). Thus separate female property was perhaps most apparent after a husband's death, when (as in Andrea da Corte's case) the widow could seek return of her dowry and restitution of the *fructus* on her other property (if she had any) within the terms of the law.[19] That was when what was owed her—the "debt of the family," to use Isabelle Chabot's term—came due.[20] But, though it is clear, as Chabot, among others, demonstrates, that widows were more active as legal players in various markets, married women too had reason to enter contracts or write wills, even if only to bail out their husbands, as in the Guicciardini and Morelli cases. A woman's patrimony was not limited to dowry, as she could receive property more directly (dowry generally being delivered to the husband) in the form of gifts or bequests. These would be the basis especially of what Baldo termed *res extra dotem. Parapherna* in common law were things the wife brought to her husband's house that were not otherwise computed into the value of the dowry.

In his account of spousal property, Manlio Bellomo places weight on statutes, such as that of Verona in 1276, that equated all goods *extra dotem* with *paraferna* and then went on to say that all goods brought into the marital home were to be considered "as if said things were given as dowry" ("ac si dicte res fuissent in dotem date").[21] Florence too, as Bellomo points out, treated *paraferna* as dotal property in the statutes of 1325, placing all usufruct in the hands of the husband for whatever a wife acquired during marriage. Yet, just as clearly, the same statute specified that any such property "is property of the wife and her heirs" ("sit mulieris proprietas et eius heredum"). Further, the statute said that what came to a wife by inheritance, or otherwise from her paternal or maternal line, belonged to her, not her husband, and that what came to her "as a result of any succession she can defend

[16]Kaser, Max. 1968. *Roman Private Law* (trans Rolf Dannenbring). Durban: Butterworths, 250–51.

[17]Kaser (as n. 16) 287; Borkowski, Andrew and du Plessis, Paul. 2005. *Textbook on Roman Law*. Oxford: Oxford University Press, 213.

[18]This consilium is in Baldo's, 2 cons. 366, fols. 100rb-vb.

[19]Ago 1995 (as n. 9) 126.

[20]Chabot, Isabelle. 2011. *La dette des familles. Femmes, lignage et patrimoine à Florence aux xive et xve siècles*. Rome: École Française.

[21]Bellomo 1961 (as n. 7) 139.

that against all creditors of her husband from every person and place, as a result of the husband."[22] Still, such statutes, says Bellomo, yield "an image of the medieval family founded on the figure of the husband, head of the family, and characterized by the tendency to identify with the husband the right to receive all the fruits, civil and natural, from the dotal goods as much as those that were parafernal."[23]

As ownership remained separate with the wife, however, the dominance of the *capo di famiglia* was not necessarily or always so complete. Because of her tacit hypothec on her husband's property for return of her dowry and her nominal ownership of *paraphernalia* and *res extra dotem*, a wife's kin, most notably her father (were he still alive, especially were she also unemancipated) had an interest in her and her property. Morelli certainly expressed interest, if also disappointment, in his sister's. Such interest could demand return of control and a rendering of payments that ran counter to the interests of the husband, or his heirs, mainly sons (who were also possibly her children).[24] Guarantees for return of dowry were a continuing legal obsession, and the veto of transactions by a wife like Piero Guicciardini's was one part of that. Even more particular steps were possible. Luca da Panzano and many other Florentine husbands purchased Monte shares in their wives' names, thus setting aside an income-earning fund for dowry. Transaction of any such shares required approval from her family, if they availed themselves of the opportunity to place encumbrances on such shares.[25] There were instances of Florentines who gave property to their married daughters or sisters on condition that no benefit accrue to the woman's husband. The donor instead might appropriate to himself all *fructus*. At some level such measures reeked of distrust of the husband, but they also expressed some trust and support for a wife by her family of origin.[26] Such bequests, from parents or any other kin, were a prime source of women's nondotal property, even when intended by the testator or donor as supplement to dowry.[27]

3 Women's Property in Statutory Law

The situation in the learned common law as traced out by the jurists (above) was modified by local statutes, which tended, in some regards, to rein in the separateness of female property. Florence's statutes addressed spousal property relations at a

[22]"Occasione alicuius successionis possit ea defendere contra omnes creditores viri ab omni persona et loco, occasione viri" (quoted in Bellomo 1961 (as n. 7) 140–41).

[23]Bellomo 1961 (as n. 7) 142.

[24]Chabot 2011 (as n. 20) 146–62.

[25]Kirshner, Julius. 2015. The Seven Percent Fund of Renaissance Florence. In *Marriage, Dowry, and Citizenship in Late Medieval and Renaissance Italy*. Toronto: University of Toronto Press, 114–30, at 127.

[26]Kuehn 1991 (as n. 6) 206.

[27]Kirshner 1991 (as n. 10) 87–90.

couple of points. One was the restitution of dowry on ecclesiastically sanctioned separations or, more regularly, death of the husband. In the earliest redaction (1325), the statutes simply mandated summary procedure to resolve the problems more rapidly, within no more than 2 months, making clear that in the eyes of civic authorities, such as the podestà, the obligation to return dowry (and any bequests to a wife beyond dowry) was a real debt that could even incur incarceration to coerce payment.[28] The more precise and long-winded version of the same provision in the last redaction of 1415 essentially added nothing. The sole exception was the brief remark that restitution of dowry (other than on ecclesiastical separation) was to be allowed "on account of the natural death of the other spouse only, and for no other reason" ("propter mortem naturalem tantum alterius coniugis, et nulla alia ratione").[29]

The legal logic for such a specification was to preclude, or at least distinguish, a legal measure that arose in the course of the fourteenth century, mainly as a result of juristic interpretation, that some litigants in Florence were attempting to use in the late fourteenth and early fifteenth centuries. This was the surrender into the wife's control of her dowry from the hands of a husband verging on insolvency.[30] There was some resistance to allowing this recourse in Florence (and elsewhere), as it brought into focus both the failings of men and the unwonted prospect of a woman actually controlling her dowry. As Julie Hardwick has remarked, on the basis of judicial settlements involving non-elite propertied Frenchmen,

> Separate property alone muddied the categories of husband and wife, along with the rights, privileges, and reputations they bestowed. Separate property came with a price for both spouses. Men lost the right to manage household property, and saw news of their financial difficulties publicized in their parish and marketplace. Wives' separate property eroded a defining pillar of adult masculinity, and effectively emasculated married men for whom the link between property and potency was severed, as well as damaging their credit. Moreover, while honourable failure could happen to anyone, separate property carried the slap of mismanagement, and not just bad luck or hard times.[31]

Hardwick is concerned more with actual separation of holdings, including by means of a legal marital separation, but she is alive to the effects of a "merely" legal separation of property. After all, husband and wife probably continued to live together. And given the legal distinctions among categories of spousal property as

---

[28]1999. *Statuti della repubblica fiorentina*, ed. Romolo Caggese, 2 vols, ed. Giuliano Pinto, Francesco Salvestrini, and Andrea Zorzi 2, *Statuti del podestà dell'anno 1325*. Firenze: Olschki, 91–93.

[29]1778–83. *Statuta communis Florentiae anno salutis mccccxv*, 1. Friburgi: apud Michaelem Kluch, 156–59.

[30]Kirshner, Julius. 1985. *Wives' Claims against Insolvent Husbands in Late Medieval Italy*, now in Kirschner 2015 (as n. 25) 131–60; Kuehn, Thomas. 2016. Protecting Dowries in Law in Renaissance Florence. In *Studies on Florence and the Italian Renaissance in honour of F. W. Kent*, ed. Peter Howard and Cecilia Hewlett. Turnhout: Brepols.

[31]Hardwick, Julie. 2009. *Family Business: Litigation and the Political Economies of Daily Life in Early Modern France*. Oxford and New York: Oxford University Press, 49.

laid out by Baldo, it was mainly the dowry and *parapherna* that were effected by a judicially ordered separation of assets.

Eventually such *consignatio dotis* was accepted in Florence and other communities, with the provision (in Florence) that such reversions be recorded and registered with civic authorities to provide some means of protection to a husband's other creditors in the face of the powerful hypothec being enforced for wives' dowries. Such thorough distinction between husband's and wife's patrimonies during marriage was about the most extreme statement of that, and of the hypothec for dowry on the husband's patrimony. In fact, the statutes of 1415 went so far as to affirm, after describing the hypothec, that it was not hurt by any consensual renunciation a woman might make to sale or alienation of her dowry (the Morelli problem).[32]

That statutory reassurance held up because another feature of Florence's laws was a prohibition on wives coming to the financial rescue of their husbands. The rubric "Quod nulla mulier vivente viro possit defendere bona viri" said it all. The statutory exception, of course, was to protect the wife's dowry, which was amorphously part of her husband's property if her dowry was "inextimata" (not given a precise value).[33] The sole substantial addition to that statute in 1415 was to concede the right to protect one's dowry from the husband "vergente ad inopiam."[34] There was also a statute precluding wives from being held liable for taxes and forced loans falling on their husbands, directly exempting nondotal goods.[35] In another statute that broadly equated women and minors, no confirmatory oath concerning alienation of dotal property by a woman could be upheld, on suspicion it was done from fear or to defraud, unless it was very formally taken before communal judges, with father or guardian present (here, acting as a *curator* and not a mere *mundualdus*). Hence also no such oath would be accepted if supposedly made outside Florentine territory.[36]

A third area of concern was about property a wife might acquire during marriage. In 1325 any objects, lands, or houses, or vineyards that might come to her generated a right for the husband to *fructus*, with or without his wife's leave, unless he were to mistreat her or expel her from the house or were an incompetent manager. Anything the wife gained by way of succession from her paternal or maternal kin was understood to be her property, however, and she could defend it from claims of any creditors. The only exception otherwise to the husband's claims to enjoy and use his wife's property was if it came to her with the express condition that no *fructus* come to him, and we have seen that Florentines were willing to use such conditions.[37] In 1415 there was added the specification that the wife could not alienate her property

[32]Statuta (1415) 1, 160.

[33]Statuti (1325), 93.

[34]Statuta (1415) 1, 161.

[35]Kirshner 1991 (as n. 10) 84.

[36]Statuta (1415) 1, 206.

[37]Statuti (1325), 103; Kirshner 1991 (as n. 10) 82–83.

without her husband's consent; and the distinction regarding inherited property coming to her disappeared.[38] In effect, this measure reduced such extra-dotal property to the status of *parapherna* (again, a term not found in Florence's statutes), eliminating Ubaldi's and Albergotti's third form of female patrimony.[39] In essence Florence's statutes (and more systematically from 1415) helped husbands exercise some control over nondotal properties and *fructus*, with or without their spouses' consent, keeping clear only that title to such properties lay with the wife.[40] Chabot has concluded that this statutory equation of a wife's non-dotal property to dowry, under the husband's control and for his enjoyment, "consecrated the concentration in the husband's hands of the entirety of female goods acquired during marriage," and that, in turn, "participated in a vaster design to guarantee the incorporation of the spouse's property in an axis of succession of her husband. Assimilated immediately to the marital patrimony, the property of the woman herself remains, as her dowry, in the form of credits even after the death of the spouse, and it is often the death of the widow which imperceptibly extinguished the debt."[41]

As the wife held nominal *dominium* on her property, one mode in which her husband's control might be limited or even undercut was by her will, directing portions of her belongings to those she chose. Florence's statutes moved to limit the damage that might strike the husband from his wife's testament. As was the case in some other cities, in Florence a husband gained his wife's dowry on her predecease, while remaining *fructus* on nondotal assets were recoverable by her heirs (or part of it in other cities). If there were children they got the dowry, though he retained usufruct. If she made a will, he still gained a third of her nondotal property, unless there were children; and if she died intestate, he still got a third.[42] Children of any prior marriage were left out. In 1415 were added a simple definition of what was dowry (what had been "confessed" as such) and the proviso that no woman could concoct a testament that harmed the rights of her husband or children or their descendants in her property.[43] As Julius Kirshner has concluded, "although no rationale accompanied the innovation that made the Florentine husband part successor to his wife's nondotal assets, it should be understood as a calculated extension of the legislation that had permitted husbands to enjoy usufruct of non-dotal fruits in an ongoing marriage."[44]

Another mode to limit a wife's attempts to manage and control her property, although it was also a potentially porous mode, was the peculiar Florentine requirement that any woman conducting a legal transaction needed a male guardian, a *mundualdus*. If a married woman entered a contract with her husband's consent,

---

[38]Statuta (1415) 1, 161–62.

[39]Kirshner 1991 (as n. 10) 75.

[40]Kirshner 1991 (as n. 10) 79.

[41]Chabot 2011 (as n. 20) 176–77.

[42]Statuti (1325), 130.

[43]Statuta (1415) 1, 222–23; Chabot 2011 (as n. 20) 51–56.

[44]Kirshner 1991 (as n. 10) 83.

he was held to be her *mundualdus* and her act was valid and unrevokable. Her right to protect her interests in the face of payments to her husband's creditors was upheld in the same statute, which did not otherwise raise a problem of conflict of interest if a husband gave consent to an act that was to his advantage. The wife could not cede a right to her dowry to someone other than her husband. If he gave away the property that was originally in her dowry and the creditor who had received it wanted to keep it, she had to be content with what was repaid her as an equivalent value.[45] But her consent to any alienation of property obligated for her dowry or renunciation of her hypothecary rights did not hold unless, at the time, there was sufficient *immobilia* to cover her dowry.

While it was thus the case that a woman would always have to have a male guardian, Florentine law—except for the presumption in favor of the spouse—allowed that anyone could be that guardian. The *mundualdus* was "electus" by the woman, in theory. Such a guardian had no real or personal liability for the consequences of the woman's acts, so any real control, guidance, or concern may have been minimal.[46] For widows, lacking a husband and quite probably a father, that seems especially to have been the case. But married women transacting nondotal goods were more than likely to employ husbands as *mundualdi*, though there were instances when others, including a kinsman of the husband, might serve as guardian.[47]

Statutes refined and "Florentinized" the rules of law, but they hardly erased all ambiguities of the two patrimonies. In some regards they made them more opaque. If they did not, the ever-changing and inventive acts of residents of Florence complicated things inevitably. Whatever the dictates of law, surely the unity of the patrimony was most apparent in the way Florentines saw women's property and treated it. In that regard it has to be noted that the officials entrusted with compilation of the first Florentine catasto declared that "wives were not allowed to declare separately from their husbands; husbands had to assume fiscal responsibility for their wives."[4] Husbands' declarations rarely distinguished wifely property from any other household assets for fiscal purposes. But husbands were otherwise highly aware of their obligations in regard to the property wives brought into the marital home.

4 A Florentine Householder

The distinctness of spousal patrimonies and the blurred edges around them are apparent in that most Florentine of sources, *ricordanza* (or other records similar to those of Guicciardini and Morelli, with which we opened). We will concentrate on

[45]Statuti (1325), 107; Statuta (1415) 1, 203–4.

[46]Kuehn 1991 (as n. 6) 212–37. See also Feci, Simona. 2004. *Pesci fuor d'acqua. Donne a Roma in età moderna: diritti e patrimoni*. Roma: Viella.

[47]Kirshner 1991 (as n. 10) 86.

one for now, but it is rich in references to dowries in a number of contexts—the *ricordanze* of Luca da Panzano.[48] Dowries figured into his text at many points, from mother, wife, daughters, and others, beginning with an early reference to his mother, Mattea, making her will in the plague year of 1400, in which she left her 1200 florin dowry to her sons, but if they all died without legitimate children, it was to go to her brothers (she was staying at the house of one of them in San Gimignano at the time) (4–5). Luca's mother, with his help as legal agent, also succeeded in lodging a claim on Antonio's property for 400 florins still owed her for her dowry and ended up with a farm (7, 144–45). Striking also is Luca's account of maneuvers by his cousins, Totto and Mea d'Antonio, such that Mea took possession of her mother's dowry as her heir (Totto having refused it), despite her father being alive still, "in truth to defend the goods of her father Antonio because the conditions of his bank were bad" ("in verità per difendere i beni d'Antonio suo padre perch'e fatti del suo bancho istavano male") (6). Here there was deliberate use of the distinctness of female titles to protect men and the family as a whole.

Luca was involved as surety on dowries received by others (examples, 214, 253), relatives and associates, including in restoring dowries to widows. But for our purposes the more interesting points concern dowries that came to him or that he arranged. His wife, Lucrezia di Salvadore del Caccia, brought him a dowry of 1018 florins in 1425. And that is how Luca saw it: "I should have **my** dowry of said Lucrezia" ("debbo avere per **mia** [emphasis added] dota di detta Luchrezia") (52). His text next records the children he had ("arò") from her. Like so many other Florentines who kept such registers of their doings, Luca da Panzano nowhere noted any other property, including the contents of her trousseau, that his wife may have brought into the home.[49] There was no category of *parapherna* to keep track of in his mind.[50] Later he jotted down that he had taken his own money and bought shares in Florence's public debt (Monte) in Lucrezia's name, at six percent interest. He added:

> Said moneys have been thus described because, should it happen that my wife want her dowry after my death, my sons may not have to unload all their possessions and that it remain to support them.[51]

In 1432 he moved the sum to another fund, still as security for her dowry, with condition that he enjoyed the interest ("ch'io possi pigliare le paghe") (120). Other Florentines similarly converted dowries into annuities based on shares in the public

---

[48]Herlihy, David and Klapisch-Zuber, Christiane, *Tuscans and Their Families* (New Haven: Yale University Press, 1985), 12.

[49]Panzano, Luca da. 2010. "*Brighe, affanni, volgimenti di stato*": *le ricordanze quattrocentesche di Luca di Matteo di messer Luca dei Firidolfi da Panzano*, ed. Anthony Molho and Franek Sznura. Firenze: SISMEL-Edizioni del Galluzzo.

[50]Kirshner 1991 (as n. 10) 75.

[51]"I detti danari ò fatti dire chosì perché ischadendo che detta mia donna volesse suo dota manchando io, ch'e miei figliuoli non s'abino a ischorporare tutte loro possisione e che rimanghi loro da vivere" (Panzano 2010 (as n. 48) 82–83).

debt. Of course he also remembered to accord her dowry and *alimenta* when he made his will, but he added no other (nondotal) assets to it (168–69).

Luca also fashioned an agreement with Michele de' Benenati da San Gimignano and his wife Bartolomea, that once both of them had died Luca would receive 1500 florins in Monte holdings in return for a payment of 360 florins to the Innocenti and the Arte di Por Santa Maria. Benenati was a fellow silk merchant and business associate, after whom Luca named one of his sons.[52] Bartolomea named Luca's sons as her heirs years later (362). A house in San Gimignano was bought in her name "with condition that after the death of monna Bartolomea said farm would be monna Lucrezia's, with condition that she not have other husband than she has today, either by monna Lucrezia's death or by taking another husband it be their sons' that he has or might have from said Luca da Panzano today her husband."[53]

In 1436 Luca scrupulously recorded that, though he and his brothers held properties in common, his wife's dowry "and clothes that I have expended from my money or from money of the dowry that I have had are mine, Luca, and that the dowry cannot be demanded by them."[54] Her death led him to remark that she "fu una valente e buona donna," "dolcie," and "costumata, " and he saw to appropriate obsequies (225, 241–42). He waited nine years to designate his five sons as his wife's intestate heirs and despatch them to retrieve the credits in her name in the Monte (330). There is no mention of any nondotal goods coming to him.

When Luca's son Antonio married, the dowry amount and payments were set forth, along with other legal adjustments between father and son (383–85). The Monte credits to indemnify this dowry were also set down, as well as amounts of grain, oil, wine, and other victuals (389–90). Mattea's husband, who did not immediately realize the 1000 florins in the Monte, once he did receive the last payment in August 1460, bought a farm near Pistoia, declaring that he used his wife's dowry (400 **lire** of it, at any rate), "and he designated the buyer as Gualterotto and that it stood for part of my Mattea's dowry" ("disse compera in Ghualterotto e che stesse per parte di dota de la Mattea mia"). It was purchased from a woman with the consent of her male guardian and her mother (425).

There is far too much careful accounting of sums, attributing of names in title of ownership, and general awareness that dowry was a special type of property and title, to allow simple assertions of "my dowry" to slip by unqualified. Yes, Luca called his wife's dowry "mia," just as he called his children "mia." But that did not define how he could and did act in so many situations. This was a man, given all the

---

[52]Because "ffui di più soleciti merchatanti del mondo e per mare [e] per terra e di nonnulla con gran chredito e infine gran limosiniere e fé gran defici per Dio di muragllie" (180).

[53]"Con condizione che dopo la mor te di detta monna Bartolomea il detto podere fussi di monna Luchrezia di Salvadore del Chaccia, con condizione che ella non abi altro marito che oggi à, o per morte di detta Luchrezia o per altro marito togliesse sia de' suoi figliuoli che à o che avesse del detto Lucha da Panzano oggi suo marito" (190).

[54]"e' panni che io avessi ispesi di miei danari o di danari di dota che abbi auti si sieno di me Lucha, e che la dota non possi loro adomandare" (199).

legal transactions he compiled in his records, who was keenly aware of the impact of law and its procedures.[55] When he acted as agent and surety for two distant cousins on a dowry, he declared that he did so "secondo gli Statuti del Comune di Firenze" (214).

5 Cases

Statutes gave a man like Luca a great deal of latitude, but they did not free him of all the complications engendered by the legal distinctions of spousal property. We can get a sense of some of these complications from the case *consilia* of attorneys active in and around Florence, on Florentine cases but also some from elsewhere.

It was a case from Trieste that holds our attention first. There a statute gave husbands usufruct on all their wives' property "those given in dowry as well as acquired [during marriage]" ("tam datorum in dotibus quam acquisitorum"). On a husband's death it was all to revert "immediately" to his wife. Baldo, however, said the statute did not wipe out the required waiting period before the wife could claim what had been left her in her husband's will. Trieste's statute also attributed ownership of acquests during marriage to both husband and wife, though only he had direct use. He could dispose of them with her consent, and so for a long time the customary sense of the statute was that he was free to do so. Could he give it away? Here Baldo degli Ubaldi equivocated a bit, but held that the statute interpretation in customary practice returned the situation to that of common law: "the husbands do not acquire for the wife but the wives for the husbands." Husbands could alienate only their share of the property. As things might be gained by testamentary bequest or full-out inheritance by one or the other spouse, husbands were not free to alienate what wives brought in by those means. Acquests of other sorts in marriage were his in full by his presumed industry, but not if by use of their common money, for then some part of it was hers.[56]

Baldo's brother Angelo (1323–1400) faced a similar case in hypothetical form and determined that the statutes of Florence advantaged husbands. If a woman received two houses as bequests from her mother, could her husband appropriate the rents obtained from them? Florence's statutes of 1355 had given women operative custody of property inherited from either parent. Angelo saw the statutes otherwise trying to give control of nondotal assets to the husband. As the distinction about inherited property contradicted the first assertion about spousal control, landing the statutes back in line with *ius commune*, Angelo had to work hard to find a coherent line of interpretation. He hit on a strange distinction, placing usufruct with the husband on bequests from the wife's paternal line but with the wife on

[55]In parallel, see Hardwick 2009 (as n. 31) 71–72.

[56]Baldo, 2 cons. 234 and 235, fol. 66rb-vb.

bequests from her maternal line.[57] In the case before him the property came from the maternal line, so the rents were to stay with the wife. Whatever the husband had appropriated had to be returned.[58] The later removal of the distinction about bequests from the statutes of 1415 should have firmly ended any doubt about the husband's active *administratio* of his wife's assets acquired during marriage.

Curiously, in a closely similar case from Bologna, Angelo offered more direct support of the wife's right to dispose of property acquired in marriage, though this time in effect securing a house to the person who bought it from the wife. The statute protected *immobilia* given in the dowry. A woman who during marriage acquired a house by succession, who treated it as her home (*inquilinum suum*) and kept it in her own name, later sold it and the purchaser wanted to know that his title was secure despite the statute, which varied greatly from common law, which did not so easily assume dowry and attribute it to the husband. Angelo aimed to bring both laws into conformity as much as he could, and that conformity began

> when at the time of the marriage the wife had her stable property, so that the husband believed he would possess that as dowry, otherwise he would in no way have contracted the marriage. For this our natural stimulus inclines us as much as by reason of cupidity as that the burdens of marriage may be sustained.[59]

Goods acquired during marriage did not answer to that logic, so the statute did not apply to them. Either acquired goods were common to both spouses or they were part of dowry, "which then the wife had or hoped to have, by some just cause, as otherwise there is no hope" ("que tunc mulier habebat, vel habere sperabat, aliqua iusta causa subsistente, quoniam aliter spes non esset"). The exception was if the wife knew and allowed her husband to behave like the owner. In this case the purchaser was secure because the house had never been in the husband's hands; the wife acted as *domina* and received the rents and sold it in her name alone.[60]

The impetus behind these cases seems to have been the wife's desire to recover all she could on the end of the marriage. In that case her property rights were about her needs and uses in widowhood. In other instances her rights might act as a cover to help retain some property when faced with the demands of creditors. The commune of Prato, near Florence, was the creditor in a suit against a wife whose dowry had supposedly been increased (*augmentum*) by 200 florins during marriage. Though Florentine law clearly privileged the wife's dowry credit against her husband's other creditors, that did not apply to a later increase, declared the jurist Paolo

---

[57]He may have hit on this because married women were expressly exempted by statute from liability for their fathers' debts, unless they were heirs to their fathers (Statuta (1415), 1: 205).

[58]Angelo degli Ubaldi. 1575. *Consilia*. Frankfurt, cons. 62, fols. 40rb–41ra.

[59]Angelo degli Ubaldi (as n. 58) fol. 40va: " cum tempore matrimonii mulier bona sua stabilia habet, ut sic illa vir se credat possessurum pro dote, aliter matrimonium nullatenus contracturus fuisset. Ad hoc enim naturalis stimulus noster inclinat, tam ratione cupidinis quam ut sustineri possint onera matrimonii."

[60]Angelo degli Ubaldi (as n. 58) cons. 335, fol. 236ra–va.

di Castro (ca. 1360–1441).[61] He compared Prato's statute to a new revision of Florence's. The key point was that an increase to dowry during marriage was suspicious: "one presumes fraud and machinations against creditors, because then as conjugal affection is contracted, it is easily presumed that fraud is thought of" ("praesumit fraudem et machinationem contra creditores, quia tunc cum sit contracta affectio coniugalis, faciliter praesumitur fraudem excogitatam"). Statutory priority of the wife's tacit hypothec for dowry versus the commune's express hypothec for fiscal claims gave way after marriage was consummated. Proofs that the increase was somehow genuine were rejected out of hand. There was no notarized *confessio* of the increase, leave alone one dating from before the point the husband began to slide into insolvency. The only guarantee to the wife was that she receive sufficient resources, even against claims of prior creditors, to sustain herself and her husband and children.[62]

A parallel case, and a similar jurisprudential distrust arose later and came before Bartolomeo Sozzini (1436–1506).[63] A Sienese Jew named Jacob Consilii, after his marriage began, in a publicly notarized instrument, gave Dulce 500 florins for her "great benefits and merits and gain and convenience" ("magna beneficia et merita et lucra et commoda"), and "in affectione," "lest she suffer some shame in going bankrupt or having to flee or in capture of her person" ("ne verecundiam aliquam in cessando, vel fugiendo, vel in captura personae pateretur"). Further, over the previous three years, "by industry, care, and diligence of said Dulce" another 100 florins had been realized for the family. Jacob swore by Mosaic law, on the Hebrew bible, to abide by the gift and *fructus*. This was posed as a gift between spouses, which was something generally precluded in Roman law, and thus was easy for Sozzini to dismiss. But he did not make it easy. He pedantically offered no less than 23 reasons such a gift did not hold. Behind the cascade of textual references he marshaled, the simple fact was that, no matter the assertion of merit to validate the gift, there was only the husband's word on that. His assertion seemed rather a feigned act of deceit ("facta colore fictitie simulationis"). Sozzini also dismissed the oath on Jewish scripture, as canon law's prescriptions regarding oaths did not affect Jews, who were outside the church. As the gift was not real, then, there was no real need to explore in depth the question whether Jacob could revoke the gift following Dulce's death. Were the gift real he could revoke it at any point in his life, were his wife alive or dead.[64]

61On him, see Martines, Lauro. 1968. *Lawyers and Statecraft in Renaissance Florence*. Princeton: Princeton University Press, 499–500; Biscione, Giuseppe. 2009. *Statuti del Comune di Firenze nell'Archivio di Stato. Tradizione archivistica e ordinamenti*. Roma: Ministero per i Beni e le Attività Culturali, 661–74; Tanzini, Lorenzo. 2004. *Statuti e legislazione a Firenze dal 1355 al 1415: Lo statuto cittadino del 1409*. Firenze: Olschki, 280–310.

62Paolo di Castro. 1571. *Consilia*, 3 vols., Venice, 3 cons. 37, fols. 42va–44rb.

63On him, Bargagli, Roberta. 2000. *Bartolomeo Sozzini: giurista e politico (1436–1506)*. Milano: Giuffrè.

64Sozzini, Bartolomeo and Mariano. 1579. *Consilia*, 4 vols., Venice, 1 cons. 56, fols. 121vb–25ra. The immediately following second consilium on the case added further references, including to

Acting as attorney for a Sienese man named Tommaso in another case, Sozzini argued that seizure of the household furnishings and utensils (masseritia) for a father's debts should be overturned. The fact was that those objects belonged not to the father but to his wife, and thus passed to Tommaso, their son, without obligation for the paternal debts. Here the father and mother had moved in with her mother; continued to live there with their children after the mother-in-law's death; and father and children resided there after the mother's death. But that did not mean that the property belonged to the husband. Whereas usually "when husband and wife live in the same house the furnishings are presumed to be the husband's" (quando vir et uxor habitant in eadem domo massaritiae praesumantur esse viri), the presumption here had to be that they belonged to the wife. Sozzini also took note of a teaching of Angelo degli Ubaldi that any cohabiting spouses were to be understood to each possess half.[65] In Sozzini's eyes, at least in this instance, both wife's and son's ownership stood separate from that of the husband/father.

A jurist who taught in Pisa, though originally from Milan, Filippo Decio (1545–1536), caught a case from Ferrara that was in fact emblematic of legal problems of women's contracts. Could a woman contract about dowry when local statute forbade women to make contracts without the consent of certain males? Dowry seemed a special contract, enjoying favor in law to encourage marriage, so a general statute about contracts might well not have applied to it. Decio, however, gave force to the very generality of the statute as applying universally to all contracts, including dowry. That was particularly the case given the intent of the statute:

> from the statute's preface it appears that such statute was made to preclude fraud, lest wives be deceived out of their assets, because the statute presumes and has constant that without formalities [set out by] the statute wives obligating themselves would be seduced on account of the shame of their sex and reverential fear, which sex and nature induces in them, as a statute for removing frauds, such a statute must be amplified and widely interpreted, as we see that common laws made to prevent frauds and malicious deeds are extended and receive a wide interpretation even if the material is odious.[66]

This last flourish indeed pointed to the direction from which a counter argument might be launched, to the effect that the law was harmful to women and against the common law, which usually required a restrictive interpretation. In any case, Decio went on to state that fraud and deception might as easily be perpetrated on a woman

(Footnote 64 continued)

Florentine jurists, and dealt more fully with the Jewish oath and the need to punish a Jew, nonetheless, for supposed perjury (1 cons. 57, fols. 125ra–28ra).

[65]Sozzini 1579 (as n. 64), 1 cons. 128, fols. 216vb–217rb.

[66]Decio, Filippo. 1570. *Consilia*. Venice, cons. 301, fols. 329vb–30vb: "ex proemio statuti apparet quod tale statutum fuit factum ad obviandum fraudibus ne mulieres eorum facilitate deciperentur, quia statutum presumit et habet pro constante quod absque solennitate statuti mulieres se obligantes seductae fuerint propter verecundiam sexus et timorem reverentialem, quem eis sexus et natura induxit, ut statutum ad removendum fraudes, tale statutum debet ampliari et late interpretari, sicut videmus quod iura communia facta ad occurrendum fraudibus et malitiis extenduntur et latam recipiunt interpretationem etiam si materia esset odiosa."

regarding dowry as anything else. Dowry was not accorded privileged status by the Ferrarese statute. Indeed, concluded Decio, "otherwise I advised at Florence and so at Florence was it judged at the time I was teaching there" ("alias consului Florentiae… et ita Florentiae tempore quo ibi legebam fuit iudicatum").[67]

His treatment was similar in a Pisan case that came to him after another local attorney had his say. Decio concurred. The statute that forbade a married woman from entering a contract about her dowry also covered a gift following and confirmed by death. It was true that prior to death such a gift could be simply revoked, and thus did not seem to carry the *preiudicium* the statute was concerned about. But Decio pointed to the obvious loss to her children, as her heirs, and to the fact that the same female *fragilitas* that led the law to forbid contracts on dowry would also be at work in any gift. Further, "in reality it cannot be judged otherwise that a gift made to the stepmother by said Cornelia seems made in contemplation of her father consenting and not on account of the stepmother herself, because a stepmother is hateful to a stepson or stepdaughter."[68] It was more a gift to the father, and through him to his wife. So the gift was invalid, as the father, who had been the male giving consent to Cornelia's act, was in fact acting to his own benefit. Decio's professional efforts went into establishing the "better" common opinion about the gift, as there were in fact authoritative arguments and texts on both sides about the father's consent.[69]

Sozzini, who taught at Pisa, confronted another case from that city, which at its heart concerned the statute—common to most every Italian city—by which daughters and other females were excluded from succession in favor of male agnates (provided the women were adequately dowered). He backed the claims of a niece (daughter of a son) to succeed with and not be excluded by her paternal uncle (father's brother) in her grandfather's estate. That conclusion rested in part on statutory language that seemed to allow males and females to inherit past the initial exclusion of dowered daughters. But part of the succession involved another statute dealing with dress and jewelry, where the whole problem, said Sozzini, was the meaning of the extra-legal terms *guarnimenta* (furnishing) and *corredia* (trousseau). It is hard to imagine that attorneys were not totally aware of the vernacular meanings of these words, although Sozzini insisted "nothing seems clear from the common manner of speaking" ("nec de communi usu loquendi constat aliquid clare"). Sozzini found that Baldo had taught that what a wife brought to her husband's house and was not used up was to be returned on the dissolution of the marriage. But what the statute called *corredia* might better in terms of civil law be called *dos inaestimata*. Sozzini took the two terms in the statute to be synonymous, "and they are those things that are for use and adornment of the wife" ("et sunt illa

[67]Decio 1570 (as n. 66).

[68]Decio 1570 (as n. 66), cons. 279, fols. 304rb–305rb: "quia veritate et ratione consonat, adeo quod verisimiliter aliter iudicari non possit quod donatio facta novercae per dictam Corneliam videtur facta contemplatione patris consentientis, et non propter ipsam novercam, quia noverca odiosa est privigno vel privignae."

[69]Decio 1570 (as n. 66), cons. 279, fols. 304rb–305rb.

quae sunt ad usum et ornatum mulieris"), that were brought by her, not given her by her husband. So the lady in question in the case, Pippa, was found to have a 400 florin dowry and 200 in *corredia*. She was to have what was left of that 200 (against whatever had been consumed or deteriorated by her use), whereas for *dos aestimata* she was due the full sum with no subtractions. The husband, Francesco, had declared (presumably in his will) that he had alienated half of his wife's *corredia* and *guarnimenta*. He had enumerated exactly what he had sold off and for how much, and that specificity told that there was substance to the declaration. By statute the husband got half of his wife's dowry and *donamenta* on her predecease, except for the wedding ring (*anulum sponsalitium*), which was to be returned to her heirs. As she had outlived him, however, she was due the entire value remaining in *corredia* and *ornamenta*—in other words, the half he had not alienated.[70]

A married woman could alienate whatever she had beyond dowry and *donamenta*, because it was hers and not her husband's, whereas dowry was his and by statute (of Siena?) he could realize half the value of *donamenta*. If she had children but no husband, she could alienate only half. If she had husband and children, she could dispose of a quarter. Lacking children, Pippa was free, said Sozzini, to dispose of half, for to not be able to control one's property was *odiosum*. So she could direct a gift of half *inter vivos* to her niece, as she apparently wanted to do.

The separateness of marital patrimonies was perhaps most on display precisely when it was violated, when a wife stepped up and used her property to meet her husband's debts, which would require her, in thus obligating herself, to renounce the privilege under the s.c. Velleianum, protecting women from obligating themselves for others. Otherwise she might invoke it to dissolve any such obligation for a third party. The problem Sozzini once faced revolved around the question whether the contract a woman had entered was in fact simulated. Regularly one assumed that a contract was what it said it was. One did not begin presuming a fiction. At least reasonable conjectures had to be available to conclude the contrary. A fictive contract meant the oath not to invoke Velleianum did not stand. But in his case that oath was not simply to uphold the contract but that the transfer of assets was true; and the Velleianum had been specifically waived, so it could not now be invoked (probably not by the wife, in any case, but possibly by her husband or her heir, seeking to get the property back or escape the obligation). The woman in question, a monna Giovanna, had sold off her property "so that she might save the house, and she has it as a possession, otherwise not to be sold" ("ut conservaret domum, et illam habet in locum possessionis, alias non venditura"). In fact, within a year, it seems, the couple were evicted from the home, but that had not been the doing of the creditors she had paid off but of others. Nor was preservation of the home the singular *causa* behind the wife's intervention:

> but there is another reason and so she is not given a return [of the property]… and so it is in our case, because if it is by reason of freeing the husband, lest he be held captive, beyond by reason of saving the house, rather that greater principle [helping the husband] in the

[70]Sozzini 1579 (as n. 63), 3 cons. 119, fols. 155va–57va.

> contract has to be considered, therefore saving the house was not in the end the final cause and consequently the contract must not be resolved... and especially because, as I said, she seems to have been moved by love of her husband... and that she wanted rather to save his person than his goods.[71]

Here then he ended up with an argument about affection, the oneness of the couple, to uphold the wife's acts, which, given the later eviction, seemed to have come a bit late, but also to her loss.

The opposite of a wife's contributing to pay off her husband's debts was her suit to retrieve her dowry from him lest it be lost to creditors as he verged on insolvency. This was not a legal device that came easily to anyone, if only because it fundamentally gave the lie to any sense of patrimonial solidarity in a household or between spouses. But it also gave rise to valid fears of fraud, as property that creditors might naively believe belonged to their debtor, and was thus available for their repayment, turned out not to be. Paolo di Castro was involved in the 1415 revision of Florence's statues, and he handled cases arising from *consignatio dotis*. Among them was one in which Mattea, whose husband, Andrea, was clearly in difficulty, could invoke her hypothec against her mother-in-law, Antonia, and brother-in-law, Lorenzo, who had pledged themselves for return of her dowry in a *confessio*. Certainly the husband was on the hook for the dowry, and so was any of his property in his mother's possession. But was the mother's property in jeopardy? Paolo di Castro faced the objection that her oath to return the dowry on the occasion of *restitutio* did not cover *consignatio*. He also addressed the statutory language, which allowed broad action by a wife, though he admitted that creditors might have claim to see demonstration of the husband's true circumstances and the wife's exigencies. In the end he insisted that the mother-in-law's pledge on the dowry her son received did not include *consignatio*. He concluded she was not liable for a claim on the hypothec in her property or that of her sons already hypothecated for her own dowry, which was a prior and more powerful claim.[72]

Effectively di Castro was not going to save one dowry with another. Sozzini also placed one dowry ahead of another. The heirs of monna Ginevra, he said, had a better claim to the dowry of Niccolosa, Ginevra's mother, than did the heirs of Bianco, who were, they argued, creditors of Bernardo, and who were in possession. The story began back in 1407 when Bernardo formally acknowledged a 600 florin dowry. Twenty years later his difficulties provoked *consignatio*, and possession of a farm went to Niccolosa. Bernardo died in 1430. Niccolosa held the land for the rest of her life, and importantly Sozzini affirmed that *consignatio* vested ownership (*dominium*) in her. So her husband living with her, while he too enjoyed the *fructus*,

---

[71]Sozzini 1579 (as n. 63), 3 cons. 83, fol. 98ra–va: "sed est alia etiam causa et tunc non datur repetitio et non resolvitur ... et ita est in casu nostro, quia si est causa liberandi maritum ne caperetur ultra causam conservando domum, immo illa magis principalis in contractu videtur consideranda, igitur conservatio domus non fuit in totum causa finalis et per consequens non debet contractus resolvi ... et maxime quia, ut dixi, videtur quod mota fuerit amore viri ... et quod potius vellet personam conservare quam bona."

[72]Di Castro 1571 (as n. 62), 3 cons. 6, fols. 9va–10va.

had only a *ius familiaritatis* (as was the case with any other family member living in a home with no real ownership). The son, Corrado, thus also had only *familiaritas*. *Consignatio*, furthermore, was not vitiated by a subsequent recovery of wealth. Once consigned to her, the dowry stayed with her (presumably unless she relented freely and there was another *confessio* to establish her right to its return). *Consignatio* was a legitimate act that was not retracted.

Corrado was also not his father's heir, as he had repudiated the estate formally and had not taken possession of his father's property (as the house they lived in belonged to the mother, Niccolosa).[73] He thus escaped the terms of Florence's statute on the obligations of heirs. Niccolosa's heir was Ginevra by her will (though she had taken care to institute Corrado also, so the will stood for not passing him over unmentioned). Ginevra had accepted this maternal inheritance (presumably Corrado had not), so it passed from her to Girolamo and her other children. These heirs, however, faced the argument of Bianco's heirs that no right passed to them from Ginevra because, by the terms of Niccolosa's will, no rights were to go to Ginevra's husband or children. Donors did on occasion add restrictions against husbands, so that was not an unheard of stipulation. Bianco's heirs also claimed that Ginevra had not in fact accepted (*adita*) the estate of her mother. Sozzini countered that Ginevra's heirs had their right through her, and that Niccolosa's property had become "unum patrimonium" with Ginevra's. He also said that there had indeed been *aditio*, as Ginevra acted as agent of her dead mother, at least tacitly agreeing to the inheritance's terms. *Aditio* could also be presumed from the fact that the maternal estate was *lucrosa*. She transmitted right of inheritance to her children:

> Moreover, it is also responded that the testator seems to have respected the disposition of the statute wanting that a husband have usufruct of the wife's acquisitions, for which he wanted to provide lest it be sought from Ginevra's husband, as we have in similar cases. And if it is said the statute provides only about usufruct and not about ownership, so it provides only with respect to the husband, but it does not provide for sons. As therefore monna Niccolosa prohibited that right ever be sought in usufruct but also in ownership, so not just to the husband but even to the sons, she does not seem to have respected the aforesaid statute on acquisition of usufruct being made to the husband, for as the prohibition respects ownership, the words of the prohibition do nothing.[74]

Bianco's heirs were also precluded by the passage of time. As it had been decades since Bernardo's death, and as Corrado had not been his father's heir, his knowledge of the debts and the estate did not prevent the clock from beginning to

---

[73]Cf. Kuehn, Thomas. 2008. *Heirs, Kin, and Creditors in Renaissance Florence*. Cambridge and New York: Cambridge University Press, 68–69, 165.

[74]Sozzini 1579 (as n. 64), 1 cons. 61, fols. 113rb–15va: "Preterea etiam respondetur quod testator videtur respexisse ad dispositionem statuti volentis quod vir habeat ususfructum acquisitorum uxori, cui voluit providere ne quaeretur viro dominae Ginevrae, sicut in simili habemus … Et si dicatur statutum tantum providet circa ususfructum et non circa proprietatem ita tantum providet respectu viri, non autem providet quo ad filios. Cum ergo domina Nicolosa prohibuerit nedum quaeri ius in usufructu sed etiam in proprietate, item nedum viro sed etiam filiis, non videtur respexisse ad praedictum statutum de acquisitione ususfructus fienda viro, nam cum prohibitio respeciat proprietatem, verba prohibitionis nihil operarentur."

run. The son was not subject to the father's obligations in all regards. Thus, as Domenico da San Gimignano (d. 1424) had said, though heir and deceased "censeantur eadem persona", in fact they were different in person and soul, so what struck one did not strike the other (at least in canon law). When *consignatio* retrieved the dowries of Francesca and her daughter-in-law Antonia from ser Lodovico, his other creditors sought to exchange cash for the properties assigned to the two women. There were several reasons that option seemed licit, including that *consignatio* "is done to the effect that a wife can support herself, her husband and children… and that the dowry in entirety be placed for the end that it may easily provide for this effect, placing the dowry with honest merchants."[75] Sozzini, however, sided with the women, though ordinarily creditors might offer the swap of cash for real dotal assets. *Consignatio* was not like restitution, as it had the limited end of furnishing *alimenta* to a woman otherwise in danger of losing wherewithal to her husband's debts. That was not the case when a marriage ended and restitution was at issue. Above all, the properties were safer than cash, "by which is not easily found one with whom money lies in safety and may realize *fructus*, as often these merchants become bankrupt, as experience teaches."[76] It would hardly seem that a woman having *consignatio* due to her own husband's insolvency needed reminding that merchants often went bankrupt. Sozzini piled up citations to authoritative jurists to substantiate that this was by far the common opinion, and he could not go contrary to that. It is interesting that the case of *consignatio*, when the woman was still married and living with her husband, was treated as distinct. Creditors could not simply buy them out of home, shop, farm, vineyard, or whatever. When it was a matter of restitution and inheritance at the end of marriage, it was different, perhaps because the household then was necessarily being reconstituted.

6 Conclusion

In all these situations marital patrimonial separation was maintained, though in some instances augmented and in others decreased. There was a functioning household to keep in mind, or that certainly was in the minds of legislators and litigants. Suits were about keeping households more or less together, or letting them come apart on the basis of individual legal rights and claims. Luca da Panzano was one such householder. He kept careful accounts of his mother's, wife's, and daughters' dowries. While these sums were recorded in the same ledgers with his business deals and contracts on family holdings, they were always separately

[75]Sozzini 1579 (as n. 64), 3 cons. 111, fols. 142va–43ra. The quotation is: "fiat ad effectum ut mulier alere possit se, maritum, et liberos … et ut dos ponatur in tuto ad finem, poterit faciliter provideri huic effectui, ponendo dotem apud mercatores ad honestum lucrum."

[76]Sozzini 1579 (as n. 64), 3 cons. 111, fols. 142va–43ra: "ex quo non de facili invenitur apud quem pecuniae sint in tuto et possit fructus percipere cum saepe isti mercatores efficiantur falliti, ut experientia docet."

ascribed. Except for a few weak hints about input or concurrence from his wife and the desires of his mother, there is little sense in his pages that the women around his house were active in managing property or influencing his management. But he also dealt with widows who seemed to have an active command of their resources, and he had to know, as with his mother and one daughter, that they had to be able to rely on resources.

The jurists, who themselves lived in such households, upheld property distinctions, even while aware that female patrimony might help preserve households, if not male patrimony more generally. None of the cases we examined resulted in a woman losing her property (in title, vs. *fructus*), except where there was doubt any such title licitly existed, or where affection was seen to underwrite a loss to her. Though statutes seem intent at times with amalgamating wives' assets with their husbands', and account books gravitated about the figure of the husband and father as property manager, the patrimony was in fact fractured. "What remains beyond doubt is the rarity of the phenomenon of assets held jointly by spouses, which confirms that, in harmony with Roman law, the patrimonies of wife and husband continued to be reckoned as distinct legal entities."[77]

References

Sources

1778–83. *Statuta communis Florentiae anno salutis mccccxv*, 3 vols. Friburgi: apud Michaelem Kluch.

1999. *Statuti della repubblica fiorentina*, ed. Romolo Caggese, 2 vols, ed. Giuliano Pinto, Francesco Salvestrini, and Andrea Zorzi, 2, *Statuti del podestà dell'anno 1325*. Firenze: Olschki.

Angelo degli Ubaldi. 1575. *Consilia*. Francofurti: typis Andreae Wecheli sumptibus Sig. Feyrabend, cons. 62, fols. 40rb–41ra.

Baldo degli Ubaldi. 1575. *Consilia*. Venetiis: Francesco de'Franceschi, Gaspare Bindoni, eredi di Nicolo Bevilacqua, Damiano Zenaro, 5 vols., 5, cons. 478.

Bartolomeo and Mariano Sozzini. 1579. *Consilia*, 4 vols. Venetiis, apud Franciscum Zilettum, 1 cons. 56.

Filippo Decio. 1570. *Consilia*. Venetiis: ad Candentis Salamandrae insigne. cons. 301.

Paolo di Castro. 1571. *Consilia*, 3 vols., Venetiis: apud Io. Baptistam Somascum, & fratres, 3 cons. 37.

Panzano, Luca da. 2010. "*Brighe, affanni, volgimenti di stato": le ricordanze quattrocentesche di Luca di Matteo di messer Luca dei Firidolfi da Panzano*, ed. Anthony Molho and Franek Sznura, Firenze: SISMEL–Edizioni del Galluzzo.

[77]Kirshner 1991 (as n. 10) 87.

Literature

Ago, R. (1995). Ruoli familiari e statuto giuridico. *Quaderni storici, 88*, 111–133.
Alberti, L. B. (1969). *The family in renaissance Florence* (trans. Renee Neu Watkins). Columbia: University of South Carolina Press.
Barbaro, F. (1978). On Wifely Duties (trans. Benjamin G. Kohl). In B. G. Kohl & R. G. Witt (Eds.), *The earthly republic: Italian humanists on government and society* (189–228). Philadelphia: University of Pennsylvania Press.
Bargagli, R. (2000). *Bartolomeo Sozzini: giurista e politico (1436–1506)*. Milano: Giuffrè.
Bellavitis, A., & Chabot, I. (2005). A proposito di 'Men and Women in Renaissance Venice' di Stanley Chojnacki. *Quaderni storici, 118*, 203–229.
Bellomo, M. (1961). *Ricerche sui rapporti patrimoniali tra coniugi: contributo alla storia della famiglia medievale*. Milano: Giuffrè.
Biscione, G. (2009). *Statuti del Comune di Firenze nell'Archivio di Stato. Tradizione archivistica e ordinamenti* (pp. 661–674). Roma: Ministero per i Beni e le Attività Culturali.
Borkowski, A., & du Plessis, P. (2005). *Textbook on Roman Law*. Oxford: Oxford University Press.
Boschetto, L. (2000). *Leon Battista Alberti e Firenze*. Firenze: Olschki.
Casey, J. (1989). *The history of the family*. Oxford and New York: Blackwell.
Chabot, I. (2011). *La dette des familles. Femmes, lignage et patrimoine à Florence aux xiv*[e] *et xv*[e] *siècles*. Rome: École Française.
Chojnacki, S. (2000). *Women and men in renaissance Venice: Twelve essays on patrician society*. Baltimore: John Hopkins University Press.
Feci, S. (2004). *Pesci fuor d'acqua. Donne a Roma in età moderna: diritti e patrimoni*. Roma: Viella.
Fubini Leuzzi, M. (1999). *"Condurre a onore": Famiglia, matrimonio e assistenza a Firenze in età moderna*. Firenze: Olschki.
Guicciardini, F. (1981). *Ricordi, diari, memorie*, ed. Marco Spinella. Roma: Riuniti.
Hardwick, J. (2009). *Family business: Litigation and the political economies of daily life in early modern France*. Oxford and New York: Oxford University Press.
Heather, G. (1987). Daughters, dowries and family in fifteenth-century Florence. *Rinascimento, 27*, 217–237.
Herlihy, D., & Klapisch-Zuber, C. (1985). *Tuscans and their families: A study of the Florentine Catasto of 1427*. New Haven and London: Yale University Press.
Kaser, M. (1968). *Roman Private Law* (trans Rolf Dannenbring). Durban: Butterworths.
Kirshner, J. (1985). *Wives' claims against insolvent husbands in late medieval Italy, now in his, 2015. Marriage, dowry, and citizenship in late medieval and renaissance Italy* (pp. 131–160). Toronto: University of Toronto Press.
Kirshner, J. (1991). Materials for a Gilded Cage: Nondotal Assets in Florence, 1300–1500. In D. I. Kertzer & R. P. Saller (Eds.) *The family in Italy from antiquity to the present* (pp. 184–227). New haven and London: Yale University Press.
Kirshner, J. (2015). *Marriage, dowry, and citizenship in late medieval and renaissance Italy*. Toronto: University of Toronto Press.
Kirshner, J., & Pluss, J. (1979). Two fourteenth-century opinions on dowries, paraphernalia and non-dotal goods. *Bulletin of Medieval Canon Law, 9*, 65–77.
Kuehn, T. (1991). *Law, family, and women: Toward a legal anthropology of renaissance Italy*. Chicago: University of Chicago Press.
Kuehn, T. (2008). *Heirs, kin, and creditors in renaissance Florence*. Cambridge and New York: Cambridge University Press.
Kuehn, T. (2016). Protecting Dowries in Law in Renaissance Florence. In P. Howard & C. Hewlett (Eds.), *Studies on Florence and the Italian Renaissance in honour of F. W. Kent*. Turnhout: Brepols.

Martines, L. (1968). *Lawyers and Statecraft in Renaissance Florence*. Princeton: Princeton University Press.

Mayali, L. (2008). Duo erunt in carne una and the Medieval Canonists. In V. Colli & E. Conte (Eds.), *Iuris Historia: Liber Amicorum Gero Dolezalek* (pp. 161–175). Berkeley: Robbins Collection.

Morelli, G. (1956). *Ricordi*, ed. Vittore Branca. Firenze: Le Monnier.

Pluss, J. A. (1984). Baldus de Ubaldis of Perugia on Dominium over Dotal Property. *Tijdschrift voor Rechtsgeschiedenis, 52*, 399–411.

Signori, G. (2012). Similitude, égalité et réciprocité: l'économie matrimoniale dans les sociétés urbaines de l'Empire à la fin du Moyen Âge. *Annales: Histoires, Sciences Sociales, 67*, 657–678.

Tanzini, L. (2004). *Statuti e legislazione a Firenze dal 1355 al 1415: Lo statuto cittadino del 1409* (pp. 280–310). Firenze: Olschki.

The English Law of Marriage and the Family (1500–1640)

R.H. Helmholz

Abstract This paper provides a survey of English matrimonial law and practice between 1500 and 1640. Throughout this period, the English church retained its hold on this aspect of human life. The Reformation did not lead to eclipse of the canon law or the end of ecclesiastical jurisdiction over marriage and divorce, as happened in Scotland and in parts of Germany. That jurisdiction included a criminal side—prosecution of lay men and women who had offended against principles of Christian morality—as well as a civil side—disputes over the validity of marriage contracts and impediments to existing marriages. Based on the surviving records of the ecclesiastical courts, the chapter shows how practice was touched by both stability and change during this period. The former predominated. Most important, the Church of England rejected the Council of Trent's decree *Tametsi*. Private exchanges of words of present consent continued to be specifically enforceable as valid marriages. Some tightening of the requirements necessary to prove their legal existence did occur, but no change in the substantive law took place. The church also continued to exercise its ex officio jurisdiction; in fact the courts slightly expanded its scope, punishing some offenses that had been left to the penitential forum during the Middle Ages. Whether this continuity was the result of lawyerly inertia or instead a product of increasing moral seriousness among the English people during these years remains an open question.

1 Introduction

The years between 1500 and 1640 witnessed dramatic events in English religious life. The Protestant Reformation stands at one end of the period. It brought an end to the ties that had linked the English church and the papacy. The English Civil War stands at the other end. It brought abolition of the monarchy and with it suppression of episcopacy and the courts of the church. These dramatic events provide

R.H. Helmholz (✉)
University of Chicago, 1111 E. 60th Street, Chicago, IL 60637, USA
e-mail: dick_helmholz@law.uchicago.edu

M.G. di Renzo Villata (ed.), *Family Law and Society in Europe from the Middle Ages to the Contemporary Era*, Studies in the History of Law and Justice 5,
DOI 10.1007/978-3-319-42289-3_6

necessary background for any history of the period. However, the essay has a more limited goal. It seeks to describe both the legal changes and the continuities that occurred within a particular area of English life: regulation of marriage and family life. It assesses the formal developments that took place and explores what the law meant to the men and women who came into contact with the law. The principal sources upon which it is based are the formal records of the ecclesiastical courts and other documents compiled by the men whose careers were spent in them.[1] These sources have been studied with care in recent years, and with good results. Among other things, they improve our understanding of the history of family life.

2 Jurisdiction and the Law of Marriage and Divorce

During the Middle Ages, the church held jurisdiction over enforcement of the law of marriage and divorce in England. The church also regulated several other aspects of family life, and it held onto its jurisdiction throughout the period covered by this essay, maintaining its hold despite criticism of its courts and occasional attempts to rein in its jurisdiction. With few exceptions, the royal courts in England made no effort to gain control of these aspects of human life.[2] The conflicts that occurred—and there were some—mostly concerned how far the temporal law should enter into collateral matters relating to regulation of family life.[3] Defining illegitimacy of birth was the textbook example. Who counted as an illegitimate child was long contested. The subject was related to the definition of marriage. That much was admitted by all. But it also had temporal consequences in the law of succession. Illegitimacy precluded inheritance. In this situation each court system simply went its own way. When a conflict arose, secular and spiritual courts simply defined illegitimacy as they saw fit. There was disagreement, no doubt, but it was one each

[1]Citations of cases and court records below are given by diocese or archdeaconry in the notes; the manuscript records so identified are found in the following archive repositories:
Canterbury—Cathedral Library and Archives, Canterbury; York—Borthwick Institute of Historical Research, York; Bath & Wells—Somerset Record Office, Taunton; Berkshire (archdeaconry)—Berkshire Record Office, Reading; Buckingham (archdeaconry)—Buckinghamshire Record Office, Aylesbury; Chester—Cheshire Record Office, Chester; Durham—Durham University Library; Ely—Cambridge University Library; Exeter—Devonshire Record Office, Exeter; Hereford—Herefordshire Record Office, Hereford; Essex (archdeaconry)—Essex Record Office, Chelmsford; Gloucester—Gloucestershire Record Office, Gloucester; London—London Metropolitan Archives, London; Salisbury—Wiltshire Record Office, Trowbridge; Winchester—Hampshire Record Office, Winchester; Worcester—Worcestershire Record Office, The Hive, Worcester.

[2]The major exception was the regime of the Interregnum; it instituted civil registration of marriage in 1653. See Firth, C. H. and Rait, R. S. (eds). 1911. *Acts and Ordinances of the Interregnum 1642–1660*. London: Stationary Office, ii, pp. 715–18. However, this change was swept aside in 1660.

[3]See Stone, Lawrence. 1992. *Uncertain Unions: Marriage in England 1660–1753*. Oxford: Oxford University Press, p. 31.

side could tolerate in practice. So it continued when the ecclesiastical courts were restored after 1660. Not until 1857 did the Matrimonial Causes Act bring ecclesiastical jurisdiction over marriage disputes to a close by transferring jurisdiction to the temporal forum.[4]

How did the church manage to hold onto this jurisdiction for so long? One examination of this question concluded that the longevity is best explained by a widespread acceptance among the people affected by it. The English people, the scholar concluded, "did not complain, because the church's marriage law worked for them."[5] This view may concede more power to public opinion than is likely under the circumstances. Formally at least, the retention of the English Church's medieval jurisdiction was secured by a combination of other factors—the enactment of a Parliamentary statute in the 1530s preserving the status quo,[6] the repeated failure of attempts at reform,[7] and the weight of inertia characteristic of lawyers.[8]

In a broader sense, however, there is surely real merit to the favorable view. The medieval canon law itself left room for local custom, even in questions involving the formation of marriage, and this would have softened resistance to ecclesiastical control among the people. Their opinions could count in marriage cases when the necessity of avoiding scandal among the people arose,[9] and their opinions were also one means of determining whether specific actions of a couple had amounted to consent to a marriage.[10] Under customary assumptions, for instance, the exchange of gifts between a man and woman was incompatible with anything but an intent to marry, and evidence about such exchanges appears in the formal records as a means of proving a marriage.[11] Similarly, "handfasting" in contracting marriage was customarily done with the right hand; where the woman had first used her left hand, it was argued in one London cause, she could not have done so *integro animo spondendi*.[12] Hence she had given no real consent. Under the canon law, custom

[4]20 & 21 Vict. c. 85.

[5]Carlson, Eric Josef. 1994. *Marriage and the English Reformation*. Oxford and Cambridge, MA: Blackwell Publishers, p. 141.

[6]25 Hen. VIII, c. 19 § 7.

[7]Most notably the failure of the ambitious *Reformatio Legum Ecclesiasticrum* to achieve statutory recognition. See Bray, Gerald. 2000. *Tudor Church Reform: the Henrician Canons of 1535 and the Reformatio Legum Ecclesiasticarum*, Church of England Record Society, Vol. 8, pp. 150–743.

[8]See the letter of Archbishop Matthew Parker (1569), In Bruce, John and Perowne, Thomas (ed). 1853. *Correspondence of Matthew Parker*. London: Parker Society, pp. 351–52.

[9]See X 4.14.3.

[10]For Continental parallels see the discussion in Lombardi, Daniela. 2008. *Storia del matrimonio: Dal Medioevo a oggi*. Bologna: Mulino, pp. 33–38.

[11]Gilbert c. Greene (ca. 1600), Civilian's Casebook, LMA, MS. 011448, f. 2v: "Donariis igitur, consensu partium, carnali copula assensuque parentis etc. precedentibus iustissime contrahatur matrimonium". *See* also Gottlieb, Beatrice. 1993. *The Family in the Western World from the Black Death to the Industrial Age*. Oxford and New York: Oxford University Press, pp. 79-83.

[12]Lee c. Diggins (ca. 1600), Civilian's Casebook, LMA, MS. 011448, f. 36v.

could not change the definition of marriage, but it could help interpret human behavior for judges required to discern whether one had been contracted.

Moreover, as it was put into practice, the canon law in England left more room for greater active participation by the laity than the formal law allowed. Although the canon law formally prohibited compromise of matrimonial litigation,[13] in practice arbitration and settlement occurred throughout this period. In the medieval court records, Frederik Pedersen uncovered many examples of meetings being held between representatives of the community and the families of the young men and women involved. The meetings were convoked to settle disputes about marriage.[14] No doubt they were normally held "in the shadow of the law." They were intended to explore the issues involved and to seek a just and lawful solution. In most cases, the process was not undertaken to flout the law, but it did take place outside the courts. Probably everyone involved wished to avoid litigation if they could. Going to an ecclesiastical court was thus a last resort, something to be done when initial efforts at settlement had failed. Moreover, it is evident in the records themselves that other secular officials could intervene to sort out matrimonial tangles. When in 1595, for example, Edmund Lowes was cited before an ecclesiastical court in Canterbury for unlawfully living apart from his wife, he answered that he had left her company only after being authorized to do so by an agreement made before the mayor of Maidstone.[15] The mayor cannot have been a canonist, but he must have had the respect of the couple and their families. Evidence like this suggests that the law of the Church was not always applied fully in practice. If so, English men and women may have found the Church's jurisdiction more compatible with their own interests and assumptions than appears on the pages of the Gregorian Decretals.

This continuity of practice mattered. It nonetheless remains true that one basic change did occur during the sixteenth century, one that led to occasional dispute. This was the enactment by Parliamentary legislation of rules to be applied in the ecclesiastical courts. The English Parliament asserted, and in fact exercised, the power to change the canon law applied in practice. In 1540, for instance, Parliament enacted a statute prohibiting dissolution of existing marriages on grounds of pre-contract, a step that would have restricted enforcement of clandestine marriage contracts. The statute was repealed 8 years later,[16] but the precedent had been established. Legislation enacted under King Edward VI abolished laws and canons that prohibited the marriage of the clergy.[17] And several statutes amended the medieval law that defined the prohibited degrees of consanguinity and affinity, their

---

[13]Gl. ord. ad X 1.36.11, v. *sacramentum*.

[14]See Pedersen, Frederik. 2000. *Marriage Disputes in Medieval England*. London and Rio Grande: Hambledon Press, pp. 105–118.

[15]Ex officio c. Lowes (Canterbury 1595), Act book X.8.15, f. 52v: "[F]atetur that by consent ex utraque parte before the mayor of Maydstone he and his wife doe lyve aparte."

[16]32 Hen. VIII, c. 38, repealed by 2 & 3 Edw. VI, c. 23.

[17]2 & 3 Edw. VI, c. 21 (1550).

object being to curtail the scope of those prohibitions.[18] Something more about the fate of the kinship impediments to marriage will be said below, and it should also be noted that the existence of secular legislation by no means precluded new ecclesiastical legislation. Convocation, the official legislative body of the English church, itself enacted statutes regulating marriage and divorce.[19] The new element was that the clergy had to share that law-making power with the Parliament. In cases of direct conflict, the latter normally prevailed. More significant than this potential for conflict and confusion was the fact that most Parliamentary legislation expressly left the jurisdiction of the ecclesiastical courts intact, that is until the fundamental legislation of the nineteenth century.[20] "Savings clauses" were frequent. Thus it was that the ecclesiastical courts kept to most of their old paths. Their matrimonial jurisdiction seems to have been subject to a diminishing demand over time, although much remains to be learned from post-1660 records.[21]

3 The Law and Practice of Marriage and Divorce

The principal features of the substantive law of marriage and divorce did not change markedly as a result of the Reformation. Except at the outer margins, the secular courts did not assume jurisdiction over the matrimonial causes that belonged to the church. The substantive law on the subject was also left largely unchanged. Most famously, whereas the Council of Trent changed the definition of a valid marriage by requiring the presence of the parish priest as a condition for a marriage's validity, the medieval law was retained in England. Couples who had privately exchanged words of present consent could (and did) consider themselves to be lawful man and wife before God. They also continued to have the right to enforce the marriage if they could prove it.[22] Many of the Protestant churches on the Continent moved towards permitting remarriage of the innocent party after securing a divorce *a mensa et thoro* ("from bed and board," a judicial separation). In England the prohibition against it was retained.

These refusals to change had results that appear in the surviving court records. One was that the cause brought to enforce a contract of marriage—usually a

---

[18]25 Hen. VIII, c. 22:4 (1533–34); 28 Hen. VIII, c. 7 (1536); 32 Hen. VIII, c. 38 (1540).

[19]See Canons of 1604, c. 62 (on marriage by banns or license), in Bray, Gerald. 1989. *The Anglican Canons 1529–1947*. London: Church of England Record Society, Vol. 6, pp. 352–353.

[20]The greatest exception was Lord Hardwicke's Marriage Act, 26 Geo. II, c. 33 (1753), and it operated only by indirection to curb the jurisdiction of the courts. *See also* Parker, Stephen. 1990. *Informal Marriage: Cohabitation and the Law, 1750–1989*. New York: St. Martin's Press.

[21]For the current state of knowledge, see Outhwaite, R. B. 2006. *The Rise and Fall of the Ecclesiastical Courts, 1500–1860*. Cambridge: Cambridge University Press, 47–56.

[22]See, *e.g.*, Rame c. Mende (Archdeaconry of Essex 1577), in Hale, William (ed). 1847 repr. 1973. *A Series of Precedents and Proceedings in Criminal Causes, 1475–1640*. Edinburgh: Bratton Publishing, No. 515.

clandestine marriage entered into by *verba de praesenti*—remained the most frequent kind of *causa matrimonialis* that came before the courts throughout the sixteenth and early seventeenth centuries. Most of the same problems also arose. For example, one London marriage was contracted under the stated condition "if God so wills." Was it binding upon the parties? To find out, they went to law. On the one hand, it was said that every human action depends on God's will in some sense, so that no real conditional element would have been added by these words. They should therefore be disregarded and the marriage should stand. On the other hand, it was contended that the requirement of freedom in entering marriage meant that the addition of any condition, at least any honest condition, rendered this contract inoperative in law. The person who used these words cannot have meant to contract an absolutely binding marriage, and since intent was what mattered, he was not bound by them. It was a problem, and it made a contentious case. How could one know whether God in fact willed that the marriage should go ahead? The ensuing debate was recorded in a manuscript report now in the London Metropolitan Archives.[23] The lawyers in it cited the opinions of two Spanish civilians, Didacus Covarrubias (d. 1577) and Tomás Sanchez (d. 1610), as well as some older authorities. Unfortunately, we do not know the outcome. We know only that this example raised a characteristic problem in English litigation. Cases based upon marriages contracted *in verbis dubiis*, as one observer aptly described them, continued to vex the courts, confuse the people, and enrich the ecclesiastical lawyers throughout the post-Reformation years.[24]

This all meant that litigation brought to secure a full divorce, that is a declaration of nullity *a vinculo* remained, if not a rarity, at least a smaller part of English court practice than historians once supposed. There was some greater uncertainty about the impediments to marriage, a subject to be discussed below, and it did lead to litigation. But it did not oust the dominance of the ordinary *causa matrimonialis*. The same can be said of judicial separation. For a time, it looked as though more efforts to secure a divorce *a mensa et thoro* would be brought before the courts. However, there were built-in limits. The numbers might have grown dramatically in numbers had they become a path to remarriage. However, any hopes raised in that direction came to naught. Even innocent parties in successful judicial separations were not permitted to remarry in England. The judges enforced this prohibition. They issued specific mandates prohibiting remarriage, sometimes even requiring that the parties enter into a penal bond not to do so.[25] Reconciliation of a couple after adultery also continued to stand in the way of divorce between them.[26] Somewhat surprisingly, so did mutual adultery. If one spouse committed adultery,

---

[23]Anon., Civilian's Casebook, LMA, MS. 011448, f. 189.

[24]Gilbert c. Greene (c. 1600), *ibid*., f. 1.

[25]See Canons of 1604, cc. 3, 100, 107, in *Anglican Canons*, above note 19, at 190–01, 224–25, 400–07.

[26]Thorsby c. Thorsby (ca. 1600), Civilian's Casebook, LMA, MS. 011448, f. 2v: "Dr Crompton sayd that reconciliatio impedit causam et intentionem divortii."

he or she could secure a divorce *a mensa et thoro*, but if both did, neither could.[27] These had been the medieval rules, and they remained in place. They discouraged litigation.

4 Extent of Matrimonial Litigation

Stability in substantive law did not preclude change in the numbers of cases brought before the courts. In fact, it did take place. A gradual but steady decline in the numbers of matrimonial cases brought before the courts occurred. Whether this was a European-wide phenomenon or not, we do not yet know, but it is likely to have been so, and it certainly was true throughout England.[28] Both in percentage of total cases and in absolute numbers, matrimonial litigation occupied a smaller part of court practice in 1500 than it had in 1300. Martin Ingram, who carried out extensive research on the records of the diocese of Salisbury, concluded that "in the period 1570–1640 the flow of marriage contract cases was… reduced from a fairly low incidence to the merest trickle."[29] The same decline seems to have occurred generally elsewhere in England. Suits brought to enforce marriages entered into by *verba de praesenti* remained the norm, but there were fewer of them.

Probably the decline reflected a gradual and increasing acceptance among the laity of the Church's rules about marriage—more compliance with the church's requirements that the banns be read and more care that solemnization of a marriage occur *in facie ecclesie*. Common disregard for these formalities had long led to uncertainty and consequent litigation brought to establish the fact of a marriage's existence. Greater regard for these formal rules led to a decrease in the frequency of disputes that ended up in the external forum.

However, there were also other factors within court practice that themselves worked to diminish the number of matrimonial disputes before the courts. In day-to-day practice, these suits became harder to win. The evidence from the records demonstrates a growing unwillingness on the part of English ecclesiastical lawyers to enforce doubtful matrimonial contracts, and in this climate of opinion the decline in number of cases brought before the courts resulted. Men and women did not sue to enforce matrimonial contracts when they knew they were unlikely to prevail. In doubtful cases they would have been advised by professional lawyers, who would have told potential litigants how slight their chances of securing a favorable sentence in litigation were.

---

[27]Anon. (ca. 1600), Civilian's Casebook, LMA, MS. 011448, f. 69.

[28]Accord Houlbrooke, Ralph. 1979. *Church Courts and the People during the English Reformation 1520–1570*. Oxford: Oxford University Press, pp. 64–67.

[29]Ingram, Martin. 1987. *Church Courts Sex and the People during the English Reformation.* Oxford: Oxford University Press, p. 192. *See* also Wunderli, Richard. 1981. *London Church Courts and Society on the Eve of the Reformation*. Cambridge, MA: Medieval Academy of America, pp. 118–121.

Several specific changes in English court practice led to this result. The first treating as excommunicate the bystanders (and potential witnesses) who had been present at clandestine marriages. A common objection made against the ecclesiastical courts at the time was that they wielded the sword of excommunication unadvisedly and for trivial causes.[30] Of the justice of this objection, there is scarcely a better example than this practice. It meant a person could be excommunicated for helping a friend by testifying to the truth of what had occurred. The new policy was not implemented uniformly, and so far as one can tell it was not applied to those who had been present at the early stages of matrimonial negotiations. However, it was widely applied in practice. A seventeenth century notebook now in the Suffolk Record Office states the rule as part of then current law.[31] Many prosecutions for having been present at a clandestine marriage are found in the act books.[32]

This was a change from the medieval practice, when disciplinary action was normally taken only against the couple and (if there were one) the cleric who had joined them together in marriage. The witnesses to the union were not troubled. The indirect but inevitable result of the change was to make it harder to prove the existence of marriages. Not only would fear of their own excommunication deter witnesses from coming forward, under the formal canon law the testimony of an excommunicated person could not be admitted as legitimate proof.[33] Without proof, there was no way to enforce a contract of marriage. It is true that the canon law made it possible to absolve such persons temporarily (*ad cautelam*) and thus to allow judges to treat their testimony as valid proof.[34] However, temporary absolution was never a matter of right. The medieval canonists were only enthusiastic about using it as a way of proving the guilt of those they classed as heretics. And at least as it appears in a case recorded in a proctor's notebook now found in the Worcester Record Office, most English courts were unwilling to exercise their discretion in favor of making an exception to the rule excluding the testimony of excommunicates in marriage litigation.[35]

A second cause of the decline in matrimonial litigation was the partial exclusion from the category of lawful proof of extra-judicial confessions made by the parties.

[30]*E.g.*, The Hampton Court Conference (1604), in Cressy, David and Ferrell, Liri Anne (eds). 2005. *Religion & Society in Early Modern England: A Sourcebook* (2d ed). New York and London: Routledge, pp. 147–50.

[31]Ecclesistical Precedent book (ca. 1610), Suffolk Record Office, Bury St. Edmunds, MS. E 14/11/7, No. 20: 'All those that are present at a clandestine marriage are ipso facto excommunicated as well as those that were married."

[32]*E.g.*, Ex officio c. William Danbye, (Gloucester 1600), Act book GDR 86, f. 156: "for being presented at Mr. Birchhis marriadge being solemnized without bannes asking or a lawful dispensacion from the ordinary".

[33]Hostiensis, *Summa aurea*, Lib. II, tit. *de testibus*, no. 2: "[N]on admittitur aliquis, nisi sit fidelis conversationis, (citing X 2.20.23), inde est quod excommunicatus testificari non potest."

[34]X 2.20.38.

[35]Barniston c. Barniston, in Civilian's Notebook Collectanea B (Worcester ca. 1600), MS. 794.093, BA 2470, p. 3.

Informal confessions were given less scope than they seem to have been in medieval practice. One of the parties to a clandestine marriage contract might later have spoken words suggesting that he (or she) had entered into a marriage contract. Could what they said during an unguarded moment be introduced as evidence to prove the existence of the marriage when the same person later denied its truth? This question was not squarely raised in the English common law, where juries were left to give such weight to evidence like this as they thought proper. By contrast, in the civilian's world, there had to be proof by two lawful witnesses or the equivalent. In court tests, the question raised was whether such statements were legally sufficient to prevent the party from later denying the substance of the confession. The evidence—most of it from the notebooks of proctors and advocates—suggests that at least where either of the parties had entered into another marriage contract (as they often did), an extra judicial confession did not count as conclusive evidence.[36] No decision could be based upon its value. An example will illustrate the common situation. In a case from the diocese of Durham the man sent a letter to a woman signed, "Your loving dnabsuh."[37] The word "dnabsuh" spelled backwards is "husband" and the question in the case was whether its use counted as proof of a marriage between them. One might have thought so. What else could it have meant? However, the English ecclesiastical lawyers did not draw that obvious conclusion. In the words of the manuscript, "[T]he counsayle of the *doctores* of the Arches [was] that the marriage was not proved." There was support among contemporary commentators for taking a hard line against according conclusive validity to such evidence,[38] and during the late sixteenth century, the English courts seem to have followed that line.[39]

A third means adopted in English court practice that discouraged bringing suit upon clandestine marriages lay in stricter application of rule that the burden of proof lay upon the party seeking relief. The judges more fully exploited the canonical rule that marriage causes required proof of the clearest kind. Such evidence was not easily uncovered. As an opinion in an early seventeenth century proctor's notebook now in the Cathedral library at Canterbury put it, "because marriage causes are arduous and serious," proof in them must be "clearer than the mid-day sun."[40]

---

[36]Civilian's Casebook, LMA, MS. 011448, f. 38 "Donaria, cohabitatio, prolis susceptio, nominatio probant matrimonium sed non ad dirimendum sequens matrimonium solemnizatum." There is a full consideration of difficulties that stemmed from clandestine marriages, in Matthew Tabor's book, 1627–29, (Bath & Wells ca. 1628), MS. D/D/O, fols. 45–50v.

[37]Clement Colmore's Book (Durham c. 1600), DDR/ XVIII/3, fols. 231–31v.

[38]See Josephus Mascardus, *De praesumptionibus, coniecturis, signis et indiciis commentaria* (Frankfurt 1593), Lib. II, concl. 1029.

[39]Killingworthe c. Harries (ca. 1600), Civilian's Casebook, LMA, MS. 011448, f. 37: opinion that a confession of a contract was not sufficient proof of marriage where the contract itself was not sufficiently proved.

[40]Taken from Precedent book (Canterbury ca. 1600) Z.3.27, fols. 70–74, taken from a suit to establish a marriage: Toby Andrews c. Agnes Bylle, with William Prynne intervening *pro interesse suo*.

Some of the sentences given now seem quite hard—indeed impossible—to justify except on the basis of a failure of exacting standards of proof. The lawyer for a defendant in a marriage case pointed out that one witness testified that his client had said, "I like you", whereas the other witness remembered the words as "I thee like."[41] The difference meant, he argued, that their depositions did not meet the law's basic requirements of valid proof, two reliable witnesses whose testimony agreed in all relevant particulars. For many of English judges in the sixteenth century, that led to an unwillingness to enforce a marriage contract unless proof of its existence was wholly clear.

Such an approach was by no means unauthorized under the traditional canon law. A commonplace of the *ius commune* held that in cases of doubt "it was better to elect the more cautious course."[42] The question was always whether the parties had formed an intent to marry and openly expressed that intent. The surrounding circumstances and the character of the parties could count in deciding the first part of that question.[43] One may also be sympathetic with the English judges in their desire not to force young people into marriage unless they had clearly intended to enter into a lifelong union. The *favor matrimonii* of the canon law was not meant to make it easy to prove the existence of clandestine marriage contracts. There is no denying that one of the by-products of this policy was to create dilemmas of conscience for the parties involved. From a policy perspective, one would conclude that the Council of Trent was helpful in enacting the simpler rule: no parish priest, no valid marriage. Whether it was also doing right is a different question. Not everyone took an "instrumentalist" view of the subject. These conflicting results are apparent in the court records.

5 The Prohibited Degrees of Consanguinity and Affinity

A second substantive change in the English church's marriage law grew out of the reduction in the prohibited degrees of consanguinity and affinity—the medieval rules prohibited marriages between kin too closely related by blood and marriage unless the man and woman secured a papal dispensation. The old law forbade marriages up to the fourth degree, and added a few other prohibitions for good measure. A desire to abridge and simplify these prohibitions was shared by many of the Protestant reformers in England. They particularly desired to end the trafficking

[41]Green c. Pashal (c. 1600), Civilian's Casebook, Bodl. Tanner MS. 427, f. 202v.

[42]Gilbert c. Greene (London ca. 1605), Civilian's Casebook, LMA, MS. 011448, f. 1.

[43]Other examples: Smart c. Rowe (1602), Civilian's Casebook, Bodl. Tanner MS. 427, f. 212 (marriage contract, although proved, held not to bind because made *iocose*); Curson c. Jaxson (1601), ibid. fols. 188v–89 (marriage contract, although admitted, attacked as invalid because one of the parties was of "very weak and simple witte not understanding what a contract meanithe"); Zinzan c. Skelley (c. 1627), Bodl. Tanner MS. 176, f. 168 (marriage contract attacked as having been made while one party was drunk).

in dispensations to which the old system had led. An Henrician statute, repealed under Queen Mary but revived under Queen Elizabeth, therefore enacted that all voluntary marriages were lawful unless they were forbidden by the law of God or the Book of Leviticus.[44] It was a bold and in some ways a quite admirable step. The change promised an end to dispensations and the necessity of paying for them. Some scholars think otherwise, but it requires some explaining to show that there is nothing wrong with declaring a marriage to be contrary to the tenets of the Christian religion but then upholding it as a valid and indissoluble union if the parties are willing (and able) to pay money for it. Under the new regime, that system was expected to disappear.

To some extent, this laudable aim was achieved. A few dispensations permitting marriages within the prohibited degrees were issued by the individual bishops or by the Faculty Office in London, but there were very few.[45] Perhaps it was thought that the authority to issue them at all had disappeared along with papal jurisdiction. However, there was also an unfortunate result. The law of unintended consequences applied here, since the result of the change was to render English ecclesiastical law quite uncertain about what marriages between kin were unlawful. The "Trees (*Arbores*) of consanguinity and affinity" familiar in the medieval law had been cast out, but what would take their place? No one knew for sure. The "law of God" on this subject lacked a clear meaning and the proscriptions in the Book of Leviticus were incomplete at best. It became difficult to know who could marry whom when anything but the closest ties of kinship existed between a man and woman. The absence of a system of dispensation only exacerbated the difficulty.

Remedial measures were taken. Most notably, a Table of the Prohibited Degrees was issued by Archbishop Parker in 1564.[46] The Table helped. It did make some things clear, but it left others uncertain. It was also not treated as a complete statement of the English church's law on the subject. In one doubtful case, the couple in question were instructed to "consult men learned in the law; to understand what is lawful, what honest and expedient." This could certainly be done in practice, but what standards were they to use in providing an answer? No clear answer was forthcoming. One supposes they might even have consulted an *arbor consanguinitatis* if they wished. Certainly some hard cases arose in fact. They have left traces in the act books and other professional literature of the time, and they reflect widespread uncertainty among the laity whose marriages were affected by the law.

One example comes from a manuscript that once was part of a collection in the Berkshire Record Office.[47] The question in it was whether it was lawful for a man to

---

[44] 32 Hen. 8 c. 38 (1540); 1 Eliz. 1, c. 1 § 3 (1559).

[45] See Wilfrid Hooper. 1910. The Court of Faculties. *English Historical Review* 25: 670–86.

[46] Cardwell, Edward. 1844. *Documentary Annals of the Reformed Church of England*. Oxford: Oxford University Press, i, pp. 316–20.

[47] It was Trumbull MS. (1588–1617), D/ED O 48, p. 155. It has now gone either to the Cambridge University Library or the British Library.

marry the aunt of his deceased wife. Under the medieval law, they would have been related in the second and third degree of affinity so that their union would clearly have been unlawful. However, the relationship was not listed in the Book of Leviticus or even in Archbishop Parker's Table. As just noted, that omission alone was not determinative. The question remained. Was such a marriage contrary to God's law? It was not easy to know, and it is no wonder that contemporaries were themselves perplexed. The families may have had other reasons for favoring or opposing the match, but validity depended on the law. Ultimately, two eminent civilians, Sir Julius Caesar and Dr. John Hammond, were consulted. They concluded that the marriage was lawful. How they reached this opinion, however, the Notebook does not provide even a hint. Nor does other civilian literature from the time help very much; unhappily, Henry Swinburne (d. 1624) did not deal with this question in his work on the English law of marriage.[48] Only the existence of a strong movement towards diminishing the scope of the prohibited degrees, a direction also taken (more timidly) by the Council of Trent,[49] is at all certain. From the perspective of the couple involved in the Trumbull Notebook's case, the opinion of counsel found in it may have been the cause for relief, perhaps even for joy. They could be married, and one hopes, live happily together. On the other hand, an opinion of counsel, at least counsel like Sir Julius Caesar, did not come cheap. The couple, or their parents, would have had to pay for it. My own guess—and it is no more than a guess—is that it would have been no less expensive than a papal dispensation.

In an additional sense, the new regime did not fully end the need for dispensations. Marriages begun without calling of the banns and marriages conducted during the prohibited seasons of Lent and Advent required licenses from the Office of Faculties, and these licenses had to be purchased. Without them, men and women who married would be subject to prosecution in the spiritual forum. The records show this happening with some frequency.[50] No doubt a 1640 petition from Kent was exaggerating when it claimed that "almost halfe the yere" had become a forbidden season for marriage.[51] No doubt the drafters were also exaggerating when they claimed the English bishops had "made and contrived illegal canons and constitutions [to] prohibite and grant marriages, neither of them by the rule of Law or Conscience."[52] No doubt there is also some justice in King James I's description of the petitioners as men "whose heat tendeth rather to combustion than

[48]Henry Swinburne (d. 1624), *Treatise of Spousals or Matrimonial Contracts* (London 1686).

[49]Sess. 24, De Reform. cc. 2–4, in Tanner, Norman (ed). 1990. *Decrees of the Ecumenical Councils*. Washington DC: Georgetown University Press, ii, p. 757.

[50]E.g., Ex officio c. Longe and Knowles (Buckingham 1600), Act book D/A C 25, f. 166: "for being married upon Shrove Monday last without licence being time prohibited".

[51]Kent Petition against Episcopacy (No. 20), in Larking, Lambert B. (ed). 1862. *Proceedings, principally in the county of Kent, in Connection with the Parliaments called in 1640*. (Camden Society, 1st ser. Vol. 80, p. 35. An earlier example from 1580 is noted (Art. 13), in Strype, John. 1822. *Life and Acts of John Whitgift*. Oxford: Oxford University Press.

[52]"Kent Petition," prior note, at p. 30.

reformation."[53] However, the drafters of these petitions were not wholly wrong. Money was changing hands for securing permission to marry. There was something more than religious idealism or simple anti-clericalism standing behind the decision taken in 1653 to replace the law of the church with a regime of purely civil marriages.[54] It is ironic that this forward looking step scarcely mattered after 1660. In that year the old regime was brought back. The demand for dispensations returned.

6 Regulation of Domestic Life

The jurisdiction related to domestic relations held by the courts of the English church always extended beyond matrimonial causes strictly defined. It dealt with offenses against morality. It encompassed efforts to promote harmony within families. It included regulation of relations between spouses and also between children and their parents. It extended even to aspects of property held within a family. In other words, the courts of the church sought to promote what we would call "family values" by entering into the lives of individual families. This happened in several different ways. They led to an expansion in the numbers and kinds of ex officio cases that were brought before the ecclesiastical courts in the years between 1500 and 1640.

7 Offenses Against Morality

One instance of expansion of the coverage of offences against morality in the ecclesiastical courts was the prosecution of newly married couples for having had sexual relations before marriage. The medieval courts had rarely taken any notice of this offense. They reversed course, however. Many prosecutions for "pre-matrimonial" fornication are found in the surviving act books of the sixteenth and seventeenth centuries.[55] There is an interesting account of this new offense in a

---

[53]No. 30, in Larkin, James and Hughes, Paul (eds). 1973. *Stuart Royal Proclamations.* Oxford: Oxford University Press, i, p. 62.

[54]The point is well made by Eales, Jacqueline. 1996. A Road to Revolution: The Continuity of Puritanism, 1559–1642. In *The Culture of English Puritanism, 1560–1700,* Christopher Durston and J. Eales (eds). New York: St. Martin's Press, pp. 215–16.

[55]*E.g.*, Ex officio c. John Gortlie (Berkshire 1599), Act book D/A 2/c 42, f. 56v: the defendant admitted that he and his wife "being man and wife between themselves he had carnal knowledge of her body about half a year before he was openly married unto her in the church." He was assigned public penance upon this confession; Ex officio c. John Bennett (Gloucester 1639), Act book GDR 203, s.d. 22 November: "for incontinency with his wife before marriage she being delivered within 2 days after her marriage."

civilian's notebook from about 1660 now preserved at the Borthwick Institute in York. Two proctors pointed out that there was little textual support for the practice in the ecclesiastical law; in fact the *glossa ordinaria* to the Gregorian Decretals stated: "Matrimony purges all that has gone before."[56] The objection was met by saying that this was the common practice, and therefore one easily dislodged, for the prosecution of the offence to be undertaken in the English courts. It was also contended that in this practice the English courts were actually following the common law, which since the council of Merton in 1234 had accorded less force to subsequent marriage than did the *ius commune*. In other words, if there were any illegality involved, the English common law was the culprit. A more overtly spiritual defense of the practice, however, is contained in a manuscript now in Worcester, where the author described pre-nuptial intercourse as a "secrete poyson which lurkes within marriage" and leads to the encouragement of adultery.[57] Opinions differed. Practice was later returned to its medieval pattern, but only by virtue of a statute that Parliament enacted in 1787.[58]

A second example of the increase in regulation was the rise of an offense for "soliciting the chastity" of a maiden. It began to figure for the first time in the pages of the church's ex officio act books during the second half of the sixteenth century. That the development was encouraged in any sense by Pope Pius IV's decree of 1561 against clerical solicitation of women, one cannot confidently assert, though it is possible.[59] The language used in the act book prosecutions was designedly archaic—"Thou, Roger Bowyer, at the instigation of the devil, didst attempt to violate the chastity and didst by divers and sundry ways and means attempt to have carnal knowledge of the body of the said Anna."[60] A modern reader cannot avoid being reminded of the modern offense of sexual harassment in reading some of the act book entries. There is unlikely to be any causal link between the two. All the same, the coincidence is thought-provoking, because the substance of the legal wrong was not greatly different. In a sense, it was also connected with the English church's jurisdiction over defamation, for one result of the unwelcome solicitation of a young girl's chastity was to injure her chances of making the match she desired.

A third example is that the offense of harboring sexual offenders was expanded to encompass the harboring of pregnant women about to give birth to an illegitimate child. In other words, the jurisdiction of the ecclesiastical tribunals was expanded to

---

[56]See Prec.Bk.11, f. 31, and *gl. ord.* ad X 4.17.6s.v. legitimi: "[M]atrimonium omnia praecedentia purgat."

[57]Civilian's Notebook Collectanea B (Worcester ca. 1600), MS. 794.093, BA 2470, p. 179.

[58]27 Geo. III, c. 44 § 2.

[59]See Haliczer, Stephan. 1996. *Sexuality in the Confessional.* New York and Oxford: Oxford University Press, pp. 42–45.

[60]Precedent book (Ely ca. 1600), MS. EDR F/5/43, f. 67.

make unlawful the *result* of illicit sexual relations, not just the sexual relations themselves. It also encompassed those who aided the offending couple.[61] Householders were required to see to it that women about to give birth to an illegitimate child were turned out and punished. Surviving post-Reformation records from English dioceses contain prosecutions for failures on the part of householders in this circumstance; whereas the surviving medieval act books by and large do not. Some of the stories are quite sad—women about to give birth being turned out into the night. No doubt this development was connected with the sixteenth century mania about illegitimate children and also has something to do with the parish's responsibilities for them under the English Poor laws.[62] However, it was not limited to those concerns, since there were prosecutions begun in which the child was dead at the time of the prosecution or in which the mother and child had fled to a place far away.

A fourth example was expansion of ecclesiastical jurisdiction to provide a remedy for jactitation of marriage. Jactitation meant boasting falsely that one person (the defendant) had entered into a marriage contract with another (the plaintiff). It was an expansion only; a few similar cases are to be found in the medieval act books, and the subject was already in place in at least some courts on the Continent.[63] It was a change nonetheless—a large increase in the incidence of prosecution. Why so many more brought were in England during the early modern period is not easy to say. They were a source of discord and legal uncertainty. If successful, defendants were ordered to keep "perpetual silence" and never to repeat the prior boast.[64] The theory was that the boasting was a legal wrong because it damaged the reputation and hindered the marriage prospects of the plaintiff.[65] It raised a controversial question among the advocates early in the seventeenth century—Whether a person sued in jactitation could bring a separate action to enforce the marriage contract, or was limited to pleading it in response to the *causa jactitationis*?[66] There was potential overlap, no doubt, but the two remedies seem both to have continued alongside each other in court practice. The wider question of the subsequent history of this remedy remains to be investigated.

[61]For medieval practice, see Poos, L.R.. 2001. *Lower Ecclesiastical Jurisdiction in late-medieval England*. Oxford: Oxford University Press, Index, v. harboring, fostering, enabling illicit sexual activity.

[62]The legislation on the subject for the period covered by this essay is usefully reviewed in Eden, F. M. 1929. *The State of the Poor* (A. G. L. Rogers ed). New York: Dutton, pp. 1–28.

[63]See Donahue, Charles Jr. 2007. *Law, Marriage, and Society in the Later Middle Ages*. Cambridge: Cambridge University Press, p. 308.

[64]See Ingram, *Church Courts*, above note 29, at 59–60.

[65]Conset, Henry. 1685. *Practice of the Spiritual or Ecclesiastical Courts*. London: T. Basset, Pt. 6, ch. 1, no. 3.

[66]Discussion of the controversial point is contained in "Proctor's Summary of Procedural Law" (Salisbury ca. 1600), MS. D 5/24/18, fols. 34–34v.

8 Regulation of Life Within the Family

The courts of the English church sought to secure harmony within individual families and respect for traditional family values. The canon law itself encouraged, if it did not require, some entry into the private life of individual households. Texts in Gratian's *Decretum* provided an adequate basis for it. Children were duty bound to honor their parents (Dist. 30 c. 1). Parents were also required to nurture and support their offspring (C. 16 q. 1 c. 64). Husbands and wives were to show respect towards one another (Dist. 31 c. 11). The coming of sixteenth century did not bring an end to general acceptance of these commonplace ideals of domestic life. Far from it. Some scholars have concluded that they actually intensified during the years covered by this essay. The relevant evidence from English court records is not thick enough to establish any firm conclusions about such large and disputed questions, but certainly it is sufficient to show that these were more than merely pious admonitions. Regular concern for the protection of family values was undertaken by the courts of the church. This was not all a recent development. The medieval records show similar concerns. Moreover, some of it was also the shared concern of the temporal courts of the sixteenth and seventeenth centuries. On this subject the two court systems overlapped in making a common effort at social control.

One example of that concern was the enforcement of parental duties to nurture and support their children. Based upon a principle of natural law (Dig. 1.1.3), the obligation extended even to illegitimate children. So, for example, the judge of the court of the Dean and Chapter of York Minster ordered a man from Ulleskelf to provide 3d. weekly to provide for the child born to a single woman as part of the prosecution brought against him for fathering a child by her.[67] He was given a choice, however. He could marry her instead. Which alternative he chose we do not know. One hopes that the wishes of the woman figured in his decision. In either case, the father could not ignore the child. Similar orders were made (without a similar choice) when the parents lived apart, as where they had been divorced *a mensa et thoro*. The obligation of support came before the English ecclesiastical courts regularly enough to have been given a specific name—the *causa alimentationis prolis*. For a time during the Middle Ages, this support obligation had extended even to the consequences of a father's death. It required him to leave a part of his property (usually a third or a fourth) for his children, even if they were adults—the so called *legitima pars*. However, by the late sixteenth century, what had once been an obligation had been reduced to the status of a local custom. It was enforced in the North of England and in a few parts of the South as well. In most of England, however, it had been displaced in favor of a regime of freedom of testation.[68]

[67]Ex officio c. Bedell (York 1523), Act book D/C/AB.2, f. 326.

[68]The history of this subject was lucidly discussed by Maitland; see Pollock, F. and Maitland, F. W. 1998. *History of English Law* (2d ed. reissued). Cambridge: Cambridge University Press,

A second example of the care for family values that is found regularly in the records of the ecclesiastical courts might be described as the reverse side of the parental duty to support their children. It was the duty of the children to respect their parents. This too was considered a requirement founded upon natural law, and it was expressed in concrete form in court proceedings brought against the children themselves. We rarely know how the cases came to the attention of the judges. The records do not say.[69] We do see the results. Some tracked the language of the canon law's prohibition against assaults upon clerics (C. 17 q. 4 c. 29); so, for example, the court of the archdeacon of Rochester prosecuted Elena Horsley in 1529 because she had "laid violent hands" upon her mother. Others entries were fuller; a daughter at Winchester in 1527 was disciplined because she "called her mother a whore."[70] Two children in Chester were prosecuted in 1635 "for violating the laws of God and nature in abusing their father, an aged and impotent man, withholding food and lodging from him and suffering him [to starve and die]."[71] The normal remedy allotted to the children in such cases was some sort of public penance, including an apology to the parent. For example, a daughter who had abused her father "in hard speeches" was required to appear in her parish church and "to ask her father's forgiveness before the minister and others of the parishioners."[72] Monetary fines or corporal punishments were not imposed for these offences in English ecclesiastical court practice. Only such spiritual sanctions were. Their effectiveness are difficult to assess, but the motivation behind them is clear.

A third example of regular efforts in familial regulation was the attempt to secure peace between husbands and wives.[73] Divorce *a mensa et thoro* was a last resort, and in a society with a very restricted right to divorces annulling existing unions, perhaps formal efforts to secure marital harmony were desirable. So we find prosecutions against husbands who were said to have beaten their wives,[74] and equally (but slightly less frequently) cases in which wives were required give a formal undertaking that they would receive their husbands and to treat them "honestly" in the future.[75] Orders like these must have seemed necessary even if the

(Footnote 68 continued)

pp. 349–56. See also the evidence presented in Helmholz, R. H. 1984. Legitim in English Legal History. *University of Illinois Law Review* 659–74.

[69]See, however, the discussion of possibilities in Quaife, G. R. 1979. *Wanton Wenches and Wayward Wives: Parents and Illicit Sex in early seventeenth century England.* New Brunswick, NJ: Rutgers University Press, pp. 48–56.

[70]Ex officio c. Love (Winchester 1529), Act book B/1/A 4, f. 117v: "vocavit matrem suam meretricem".

[71]Ex offico c. Ditchfield (Chester 1635), Act book EDC/1/52, s.d. 17 January.

[72]Ex offico c. Gyles (Oxford 1598), Act book MS. Oxf. Dioc. Papers d.6, f. 46v.

[73]Hanawalt, Barbara. 1986. *The Ties that Bound.* New York and Oxford: Oxford University Press, pp. 206–26.

[74]Ex officio c. Fisher (Ely 1600), Act book B/2/21, f. 118v.

[75]Ex officio c. Higons (Winchester 1518), Act book B/1/A 1, f. 73: "Dominus monuit quod recipiat maritum quando venerit in domum suam et honeste eum tractabit."

chances of their being fully obeyed were uncertain. The English courts sometimes ordered husbands and wives who had been living part, apparently by choice, to live together in harmony,[76] but there were limits to what could actually be accomplished by such orders. Two people who have come to hate each other cannot be forced to share the same bed and table for very long, no matter what the formal law may say. The judges of the ecclesiastical courts recognized this fact of life. Their response—a change from medieval practice—was tacitly to permit the separation to continue, but to provide that an alimony payment be made from husband to the separated wife. The otherwise notorious courts of High Commission led the way in taking this sensible step forward in dealing with one of the most difficult areas of family law.[77]

A fourth example of regular entry by the ecclesiastical courts into family life was the effort they made during this period to compel masters of households to secure proper order among their children and servants. This was something new. Men at least nominally in charge of households were brought before the courts charged with having allowed "misrule" within them. Normally this meant having allowed some type of sexual license by occupants of the house. For instance, in 1588 a London householder was prosecuted for having "kept evil rule in [his] house by receiving of incontinent persons suspected of bawdry."[78] Taking pregnant women into a house, even for the sake of charity, and allowing them to depart unpunished after having given birth was also a frequent entry in court books of the sixteenth and seventeenth centuries.[79] However, the obligations of the master of a household did not end there. Masters were required to see to it that members of the household obeyed the precepts of religion and decorum. The act books contain prosecutions for having "suffered people to drink, wrangle, and talk" on Sundays, for having permitted drinking and card playing within their house at time of divine services, and for having allowed his servants to work on holy days.[80] At least in their intention, the judges of the English courts had high ambitions. They sought to secure the observance of clear moral rules even inside the family circle.

[76]E.g., Ex officio c. Langrigg (Carlisle 1608), Act book DRC 5/1, s.d. 1 July: "for not keeping house together with his wife."

[77]E.g., Moore c. Moore (Exeter 1629), Chanter MS. 57, f. 5 (an award of the right to live in the marital house and possession of four cows, a horse for field work, and fourteen sheep); Ex officio c. Ellis (York 1612), MS. HC.AB.16, f. 13 (five shillings a week for a restricted period). A formulary from the 1630s now in the University of Nottingham Library contains standards for making such alimony awards; see MS. A 43.

[78]Ex officio c. Darry (London 1587), MS. 9064/13, f. 12v.

[79]E.g., Ex officio c. Jamesdon (Chester 1598), Act book EDV 1/12a, f. 83v: "[He] harbored a woman incontinent and suffered her to escape unpunished the childe being not baptized." In Ex officio c. White (Berkshire Archdeaconry 1583), Act book D/A 2/c.20, f. 23, the defendant answered the charge by saying that he had been "moved with pitie" and the woman "had noe friends to help her" so that he had been afraid she would leave the child to die upon its birth. He was dismissed with a warning.

[80]Ex officio c. Bowker (Chester 1619), Act book EDV 1/21, f. 20v; Ex officio c. Younger (Durham 1600), Act book DDR VIII/1, f. 40; Ex officio c. Blomefield (Archdeaconry of Essex 1638), Act book D/ABA 9, f. 5.

9 Conclusion

Prosecutions like these for offences against morality and judicial efforts to regulate life within households expressed common assumptions of the times. They were not merely medieval hold-overs, although like the law of marriage and divorce itself, they did continue in paths laid out in the Middle Ages. They were also part of a joint effort with the temporal law. The English Poor Laws encouraged the same kind of entry into what today may seem like purely private matters, and throughout England Justices of the Peace and local courts exercised a concurrent disciplinary jurisdiction in some of the areas entered first by the church. In time, these secular efforts would eclipse ecclesiastical jurisdiction, but that had not occurred by 1640. In the years between 1500 and then the role in the regulation of English domestic life exercised by the church was consequential in many ways.

References

Bray, G. (1989). *The Anglican Canons 1529–1947* (Vol. 6). London: Church of England Record Society.

Bray, G. (2000). *Tudor church reform: The Henrician Canons of 1535 and the Reformatio Legum Ecclesiasticarum* (Vol. 8). London: Church of England Record Society.

Cardwell, E. (1844). *Documentary annals of the reformed church of England*. Oxford: Oxford University Press.

Carlson, Eric Josef. (1994). *Marriage and the English reformation*. Oxford and Cambridge, MA: Blackwell Publishing.

Conset, H. (1685). *Practice of the spiritual or Ecclesiastical Courts*. London: T. Basset.

Cressy, D., & Ferrell, L. A. (Eds.). (2005). *Religion & society in early modern England: A sourcebook* (2d ed.). New York and London: Routledge.

Donahue, Charles Jr. (2007). *Law, marriage, and society in the later middle ages*. Cambridge: Cambridge University Press.

Eales, J. (1996). A road to revolution: The continuity of puritanism, 1559–1642. In C. Durston, & J. Eales (Eds.), *The Culture of English Puritanism, 1560–1700*. New York: St. Martin's Press.

Gottlieb, B. (1993). *The family in the western world from the black death to the industrial age*. Oxford and New York: Oxford University Press.

Hale, W. (Ed.). (1847). *A series of precedents and proceedings in criminal causes, 1475–1640*. Edinburgh: Bratton Publishing. repr. 1973.

Haliczer, S. (1996). *Sexuality in the confessional*. New York and Oxford: Oxford University Press.

Hanawalt, B. (1986). *The ties that bound*. New York and Oxford: Oxford University Press.

Helmholz, R. H. (2004). *Oxford history of the laws of England, volume I: The Canon law and Ecclesiastical jurisdiction from 597 to the 1640s*. Oxford: Oxford University Press.

Houlbrooke, R. (1979). *Church courts and the people during the English reformation 1520-1570*. Oxford: Oxford University Press.

Ingram, M. (1987). *Church courts, sex and marriage in England, 1570–1640*. Cambridge: Cambridge University Press

Larkin, J., & Hughes, P. (Eds.). (1973). *Stuart royal proclamations*. Oxford: Oxford University Press.

Lombardi, D. (2008). *Storia del matrimonio: Dal Medioevo a oggi*. Bologna: Il Mulino.

Mascardus, J. (1593). *De praesumptionibus coniecturis signis et indiciis commentaria*. Frankfurt: Sigismund Feyrabendius.

Outhwaite, R. B. (2006). *The rise and fall of the Ecclesiastical Courts, 1500–1860*. Cambridge: Cambridge University Press.

Parker, S. (1990). *Informal marriage: Cohabitation and the law, 1750–1989*. New York: St. Martin's Press.

Pedersen, F. (2000). *Marriage disputes in medieval England*. London and Rio Grande, OH: Hambledon Press.

Pollock, F., & Maitland, F. W. (1998). History of English Law. 2nd ed. 1898, reissued. Cambridge: Cambridge University Press.

Poos, L. R. (2001). *Lower ecclesiastical jurisdiction in late-medieval England*. Oxford: Oxford University Press.

Quaife, G. R. (1979). *Wanton Wenches and Wayward Wives: Parents and illicit sex in early seventeenth century England*. New Brunswick, NJ: Rutgers University Press.

Seidel Menchi, S., & Quaglioni, D. (Eds.). (2006). I tribunali del matrimonio (secoli XV–XVIII). Bologna: Il Mulino.

Stone, L. (1992). *Uncertain unions: Marriage in England 1660–1753*. Oxford: Oxford University Press.

Strype, J. (1822). *Life and acts of John Whitgift*. Oxford: Oxford University Press.

Swinburne, H. (1686). *Treatise of spousals or matrimonial contracts*. London: S. Roycroft.

Tanner, N. (Ed.). (1990). *Decrees of the ecumenical councils*. Washington DC: Georgetown University Press.

Wunderli, R. (1981). *London Church Courts and society on the eve of the reformation*. Cambridge, MA: Medieval Academy of America.

Towards a New Era of Modernity? Late Scholastic Speculation on Bigamy and Polygamy

Stefania T. Salvi

Abstract By the 16th century, canon law had long established a regulatory structure for the institution of marriage. Likewise, jurisprudence had developed a solid doctrinal system to deal with the numerous legal issues that marriage presented. Thus, it should come as no surprise that late Scholasticism offered very little in terms of totally new solutions to the most relevant problem areas. Nonetheless, the late Scholastic contribution to the specific area of family law was anything but trivial, not only because of its influence on the practice of law during that time, but also because of its importance in the history of legal thought. From this point of view, the jurists/theologians of the *siglo de oro* left a fundamental legacy to the subsequent doctrines of natural law and the Enlightenment through the methodology they employed. The aim of this article is to provide an initial account of how exponents of the *siglo de oro* examined the complex issue of bigamy (more correctly, polygamy), which was of enormous practical impact in an era that was characterized by a high number of secret marriages. As innovators of Thomistic thought during the Counter-Reformation, they reflected on the problematic contrast between *pluralitas uxorum* and the natural ends of marriage. While they primarily relied on biblical texts and the word of Saint Thomas Aquinas, to a lesser extent they also considered the *auctoritates* of the *ius commune*. Though there were some differences of opinion to be found among the various authors, late Scholastic speculation on this issue generally came to defend the traditional stances of the Church. As such, it was not the formulation of particularly original solutions that characterized this period, but rather the skill and insight that thinkers exhibited in philosophizing on what was rationally justifiable and in discussing the pros and cons of the issue.

S.T. Salvi (✉)
University of Milan, Via Festa del Perdono 7, 20122 Milan, Italy
e-mail: stefania.salvi@unimi.it

M.G. di Renzo Villata (ed.), *Family Law and Society in Europe from the Middle Ages to the Contemporary Era*, Studies in the History of Law and Justice 5,
DOI 10.1007/978-3-319-42289-3_7

1 Preliminary Remarks. Marriage and Bigamy in the Sixteenth Century

The sixteenth century was a troubled period for the institution of marriage, a battlefield of legal and theological reflections with various overtones.[1]

Different sides raised voices of criticism against the marriage rules of the time, which had been the Church's exclusive prerogative for centuries. The Church was struck with the unsettling phenomena of the Protestant Reformation[2] and the subsequent Counter-Reformation, fraught with consequences and leading to the important changes set forth in the measures taken by the Council of Trent.[3]

Until the end of the fifteenth century, marriage was essentially a private act that was not always announced publicly. Though there were provisions in ecclesiastical law that aimed to include its public announcement in the definition of marriage,[4] there was no binding provision whatsoever in marriage law that dictated a particular

---

[1]There are countless examples of historiographical studies on this topic. Recent work includes: Melchior-Bonnet, Sabine and Salles, Catherine (Eds.). 2009. *Histoire du marriage*. Paris: Éditions Robert Laffont, 433–624; di Renzo Villata, Maria Gigliola. 2010. Il matrimonio tra sacro e profano. Dalla lezione giusnaturalistica al giurisdizionalismo. In Amato Mangiameli, Agata C. and Di Simone, Maria Rosa (Eds.), *Diritto e religione tra passato e futuro*, Atti del Convegno internazionale Villa Mondragone-Monte Porzio Catone (Roma) 27–29 novembre 2008, Roma: Aracne, 259–325, especially 261–262.

[2]On the effects of the Protestant Reformation on law, see Bergman, Harold J. 2010. *Diritto e rivoluzione* 2, *L'impatto delle riforme protestanti sulla tradizione giuridica occidentale*. Edizione italiana a cura di Diego Quaglioni. Bologna: il Mulino; Schmoeckel, Mathias. 2014. *Das Recht der Reformation*. Tübingen: Mohr Siebeck. About marriage see Tejero, Eloy. 1971. *El matrimonio. Misterio y signo. Siglos XIV–XVI*. Pamplona: Ediciones Universidad de Navarra, 223–324; Brundage, James A. 1987. *Law, Sex, and Christian Society in Medieval Europe*. Chicago and London: The University of Chicago Press. 551–575; Bethery de La Brosse, Arnould. 2011. *Entre amour et droit: le lien conjugal dans la pensée juridique moderne (XVIe–XXIe siècles)*. Préface de Anne Lefebvre-Teillard. Paris: Lextenso éditions, 39–52.

[3]There is boundless literature on the Council of Trent. It suffices to mention Esmein, Adhemar. 1891. *Le mariage en droit canonique* 2. Paris: L. Larose et Forcel, 151–207; Jemolo, Arturo Carlo. 1948. La riforma tridentina nell'ambito matrimoniale. *Quaderni di Belfagor* 1: 45–51; Jemolo, Arturo Carlo. 1993. *Il matrimonio nel diritto canonico. Dal Concilio di Trento al Codice del 1917*. Prefazione di Jean Gaudemet. Bologna: il Mulino; Jedin, Hubert. 1973–1981. *Storia del Concilio di Trento*. 4 voll. Brescia: Morcelliana; Cristiani, Leone. 1977. *La Chiesa al tempo del Concilio di Trento* (trans. A. Galuzzi). Torino: S.A.I.E. See also Quaglioni, Diego. 2001. «Sacramenti detestabili». La forma del matrimonio prima e dopo Trento. In Seidel Menchi, Silvana and Quaglioni, Diego (Eds.), *Matrimoni in dubbio. Unioni controverse e nozze clandestine in Italia dal XIV al XVIII secolo*, Bologna: il Mulino, 61–79; Bernhard, Jean, Lefebvre Charles and Rapp, Francis. 1990. *L'époque de la réforme et du Concile de Trente*. Paris: Éditions Cujas.

[4]The requirement to publicly announce a marriage was sanctioned in particular by the Fourth Council of the Lateran in 1215, as a way to combat against clandestine marriages (Gaudemet, Jean. 1987. *Le mariage en Occident. Les moeurs et le droit*. Paris: Les éditions du cerf, 233).

form to be followed.[5] The marriage was sometimes recorded by a notary public—a custom that could be traced to both the aristocracy and the middle class—but in most cases it was celebrated with an informal ceremony, and such a situation in reality led to many cases of bigamy and illegitimate births. The uncertainty surrounding the institution of marriage—what with it not being bound by mandatory public formalities—often made it difficult to ascertain whether two people were joined in wedlock.

The need for an overall reform was becoming increasingly apparent between the Middle Ages and the Modern Era: such reform would be painstakingly set in motion[6] at the twenty-fourth session of the Council of Trent, a real watershed in the history of marriage.[7] In broaching the thorny subject of clandestine marriages celebrated without any witnesses or without parents' consent,[8] the decree *de reformatione matrimonii* expressly condemned multiple marriages, which were often precisely the result of a marriage celebrated clandestinely.[9]

---

[5]On the laws governing marriage before the Council of Trent, which based its validity primarily on custom, and on the practical problems of proving that a marriage had taken place, see Rasi, Piero. 1943. *La conclusione del matrimonio nella prassi prima del concilio di Trento*. Bologna: Zanichelli; Rasi, Piero. 1958. *La conclusione del matrimonio nella dottrina prima del Concilio di Trento*. Napoli: Jovene; Valsecchi, Chiara. 1999. «Causa matrimonialis est gravis et ardua». Consiliatores e matrimonio fino al Concilio di Trento. In *Studi di storia del diritto* 2, Milano: Giuffrè, 407–580; Seidel Menchi, Silvana. 2001. Percorsi variegati, percorsi obbligati. Elogio del matrimonio pre-tridentino. In Seidel Menchi, Silvana and Quaglioni, Diego (Eds.), *Matrimoni in dubbio. Unioni controverse e nozze clandestine in Italia dal XIV al XVIII secolo*. Bologna: il Mulino, 17–60.

[6]It suffices to mention here Rasi, Piero. 1941. L'applicazione delle norme del concilio di Trento in materia matrimoniale. In *Studi in onore di Arrigo Solmi* 1, Milano: Giuffrè, 235–281; Gismondi, Pietro. 1953. L'attuazione dottrinaria e pratica delle norme tridentine sulla forma del matrimonio. *Rivista italiana per le scienze giuridiche* 6.3: 250–284; Tejero 1971 (as n. 2) 325–358; Zarri, Gabriella. 1996. Il matrimonio tridentino. In Prodi, Paolo and Reinhard, Wolfgang (Eds.), *Il concilio di Trento e il moderno*. Bologna: il Mulino, 437–483.

[7]Tamassia, Nino. 1910. *La famiglia italiana nei secoli decimoquinto e decimosesto*. Milano-Palermo-Napoli: Sandron, 150.

[8]On the problem of clandestine marriages, see Lombardi, Daniela. 1996. Fidanzamenti e matrimoni dal Concilio di Trento alle riforme settecentesche. In De Giorgio, Michela and Klapisch-Zuber, Christiane (Eds.), *Storia del matrimonio*. Roma-Bari: Laterza, 215–250; Lombardi, Daniela. 2001. *Matrimoni di antico regime*. Bologna: il Mulino, 27–126; Lombardi, Daniela. 2008. *Storia del matrimonio. Dal Medioevo a oggi*. Bologna: il Mulino, 38–45; Cozzi, Gaetano. 2000. Padri, figli e matrimoni clandestini (metà secolo XVI–metà secolo XVIII). In Cozzi, Gaetano. 2000. *La società veneta e il suo diritto. Saggi su questioni matrimoniali, giustizia penale, politica del diritto, sopravvivenza del diritto veneto nell'Ottocento*. Venezia: Marsilio, 19–64; Aznar Gil, Federico. 2003. Penas y sanciones contra los matrimonios clandestinos en la península ibérica durante la baja edad media. *Revista de Estudios Histórico-Jurídicos* 25: 189–230. About the fight against clandestine marriages in previous centuries see Dauvillier, Jean. 1933. *Le mariage dans le droit classique de l'Église depuis le décret de Gratien (1140) jusqu'à la mort de Clément V (1314)*. Paris: Librairie du Recueil Sirey, 102–121.

[9]For a recent study of this topic, see Garlati, Loredana. 2011. La famiglia tra passato e presente. In Patti, Salvatore and Cubeddu, Maria Giovanna (Eds.), *Diritto della famiglia*. Milano: Giuffrè, 1–48, especially 15–18.

The first of its ten chapters, better known as the *Tametsi* decree (1563), set forth some necessary formalities in order for the marriage to be valid.[10] The so-called ordinary form of marriage transformed the deed from a private union entered into inside one's home to a public ceremony celebrated in Church—in short, making it sacred. This was aimed at safeguarding the indissolubility and stability of the union, in accordance with the express condemnation of the *pluralitas uxorum* ("Si quis dixerit licere christianis plures simul habere uxores, et hoc nulla lege divina esse prohibitum, Anathema sit").[11]

In contrast with Protestantism, which equated marriage to a contract which could be dissolved in certain cases, the Counter-Reformation once again made a strong appeal to the sacramental doctrine of marriage, which was to be monogamous and indissoluble. From this perspective, polygamy was considered the ultimate infringement of the unity and indissolubility of the bond of marriage, and as such it became one of the preferred targets of Counter-Reformation doctrine towards the end of the sixteenth-century. Exponents of such doctrine were mainly the jurists and theologians of second scholasticism, who acted on the lesson of Trent and stigmatized the illicit nature of polygamy in the eyes of natural law.

Nevertheless, the Tridentine rules were only partially effective when it came to the age-old problem of clandestine marriages. The following decades would witness a significant decrease in the cases of bigamy, but it would not completely disappear from the Catholic world; this was partly a result of the fact that, in many regions of Europe, the text of the *Tametsi* decree was neither published nor explained for a long time after its adoption.[12]

Bigamy has aroused certain historiographical interest in recent decades, not only as a social phenomenon studied both within and outside of Europe,[13] but also as

---

[10]Formalities included the official announcement that had to precede the ceremony, the role of the parish priest, the two witnesses, who had to be present when consent was exchanged, and the recording of the deed in the parish registers (1991. *Conciliorum Oecumenicorum Decreta*. Bologna: Edizioni dehoniane, 755–757).

[11]1991. *Conciliorum Oecumenicorum Decreta* (as n. 10) 754. The *Tametsi* decree established the ordinary form of celebrating marriage, but it did not account for those cases in which this provision could not be observed because there were no priests present. On the so-called extraordinary form of marriage, see Saje, Andrej. 2003. *La forma straordinaria e il ministro della celebrazione del matrimonio secondo il Codice latino e orientale*. Roma: Editrice Pontificia Università Gregoriana.

[12]Brundage 1987 (as n. 2) 565.

[13]Frost, Ginger. 1997. Bigamy and Cohabitation in Victorian England. *Journal of Family History* 22.3: 286–306; Prasada Rao, Kande. 2003. *Bigamy in Christian Law*. New Delhi: Orient Law House; Scaramella, Pierroberto. 2005. Controllo e repressione ecclesiastica della poligamia a Napoli in Età moderna: dalle cause matrimoniali al crimine di fede (1514–1799). In Scaramella, Pierroberto. 2005. *Inquisizioni, eresie, etnie, dissenso religioso e giustizia ecclesiastica in Italia (secc. XVI–XVIII)*. Bari: Cacucci Editore, 239–294; McDougall, Sara. 2012. *Bigamy and Christian Identity in Late Medieval Champagne*. Philadelphia: University of Pennsylvania; Witte, John jr. 2015. *The Western Case for Monogamy Over Polygamy*. New York: Cambridge University Press. See also Sertoli Salis, Renzo. 1962. *La poligamia nella storia e nel costume*. Roma: Accademia internazionale Leonardo da Vinci di scienze, lettere ed arti.

regards its specific criminal repercussions.[14] The Council of Trent's decrees on marriage meant that this conduct was seen as a heretical action with devastating social effects, and analysis of its criminal repression highlights a series of issues that were typical of the Modern Era: from the control exercised over mobility and civic individuality to problems concerning the citizenry, to the spread of the parish register system and the simultaneous development of forgery in certificates and witness evidence. Indeed, forging one's identity was the most widespread practice amongst polygamists, often men who were constantly attracted to the idea of creating a new life for themselves.[15]

Nonetheless, they were not always aware of the fact that they were perpetrating a crime: a spouse who had been absent for an extended period of time was sometimes presumed dead, and in good faith the surviving spouse could be tempted by the possibility of a second marriage. Precisely to avoid the risk of bigamy, canon law authorized a second marriage—thus granting the *licentia nubendi*—only if there were well-founded reasons for presuming the death of the husband (or wife).[16]

By the 16th century, canon law had long established a regulatory structure for the institution of marriage. Likewise, jurisprudence had developed a solid doctrinal system to deal with the numerous legal issues that marriage presented. Thus, it should come as no surprise that late Scholasticism[17] offered very little in terms of totally new

---

[14]Vega Gutiérrez, Ana María. 1997. *La unidad del matrimonio y su tutela penal: precedentes romanos y canonicos del delito de bigamia*. Prólogo de Javier Ferrer Ortiz. Granada: Comares. See Gacto Fernández, Enrique. 1987. El delito de bigamia y la Inquisición española. *Anuario de historia del derecho español* 57: 465–492, also in Tomas y Valiente, Francisco. 1990. *Sexo barroco y otras transgresiones premodernas*, Madrid: Alianza, 27–152; Torres Aguilar, Manuel. 1997. Algunos aspectos del delito de bigamia en la Inquisición de Indias. *Revista de la Inquisición* 6: 117–138, also in Levaggi, Abelardo (Ed.). 1997. *La Inquisición en Hispanoamérica. Estudios*. Bueons Aires: Ediciones Ciudad Argentina, 65–104; Torres Aguilar, Manuel. 1997. El delito de bigamia: estudio general y especial perspectiva en el Tribunal de la Inquisición de Sevilla en el siglo XVIII. In Gacto Fernández, Enrique (Ed.), *El centinela de la fe: estudios jurídicos sobre la Inquisición de Sevilla en el siglo XVIII*. Sevilla: Universidad de Sevilla, 173–232. About in particular Republic of Venice cf. Andreato, Claudia. 2004. Il reato di bigamia nella Repubblica di Venezia (secoli XVI e XVII). In Chiodi, Giovanni and Povolo, Claudio (Eds.), *L'amministrazione della giustizia penale nella Repubblica di Venezia (secoli XVI–XVIII)* 2, *Retoriche, stereotipi, prassi*. Verona: Cierre Edizioni, 413–464; Andreato, Claudia. 2007. Il reato di bigamia nella Repubblica di Venezia da un processo del 1630. *Acta Histriae* 15.2: 471–492.

[15]McDougall, Sara. 2010. Bigamy: A Male Crime in Medieval Europe? *Gender & History* 22: 430–446.

[16]Esmein, Adhemar. 1891. *Le mariage en droit canonique* 1. Paris: L. Larose et Forcel, 267–269; Gaudemet 1987 (as n. 4) 200.

[17]There are countless examples of historiographical studies on this topic. Though it is by no means a comprehensive list, the following can be cited: Beltrán de Heredia, Vicente. 1953. *Los orígenes de la Universidad de Salamanca*. Salamanca: Ediciones Universidad de Salamanca; Grossi, Paolo (Ed.). 1973. *La Seconda Scolastica nella formazione del diritto privato moderno*, Incontro di studio (Firenze, 16–19 ottobre 1972). Milano: Giuffrè; Férnandez Álvarez, Manuel, Robles, Laureano and Rodríguez-San Pedro Bezares, Luis Enrique (Eds.). 1990. *La Universidad de Salamanca* 2, *Atmósfera intelectual y Perspectivas de investigación*, Salamanca: Ediciones

solutions to the most relevant problem areas. Nonetheless, the late Scholastic contribution to the specific area of family law was anything but trivial, not only because of its influence on the practice of law during that time,[18] but also because of its importance in the history of legal thought. From this point of view, the jurists/theologians of the *siglo de oro*[19] left a fundamental legacy to the subsequent doctrines of natural law and the Enlightenment through the methodology they employed.

The aim here is to provide an initial account of how the leading exponents of late Scholasticism reflected on the complex issue of bigamy (*rectius* polygamy). On the one hand, it will be shown how they were indebted to previous doctrine, in particular Thomistic thought; yet on the other hand, the originality of their methodology shall become clear, as well as the insight provided by their legal and theological reasoning. Indeed, they explored in depth a centuries-old problem, going so far as to the extreme boundaries of the rational and thinkable.

2 The Problem of Polygamy and the Justification of Its Prohibition in Sixteenth-Century Scholasticism

The fact that Christians were not allowed to practice polygamy is one of the indisputable foundations of medieval marriage law.

(Footnote 17 continued)

Universidad de Salamanca; Belda Plans, Juan. 2000. *La Escuela de Salamanca y la renovación de la teología en el siglo XVI*. Madrid: BAC; Rodríguez San Pedro Bezares, Luis Enrique (Ed.). 2002–2006. *Historia de la Universidad de Salamanca*, 4 vol. Salamanca: Ediciones Universidad de Salamanca; Alonso Romero, Maria Paz. 2012. *Salamanca, escuela de juristas. Estudios sobre la enseñanza del derecho en el Antiguo Régimen*, Madrid: Universidad Carlos III de Madrid; Villey, Michel. 2013. *La formation de la pensée juridique moderne*. Paris: PUF, 326–368. See also, though dated, Giacon, Carlo. 1944. *La Seconda Scolastica* 1, *I grandi commentatori di San Tommaso*. Milano: Bocca; Giacon, Carlo. 1947. *La Seconda Scolastica* 2, *Precedenze teoretiche ai problemi giuridici: Toledo, Pereira, Fonseca, Molina, Suarez*. Milano: Bocca; Giacon, Carlo. 1950. *La Seconda Scolastica* 3, *I problemi giuridico–politici. Suarez, Bellarmino, Mariana*. Milano: Bocca. Recent works: Frank and Seelmann, Kurt (Eds.). 2001. *Die Ordnung der Praxis. Neue Studien zur spanischen Spätscholastik*. Tübingen: Niemeyer; Pena González, Miguel Anxo (Ed.). 2009. *La Escuela de Salamanca. De la Monarquía hispánica al Orbe católico*. Madrid: BAC; Riverso, Roberta. 2011. *La nascita del concetto dei diritti umani nella Seconda Scolastica*. Roma: Albatros; Brunori, Luisa. 2015. *Societas quid sit. La société commerciale dans l'élaboration de la Seconde Scolastique*. Préface de Jean Hilaire. Paris: Mare & Martin; Poncela González, Ángel. 2015. *La Escuela de Salamanca. Filosofía y Humanismo ante el mundo moderno*. Madrid: Editorial Verbum.

[18]As regards marriage law, see the recent work of Donahue, Charles jr. 2014. The Role of the Humanists and the Second Scholastic in the Development of European Marriage Law from the Sixteenth to the Nineteenth Centuries. In Decock, Wim, Ballor, Jordan, Germann, Michael and Waelkens, Laurent (Eds.), *Law and Religion. The Legal Teachings of the Protestant and Catholic Reformations*. Göttingen: Vandenhoeck & Ruprecht, 45–62.

[19]Lamacchia, Ada. 1995. *La Filosofia nel Siglo de Oro. Studi sul tardo Rinascimento spagnolo*. Bari: Levante.

The starting point of sixteenth-century Scholasticism in facing the issue was the letter of the Holy Scriptures, which bear witness to the divine propensity for monogamy. Indeed, marriage is described with the use of the singular starting from the well-known passage in Genesis ("For this reason a man shall leave his father and his mother, and be joined to his wife; and they shall become one flesh"),[20] which is referred to numerous times in the New Testament.[21] The message of conjugal solidarity is strengthened by St Paul's words, who likens the bond of marriage to that between Christ and the Church, bidding spouses to love and support each other ("Nevertheless each of you must also love his own wife even as himself; and let the wife see that she respects her husband").[22]

Therefore, it was clear that polygamy went against divine positive law, and as such, moral theologians utterly condemned it.

On the contrary, it would be more complicated to declare it against divine natural law: indeed, St. Augustine in *De civitate Dei* and St. Thomas in *Summa Theologiae*,[23] among others, had testified to the fact that many patriarchs from ancient times had several wives without this leading to any divine disapproval.

It is well known that in Biblical times the Hebrews generally practised polygamy, but it would be more correct to speak about polygyny: since the days of Lamech, which was the first case recalled by the Bible, the custom of having two or more wives was tolerated as a sign of a man's power and wealth, as well as a useful remedy for sterility problems, which would have inevitably led to the weakening—and perhaps even total extinction—of a family group.[24] Therefore, just like levirate, which was the Hebrew custom by which a man was obliged to marry his brother's childless widow, polygamy was normal practice. Notwithstanding the sharp contrast with Christian principles, the Church did not ban the Jews from practising

[20]Gen. 2.24. Cf. Legendre, Pierre (Ed.). 2004. *"Ils seront deux en une seule chair". Scénographie du couple humain dans le texte occidental. Travaux du Laboratoire Européen pour l'étude de la filiation*. Brussels: E. Van Balberghe; Mayali, Laurent. 2008. "Duo erunt in carne una" and the Medieval Canonists. In Colli, Vincenzo and Conte, Emanuele (Eds.), *Iuris Historia. Liber Amicorum Gero Dolezalek*. Berkley: University of California, 161–175.

[21]Matteo 19.4-6; Marco 10.6-8; Prima lettera ai Corinzi 6.16; Lettera agli Efesini 5.31.

[22]Lettera agli Efesini 5.33.

[23]Sant'Agostino. 1981. *De civitate Dei libri XXI* 2. Stuttgart: B. G. Teubner, 187. L. XVI. Cap. XXXVIII: "...eo tempore, quando multiplicandae posteritatis causa plures uxores lex nulla prohibebat". See also San Tommaso d'Aquino. *Summa Theologiae, Supplementum tertiae partis* (ST, *Suppl.*). Quaestio LXV, *De pluralitate uxorum.*. Articulus II, *Utrum habere plures uxores potuerit aliquando esse licitum*, n. 2, § *Praeterea, hoc idem videtur* (San Tommaso d'Aquino. 1986. La Somma teologica, traduzione e commento a cura dei domenicani italiani, testo latino dell'edizione leonina 31 (Suppl., qq. 41–68). Bologna: Edizioni Studio Domenicano, 421).

[24]See Colorni, Vittore. 1945. *Legge ebraica e leggi locali. Ricerche sull'ambito d'applicazione del diritto ebraico in Italia dall'epoca romana al secolo XIX*. Milano: Giuffrè, 159–197; Biale, Rachel. 1995. *Women and Jewish Law. The essential texts, their history and their relevance for today*. New York: Schocken books; Colafemmina, Cesare. 1992. La poligamia presso gli ebrei nel Medioevo. *Quaderni medievali* 34: 114–122; Schereschewsky, Ben-Zion and Elon, Menachem. 2007. Bigamy and Polygamy. In Berenbaum, Michael and Skolnik, Fred (Eds.), *Encyclopaedia Judaica* 3. Detroit: Macmillan Reference USA, 691–694.

polygamy during the Middle Ages, even though the Councils of Elvira, Ancyra and Laodicea had included it in the category of *delicta carnis*, with strict punishments.[25]

Medieval legal science had already clashed with this large difficulty and was able to overcome it through the divine dispensation theory, which was developed on the following principle expressed in the decretal *Gaudemus* issued by Innocent III: "Nec ulli unquam licuit insimul plures uxores habere, nisi cui fuit divina revelatione concessum".[26] Second Scholasticism adopted the same solution, specifying that at this point, since Christ had taken marriage back to its original purity by revoking such divine *dispensatio* in the Gospel, the bond of marriage was essentially monogamous not only for Christians, but also for the Hebrews and the other *infideles*, in accordance with natural law.[27]

All late Scholastic reasoning was aimed at proving the unlawfulness of the *habere plures uxores*, and it was centred on the text of the Old and New Testaments: any references made to sources of positive law was only by chance. There were no particularly relevant legal precedents in this respect.

In classical Roman law, bigamy was not an independent legal offence prior to being defined *crimen extraordinarium* in an edict of Diocletian.[28]

Barbaric laws made scanty and vague mention of the issue, and when they did it was sometimes considered the most serious and aggravated type of adultery.[29] Furthermore, there were not many statutes governing the crime of bigamy when it fell within the jurisdictional authority of a canonical judge:[30] some of the strictest statutory sanctions were those set forth by the legislators in Cremona, who punished

---

[25]Cf. Colafemmina 1992 (as n. 24); Aboi Rubio, Diego. 2012. Bigamia. In *Diccionario general de derecho canónico*, Obra dirigida y coordinada por Javier Otaduy, Antonio Viana, Joaquín Sedano 1. Navarra: Thomson Reuters Aranzadi, 708–711.

[26]X 4.19.8.

[27]de Ledesma, Pedro. 1595. *Tractatus de magno matrimonii sacramento*. Venetiis: apud Marcum Antonium Zalterium. Quaestio LXV, *De bigamia*. Articulus II, *Utrum aliquando licitum fuerit habere plures uxores*, 702, § *Tertia conclusio*; Sanchez, Thomas. 1693. *De sancto matrimonii sacramento disputationum tomi tres* 2. Venetiis: typis, et sumptibus Antonij Tivani. Liber VII, *De impedimentis matrimonii. De impedimento ligaminis*. Disputatio LXXX, *An secundae nuptiae primis non dissolutis, sed consistentibus, sint iure naturae interdictae atque irritae?*, 251, n. 8. See also Bonacina, Martino. 1629. *De magno matrimonii sacramento tractatus*. Venetiis: sumptibus disiunctae societatis. Quaestio III, *De impedimentis matrimonii*. Punctum X, *De impedimento ligaminis*, 160 n. 4.

[28]Volterra, Edoardo. 1934. Per la storia del reato di bigamia in diritto romano. In Albertario, Emilio (Ed.), *Studi in memoria di Umberto Ratti*. Milano: Giuffrè, 387–447; Pisapia, Gian Domenico. 1958. Bigamia. In *Novissimo Digesto Italiano* 2, Torino: UTET, 396–409. See also Volterra, Edoardo. 1975. Matrimonio (diritto romano). In *Enciclopedia del diritto* 25. Milano: Giuffrè, 726–807, 795.

[29]Marongiu, Antonio. 1959. Bigamia (storia). In *Enciclopedia del diritto* 5. Milano: Giuffrè, 361–362.

[30]There is some mention of this issue in Esposito, Anna. 2004. Adulterio, concubinato, bigamia: testimonianze dalla normativa statutaria dello Stato pontificio (secoli XIII–XVI). In Seidel Menchi, Silvana and Quaglioni, Diego (Eds.), *Trasgressioni. Seduzione, concubinato, adulterio, bigamia (XIV–XVIII secolo)*. Bologna: il Mulino, 21–42, especially 40–41.

bigamists with ruthless corporal punishment.[31] A broader examination of the rest of Europe reveals similar situations.[32]

On the other hand, the *ius commune* doctrine made more convincing reference to the problem and fully formulated the criminal offence of bigamy (*simul habere plures uxores*). Glossators applied their exegetical skills to the few rules on the subject-matter that could be found in Justinian's compilation, and great commentators such as Baldo degli Ubaldi and Bartolomeo da Saliceto provided important analysis which would pave the way for the masters of the mature *ius commune* to address the offence. One such master was Giulio Claro,[33] who at that point came to define the conduct of someone who celebrates more than one marriage as an independent illegal act.[34]

However, even before considering it a crime of contracting different marriages at the same time,[35] *ius commune* literature construed the term «bigamy» as indicating that irregular situation which prevented a person from being promoted to Holy Orders if said individual had lawfully contracted marriage multiple times successively; had had multiple wives at the same time or had married a widow or a woman who was no longer a virgin; or finally, had contracted marriage despite being a clergyman. Corroboration of such may also be found in Alberico da Rosciate's *Dictionarium iuris*, wherein he only explains the meaning of *irregularitas ex defectu sacramenti*.[36]

Graziano himself had dealt with bigamy from the point of view of the *irregularitates*, though he did not formulate a true treatment of this impediment.[37]

Even though references to the *communis opinio doctorum* are rather frequent, the jurists/theologians of the sixteenth century organized their treatment of polygamy by following the model outlined by St. Thomas, who was the fundamental cornerstone of all sixteenth-century Spanish doctrine. Therefore, it is worth

[31]"Et quod si aliquis, habens uxorem, aliam acceperit, testiculi sibi incidantur, ita quod penitus a corpore separentur" (1952. *Statuta et ordinamenta Comunis Cremonae facta et compilata currente anno Domini MCCCXXXIX*, curati e aggiornati con le riforme del decennio successivo da Ugo Gualazzini. Milano: Giuffrè, Rub. XLII, 46–47). Cf. Brundage 1987 (as n. 2) 539–540.

[32]A sentence issued in Paris in 1387 ordered imprisonment for a bigamous woman (Donahue, Charles jr. 2007. *Law, Marriage, and Society in the Later Middle Ages. Arguments About Marriage in Five Courts*. New York: Cambridge University Press, 372). On Charles Donahue jr.'s powerful study, see Lefebvre-Teillard, Anne. 2009. *Law and History Review* 27.2: 451–453.

[33]On Giulio Claro, see Massetto, Gianpaolo. 1985. *Un magistrato e una città nella Lombardia spagnola. Giulio Claro pretore a Cremona*. Milano: Giuffrè; Massetto, Gianpaolo. 1994. *Saggi di storia del diritto penale lombardo (Secc. XVI-XVIII)*. Milano: LED, 11–227.

[34]Marchetto, Giuliano. 2004. «Primus fuit Lamech». La bigamia tra irregolarità e delitto nella dottrina di diritto comune. In Seidel Menchi, Silvana and Quaglioni, Diego (Eds.), *Trasgressioni. Seduzione, concubinato, adulterio, bigamia (XIV–XVIII secolo)*. Bologna: il Mulino, 43–105.

[35]On bigamy as a crime in canon law, see Naz, Raoul. 1937. Bigamie (Le délit de). In *Dictionnaire de droit canonique* 12. Paris: Letouzey et Ané, 888–889.

[36]Alberici a Rosate. 1548. *Dictionarium*. Lugduni: Compagnie des libraires de Lyon, *ad vocem*.

[37]d'Avack, Pietro Agostino. 1965. Il «ligamen seu vinculum prioris matrimonii» nelle fonti e nella dottrina classica della Chiesa. In *Studi in memoria di Guido Zanobini* 4. Milano: Giuffrè, 191–229.

examining the observations made on the matter by *Doctor Angelicus* in *Summa Theologiae*, which are very similar to the remarks contained in his famous comment on the *Sentenze* by Pietro Lombardo.[38]

In quaestio LXV of the *supplementum* to the *tertia pars* of the *Summa Theologiae*—drafted by Reginaldo da Piperno immediately after his master's death[39]—the first point analysed concerns the contrariness of polygamy with natural law. Though the expression «ius naturae» may take on different meanings, and such semantic heterogeneity impacts the solution of the query at issue, and though it is true that the *habere plures uxores* does not hinder the main aim of marriage in its duel meaning of procreation and raising children,[40] it nonetheless prevents the achievement of the secondary aims of the bond of marriage (namely the collaboration between husband and wife, and the symbolic realisation of the relationship between Christ and the Church through the *sacramentum*). As a matter of fact, even if the goal of reproduction may be easily reached by a man with many wives, the aim of cooperating as spouses to fulfil family duties is bound to fall short. This is because, as explained by St. Thomas, a plurality of wives upsets family harmony ("…non facile potest esse pax in familia ubi uni viro plures uxores iunguntur, cum non possit unus vir sufficere ad satisfaciendum pluribus uxoribus ad votum").[41] Lastly, the third aim is completely nullified, since there is only one Christ and only one Church, and the presence of more than one spouse is utterly incompatible with the monogamous and indissoluble bond between Christ and the Church.

This model would be used again in the sixteenth-century works examined herein, whereby the authors provided an initial analysis (of varying depth) of the lawfulness of polygamous conduct, a concept which was once again strictly linked to its incompatibility with the ends of marriage as set out by St. Thomas.

---

[38]San Tommaso d'Aquino. 1660. *Praeclarissima commentaria in quartum librum sententiarum Petri Lombardi*. Parisiis: apud societatem bibliopolarum. Distinctio XXXIII, *De diversis coniugij legibus*. Quaestio I, *Hic est triplex quaestio*. Articulus I, *Utrum habere plures uxores sit contra legem naturae*, 516.

[39]The Dominican theologian lived in the thirteenth century and was a disciple and secretary of St. Thomas. He finished the third part of *Summa Theologiae* (after quaestio 90) in his master's place, adding a *Supplementum* based on St. Thomas' notes. Cf. Corvino, Francesco. 1957. Reginaldo da Piperno. In *Enciclopedia filosofica* 3. Venezia-Roma: Istituto per la collaborazione culturale, col. 1921.

[40]ST, *Suppl.* (as n. 23) Quaestio LXV, *De pluralitate uxorum*. Articulus I, *Utrum habere plures uxores sit contra legem naturae*, 413 § *Matrimonium*: "Matrimonium ergo habet pro fine principali prolis procreationem et educationem"; Quaestio LXV, *De pluralitate uxorum*, Articulus III, *Utrum habere concubinam sit contra legem naturae*, 425 § Respondeo: "Finis autem quem natura ex concubitu intendit est proles procreanda et educanda". See Burguière, André, Klapisch-Zuber, Christiane, Segalen, Martine and Zonabend, Françoise (Eds.). 1986. *Histoire de la famille*. Préface de Jack Goody 2, *Le choc des modernités*. Paris: Armand Colin Editeur, 96–99.

[41]ST, *Suppl.* (as n. 23) Quaestio LXV, *De pluralitate uxorum*. Articulus I, *Utrum habere plures uxores sit contra legem naturae*, 413 § *Pluralitas*.

Reflection on this matter was certainly not new: in those same years, even a champion of the *mos italicus* like Jacopo Menochio, jurisconsult from Pavia who lived between the sixteenth and seventeenth centuries,[42] made similar remarks in his *De arbitrariis iudicum quaestionum*. While it is true that, on the one hand, polygamy does not jeopardise, but rather favours, the first aim of marriage—as proven by the example of the patriarchs, who were exempt from the prohibition to have multiple wives precisely for this purpose—on the other hand, it is clear that it is irremediably detrimental to the second aim, that of the assistance that the spouses must give to each other, as well as to the third, namely the realisation of the sacrament, symbol of the bond between Christ and the Church and origin of the principle of indissolubility.[43]

It is indisputable that second Scholasticism reproposed the thought of *Doctor Angelicus*, mainly by focusing on the concept of *ius naturae*, which, as is well known, was already of great significance to medieval Scholasticism. Indeed, medieval Scholasticism had founded a new cognitive approach to political and social phenomena such as the State, family and law, based on the law of nature. In this way, each single rule of human and positive law could be critically analysed, by examining whether it complied with nature or whether it could be justified based on a rational aim.[44]

Following previous tradition, late Scholasticism reproposed an argumentative process in which objections were formulated against the theory that the author wanted to prove as true—this was the case for the passages concerning polygamy as well. Such *modus procedendi* allowed the author to present the opposing position to that which was held as rationally justifiable, in order to then reach the shared solution.

This is what Domingo de Soto did, for instance.[45] Quoting the definition of natural law taken from Roman law (*ius naturale est quod natura omnia animalia*

[42]Valsecchi, Chiara. 1994. L'istituto della dote nella vita del diritto del tardo Cinquecento: i "Consilia" di Jacopo Menochio. *Rivista di Storia del Diritto Italiano* 67: 205–282; Valsecchi, Chiara. 2000. Jacopo Menochio e il giurisdizionalismo tra Cinque e Seicento. *Studia Borromaica. Saggi e documenti di storia religiosa e civile della prima età moderna* 14: 93–116; Valsecchi, Chiara. 2009. Menochio, Giacomo (Jacopo). In *Dizionario Biografico degli Italiani* 73. Roma: Istituto della Enciclopedia Italiana, 521–524; Valsecchi, Chiara. 2013. Dar ordine al caos. Il processo del tardo diritto comune nelle opere di Jacopo Menochio. In di Renzo Villata, Maria Gigliola (Ed.), *Lavorando al cantiere del 'Dizionario biografico dei giuristi italiani (XII–XX sec.)'*. Milano: Giuffrè, 217–238.

[43]Menochio, Iacopo. 1587. *De arbitrariis iudicum quaestionibus et causis libri duo*. Coloniae Agrippinae: apud Ioannem Gymnicum. Liber II. Centuria V. Casus CCCCXX. *Uxorum ac maritorum pluralitatem improbari lege antiqua divina, lege Evangelica, naturali, civili, et pontificia et inibi de poenis eorum, qui duas uno tempore ducunt, vel duos viros habent*, n. 34, 572, nn. 56–58, 574.

[44]Schwab, Dieter. 1973. Ehe und Familie nach den Lehren der Spätscholastik. In Grossi, Paolo (Ed.), *La Seconda Scolastica nella formazione del diritto privato moderno*, Incontro di studio (Firenze, 16–19 ottobre 1972). Milano: Giuffrè, 73–116.

[45]Domingo de Soto (1495–1560), a Dominican theologian born in Segovia, was one of the main exponents of the School of Salamanca. He studied at Alcalà and taught theology at Salamanca, and

docuit),[46] he argues that polygamy is also permitted for men, since the union with different partners is permitted amongst animals. Thus, in so far as the procreation and raising of children are concerned, we start from the assumption that this is a law of nature partially shared by man and animals. Nonetheless, while it is true that the "uxorum multitudo" does not hinder, but rather favours, the aim of the "prolis generatio" by man, it is also true that it is very harmful, as it would prevent him from satisfying the requests of different wives at the same time, and thus from correctly fulfilling his own conjugal duties. The consequences are disastrous, to say the least: inevitably, the marriage would end up not constituting a valid "remedium contra concupiscentiam", with predictable consequences to the detriment of the unsatisfied women's morality. Furthermore, in such a situation, rows and squabbles would fill the house, making a peaceful life in common impossible.[47] Consequently, since the aim of the marriage between a man and a woman is not solely procreation, but also the equally important "communicatio in officiis domesticis", the theologian from Segovia concludes by asserting the irremediable contrast between polygamy and the law of nature.

Marriage would be the subject-matter of many subsequent digests. In his famous treatise on the matter, Thomas Sanchez[48] also goes back over the line of reasoning in St. Thomas' arguments, tracing the prohibition to *habere plures uxores* back to

(Footnote 45 continued)

he took on powerful roles such as representative of the emperor at the Council of Trent (Ramos-Lissón, Domingo. 2004. Domingo de Soto (1495–1560). In Domingo, Rafael (Ed.), *Juristas universales* 2, *Juristas modernos*. Madrid-Barcelona: Marcial Pons, 160–165). See also Cruz Cruz, Juan (Ed.). 2007. *La Ley natural como fundamento moral y jurídico en Domingo de Soto*. Pamplona: EUNSA.

[46]D. 1.1.1.3; Inst. 1.2.1.

[47]de Soto, Domingo. 1569. *Commentariorum Fratris Dominici Soto Segoviensis ... in Quartum Sententiarum* 2. Salmanticae: apud Ioannes Baptista a Terranova. Distinctio XXXIII, *De polygamia et repudio*. Quaestio I, *De uxoribus pluribus unius viri*. Articulus I, *Utrum habere plures uxores sit iuri naturae contrarium*, 209–210, § *Secunda conclusio*.

[48]Thomas Sanchez (1550–1610), Jesuit theologian who in 1602 published the first volume of his famous treatise on marriage. The work was placed on the Index in 1627, above all thanks to book IX libro (*De debito coniugali*), which was largely dedicated to the intimate realm of conjugal relations. See Carrodeguas, Celestino. 2003. *La sacramentalidad del matrimonio. Doctrina de Tomás Sanchez, S.J.* Madrid: Universidad pontificia Comillas; Alfieri, Fernanda. 2010. *Nella camera degli sposi. Tomás Sánchez, il matrimonio, la sessualità (secoli XVI–XVII)*. Bologna: il Mulino. On the life and work of the author, see, among others: Brouillard, René. 1939. Sanchez Thomas. In *Dictionnaire de théologie catholique* 14. Paris: Letouzey et Ané, 1075–1085; Naz, Raoul. 1965. Sanchez (Thomas). In *Dictionnaire de droit canonique* 7. Paris: Letouzey et Ané, 864–870; Viejo-Ximénez, José Miguel. 2006. Sánchez, Tomás (1550–1610). In *Diccionario crítico de juristas españoles, portugueses y latinoamericanos* 2. Zaragoza-Barcelona: Cátedra de Historia del Derecho y de las Instituciones, 480–481; Viejo-Ximénez, José Miguel. 2012. Sánchez, Tomás. In *Diccionario general de derecho canónico*, Obra dirigida y coordinada por Javier Otaduy, Antonio Viana, Joaquín Sedano 7. Navarra: Thomson Reuters Aranzadi, 144–146.

the New Testament: "Et ea quidem veritas tanquam Catholica praemittenda est, nunc in lege Evangelica prohibitum esse iure divino plures simul habere uxores".[49] This prohibition by divine law is expressly corroborated in the Tridentine canon *Si quis dixerit licere christianis plures simul habere uxores, et hoc nulla lege divina esse prohibitum, Anathema sit*, which the author unequivocally cites.

Throughout his long treatment, the Jesuit resolves the problem of the nature of this prohibition by resorting to the same instruments used by St. Thomas, that is by analysing the contrast between the *pluralitas uxorum* and the fundamental ends of marriage.[50] Even if the *procreatio prolis* is actually facilitated should a man have different wives at the same time (this could not be said were a woman to have different husbands, as such circumstance would not allow a clear ascertainment of paternity—"incerta erit proles"),[51] the *domestica societas*, that is peaceful conjugal cohabitation, and the correct management of the household would be irremediably jeopardised by the presence of many *uxores* ("Quod uxorum pluralitas adversetur secundario matrimonij fini, nimirum, tranquillae ac pacificae cohabitationi coniugum, ac gubernationi domesticae: qui finis est secundarius").[52] Finally, a wife's very chastity is also put at risk if the polygamous husband is not capable of satisfying his conjugal duty, and such a danger was anything but minor: "Non enim vir poterit satisfacere concupiscentiae uxorum plurium. Et contingit illas simul debitum petere, et cum vir nequeat illis correspondere, periclitabitur continentia illius, cui debitum negatur".[53] Therefore, the theory supporting polygamy—which was defended by Luther, the Anabaptists and Mohammed—is clearly heretical[54] and is to be rejected without hesitation. Thus, Sanchez confirms the nullity "naturae iure" of any marriage celebrated "cum alia uxore … priori superstite".[55]

[49] Sanchez 1693 (as n. 27) 2. Liber VII, *De impedimentis matrimonii. De impedimento ligaminis.* Disputatio LXXX, *An secundae nuptiae primis non dissolutis, sed consistentibus, sint iure naturae interdictae atque irritae?*, 249, n. 1.

[50] On this topic, see the analysis conducted by Marchetto 2004 (as n. 34) 68–78.

[51] Sanchez 1693 (as n. 27) 2. Liber VII, *De impedimentis matrimonii. De impedimento ligaminis.* Disputatio LXXX, *An secundae nuptiae primis non dissolutis, sed consistentibus, sint iure naturae interdictae atque irritae?*, 250, n. 4.

[52] Sanchez 1693 (as n. 27) 2. Liber VII, *De impedimentis matrimonii. De impedimento ligaminis.* Disputatio LXXX, *An secundae nuptiae primis non dissolutis, sed consistentibus, sint iure naturae interdictae atque irritae?*, 251, n. 8.

[53] Sanchez 1693 (as n. 27) 2. Liber VII, *De impedimentis matrimonii. De impedimento ligaminis.* Disputatio LXXX, *An secundae nuptiae primis non dissolutis, sed consistentibus, sint iure naturae interdictae atque irritae?*, 251, n. 8.

[54] Sanchez 1693 (as n. 27) 2. Liber VII, *De impedimentis matrimonii. De impedimento ligaminis.* Disputatio LXXX, *An secundae nuptiae primis non dissolutis, sed consistentibus, sint iure naturae interdictae atque irritae?*, 251, n. 2.

[55] Sanchez 1693 (as n. 27) 2. Liber VII, *De impedimentis matrimonii. De impedimento ligaminis.* Disputatio LXXX, *An secundae nuptiae primis non dissolutis, sed consistentibus, sint iure naturae interdictae atque irritae?*, 251, n. 8.

Cardinal Roberto Bellarmino[56] was loyal to St. Thomas' reasoning, and in his monumental *Disputationes de controversiis christianae fidei, adversus huius temporis haereticos*, he dealt with polygamy in the book dedicated to marriage, distinguishing between "polygamia multarum uxorum successive", which prevented the promotion to Holy Orders,[57] and "polygamia multarum uxorum simul".[58]

His firm condemnation of polygamous practices was vehemently developed through broad and precisely-reasoned arguments which could essentially be traced back to the irremediable divergence between such conduct and divine, natural and evangelic law (in particular, the four aims of marriage). It represented an opportunity to thwart Luther's word that the cardinal did not want to miss, after Luther's sensational involvement with Henry VIII and the less well-known episode with Philip I of Hesse.[59]

The founder of Protestantism, who also acknowledged the sacredness of the bond of marriage, developed a rather pragmatic concept of marriage and declared himself in favour of polygamy in certain cases, even if the general rule—in his opinion—should have been monogamy. His profound aversion to divorce made him open to compromise on polygamous conduct, which was not prohibited by the Old Testament and which was therefore an old custom that had never been abrogated.[60] Nonetheless, Luther's stance on the lawfulness of bigamy always remained rather unclear: in a letter of 1526 he declared that even though the patriarchs were polygamous, such an example was not to be followed by Christians since there was no need to do so, nor was there any benefit whatsoever; and above all, there was no divine commandment compelling a man to marry two women.[61]

A second argument, analysed by St. Thomas and taken up again by second Scholasticism, concerned the power to dispense men from the prohibition on

[56]A Jesuit theologian, Cardinal Roberto Bellarmino (1542–1621) was an advisor to Paul V on the main issues of the day. He authored numerous polemical texts on Protestant doctrine, such as the famous *Disputationes de controversiis christianae fidei adversus huius temporis haereticos*. For a more recent study on the life and personality of Cardinal Bellarmino, see Motta, Franco. 2005. *Bellarmino. Una teologia politica della Controriforma*. Brescia: Morcelliana.

[57]Bellarmino, Roberto. 1721. *Disputationes de controversiis christianae fidei, adversus huius temporis haereticos* 3. Pragae: typis Wolffgangi Wickhart. *De sacramento matrimonii liber unicus*. Controversia tertia, *De unitate conjugii*. Caput IX, *De polygamia multarum uxorum successive*, 747.

[58]Bellarmino 1721 (as n. 57) Caput X, *De polygamia multarum uxorum simul*, 748.

[59]Grisar, Hartmann. 1917. *Luther* 5 (trans. E. M. Lamond). London: Kegan Paul, Trench, Trübner & Co, 86; Villa, Luigi. 2011. *La riforma protestante*. Brescia: Editrice Civiltà, 29; Dall'Olio, Guido. 2013. *Martin Lutero*. Roma: Carocci editore, 141–143; Whitford, David. 2014. "It Is Not Forbidden that a Man May Have More Than One Wife". Luther's Pastoral Advide on Bigamy and Marriage. In Luebke, David, and Lindemann, Mary (Eds.). Mixed Matches. Transgressive Unions in Germany from the Reformation to the Enlightenment. New York-Oxford: Berghahn, 14–30; Witte 2015 (as n. 13) 209.

[60]See Witte, John jr. 2002. *Law and Protestantism. The Legal Teachings of the Lutheran Reformation*. Cambridge: Cambridge University Press.

[61]1960. *Luther: Letters of Spiritual Counsel* (trans. T. G. Tappert). Vancouver: Regent College Publishing, 276.

polygamy. St. Thomas was very clear in this respect: only God may exercise such power, as proven by the vicissitudes of the holy patriarchs, who were allowed to have more than one wife.[62] By contrast, the prohibition on promoting a bigamist to the Holy Orders, being a rule "de iure positive", did not need any divine dispensation: the Pope—and for minor orders, even a bishop—may lawfully dispense with such an irregularity.[63]

Sanchez took up this precise point: no human authority, not even the Pope, has the power to dispense men;[64] only God may do so, as happened at the time of the patriarchs, who were polygamous by divine concession.[65] The theologian goes further by asking himself "An Deus possit dispensare, ut una uxor pluribus viris nubat?".[66] In diverging from the judgment of the majority of the *doctores*, who deemed it unlikely, or even impossible, for there to be a divine dispensation in favour of a woman to have different husbands, Sanchez demonstrated his aspirations towards a more equal treatment of men and women. By challenging the conventions of the time, the Spanish Jesuit was not afraid of openly declaring that there would not be any "repugnantia" towards the principles of natural law were God to decide to allow different husbands to one woman.[67]

The one element which is undoubtedly worth highlighting in Sanchez's thought is precisely this proclaimed equality between spouses within a marriage. This concept was shared by other exponents of the same school of thought. Following Pietro Lombardo's lesson,[68] the *Doctor Cordubensis* rejects the traditional idea of the subordination of the wife to the husband. Thus, because the wife is entitled to

[62]"Lex autem de unitate uxoris non est humanitus, sed divinitus instituta: nec unquam verbo aut litteris tradita, sed cordi impressa, sicut et alia quae ad legem naturae qualitercumque pertinent. Et ideo in hoc a solo Deo dispensatio fieri potuit per inspirationem internam" (ST, *Suppl.* (as n. 23) Quaestio LXV, *De pluralitate uxorum.* Articulus II, *Utrum habere plures uxores potuerit aliquando esse licitum*, 421 § *Lex autem*).

[63]ST, *Suppl.* (as n. 23) Quaestio LXVI, *De bigamia et irregularitate ex ea contracta.* Articulus V, *Utrum cum bigamo liceat dispensare*, 451 § *Respondeo dicendum.*

[64]Sanchez 1693 (as n. 27) 2. Liber VII, *De impedimentis matrimonii. De impedimento ligaminis.* Disputatio LXXX, *An secundae nuptiae primis non dissolutis, sed consistentibus, sint iure naturae interdictae atque irritae?*, 252, n. 16.

[65]Sanchez 1693 (as n. 27) 2. Liber VII, *De impedimentis matrimonii. De impedimento ligaminis.* Disputatio LXXX, *An secundae nuptiae primis non dissolutis, sed consistentibus, sint iure naturae interdictae atque irritae?*, 251–252, n. 12.

[66]Sanchez 1693 (as n. 27) 2. Liber VII, *De impedimentis matrimonii. De impedimento ligaminis.* Disputatio LXXX, *An secundae nuptiae primis non dissolutis, sed consistentibus, sint iure naturae interdictae atque irritae?*, 252, n. 14 [but 15].

[67]Sanchez 1693 (as n. 27) 2. Liber VII, *De impedimentis matrimonii. De impedimento ligaminis.* Disputatio LXXX, *An secundae nuptiae primis non dissolutis, sed consistentibus, sint iure naturae interdictae atque irritae?*, 252, n. 14 [but 15].

[68]Pietro Lombardo. 1757. *Sententiarum Libri Quatuor.* Antverpiae: sumptibus Marci-Michael Bousquet et socior. Liber IV. Distinctio XXVIII, *Si consensus de futuro cum juramento faciat conjugium*, n. 3, 533–534.

the same level of dignity, it becomes impossible to reconcile multiple spouses with the good management of a household characterized by a peaceful family life: "Uxor enim non subditur viro ut famula, sed ut socia, et collateralis, ac in domestica gubernatione principatum tenens".[69]

Francisco de Vitoria—a famous Spanish theologian in the first half of the sixteenth century and leading exponent of late Scholasticism[70]—was also a fervent supporter of the equal dignity between spouses, even though he did not dwell upon the issue of polygamy very extensively.

It is well known that his *Relectiones theologicae*, which were collected by his pupils and published posthumously, offer a more substantial contribution to public law than to private law. However, there are arguments in the *Relectio de matrimonio* (1531)[71] concerning family law which are worth highlighting for their undoubted modernity, once again showing how second Scholasticism truly identified the fundamental principles not only of Roman law of the time, but also of modern private law.[72] In particular, I am referring to the emphasis placed on the reciprocal obligations by which spouses must abide in their relationship ("mutua

[69]Sanchez 1693 (as n. 27) 2. Liber VII. *De impedimentis matrimonii. De impedimento ligaminis.* Disputatio LXXX. *An secundae nuptiae primis non dissolutis, sed consistentibus, sint iure naturae interdictae atque irritae?*, 251. n. 8.

[70]Francisco de Vitoria (1483–1546) was a Dominican who started teaching theology in Paris at the Dominican college at the Sorbonne. In 1523 he returned to Valladolid, in Spain, and in 1526 he became the first chair of Theology at the prestigious University of Salamanca. Some of the most recent studies on the life and work of Francisco de Vitoria include (the list is by no means comprehensive): Hernández Martín, Ramón. 1999. *La lezione sugli Indios di Francisco de Vitoria* (trans. S. Casabianca). Milano: Jaca Book; Barbier, Maurice. 1999. La notion de *respublica* chez Vitoria. In Zarka, Yves Charles (Ed.), *Aspects de la pensée médiévale dans la philosophie politique moderne.* Paris: Presses Universitaires de France, 83–101; Brown Scott, James. 2000. *The Spanish Origin of International Law: Francisco de Vitoria and His Law of Nations*. Union. New Jersey: The Lawbook Exchange, LTD, especially 68–93 for some biographical details; Cruz Cruz, Juan (Ed.). 2008. *Ley y dominio en Francisco de Vitoria*. Pamplona: EUNSA; Palamidessi, Andrea Maria. 2010. *Alle origini del diritto internazionale: il contributo di Vitoria e Suarez alla moderna dottrina internazionalistica*. Roma: Aracne; Bunge, Kirstin, Spindler, Anselm and Wagner, Andreas (Eds.). 2011. *Die Normativität des Rechts bei Francisco de Vitoria.* Stuttgart-Bad Cannstatt: Fromman-holzboog; Milazzo, Lorenzo. 2012. *La teoria dei diritti di Francisco de Vitoria*. Pisa: Edizioni ETS and bibliography.

[71]See de Vitoria, Francisco. 2005. *Sobre el matrimonio. Estudio preliminar, traducción y notas de Luis Frayle Delgado.* Salamanca: Editorial San Esteban. See also Brown Scott 2000 (as n. 70) 242–252; Bethery de La Brosse 2011 (as n. 2) 54–61. See also the italian version: de Vitoria, Francisco. 2015. *Sul matrimonio. Introduzione, traduzione e commento di Mauro Mantovani.* Roma: Aracne. Another valid—though dated—source is Otte, Gerhard. 1964. *Das Privatrecht bei Francisco de Vitoria.* Köln Graz: Böhlau Verlag, 121–129.

[72]Gordley, James. 2006. *Foundations of Private Law. Property, Tort, Contract, Unjust Enrichment*. Oxford: Oxford University Press. 5. On the fundamental role played by second Scholasticism in the field of private law, see Grossi, Paolo (Ed.). 1973. *La Seconda Scolastica nella formazione del diritto privato moderno*, Incontro di studio (Firenze, 16–19 ottobre 1972). Milano: Giuffrè.

obsequia, et officia inter virum et foeminam"),[73] which are only possible within the scope of monogamy, in a *consortium vitae* in which husband and wife totally belong to each other.[74] I am also referring to the emphasis placed on recognizing equal rights among the sexes, from a perspective that does not call for the woman's automatic submission to the man ("Nam esto, quod vir caput sit mulieris, tamen mulier socia est, non serva").[75] After clarifying the inadmissibility of *pluralitas uxorum*, Vitoria specifies that he does not, however, deem it to be against the law of nature as such, but only because it prevents the aims of marriage from being achieved.

Naturally, the sacrament of marriage was also treated in the *Summa sacramentorum ecclesiae*, wherein Thomas Chaves cites his master's thought: one of the first issues covered concerns the lawfulness of polygamy ("Quaeritur, an liceat fidelibus plures simul habere uxores?"). The answer is obviously negative, even though in this case the expository reasoning is much more circumscribed, with simply a reference to the above-mentioned Tridentine canon *Si quis dixerit licere christianis plures simul habere uxores, et hoc nulla lege divina esse prohibitum, Anathema sit.*[76]

The observations of the eclectic Basilio Ponce de León, Theology Professor in Salamanca in the first decades of the seventeenth century,[77] are much more substantial. His thoughts were focused on the *impedimentum ligaminis*, both within the scope of his *Tractatus de impedimentibus matrimonii sive commentarius ad decem Gratiani causas a 27* and the more wide-ranging *Tractatus de sacramento matrimonii*. He developed the same line of reasoning in both works.

The unlawfulness of polygamy is once again connected to its incompatibility with the ends of marriage, the first and most important of which is the *procreatio prolis*: in this case the author believes this aim is hindered by the supposed infertility of he who has different partners ("luxuriosi et pluribus foeminis vacantes minus foecundi esse solent"). Thus, he does not closely adhere to the words of St. Thomas on this point.

But the treatment continues, and he cites other rational reasons that are just as serious in nature and that require a man to refrain from the temptation of marrying different women. The *socialis cohabitatio* is irremediably jeopardised by the *multitudo uxorum*, which at its outset is a very mortifying situation for each of the

[73]de Vitoria, Francisco. 1765. *Relectio de matrimonio* 1. n. 2. In de Vitoria, Francisco. 1765. *Relectiones theologicae*. Matriti: en la Oficina de Manuel Martin.

[74]"Mulier sui corporis potestatem non habet, sed vir: similiter autem, et vir potestatem sui corporis non habet, sed mulier. Ergo requiritur obligatio" (de Vitoria 1765 (as n. 73) 1. n. 3).

[75]de Vitoria 1765 (as n. 73) 2. n. 7.

[76]Chaves, Thomas. 1594. *Summa sacramentorum ecclesiae, ex doctrina fratris Francisci a Victoria, ordinis Praedicatorum et olim Primarii Cathedratici,* Antverpiae: in aedibus Petri Belleri, f. 124r.

[77]Born in Granada in 1569, Basilio Ponce de León (1569–1629) was a professor of theology at the Royal College of Alcalà starting in 1602, and between 1603 and 1623 at the University of Salamanca. He authored numerous theological treatises.

wives. Just like Sanchez and Vitoria, Ponce de León does not underestimate the fundamental role of women in the good management of the household and in preserving long-lasting family harmony. A woman is not her husband's "servant", but rather her "partner", thus he believes that none of the wives deserve to be treated as the former.

Once it becomes so distorted and deprived of its essential features, the bond of marriage no longer constitutes the "remedium concupiscentiae" it should represent, since "unus vir pluribus uxoribus minus valeat debitum reddere".

Finally, the *defectus sacramenti*—caused by the plurality of wives (or husbands)—makes polygamy a condition abhorred by divine law, since the bond between one individual with more than one person is so far from the bond between Christ and the Church.[78]

The theological disputes of the Augustinian Ponce de León are well known for offering an excellent overall picture of the debates of the time,[79] and his nonconformism is corroborated by the reflections of the Dominican theologian Pedro de Ledesma.[80] Ledesma presents a modernity of thought worth noting both here and elsewhere,[81] though not so much as regards the woman's role within the family but rather the importance of the parents' task in educating their children. He presented his analysis in the quaestio LXV of the *Tractatus de magno matrimonii sacramento*, covering five fundamental points that essentially focused on the unlawfulness of polygamy and concubinage, as well as their contrariness to natural law.

The author summarises the fundamental principles concerning *pluralitas uxorum*, ranging from the decretal *Gaudemus* of Innocent III and canon 2 of the twenty-fourth session of the Council of Trent, to the Holy Scriptures and St. Thomas' doctrine. Unlike *Doctor Angelicus* and most of his contemporaries, Ledesma argues that polygamy is also against the first aim of marriage, in particular, the education of the children, which is a privilege of the human species "in qua

---

[78]Ponce de León, Basilio. 1613. *Tractatus de impedimentibus matrimonii sive commentarius ad decem Gratiani causas a 27*. Salmanticae: apud Antoniam Ramirez viduam. Quaestio II, *De impedimento ligaminis ad quaestionem secundam*. Caput XIII, § I, 143–144. Cf. Ponce de León, Basilio. 1640. *De sacramento matrimonii tractatus*. Lugduni: sumptibus haeredis Gabr. Boissat et Laurentij Anisson. Liber VII, *De impedimento ligaminis*. Caput XLIX, *Pluralitatem uxorum simul illicitam nisi ex Dei revelatione*, 420–423.

[79]Ardito, Sabino. 1981. La dottrina matrimoniale di Basilio Ponce de León (1570–1629) e la letteratura ecclesiastica posteriore fino al Concilio Vaticano II. Contributo alla storia della rilevanza giuridica dell'amore coniugale. *Salesianum* 43: 757–815.

[80]Pedro de Ledesma (1544–1616) was a Dominican theologian and professor at Salamanca, Segovia and Avila: see Chenu, Marie Dominique. 1926. Ledesma (Pierre de). In *Dictionnaire de théologie catholique* 9. Paris: Letouzey et Ané, 126–127. See also Hernández, Ramón. 1991. La Escuela de Salamanca del siglo XVII y los problemas de Indias: fray Pedro de Ledesma. In *Congreso Internacional sobre los dominicos y el nuevo mundo* 3. Granada-Madrid: Deimos, 645–667, which highlighted his thought on the state of the *indios*.

[81]If I may, please refer to Salvi, Stefania T. 2015. Luci e ombre nella famiglia del *siglo de oro*: filiazione illegittima e seconda scolastica. *Rivista di Storia del Diritto Italiano* 88: 175–202.

pater solicitus est de prole".[82] Unlike animals, human beings do not limit themselves to generating their own progeny, but also dedicate themselves with great care to the personal growth of their children, nurturing them and ensuring that all of their material and spiritual needs are met.

The potential presence of multiple wives (or husbands) would make it impossible not so much to procreate, but to correctly educate the children, which is an integral part of the primary aim of marriage. Indeed, Ledesma expresses the opinion that such *educatio*, from a moral and material standpoint, cannot disregard the unity and indissolubility of the parents' union, bound in lawful marriage: "Impossibile est moraliter loquendo unum patrem providere in educatione, et institutione filiis, qui ex pluribus uxoribus haberi possunt, ergo est contra primum finem".[83]

The importance ascribed to the parents' educational duty emerges again in the part in which Pedro de Ledesma describes the second aim of marriage, namely the "communicatio operum inter coniuges"; said aim, the achievement of which is prevented by bigamy, must actually be safeguarded, as it is a necessary condition for the children's correct educational growth.[84]

An additional element that was studied in-depth by most theologians was the degree of certainty required on the death of a husband (or wife) in order for a second marriage to be valid if it were celebrated by the surviving spouse.[85]

The principle according to which the second marriage was to be irremediably null and void "sine certo nuntio de morte prioris coniugis" was certainly not an invention of the School of Salamanca. Just like Domingo de Soto, Basilio Ponce de León discloses his own reasoning by making reference to the decretal *In praesentia* of Clement III,[86] in which it is clearly stated that, regardless of the years a husband is absent, in no way will a woman be lawfully entitled to marry again "donec certum nuncium recipiant de morte virorum"[87]—this principle was confirmed by the great masters of *ius commune* such as Bartolus de Saxoferrato and

[82]de Ledesma 1595 (as n. 27) Quaestio LXV, *De bigamia.* Articulus I, *Utrum habere plures uxores sit contra legem naturae*, 697 § *Sit nihilominus quarta conclusio.*

[83]de Ledesma 1595 (as n. 27) Quaestio LXV, *De bigamia.* Articulus I, *Utrum habere plures uxores sit contra legem naturae*, 697 § *Sit nihilominus quarta conclusio*, 697 § *Secundo probatur conclusio.*

[84]de Ledesma 1595 (as n. 27) Quaestio LXV, *De bigamia.* Articulus I, *Utrum habere plures uxores sit contra legem naturae*, 697 § *Sit nihilominus quarta conclusio*, 697 § *Ultimo probatur.*

[85]Ponce de León 1613 (as n. 78) Quaestio II, *De impedimento ligaminis ad quaestionem secundam.* Caput XIII. § V, 164; Ponce de León 1640 (as n. 78) Liber VII, *De impedimento ligaminis.* Caput LIII, *Quae fama requiratur de prioris coniugis obitu, ut ad secundum matrimonium transeat alter?*, 427.

[86]X. 4.1.19.

[87]de Soto 1569 (as n. 47) Distinctio XXXVII, *De alijs criminibus, quae sunt matrimonij impedimenta.* Quaestio unica. Articulus V, *Utrum ligamen sit impedimentum matrimonium dirimens*, 280, § *Sit ergo quarta conclusio*; Ponce de León 1613 (as n. 78) Quaestio II, *De impedimento ligaminis ad quaestionem secundam.* Caput XIII. § V, 165; Ponce de León 1640 (as n. 78) Liber VII, *De impedimento ligaminis.* Caput LIII, *Quae fama requiratur de prioris coniugis obitu, ut ad secundum matrimonium transeat alter?*, 428.

Panormitanus. Once again, it is not the outcomes of late Scholastic speculation that are worthy of note, but rather the keen deductive reasoning that was employed, which further developed the conclusions of past *auctoritates* and at the same time constituted a model for subsequent doctrine to follow.

The issue was also examined with a certain degree of thoroughness by the less well-known Alonso de la Vera Cruz, an Augustinian theologian who was trained in Salamanca.[88] He explores the *impedimentum ligaminis* in the *Speculum conjugiorum* (1572), a work which was famous mainly for having looked into the validity of marriage with the *indios*. He makes use of the Aristotelian and Thomistic traditions, as well as canonist doctrine, in order to draw a constant comparison between Christian marriage and American Indian marriage: the former was founded on the freely given consent of the spouses, the premise of monogamy and the indissolubility of the bond of marriage; the latter was observed in the customs of the natives and permitted polygamy.[89]

In particular, the author examines the risk of unwittingly becoming bigamous as a result of having celebrated a second marriage while the first is still valid. In this respect, he insists many times on the need to assess whether the news of the spouse's death has been ascertained "a fide dignis" before getting married again—Covarrubias himself deems it necessary for the "uxorem certam esse oportere de

[88]The theologian, philosopher and jurist Alonso de la Vera Cruz (1504–1584), whose original name was Alonso Gutiérrez, was born in Toledo, Spain, in 1504 (or perhaps 1507). He studied grammar and rhetoric at Alcalà and philosophy and theology at Salamanca, where he was a disciple of Vitoria. As a member the Hermits of St. Augustine, in 1563 he was sent to the Augustinian school in Vera Cruz, Mexico. He actively contributed to the foundation of the Universidad Nacional Autónoma de Mexico, where he held the chair of Holy Scripture and Scholastic Theology. For a biographical history, see Reinhardt, Kurt Frank. 2003. Vera Cruz, Alonso de la, Fray. In *New Catholic Encyclopedia* 14, Detroit-New York: Gale, 443–444; Lazcano, Rafael. 2007. *Fray Alonso de Veracruz (1507–1584). Misionero del saber y protector de indios*. Madrid: Ed. Revista Agustiniana. His commitment to spreading Salamancan culture in Mexico and to defending the rights of indigenous peoples as an crucial intercultural mediator has recently been highlighted in a historiographical study: cf. Ponce Hernández, Carolina (Ed.). 2007. *Innovación y tradición en Fray Alonso de la Veracruz*. Prólogo de A. Velasco Gómez. Ciudad Universitaria: Facultad de Filosofía y Letras Universidad Nacional Autónoma de México. His writings were collected in a multi-volume series edited by Burrus, Ernest. 1967–1972. *The Writings of Fray Alonso de la Vera Cruz*. Saint Louis: Jesuit Historical Institute.

[89]On this work, which can be considered the first implementation of the new marriage laws established by the Council of Trent, see especially Castro Corona, Saraí. 2007. Los argumentos aristotélicos en el Speculum coniugiorum de Alonso de la Veracruz. In Ponce Hernández, Carolina (Ed.) 2007 (as n. 88) 235–245; Barp Fontana, Luciano. 2007. Fundamentos filosóficos de los derechos humanos en el Speculum coniugiorum de Alonso de la Veracruz. In Ponce Hernández, Carolina (Ed.) 2007 (as n. 88) 247–269. See also Noonan, John jr. 1973. Power to Choose. *Viator. Medieval and Renaissance Studies* 4: 419–439.

morte viri priusquam alteri nubat"[90]—and whether the messenger is a "nuntium certum", whose words need to be considered with care.[91]

A woman "certificata de morte proprij viri" does not commit a sin by celebrating a second marriage, and any children who may be born will be legitimate. But if the first husband is found to still be alive, the marriage becomes irremediably null and void,[92] the woman must immediately go back to her original husband as soon as she takes cognisance of this fact, otherwise she shall be considered an adulteress.[93]

On the other hand, should the second marriage be celebrated whilst the first husband is effectively dead, but the woman is acting "putans virum suum vivere" and thus not in good faith, then the second marriage shall be valid provided that "adsit verus consensus". By contrast, if the woman "credens impedimentum", even though she has solemnly sworn, "non intendebat contrahere", "non esset matrimonium".[94]

The indisputable practical impact of these issues spurred many jurists and theologians of the time to take an interest therein, thus leading to some fundamental points of reference. One of these was the Milanese Martino Bonacina, who lived between the end of the sixteenth century and the first half of the seventeenth century. His answer to the query "Qualis certitudo de morte coniugis requiratur, ut superstes possit cum alio matrimonium inire?"[95] relied on the help of two outstanding authorities of second Scholasticism, namely Soto and Sanchez.[96] Bonacina also believed that the required degree of certainty could be none other than the

[90]de Covarrubias, Diego. 1581. *Opera omnia* 1. Venetiis: apud haeredem Hieronymi Scoti. *Epitome in quartum librum decretalium*. Secunda Pars. Caput VII, § 3, n. 3, 212.

[91]de la Vera Cruz, Alonso. 1572. *Speculum coniugiorum*. Compluti: ex officina Ioannis Graciani. Articulus XLII, *De impedimento ligaminis*, 220–223, § *Prima conclusio*.

[92]de la Vera Cruz 1572 (as n. 91) Articulus XLII, *De impedimento ligaminis*, 221, § *Secunda conclusio*. See also degli Ubaldi, Baldo. 1575. *Consiliorum sive responsorum* 1. Venetiis: Francesco de' Franceschi & Gaspare Bindoni & Nicolo Bevilacqua & Damiano Zenaro [1970. Torino: Bottega d'Erasmo]. Consilium 488, 156–157.

[93]de la Vera Cruz 1572 (as n. 91) Articulus XLII, *De impedimento ligaminis*, 222, § *Quarta conclusio*.

[94]de la Vera Cruz 1572 (as n. 91) Articulus XLII, *De impedimento ligaminis*, 222, § *Quinta conclusio*.

[95]Bonacina 1629 (as n. 27) Quaestio III, *De impedimentis matrimonii*. Punctum X, *De impedimento ligaminis*, 161, n. 12. Martino Bonacina (1585–1631) came from a noble Milanese family, and taught canon law and civil law at the Ambrosian seminary. He authored several works, including the treatises *De sacramentis, De magno matrimonii sacramento, De morali theologia, De simonia, De contractibus et restitutione*, in which he combined theological, legal and economic interests (Castronovo, Valerio. 1969. Bonacina, Martino. In *Dizionario Biografico degli Italiani* 11. Roma: Istituto della Enciclopedia Italiana, 466–468).

[96]de Soto 1569 (as n. 47) Distinctio XXXVII, *De alijs criminibus, quae sunt matrimonij impedimenta*. Quaestio unica. Articulus V, *Utrum ligamen sit impedimentum matrimonium dirimens*, 280, § *De hac vero certitudine*; Sanchez, Thomas. 1693. *De sancto matrimonii sacramento disputationum tomi tres* 1. Venetiis: typis, et sumptibus Antonij Tivani. Liber II, *De essentia et consensu matrimonii*. Disputatio XLI [but XLVI], *Qualiter constare debeat de alterius coniugis obitu ut possit superstes aliud inire matrim*, n. 6, 181–182.

"moralis certitudo", as those who married in any different way would expose themselves to the danger of adultery.[97] Consequently, his reasoning follows that a wife cannot marry again even when her husband has been absent for many years, since an absence without any news of the absentee—even when much time has passed—does not provide sufficient guarantees, just as a spouse's death cannot be considered proved if there is just one witness.[98] However, there is one particular case in which a woman may marry again: if she is the only one to know with certainty that her husband is dead, even if she is not capable of proving it. This could happen, for instance, if she personally witnessed his death without any other witnesses present.[99]

The tendency to relativize the law of nature, which was already clearly perceivable in Thomas Aquinas, was markedly present in the works of those theologians and jurists who, from their university chairs, innovated Thomistic thought under the influence of the Counter-Reformation. Their conclusion was that polygamy was totally contrary to the law of nature, but not in absolute terms: as stated above, God had allowed marriage with different women in the Old Testament.

While it is true that all the masters from Salamanca agreed in clarifying that the *pluralitas uxorum* was permitted at the time of the ancient patriarchs, it was Diego de Covarrubias y Leiva—eminent jurisconsult of the sixteenth century, judge of the *Audiencia* in Granada and professor in Salamanca[100]—who studied the issue in depth in his *Epitome in quartum librum decretalium*, explaining why polygamy was lawful in the Old Testament while at the same time formally prohibited by Christian marriage. A marriage celebrated based on the model of the bond between Christ and the Church obliges monogamy, as it was established precisely for the purpose of

[97]Bonacina 1629 (as n. 27) Quaestio III, *De impedimentis matrimonii*. Punctum X, *De impedimento ligaminis*, 161, n. 12.

[98]Bonacina 1629 (as n. 27) Quaestio III, *De impedimentis matrimonii*. Punctum X, *De impedimento ligaminis*, 161, n. 16.

[99]Bonacina 1629 (as n. 27) Quaestio III, *De impedimentis matrimonii*. Punctum X, *De impedimento ligaminis*, 162, n. 16.

[100]Although Diego de Covarrubias y Leiva (1512–1577) was best remembered for his work as a criminal law expert, civil law expert and economist—work that was not without important internationalist connotations—he did also deal with filiation, albeit marginally, above all in the note *Epitome in quartum librum decretalium*. On his contribution to the field of criminal law, please refer to Pereda, Julián. 1959. *Covarrubias penalista*. Barcelona: Bosch. There is much historiographical information available in Piano Mortari, Vincenzo. 1980. *Gli inizi del diritto moderno in Europa*. Napoli: Liguori Editore, 412–413 and 416–417. See also the recent work by Alvarado, Javier. 2004. Diego de Covarrubias y Leyva (1512–1577). In Domingo, Rafael (Ed.), *Juristas universales* 2, *Juristas modernos*. Madrid-Barcelona: Marcial Pons, 202–206; Codes, Guadalupe. 2012. Covarrubias y Leiva, Diego de. In *Diccionario general de derecho canónico*, Obra dirigida y coordinada por Javier Otaduy, Antonio Viana, Joaquín Sedano 2. Navarra: Thomson Reuters Aranzadi, 808–809; Rodríguez San Pedro Bezares, Luis Enrique. 2013. El canonista Diego de Covarrubias y Leiva (1512–1577) y la Universidad de Salamanca. *Revista española de derecho canónico* 70.174: 41–65.

fighting concupiscence: it would therefore be against its own aims to grant a man the possibility of having more than one spouse.[101]

The jurist from Toledo also reserved a rather negative opinion of a woman bound to different men, which he considered a despicable situation. This interpretation would pave the way for the observations of the German natural law scholar Christian Thomasius in his *Disputatio de crimine bigamiae* (1685) more than a century later.[102] To Diego de Covarrubias y Leiva, the reason for prohibiting such a situation not only stems from its contradiction with the law of nature, but also from the potential risks polyandry poses for ascertaining paternity.[103]

In reading the words that the 'Spanish Bartolus' dedicates to the subject, it must be emphasized that while his argumentation reveals itself to be lucid and rational as always, it is nonetheless only directed at the fortuitous element of marriage, thus failing to mention its spiritual connotation or any reference to that *consensus* which for centuries canonist doctrine had held was the cornerstone of the bond of marriage.[104]

Bigamy's contrariness to the ends of marriage had important repercussions not only from a legal standpoint but also from a spiritual standpoint, given its considerable dangerousness for the soul. This led the Spaniard Diego García de Trasmiera, general inquisitor of Sicily during the revolt of Palermo in 1647,[105] to dedicate a specific treatise on the matter, revealing the weight and the jurisdictional scope of the Tribunal of the Holy Office.[106] Just like the masters of second Scholasticism, he also connects the unlawfulness of polygamous conduct exclusively with the ends of marriage, which he identifies based on Bellarmino. The "domestica societas et communicatio operum, quae ad vitam necessaria sunt", the "remedium contra concupiscentiam" and the "repraesentatio unitatis Sacramenti sponsi Christi cum Ecclesia" are added to the main aim of the "susceptio et educatio

[101]de Covarrubias 1581 (as n. 90) Secunda Pars. Caput VII, § 3, 212.

[102]Dufour, Alfred. 1972. *Le mariage dans l'école allemande du droit naturel moderne au XVIIIe siècle. Les sources philosophiques de la Scolastique aux Lumières. La doctrine.* Paris: Librairie générale de droit et de jurisprudence, 317–321.

[103]de Covarrubias 1581 (as n. 90) Secunda Pars. Caput VII, § 3, n. 2, 212.

[104]de Covarrubias 1581 (as n. 90) Secunda Pars. Caput VII, § 3, n. 3, 212–214. Cf. Ruiz-Galvez Priego, Estrella. 1990. *Statut socio-juridique de la femme en Espagne au XVIe siècle. Une étude sur le mariage chretien faite d'après l'Epitome de matrimonio de Diego de Covarrubias y Leiva, la legislation royale et les moralistes.* Paris: Diffusion Didier Érudition, especially 408–412.

[105]Rivero Rodríguez, Manuel. 2004. Técnica de un golpe de Estado: el inquisidor García de Trasmiera en la revuelta siciliana de 1647. In Aranda Pérez, Francisco José (Ed.), *La declinación de la Monarquía Hispánica en el Siglo XVII*, Cuenca: Ediciones de la Universidad de Castilla-La Mancha, 129–153.

[106]García de Trasmiera, Diego. 1638. *De polygamia, et polyviria libri tres.* Panhormi: apud Decium Cyrillum. On this work, in the field of historiography, see Canosa, Romano. 1994. *Sessualità e Inquisizione in Italia tra Cinquecento e Seicento.* Roma: Sapere 2000, 25–36. See also Brambilla, Elena. 2000. *Alle origini del Sant'Uffizio. Penitenza, confessione e giustizia spirituale dal medioevo al XVI secolo.* Bologna: il Mulino.

prolis". Since polygamy is against all four aims, including the main aim of procreation due to the fact that, as Ponce de León had stated, "luxuriosi minus foecundi esse solent",[107] it is thus clear "quam graviter peccent hi, qui simul plures ducunt uxores, et non leviter quidem".[108]

3 Conclusions

To conclude, an initial analysis of the stances held by second Scholasticism reveals some common explanations and some fundamental tendencies in lines of reasoning.

First of all, it should be of no surprise that many authors who are normally traced back to late Scholasticism justify—to a greater or lesser extent—the prohibition on polygamy by showing its incompatibility with the principles of natural law (as well as with divine and human law) through solid rational arguments. The subversive potential of bigamy—very dangerous for the stability of the institution of marriage and for the entire social order—was influenced by new developments in that delicate phase for the Catholic Church that was the sixteenth century, an era that in many ways marked the beginning of the collapse of the traditional world.[109]

These decades saw the epistemological theories of Protestantism and the dogmas of the Counter-Reformation face off on the shaky ground that was the sacrament of marriage, and by examining this period it becomes clear just how important the jurists and theologians of the sixteenth-century were in developing the post-Tridentine marriage doctrine.

These thinkers were poised between the decline of medieval subject-matter and the emergence modern currents of thought, in what has been defined as a role 'of transition' for late scholastic thought.[110] Thus, the greatest difficulty they encountered was their attempt to rationally provide grounds for the rules of the law of nature, and in particular for the natural prohibition of polygamy. Indeed, they sometimes engaged in subtle dialectic 'acrobatics', which led these keen supporters of reformed Catholicism down impassable paths, thus compounding doubts and causing them to dangerously slip towards voluntaristic explanations.

As such, it was not the formulation of particularly original solutions that characterized this period, but rather the skill and insight that the thinkers exhibited in philosophizing on what was rationally justifiable and in discussing the pros and

---

[107]García de Trasmiera, Diego 1638 (as n. 106) Liber I. Quaestio VI, *De gravitate delicti Bigamiae apud Christianos*, 15, n. 12.

[108]García de Trasmiera, Diego 1638 (as n. 106) Liber I. Quaestio VI, *De gravitate delicti Bigamiae apud Christianos*, 16, n. 20.

[109]Hespanha, António Manuel. 2013. *La cultura giuridica europea*. Bologna: il Mulino, 171.

[110]Todescan, Franco. 2011. «Nolite silere theologi in munere alieno». Il perché di una ricerca sulla Seconda Scolastica. In Ferronato, Marta and Bianchin, Lucia (Eds.), Silete theologi in munere alieno. *Alberico Gentili e la Seconda Scolastica*, Atti del Convegno Internazionale (Padova, 20–22 novembre 2008). Padova: Cedam, 185–217, especially 196–203.

cons of the issue. There was a palpable contrast between the apologetic duty of consolidating European Catholicism and the willingness to push the boundaries of thought at the time.

Even though late Scholasticism only reproduced the theory contrasting *pluralitas uxorum* with *lex naturalis* and the theory of divine dispensation (to justify the ancient lawfulness of polygamy), new horizons of thought were explored that paved the way for future assertions of natural law scholars and Enlightenment thinkers. Indeed, though these future thinkers would tackle the problem of polygamy with partially different results, they would not abandon the arguments developed in sixteenth-century Scholasticism.

The Scholastic authors were faithful to Thomism and to the traditional stances of the Church, but at the same time influenced by modern cultural and philosophical developments such as the empirical observation of reality and the exercise of logical reasoning. Thus, they became the bearers of a markedly rational knowledge of the law, opening themselves up to the challenges of the world with a deep feeling of independence.

References

Literature

1952. *Statuta et ordinamenta Comunis Cremonae facta et compilata currente anno Domini MCCCXXXIX*, curati e aggiornati con le riforme del decennio successivo da Ugo Gualazzini. Milano: Giuffrè.

1991. *Conciliorum Oecumenicorum Decreta*. Bologna: Edizioni dehoniane.

Aboi Rubio, D. (2012). Bigamia. In *Diccionario general de derecho canónico*, Obra dirigida y coordinada por Javier Otaduy, Antonio Viana, Joaquín Sedano 1. Navarra: Thomson Reuters Aranzadi, 708–711.

Alberici a Rosate. (1548). *Dictionarium*. Lugduni: Compagnie des libraires de Lyon.

Alfieri, F. (2010). *Nella camera degli sposi. Tomás Sánchez, il matrimonio, la sessualità (secoli XVI–XVII)*. Bologna: il Mulino.

Alonso, R., Maria, P. (2012). *Salamanca, escuela de juristas. Estudios sobre la enseñanza del derecho en el Antiguo Régimen*, Madrid: Universidad Carlos III de Madrid.

Alvarado, J. (2004). Diego de Covarrubias y Leyva (1512–1577). In Domingo, R. (Ed.), *Juristas universales* 2, *Juristas modernos* (pp. 202–206). Madrid-Barcelona: Marcial Pons.

Andreato, C. (2004). Il reato di bigamia nella Repubblica di Venezia (secoli XVI e XVII). In Chiodi, G. & Povolo, C. (Eds.), *L'amministrazione della giustizia penale nella Repubblica di Venezia (secoli XVI–XVIII)* 2, *Retoriche, stereotipi, prassi* (pp. 413–464). Verona: Cierre Edizioni.

Andreato, C. (2007). Il reato di bigamia nella Repubblica di Venezia da un processo del 1630. *Acta Histriae 15*(2), 471–492.

Ardito, S. (1981). La dottrina matrimoniale di Basilio Ponce de León (1570–1629) e la letteratura ecclesiastica posteriore fino al Concilio Vaticano II. Contributo alla storia della rilevanza giuridica dell'amore coniugale. *Salesianum 43*, 757–815

Aznar Gil, F. (2003). Penas y sanciones contra los matrimonios clandestinos en la península ibérica durante la baja edad media. *Revista de Estudios Histórico-Jurídicos 25*, 189–230.

Barbier, M. (1999). La notion de *respublica* chez Vitoria. In Zarka, Y. C. (Ed.), *Aspects de la pensée médiévale dans la philosophie politique moderne* (pp. 83–101). Paris: Presses Universitaires de France.

Barp Fontana, L. (2007). Fundamentos filosóficos de los derechos humanos en el Speculum coniugiorum de Alonso de la Veracruz. In Ponce Hernández, C. (Ed.). *Innovación y tradición en Fray Alonso de la Veracruz* (pp. 247–269). Ciudad Universitaria: Facultad de Filosofía y Letras Universidad Nacional Autónoma de México.

Belda Plans, J. (2000). *La Escuela de Salamanca y la renovación de la teología en el siglo XVI*. Madrid: BAC.

Bellarmino, R. (1721). *Disputationes de controversiis christianae fidei, adversus huius temporis haereticos* 3. Pragae: typis Wolffgangi Wickhart.

Beltrán de Heredia, V. (1953). *Los orígenes de la Universidad de Salamanca*, Salamanca: Ediciones Universidad de Salamanca.

Bergman, H. J. (2010). *Diritto e rivoluzione* 2, *L'impatto delle riforme protestanti sulla tradizione giuridica occidentale*. Edizione italiana a cura di Diego Quaglioni. Bologna: il Mulino.

Bernhard, J., Lefebvre, C. & Rapp, F. (1990). *L'époque de la réforme et du Concile de Trente*. Paris: Éditions Cujas.

Bunge, K., Spindler, A. & Wagner, A. (Eds.). 2011. *Die Normativität des Rechts bei Francisco de Vitoria*. Stuttgart-Bad Cannstatt: Fromman-holzboog

Bethery de La Brosse, A. (2011). *Entre amour et droit: le lien conjugal dans la pensée juridique moderne (XVIe–XXIe siècles)*. Préface de Anne Lefebvre-Teillard. Paris: Lextenso éditions.

Biale, R. (1995). *Women and Jewish Law. The essential texts, their history and their relevance for today*. New York: Schocken books.

Bonacina, M. (1629). *De magno matrimonii sacramento tractatus*. Venetiis: sumptibus disiunctae societatis.

Brambilla, E. (2000). *Alle origini del Sant'Uffizio. Penitenza, confessione e giustizia spirituale dal medioevo al XVI secolo*. Bologna: il Mulino.

Brouillard, R. (1939). Sanchez Thomas. In *Dictionnaire de théologie catholique* 14 (pp. 1075–1085). Paris: Letouzey et Ané.

Brown Scott, J. (2000). *The spanish origin of international law: Francisco de vitoria and his law of nations*. Union. New Jersey: The Lawbook Exchange, LTD.

Brundage, J. A. (1987). *Law, Sex, and Christian Society in Medieval Europe*. Chicago and London: The University of Chicago Press.

Brunori, L. (2015). *Societas quid sit. La société commerciale dans l'élaboration de la Seconde Scolastique*. Préface de Jean Hilaire. Paris: Mare & Martin.

Burguière, A., Klapisch-Zuber, C., Segalen, M. & Zonabend, F. (Eds.). (1986). *Histoire de la famille*. Préface de Jack Goody 2, *Le choc des modernités*. Paris: Armand Colin Editeur.

Burrus, E. (1967–1972). *The Writings of Fray Alonso de la Vera Cruz*. Saint Louis: Jesuit Historical Institute.

Canosa, R. (1994). *Sessualità e Inquisizione in Italia tra Cinquecento e Seicento*. Roma: Sapere 2000.

Carrodeguas, C. (2003). *La sacramentalidad del matrimonio. Doctrina de Tomás Sanchez, S.J.*. Madrid: Universidad pontificia Comillas.

Castro Corona, S. (2007). Los argumentos aristotélicos en el Speculum coniugiorum de Alonso de la Veracruz. In Ponce Hernández, C. (Ed.). *Innovación y tradición en Fray Alonso de la Veracruz* (pp. 235–245). Ciudad Universitaria: Facultad de Filosofía y Letras Universidad Nacional Autónoma de México.

Castronovo, V. (1969). Bonacina, Martino. In *Dizionario Biografico degli Italiani* 11 (pp. 466–468). Roma: Istituto della Enciclopedia Italiana.

Chaves, T. (1594). *Summa sacramentorum ecclesiae, ex doctrina fratris Francisci a Victoria, ordinis Praedicatorum et olim Primarii Cathedratici*. Antverpiae: in aedibus Petri Belleri.

Chenu, M. D. (1926). Ledesma (Pierre de). In *Dictionnaire de théologie catholique* 9 (pp. 126–127). Paris: Letouzey et Ané.
Codes, G. (2012). Covarrubias y Leiva, Diego de. In *Diccionario general de derecho canónico*, Obra dirigida y coordinada por Javier Otaduy, Antonio Viana, Joaquín Sedano 2 (pp. 808–809). Navarra: Thomson Reuters Aranzadi.
Colafemmina, C. (1992). La poligamia presso gli ebrei nel Medioevo. *Quaderni medievali* 34, 114–122.
Colorni, V. (1945). *Legge ebraica e leggi locali. Ricerche sull'ambito d'applicazione del diritto ebraico in Italia dall'epoca romana al secolo XIX*. Milano: Giuffrè.
Corvino, F. (1957). Reginaldo da Piperno. In *Enciclopedia filosofica* 3. Venezia-Roma: Istituto per la collaborazione culturale, col. 1921.
Cozzi, G. (2000). Padri, figli e matrimoni clandestini (metà secolo XVI–metà secolo XVIII). In Cozzi, Gaetano. 2000. *La società veneta e il suo diritto. Saggi su questioni matrimoniali, giustizia penale, politica del diritto, sopravvivenza del diritto veneto nell'Ottocento* (pp. 19–64). Venezia: Marsilio.
Cristiani, L. (1977). *La Chiesa al tempo del Concilio di Trento* (trans. A. Galuzzi). Torino: S.A.I.E.
d'Avack, Pietro Agostino. (1965). Il «ligamen seu vinculum prioris matrimonii» nelle fonti e nella dottrina classica della Chiesa. In *Studi in memoria di Guido Zanobini* 4 (pp. 191–229). Milano: Giuffrè.
Cruz Cruz, J. (Ed.). (2007). *La Ley natural como fundamento moral y jurídico en Domingo de Soto*. Pamplona: EUNSA.
Cruz Cruz, J. (Ed.). (2008). *Ley y dominio en Francisco de Vitoria*. Pamplona: EUNSA.
Dall'Olio, G. (2013). *Martin Lutero*. Roma: Carocci editore.
Dauvillier, J. (1933). *Le mariage dans le droit classique de l'Église depuis le décret de Gratien (1140) jusqu'à la mort de Clément V (1314)*. Paris: Librairie du Recueil Sirey.
de Covarrubias, D. (1581). *Opera omnia* 1. Venetiis: apud haeredem Hieronymi Scoti. *Epitome in quartum librum decretalium*.
de la Vera Cruz, A. (1572). *Speculum coniugiorum*. Compluti: ex officina Ioannis Graciani.
de Ledesma, P. (1595). *Tractatus de magno matrimonii sacramento*. Venetiis: apud Marcum Antonium Zalterium.
de Soto, D. (1569). *Commentariorum Fratris Dominici Soto Segoviensis ... in Quartum Sententiarum* 2. Salmanticae: apud Ioannes Baptista a Terranova.
de Vitoria, F. (1765). *Relectio de matrimonio*. In de Vitoria, Francisco. 1765. *Relectiones theologicae*. Matriti: en la Oficina de Manuel Martin.
de Vitoria, F. (2005). *Sobre el matrimonio. Estudio preliminar, traducción y notas de Luis Frayle Delgado*. Salamanca: Editorial San Esteban.
de Vitoria, F. (2015). *Sul matrimonio. Introduzione, traduzione e commento di Mauro Mantovani*. Roma: Aracne.
degli Ubaldi, B. (1575). *Consiliorum sive responsorum* 1. Venetiis: Francesco de' Franceschi & Gaspare Bindoni & Nicolo Bevilacqua & Damiano Zenaro [1970. Torino: Bottega d'Erasmo].
di Renzo, V., Maria, G. (2010). Il matrimonio tra sacro e profano. Dalla lezione giusnaturalistica al giurisdizionalismo. In Amato Mangiameli, A. C. & Di Simone, M. R. (Eds.), *Diritto e religione tra passato e futuro*, Atti del Convegno internazionale Villa Mondragone-Monte Porzio Catone (Roma) 27–29 novembre 2008 (pp. 259–325). Roma: Aracne.
Donahue, C. (2007). *Law, marriage, and society in the later middle ages. Arguments about marriage in five courts*. New York: Cambridge University Press.
Donahue, C. (2014). The Role of the humanists and the second scholastic in the development of european marriage law from the sixteenth to the nineteenth centuries. In Decock, W., Ballor, J., Germann, M., & Waelkens, L. (Eds.), *Law and religion. The legal teachings of the protestant and catholic reformations* (pp. 45–62). Göttingen: Vandenhoeck & Ruprecht.
Dufour, A. (1972). *Le mariage dans l'école allemande du droit naturel moderne au XVIIIe siècle. Les sources philosophiques de la Scolastique aux Lumières. La doctrine*. Paris: Librairie générale de droit et de jurisprudence.

Esmein, A. (1891). *Le mariage en droit canonique* 1. Paris: L. Larose et Forcel.

Esmein, A. (1891). *Le mariage en droit canonique* 2. Paris: L. Larose et Forcel.

Esposito, A. (2004). Adulterio, concubinato, bigamia: testimonianze dalla normativa statutaria dello Stato pontificio (secoli XIII–XVI). In Seidel Menchi, S. & Quaglioni, D. (Eds.), *Trasgressioni. Seduzione, concubinato, adulterio, bigamia (XIV–XVIII secolo)* (pp. 21–42). Bologna: il Mulino.

Férnandez Á. M., Robles, L. & Rodríguez-San, Pedro Bezares, L. E. (Eds.). (1990). *La Universidad de Salamanca* 2, *Atmósfera intelectual y Perspectivas de investigación*. Salamanca: Ediciones Universidad de Salamanca.

Frost, G. (1997). Bigamy and Cohabitation in Victorian England. *Journal of Family History* *22*(3): 286–306.

Gacto Fernández, E. (1987). El delito de bigamia y la Inquisición española. *Anuario de historia del derecho español* 57: 465–492, also in Tomas y Valiente, Francisco. 1990. *Sexo barroco y otras transgresiones premodernas* (pp. 27–152). Madrid: Alianza.

García de Trasmiera, D. (1638). *De polygamia, et polyviria libri tres*. Panhormi: apud Decium Cyrillum.

Garlati, L. (2011). La famiglia tra passato e presente. In Patti, S. & Cubeddu, M. G. (Eds.), *Diritto della famiglia* (pp. 1–48). Milano: Giuffrè.

Gaudemet, J. (1987). *Le mariage en Occident. Les moeurs et le droit*. Paris: Les éditions du cerf.

Giacon, C. (1944). *La Seconda Scolastica* 1, *I grandi commentatori di San Tommaso*. Milano: Bocca.

Giacon, C. (1947). *La Seconda Scolastica* 2, *Precedenze teoretiche ai problemi giuridici: Toledo, Pereira, Fonseca, Molina, Suarez*. Milano: Bocca.

Giacon, C. (1950). *La Seconda Scolastica* 3, *I problemi giuridico–politici. Suarez, Bellarmino, Mariana*. Milano: Bocca.

Gismondi, P. (1953). L'attuazione dottrinaria e pratica delle norme tridentine sulla forma del matrimonio. *Rivista italiana per le scienze giuridiche* *6*(3), 250–284.

Gordley, J. (2006). *Foundations of Private Law. Property, Tort, Contract, Unjust Enrichment*. Oxford: Oxford University Press.

Grisar, H. (1917). *Luther* 5 (trans. E. M. Lamond). London: Kegan Paul, Trench, *Trübner* & Co.

Grossi, P. (Ed.). (1973). *La Seconda Scolastica nella formazione del diritto privato moderno*, Incontro di studio (Firenze, 16–19 ottobre 1972). Milano: Giuffrè.

Grunert, F. & Seelmann, K. (Eds.). (2001). *Die Ordnung der Praxis. Neue Studien zur spanischen Spätscholastik*. Tübingen: Niemeyer.

Hernández, R. (1991). La Escuela de Salamanca del siglo XVII y los problemas de Indias: fray Pedro de Ledesma. In *Congreso Internacional sobre los dominicos y el nuevo mundo* 3 (pp. 645–667). Granada-Madrid: Deimos.

Hernández Martín, R. (1999). *La lezione sugli Indios di Francisco de Vitoria* (trans. S. Casabianca). Milano: Jaca Book.

Hespanha, António Manuel. 2013. *La cultura giuridica europea*. Bologna: il Mulino.

Jedin, H. (1973–1981). *Storia del Concilio di Trento*. 4 voll. Brescia: Morcelliana.

Jemolo, A. C. (1948). La riforma tridentina nell'ambito matrimoniale. *Quaderni di Belfagor 1*, 45–51.

Jemolo, A. C. (1993). *Il matrimonio nel diritto canonico. Dal Concilio di Trento al Codice del 1917*. Prefazione di Jean Gaudemet. Bologna: il Mulino.

Lamacchia, A. (1995). *La Filosofia nel Siglo de Oro. Studi sul tardo Rinascimento spagnolo*. Bari: Levante.

Lazcano, R. (2007). *Fray Alonso de Veracruz (1507–1584). Misionero del saber y protector de indios*. Madrid: Ed. Revista Agustiniana.

Lefebvre-Teillard, A. (2009). *Law and History Review* *27*(2), 451–453.

Legendre, P. (Ed.). (2004). *"Ils seront deux en une seule chair". Scénographie du couple humain dans le texte occidental. Travaux du Laboratoire Européen pour l'étude de la filiation*. Brussels: E. Van Balberghe.

Lombardi, D. (1996). Fidanzamenti e matrimoni dal Concilio di Trento alle riforme settecentesche. In De Giorgio, M. & Klapisch-Zuber, C. (Eds.), *Storia del matrimonio* (pp. 215–250). Roma-Bari: Laterza.

Lombardi, D. (2001). *Matrimoni di antico regime*. Bologna: il Mulino.

Lombardi, D. (2008). *Storia del matrimonio. Dal Medioevo a oggi*. Bologna: il Mulino.

Lutero, M. (1960). *Luther: Letters of Spiritual Counsel* (trans. T. G. Tappert). Vancouver: Regent College Publishing.

Mayali, L. (2008). "Duo erunt in carne una" and the Medieval Canonists. In Colli, V. & Conte, E. (Eds.), *Iuris Historia. Liber Amicorum Gero Dolezalek* (pp. 161–175). Berkley: University of California.

Melchior-Bonnet, S. & Salles, C. (Eds.). (2009). *Histoire du marriage*. Paris: Éditions Robert Laffont.

Milazzo, L. (2012). *La teoria dei diritti di Francisco de Vitoria*. Pisa: Edizioni ETS.

Marchetto, G. (2004). «Primus fuit Lamech». La bigamia tra irregolarità e delitto nella dottrina di diritto comune. In Seidel Menchi, S. & Quaglioni, D. (Eds.), *Trasgressioni. Seduzione, concubinato, adulterio, bigamia (XIV–XVIII secolo)* (pp. 43–105). Bologna: il Mulino.

Marongiu, A. (1959). Bigamia (storia). In *Enciclopedia del diritto* 5 (pp. 361–362). Milano: Giuffrè.

Massetto, G. (1985). *Un magistrato e una città nella Lombardia spagnola. Giulio Claro pretore a Cremona*. Milano: Giuffrè.

Massetto, G. (1994). *Saggi di storia del diritto penale lombardo (Secc. XVI–XVIII)*. Milano: LED.

Menochio, I. (1587). *De arbitrariis iudicum quaestionibus et causis libri duo*. Coloniae Agrippinae: apud Ioannem Gymnicum.

McDougall, S. (2010). Bigamy: a male crime in medieval Europe? *Gender & History 22*: 430–446.

McDougall, S. (2012). *Bigamy and christian identity in late medieval champagne*. Philadelphia: University of Pennsylvania.

Motta, F. (2005). *Bellarmino. Una teologia politica della Controriforma*. Brescia: Morcelliana.

Naz, R. (1937). Bigamie (Le délit de). In *Dictionnaire de droit canonique* 12 (pp. 888–889). Paris: Librairie Letouzey et ané.

Noonan, J. (1973). Power to Choose. *Viator. Medieval and Renaissance Studies 4*, 419–439.

Otte, G. (1964). *Das Privatrecht bei Francisco de Vitoria*. Köln Graz: Böhlau Verlag.

Palamidessi, A. M. (2010). *Alle origini del diritto internazionale: il contributo di Vitoria e Suarez alla moderna dottrina internazionalistica*. Roma: Aracne.

Pena González, M. A. (Ed.). (2009). *La Escuela de Salamanca. De la Monarquía hispánica al Orbe católico*. Madrid: BAC.

Pereda, J. (1959). *Covarrubias penalista*. Barcelona: Bosch.

Piano Mortari, V. (1980). *Gli inizi del diritto moderno in Europa*. Napoli: Liguori Editore.

Pietro, L. (1757). *Sententiarum Libri Quatuor*. Antverpiae: sumptibus Marci-Michael Bousquet et socior.

Pisapia, G. D. (1958). Bigamia. In *Novissimo Digesto Italiano* 2 (pp. 396–409). Torino: UTET.

Ponce de León, B. (1613). *Tractatus de impedimentibus matrimonii sive commentarius ad decem Gratiani causas a 27*. Salmanticae: apud Antoniam Ramirez viduam.

Ponce de León, B. (1640). *De sacramento matrimonii tractatus*. Lugduni: sumptibus haeredis Gabr. Boissat et Laurentij Anisson.

Ponce Hernández, C. (Ed.). (2007). *Innovación y tradición en Fray Alonso de la Veracruz*. Prólogo de A. Velasco Gómez. Ciudad Universitaria: Facultad de Filosofía y Letras Universidad Nacional Autónoma de México.

Poncela González, Á. (2015). *La Escuela de Salamanca. Filosofía y Humanismo ante el mundo moderno*. Madrid: Editorial Verbum.

Prasada Rao, K. (2003). *Bigamy in Christian Law*. New Delhi: Orient Law House.

Quaglioni, D. (2001). «Sacramenti detestabili». La forma del matrimonio prima e dopo Trento. In Seidel Menchi, S. & Quaglioni, D. (Eds.), *Matrimoni in dubbio. Unioni controverse e nozze clandestine in Italia dal XIV al XVIII secolo* (pp. 61–79). Bologna: il Mulino.

Ramos-Lissón, D. (2004). Domingo de Soto (1495–1560). In Domingo, R. (Ed.), *Juristas universales* 2, *Juristas modernos* (pp. 160–165). Madrid-Barcelona: Marcial Pons.

Raoul, N. Sanchez (Thomas). In *Dictionnaire de droit canonique* 7 (pp. 864–870). Paris: Letouzey et Ané.

Rasi, P. (1941). L'applicazione delle norme del concilio di Trento in materia matrimoniale. In *Studi in onore di Arrigo Solmi* 1 (pp. 235–281). Milano: Giuffrè.

Rasi, P. (1943). *La conclusione del matrimonio nella prassi prima del concilio di Trento*. Bologna: Zanichelli.

Rasi, P. (1958). *La conclusione del matrimonio nella dottrina prima del Concilio di Trento*. Napoli: Jovene.

Reinhardt, K. F. (2003). Vera Cruz, Alonso de la, Fray. In *New Catholic Encyclopedia* 14 (pp. 443–444). Detroit-New York: Gale.

Rivero Rodríguez, M. (2004). Técnica de un golpe de Estado: el inquisidor García de Trasmiera en la revuelta siciliana de 1647. In Aranda Pérez, F. J. (Ed.), *La declinación de la Monarquía Hispánica en el Siglo XVII* (pp. 129–153). Cuenca: Ediciones de la Universidad de Castilla-La Mancha.

Riverso, R. (2011). *La nascita del concetto dei diritti umani nella Seconda Scolastica*. Roma: Albatros.

Rodríguez San Pedro Bezares, L. E. (Ed.). 2002–2006. *Historia de la Universidad de Salamanca*, 4 voll. Salamanca: Ediciones Universidad de Salamanca.

Rodríguez San Pedro Bezares, L. E. (2013). El canonista Diego de Covarrubias y Leiva (1512–1577) y la Universidad de Salamanca. *Revista española de derecho canónico 70*(174), 41–65.

Ruiz-Galvez Priego, E. (1990). *Statut socio-juridique de la femme en Espagne au XVIe siècle. Une étude sur le mariage chretien faite d'après l'Epitome de matrimonio de Diego de Covarrubias y Leiva, la legislation royale et les moralistes*. Paris: Diffusion Didier Érudition.

Salvi, S. T. (2015). Luci e ombre nella famiglia del *siglo de oro*: filiazione illegittima e seconda scolastica. *Rivista di Storia del Diritto Italiano 88*, 175–202.

San Tommaso d'Aquino. (1986). *La Somma teologica*, traduzione e commento a cura dei domenicani italiani, testo latino dell'edizione leonina 31 (Suppl., qq. 41–68). Bologna: Edizioni Studio Domenicano.

San Tommaso d'Aquino. (1660). *Praeclarissima commentaria in quartum librum sententiarum Petri Lombardi*. Parisiis: apud societatem bibliopolarum.

Sanchez, T. (1693). *De sancto matrimonii sacramento disputationum tomi tres*. Venetiis: typis, et sumptibus Antonij Tivani.

Sant'Agostino. (1981). *De civitate Dei libri XXII* 2. Stuttgart: B. G. Teubner.

Saje, A. (2003). *La forma straordinaria e il ministro della celebrazione del matrimonio secondo il Codice latino e orientale*. Roma: Editrice Pontificia Università Gregoriana.

Scaramella, P. (2005). Controllo e repressione ecclesiastica della poligamia a Napoli in Età moderna: dalle cause matrimoniali al crimine di fede (1514–1799). In Scaramella, Pierroberto. 2005. *Inquisizioni, eresie, etnie, dissenso religioso e giustizia ecclesiastica in Italia (secc. XVI–XVIII)* (pp. 239–294). Bari: Cacucci Editore.

Schereschewsky, B.-Z. & Elon, M. (2007). Bigamy and Polygamy. In Berenbaum, M. & Skolnik, F. (Eds.), *Encyclopaedia Judaica* 3 (pp. 691–694). Detroit: Macmillan Reference USA.

Schmoeckel, M. (2014). *Das Recht der Reformation*. Tübingen: Mohr Siebeck.

Schwab, D. (1973). Ehe und Familie nach den Lehren der Spätscholastik. In Grossi, P. (Ed.), *La Seconda Scolastica nella formazione del diritto privato moderno*, Incontro di studio (Firenze, 16–19 ottobre 1972) (pp. 73–116). Milano: Giuffrè.

Seidel Menchi, S. (2001). Percorsi variegati, percorsi obbligati. Elogio del matrimonio pre-tridentino. In Seidel Menchi, S. & Quaglioni, D. (Eds.), *Matrimoni in dubbio. Unioni controverse e nozze clandestine in Italia dal XIV al XVIII secolo* (pp. 17–60). Bologna: il Mulino.

Sertoli Salis, R. (1962). *La poligamia nella storia e nel costume*. Roma: Accademia internazionale Leonardo da Vinci di scienze, lettere ed arti.

Tamassia, N. (1910). *La famiglia italiana nei secoli decimoquinto e decimosesto.* Milano-Palermo-Napoli: Sandron.

Tejero, E. (1971). *El matrimonio. Misterio y signo. Siglos XIV–XVI.* Pamplona: Ediciones Universidad de Navarra.

Todescan, F. (2011). «Nolite silere theologi in munere alieno». Il perché di una ricerca sulla Seconda Scolastica. In Ferronato, M. & Bianchin, L. (Eds.), Silete theologi in munere alieno. *Alberico Gentili e la Seconda Scolastica,* Atti del Convegno Internazionale (Padova, 20–22 novembre 2008) (pp. 185–217). Padova: Cedam.

Torres Aguilar, M. (1997). Algunos aspectos del delito de bigamia en la Inquisición de Indias. *Revista de la Inquisición* 6: 117–138, also in Levaggi, A. (Ed.). 1997. *La Inquisición en Hispanoamérica. Estudios* (pp. 65–104). Bueons Aires: Ediciones Ciudad Argentina.

Torres Aguilar, M. (1997). El delito de bigamia: estudio general y especial perspectiva en el Tribunal de la Inquisición de Sevilla en el siglo XVIII. In Gacto Fernández, E. (Ed.), *El centinela de la fe: estudios jurídicos sobre la Inquisición de Sevilla en el siglo XVIII* (pp. 173–232). Sevilla: Universidad de Sevilla.

Valsecchi, C. (1994). L'istituto della dote nella vita del diritto del tardo Cinquecento: i "Consilia" di Jacopo Menochio. *Rivista di Storia del Diritto Italiano 67,* 205–282.

Valsecchi, C. (1999). «Causa matrimonialis est gravis et ardua». Consiliatores e matrimonio fino al Concilio di Trento. In *Studi di storia del diritto* 2 (pp. 407–580). Milano: Giuffrè.

Valsecchi, C. (2000). Jacopo Menochio e il giurisdizionalismo tra Cinque e Seicento. *Studia Borromaica. Saggi e documenti di storia religiosa e civile della prima età moderna 14,* 93–116.

Valsecchi, C. (2009). Menochio, Giacomo (Jacopo). In *Dizionario Biografico degli Italiani* 73 (pp. 521–524). Roma: Istituto della Enciclopedia Italiana.

Valsecchi, C. (2013). Dar ordine al caos. Il processo del tardo diritto comune nelle opere di Jacopo Menochio. In di Renzo Villata, M. G. (Ed.), *Lavorando al cantiere del 'Dizionario biografico dei giuristi italiani (XII–XX sec.)'* (pp. 217–238). Milano: Giuffrè.

Vega Gutiérrez, A. M. (1997). *La unidad del matrimonio y su tutela penal: precedentes romanos y canonicos del delito de bigamia.* Prólogo de Javier Ferrer Ortiz. Granada: Comares.

Viejo-Ximénez, J. M. (2006). Sánchez, Tomás. (1550–1610). In *Diccionario crítico de juristas españoles, portugueses y latinoamericanos* 2 (pp. 480–481). Zaragoza-Barcelona: Cátedra de Historia del Derecho y de las Instituciones.

Viejo-Ximénez, J. M. (2012). Sánchez, Tomás. In *Diccionario general de derecho canónico,* Obra dirigida y coordinada por Javier Otaduy, Antonio Viana, Joaquín Sedano 7 (pp. 144–146). Navarra: Thomson Reuters Aranzadi.

Villa, L. (2011). *La riforma protestante.* Brescia: Editrice Civiltà.

Villey, M. (2013). *La formation de la pensée juridique moderne.* Paris: PUF.

Volterra, E. (1934). Per la storia del reato di bigamia in diritto romano. In Albertario, E. (Ed.), *Studi in memoria di Umberto Ratti* (pp. 387–447). Milano: Giuffrè.

Volterra, E. (1975). Matrimonio (diritto romano). In *Enciclopedia del diritto* 25 (pp. 726–807). Milano: Giuffrè.

Zarri, G. (1996). Il matrimonio tridentino. In Prodi, P. & Reinhard, W. (Eds.), *Il concilio di Trento e il moderno* (pp. 437–483). Bologna: il Mulino.

Whitford, D. (2014). It is not forbidden that a man may have more than one wife. Luther's pastoral advice on bigamy and marriage. In D. Luebke & M. Lindemann (Eds.), *Mixed matches. Transgressive unions in Germany from the reformation to the enlightenment* (pp. 14—30). New York-Oxford: Berghahn.

Witte, J. (2002). *Law and Protestantism. The Legal Teachings of the Lutheran Reformation.* Cambridge: Cambridge University Press.

Witte, J. (2015). *The Western Case for Monogamy Over Polygamy.* New York: Cambridge University Press.

The Father's Right to Kill His Adulterous Daughter in the Late *Ius Commune*

Andrea Massironi

Abstract The father's right to kill his adulterous daughter that had been introduced by Roman law aroused some interesting discussions among law scholars even in the Modern Age. They accepted the idea that the father could kill his daughter and her lover with impunity in the case of flagrant adultery. This right could be deemed as connected to paternal authority. It was a relic of the ancient *ius vitae ac necis* which, meanwhile, had developed into a milder right to chastise a disobedient child. Some law scholars dealing with father's powers between the 16th and the 17th centuries dedicated entire chapters of their works to this considerably interesting topic. The father would be granted impunity only if he had killed his adulterous daughter on certain conditions required by Roman law. The legacy of Roman law on this matter was very clear indeed, but the law scholars of the late *ius commune* had to update those conditions and to clarify them. Furthermore, law scholars discussed some aspects of the father's right to kill his adulterous daughter that were still disputed and had not received a definitive solution, such as the father's possibility to ask someone for help or to kill his daughter despite the fact that she was pregnant. Other important subjects were also dealt with, e.g. presumptions and circumstantial evidences in adultery, which was a hard-to-prove crime. The father's right to kill his adulterous daughter also caused moral problems because, although it was lawful, it did not prevent the father from committing a mortal sin: in this way, the relationship between internal forum and external forum was often dealt with as a pivotal topic.

A. Massironi (✉)
University of Milano-Bicocca, Piazza dell'Ateneo Nuovo 1, 20126 Milan, Italy
e-mail: andrea.massironi1@unimib.it

M.G. di Renzo Villata (ed.), *Family Law and Society in Europe from the Middle Ages to the Contemporary Era*, Studies in the History of Law and Justice 5,
DOI 10.1007/978-3-319-42289-3_8

1 The Father Murderer of His Daughter in the *Ius Commune*

In the imagination of some scholars, in the Middle Ages as well as in the modern period, with regards to the people living in the family home the father had the right to behave as a prince ruling over his reign and subjects.[1] Pursuant to this authority he had, recognized by Roman law, he would have had an actual "autorità monarchica" ("monarchic authority"), taking on the essence of the family itself.[2] The right of the *paterfamilias* to be the head of the family respected a natural order, that the hierarchies within the family reflected: father and prince embodied the idea that superior and inferior existed in all things in nature.[3]

This, however, did not mean that the father possessed a kind of omnipotence. The sources of the *ius commune* emphasized the differences from a ruthless past, in which the legislators of a distant and almost mythical time (dating back even to Romulus) had granted the father the power that could, in theory, even lead to the killing of his children. The deep trust in fatherly love and mercy, that would have mitigated its use, made the introduction of this right acceptable. However, both in

[1]On this topic and with regards to the entanglement between private law and public law in the *ius commune* see Calasso, Francesco. 1951 (2nd edition). *I glossatori e la teoria della sovranità. Studio di diritto comune pubblico*. Milano: Giuffrè, 172–175; Quaglioni, Diego. 1977. «Quilibet in domo sua dicitur rex» (in margine ad alcune pagine di Francesco Calasso). *Studi senesi* 26: 344–358; Quaglioni, Diego. 1983. *Politica e diritto nel Trecento italiano. Il «De Tyranno» di Bartolo da Sassoferrato (1314–1357). Con l'edizione critica dei trattati «De Guelphis et Gebellinis», «De Regimine civitatis» e «De Tyranno»*. Firenze: Olschki, 42, who refers to the treatise of Bartolus who stated that the *paterfamilias* had "aliquid iuris regalis" in ruling his home (see *De Tyranno*, quaestio 4, 183); Cavina, Marco. 1997. *Paterfamilias-Princeps* nella tradizione teologica e giuridica bassomedievale. Alcuni sondaggi nelle fonti e nella storiografia. In Landau, Peter, and Mueller, Joers (eds.), *Proceedings of the Ninth International Congress of Medieval Canon Law* (Munich, 13–18 July 1992), 1137–1153. Città del Vaticano: Biblioteca Apostolica Vaticana; Bonfield, Lloyd. 2002. Gli sviluppi del diritto di famiglia in Europa. In Barbagli, Marzio, and Kertzer, David I. (eds.), *Storia della famiglia in Europa. Dal Cinquecento alla Rivoluzione francese*, 121–175. Bari-Roma: Laterza, 166; Cavina, Marco. 2007. *Il padre spodestato. L'autorità paterna dall'antichità a oggi*. Bari-Roma: Laterza, 50–54.

[2]Vismara, Giulio. 1956. L'unità della famiglia nella storia del diritto in Italia. *Studia et Documenta Historiae et Iuris* 22: 228–265, also in Vismara, Giulio. 1988. *Scritti di storia giuridica. 5. La famiglia*, 1–44. Milano: Giuffrè, 32 and 36–37.

[3]Frigo, Daniela. 1985. *Il padre di famiglia. Governo della casa e governo civile nella tradizione dell'"economica" tra Cinque e Seicento*. Roma: Bulzoni, 75–81.

the Digest (Paulus, in the second book *ad Sabinum*)[4] and in the *Codex* (Constantine)[5] it was indicated as a vestige of concluded and past experiences.[6]

The father's right of life or death over his children was therefore a relic of ancient times: for this reason, the Gloss referred to it as a chapter of the historical past, positioned in an undefined time-frame (*olim*), but which surely did not have anything to do with the present.[7]

In any case, if there had been an acceptable and serious cause of justification, a father could be the unpunished murderer of his children, even in the modern period. For example, if the son or daughter were recognized as being *rebellis patriae*, the father could kill him or her without being subject to any kind of punishment. Indeed, he was held in consideration by society for this.[8] However, this was a situation without particular significance, considering that the response of the father could have—indeed should have—been that of any member of the community towards a traitor.

Children could be killed with impunity also when they dared react to the beatings that the father legitimately inflicted upon them in the exercise of his right to correction.[9] The objection of the children was an intolerable lack of respect (which was also imposed by divine law, especially by the fourth commandment of

---

[4]D. 28.2.11: "... licet eos exheredare, quod et occidere licebat".

[5]C. 8.46(47).3: "... patribus, quibus ius vitae in liberos necisque potestas olim erat permissa...".

[6]The father's right of life or death over his children developed during the history of Rome. The further back in time studies go, towards the origins of the city, the more extended it appears. However, it was not a power completely free from limits, even during a more archaic age, since the ancient *mores* obliged the father to consult with his family and friends before carrying out such an irreparable deed. From the early monarchy onwards, the killing of children under three years was prohibited (but the exposure of infants born deformed remained acceptable) as well as that of the first born daughter. The *ius vitae ac necis* underwent significant restrictions during the imperial age and disappeared during post-classical period (Adrian punished a father who had killed his son for misconduct with deportation to an island: D. 48.9.5; Constantine considered the killing of a son as parricide: C. 9.17.1; Valentinian and Valens sanctioned the exposure of infants: C. 8.51[52].2). See Yaron, Reuven. 1962. Vitae necisque potestas. *Tijdschrift voor Rechtsgeschiedenis* 30: 243–251, 243–244, 248–250; Capogrossi Colognesi, Luigi. 1982. Patria potestà (diritto romano). In *Enciclopedia del diritto* 32, 242–249. Milano: Giuffrè, 242–243; Capogrossi Colognesi, Luigi. 1984. Idee vecchie e nuove sui poteri del *pater familias*. In *Poteri* negotia actiones *nella esperienza romana arcaica*, Atti del Convegno di diritto romano (Copanello, 12–15 maggio 1982) 53–76. Napoli: Edizioni scientifiche italiane, 56–57; Talamanca, Mario. 1990. *Istituzioni di diritto romano*. Milano: Giuffré, 120–121.

[7]Gl. *licebat ad* D. 28.2.11, *de liberis et postumis heredibus instituendis vel exheredandis* l. *in suis*, that recalled the parallelism with the situation of *servi*, *olim* subject to the *potestas vitae ac necis* of the *dominus* and *hodie* subject to a regime at least theoretically more favourable.

[8]Clementinus, Ascanius. 1572–1573. *De patria potestate*. Francoforti ad Moenum: impressum per Nicolaum Bassee, impensis Hieronymi Feyerabend, cap. 6, effectus I, n. 19, 48v.

[9]See, for example, de Marsiliis, Hippolytus. 1574. *Practica criminalis ... Averolda nuncupata*. Venetiis: ex Typographia Bartholomei Rubini, § *aggredior*, n. 79, 252v; Pascalis, Philippus. 1619. *De viribus patriae potestatis*. Genevae: apud Philippum Albertum, pars 3, cap. 4, n. 7, 530b; Bossius, Ioannes Angelus. 1667. *De effectu contractus matrimonii*. Lugduni: sumptibus Philippi Borde, Laur. Arnaud et Petri Borde, cap. 3, § 3, 90b.

the Decalogue). Failing in *reverentia* and obedience due was one of the worst violations that a child could be responsible for towards his parents.[10] If the punishment of the father was deemed lawful, the reaction and response of the children was unlawful.[11] This was sufficient cause to proceed with the killing of the disobedient child who wanted to object to the chastisement, presumed aimed at his correction and therefore just.[12]

Finally, there was also a situation specifically concerning the daughter. It came directly from and was deeply rooted in Roman law, in the second chapter of the *Lex Julia de adulteriis*[13]: the father was entitled to kill his married daughter and her lover caught in flagrant adultery.[14]

---

[10]Obedience and respect were the first duties of a son towards his father: see the gl. *parentibus ad* D. 1.1.2, *de iustitia et iure* l. *veluti* ("nota filium debere patri obedire"), also mentioned by Boari, Marco. 2007. *La coercizione privata nella Magna Glossa. Tracce fra diritto e violenza*. Milano: Giuffrè, 24. The father figure was always considered sacred and inviolable: Bellomo, Manlio. 1966 (reprint 1986). *Profili della famiglia italiana nell'età dei comuni*. Catania: Giannota, 42–44; Bellomo, Manlio. 1984. Die Familie und ihre rechtliche Struktur in den italienischen Stadtkommunen des Mittelalters (12.–14. Jahrhundert). In Haverkamp, Alfred (ed.), *Haus und Familie in der spätmittelalterlichen Stadt*, 99–135. Köln-Wien: Böhlau, 107. See also reference by di Renzo Villata, Maria Gigliola. 1995. Persone e famiglia nel diritto medievale e moderno. In *Digesto delle discipline privatistiche. Sezione civile* 13, 457–527. Torino: Utet, 501, 506.

[11]"Erat licita offensio, ergo erat illicita defensio", stated the golden rule in a logically flawless way, repeated by each author to justify such a terrible fatherly reaction. See, for example, among many others, Bartolus de Saxoferrato. 1555. *Prima in Digestum vetus*. Lugduni: excudebat Blasius Guido, *ad* D. 1.1.3, *de iustitia et iure* l. *ut vim*, n. 4, 7va, and the beginning of the commentary, which posed the general principle "illud est licitum, cuius contrarium est illicitum". See also Monticulus, Sebastianus. 1584. Tractatus de patria potestate. In *Tractatus illustrium, in utraque, tum Pontificii, tum Caesarei iuris facultate Iurisconsultorum. De ultimis voluntatibus... Tomi VIII Pars II*. Venetiis: Franciscus Zilettus, § *patri ergo tantum*, n. 26, 128va.

[12]Menochius, Iacobus. 1615. *De Praesumptionibus, Coniecturis, Signis, et Indiciis Commentaria*: Coloniae Agrippinae: ex officina Antonii Hierat bibliopolae, lib. 5, praes. 14, n. 1, 978b.

[13]See Coll. 4.2.3: "Secundo vero capite permittit patri, si in filia sua, quam in potestate habet, aut in ea, quae eo auctore, cum in potestate esset, viro in manum convenerit, adulterum domi suae generive sui deprehenderit, isve in eam rem socerum adhibuerit, ut is pater eum adulterum sine fraude occidat, ita ut filiam in continenti occidat". See Capogrossi Colognesi 1982 (as n. 6) 243; Talamanca 1990 (as n. 6) 144; Rizzelli, Giunio. 1997. Lex Iulia de adulteriis. *Studi sulla disciplina di* adulterium, lenocinium, stuprum. Lecce: Edizioni del Grifo, 19.

[14]On the subject of adultery in medieval and modern age there is an abundant historiography, which has analysed both *ius civile* and canon law. It is usually focused on important topics regarding the configuration of adultery as a crime, the violation of religious and moral principles, the consequences—also juridical—of this action in the relationship between husband and wife. For these different aspects, obviously without claiming to be complete, see, for example, Brundage, James A. 1980. Carnal Delight: Canonistic Theories of Sexuality. In Kuttner, Stephan, and Pennington, Kenneth (eds.), *Proceedings of the Fifth International Congress of Medieval Canon Law*, 361–385. Città del Vaticano: Biblioteca Apostolica Vaticana, also in Brundage, James A. 1993. *Sex, Law and Marriage in the Middle Ages*, I. Aldershot: Ashgate, 370–377; Brundage, James A. 1986. Marriage and Sexuality in the Decretals of Pope Alexander III. In Liotta, Filippo (ed.), *Miscellanea Rolando Bandinelli Papa Alessandro III*, 59–83. Siena: Accademia Senese degli Intronati, also in Brundage, James A. 1993. *Sex, Law and Marriage in the Middle Ages*, IX. Aldershot: Ashgate, 71–72; Brundage, James A. 1987. *Law, Sex, and Christian Society in*

The father's impunity in this situation reached widespread consensus. Julius Clarus, to name an undisputed authority among criminal law scholars in the Modern Age, also supported this. The killing of the adulterous daughter caught committing adultery was listed among the causes of murder allowed by the law and was therefore not punishable. For this reason, Clarus put it at the same level as the murder of a thief caught red-handed or of a bandit encountered on public streets:[15] the comparison—sensational in our way of thinking—gives a good idea of the legitimacy of paternal actions in the perspective of that period.

The murder of an adulterous daughter could be considered a corrective action of the father in response to his daughter's immoral conduct. This was a perfect example of paternal prerogatives. Indeed, it was commonly considered by lawyers

(Footnote 14 continued)

Medieval Europe. Chicago and London: The University of Chicago Press, 30–32, 207–209, and 248; Brundage, James A. 1990. Sexual Equality in Medieval Canon Law. In Rosenthal, Joel T. (ed.), *Medieval Women and the Sources of Medieval History,* 66–79. Athens: University of Georgia Press, also in Brundage, James A. 1993. *Sex, Law and Marriage in the Middle Ages,* VI. Aldershot: Ashgate, 61–70; Davidson, Nicholas. 1994. Theology, Nature and the Law: Sexual Sin and Sexual Crime in Italy from the Fourteenth to the Seventeenth Century. In Dean, Trevor, and Lowe, Kate J.P. (eds.), *Crime, Society and the Law in Renaissance Italy,* 74–98. Cambridge: Cambridge University Press, 89 and 94; Minnucci, Giovanni. 1994. *La capacità processuale della donna nel pensiero canonistico classico. 2. Dalle scuole d'Oltralpe a S. Raimondo di Pennaforte.* Milano: Giuffrè, 267–279; Minnucci, Giovanni. 1998. Processo e condizione femminile nel pensiero dei primi glossatori civilisti. *Studia Gratiana* 30: 641–660, 652–653, and 657–660; Minnucci, Giovanni. 1999. Processo e condizione femminile nella canonistica classica. In Liotta, Filippo (ed.), *Studi di storia del diritto medioevale e moderno,* 129–183. Bologna: Monduzzi, 170–183; Marchisello, Andrea. 2004. "Alieni thori violatio": l'adulterio come delitto carnale in Prospero Farinacci (1544–1618). In Seidel Menchi, Silvana, and Quaglioni, Diego (eds.), *Trasgressioni. Seduzione, concubinato, adulterio, bigamia (XIV–XVIII secolo),* 133–183. Bologna: il Mulino; Dean, Trevor. 2010. *Crime and Justice in Late Medieval Italy.* Cambridge: Cambridge University Press, 138–141; Cavina, Marco. 2011. *Nozze di sangue. Storia della violenza coniugale.* Bari–Roma: Laterza, 68–81; di Renzo Villata, Maria Gigliola. 2014. "Crimen adulterii est gravius aliis delictis…". L'adultera tra diritto e morale nell'area italiana (XIII–XVI secolo). In Cavina, Marco, Ribémont, Bernard, and Hoxha, Damigela (eds.), *Le donne e la giustizia fra Medioevo ed età moderna. Il caso di Bologna a confronto,* 11–45. Bologna: Patron; di Renzo Villata, Gigliola. 2015. Dall'amore coniugale 'proibito' all'infedeltà. L'adulterio nelle Summae confessorum italiane (XIV–XVI secolo). *Italian Review of Legal History* 1: 02, 1–41. The problem from the point of view of the relationship between father and daughter in adultery is mentioned in Cavina 2007 (as n. 1) 86; Cavina 2011, 68–69; di Renzo Villata 2014, 16–17, 35; di Renzo Villata 2015, 19–20.

[15]Clarus, Julius. 1587. *Sententiarum receptarum liber quintus.* Venetiis: apud Cornelium Arrivabenum, § *homicidium*, vers. *ultima est defensio*, 34ra.

of the late *ius commune* as the actual residual case of the ancient *ius vitae ac necis*, which, over time, had shrunk and had evolved in the milder *ius corrigendi*.[16]

Authoritative Roman law scholars demonstrated that it is not possible to put in such close relationship this option granted to the father by the Augustan legislation with paternal authority and the ancient right of life and death.[17] However, the formulation and conclusions of some works of the late *ius commune* seem to show that this may be the prevailing conception of law scholars in the Modern Age.

To better understand this, it may be useful to refer to the treatises of some authors who, between the 16th and the 17th centuries, investigated the issue of paternal authority. For example, Sebastianus Monticulus (1538–1612/13)[18] expressly recognized a case of survival of the ancient right of life and death over children in the possibility of the father to kill his adulterous daughter.[19] In the works

[16]The right of *emendatio* and *correctio* of the son was, in fact, conceived as the evolution of the powers which were once much more penetrating and incisive, such as a reduction of the original extensive *patria potestas* which could also be expressed in a harsh and cruel way. Hence, the right of life and death was put into direct relationship with the different way of understanding the *ius corrigendi* and its putting into practice. Once the *ius vitae ac necis* was eliminated, parents could apply "quaedam decens emendatio" in the correction of their children. Cf. Clementinus 1572 (as n. 8) cap. 6, effectus I, n. 11, 47v; Monticulus 1584 (as n. 11) § *patri ergo tantum*, nn. 22–25, 128rb; Pascalis 1619 (as n. 9) pars 3, cap. 4, n. 1, 529b–530a.

[17]Thomas, Yan. 1984. *Vitae necisque potestas*. Le père, la cité, la mort. In *Du châtiment dans la cité. Supplices corporels et peine de mort dans le monde antique*. Table ronde de Rome (9–11 novembre 1982), 499–548. Rome: École Française de Rome, 501; Cantarella, Eva. 1991. Homicides of Honor. The Developement of Italian Adultery Law over two Millennia. In Kertzer, David I., and Saller, Richard P. (eds.), *The Family in Italy, from Antiquity to the Present*, 229–244. New Haven-London: Yale University Press; Italian translation: Cantarella, Eva. 1995. L'omicidio d'onore: lo sviluppo della legislazione italiana attraverso due millenni. In Kertzer, David I., and Saller, Richard P. (eds.), *La famiglia in Italia dall'antichità al XX secolo*, 255–272. Firenze: Le Lettere, with some modifications also Cantarella, Eva. 1992. La causa d'onore dalla «Lex Iulia» al codice Rocco. In *Testimonium amicitiae*, 73–94. Milano: Giuffrè, also in Cantarella, Eva. 2011. *Diritto e società in Grecia e a Roma. Scritti scelti*, Maffi, Alberto, and Gagliardi, Lorenzo (eds.), 555–576. Milano: Giuffrè 256–259. Benke, Nikolaus. 2012. On the Roman Father's Right to Kill His Adulterous Daughter. *The History of the Family* 17.3: 284–308, 286–288, does not share this opinion. The connection between *ius adulterum cum filia occidendi* and paternal *ius vitae ac necis* is also discussed by Rizzelli 1997 (as n. 13) 32–35.

[18]Monticulus was born in Vicenza and was one of the most famous scholars of the second part of the 16th century in Padua. He wrote several treatises, including a short *Tractatus seu commentarius de patria potestate* (1576) also included in the *Tractatus universi iuris* (*De ultimis voluntatibus*, tomus VIII, pars II). Cf. Faggion, Lucien. 2013. Montecchio (Monticelli), Sebastiano. In Birocchi, Italo, Cortese, Ennio, Mattone, Antonello, and Miletti, Marco Nicola (eds.), *Dizionario biografico dei giuristi italiani (XII–XX secolo)* (*DBGI*) 2, 1368. Bologna: il Mulino.

[19]Monticulus 1584 (as n. 11) § *patri ergo tantum*, n. 26, 128rb, and § *ius autem*, n. 24, 134va.

of Philippus Pascalis (1545–1625)[20] and Ioannes Angelus Bossius (1590–1665),[21] who, in that period, probably provided a better synthesis of *ius commune* regarding paternal powers of correction,[22] this topic took up extensive and detailed chapters.[23] This may be significant in itself. Pascalis also indicated the possibility of a father to kill his adulterous daughter as a direct consequence of paternal authority.[24] Franciscus Maria Pratus, a lawyer working in Naples who provided *adnotationes* to the treatise of Pascalis starting from the 1653 edition, put even more emphasis on this issue, defining this consequence as a primary effect of paternal authority.[25] Bossius, on the other hand, underlined that the ancient right to kill sons and daughters persisted only in this situation, which was allowed on the basis of the right connected to paternal authority.[26] The matter therefore had to be, at least theoretically, of particular interest to those involved in the discipline and the implications of the power of the father over his children.[27]

The same justification supported the idea of the relationship between this right and the ancient father's power to kill his children. Roman lawyers had acknowledged only to the father the opportunity to physically eliminate the adulteress,[28] trusting in the great love, sense of justice and inclination to mercy that would have guided and inspired him in such a delicate situation. The explanation takes on even

[20]Pascalis studied as a lawyer in Naples. He served as a magistrate in some towns of the Kingdom. He was a judge of the Great Court of the *Vicaria* as well as a member of the Sacred Royal Council. He published his only work in 1618, *De viribus patriae potestatis*, the most extensive and complete monographic study dedicated by jurists of the late *ius commune* to the numerous problems connected to the institution of parental authority. See Sinisi, Lorenzo. 2013. Pascali, Filippo. In *DBGI* 2 (as n. 18) 1516.

[21]Bossius was born in Milan and was sent to study humanistic, philosophical and legal subjects. He was a Barnabite (and general of the Order starting from 1653), and Councillor in law of Grand Duke Ferdinando II de' Medici. He wrote essays regarding theology and Christian morals, which earned him solid reputation as a writer of treatises and authoritative interpreter of canon law. Among these we can name *De effectibus contractus matrimonii*: see Castronovo, Valerio. 1971. Bossi, Giovanni Angelo. In *Dizionario biografico degli italiani* 13, 309–310. Roma: Istituto della Enciclopedia italiana.

[22]Cavina 2007 (as n. 1) 85.

[23]See Pascalis 1619 (as n. 9) pars 1, cap. 5, nn. 1–34, 92–98; Bossius 1667 (as n. 9) cap. 3, § 2, 60b–80b.

[24]Pascalis 1619 (as n. 9) pars 1, cap. 5, n. 1, 92.

[25]Pratus, Franciscus Maria. 1655. *Adnotationes ad* Pascalis, Philippus, *Tractatus amplissimus de viribus patriae potestatis*. Venetiis: Bertanorum sumptibus, pars 1, cap. 5, 21a: "inter effectus patriae potestatis, ille uti praecipuus sit adnumerandus, nempe, Genitori licitum fieri filiam in adulterio deprehensam insimul cum adultero interficere, nullius poenae obnoxio".

[26]Bossius 1667 (as n. 9) cap. 3, § 2, n. 46, 63b.

[27]To those theologians who had supported the repeal of these provisions in everyday use and who, therefore, did not acknowledge any—civil, natural or divine—right to the father to kill his daughter caught committing adultery, Bossius 1667 (as n. 9) cap. 3, § 2, n. 46, 63b, replied highlighting that if the *doctores* had never spoken about the repeal, then it was assumed that they considered the father's right still applicable.

[28]Rizzelli 1997 (as n. 13) 10–11.

more importance if considered with regards to the mistrust that surrounded the figure of the husband. Indeed, Roman law had entitled him to kill the adulterer but not his wife, because it was thought that his judgement, faced with the adulteress caught in flagrant adultery, would be affected by the wish for revenge.[29] The father, even if pained, would instead be able to better evaluate his reaction thanks to the *pietas* that would have guided him.[30] "Patria potestas in pietate debet, non atrocitate consistere", as stated by the Roman jurist Marcianus (D. 48.9.5).[31]

The *doctores* of the *ius commune* hence highlighted the differences in the prerogatives of the husband and the father in this situation. Often not originally, even using the same words as those of Roman law, or expressions which rephrased the contents.[32] However, statutory laws were sometimes more favourable to the husband, giving him the possibility of killing his wife.[33] From the theoretical point of view, trusting in the power of the father was absolutely understandable because,

---

[29]However, the right to kill the lover of the unfaithful wife was subject to some restrictions relating to the man's personal condition (he had to be *vilis*) and the place of the crime (only in the husband's house). Subsequent legislations, especially the Nov. 117.15 (= Coll. 8.13), extended this power. See Cantarella, Eva. 1976. *Studi sull'omicidio in diritto greco e romano*. Milano: Giuffrè, 171–174, 183–189; Cohen, David. 1991. The Augustan Law on Adultery. The Social and Cultural Context. In Kertzer, David I., and Saller, Richard P. (eds.), *The Family in Italy, from Antiquity to the Present*, 109–126. New Haven-London: Yale University Press; Italian translation: Cohen, David. 1995. Le leggi augustee sull'adulterio: il contesto sociale e culturale. In Kertzer, David I., and Saller, Richard P. (eds.), *La famiglia in Italia dall'antichità al XX secolo*, 123–142. Firenze: Le Lettere, 125. These rules then evolved a little in favour of the husband: see Rizzelli 1997 (as n. 13) 12–18.

[30]These reasons are given by Papinian (D. 48.5.23[22].4). Cf. Cantarella 1976 (as n. 29) 171; Thomas 1984 (as n. 17) 502; Cohen 1991 (as n. 29) 133; Rizzelli 1997 (as n. 13) 65; Cantarella, Eva. 2014 (4th edition). *L'ambiguo malanno. Condizione e immagine della donna nell'antichità greca e romana*. Milano: Feltrinelli, 184–186.

[31]Bossius 1667 (as n. 9) cap. 3, § 2, n. 37, 61a. See also Clementinus 1572 (as n. 8) cap. 4, nn. 11–12, 14v–15r, and cap. 6, effectus I, n. 10, 47v; Pascalis 1619 (as n. 9) pars 3, cap. 4, n. 2, 530a.

[32]For example, the differences between the rights of the husband and of the father over the adulteress were already clearly pointed out in Minnucci, Giovanni (ed.). 1997. *Tractatus criminum saeculi XII*. Bologna: Monduzzi, 28–29. Franciscus Accursii in the *casus ad* D. 48.5.21(20), *ad legem Juliam de adulteriis coercendis* l. *patri*, distinguished a "paternus furor", which could be controlled, from a "viri furor", which, on the other hand, could not be held back: this was sufficient to establish the different disciplines. For a synthesis in the Gloss see Boari 2007 (as n. 10) 90–93. For an overview of the differences between the two disciplines by an author of the late *ius commune* see Bossius 1667 (as n. 9) cap. 3, § 2, nn. 78–82, 72ab.

[33]For example, Carerius, Ludovicus. 1562. *Practica causarum criminalium*. Lugduni: apud Gulielmum Rovillium, *Tractatus de homicidio et assassinio*, § *nono excusatur*, nn. 7–8, 197r, indicated that despite being inconsistent with the provisions of the *ius commune*, in the Kingdom of Naples a constitution allowed the husband to do what Roman law only authorized the father to do, that is to kill both lovers caught in the act of adultery, without taking into consideration the social status of the man ("si maritus uxorem in ipso actu adulterij deprehenderit, tam adulterum, quam uxorem occidere licebit, nulla tamen mora protracta": cf. 1568. *Constitutiones Regni utriusque Siciliae*. Lugduni: apud haeredes Iacobi Iunctae, tit. 90, 277b). The ordinary gloss and the comment of Andrea de Isernia annotating the text confirmed that it was an exception to the

however extensive, it was restricted by its own nature. Connoting it as *pietas* rather than as a tyrannical right to dispose of the existence of a daughter showed in this perspective the coherence of the choice.[34]

2 The Impunity of the Father Murderer of His Adulterous Daughter

The father would be granted impunity only if he had killed his adulterous daughter on certain conditions, which distinguished the event from the indiscriminating *ius vitae ac necis* of the very early Roman law, firmly denied and confined to a past so distant from *hodie*. This right therefore had to be contained within the field of exceptionality, a so to speak almost necessary constraint for superior reasons—certainly including the protection of family honour—which inevitably led to the extreme solution. Roman law had already considered this aim,[35] introducing a series of quite stringent conditions that the father had to respect so as to avoid being punished for the murder of his adulterous daughter: that the father was *paterfamilias* at the relevant time; that the lovers were caught in flagrant adultery in the father's house or in the husband's; that the murder took place *incontinenti*; that both the daughter and the adulterer were killed.[36] The *Lex Julia de adulteriis* was introduced for an evident moralizing purpose as well as to prevent the possible use of the power to kill: the prediction of these conditions seemed aimed at limiting the father's right to a small number of cases.[37]

In the *corpus iuris* it was therefore possible to find the conditions thanks to which the father could go unpunished for the killing of his adulterous daughter. The possibilities for the interpreters of the *ius commune* to examine this topic seemed to be limited. Nevertheless, it was not so. Said conditions could be read in random order in different parts of the Digest, particularly in the title *Ad legem Juliam de adulteriis coercendis* (D. 48.5). This alone enabled to have a differently structured enumeration, or even an integration of it. Thus, for example, for Angelus de

(Footnote 33 continued)

rules of the *ius commune*. For this and other similar derogations from the *ius commune* by statutory laws see di Renzo Villata 2014 (as n. 14) 21–29.

[34]Monticulus 1584 (as n. 11) § *patri ergo tantum*, n. 26, 128rb, on this occasion spoke of a "pietas, et charitas" which "omne odium removet". It was an attempt to characterize this remnant of the ancient *ius vitae ac necis* as exceptional. The insistence on the endless kindness and virtues of the father seems to reinforce the idea that the parent who had made such a choice could only be in the right.

[35]D. 48.5.21(20), D. 48.5.22(21), D. 48.5.23(22), D. 48.5.24(23), D. 48.5.25(24), D. 48.5.33(32).

[36]See Cantarella 1976 (as n. 29) 164–170; Cantarella 1991 (as n. 17) 257–258; Rizzelli 1997 (as n. 13) 19–22.

[37]Cf. Cantarella 1991 (as n. 17) 260; Cohen 1991 (as n. 29) 139; Rizzelli 1997 (as n. 13) 66.

Gambilionibus there were seven conditions,[38] for Clarus five,[39] for Pascalis five, but a sixth could be added,[40] and there were also six for Bossius.[41]

The contribution of the authors of the late *ius commune* did not end with the different method used to create the list of conditions for the case in question. They actually gave instructions to explain how said conditions had to be interpreted and given meaning. In other words, they tried to give them content. In this way, they could suggest solutions to the numerous problems that they had to face in everyday life. These operations certainly deeply investigated and updated the Justinian legacy, as well as resumed and increased the considerations carried out by the previous law scholars who had had the chance to deal with the subject.

Some of these conditions stimulated more than others the imagination and propensities of the law scholars of the *ius commune*. For instance, the immediacy—the concomitance between the discovery of the adultery and the murder required by D. 48.5.24(23).4—was understood in a very broad sense.[42] The psychological aspects of the offended father were considered with more importance than the time-scale in which the events took place and concluded: even if some hours had gone by since the event, the father could still kill his daughter without being punished, provided that he had not carried out any other actions than the pursuit of justice in order to wash away the insult. The father had to dedicate his efforts and intentions only to reach his daughter and kill her, if he had not been able to do it immediately.[43] The daughter, in fact, could have escaped at least temporarily from her tragic destiny. Nevertheless, the father could not be deprived of his right. This remained even if it took months to find her, also overcoming harsh difficulties. Law

---

[38]de Gambilionibus, Angelus. 1555. *De maleficiis*. Lugduni: apud haeredes Iacobi Iuntae, § *che hai adulterato la mia donna*, nn. 8–15, 366a–367a: that the father killed his daughter 1. caught in the act of committing adultery; 2. in the father's house or in the husband's; 3. together with her lover; 4. still under his authority; 5. personally, without handing over the work to others; 6. under his authority at the time of the murder, regardless of the condition at the time of marriage; 7. who was married.

[39]Clarus 1587 (as n. 15) § *homicidium*, vers. *dixi etiam*, 34rb: that the father killed his daughter 1. in one go; 2. under his authority; 3. who was committing adultery in the father's house or in the husband's; 4. who was married; 6. caught in the act of committing adultery. For this passage see Massetto, Gian Paolo. 1979. I reati nell'opera di Giulio Claro. *Studia et Documenta Historiae et Iuris* 45: 328–503, also in Massetto, Gian Paolo. 1994. *Saggi di storia del diritto penale lombardo (secc. XVI–XVIII)*, 61–227. Milano: LED, 371.

[40]Pascalis 1619 (as n. 9) pars 1, cap. 5, n. 2, 92a: that the father killed his daughter 1. immediately after discovering the event; 2. under his authority; 3. who was committing adultery in the father's house or in the husband's; 4. who was married; 5. caught in the act of committing adultery; 6. and her lover at the same time.

[41]Bossius 1667 (as n. 9) cap. 3, § 2, n. 48, 64a: that the father killed his daughter 1. immediately after discovering the event; 2. if possible, with the adulterer; 3. under his authority; 4. who was committing adultery in the father's house or in the husband's; 5. who was married; 6. caught in the act of committing adultery.

[42]Bossius 1667 (as n. 9) cap. 3, § 2, n. 49, 64b: "hoc verbum *incontinenti*, non significat semper idem tempus, sed modo maius, modo minus intervallum".

[43]Pascalis 1619 (as n. 9) pars 1, cap. 5, n. 3, 92b.

scholars often repeated the example of the daughter looking for refuge in a castle that was difficult to enter. It was important that the father continued to be convinced in his idea of achieving his goal. Even if he had to use a siege or some kind of trick or ploy to enter this imaginary fortress, this action would be deemed as immediate with regards to the discovery of the adultery.[44] In short, it was necessary that the father had not put aside his anger towards his daughter, as Augustinus Ariminensis stated in his commentary on the work of Angelus de Gambilionibus.[45] The observation is particularly significant if the implications are considered, which were stressed by the law scholar: the father who had decided to kill his daughter the following day was guilty of murder (and as such punishable) if he did not want to do it immediately and had had second thoughts; on the other hand the father was not punished if he wanted to do it immediately but had been physically impeded. Despite being successful in his intentions after a considerable lapse of time, he could not be convicted of any crime.

Moreover, Roman law required the father expressly to kill the two lovers (D. 48.5.21[20]; D. 48.5.24[23].4; D. 48.5.33[32]pr.), no matter in what order: Ulpian even spoke about the same and single action and the same and unique momentum (D. 48.5.24[23].4: "uno ictu et uno impetu") with which the father had to eliminate the two lovers. The father had the possibility of choosing: killing only the daughter or killing the adulterer and necessarily the daughter. This was to limit the exercise of the father's right to kill.[46] Pascalis, borrowing the idea from Pierre de Belleperche, justified this choice with the fact that if the father was able to kill the adulterer but let his daughter go because of his *paterna pietas*, he could have also avoided killing the lover.[47]

The father therefore would not have been exempt from punishment if he had killed the adulterer but not his daughter. He could not let her escape or just wound her, unless the wound could be considered deadly, but which she recovered from. All efforts made to kill her had to be taken into account. The results achieved were not important, while the intentions to reach these results were: if the father did not succeed in his intentions, it was not because of lack of will, but because fate wanted otherwise. Behind these considerations, which can seem quite cruel, there was the pursuit of an idea of justice unrelated to our sensibility, and the attempt to limit

---

[44]de Gambilionibus 1555 (as n. 38) § *che hai adulterato la mia donna*, n. 17, 367b; Pascalis 1619 (as n. 9) pars 1, cap. 5, n. 3, 92b. The *casus* of Franciscus Accursii *ad* D. 48.5.21[20], *ad legem Juliam de adulteriis coercendis* l. *patri*, had already clarified this idea believing that the father "quasi incontinenti videatur occidere".

[45]Augustinus Ariminensis. 1555. *Additio ad* Angelus de Gambilionibus, *De maleficiis*, Lugduni: apud haeredes Iacobi Iuntae, § *che hai adulterato la mia donna*, n. 21, 369a.

[46]Cf. Rizzelli 1997 (as n. 13) 19; Cantarella 2014 (as n. 30) 185.

[47]Pascalis 1619 (as n. 9) pars 1, cap. 5, n. 13, 94ab. The Gloss had already clearly indicated how the double murder was a condition for the impunity of the father: see gl. *occidi potuerit ad* C. 9.9.4pr., *ad legem Juliam de adulteriis et stupro* l. *Gracchus*, which authorized the father to kill the adulterer "dummodo et filiam occidat". See also the gl. *adulterum cum filia ad* D. 48.5.21(20), *ad legem Juliam de adulteriis coercendis* l. *patri*: "eum et filiam, non adulterum tantum".

murders, paradoxically forcing to commit two instead of one. The idea of having to kill his daughter should have stopped the father from killing the adulterer. It was a point of view also shared by some leading criminal law scholars in the Modern Age who expressed their opinions on this topic: among them Angelus de Gambilionibus, Tiberius Decianus and Prosperus Farinaccius.[48]

With regards to the condition that the daughter had to be under her father's authority, lawyers developed thorough examples. The rule was valid both for the natural and legitimate father and the adoptive father. From this point of view, there was no recognized difference among them.[49] The adulterous emancipated daughter could not, therefore, be killed by her father.[50] Consequently, the *filiusfamilias* father could not benefit from this right: since he was still subject to the *potestas* of his own father, he did not have the *potestas* over his daughter.[51]

The law scholars of the late *ius commune* also repeated with conviction the condition dictated clearly by the Justinian's body of civil law (Papinian in D. 48.5.23[22].2 and Ulpian in D. 48.5.24[23].2) that the fact had to take place and be discovered in the house of the father or of the husband of the adulteress. The foundation of this requirement was also restated, thus confirming its effect even in the Modern Age: such an action caused greater offence in that place (as specified by Ulpian in D. 48.5.24[23].2). Tiberius Decianus believed that the outrage was not even comparable if the adultery had been consumed under another roof.[52] Prosperus Farinaccius, quoting the extensive doctrine related to this idea,[53] with his typical way of writing that accumulated "una straripante catena di *auctoritates*" ("an overwhelming chain of *auctoritates*") and specified (extending and limiting)

[48]de Gambilionibus 1555 (as n. 38) § *che hai adulterato la mia donna*, n. 11, 366b–367a; Decianus, Tiberius. 1591. *Tractatus criminalis ... Tomus secundus*, Francofurti ad Moenum: impensis Petri Fischeri, lib. 9, cap. 15, n. 17, 106b; Farinaccius, Prosperus. 1631. *Praxis et theoricae criminalis pars quarta*, Lugduni: sumptibus Iacobi Cardon, pars 4, q. 121, nn. 31–32, 148b–149a.

[49]Cf. D. 48.5.23(22)pr. See de Gambilionibus 1555 (as n. 38) § *che hai adulterato la mia donna*, n. 16, 367b; Carcrius 1562 (as n. 33) *Tractatus de homicidio et assassinio*, § *octavo excusatur*, n. 11, 196r; Farinaccius 1631 (as n. 48) pars 4, q. 121, nn. 2–3, 146a. A father retained his *potestas* over a married daughter, so that paternal authority coexisted with the control over the daughter wielded by her husband: Kuehn, Thomas. 1981. Women, Marriage, and *Patria Potestas* in Late Medieval Florence. *Tijdschrift voor Rechtsgeschiedenis* 49: 127–147, also in Kuehn, Thomas. 1991. *Law, Family, & Women. Toward a Legal Anthropology of Renaissance Italy*, 197–211. Chicago-London: The University of Chicago Press, 210.

[50]Farinaccius 1631 (as n. 48) pars 4, q. 121, n. 3, 146a; Bossius 1667 (as n. 9) cap. 3, § 2, n. 51, 65a.

[51]D. 48.5.21(20) and D. 48.5.22(21) were explicit from this point of view. Cf. Farinaccius 1631 (as n. 48) pars 4, q. 121, n. 35, 149a; Bossius 1667 (as n. 9) cap. 3, § 2, n. 52, 65a.

[52]Decianus 1591 (as n. 48) lib. 9, cap. 15, n. 14, fol 106a: "quia non tanta est iniuria, si alienam domum foedavit". Bossius 1667 (as n. 9) cap. 3, § 2, n. 56, 65b, informed that justice of Roman law was also shared by theologians, who he never failed to mention, attentive as he was towards both moral and legal aspects of each issue.

[53]Farinaccius 1631 (as n. 48) q. 121, n. 26, 148a.

the *regulae*,[54] provided the consolidated definition of what could be intended as the father's domicile: it was where he lived or rented, not a house that he owned but did not live in. Then, however, he expanded the boundaries: just like a 'time fiction', so one could presume a 'spatial fiction'. All the *doctores* believed that the daughter could be considered killed at home even if she was able to flee after being caught in flagrant adultery and was wounded mortally in another place.[55] This interpretation, indeed, seemed almost necessary to coordinate this condition with that of the immediacy of the murder: just think of the said example of an escaping daughter who found refuge far from home. The place where the murder was committed was therefore not important, but where the person was discovered was significant: for these purposes he who was seen at home was said to be discovered in the house, even if it was not possible to capture him.[56] Immediacy of time and identity of the place could be evidently assumptions justifying the murder committed by the father: the lovers could be considered "interfecti in actu venereo et in domo patris, vel generi".[57] In this case too, it was the father's perspective to prevail, instead of the objectivity of the situation. Everything was immediately brought back to the discovery of the adultery: that moment was halted and its effects were extended until justice was finally done.

Furthermore, the daughter had to be married: a widowed daughter found committing adultery could not therefore be killed by her father. Roman law (D. 48.5.23 [22].1) had forbidden the father to accuse of adultery his widowed daughter. Even more so, the *doctores* argued, the father could not exercise against her any power more awful than simple accusation, and therefore he could not kill her.[58] Moreover, he could not exercise this right towards his unmarried daughter (*virgo*).[59]

Perhaps the most heated (and certainly the liveliest) debate in which the legal scholars of the *ius commune* were involved was related to the attempt to define the notion of 'venereal things' which were recalled by Pomponius in the Digest (D. 48.5.24[23]pr.) to indicate the very performance of the sexual act. They represented another of those conditions in the absence of which the father murder of his daughter and her lover had to be punished. This is an example showing how the scholars' interpretation could provide several different readings of the same passage

---

[54]Mazzacane, Aldo. 2013. Farinacci, Prospero. In *DBGI* 1 (as n. 18) 822–825, 824.

[55]Farinaccius 1631 (as n. 48) pars 4, q. 121, nn. 27–28, 148ab. He also referred to some scholars' point of view, who considered as 'home' a place different from the family home only if it was located in the same territory or district.

[56]Bossius 1667 (as n. 9) cap. 3, § 2, n. 56, 65b.

[57]de Gambilionibus 1555 (as n. 38) § *che hai adulterato la mia donna*, n. 17, 367b.

[58]de Gambilionibus 1555 (as n. 38) § *che hai adulterato la mia donna*, n. 15, 367a; Baiardus, Iohannes Baptista. 1617. *Additiones et adnotationes … ad Julii Clari Receptarum Sententiarum Libros V.* Francofurti: officina typographica Nicolai Hoffmanni, impensis Ioannis Bassaei, § *homicidium*, n. 169, 59b; Farinaccius 1631 (as n. 48) pars 4, q. 121, n. 37, 149a; Bossius 1667 (as n. 9) cap. 3, § 2, n. 57, 66a.

[59]Baiardus 1617 (as n. 58) § *homicidium*, n. 169, 59b; Farinaccius 1631 (as n. 48) pars 4, q. 121, n. 38, 149b; Bossius 1667 (as n. 9) cap. 3, § 2, n. 58, 66a.

of Roman law, in this way revitalizing it and, at the same time, highlighting how the *ius commune* worked and developed.

The disagreements focused on the interpretation to be given to the expressions used in the Justinian text (which spoke about *res Veneris*). It was necessary to understand if the father was granted impunity only if he had discovered his daughter during sexual intercourse or if it was sufficient that the daughter had been caught in ambiguous behaviour which preceded the act of adultery.

The second hypothesis resulted in abundant examples, with which the law scholars of the late *ius commune* used to develop their ideas. This interpretation was evidently marked by greater severity. The advocates of this point of view considered sufficient that the father had caught his daughter "in praeludiis adulterii". They must, however, explain what was meant by act preceding adultery. The discussion was part of a more general discourse regarding the presumptive proof of adultery, a hard-to-prove crime, which scholars working on these topics were really interested in.[60]

Among the supporters of a particularly broad concept of *res Veneris*, also including behaviour far distant from sexual intercourse, there were highly authoritative scholars of the past, whose ideas the law scholars of the late *ius commune* also had to deal with. For example, this was the position of the Gloss, which among the "antecedentia ipsum scelus" included "apparatus, colloquia ... locus constitutus convivia, basia, tactus".[61] Some of these elements could not immediately be related to the completion of the adulterous act and gave the offended father who wanted to do justice for himself a certain level of discretion in the assessment. Elsewhere, however, the Gloss tried to be a little more precise and limited the semantic sphere of the *res Veneris*: the daughter's lover could be killed if caught "in lecto cum ea, vel osculando eam" (behaviour clearly closer to adultery compared to some of those previously indicated).[62] Bartolus de Saxoferrato agreed with the Gloss and added that the statute of the town he was in ("in civitate ista"), which allowed the husband to kill his wife's lover, had to be interpreted as if the *res Veneris* were those in preparation for the final act. In any case, they were useful to prove adultery.[63] Since in this case the subject of the discussion was the proof of the adultery, it was not so important to speak about husband or father: the overlapping of the issues did not cause any type of problem.

Angelus de Gambilionibus also shared the idea that actions prior to adultery were sufficient, since the definition of the *res Veneris* could not just be limited to the situation in which the two lovers were discovered naked having sexual intercourse: it was just necessary that they had been seen together in a bedroom exchanging

[60]With regards to circumstantial evidences able to prove the act of adultery see, for example, di Renzo Villata 2014 (as n. 14) 17–18, 31; di Renzo Villata 2015 (as n. 14) 9–10, 16.

[61]Gl. *in ipsis rebus ad* D. 48.5.24(23)pr., *ad legem Juliam de adulteriis coercendis* l. *quod ait lex*.

[62]Cf. the *casus ad* D. 48.5.21(20), *ad legem Juliam de adulteriis coercendis* l. *patri*.

[63]Bartolus de Saxoferrato. 1555. *Commentaria in secundam Digesti novi partem*. Lugduni: [Compagnie des libraires de Lyon], *ad* D. 48.5.24(23)pr., *ad legem Juliam de adulteriis coercendis* l. *quod ait lex*, nn. 1–2, 190rb–191va.

loving words or actions[64] ("verbis blandis, lascivis, vel cum basiis, vel cum tactu mamillarum", resuming the words also used by Rolandus a Valle[65]). This was in any case a presumption.

The same presumption did not apply, on the other hand, if the man involved was a cleric, since it was assumed that he was not kissing and putting his arms around a woman before committing adultery, but "charitate et bono zelo": in practice in the fulfilment of his pastoral duty.[66] Stronger presumptions were therefore needed to prove the act of adultery with a churchman.

Bossius showed indulgence towards the father who had killed his daughter caught during *praeludia adulterii*, above all if almost having sexual intercourse, because it was really very difficult to state with certainty that it would not lead to actual adultery, especially if the two lovers were given the time to do it.[67]

Other interpretations, on the other hand, were less severe and tried to be as close as possible to the words of the rules. Decianus repeated that the words of D. 48.5.24 (23) were "in ipsis rebus Venereis" and therefore did not really leave much discretion to the interpreter: for this reason, in order to grant the father's impunity, it was necessary to catch the couple "in ipso actu adulterii". Simple preliminary actions could have only enabled him to have a lighter punishment, but not to escape justice.[68] Others required at least an extremely explicit and unequivocally interpretable action, which was much more than just the suspicious behaviour such as kissing or being alone together in a room: this was, for example, the opinion of Farinaccius, who, with a more pragmatic approach, referred explicitly to cases in which excesses so close to the fulfilment of adultery itself could take place.[69]

The father, therefore, if every required condition was met, was entitled to kill his daughter and not to be punished by the law. This was also possible if she were pregnant, as claimed by some scholars, since the pain felt by the father on seeing the act of adultery of his daughter would be the same, independently from her

[64]de Gambilionibus 1555 (as n. 38) § *che hai adulterato la mia donna*, n. 9, 366ab.

[65]Rolandus a Valle. 1584. *Consiliorum seu mavis responsorum ... volumen secundum*. Francoforti: apud Martinum Lechlerum, impensis Sigismundi Feyrabendii, cons. 34, nn. 6–7, 115ab.

[66]For further presumptions of adultery Pascalis 1619 (as n. 9) pars 1, cap. 5, n. 8, 93b, referred to the numerous authorities cited by Mascardus, Ioseph. 1593. *De probationibus ... volumen primum*. Francofurti ad Moenum: impensis haeredum Sigismundi Feyrabendii, concl. 64, n. 1, 68vb, and by Caballus, Petrus. 1613. *Resolutionum criminalium ... centuriae tres*. Francoforti: e Collegio Paltheniano, cent. 3, casus 300, nn. 28–29, 281b–282a.

[67]Bossius 1667 (as n. 9) cap. 3, § 2, n. 76, 71b.

[68]Decianus 1591 (as n. 48) lib. 9, cap. 15, n. 15, 106b. Pascalis 1619 (as n. 9) pars 1, cap. 5, n. 9, 93b, for the evidence of the committing of adultery referred to Baldus de Ubaldis. 1589. *Consiliorum, sive responsorum ... volumen secundum*. Francofurti ad Moenum: impensis Sigismundi Feyrabendij, cons. 445, n. 1, 108ra, reference point of the subject, as demonstrated by the numerous citations that he received from subsequent scholars.

[69]Cf. Farinaccius 1631 (as n. 48) pars 4, q. 121, nn. 42–43, 149b–150a, always generous with citations. Bossius 1667 (as n. 9) cap. 3, § 2, nn. 60–76, 66a–71b, was also comprehensive in retracing all the nuances of the debate (including an *excursus* about hard-to-prove crimes and the function and probative value of presumptions).

physical conditions.[70] The anger of the father was aimed exclusively at his daughter. He intended only to remove the insult. Killing his unborn grandchild was a collateral effect of his impulsive action.[71] It was another rather cynical remark, but it was absolutely coherent with this point of view.

However, not everyone agreed with this idea. The honour of the family, and of the father in particular, was damaged by a pregnant daughter as much as by a daughter who was not expecting a baby. Nevertheless, in the situation in question it was not only the life of the adulteress to be at stake, but also that of the baby in her womb. For this reason, according to some scholars, the pain experienced by the father could have saved him from being subject to an ordinary punishment, but not from being sentenced to extraordinary punishment,[72] because of the killing of the unborn child: despite it was inevitable and understandable, the pain should not have prevented the father from having an *animus*.[73]

The father's impunity depended on the fulfilment of a series of conditions. If those conditions were met, his right not to be punished was so extensive that according to the *communis opinio* he could not be excommunicated even if he had killed the cleric who was committing adultery with his daughter. It was an important exception to the discipline provided for by canon law to preserve the physical inviolability of consecrated men. Indeed, the sanction of excommunication against those who dared lay his hands on a churchman had been introduced by the fundamental c. *si quis suadente* (included in Gratian's *Decretum*[74]). Papal decretals had then implemented said rule. These also included an intervention of Pope Alexander III (1Comp. 5.34.4 = X. 5.39.3) which exempted from such a severe sanction the father who had hit a cleric who was committing adultery with his

[70]de Gambilionibus 1555 (as n. 38) § *che hai adulterato la mia donna*, n. 11, 366a; Decianus 1591 (as n. 48) lib. 9, cap. 15, n. 16, 106b; Cephalus, Iohannes. 1624. *Consiliorum sive responsorum iuris liber tertius*. Francofurti: sumptibus Godefridi Tampachii bibliopolae, cons. 305, n. 8, 36b.

[71]Bossius 1667 (as n. 9) cap. 3, § 2, n. 83, 72b, who reported the opinion of others.

[72]Meccarelli, Massimo. 1998. Arbitrium. *Un aspetto sistematico degli ordinamenti giuridici in età di diritto comune*. Milano: Giuffrè, 195–254.

[73]Grammaticus, Thomas. 1562. *In Constitutionibus, Capitulis, et Pragmaticis Regni Neapolitani et Ritibus Magnae Curiae Vicariae Additiones, et Apostillae*. Venetiis: impressum apud Ioannem Variscum, expensis D. Baptistae de Christophoro Bibliopolae Parthenopei, const. *si maritus*, n. 8, 110rb; Baiardus 1617 (as n. 58) § *homicidium*, n. 167, 59b; Farinaccius 1631 (as n. 48) pars 4, q. 121, nn. 4–5, 146ab, who reported perfectly all 'sides' on the point, starting from the fundamental Bartolus de Saxoferrato 1555 (as n. 11) *ad* D. 1.5.8, *de statu hominum* l. *Imperator*, n. 2, 28ra, who had set out the line to follow, becoming essential reference point for the advocates of the father's impunity. Caballus 1613 (as n. 66) cent. 3, casus 300, n. 83, 286a, stated that he would have solved the case this way if he had ever had to be the judge. Pascalis 1619 (as n. 9) pars 1, cap. 5, n. 14, 94b, on his part, approved the slightly more strict interpretation towards the father who killed his pregnant daughter.

[74]C. 17 q. 4 c. 29, on which see Helmholz, Richard. 1988. 'Si quis suadente': Theory and Practice. In Linehan, Peter (ed.), *Proceedings of the Seventh International Congress of Medieval Canon Law* (Cambridge, 23–27 July 1984): 425–438. Città del Vaticano: Biblioteca Apostolica Vaticana.

daughter.[75] It was therefore easy for scholars of the *ius commune* to coordinate this concession with the case of killing the cleric.[76] The text of the decretal only allowed the possibility of wounding, but it was not difficult to assert that said wounds could also be mortal. It was, however, important that all the required conditions were respected, above all those regarding the immediacy of the action. In this way, it could not be the devil suggesting to the father what to do (as claimed by the c. *si quis suadente* for those who hit clerics). The father, on the other hand, acted driven by his pain, difficult to keep in check in such a situation. The *ius civile* did not inflict a punishment on the father in this circumstance, and canon law did not intervene with excommunication.[77]

3 The Murder of the Adulterous Daughter: A Personal Matter

The father's privilege was extremely personal: he alone could kill his adulterous daughter. No other member of the family could do it, certainly not a female member—such as the mother—and neither could one of the male members of the family. They were all excluded from this right, which was a matter of the father alone. It did not include brothers, grandfathers, not even if they had the *potestas* over the grandchildren.[78] We can deduct that this was not a privilege connected only to the power that one had over the subjects under his authority, since the question also regarded the people involved and their ties.

On the other hand, if the father had ordered his son to murder on his behalf, that is to be the perpetrator of his order, the son could not be punished: this was the broad interpretation that was given to a rescript by Alexander Severus (the l. *Gracchus*: C. 9.9.4), which authorized the murder of the adulterer in this way.

---

[75]The v. *turpiter ad* X. 5.39.3, *de sententia excommunicationis* c. *si vero*, justified the exception to this rule in the usual way: "parcit canon, quia tam iustum dolorem compescere non posset".

[76]Clarus 1587 (as n. 15) § *homicidium*, vers. *dixi etiam*, 34rb; Baiardus 1617 (as n. 58) § *homicidium*, n. 174, 59b–60a; Farinaccius 1631 (as n. 48) pars 4, q. 121, nn. 6–7, 146b; Caballus 1613 (as n. 66) cent. 3, casus 300, n. 42, 282b; Bossius 1667 (as n. 9) cap. 3, § 2, n. 102, 78b–79a. Pascalis 1619 (as n. 9) pars 1, cap. 5, n. 15, 94b, informed that many times the father had preferred to evirate the cleric caught during ambiguous behaviour with his daughter.

[77]Bossius 1667 (as n. 9) cap. 3, § 2, n. 102, 78b.

[78]de Gambilionibus 1555 (as n. 38) § *che hai adulterato la mia donna*, n. 13, 367a; Carerius 1562 (as n. 33) *Tractatus de homicidio et assassinio*, § *nono quaero*, n. 18, 120r, and § *octavo excusatur*, n. 8, 196r; Decianus 1591 (as n. 48) lib. 9, cap. 15, n. 18, 106b; Baiardus 1617 (as n. 58) § *homicidium*, n. 170, 59b; Farinaccius 1631 (as n. 48) pars 4, q. 121, n. 48, 150b; Pascalis 1619 (as n. 9) pars 1, cap. 5, n. 19, 95a; Bossius 1667 (as n. 9) cap. 3, § 2, n. 53, 65a. The question of whether it was lawful for the brother to kill his adulterous sister caught in the act of committing adultery was the only topic dealt with by Pratus in his *adnotationes* to this chapter of Pascalis's work (Pratus 1655 [as n. 25] 21b), before concentrating his attention to the more frequent problem of the betrayed husband.

The interpretation given to the l. *Gracchus* was, in reality, necessary, since when the father killed the lover he was also obliged to kill his daughter (coherently with the provisions of D. 48.5.33[32]pr.). Therefore, a provision that allowed the son to kill his sister's lover on behalf of his father entitled (and so to say forced) him to kill his sister too. This was the common opinion among law scholars.[79]

Although the son was not usually obliged to obey his father who ordered him to carry out violent actions, in this situation it was the actual realization of something that the father was legally authorized to do: this was the reason of a similar discipline according to the Gloss,[80] as also reported by Farinaccius. Franciscus Vivius and Petrus Caballus referred to the famous belief (also founded on legal bases) according to which father and son had to be considered the same person[81] due to the blood ties and intense love that they shared.[82] Therefore, on the one hand the son would have certainly felt the same disdain as his father and the insult would have offended him in the same way. On the other hand, the murder of the unfaithful sister by the *filiusfamilias* would have been considered as having been carried directly by the father instigator.[83]

The exception to the general rule was valid only for the brother who had proceeded respecting the order received from his father. In any case, if the grandfather, uncle or brother had independently killed the granddaughter, niece or sister caught in flagrant adultery, they would not been subject to ordinary punishment provided for by the law, but to a milder extraordinary punishment. The suffering caused by the appalling scene of their kinswoman's adultery would have been considered the

---

[79]For the *communis opinio* about this point, see Vivius, Franciscus. 1582. *Sylvae communium opinionum doctorum utriusque censurae ... liber primus*. Aquilae: apud Georgium Daghanum Monteripellium Sabaudium, opinio 33, n. 11, 27b; Farinaccius 1631 (as n. 48) pars 4, q. 121, nn. 18–19, 147ab, and n. 79, 154ab; Caballus 1613 (as n. 66) cent. 3, casus 300, nn. 54–55, 283b–284a, and the numerous authorities cited by them.

[80]Gl. *occidi potuerit ad* C. 9.9.4pr., *ad legem Juliam de adulteriis et stupro* l. *Gracchus*.

[81]C. 6.26.11.1: "natura pater et filius eadem persona paene intelleguntur". "Pater et filius una identitas sunt": Baldus de Ubaldis. 1589. *Consiliorum, sive responsorum ... volumen primum*. Francofurti ad Moenum: impensis Sigismundi Feyrabendij, cons. 234, n. 1, 62rb. On this matter see Lobrano, Giovanni. 1984. Pater et filius eadem persona. 1. *Per lo studio della* patria potestas. Milano: Giuffrè.

[82]Due to a presumption going far back and commonly accepted, the love of the father towards his son was thought to be greater than the love of the son towards his father. Cf. gl. *magis ad* D. 4.2.8, *de eo quod metus causa* l. *isti quidem*: "pater plus diligit filium quam seipsum. Illud constat quod plus pater filium quam filius patrem diligit"; gl. *diximus ad* D. 28.1.20.3, *qui testamenta facere possunt, et quemadmodum testamenta fiant* l. *qui testamento* § *quae autem*: "[pater] plus diligit filium, quam econtra filius patrem". See also the gl. *institueret ad* D. 28.5.46, *de haeredibus instituendis* l. *quidam*, which stated that "filium non posse invenire meliorem amicum quam patrem". Albericus de Rosate. 1572. *Dictionarium iuris tam civilis, quam canonici*. Venetiis: apud Guerreos fratres, et socios, *sub voce Filius*, explained the reason for this preferential love, using a 'bucolic' metaphor: "Filius plus diligitur a patre, quam econtra. Humor enim ascendit a trunco ad ramos". See Bellomo 1984 (as n. 10) 108.

[83]All these reasons were summarized with numerous citations by Bossius 1667 (as n. 9) cap. 3, § 2, nn. 87–88, 73b–74a.

same as a mitigating circumstance. For this reason, they deserved to be treated with mercy. Moreover, on the basis of a fragment of Papinian (D. 48.5.39[38].8) a certain leniency was also used in judging the betrayed husband who, blinded by his anger, had violated the prohibition of the *ius commune* of committing the uxoricide of his adulterous wife. He was not sentenced to death, but to a less severe punishment.[84] Actually, however, husbands were often not punished, in the indifference of practice or thanks to particular legislations that allowed the murder of adulteresses or presumed adulteresses, also considering that sometimes the physical elimination was the only way to be free of a wife from whom you could not divorce.[85]

The opinions of lawyers differed, on the other hand, with regards to the question whether the father could entrust the murder of the adulterous daughter also to a person who was not a member of his family. Many gave negative answer to this question, referring above all to the words of the text of the l. *Gracchus*, for which this act could be entrusted only to the son: since it was *materia odiosa*, it was not subject to broad interpretation. Augustinus Ariminensis also noted that the law allowed the father to take his immediate revenge, that is while his anger was still strong;[86] this was difficult to combine with the idea of recruiting someone to carry out his wishes (above all being paid for it, added Farinaccius). In this way, the boundaries that limited the impulsiveness of his reaction, the only to be justified in this context, were not so clear.

According to Clarus, refusing the possibility of paying someone to kill an adulterous daughter was the *communis opinio*, even if the opposite solution was followed in practice.[87] These exceptions were confirmed especially when the father was not in the physical condition of doing it by himself because he was weak, ill or old.[88] Lawyers often argued this case by analogy with the discipline of the betrayed husband who had paid someone to eliminate his wife's lover: a passage of the commentary of Matthaeus de Afflictis on the Constitutions of the Sicilies and Naples[89] regarding this circumstance was quoted by Clarus and other lawyers to

[84] Koch, Elisabeth. 1991. *Maior dignitas est in sexu virili. Das weibliche Geschlecht im Normensystem des 16. Jahrhunderts*. Frankfurt am Main: Vittorio Klostermann, 121–122; di Renzo Villata 2014 (as n. 14) 15–18.

[85] Cavina 2011 (as n. 14) 73–81.

[86] Augustinus Ariminensis 1555 (as n. 45) § *che hai adulterato la mia donna*, n. 24, 370a.

[87] Clarus 1587 (as n. 15) § *homicidium*, vers. *dubium est*, 34vab. See also Vivius 1582 (as n. 79) opinio 33, n. 10, 27b, and above all Caballus 1613 (as n. 66) cent. 3, casus 300, nn. 45–53, 283a–284a, who reconstructed the broad debate referring to the different positions.

[88] de Gambilionibus 1555 (as n. 38) § *che hai adulterato la mia donna*, n. 24, 369b; Caballus 1613 (as n. 66) cent. 3, casus 300, n. 72, 285a.

[89] de Afflictis, Matthaeus. 1580. *In utriusque Siciliae, Neapolisque Sanctiones, et Constitutiones novissima Praelectio ... Secunda Commentarii Pars in Secundum et Tertium earundem constitutionum Librum*. Venetiis: apud Ioannem Variscum, et Socios, rubr. 46, *ad* const. *si maritus*, nn. 3–4, 175rb–175va.

demonstrate how practice often differed from the opinion that was more established among scholars.[90]

A further question was that of the father who did not consider himself able to kill his daughter and her lover by himself, and therefore asked relatives and friends to assist him. In this case they would all go unpunished because they were deemed as the tool used by the father who was not able to do it by himself. Farinaccius emphasized that this solution was also shared by those who denied the father the possibility of entrusting others with the task of killing his daughter: but this was evidently a different situation.[91] The accomplices certainly could not be subject to a more severe punishment than that of their instigator and partner in the murder. If the father had fulfilled every required condition, he would not have been punished. Therefore his accomplices could also not be subject to any punishment.[92] Some scholars claimed that the accomplices who took part in the punitive expedition aimed at the murder of the daughter and her lover, had to refrain from committing physical actions, but had only to provide assistance and help, so as the father could take his revenge in complete safety.[93] All things considered, Pascalis thought that this was a fair and acceptable opinion.[94]

4 The Murder of the Adulterous Daughter: Also a Matter of Conscience

As already said, if the father killed his daughter and her lover respecting the conditions set out by the *Lex Julia de adulteriis* and revised by the law scholars of the *ius commune*, he would go unpunished. The common opinion was that the father would be "tutus"—this was the recurrent term used by the sources—thanks to the provisions in the *leges civiles*.[95] This also happened according to canon law and even if the fact had taken place *in terris Ecclesiae*.[96]

[90]The debate was well reconstructed, as usual, by Farinaccius 1631 (as n. 48) pars 4, q. 121, nn. 83–85, 154b, and by Bossius 1667 (as n. 9) cap. 3, § 2, nn. 88–89, 74b–75a.

[91]Farinaccius 1631 (as n. 48) pars 4, q. 121, n. 20, 147b.

[92]Baiardus 1617 (as n. 58) § *homicidium*, n. 185, 60a; Caballus 1613 (as n. 66) cent. 3, casus 300, nn. 58–60, 284ab.

[93]Caballus 1613 (as n. 66) cent. 3, casus 300, n. 73, 285a.

[94]Pascalis 1619 (as n. 9) pars 1, cap. 5, n. 26, 96b. This opinion was also shared by Bossius 1667 (as n. 9) cap. 3, § 2, n. 91, 75b.

[95]Sorice, Rosalba. 2012. "Impune occidetur, licite occidetur?". La non punibilità dell'omicidio nella dottrina medievale e moderna. In Schmoeckel, Mathias, Condorelli, Orazio, and Roumy, Frank (eds.), *Der Einfluss der Kanonistik auf die Europäische Rechtskultur.* 3. *Straf- und Strafprozessrecht*, 99–106. Köln Weimar Wien: Böhlau.

[96]Cephalus 1624 (as n. 70) cons. 305, 36a–37a, who suggested to solve in this sense the case "miseratione digno, ac pietate" regarding a father who had killed his only daughter caught committing flagrant adultery with one of his servants; Baiardus 1617 (as n. 58) § *homicidium*,

On the other hand, if the father was overwhelmed by his emotions and had not respected the required conditions, only an extraordinary punishment should be imposed on him, since the great difficulty of "iustum dolorem temperare" served as a mitigating factor.[97] Hence, for the father there was a particularly comprehensive set of rules.

The debate regarding the impunity of the father, however, also involved moral implications, which were connected to legal reasons, causing lively discussions among lawyers (and not only). It was a topic that included considerably controversial points, as explained by Bossius, who studied it in depth.[98] It was, indeed, on the boundary between law and ethics and introduced the topic of the dialectical relationship between internal forum and external forum.[99] Human standards which allowed an evident violation of the divine rules (the fifth commandment) did not cancel the negative religious and moral value of the action, which nevertheless represented a mortal sin. The provisions of Justinian's text had to be compared with the principles of Christian ethics. Lawyers therefore had to reckon with more intransigent opinions put forward by some canonists and more frequently from theologians. In fact, even if he could not be affected by temporal punishment, the father still risked a punishment of a spiritual nature, since the compliance of his actions with the secular rules and the *communis opinio* could not go so far as to exclude sin.

(Footnote 96 continued)

n. 173, 59b, nn. 179–180, 60a; Farinaccius 1631 (as n. 48) pars 4, q. 121, nn. 53–55, 150b–151a; Pascalis 1619 (as n. 9) pars 1, cap. 5, n. 28, 96b; Bossius 1667 (as n. 9) cap. 3, § 2, nn. 84–86, 73ab. For the opposite opinion, see Caballus 1613 (as n. 66) cent. 3, casus 300, n. 43, 282b, who related to Clarus (see the following notes).

[97]Bossius 1667 (as n. 9) cap. 3, § 2, n. 49, 64b (killing *ex intervallo*); n. 50, 64b (killing of either the daughter or her lover); n. 56, 65b (killing of the daughter in the father's house, in which the father, however, did not live); n. 58, 66a (killing of the widowed or unmarried daughter); n. 60, 66b (killing of the daughter caught committing acts that are preliminary to adultery, given the interpretation that recognized the *res Veneris* mentioned by Roman law only in the consummation of the sexual act itself); n. 76, 71b (killing of the daughter caught committing acts that are preliminary to adultery in the absence of other circumstances required to supplement the presumption that adultery was consumed, given the interpretation that recognized the *res Veneris* mentioned in Roman law in the *praeludia adulterii*); 77, 71b–72a (where the general rule was repeated).

[98]Cf. Bossius 1667 (as n. 9) cap. 3, § 2, n. 84, 73a, and nn. 92–101, 75b–78b.

[99]With regards to the relationship between the two courts see Prodi, Paolo. 2000. *Una storia della giustizia. Dal pluralismo dei fori al moderno dualismo tra coscienza e diritto*. Bologna: il Mulino, 155–267; Minnucci, Giovanni. 2011b. Foro della coscienza e foro esterno nel pensiero giuridico della prima età moderna. In Dilcher, Gerhard, and Quaglioni, Diego (eds.), *Gli inizi del diritto pubblico. 3. Verso la costruzione del diritto pubblico tra medioevo e modernità* (= *Die Anfänge des öffentlichen Rechts. 3. Auf dem Wege zur Etablierung des öffentlichen Rechts zwischen Mittelalter und Moderne*), 54–86. Bologna: il Mulino; Berlin: Duncker & Humblot; Müller, Wolfgang P. 2015. The Internal Forum of the Later Middle Ages. A Modern Myth? *Law and History Review* 33.04: 887–913. doi: 10.1017/S0738248015000486.

This aspect troubled Clarus, who revealed his unease: in the opinion of the learned criminal law scholar it was even unholy to claim that a law in force would allow to incur in eternal damnation.[100] The question therefore became whether the father could be granted impunity, not only in the law courts, but also in the forum of conscience. Some scholars gave an affirmative answer to the question, provided that the father had acted for the sake of justice, not only with vindictive feelings for the offence he had suffered. According to this school of thought, the father did not kill his daughter and her lover on the basis of his private authority, but also on that of the law, thus becoming perpetrator of justice. The father who therefore acted in defence of the public weal, could not commit a sin.[101] Clarus can be included among those who worked on this explanation. He looked for the solution of the dilemma examining another case of legitimate murder: that of a bandit (as already seen, the killing of an adulterous daughter was considered as lawful as the killing of a bandit). It was necessary to investigate the *animus* of the subject when he acted because he was also pardoned *in foro conscientiae* if driven by "zelo reipublicae", while he was not if driven by the mere vengeful desire.[102]

The level of importance of the issue of the conflict between the two courts is also given by the fact that Albericus Gentilis dealt with this topic in his commentary on the *Lex Julia de adulteriis*, although he had adhered to the Reformation. Moreover, he tried to find a solution to the problem in a long-distance discussion with Clarus.[103]

Farinaccius very pragmatically repelled the objections of the canonists who thought that the father had to be subject to punishment for the murder of his daughter and her lover. They were surely referring only to the consequences concerning the forum of conscience: in Farinaccius's opinion the moral aspect, which was compromised, was evidently not so fundamental. It was important that the legal solution was not jeopardized.[104]

---

[100]Clarus 1587 (as n. 15) § *homicidium*, vers. *sed haec quidem*, 34va. According to Massetto 1979 (as n. 39) 497, this passage demonstrates an "evidente senso di religiosità e di osservanza dell'autorità della Chiesa" ("evident sense of religiousness and observance of the authority of the Church") by Clarus.

[101]See the detailed reconstruction by Bossius 1667 (as n. 9) cap. 3, § 2, n. 92, 75b–76b.

[102]Clarus 1587 (as n. 15) § *homicidium*, vers. *sed nunquid*, 35rb, who also expanded the discussion to the evaluation of the behaviour of the husband who killed his wife's lover. With regards to this passage and the solution suggested by Clarus (who was inspired by Gomez) see Massetto 1979 (as n. 39) 443–444; Sorice 2012 (as n. 95) 103.

[103]Minnucci, Giovanni. 2002. *Alberico Gentili tra* mos italicus *e* mos gallicus. *L'inedito commentario* Ad legem Juliam de adulteriis. Bologna: Monduzzi, 184. Gentilis, in reality, dealt with the situation of the betrayed husband, as it took into consideration l. *Gracchus*. Nevertheless, this did not prevent him from having the same problems of moral order. For this topic, see also ibidem 89–96. Gentilis also dealt with this subject in *De nuptiis*: see Minnucci, Giovanni. 2011a. *Alberico Gentili* iuris interpres *della prima età moderna*. Bologna: Monduzzi, 40–46; Minnucci 2011b (as n. 99) 67–73.

[104]Farinaccius 1631 (as n. 48) pars 4, q. 121, n. 55, 151a.

Keeping these two different levels separate seems in any case to have been the most used (and usable) solution. Many lawyers and theologians therefore gave a negative answer to the question regarding the possibility of not considering the murder of an adulterous daughter as a sin.[105] In the forum of conscience and before God the father could never kill his daughter and her lover caught in flagrant adultery without incurring in mortal sin, even though laws and statutes allowed to do this granting impunity in the external forum: in this way, Bossius introduced the debate, as always attentive to the moral implications of each question, since he also studied as a moralist.[106] Several passages of canon law could have been used to justify this position.[107] The father's action then blatantly violated divine law. The prohibition to kill sanctioned by the Decalogue was certainly valid also in this case, since the father killed by virtue of his private authority and not of any special indiscriminate power received from the *leges*.

Eventually, the negative answer to this question could also be based on the consideration that laws and statutes did not grant the father a general right to kill his daughter and her lover caught in the act of committing adultery, but only to kill them on fulfilment of a just cause. Laws and statutes therefore prevented the father only from being subject to the punishment of the judicial forum due to the great suffering caused by the insult. The law indicated that the father acted impulsively, driven by the anger caused by the discovery of the act of adultery and in such a state that he could not control his reactions. The laws that allowed to do something without being punished did not, however, excuse from the sin, as they were minimal concessions to avoid major sins and scandals. Bossius completed the argumentation with an illuminating example: the *leges civiles* allowed within the *respublica Christiana* prostitution to avoid major sins and scandals (such as

[105]For the thought of some modern age theologians about the murder committed by the husband of the adulteress—but in their works the subject goes hand in hand with that of the adulterous daughter by the father—see Cavina 2011 (as n. 14) 80.

[106]Bossius 1667 (as n. 9) cap. 3, § 2, n. 93, 76b.

[107]The *sedes materiae* that aroused the problem was mainly C. 33 q. 2 c. 6, c. *inter haec* (partly referred to as an exception to the discipline of Justinian law: see, for example, Antonius de Butrio. 1578. *Super prima secundi Decretalium Commentarij*. Venetiis: apud Iuntas, *ad* X. 2.2.13, *de foro competenti* c. *cum contingat*, n. 11, 43rb). It was an epistle of Pope Nicholas I treating only the murder of the adulteress by her husband. This option had been permitted by a *lex mundana*, which did not, however, bind the Church. The canon is, however, to be read together with the v. *inter haec*, without which the connection to this context would not be understood. In fact, the Gloss specified that the *lex mundana* to which it referred was not Roman law, but it was *Lombarda*. It then referred directly to the passages of the Justinian *corpus* that ruled this matter to highlight the role that only the father could have in chastising his daughter. What is more important, however, is that it marked the difference between *ius civile* and *ius canonicum*: the authorization given by the secular law, which also excluded the imposition of a punishment, did not dispense from falling into mortal sin (in fact, to use the terminology of that time, the civil law was *nutritiva peccati*). The only way not to violate the fifth commandment of the Decalogue would have been to obtain a special canonical concession to guarantee immunity from the sin.

adultery and sodomy),[108] but prostitutes were not excused from their sin. Nevertheless, it was not possible to say that these laws had to be considered unjust or had to be abrogated.[109] The fact that something was lawful and conformed to the provisions of the law did not necessarily imply that it was also right and would preserve from sin.

5 Conclusions

The father's right to kill his adulterous daughter caught in the act of committing adultery was surrounded by the ancient taste of revenge and by the idea that the insult had to be washed away immediately with blood. In the scholars' debate of the late *ius commune*, it also led to some interesting discussions.

The law scholars of the late *ius commune* did not question its existence. They also had to face theologians and moralists of their time, who opposed the idea of granting the father the right to commit such a serious crime and go unpunished, considering that the victim was a close relative. The continuation of this case in the debates of the law scholars, who accepted and justified its premises, bears witness to the survival (and acceptance) even in the Modern Age of a power that could be carried out in a bloody manner inside the family home.

The same law scholars remarked, where possible, the differences between the provisions of Roman law for the father and the betrayed husband, who was not allowed to kill his wife, but who was granted a conditional *ius occidendi* towards her lover. The scholars reaffirmed the *ius commune*, while practice and statutory laws, on the other hand, had begun to accept the killing of adulterous wives by their husbands, who often used this right as a pretence.

The legacy of Roman law was clear in the discipline of this matter. Lawyers in the modern period, pursuant to the scholars' elaborations of previous centuries, tried to exploit the possible interpretations that the Justinian's texts had left them, to adapt those rules to the reality of their times, and fill them with content. This could be clearly seen thanks to the way in which the lawyers dealt with the conditions that the *Lex Julia de adulteriis* had introduced at the end—not expressed, but in any case evident—to limit the violence of the father that had caught his daughter in flagrant adultery, and to favour, instead, the intervention of the public authorities. These conditions, aimed at granting the father's impunity for the murder of his adulterous daughter, would have had to restrict the possibilities of killing the daughter and her lover.

[108]Cf. Dean 2010 (as n. 14) 151–152; Tavilla, Elio. 2014. Cinquecento postribolare: dilemmi morali e giuridici in tema di *meretrices* e *meretricium*. In Cavina, Marco, Ribémont, Bernard, and Hoxha, Damigela (eds.), *Le donne e la giustizia fra Medioevo ed età moderna. Il caso di Bologna a confronto*, 91–106. Bologna: Patron.

[109]Cf. Bossius 1667 (as n. 9) cap. 3, § 2, nn. 93–94, 76b–77a, extremely detailed in the citation of sources—both juridical and theological.

In any case, in giving substance to each single condition, the law scholars of the late *ius commune* decreased in fact the limiting effect: just think of how the time and space limitations were intended with regards to the father's actions; or how the *res Veneris* were interpreted, which could also indicate actions that were not so closely connected to the act of adultery. It seems that where Roman law had tried to stem the private spaces to grant more to the public authority, the law scholars of the *ius commune*, on the other hand, wanted to keep the private sphere of adultery. From this point of view, the autonomy and powers of the father were strengthened, on the basis of the solid theoretical implications of the *ius commune*.

In this way, it was possible to confirm the exclusivity of the right to kill the adulteress that Roman law had granted only to the *paterfamilias*. The 'external' limits (the conditions required for impunity) were reconsidered, but trust was placed in the 'internal' limits, that is in the *pietas* that founded and characterized the exercise of parental authority. This framework also included the configuration of the right to kill an adulterous daughter as a right connected to the ancient *ius vitae ac necis* and the father's powers within his family.

References

(1568). *Constitutiones Regni utriusque Siciliae*. Lugduni: apud haeredes Iacobi Iunctae.

Albericus de Rosate. (1572). *Dictionarium iuris tam civilis, quam canonici*. Venetiis: apud Guerreos fratres, et socios.

Antonius de Butrio. (1578). *Super prima secundi Decretalium Commentarij*. Venetiis: apud Iuntas.

Augustinus Ariminensis. (1555). *Additiones ad* Angelus de Gambilionibus, *De maleficiis*. Lugduni: apud haeredes Iacobi Iuntae.

Baiardus, I. B. (1617). *Additiones et adnotationes ... ad Julii Clari Receptarum Sententiarum Libros V*. Francofurti: officina typographica Nicolai Hoffmanni, impensis Ioannis Bassaei.

Baldus de Ubaldis. (1589). *Consiliorum, sive responsorum ... volumen primum*. Francofurti ad Moenum: impensis Sigismundi Feyrabendij.

Baldus de Ubaldis. (1589). *Consiliorum, sive responsorum ... volumen secundum*. Francofurti ad Moenum: impensis Sigismundi Feyrabendij.

Bartolus de Saxoferrato. (1555). *Prima in Digestum vetus*. Lugduni: excudebat Blasius Guido.

Bartolus de Saxoferrato. (1555). *Commentaria in secundam Digesti novi partem*. Lugduni: [Compagnie des libraires de Lyon].

Bossius, I. A. (1667). *De effectu contractus matrimonii*. Lugduni: sumptibus Philippi Borde, Laur. Arnaud et Petri Borde.

Caballus, P. (1613). *Resolutionum criminalium ... centuriae tres*. Francoforti: e Collegio Paltheniano.

Carerius, L. (1562). *Practica causarum criminalium*. Lugduni: apud Gulielmum Rovillium.

Cephalus, I. (1624). *Consiliorum sive responsorum iuris liber tertius*. Francofurti: sumptibus Godefridi Tampachii bibliopolae.

Clarus, J. (1587). *Sententiarum receptarum liber quintus*. Venetiis: apud Cornelium Arrivabenum.

Clementinus, A. (1572–1573). *De patria potestate*. Francoforti ad Moenum: impressum per Nicolaum Bassee, impensis Hieronymi Feyerabend.

de Afflictis, M. (1580). *In utriusque Siciliae, Neapolisque Sanctiones, et Constitutiones novissima Praelectio ... Secunda Commentarii Pars in Secundum et Tertium earundem constitutionum Librum*. Venetiis: apud Ioannem Variscum, et Socios.
Decianus, T. (1591). *Tractatus criminalis ... Tomus secundus*, Francofurti ad Moenum: impensis Petri Fischeri.
de Gambilionibus, A. (1555). *De maleficiis*. Lugduni: apud haeredes Iacobi Iuntae.
de Marsiliis, H. (1574). *Practica criminalis ... Averolda nuncupata*. Venetiis: ex Typographia Bartholomei Rubini.
Farinaccius, P. (1631). *Praxis et theoricae criminalis pars quarta*. Lugduni: sumptibus Iacobi Cardon.
Grammaticus, T. (1562). *In Constitutionibus, Capitulis, et Pragmaticis Regni Neapolitani et Ritibus Magnae Curiae Vicariae Additiones, et Apostillae*. Venetiis: impressum apud Ioannem Variscum, expensis D. Baptistae de Christophoro Bibliopolae Parthenopei.
Mascardus, I. (1593). *De probationibus ... volumen primum*. Francofurti ad Moenum: impensis haeredum Sigismundi Feyrabendii.
Menochius, I. (1615). *De Praesumptionibus, Coniecturis, Signis, et Indiciis Commentaria*: Coloniae Agrippinae: ex officina Antonii Hierat bibliopolae.
Minnucci, G. (Ed.). (1997). *Tractatus criminum saeculi XII*. Bologna: Monduzzi.
Monticulus, S. (1584). Tractatus de patria potestate. In *Tractatus illustrium, in utraque, tum Pontificii, tum Caesarei iuris facultate Iurisconsultorum. De ultimis voluntatibus... Tomi VIII Pars II*. Venetiis: Franciscus Zilettus.
Pascalis, P. (1619). *De viribus patriae potestatis*. Genevae: apud Philippum Albertum.
Pratus, F. M. (1655). *Adnotationes ad* Pascalis, Philippus, *Tractatus amplissimus de viribus patriae potestatis*. Venetiis: Bertanorum sumptibus.
Rolandus a Valle. (1584). *Consiliorum seu mavis responsorum ... volumen secundum*. Francoforti: apud Martinum Lechlerum, impensis Sigismundi Feyrabendii.
Vivius, F. (1582). *Sylvae communium opinionum doctorum utriusque censurae ... liber primus*. Aquilae: apud Georgium Daghanum Monteripellium Sabaudium.

Literature

Bellomo, M. (1966, reprint 1986). *Profili della famiglia italiana nell'età dei comuni*. Catania: Giannota.
Bellomo, M. (1984). Die Familie und ihre rechtliche Struktur in den italienischen Stadtkommunen des Mittelalters (12.–14. Jahrhundert). In A. Haverkamp (Ed.), *Haus und Familie in der spätmittelalterlichen Stadt* (pp. 99–135). Köln-Wien: Böhlau.
Benke, N. (2012). On the Roman Father's Right to Kill His Adulterous Daughter. *The History of the Family, 17*(3), 284–308.
Boari, M. (2007). *La coercizione privata nella Magna Glossa. Tracce fra diritto e violenza*. Giuffrè: Milano.
Bonfield, L. (2002). Gli sviluppi del diritto di famiglia in Europa. In M. Barbagli & D.I. Kertzer (Eds.), *Storia della famiglia in Europa. Dal Cinquecento alla Rivoluzione francese* (pp. 121–175). Bari-Roma: Laterza.
Brundage, J. A. (1980). Carnal Delight: Canonistic Theories of Sexuality. In S. Kuttner & K. Pennington (Eds.), *Proceedings of the Fifth International Congress of Medieval Canon Law* (Salamanca, 21-25 September 1976) (pp. 361–385). Città del Vaticano: Biblioteca Apostolica Vaticana, also in Brundage, J. A. 1993. *Sex, Law and Marriage in the Middle Ages*, I. Aldershot: Ashgate.
Brundage, J. A. (1986). Marriage and Sexuality in the Decretals of Pope Alexander III. In F. Liotta (Ed.), *Miscellanea Rolando Bandinelli Papa Alessandro III* (pp. 59–83). Siena: Accademia Senese degli Intronati, also in Brundage, J. A. 1993. *Sex, Law and Marriage in the Middle Ages*, IX. Aldershot: Ashgate.

Brundage, J. A. (1987). *Law, Sex, and Christian Society in Medieval Europe*. Chicago-London: The University of Chicago Press.

Brundage, J. A. (1990). Sexual Equality in Medieval Canon law. In J.T. Rosenthal (Ed.), *Medieval Women and the Sources of Medieval History* (pp. 66–79). Athens: University of Georgia Press, also in Brundage, J. A. (1993). *Sex, Law and Marriage in the Middle Ages*, VI. Aldershot: Ashgate.

Calasso, F. (1951). *I glossatori e la teoria della sovranità. Studio di diritto comune pubblico* (2nd ed.). Milano: Giuffrè.

Cantarella, E. (1976). *Studi sull'omicidio in diritto greco e romano*. Milano: Giuffrè.

Cantarella, E. (1991). Homicides of Honor. The Development of Italian Adultery Law over Two Millennia. In D.I. Kertzer & R.P. Saller (Eds.), *The Family in Italy, from Antiquity to the Present* (pp. 229–244). New Haven-London: Yale University Press; Italian translation: Cantarella, E. (1995). L'omicidio d'onore: lo sviluppo della legislazione italiana attraverso due millenni. In D.I. Kertzer & R.P. Saller (Eds.), *La famiglia in Italia dall'antichità al XX secolo* (pp. 255–272). Firenze: Le Lettere, with some modifications also Cantarella, Eva. 1992. La causa d'onore dalla «Lex Iulia» al codice Rocco. In *Testimonium amicitiae* (pp. 73–94). Milano: Giuffrè, also in Cantarella, Eva. 2011. *Diritto e società in Grecia e a Roma. Scritti scelti*, A. Maffi & L. Gagliardi (Eds.), 555–576. Milano: Giuffrè.

Cantarella, E. (2014). *L'ambiguo malanno. Condizione e immagine della donna nell'antichità greca e romana* (4th ed.). Milano: Feltrinelli.

Capogrossi Colognesi, L. (1982). Patria potestà (diritto romano). In *Enciclopedia del diritto* (Vol. 32, pp. 242–249). Milano: Giuffrè.

Capogrossi Colognesi, L. (1984). Idee vecchie e nuove sui poteri del *pater familias*. In *Poteri* negotia actiones *nella esperienza romana arcaica*, Atti del Convegno di diritto romano (Copanello, 12–15 maggio 1982) (pp. 53–76). Napoli: Edizioni scientifiche italiane.

Castronovo, V. (1971). Bossi, Giovanni Angelo. In *Dizionario biografico degli italiani* (Vol. 13, pp. 309–310). Roma: Istituto della Enciclopedia italiana.

Cavina, M. (1997). *Paterfamilias-Princeps* nella tradizione teologica e giuridica bassomedievale. Alcuni sondaggi nelle fonti e nella storiografia. In P. Landau & J. Mueller (Eds.), *Proceedings of the Ninth International Congress of Medieval Canon Law* (Munich, 13–18 July 1992) (pp. 1137–1153). Città del Vaticano: Biblioteca Apostolica Vaticana.

Cavina, M. (2007). *Il padre spodestato. L'autorità paterna dall'antichità a oggi*. Bari–Roma: Laterza.

Cavina, M. (2011). *Nozze di sangue. Storia della violenza coniugale*. Laterza: Bari-Roma.

Cohen, D. (1991). The Augustan Law on Adultery. The Social and Cultural Context. In D. I. Kertzer & R. P. Saller (Eds.), *The Family in Italy, from Antiquity to the Present* (pp. 109–126). New Haven-London: Yale University Press; Italian translation: Cohen, D. (1995). Le leggi augustee sull'adulterio: il contesto sociale e culturale. In D. I. Kertzer & R. P. Saller (Eds.), *La famiglia in Italia dall'antichità al XX secolo* (pp. 123–142). Firenze: Le Lettere.

Davidson, N. (1994). Theology, Nature and the Law: Sexual Sin and Sexual Crime in Italy from the Fourteenth to the Seventeenth Century. In T. Dean & K. J. P. Lowe (Eds.), *Crime, Society and the Law in Renaissance Italy* (pp. 74–98). Cambridge: Cambridge University Press.

Dean, T. (2010). *Crime and Justice in Late Medieval Italy*. Cambridge: Cambridge University Press.

di Renzo Villata, M. G. (1995). Persone e famiglia nel diritto medievale e moderno. In *Digesto delle discipline privatistiche. Sezione civile* (Vol. 13, pp. 457–527). Torino: Utet.

di Renzo Villata, M. G. (2014). "Crimen adulterii est gravius aliis delictis…". L'adultera tra diritto e morale nell'area italiana (XIII–XVI secolo). In M. Cavina, B. Ribémont & D. Hoxha (Eds.), *Le donne e la giustizia fra Medioevo ed età moderna. Il caso di Bologna a confronto* (pp. 11–45). Bologna: Patron.

di Renzo Villata, G. (2015). Dall'amore coniugale 'proibito' all'infedeltà. L'adulterio nelle Summae confessorum italiane (XIV–XVI secolo). *Italian Review of Legal History, 1*(02), 1–41.

Faggion, L. (2013). Montecchio (Monticelli), Sebastiano. In I. Birocchi, E. Cortese, A. Mattone & M. N. Miletti (Eds.), *Dizionario biografico dei giuristi italiani (XII–XX secolo)* (Vol. 2, p. 1368). Bologna: il Mulino.

Frigo, D. (1985). *Il padre di famiglia. Governo della casa e governo civile nella tradizione dell'"economica" tra Cinque e Seicento*. Roma: Bulzoni.

Helmholz, R. (1988). 'Si quis suadente': Theory and Practice. In P. Linehan (Ed.), *Proceedings of the Seventh International Congress of Medieval Canon Law* (Cambridge, 23–27 July 1984) (pp. 425–438). Città del Vaticano: Biblioteca Apostolica Vaticana.

Koch, E. (1991). Maior dignitas est in sexu virili. *Das weibliche Geschlecht im Normensystem des 16. Jahrhunderts*. Frankfurt am Main: Vittorio Klostermann.

Kuehn, T. (1981). Women, Marriage, and *Patria Potestas* in Late Medieval Florence. *Tijdschrift voor Rechtsgeschiedenis, 49*, 127–147, also in Kuehn, T. (1991). *Law, Family, & Women. Toward a Legal Anthropology of Renaissance Italy* (pp. 197–211). Chicago: The University of Chicago Press.

Lobrano, G. (1984). Pater et filius eadem persona. 1. *Per lo studio della* patria potestas. Milano: Giuffrè.

Marchisello, A. (2004). "Alieni thori violatio": l'adulterio come delitto carnale in Prospero Farinacci (1544–1618). In S. Seidel Menchi & D. Quaglioni (Eds.), *Trasgressioni. Seduzione, concubinato, adulterio, bigamia (XIV–XVIII secolo)* (pp. 133–183). Bologna: il Mulino.

Massetto, G.P. (1979). I reati nell'opera di Giulio Claro. *Studia et Documenta Historiae et Iuris, 45*, 328–503, also in Massetto, G.P. (1994) *Saggi di storia del diritto penale lombardo (secc. XVI–XVIII)* (pp. 61–227). Milano: LED.

Mazzacane, A. (2013). Farinacci, Prospero. In: I. Birocchi, E. Cortese, A. Mattone & M. N. Miletti (Eds.), *Dizionario biografico dei giuristi italiani (XII–XX secolo)* (Vol. 1, pp. 822–825). Bologna: il Mulino.

Meccarelli, M. (1998). Arbitrium. *Un aspetto sistematico degli ordinamenti giuridici in età di diritto comune*. Milano: Giuffrè.

Minnucci, G. (1994). *La capacità processuale della donna nel pensiero canonistico classico*. 2. *Dalle scuole d'Oltralpe a S. Raimondo di Pennaforte*. Milano: Giuffrè.

Minnucci, G. (1998). Processo e condizione femminile nel pensiero dei primi glossatori civilisti. *Studia Gratiana, 30*, 641–660.

Minnucci, G. (1999). Processo e condizione femminile nella canonistica classica. In F. Liotta (Ed.), *Studi di storia del diritto medioevale e moderno* (pp. 129–183). Bologna: Monduzzi.

Minnucci, G. (2002). *Alberico Gentili tra mos italicus e mos gallicus. L'inedito commentario Ad legem Juliam de adulteriis*. Bologna: Monduzzi.

Minnucci, G. (2011a). *Alberico Gentili iuris interpres della prima età moderna*. Bologna: Monduzzi.

Minnucci, G. (2011b). Foro della coscienza e foro esterno nel pensiero giuridico della prima età moderna. In G. Dilcher & D. Quaglioni (Eds.), *Gli inizi del diritto pubblico*. 3. *Verso la costruzione del diritto pubblico tra medioevo e modernità* (= *Die Anfänge des öffentlichen Rechts*. 3. *Auf dem Wege zur Etablierung des öffentlichen Rechts zwischen Mittelalter und Moderne*) (pp. 54–86). Bologna: il Mulino; Berlin: Duncker & Humblot.

Müller, W. P. (2015). The Internal Forum of the Later Middle Ages. A Modern Myth? *Law and History Review, 33*(04), 887–913. doi:10.1017/S0738248015000486.

Prodi, P. (2000). *Una storia della giustizia. Dal pluralismo dei fori al moderno dualismo tra coscienza e diritto*. Bologna: il Mulino.

Quaglioni, D. (1977). «Quilibet in domo sua dicitur rex» (in margine ad alcune pagine di Francesco Calasso). *Studi senesi, 26*, 344–358.

Quaglioni, D. (1983). *Politica e diritto nel Trecento italiano. Il «De Tyranno» di Bartolo da Sassoferrato (1314–1357). Con l'edizione critica dei trattati «De Guelphis et Gebellinis», «De Regimine civitatis» e «De Tyranno»*. Firenze: Olschki.

Rizzelli, G. (1997). Lex Iulia de adulteriis. *Studi sulla disciplina di* adulterium, lenocinium, stuprum. Lecce: Edizioni del Grifo.

Sinisi, L. (2013). Pascali, Filippo. In I. Birocchi, E. Cortese, A. Mattone & M. N. Miletti (Eds.), *Dizionario biografico dei giuristi italiani (XII–XX secolo)* (Vol. 2, p. 1516). Bologna: il Mulino.

Sorice, R. (2012). "Impune occidetur, licite occidetur?". La non punibilità dell'omicidio nella dottrina medievale e moderna. In M. Schmoeckel, O. Condorelli & F. Roumy (Eds.), *Der Einfluss der Kanonistik auf die Europäische Rechtskultur. 3. Straf- und Strafprozessrecht* (pp. 99–106). Köln-Weimar-Wien: Böhlau.

Talamanca, M. (1990). *Istituzioni di diritto romano*. Milano: Giuffré.

Tavilla, E. (2014). Cinquecento postribolare: dilemmi morali e giuridici in tema di *meretrices* e *meretricium*. In M. Cavina, B. Ribémont & D. Hoxha (Eds.), *Le donne e la giustizia fra Medioevo ed età moderna. Il caso di Bologna a confronto* (pp. 91–106). Bologna: Patron.

Thomas, Y. (1984). Vitae necisque potestas. Le père, la cité, la mort. In *Du châtiment dans la cité. Supplices corporels et peine de mort dans le monde antique*. Table ronde de Rome (9–11 novembre 1982) (pp. 499–548). Rome: École Française de Rome.

Vismara, G. (1956). L'unità della famiglia nella storia del diritto in Italia. *Studia et Documenta Historiae et Iuris, 22*, 228–265, also in Vismara, G. (1988). *Scritti di storia giuridica*. 5. *La famiglia* (pp. 1–44). Milano: Giuffrè.

Yaron, R. (1962). Vitae necisque potestas. *Tijdschrift voor Rechtsgeschiedenis, 30*, 243–251.

Duæ Animæ in Una Carne. The Disqualification of the Spouses in *Common Law*

Yves Mausen

Abstract In modern common law the disqualification of witnesses for family reasons is more or less restricted to the spouse. The first two treatises on evidence law, *The Law of Evidence* by William Nelson (1717) and *The Law of Evidence* by Jeffrey Gilbert (1754), offer a twofold explanation of the prohibition: The identity of interests between spouses and the interest of marriage as such. Coherently the principle does not apply if the wife's testimony is brought forth for the good of the couple or for her own sake as opposed to the wish of her husband. These reasons are not based on any specific English social context but on ancient conceptions of the nature of the union between two human people and on timeless considerations of human psychology. Similarly the absence of the other Roman-canonical relative motives for refusing witnesses (affinity, dependence) cannot be reduced to social or intellectual choices but must be seen as the consequence of the freedom left to the jurors to appreciate the quality of the evidence.

Y. Mausen (✉)
Legal History and Religious Law, University of Fribourg, Av. de l'Europe 20,
1700 Fribourg, Switzerland
e-mail: yves.mausen@unifr.ch

M.G. di Renzo Villata (ed.), *Family Law and Society in Europe from the Middle Ages to the Contemporary Era*, Studies in the History of Law and Justice 5,
DOI 10.1007/978-3-319-42289-3_9

1 Introduction

Contrary to the thesis of the still dominant Anglophone historiography,[1] in common law the law of evidence did not develop only since the modern era. As early as the 14th century, under Edward III, the Londoner judges presiding assizes of novel disseisin combined the verdict of the jury with the evidence given by witnesses.[2] The *Year Books* and their *Abridgments* identify numerous cases. However it is true that the first monographic treatises on the subject appear only at the beginning of the 18th century. One was *The Law of Evidence* by William Nelson, edited in London in 1717,[3] followed by a work with the same title by Sir Jeffrey Gilbert, Lord Chief Baron of the Exchequer, published posthumously in 1754 in Dublin and 2 years later in London.[4] Until the 20ies of the 19th century other ones were edited.[5] They were all destined to be the target of Jeremy Bentham's criticism. His

---

[1]Cf. Pollock, Frederick and Maitland, Frederic W. 1895. *The History of English Law Before the Time of Edward I*. Cambridge: University Cambridge Press; Thayer, James B. 1898. *A Preliminary Treatise on Evidence at the Common Law*. Boston: Little, Brown. From there on the positions become gradually even more radical and postpone more and more the time where testimonial evidence and thus systematic law of evidence are supposed to have developed: Wigmore, John H. 1905. *A Treatise on the System of Evidence in Trials at Common Law*. Boston: Little, Brown and Company, 1, ch. 1, § 8: "A General Survey of the History of the Rules of Evidence"; Morgan, Edmund M. and Maguire, John. 1934. *Cases on Evidence*. Chicago: The Foundation Press, Inc. (based on another work by Thayer, James B. 1892. *Select Cases on Evidence at the Common Law*. Cambridge: Cambridge University Press); Morgan, Edmund M. 1937. The Jury and the Exclusionary Rules of Evidence. *The University of Chicago Law Review* 4.2: 247–258; Langbein, John H. 1996. Historical Foundations of the Law of Evidence: A View from the Ryder Sources. *Columbia Law Review* 96: 1168–1202. To these works may be added Macnair, Michael R. T. 1999. *The Law of Proof in Early Modern Equity* (*Comparative Studies in Continental and Anglo–American Legal History*, 20). Berlin: Duncker & Humblot. The work is remarkable because the author does not close his mind to the influence of the learned law (see infra, conclusion) but his view remains incomplete because he limits himself to equity and so to the modern era, which does not allow for any reconsideration of the chronology established by Wigmore (p. 25).

[2]See for a particularly striking example: Mausen, Yves. 2016 (to be published). Sans lour scient de veritie dire. Aux origines de l'interdiction de l'*opinion evidence* en *common law*. In *La culture judiciaire anglaise au moyen âge. Première partie*, ed. Yves Mausen. Paris: Mare & Martin.

[3]Anon. 1717. *The Law of Evidence: wherein All the Cases that have yet been printed in any of our* Law Books *or* Tryals, *and that in any wise relate to Points of Evidence, are collected and methodically digested under their proper Heads*. In the Savoy: Printed by Eliz. Nutt and R. Gosling for R. Gosling.

[4]Anon. (By a late Learned Judge). 1756. *The Law of Evidence*. London: Printed by Henry Lintot for W. Owen. Gilbert died in 1726 and may have written his treatise before 1710.

[5]Bathurst, Henry J. 1761. *The Theory of Evidence*. Dublin: Cotter; Buller, Francis. 1772. *An Introduction to the Law Relative to Trials at Nisi Prius*: Dublin: Eliz. Lynch; Morgan, John. 1789. *Essays upon the Law of Evidence*: E. Lynch, H. Chamberlaine, et al.; Peake, Thomas. 1801. *A Compendium of the Law of Evidence*: E. & R. Brooke & T. Rider; McNally, Leonard. 1802. *The Rules of Evidence on Pleas of the Crown*. London and Dublin; Evans, William D. 1806. On the Law of Evidence. In Pothier, Robert Joseph. *A Treatise on the Law of Obligations, or Contracts*. London: A. Strahan; Phillipps, Samuel March. 1814. *Treatise on the Law of Evidence*. London:

Traité des preuves judiciaires was published in 1823 in Paris, translated by Etienne Dumont, and in 1825 in London (*A Treatise on Judicial Evidence*). In 1827, he published the *Rationale of Judicial Evidence, Specially Applied to English Practice*, written probably between 1802 and 1812. Bentham's will of modernization and rationalization of the subject was continued by his followers, in particular by Henry Brougham and Thomas Denman. It lead directly to the *Common Law Procedure Acts* in 1852 and 1854. That part of the history of the common law is so well known that it marked the historiography itself lastingly: Bentham's judgement on the previous treatises was simply adopted.

As a matter of fact the first books, which are so badly reputed today, describe a system which is essentially based on practice and insofar a law of evidence which seems elementary or even different.[6] Nelson and Gilbert are unable to separate procedure and substantial law clearly and present the evidence from the perspective of the different issues and forms of action.[7] Still, their works contain also some general considerations, in Nelson's in particular in the two first chapters, named "Of Evidence in general" and "Of Witnesses in general",[8] and in Gilbert's in an initial presentation of the subject much inspired by the philosophy of John Locke[9] and in a more disseminated way throughout the treatise. On the question of testimonial evidence, Nelson is particularly interested by the motives for disqualifying witnesses. He dedicates most of his developments to the "Witnesses that are interested in the Event of the Cause".[10] So does Gilbert.[11] It shows that, at least in the practice of the first half of the 18th century, that means of defence remained essential.

At first glance this situation is not much different from the *ius commune* of the Middle Ages. Its authors indulged already in long enumerations of *reprobationes* and among the relative motives (those based not on the personal status of the witness but on his relationship with one of the parties), the personal direct interest as well as friendship, family and domesticity were of great importance.[12] However,

(Footnote 5 continued)

J. Butterworth and Son; Starkie, Thomas. 1824. *Practical Treatise on the Law of Evidence*. London: J. & W.T. Clarke.

[6]Edmund Burke's outburst during the trial of Warren Hastings in the *House of Lords* on February 25th 1794 is well known: "As to rules of law and evidence, he did not know what they meant; […] it was true, something had been written on the law of Evidence, but very general, very abstract, and comprised in so small a compass that a parrot he had known might get them by rote in one half–hour and repeat them in five minutes" (*Lords' Journal*, Feb. 25, 1794. In Wigmore (as n. 1) 26, n. 4.

[7]Cf. Nelson (as n. 3) 111–243; Gilbert (as n. 4) 161–289.

[8]Nelson (as n. 3) 1–6 and 7–19 resp.

[9]Gilbert (as n. 4) 1–6. In 1709 Gilbert published *An Abstract of Mr. Locke's Essay on Human Understanding*. London: s.n.

[10]Nelson (as n. 3) 33–62.

[11]Gilbert (as n. 4) 122–140.

[12]Cf. Mausen, Yves. 2006. Veritatis adiutor. *La procédure du témoignage dans le droit savant et la pratique française (XIIe–XIVe siècles)*. Milano: Giuffrè, 455–580.

the common law judges would only recognize certain motives, limited in number and following more or less *sui generis* rules. Their attitude towards the witnesses who are of the family of one of the parties is particularly revealing.

Extending the scope of Roman rules, the Medieval lawyers rejected not only the ascendants and descendants, but also, following canonical texts, the collaterals, especially those related by blood. Husband and wife were also barred one against the other.[13] Out of this body of rules the English common law really accepts only the prohibition concerning the spouses[14] as outlined in the clearest way by Gilbert:

> But no other Relation is excluded, because no other Relation is absolutely the same in Interest; but by the Civil Law, Servants and Children were excluded, because the Parents and Masters had an absolute Power over them, and therefore under that Law they swore with manifest Interest to themselves.[15]

On his part, Nelson considers also the case of the father but only through two precedents in which a father was allowed to testify in his son's case because he himself stayed at the origin of the commitment in question.[16] Nelson also raises the case of the cousin but only by mentioning an assize (going back to 1349 by the way) in which the exception was not granted.[17] And in the cases he lists where a mother or a father were refused this decision was justified by an additional specific interest they had.[18] It is all the more essential to analyse the situation of the spouses in order to understand the mechanisms of English and American evidence law through the reasons of their disqualification as witnesses (I) and the justification of the exceptions to this principle (II).

[13]Cf. Mausen (as n. 12) 561–567, with a detailed presentation of the discussions and the exceptions; 566–567, concerning the spouses. Cf. Mausen, Yves. 2012. La famille suspecte. Liens familiaux et motifs de récusation des témoins à l'époque médiévale. In *Histoires de famille. A la convergence du droit pénal et des liens de parenté* (*Cahiers de l'Institut d'Anthropologie Juridique de l'Université de Limoges*, 33), ed. Leah Otis-Cour, 161–171. Limoges: PULIM.

[14]Cf. Macnair (as n. 1) 185 ss. ("Exceptions to Witnesses"), 202 ss. ("Bias"), 222 ss. ("Affinity and dependance") and finally 223 sq. ("Spouses"). Cf. for an analysis of the more recent developments: Klapisch, Jutta. 1994. Duae animae in carne una? Spouses as Witnesses in the American Law of Evidence between 1839 and 1944. In *Subjektivierung des justiziellen Beweisverfahrens. Beiträge zum Zeugenbeweis in Europa und den USA (18.–20. Jahrhundert)* (*Ius Commune Sonderheft*, 64), ed. André Gouron, Laurent Mayali, Antonio Padoa-Schioppa and Dieter Simon. Frankfurt: Klostermann, 301–336.

[15]Gilbert (as n. 4) 138.

[16]Nelson (as n. 3) 54, § 54 s. The two cases go back to the 2. half of the 17th century, cited according to the *King's Bench reports* by Joseph Keble and Thomas Siderfin.

[17]Nelson (as n. 3) 59, § 68. The initial reference is wrong: "23 Ass. 12", for 23. Edw. 3, Lib. Ass. 11, f° 110.

[18]Nelson (as n. 3) 44 s, § 31; 55, § 59; 56, § 60.

2 For the Peace of Households

In order to introduce the English judge's dismissal of the wife as a witness for or against her husband, William Nelson quotes almost accurately the first part of the *Institutes of the Laws of England* by Edward Coke. He gives a double reason: the nature of the bond between the spouses on one hand, the psychology of the couple on the other:

> It has been resolved by the Justices, That the Wife cannot be produced as a Witness either against, or for her Husband, *quia sunt duæ Animæ in una Carne*; and it might be a cause of implacable Discord and Dissension between the Husband and the Wife.[19]

The common place of the one body receiving two souls, destined to a great fortune in the common law, was already present in the literature of the Medieval *ius commune*.[20] Originally it comes from the *Book of Genesis* and is mentioned in the *Gospel* according to Saint Mark by Christ himself.[21] Jeffrey Gilbert, whose treatise shows the same marginal reference to Coke's work, also is of the opinion that the impossibility for the spouses to testify for or against each other is due to the identity of their personal interests and the interest of marriage as such:

> Husband and Wife cannot be admitted to be Witnesses for or against each other, for if they swear for the Benefit of each other, they are not to be believed, because their Interests are absolutely the same, and therefore they can gain no more Credit when they attest for each other, than when any Man attests for himself. And it would be very hard that a Wife should be allowed as Evidence against her own Husband, when she cannot attest for him; such a Law would occasion implacable Divisions and Quarrels, and destroy the very legal Policy of Marriage that has so contrived it, that their Interest should be but one…[22]

Both treatises base the principle more or less on Coke's doctrine only but in their developments on the interdict they mention many cases allowing to establish the rule in question. William Nelson summarizes them one by one whereas Jeffrey Gilbert offers a more synthetic reading of them. Obviously this is not the place to go through the details of each one. Coke himself mentions a case judged "upon the Stat [ute] of Bankroute" by the Court of Common Pleas during the 10th year of the reign of James I (1603–1625). This would also have been the last year Coke was Chief

---

[19]Nelson (as n. 3) 35, § 4. Cf. Coke. Edward. 1628. *The first Part of the Institutes of the Lawes of England. Or, A Commentarie upon Littleton, not the name of a Lawyer onely, but of the Law itselfe*. London: Printed [by Adam Islip] for the Societie of Stationers. 1, ch. 1 ("Of Fee simple"), Sect. 1, f° 6 v: "*Note*, it hath beene resolved by the Justices, that a wife cannot be produced either against or for her husband, *quia sunt duæ animæ in carne una*, and it might be a cause of implacable discord and dissention beweene the husband and the wife, and a meane of great inconvenience […]".

[20]Cf. Mausen (as n. 12) 567, n. 714.

[21]Gn 2, 24: "[…] and they shall be one flesh"; Mc 10, 8: "[…] *And they twain shall be one flesh*: so then they are no more twain, but one flesh". The medieval gloss applies the argument to the father and his son (cf. Mausen, as n. 12, 562).

[22]Gilbert (as n. 4) 135s.

Justice of this Court before stepping aside for Henry Hobart in 1613. The case is not to be found in Coke's reports though and Nelson, who lists it first, quotes it word for word from the reports of Richard Brownlow and John Goldesborough:

> The Court was moved to know, Whether the Wife of a Bankrupt can be examin'd by the Commissioners upon the Statute of Bankrupts? And they were of Opinion she could not be examin'd; for the Wife is not bound in Case of High Treason to discover her Husband's Treason, altho' the Son be bound to reveal it; therefore by the Common Law she shall not be examin'd.[23]

In this case, the Court of Common Pleas apparently followed an argument running *a maiore ad minus*: since the wife is not obliged to reveal the actions of her husband in a case of high treason, she cannot be heard either as a witness in a case of bankruptcy. Gilbert retains only the first proposition of the judges' reasoning.[24] The problem does not seem to be restored in all its legal rigor for the distinction, usual in European learned law, between the prohibition to compel the witness to testify and the refusal to admit his testimony even when offered voluntarily is not operated clearly enough by the English lawyers. The Court's line of thought may be understandable from a psychological perspective (the wife is not obliged to testify in cases of high treason, she could *a fortiori* not be obliged to do so in a minor case) but its conclusion is less compelling from a purely logical point of view (the wife cannot be obliged to testify in the first case, therefore she cannot be examined at all in the second case).

In *Mary Grigg*'s case the accused, charged with bigamy, pleaded Not guilty. Her first husband was disqualified as a witness by the King's Bench on the grounds of Coke's principle "because it might occasion implacable Dissension according to I *Inst.* 6. *b.*" In the absence of any other "considerable Witness", the jury declared the prisoner innocent of the charges held against her.[25] Here Coke's original argument is misused: The ensuing conflict might have destroyed the second marriage, but not the couple in question. But because of the limitations imposed on the possibilities of evidence it was the former one which became safe. In this case treason was mentioned as the only exception to the principle that "a Wife could not be admitted to give Evidence against her Husband, nor the Husband against his Wife".[26] In order to justify this Gilbert puts forth the "publick Safety, which is to be preferred before the Interest or Peace of private Families".[27] But the distinction between the prohibition of constraint and the impossibility to interrogate the voluntary witness is still not explicitly worded.

---

[23]Nelson (as n. 3) 35, § 5. Brownlow, Richard, Goldesborough, John. 1651. *Reports of Diverse Choice Cases of Law*, I, 47. London (=*English Reports*, 123: 656 s.): Printed by Tho. Roycroft for Matthew Walbancke. The report adds: "An Infant shall not be examined".

[24]Gilbert (as n. 4) 136.

[25]Nelson (as n. 3) 38, § 10.

[26]Nelson (as n. 3) 38, § 10.

[27]Gilbert (as n. 4) 136.

Even in a case where the second marriage is not threatened a first union could still produce some effects. This is what follows *in fine* from a lawsuit the different judicial stages of which are mentioned by Gilbert. A., who had lost his second wife, was, in virtue of *curtesy* law, put into seisin of the land that his second wife had left to their common child. The inheritance was competed by a collateral heir of the deceased who wanted to produce as a witness B., the first wife of A. Against him it was said that "by the very Testimony of B. she supposes herself the Wife of A. and consequently she can depose nothing contrary to his Interest". To that the judge replied that "the Trial in this Case could be no Evidence in the Question between A. and the collateral Heir" and admitted the wife as a witness. But in a second trial between the same two parties in front of another judge the objection was risen again that "the Wife was no Evidence in this Case, because she by her Oath gains an Interest in a Husband". This time the judge agreed to the disqualification.[28]

Obviously these sources do not permit to discover the common law origins of the interdict in question. *Mary Grigg*'s case refers to Coke whose work does only give access to the contemporary practice of the Court of the Common Pleas. Michael R. T. Macnair has discovered a case judged in a Court of equity at the very end of the 16th century the manuscript report of which reads as follows: "The wife not allowed to be a wittnes for her husband *Bulwer con Levet* according to opinions of the Civilians and of the Judges also".[29] The formulation suggests that it is indeed the very introduction of this Roman-canonical rule into the English judicial world.

The other cases quoted by Nelson and Gilbert reveal some exceptions to the principle.

3 For the Salvation of Women

The first exception takes its origin in the very principle that is also at the heart of the rule itself: the marriage is an institution that deserves the favours of the justice. (The canonical principle that marriage is one of the *causæ fauorabiles* which deserve a special protection is indeed never very far away).[30] As a consequence the wife can validly testify if not only there is no risk that by doing so she instils discord between herself and her husband but the hope to save their couple. Nelson remembers a case wherein a woman was allowed as a witness against someone her husband accused of having seduced her and put for a while into a situation of adultery.[31]

---

[28]Gilbert (as n. 4) 137 s.

[29]Macnair (as n. 1) 223.

[30]Cf. Mausen, Yves. 2008. *Personae miserabiles* et *causæ fauorabiles*, victimes–nées? La réponse de la procédure médiévale. In *La victime. I. Définitions et statut* (*Cahiers de l'Institut d'Anthropologie Juridique de l'Université de Limoges*, 19), ed. Jacqueline Hoareau–Dodinau, Guillaume Métairie and Pascal Texier, 79–96. Limoges: PULIM.

[31]Nelson (as n. 3) 35 s., § 6.

On the contrary if there is no marriage to be saved the woman can validly testify. Actually she is often the one who needs protection and is therefore allowed to invalidate the claimed "union" by her testimony. Nelson notices that she is accepted as a witness against the person to whom she got "married" against her own will after having been abducted "by Force and Arms".[32] In such a case the Court will not accept the objection that "there was a Marriage proved in the Spiritual Court; and where the Consequence of the Evidence will redound to the Benefit of the Witness, he is always rejected". In the case quoted by Nelson the decision rests on two other cases where in similar circumstances and according to the statute of 1487 on the seizure of women[33] the "wife" was heard.

The first is *Brown*'s case. John Brown kidnapped Lucy Ramsey when she was 14 years old in Hide Park where he had her meet him. He took her to his home and threatened her to take her across the ocean if she would not accept to marry him. Lucy yielded. The Court doubted "Whether the Evidence of Lucy Ramsey was to be admitted, because she was his wife de facto, though not *de jure*". The judges gave several arguments in favour of her testimony: first the fact that she had been under the constant influence of violence, "wherefore whatsoever was done while she was under that Violence was not to be respected"; then the consideration that experience shows that "so heinous a Crime wou'd go unpunish'd, unless the Testimony of the Woman shou'd be receiv'd"; lastly some precedents. Eventually Brown was hung.[34]

The distinction between a de facto union and a *de jure* marriage is essential. Gilbert summarises the judicial position in terms of contract law:

> There is a great Difference between a Wife De Facto and a Wife *De Jure*; for a Wife *De Jure* cannot be an Evidence for or against her Husband; but a Wife De Facto may; as if a Woman be taken away by Force and married, she may be an Evidence against her Husband indicted on the Statute of 3 *H*. 7. against the stealing of Women; for a Contract obtained by Force, has no Obligation in Law, and therefore she is a Witness in this Case as well as in any other Case whatsoever.[35]

Finally even a wife *de jure* is allowed by criminal law to testify against her husband in some particularly dramatic circumstances, as in *Lord Audley*'s case which is mentioned by Nelson. Lord Audley was accused of having helped B. to rape his own wife. Concerning the ability of the wife to testify the judges decided unanimously "That in the Case of a common Person between Party and Party, she could not, according to the Opinion in *Coke*'s first *Inst. fol. 6*. But between the King and the Party, upon an Indictment, she may, although it concerns the Feme herself; as she may have the Peace against her Husband".[36] Gilbert points out that the reason for accepting the wife was twofold: "because it was a personal Force

[32]Nelson (as n. 3) 36, § 7.

[33]3 H VII c.2.

[34]Nelson (as n. 3) 36 s., § 8.

[35]Gilbert (as n. 4) 137.

[36]Nelson (as n. 3) 37 s., § 9.

done to her, and of such secret Violence, there could be no other Proof but by the Oath of the Wife".[37]

The aim is no more, as in *Mary Grigg*'s case, to save a marriage, be it an illegitimate one, by widening the scope of the disqualification of the husband as a witness in order to restrain the possibility of evidence, but to save a women and by facilitating the evidence. But it is not a question either, as it is in cases of kidnapping, of making possible the termination of a simple de facto union. Here we are facing a true exception to the principle. For this reason both the judges and the lawyers are in favour of its strict interpretation. Precisely in *Grigg*'s case its authority is expressly rejected.[38] On this matter Gilbert writes:

> But this Piece of Law hath since been exploded, that in a personal Wrong done to the Wife, the Wife may be Evidence against the Husband; because it may be improved to dreadful Purposes, to get rid of Husbands that prove uneasy, and must be a Cause of implacable Quarrels if the Husband chance to be acquitted.[39]

4 Conclusion

Contrary to the creators of the Roman-canonical procedure law, the English lawyers dare to operate a drastic choice among the *reprobationes* contained in abundance in the *Corpus Juris Ciuilis*. The meaning of their approach seems clear enough: to retain only what remains relevant in the social and judicial context of the common law. Michael R. T. Macnair writes on the subject:

> The absence of the exceptions for affinity and dependence was Wigmore's strongest argument against influence of the roman-canon law of proof on the evolution of the common law of evidence and on equity proof. In the case of the exclusion of spouses, however, influence is clear. [...] Why, then, were the rest of the rules about affinity and dependence not "received"? Two points may be made. The first is that several civilian authorities regard these exceptions as not completely ruling the witness out, but rather affecting their credit proportionally to the degree of the relationship. *Prima facie*, therefore, if translated into common law they would have been matters for the jury [...]. The second point is that these exceptions were inappropriate to the social context. The wider ranging romano-canonical exceptions based on affinity and dependence (and the similar jury challenges) assume that witnesses (jurors) will be so strongly governed by relationships of consanguinity and affinity, or by the influence of their employers or landlords, that they cannot be expected to tell the truth. This, however, becomes less likely to the extent that society is governed more by market relationships and the family is "nuclear" rather than extended.[40]

---

[37]Gilbert (as n. 4) 137.

[38]Nelson (as n. 3) 38, § 10.

[39]Gilbert (as n. 4) 137.

[40]Macnair (as n. 1) 227 s. ("Why were the affinity and dependence exceptions in general not 'received'?").

However, the sociological explanation forgets that the exceptions in question are admitted against the jurors as Edward Coke himself points out:

> But often times a man may be challenged to be of a Jury, that cannot be challenged to be a Witnesse; and therefore though the Witnesse be of the neerest alliance, or kindred, or of counceit, or tenant, or servant to either partie, (or any other exception that maketh him not infamous, or to want understanding, or discretion, or a partie in interest) though it be proved true, shall not exclude the witnesse to bee sworne but hee shall bee sworne, and his credit upon the exceptions taken against him left to those of the Jury, who are tryers of the fact [...].[41]

William Hawkins, author of the very popular *Abridgment of the First Part of my L[or]d Coke's Institutes*, explains the difference in a definitive manner:

> For if a Juror be challeng'd, his Room may easily be supplied by others; but it is otherwise of a Witness.[42]

Everything leads us to believe that, on this point, the Anglo-Saxon law of evidence owes its specific form to the presence of the jury. However this does not take us back to the traditional historiography which has its very development derive from the necessity to protect the jury from the parties' schemes.[43] From that perspective the main purpose of the rules would be to restrict the evidence in order to compensate for the lack of experience or even the supposed naivety of the jurors. If that assumption were to be confirmed certainly the motives for disqualifying witnesses should count amongst the more direct and simple means to achieve this goal. But quite on the contrary precisely in this area the near to total rejection of the Roman-canonical rules reflects the intention to liberate the evidence in order to make the most complete sources of information available to the jurors and to turn them into the sole "judges" of the quality of the various pieces of evidence.

References

Anon. (1711) (1. ed.). *Abridgment of the First Part of my L[or]d Coke's Institutes; with Some Additions explaining many of the difficult Cases and shewing in what Points the Law has been altered by late* Resolutions *and* Acts of Parliament. London: Printed by the assignee of Edward Sayer Esq. for John Walthoe.

---

[41]Coke (as n. 19) f°6 v.

[42]Anon. 1711 (1. ed.). *Abridgment of the First Part of my L[or]d Coke's Institutes; with Some Additions explaining many of the difficult Cases and shewing in what Points the Law has been altered by late* Resolutions *and* Acts of Parliament. London: Printed by the assignee of Edward Sayer Esq. for John Walthoe, 9. This pragmatical position is somewhat reminiscent of the common canonical gloss argumenting against the extension to the witnesses of the motives for disqualification applicable to the judges: "Et hæc est causa, quia facilius posset habere multos iudices quam unum testem" (*v° subesse*, *ad* X. 2, 7, 2; cf., for other references: Mausen (as n. 12) 455, n. 209).

[43]Cf. notably Wigmore (as n. 1).

Anon. (1717). *The law of evidence: Wherein all the cases that have yet been printed in any of our* law books *or* tryals, *and that in any wise relate to points of evidence, are collected and methodically digested under their proper Heads*. In the Savoy: Printed by Eliz. Nutt and R. Gosling for R. Gosling.

Anon. (By a late Learned Judge). (1756). *The law of evidence*. London: Printed by Henry Lintot for W. Owen.

Bathurst, H. J. (1761). *The theory of evidence*. Dublin: Cotter.

Buller, F. (1772). *An introduction to the law relative to trials at Nisi Prius*. Dublin: Eliz. Lynch;

Coke, E. (1628). *The first part of the institutes of the lawes of England, or a commentary upon littleton*... London: Printed [by Adam Islip] for the Societe of Stationers.

Klapisch, J. (1994). Duae animae in carne una? Spouses as witnesses in the american law of evidence between 1839 and 1944. In A. Gouron, L. Mayali, A. Padoa-Schioppa, D. Simon (Eds.), *Subjektivierung des justiziellen Beweisverfahrens. Beiträge zum Zeugenbeweis in Europa und den USA (18.–20. Jahrhundert)* (*Ius Commune Sonderheft*, 64) (pp. 301–336). Frankfurt: Klostermann.

Langbein, J. H. (1996). Historical foundations of the law of evidence: A view from the ryder sources. *Columbia Law Review, 96*, 1168–1202.

Macnair, M. R. T. (1999). *The law of proof in early modern equity (comparative studies in continental and anglo-American legal history, 20)*. Berlin: Duncker & Humblot.

Mausen, Y. (2006). Veritatis adiutor. *La procédure du témoignage dans le droit savant et la pratique française (XIIe-XIVe siècles)* (pp. 455–580). Milano: Giuffrè.

Mausen, Y. (2008). *Personae miserabiles* et *causæ fauorabiles*, victimes-nées? La réponse de la procédure médiévale. In J. Hoareau-Dodinau, G. Métairie, P. Texier (Eds.), *La victime. I. Définitions et statut* (*Cahiers de l'Institut d'Anthropologie Juridique de l'Université de Limoges*, 19) (pp. 79–96). Limoges: PULIM.

Mausen, Y. (2012). La famille suspecte. Liens familiaux et motifs de récusation des témoins à l'époque médiévale. In L. Otis-Cour (Ed.), *Histoires de famille. A la convergence du droit pénal et des liens de parenté* (*Cahiers de l'Institut d'Anthropologie Juridique de l'Université de Limoges*, 33) (pp. 161–171). Limoges: PULIM.

Mausen, Y. (2016) (to be published). *Sans lour scient de veritie dire*. Aux origines de l'interdiction de l'*opinion evidence* en *common law*. In Y. Mausen (Ed.), *La culture judiciaire anglaise au moyen âge. Première partie*. Paris: Mare & Martin.

Morgan, J. (1789). *Essays upon the law of evidence*: Dublin: E. Lynch.

Morgan, E. M. (1937). The jury and the exclusionary rules of evidence. *The University of Chicago Law Review, 4*(2), 247–258.

Morgan, E. M., & Maguire, J. (1934). *Cases on evidence*. Chicago: The Foundation Press Inc.

Nelson, W. (1717). *The law of evidence*. [London]: In the Savoy: Printed by Eliz. Nutt, and R. Gosling, (assignees of Edward Sayer Esq;) for R. Gosling.

Pollock, F., & Maitland, F. W. (1895). *The history of english law before the time of edward I*. Cambridge: Cambridge University Press.

Thayer, J. B. (1898). *A preliminary treatise on evidence at the common law*. Boston: Little, Brown.

Wigmore, J. H. (1905). *A treatise on the system of evidence in trials at common law*. Boston: Little, Brown and Company.

Fathers by Law, Fathers by Choice. Paternity and Illegitimacy Between *Ancien Régime* and Codification in Western Countries

Chiara Valsecchi

Abstract Paternity as a legal institute is historically marked by an instrinsical ambiguity: its aim is to acknowledge and provide judicial remedies for a natural phenomenon, which however cannot be ascertained and verified through the usual legal procedures. Legislators, therefore, never fail to evoke nature, but then they set off on a path of their own in order to regulate its different legal forms and cases. Moreover, civil law in Italy, in Europe and elsewhere, during the transition from the law system of the *ancien régime* to modern codifications, is marked by the troubled coexistence of two different and diverse elements: on one hand the tradition of the Roman and Canon law, on the other the model provided by the French revolution and the Napoleonic code. Paternity is thus caged inside the ancient Roman presumption, while bastardy is abandoned to the free will and choice of the parent: given the prohibition to investigate paternity out of wedlock, introduced in the XIX-century codes, he cannot be compelled to take responsibility. The disparity of status between legitimate offspring and bastards would shape family law for a long time.

1 The Legacy of the *Jus Commune*. The Great Watershed: Filiation and Marriage

The historical development of the legal institute of filiation is marked by an intrinsic ambiguity. On the one hand, it serves to acknowledge and protect a natural phenomenon. On the other hand, however, this phenomenon cannot be ascertained and

C. Valsecchi (✉)
University of Padua, Via 8 Febbraio 2, 35122 Padua, Italy
e-mail: valsecchi@giuri.unipd.it

M.G. di Renzo Villata (ed.), *Family Law and Society in Europe from the Middle Ages to the Contemporary Era*, Studies in the History of Law and Justice 5,
DOI 10.1007/978-3-319-42289-3_10

verified by means of the instruments the Law usually makes use of when determining rights and obligations.[1]

The tension between the value attributed to 'blood' ties (today we use the term 'genetic') and the rigorously legal nature of filiation can be seen in both ancient and medieval legislation and doctrine as well as the modern Codes, which seem to oscillate between two opposing poles. Whereas they constantly refer to natural and biological facts, they must then put them aside and somehow deny them in order to determine rules which are certain.

This contrast becomes stronger, even emotionally charged, when the relationship is to be identified and regulated between the child and that parent whose natural tie with the child depends on a 'fact' which is less evident and less 'certain', namely the father.[2]

---

[1]There are innumerable studies, both recent and old, dealing with the notion of filiation in ancient and medieval law, and the systems of rules applicable to it. As it is impossible to mention them all, I shall only list an essential bibliography: Loiseau, Jean Simon. 1811. *Traité des enfans naturels, adultérine, incestueux et abandonnés*. Paris: Antoine; Dalloz, Desiré. 1855. Paternité et filiation. *Répertoire méthodique et alphabétique de legislation de doctrine et de jurisprudence en matière de droit civil, commercial, criminel, administratif de droit des gens et de droit public* 35, Paris: Au Bureau de la Jurisprudence générale du Royaume, 145 ss.; Leoni, Giuseppe, 1892–98. Filiazione. In *Digesto Italiano* 11.2. Torino: UTET: 207–301; Marongiu, Antonio, 1958. Adulterini e incestuosi (figli) (diritto intermedio). In *Enciclopedia del diritto* 1. Milano: Giuffrè: 610–611; Volterra, Edoardo. 1961. Filiazione. Diritto romano. In *Novissimo Digesto Italiano* 7. Torino: UTET: 308–309; Pecorella, Corrado. 1968. Filiazione (parte storica). In *Enciclopedia del diritto* 17. Milano: Giuffrè: 449–456; Van de Wiel, Constant. 1992. Les différentes formes de cohabitation hors justes noces et les dénominations diverses des enfants qui en sont nés dans le droit romain, canonique, civil et byzantin jusqu'au XIII siècle. *Revue internationale des droits de l'antiquité* 39: 327–358; di Renzo Villata, Maria Gigliola. 2001. La famiglia. In *Enciclopedia Italiana. Eredità del Novecento, Roma, Istituto dell'Enciclopedia Italiana* 2: 760–776; Lefebvre-Teillard, Anne. 2008. De la théologie au droit: naissance médiévale du concept de filiation. In *Autour de l'enfant. Du droit canonique at romain médieval au Code Civil de 1804*. Leiden-Boston: Brill: 149–273; A propose d'une lettre à Guillaume: la filiation légitime dans l'ouvre d'Ives de Chartres: 239–258; L'enfant naturel dans l'ancien droit français: 259–273; Lefebvre–Teillard, Anne. 2007. Approche historique d'un grand concept juridique: la filiation. *Sartoriana* 20: 109–130, www.sartonchair.ugent.be/file/238.

[2]The history of paternity too has been amply investigated by international historiography. On this subject see, for instance: Montani, Paola. 1995. Madri nubili e tribunali. Legislazione e sentenze in età liberale. *Italia contemporanea* 200: 455–468; Cazzetta, Giovanni. 1999. Praesumitur seducta. *Onestà e consenso femminile nella cultura giuridica moderna*, Milano: Giuffrè; Conti Odorisio, Ginevra. 2005, Il divieto di ricerca della paternità nello Stato liberale. In *Ragione e tradizione. La questione femminile nel pensiero politico*. Roma: Aracne: 175–200; Baker, Katharine K. 2004. Bargaining or Biology. The History and Future of Paternity Law and Parental Status. *Cornell Journal of Law and Public Policy* 14 iss. 1, art. 1: http://scholarship.law.cornell.edu/cjlpp/vol14/iss1/1; Montesi, Barbara. 2007. *Questo figlio a chi lo do?: minori, famiglie, istituzioni (1865–1914)*. Milano: FrancoAngeli: 97–103; Cavina, Marco. 2007. *Il padre spodestato. L'autorità paterna dall'antichità ad oggi*. Bari: Laterza; Galeotti, Giulia. 2009. *In cerca del padre. Storia dell'identità paterna in età contemporanea*. Roma-Bari: Laterza.

Reference to nature has to date been the key to the legal regulation of maternity. But with regard to paternity, and its different manifestations, one has to forgo nature.

The principal dividing line in ancient, medieval, and modern law, is obviously marriage;[3] legal systems use it to place the child within the family structure and to identify and catalogue different types of filiation.

The two main categories are legitimate filiation and illegitimate filiation. The latter, however, includes situation which are quite varied.

Children born to a married woman are defined and considered as legitimate by the legal system: in these cases, the father is determined by means of the strictly legal mechanism of presumption, expressed in the adage, *pater is est quem nuptiae demonstrant*. There is a second presumption whereby a child is considered legitimate if it is born at least 180 days after the wedding and not later than 300 after the dissolution of the marriage, as these two figures represent the minimum and maximum duration of a pregnancy.

Both criteria were also present in Roman Law, which however allowed the husband to claim their inapplicability and prove that conception was not possible, on account of absence, impotence or disease.

There is no doubt that during the entire legal history of the West down to the 20th century, the only status to confer full rights was that of legitimate offspring. It is therefore not surprising that efforts were made to maximise the possibilities of obtaining that status. Gradually, from the time of Constantine onward, there emerged a new sensibility toward the protection of children born outside of *iustae nuptiae* and the first remedy to be identified was the institute of legitimation.

The spread of Christianity, which places marriage among the sacraments, strengthened the inseparable link between marriage and legitimate filiation. Even during the Middle Ages, paternity was regulated by the complex Roman legal

---

[3]Already in the Roman Republic, only if there was a legitimate union were the children subjected to the *potestas* of the *paterfamilias* and the paternity tie established. Otherwise, the *naturales* and the *spuria* acquired the legal status of the mother and were therefore deprived of legal paternity. This system has remained unchanged in medieval and modern law. Cf. Volterra, Edoardo. 1975. Matrimonio (diritto romano). In *Enciclopedia del diritto* 25. Milano: Giuffrè: 726–807; Gaudemet, Jean. 1987. *Le mariage en Occident. Les moeurs et le droit*. Paris: ed. Du Cerf; Brundage James A. 1993. Concubinage and Marriage in Medieval Canon Law. In Brundage James A. *Sex, Law and Marriage in the Middle Ages* (Variorum 397), Aldershot: Variorum; Lefebvre-Teillard, Anne. 2008. "Si mieux n'aime l'épouser": marriage et relations charnelles hors marriage (France XVIe–XVIIIe s.). In *Autour de l'enfant* (as n. 1) 31–50; "Pater is est quem nuptiae demostrant": jalons pour une histoire de la présomption de paternité: 185–197; *Bastardy and its comparative history: studies in the history of illegitimacy and marital nonconformism in Britain, France, Germany, Sweden, North America, Jamaica, and Japan*, edd. Peter Laslett, Karla Oosterveen, Richard Michael Smith. 1980 Cambridge MA: Harvard University Press; Blaikie, Andrew. 1993. *Illegitimacy, Sex, and Society: Northeast Scotland, 1750–1900*. Oxford: Clarendon press; Adair, Richard. 1996. *Courtship, Illegitimacy and Marriage in early modern England*. Manchester and New York: Manchester University press: 78 ss., 129 ss.; Reid, Charles J. 2004. *Power over the Body, Equality in the Family: Rights and Domestic Relations in Medieval Canon Law*, Grand Rapids, Michigan-Cambridge U.K.: William B. Eerdmans Publishing Co.: 69 ss., 153 ss.

edifice built on lawful marriage and presumptions which were bolstered to such a degree that they became practically impossible to overcome.

Since it became no longer possible to cast doubt on the serious disparities in treatment,[4] it became necessary to add, as soon as possible, a declaration of legitimate filiation. This was the essence of the considerations, particularly by canon lawyers seeking various means to ascertain the existence of a lawful wedding, on how to apply the presumption of the husband's paternity. The same function was carried out by the widening of legitimation.[5]

Children who could not fall within this category were inexorably destined to be qualified as illegitimate, and thus deprived of family and succession rights. If, on the other hand, they were simply 'natural' children, that is children of free persons who were not married or bound by religious vows, then they could be acknowledged by the parents thereby acquiring certain rights, even succession rights. Children born of adultery or incest, however, were not entitled to anything, and could never be acknowledged by their parents. Nevertheless, medieval doctrine did concede that they were entitled to alimony, in the name of a natural right.[6]

The same principles and objectives concerning the safeguarding of the weakest can be found, in the Middle Ages and in the Modern Era, with regard to the ascertainment of natural paternity.

Doctrine and judicial decision, following the example of the *Sacra Rota*,[7] compiled a catalogue of situations and circumstances which allowed the child, and at times the mother too, to institute an action.

[4]Jurists are aware of the fact that all distinctions between children derive from the *ius civile*. For natural law, there are no distinctions. They therefore interpret the rules seeking to decide *favor prolis* (Pecorella 1968 (as n. 1) 453–454).

[5]Cf. for instance Pecorella 1968 (as n. 1) 453–454; Pitzorno, Benvenuto. 1904. *La legittimazione nella storia delle istituzioni familiari del Medio Evo*. Sassari: Satta; Luchetti, Giovanni. 1990. *La legittimazione dei figli naturali nelle fonti tardo imperiali e giustinianee*. Milano: Giuffrè; Génestal, Robert. 1905. *Histoire de la légitimation des enfants naturels en droit canonique*. Paris: E. Leroux; Mayali, Laurent. 1990. Note on the legitimization by subsequent marriage from Alexander III to Innocent III. In *The two laws. Studies in medieval legal history dedicated to S. Kuttner*. Washington: Catholic University of America Press: 55 ss.; Lefebvre-Teillard, Anne. 2008. Histoire de la légitimation des enfants naturels en droit canonique: observations sur un ouvrage Presque centenaire, in *Autour de l'enfant*. (as n. 1) 277–286; *Tanta est vis matrimonii*: remarques sur la légitimation par mariage subséquent de l'enfant adultérin: 287–299; L'effet rétroactif de la légitimation en droit canonique médiéval: 329–341; De la rétroactivité à la fiction. Notes sur la légitimation par mariage subséquent en droit canonique: 359–373.

[6]Pecorella 1968 (as n. 1) 453 ss.

[7]With regard to this subject, and a bibliographical overview, refer to Santangelo Cordani, Angela. 2003. L'accertamento della paternità tra dottrina e prassi all'indomani del Concilio di Trento: uno sguardo alle *decisiones* della Rota romana, in Amicitiae Pignus. *Studi in ricordo di Adriano Cavanna* 3, edd. Antonio Padoa Schioppa, Gigliola di Renzo Villata and Giampaolo Massetto, 1949–1987. Milano: Giuffrè.

This is the line followed also by the courts of many European countries. The prime example would be France, where, following a royal *ordonnance* of 1579,[8] the courts and doctrine developed a flourishing current on this point.

This notwithstanding, throughout all of Europe, heavy limitations on the rights of illegitimate children were the norm. For instance, in France, such children did not have any family right, were not admitted to civil or military offices, and could ask only for alimony.[9] The same applied throughout German lands, were they were even considered as foreigners and villains.[10]

2 The Codification Instances of the 19th Century

The doctrines of the Enlightenment and the French Revolution, solemnly affirming the rights *de l'homme et du citoyen*, questioned the model of the patriarchal family. They proposed a new idea of 'natural' family, represented by a nucleus made up of the parents and minor children and based on the safeguarding of the individual rights of its members.

For this reason, in the *droit intermediaire*, the value of equality was the hallmark of the entire filiation practice. For the first time in history, marriage lost its essential importance for the classification of children's rights, and their conferment. In virtue of a 1793 law, natural children were allowed to partake in succession with equal rights.[11]

This extraordinary positive attitude, however, ceased once the revolutionary phase was over. The Civil Code, promulgated by Napoleon in 1804, returned to the central importance of the legitimate family. Natural children were once again in disfavour, and they were still defined with the derogatory term *bâtards*.[12]

---

[8]For instance, Fournel, Jean-François. 1781. *Traité de la séduction considérée dans l'ordre judiciaire*. Paris: Demonville: 244 ss.; Leoni 1892–98 (as n. 1) 221, with the bibliography cited therein.

[9]Dalloz 1855 (as n. 1) 289 ss.

[10]Glück, Christian Friedrich. 1790. *Ausführliche Erläuterung der Pandekten* 1, Erlagen (=1888. Commentario alle Pandette 1. Milano:Vallardi,499); cf. also Leoni 1892–98 (as n. 1) 221.

[11]Garaud, Marce and Szramkiewicz, Romuald. 1978. *La Révolution française et la famille*. Paris: PUF; Lévy, Jean Philippe. 1989. L'évolution du droit familial français de 1789 au Code Napoléon, in *La famille, la loi, l'État de la Révolution au code civil*. Paris: Centre G. Pompidou: 508 ss.; Cavanna, Adriano. 2005. *Storia del diritto moderno in Europa. Le fonti e il pensiero giuridico* 2. Milano: Giuffrè: 448–457; Cavanna, Adriano. 2007. Onora il padre. Storia dell'art. 315 cod. civ. (ovvero: il ritorno del flautista di Hamenlin), in *Scritti (1968–2002)* 2. Napoli: Jovene: 771–832 (804–826); Desan, Suzanne. 2004. *The Family on Trial in Revolutionary France*. Berkeley, Los Angeles, London: University of California Press, 178–219, about natural filiation, and 220–248 about paternity.

[12]The legal situation in nineteenth-century France is faithfully reconstructed, through the lively mid-century debate on these topics, by Koenigswarter, Louis-Jean. 1842. *Essai sur la législation des peuples anciens et modernes relative aux enfants nés hors mariage; suivi de quelques observations d'économie social su le même sujet*. Paris: Joubert, Libraire de la Cour de Cassation, who, after a vast analysis of ancient and medieval law, discusses the legislation of many European

The distinction between various statuses of children was still present even in the other European legal systems of the beginning of the nineteenth century, from the Austrian A. B. G. B. to the Codes of the pre-unification Italian States, to the Code of the Netherlands, and Prussian legislation. It featured with the same logic in the civil law of American States following the European model, such as Louisiana, Mexico, Argentina, Venezuela, Haiti, and others, and was also present in the Common Law system.[13]

All the legislations of Western countries, therefore, maintained marriage as the line of demarcation, and many of them proposed again also the distinction between natural children in the strict sense of the word and children born of adultery or incest.[14]

2.1 *Legitimate Filiation: An Outline of the Presumption of Paternity*

In all European codes, a child was legitimate if, either at the moment of conception or of birth, the parents were wed. This brought in its wake an optimal status from the point of view of enjoyment of rights.

(Footnote 12 continued)

countries and some American states: 78 ss.; also Accollas, Émile. 1870. *Le droit de l'enfant. L'enfant né hors mariage*. Paris: Germer Baillière, Libraire-Éditeur, who after an initial historical *excursus* deals also with the genesis of the Code and harshly criticising Napoleon's personal thoughts (in particular: 19 ss.). Indeed, the contemptuous statement made by the First Consul on November 17, 1801, much harped upon by historiography, is well-known. Refer for all of these to Cavanna, Adriano. 2007. Mito e destini del *code Napoléon* in Italia (Riflessioni in margine al *Panegirico a Napoleone legislatore* di Pietro Giordani), in *Scritti* (as n. 11) 1079–1129 (1102 ss.). Cf. *Code civil des français*. Nouvelle Édition stereotype. 1805. Paris: Fantin, Libraire.

[13]The entire picture, with precise references to legislation, in Koenigswarter 1842 (as n. 12) 78–84. Cf. *Código civil sancionado por el Congreso de los Estados Unidos de Venezuela en 1867*. Caracas: Imprenta de Josè R. Enriquez; *Código civil del imperio mexicano*. 1866. Mexico: Imprenta de Andrade y Escalante; *The civil code of the State of Louisiana, revised, arranged and amended by the hon. John Ray reviser of the statutes and codes under the supervision of the joint committee of revision*. 1869. Monroe LA: Office of the "Louisiana Intelligencer".

[14]In these cases, there was a difference both between the practice of acknowledgement and the rights conferred to these children. Under Italian civil law, say, until the mid–nineteenth century, there were still six categories of children (Cf. Leoni 1892–98 (as n. 1) 207–301). In other countries, such as Austria and Prussia, all natural children were entitled only to alimony. In such cases, there were no specific rules for children born of adultery or incest, because they were clearly superfluous. The various categories were faithfully reproduced by the Code of Lousiana (art. 197–202, renumbered as 178–183 after the 1869 revision). With regard to English law, Cf. Harris, Nicolas. 1836. *A treatise on the Law of adulterine bastardy, with a report of the Banbury case and of all other cases bearing upon the subject*. London: William Pickering, 1–289; Levene, Alysa, Williams, Samantha and Nutt, Thomas. 2005. Introduction, in *Illegitimacy in Britain, 1700–1920*, edd. Alysa Levene, Samantha Williams, Thomas Nutt. Bansingstoke: Palgrave Macmillan.

In this regard, civil-law doctrine had traditionally enunciated the principle of *favour legitimitatis*. In this historical phase, this principle prevailed more than its competing principle, *favor veritatis*.

In particular with regard to the identification of the father, the legal presumption was still universally accepted that he was always the husband of the mother.[15] Paternity was, so to speak, imposed on the married man not only and not so much by nature, but by the State itself which recognised in a solid and ordered family institution an asset worthy of protection more than individual rights.

Even though certain hypothetical situations were foreseen in which the husband could contest the legitimacy of the child, many codes imposed very short time limits and required specific proofs. The Italian Code, for instance, following the French (art. 312–313), required that the husband demonstrated that it had been 'physically impossible for him to cohabit with his wife', or that he had been legally separated from her, without there being any reconciliation, not even temporary, for the entire period during which the law presumed the conception could have taken place. Or else he had to demonstrate his own 'manifest' impotence (art. 164) or, lastly, the wife's adultery, but this only if the woman had also concealed the birth (Italian Civil Code of 1865, art.162 et seq.).

In this case, the Austrian situation was similar (§§. 100, 101, 138, 155 et seq.). The presumption was less stringent in the Code of the American State of Louisiana, which excluded it if the child was born before 180 days (art. 205, renumbered as 186), and made disavowal easier even in case of conjugal separation (art. 207, renumbered as 188). The same applied for the legislation of the Netherlands (art. 309), whereas according to Bavarian law, disavowal was allowed also for *evidentia facti*, and variations on this were foreseen even by the Prussian Code. The Code of the Canton of Ticino allowed the husband or his heirs the possibility of merely proving that "he was in the physical impossibility of being [the child's] father" (art. 77).[16]

It is significant that the force of the severy ancient rules was confirmed in English law. Not only did the Common Law "adop[t] as a fundamental principle, the maxim of civilians, that *marriage* is the *proof of paternity*". It also defended it for centuries with absolute strictness, despite the spread of opinions to the contrary,

[15]For instance, Cf. the French Civil Code, art. 312; A.B.G.B., §§. 137 and ss. Art. 159 of the 1865 Italian Civil Code does not use the verb 'to presume' either, but simply declares that "the husband is the father of the child conceived during marriage" (see Huc, Théophile. 1868. *Le code civil italien et le code Napoléon. Études de législation comparée* 1. Paris: Cotillon, Libraire du Conseil d'État: 85 ss.). On the contrary, the Code of Louisiana lays down that "The Law considers the husband of the mother as the father of all children conceived during the marriage" (art. 203, renumbered as 184), thereby acknowledging that the presumption is a *fictio iuris* even if it keeps its full force (see articles 204–211, renumbered as 185–192).

[16]For a short review, see Leoni 1892–98 (as n. 1) 224–225.

observing "with great precision, the only possible grounds upon which the paternity of a child born in wedlock, could be impeached".[17]

The *favour legitimitatis* principle featured also in the institute of legitimation. Although with wide diversity and some variations, this institute was known by nearly all the legislations of the nineteenth century.[18]

2.2 Natural Filiation

On the opposite side of legitimate filiation was the condition of those born outside lawful wedlock.

These children could be spontaneously acknowledged by their father and mother, with some exceptions (numerous Codes did not allow acknowledgement of children born of adultery and incest),[19] or else–but this matter was even more controversial and debated–the possibility was granted to institute an action to obtain a judicial declaration of maternity or paternity.

The legal effects too of spontaneous acknowledgement or of the judicial pronouncement were varied. Under the law of France, Italy and other countries following the Napoleonic model, acknowledged natural children were granted only some rights, which were heavily limited with regard to ties of kinship, to succession, and the like. Other Codes were instead more generous with safeguards or, yet again, even stricter.

The picture was outlined with remarkable clarity in the mid-nineteenth century by Jean-Louis Koenigswarter. According to this French jurist, "Trois systèmes différents se présentent dans les législations existantes: celui qui ne reconnaît aucun droit de succession aux enfants naturels, ni sur les biens du père, ni sur ceux de la

---

[17]Harris 1836 (as n. 14) 1. The reasons of law policy underlying the rule are also the same as those adopted by French or Italian ministers in their reports about the Codes. The observation was made that, "no man with a slightest power of reflection, can fail to perceive that the law which presumes that the husband is the fatherof a child born of his wife, tends to promote public morals and female chastity; and consequently in an immense majority of cases, to render the de facto, consistent with the de jure paternity" (2).

[18]With regard to France, see Lefebvre-Teillard, Anne. 2008. *Tanta est vis matrimonii*: l'écho français d'une vielle controverse, in *Autour de l'enfant* (as n. 1) 301–314; with regard to English law, from its medieval origins, Harris 1836 (as n. 14) 5 ss. With regard to Italian law, see Leoni 1892–98 (as n. 1) 291–301. Louisiana followed France closely in its practice (art. 217, renumbered as 198, and ss).

[19]According to the Italian Civil Code of 1865, for instance, the legal condition for these children was decidedly more disadvantageous: they could not even look for their mother, having only the right to alimony should paternity or maternity transpire indirectly from a civil or criminal sentence, from an explicit declaration written by the parents or by a marriage declared to be null (art. 193). On this point, Cf. Leoni 1892–98 (as n. 1) 243 and 252 ss. The prohibition to acknowledge was contemplated also by the Code of Louisiana, according to which "such acknowledgment shall not be made in favor of children, whose parents were incapable ofcontracting marriage at the time of conception" (art. 222, renumbered as 204).

mère, nous l'appelons le système *germanique*; celui qui ne fait succéder l'enfant naturel qu'à la mère et à toute la ligne maternelle, nous le désignons sous le nom de systèm *romain*; enfin, le système naturel, qui donne à l'enfant illégitime une place parmi les héritiers du sang, et le fait succéder aux biens du père aussi bien qu'à ceux de la mère".[20]

2.2.1 Acknowledgement and Its Effects

The majority of European and non-European legislations[21] conceived acknowledgment as a voluntary and freely-done act,[22] to be looked upon with moderate favour.[23]

The French Civil Code, like the many codes modelled on it, contemplated spontaneous acknowledgment, but limited it heavily with regard to form (which the doctrine of the time in fact considered to be "trop étroites").[24] If not already indicated in the deed of birth, it had to be carried out by means of an '*acte authentique*' in the presence of a notary; it could not be done by means of a private writing.[25]

Nineteenth-century French doctrine and judicial decisions were divided as to the search for possible ways to widen the interpretation. The same questions were posed in Italy where, for instance, it was also allowed that the act could be done even by a parent who was still a minor.[26]

According to this approach, however, acknowledgement remained a personal act. For this reason, the father could express himself only with regard to his

[20]Carrying on with his analysis, the author adds that "C'est surtout dans les législations qui ont consacré le dernier système, que la position des enfants naturels est nuancée différemment, selon l'ordre dans lequel ils sont appelés parmi les autres héritiers, selon qu'ils succèdent aux père et mère seuls, ou à toute leur ligne, et enfin selon la quote-part héréditaire que la loi leur attribute" (1842 (as n.) 93).

[21]Actually, according to Koenigswarter, "toutes les législations permettent aux père et mère de reconnaitre volontairement leurs enfants naturels" (Koenigswarter 1842 (as n. 12) 87).

[22]It could definitively be impugned if exorted by violence or malice or if it was the consequence of an essential error.

[23]This is also the interpretation given by contemporaries to the general principle of the 1865 Italian Civil Code, according to which "the natural child may be acknowledged by the father and the mother both together and separately" (art. 179). Cf. on this matter, Leoni 1892–98 (as n. 1) 243 ss.

[24]Thus Koenigswarter 1842 (as n. 12) 86–87. The same author examined the legislation of other European and American countries (Cf. 86–87).

[25]French Civil Code, art. 334; Italian Civil Code, art. 179 and ss.; Civil Code of the Canton of Ticino, art. 85 (*Codice civile della repubblica e Cantone del Ticino*. 1837. Bellinzona: Tipografia e Libreria patria); Civil Code of Lousiana, art. 221, renumbered as 203.

[26]"with regard to acknowledgement, the law must be benign and allow the minor to acknowledge his natural issue: what harmful consequences could there be for the minor? A bigger responsibility in life? Hasn't he already undertaken it when he engaged in amorous congress with a lass he made into a mother? Isn't the provision prohibiting enquiries about paternity already serious enough? Does one need to make it impossible for a beautiful act such as the acknowlegement to happen, simply because the natural father is still a minor?" (Leoni 1892–98 (as n. 1) 244).

paternity and the mother to her maternity, without in any way being able to commit the other parent, and without needing the consent of the other parent or even of the child itself. The latter could actually contest the acknowledgement in certain circumstances.[27]

In order to enable this act to the widest possible extent, it being the only act which could give any rights to the natural child, generally speaking there was no time-barring. Acknowledgment could take place before the birth and after, and even, according to the majority of interpretations, when the child itself was already dead, in order to extend the child's rights to its descendants.

The legal consequences of this act varied according to the different laws of Western countries.

According to the Napoleonic Civil Code, and following its example, the Dutch, Italian, and Portuguese Codes, the Codes of the Duchy of Baden and of Louisiana, and many other codes, the acknowledged child obtained the establishment of a bond of natural kinship with its parent on the basis of which the child could acquire the surname of the parent (the father's surname, if the child had been acknowledged by both parents) and the right to be maintained, educated, taught and steered towards a profession or craft, as well as receiving alimony in case of necessity.[28]

The parent (the father if both parents had acknowledged the child) was entrusted with legal tutelage[29] until the child reached major age; the parent was also given the right to alimony in case of necessity.[30]

No tie was established with the other relatives of the parent. This was reiterated, with more or less force, by all the Codes of the nineteenth century.[31]

---

[27]According to the Italian Code (art. 188), acknowledgement was to be considered null in varied cases: 1. If the *acte authentique* in which the deed of birth is found turns out to be invalid; 2. If it is false; 3. If it is vitiated by malice, violence or essential error. It could be impugned for lack of truthfulness by the author himself, the child or his/her heir, whoever might have wanted to recognise himself the child, the other parent, and so on.

[28]In reality, in France, the right to alimony for natural children was not expressly contemplated by the Code, and was introduced, after some polemics, only by judicial decisions. The Austrian Code attributed to all natural children, as has already been said, only the right to alimony (Mattei, Jacopo. 1852. *I paragrafi del codice civile austriaco avvicinati dalle leggi romane, francesi e sarde* I. Venezia: co' tipi di Pietro Naratovich: 502 ss.). See Caberlotto, Enrico. 1893. Alimenti. In *Digesto Italiano* 2, parte 2: 342–351; Petroni, Giulio. 1877. Il diritto agli alimenti dei figliuoli semplicemente naturali studiato nel codice civile italiano. *Il Filangieri* 2: 526–544; Quartarone, Melchiorre. 1884. *Il diritto agli alimenti e le azioni alimentari secondo il codice civile e il codice di procedura civile: studio teorico-pratico*. Torino: F.lliBocca.

[29]According to Italian law, tutelage was wider than that of the unrelated tutor and closer to paternal authority: it comprised the obligation of the child to remain in the house given it by the parent (art. 221), the grant to the parent of disciplinary powers (art. 222), the representation and administration of assets (art. 224–225–226), and so on.

[30]For instance, art. 187 of the Italian Civil Code of 1865 contemplated that the natural child owed alimony to the parent in the absence of legitimate ascendants or descendants or a spouse. Cf. also the Code of Louisiana, art. 256, renumbered 240.

[31]The formulation of the Code of Louisiana is particularly incisive: "Illegitimate children generally speaking, belong to no family, and have no relations; accordingly they are not submitted to the

With regard to succession rights, these were clearly treated differently, and the solutions were quite varied. Generally speaking, acknowledged natural children, even when allowed to inherit their parents, were subjected to strict bounds and limits, both quantitatively and qualitatively, particularly if there were other heirs entitled to the inheritance.[32]

In contrast to legislations modelled on the French example, one found others, particularly from the German and Northern parts of Europe, which adopted a different line.[33]

Some of them, in particular, excluded natural children, even if acknowledged, from any succession right in relation to both mother and father.[34] Others would instead seem to allow the natural child at least to inherit the mother. This was the case in Danish,[35] Prussian,[36] and Austrian legislation.

2.2.2 Actions to Establish Paternity

The panoply of solutions and openness one finds in the legislations of Western Nations with regard to the acknowledgement of natural children become a veritable rift if one looks at the regulation of the search for paternity. This search, let us remember, was the only avenue available to the unacknowledged child to obtain a minimum of tutelage and rights, even of an economic nature.

(Footnote 31 continued)

paternal authority, even when they have been legally acknowledged" (art. 254, renumbered as 238); "nevertheless nature and humanity establish certain reciprocal duties between fathers and mothers and their illegitimate children" (art. 255, renumbered as 239).

[32]In this case too, the American rule is very clear: "illegitimate children, though duly acknowledged cannot claim the rights of legitimate children" (art. 224, renumbered as 206). In the same way, the Bavarian Code lays down that "succèdent à leur mère à défaut d'enfants légitimes; ils ne succèdent à leur père qu'à défaut de tout parent au degré successible", while "le Code du canton de Vaud fait succéder l'enfant naturel à la totalité des biens de ses père et mère, si ceux-ci ne laissent aucun parent au degré successible, ni époux survivant (art. 546)" (Koenigswarter 1842 (as n. 12) 98). The 1865 Italian Code confers unto acknowledged natural children "one moiety of the share which they would be entitled to had they been legitimate" should there also be legitimate heirs (art. 744), and two-thirds in the absence of legitimate children but if there are ascendants or a spouse (art. 745). The natural child however acquired the entire inheritance if its parent left neither legitimate descendants or ascendants, nor a spouse (art.747).

[33]According to Jean-Louis Koenigswarter's reading—who cites the laws of Russia, Sweden, Denmark, and England, and the Codes of the Swiss Cantons of Bern, Fribourg, and Argau—all of these legislations were influenced by ancient German law (Koenigswarter 1842 (as n. 12) 93 ss.).

[34]Thus, for instance, the Codes of the German-speaking Swiss Cantons such as Bern (art. 206), Fribourg (art. 299 et seq.) and Argau (art. 231 et seq.). Cf. Koenigswarter (as n. 12) 94–95.

[35]In this case, the right is extended not just to the mother but to all relatives on the mother's side (Koenigswarter 1842 (as n. 12) 96).

[36]With regard to this legislation too, refer to the analysis made by Koenigswarter 1842 (as n. 12) 96–97.

The debate on these aspects was very lively among jurists all over Europe, and it frequently happened that the calls for reform were a result of the comparison with regulation in other countries which appeared more open and more inclined toward the safeguarding of individual rights.

One can actually observe that the legal systems obtaining in the world could be divided in two or three classes, depending on whether the natural child was afforded the right freely to look for its father,[37] whether the right was completely prohibited or—and this was the commonest situation—whether the action itself was allowed only in certain cases.[38]

Even among the legal systems which allowed the action at law, there were important differences with regard to the legal consequences of a judicial sentence of ascertainment.

The Napoleonic model and its dissemination

Putting an end to uncertainty, and, according to the drafters, giving an adequate reply to the 'general hue and cry' that had long been raised against a rapidly-spreading judicial ill-practice,[39] art. 340 of the French *code civil* of 1804 provided for a strict prohibition of all actions to establish paternity, the only exception being in the case of abduction.[40]

---

[37]According to Giuseppe Leoni, the search was deemed as freely permitted in Greece, England, Scotland, Finland, Sweden, Norway, Denmark, Spain, Germany, Austria-Hungary, some Cantons in German-speaking Switzerland, and some States of the United States, as well as Argentina and Peru (Leoni 1892–98 (as n. 1) 253).

[38]Italian and French jurists in particular, who were very critical of the codes of their respective countries, based their observations on a wide review of the legislative solutions adopted in Europe and America, to ask for the introduction of at least specific exceptions to the prohibition. Among the Italians: Leoni 1892–98 (as n. 1) 253; Gabba, Carlo Francesco. 1881. La dichiarazione della paternità illegittima e l'articolo 189 del Codice civile italiano, *Annuario delle scienze giuridiche, sociali e politiche*: 178–240 (190 ss.); Mori, Vincenzo. 1890. Appunti su l'azione di paternità naturale nel diritto antico e modern. *Il Filangieri* 15: 569–584, 594–631, 622–708 (a classification is proposed on pp. 576 et seq. of modern legislations which allow or do not allow the search, showing the marked prevalence of the former); Regnoli, Oreste. 1897. Prima tesi. Relazione, Parte prima "se e quali riforme siano da introdursi nel Codice civile relativamente alla ricerca della paternità, e alla condizione giuridica dei figli illegittimi", in *Atti del III Congresso Giuridico Nazionale tenutosi in Firenze l'anno 1891 pubblicati per incarico della Commissione esecutiva dall'Avv. Camillo de Benedetti, direttore della "Cassazione Unica"*. Torino: UTET: 32–51.

[39]Dalloz 1855 (as n. 1) 292 ss. According to Ahrens, however, the principle adopted by the French Code was inspired by a wrong consideration of the scandal which frequently arose from similar judicial processes and constituted a violation of a fundamental principle of justice both for the mother and the child (Ahrens, Heinrich. 1838. *Cours de droit naturel ou De philosophie du droit: complété, dans les principales matières, par des aperçus historiques et politiques*, trad.it. *Corso di diritto naturale o di filosofia del diritto completato nelle materie più importanti da alcuni schizzi storici e politici* (trans. Alberto Marghieri. Napoli 1872, 202). On the genesis of the rule Cf. also Pouzol, Abel. 1902. *La recherche de la paternité: étude critique de sociologie et de législation comparée*. Paris: V. Giard & E. Briere, 26 ss.; Azzariti, Giuseppe. 1939. Paternità (ricerca della). In *Nuovo Digesto Italiano* 9, 527–533.

[40]Jean Simon Loiseau seems to justify the harshness of the practice as a punishment for the irresponsible behaviour of natural parents (Loiseau 1811 (as n. 1) 768 ss.); Cadrès too explains

Once again, the emotionally-charged contradiction between the natural and the social fact of child-bearing came to the fore, together with the problem of ascertaining this fact using the instruments and mechanisms of the legal system. There was now the added paradox that codified law ended up being even more rigid and restrictive than the law of the *ancient régime*, than canon law and than court decisions of the eighteenth century.

Instituting actions about maternity was almost always permitted, at least for natural children in the proper sense of the word, given that the basis was a fact (the parturition) of which it was possible to have a certain proof even through witnesses. As regards paternity, however, many nineteenth-century Codes introduced the very harsh novelty of prohibiting such actions, based on the fear of possible abuses, which would pose a danger to social and family order and stability.

Following the example of France, many European and American countries opted for virtually absolute prohibition.

Whereas the Code of the Ticino of 1837, in the dry and synthetic style which characterises all its provisions, concisely laid down that "it is permitted to natural children to institute actions only to establish maternity"[41] (and the Mexican text was similar to it),[42] that of other Swiss Cantons,[43] Serbia, Romania, Bolivia and the

(Footnote 40 continued)

that, "La paternité étant un mystère de la nature, le législateur a sagement prohibé, par l'article 340, toute action qui aurait pour but de rechercher quelest le père d'un enfant" and quotes at length from the speech delivered when the draft was submitted to the French legislative body by Bigot de Préameneu (repeatedly cited also by other authors) who qualified enquiries on paternity as a veritable scourge of society (Cadrès, Émile. *Traité des enfants naturels mis en rapport avec la doctrine et la jurisprudence.* Paris: Videcoq père et fils éditeurs, 41; tradit., *Trattato dei figli naturali messo in rapporto colla dottrina e la giurisprudenza,* prima versione italiana dell'avvocato Giuseppe Puglisi. Palermo 1852, 38–39). On Napoleonic practice and its genesis, see the analysis made by Cazzetta 1999 (as n. 2) 227–243.

[41]"ai figli naturali non è permessa l'indagine che sulla maternità": Thus art. 87. The subsequent art. 88 adds in the same manner that "it shall be prohibited to children born to adultery or incest to institute an action to establish paternity or maternity".

[42]The text, which remained in force between 1845 and 1871, provided in art. 256: "Se prohibe absolutamente la investigacion de la paternidad de los hijos nacidos fuera de matrimonio. La prohibicion de investigar es absoluta, tanto en favor como en contra del hijo". The subsequent art. 257 provided on the otherhand that "Solamente el hijo tiene derecho para investigar la maternidad, á fin de obtener el reconocimiento de la madre; y únicamente podrá hacerlo, concurriendo simultáneamente todas las circunstancias siguientes: 1. Si tiene en su favor la posesion de estado de hijo natural de aquella. 2. Si la persona, cuya maternidad se reclama, no estáligada con vínculo conyugal al tiempo en que se pide el reconocimiento. La posesion de estado, para los efectos de este artículo, se justifica, probando simultáneamente que la pretendida madre cuidó de su lactancia y educacion, y que lo reconoció y trató como tal hijo. La prueba de estos hechos podrá hacerse con testigos que no sean de oídas, habiendo un principio de prueba por escrito". The new code, promulgated at the end of 1870, provides the same exceptions also to establish the identity of the father (cf. on this point Leoni 1892–98 (as n. 1) 260–261).

[43]For instance, in the Cantons of Geneva, Vaud, Fribourg, Neuchâtel, Valais (the last mentioned however allowed the action even in the case of paternal care, cohabitation of parents, written proof originating from the father, and so on). Leoni 1892–98 (as n. 1) 259.

Republic of Haiti,[44] as well as art. 342 of the Code of the Netherlands andart. 189 of the 1865 Italian Civil Code carried a literal reproduction of the Napoleonic Code and strictly affirmed that "actions to establish paternity are not allowed, except in cases of abduction or rape, when the time of their happening corresponds to that of the conception".[45]

When he was explaining his choice, which departed from the preceding national legal tradition, the Italian Minister Giuseppe Pisanelli, an expert on the civil law and the author of the draft Code which was later promulgated in 1865, defined the prohibition as "a safeguard of the stability and decorum of families".[46] The Commission appointed by the Senate to revise the draftreiterated that the principle was by then common to civilised peoples,[47] thereby showing that it did not know (or did not want to know) the different solutions which actually existed.

In reality, doubts had surfaced during the *travaux préparatoires*, also because the Italian law was being prepared when other countries had already embarked on the discussion of these themes and had even produced some reforms.

A few exceptions to the prohibition had therefore been devised, such as if a written document existed originating from the individual identified as the father of the child, a situation already contemplated in the Piedmontese Civil Code of 1837.[48]

The addition did not appear in the definitive text of the Italian Code. At the moment of promulgation, the Minister for Justice suggested that public opinion should be heard, and that "the issue be subjected to new investigations and new studies" in order to submit it to Parliament.[49]

The other Codes of the beginning of the nineteenth century: the differing Austrian model.

The policy proposed by many Italian jurists, namely maintaining the prohibition but with a reasonable series of exceptions, was the policy adopted by, say, the

---

[44]Leoni 1892–98 (as n. 1) 259.

[45]Thus the Italian text. On the Dutch text, which he proposed translated in French ("La recherche de la paternité est interdite. Dans le cas de viol ou d'enlèvement, lorsque l'époque du délit se rapportera à celle de la grossesse, le coupable pourra être, sur la demande des parties intéressées, déclaré père de l'enfant"), the advocate Verduchène simply observed that "cet article est conforme à l'art. 340 nap.": Verduchène, J. 1860. *Observations critiques sur le code civil neerlandais, comparé avec le code napoléon. Livre I, tit. I au VI*e. Maëstricht: Van Osch-America et C., 153.

[46]Cf. *Relazione sul Progetto del primo libro del Codice Civile presentato in iniziativa al Senato dal Ministro Guardasigilli (Pisanelli) nella tornata del 15 novembre 1862*, in *Codice civile preceduto dalle Relazioni Ministeriale e Senatoriale, dalle Discussioni Parlamentari e dai Verbali della Commissione coordinatrice,* ed. Sebastiano Gianzana. 1. *Relazioni.* Torino: UTET, 28.

[47]*Relazione della Commissione del Senato sul Progetto del Codice Civile presentato dal Ministro Guardasigilli (Pisanelli) nelle tornate del 15 luglio e 26 novembre 1863*, in *Codice civile* (as n. 46) 1. *Relazioni*: 152 ss. (210).

[48]*Verbali della Commissione di coordinamento*, verbale n. 12, Seduta del 27 aprile 1865, in *Codice civile* (as n. 46), 3, *Verbali*, 93–94.

[49]*Codice civile del regno d'Italia.* 1866. Torino: Stamperia reale, XIII ss. See also Aquarone, Alberto, 1960. *L'unificazione legislativa e i codici del 1865*. Milano: Giuffrè, 370–371.

Portuguese Civil Code,[50] or the Code of Louisiana, according to which "illegitimate children, who have not been legally acknowledged, may be allowed to prove their paternal descent".[51] The admitted proofs constituted a clear return to the ancient tradition of the Rota's judicial decisions. The subsequent rule, in fact, clarifies that "In the case where the proof of paternal descent is authorized by the preceding article, the proof may be made in either of the following ways:

"1. By all kinds of private writings, in which the father may have acknowledged the bastard as his child, or may have called him so";

"2. When the father, either in public or in private, has acknowledged him as his child, or has called him so in conversation, or has caused him to be educated as such";

"3. When the mother of the child was known as bring in a state of concubinage with the father, and resided as such in his house at the time when the child was conceived".[52]

At the opposite extreme of the prohibition, one found the legislations which allowed full freedom to the natural child to institute a judicial action to ascertain the identity of its father.

The fundamental model was found in §. 163 of the Austrian Code, promulgated in 1811.

On the basis of this rule, if it could be proven that a man had sexual relations with the mother between 6 and 10 months before the delivery, or if the man himself had confessed in this sense, even if extra-judicially, then it was presumed that he was the father of the child.

As observed by the most prominent among the commentators of the A. B. G. B., it was clear that this provision followed the policy of offering maximum protection to the child, opening the proof of paternity not only to all the means which the Austrian civil procedure contemplated in general, but also to the simple

[50]The exceptions carried by the Portuguese Civil Code (promulgated in 1867), in addition to abduction and rape, are a text written by the alleged father and 'possession of state' (art. 130). Cf. *Codigo civil portuguez approvado por carta de lei de 1 de Julho 1867*. Segunda ediçao official. 1868. Lisboa: Imprencia nacional.

[51]Thus art. 226, renumbered as 209.

[52]It is the text of art. 227, later renumbered as 210; whereas the subsequent provision refers to both the civil law and the common law traditions: "The oath of the mother, supported by proof of the co–habitation of the reputed father with her, out of his house, is not sufficient to establish natural paternal descent, if the mother be known as a woman of dissolute manners, or as having had an unlawful connexion with one or more men (other than the man whom she declares to be the father of the child) either before or since the birth of the child" (art. 228, then 211). It is the same line adopted by English law after 1835 (cf. also Leoni 1892–98 (as n. 1) 254).

extra-judicial confession done to anybody, whereas as a rule such a confession attained probatory value only if made to the person who had an interest in knowing the truth.[53]

To counterbalance the manifest favour toward the child, the possibility was offered to the plaintiff to submit proof to the contrary.[54]

One had also to consider the limited effects of acknowledgment, whichever way it took place.

Austrian law, in fact, excluded all illegitimate children from enjoying family rights, precluding even the use of the paternal surname.[55]

These children were only allowed to ask from their parents, in addition to alimony, that they be educated and helped to find a job or profession in proportion to their parents' economic resources.[56]

The Codes of numerous German-speaking Swiss Cantons adopted a position very similar to the Austrian one, allowing the institution of an action as a general principle. They allowed the action both to the pregnant woman (within certain limits) and to the child, but they provided that the child was entitled to maintenance, education and professional training, clarifying that in each case natural children had to carry their mother's surname and be excluded from any potential title of nobility.[57]

Some North and South American legislations too adopted principles favouring natural children, allowing for the free search of one's father's identity, but rarely did they give them more than the right to alimony.[58]

---

[53]Moreover, in the light of the *ratio* attributed to the legislative text, the judicial decisions of the first half of the nineteenth century had considered as equivalent the confession of being the father of an illegitimate child and that of having had relations with the mother. The courts had even considered valid the proof given by a minor. Cf. Mattei 1852 (as n. 28) 502, with his bibliography. See also Cavagnari, Camillo. 1891. *Nuovi orizzonti del diritto civile in rapporto colle istituzioni pupillari. Saggio di critica e riforma legislativa.* Milano: Fratelli Dumolard, 32 ss. Cf. Valsecchi, Chiara. 2015. "The determination of paternity must be admissible". post-unification civil law theory and practice and the family law reforms. transitory law issues. *Italian Review of Legal History* 1.13: 1–17.

[54]Legal authors reiterate it in no uncertain terms, clarifying that the presumption foreseen in § 163 has to be deemed a simple one (Mattei 1852 (as n. 28) 502).

[55]§. 165 of the A.B.G.B. laid down that illegitimate children did not enjoy family or kinship rights; they could not lay claim to their father's surname, nor did they have the right to nobility or other prerogatives of the parents, but merely took the name of their mother.

[56]Thus § 166 which closed with the clarification that illegitimate children were not "really subject to the paternal authority of their father, but are assisted and represented by a tutor".

[57]The detailed regulation found in the Code of Zurich of 1887 inspired subsequent ones of other cantons, such as that of Thurgau or Graubünden. The Codes of Bern (1830), Lucerne (1839), or Argau (1855) were very similar too (Leoni, Giuseppe. 1892–98: 257).

[58]This was the exceptional case of Argentina, were not only the Code permitted the proof of paternity by any means, but also granted the natural child (save those born of adultery or incest) even a share of the father's inheritance. Leoni 1892–98 (as n. 1) 258.

3 Between the Nineteenth and Twentieth Centuries: Reforms Proposed and Approved

Since the entry into force of the Codes and in particular during the last 30 years of the nineteenth century, legal doctrine was actively advocating a reform that would take the child into account. It was supported by a movement representing public opinion, sustained by intellectuals, men of letters and sociologists.

In certain cases, the insistence of the legal world and civil society brought about a quick change in the law: for instance, on February 21, 1851, the small Duchy of Baden, which had a Code modelled on the French one, enacted a specific law to allow the institution of an action to establish paternity.[59] Mexican legislation too moved in this direction.[60]

In other cases, the discussion had no concrete consequences. In the German jurisdictions, say, the doctrine was authoritatively expressed during the third congress of jurists held in 1866 in Berlin. The suggestion made by the Viennese Professor Unger was accepted, and the freedom to seek one's father as a general principle with few, limited exceptions[61] was debated.

In Belgium, already in the nineteenth century, a revision of the Civil Code was on its way but the draft carefully prepared by François Laurent, Professor at the University of Ghent, did not become law, even if on repeated occasions government authorities had recognised a profound necessity to renew the Code on this topic.[62]

Both in Belgium and the Netherlands, the new century began without any legislative change. But the solution was achieved within the first decade of the century;[63] even the Swiss Civil Code of 1912 overcame the prohibition contemplated by the previous legislation which held sway in many cantons.[64]

In France, the battle for the reform of the Code involved law experts, artists, members of social sciences circles, and even public opinion and the press. A frontline campaigner, for instance, was Alexandre Dumas *fils*, who intervened often in public fora on family-related themes while also portraying them mostly in

---

[59]Mori 1890 (as n. 38) 581.

[60]*Supra*, n. 42.

[61]The only exceptions were the case in which the mother lived a wanton life or there were clear scientific elements to demonstrate that the moment of conception was different from that in which the mother had had relations with the alleged father, and other particular cases. *Verhandlungen des Geschiten Deutschen Juristentages*, Zweiter Band. 1866. Berlin: Drud und Commissions-Verlag von G. Jansen, 41–43. Cf. Mori 1890 (as n. 38) 692.

[62]Mentioned also by Leoni 1892–98 (as n. 1) 285–286.

[63]Cf. Haanebrink, H. 1921. *Code civil néerlandais traduit en français et mis en concordance avec le code civil belge*. Bruxelles: Établissements Émile Bruylant-Paris, Librairie Générale de droit, 63; Azzariti, Giuseppe. 1939: 531.

[64]Swiss Civil Code, art. 307–323. Cf. Azzariti 1939 (as n. 39) 531.

his theatrical works.[65] Later, during the Seventies and Eighties, the experts on the problems of minors and the so-called "enfance abandonnée"[66] got involved.

Even thanks to these currents in public opinion, different bills were prepared and submitted which tried to introduce, in differing ways, exceptions to the prohibition to seek the identity of one's own father.[67]

The long battle finally reached its epilogue, in France, only as the year 1912 was coming to an end. On November 16, a law was approved allowing the judicial search for the identity of the father, even if in a limited series of situations.

New provisions on the condition of children born of adultery were then enacted during the Fifties, accompanied by a series of sentences based on the principle of equality among all children.[68]

In Italy, where the prohibition to seek paternity had been a surprising and ill-received novelty, the newly-approved Code immediately became the target of harsh criticism and numerous motions to amend.

New rules were being insistently requested which would open, at least in certain cases, the way for natural children to seek the judicial ascertainment of their father's identity and it was underlined that this was certainly no revolutionary solution, having been adopted already by the Sacra Rota and pre-unification legislation.

Each having its own undertone, many authoritative voices were raised among jurists listing a range of hypotheses in which the proof of paternity, though always

---

[65]Dumas, Alexandre, fils. 1883. *La Recherche de la paternité. Lettre à M. Rivet*. Paris: Calmann Levy. Cf. also the authors named by Leoni 1892–98 (as n. 1) 281–282.

[66]In 1876, during a conference on the rights of children, Maria Deraisme held, among other things, that "La paternité est la première application du droit de l'enfant"and that " Il est dans l'ordre, dans la justice qu'il retombe à la charge de ceux qui ont provoqué sa venue, de ses auteurs en somme. Et que si ceux-ci se dérobent à cette obligation naturelle, la loi les mette en demeure de s'exécuter". The inevitable conclusion was that "Aussi, cette interdiction de la recherche de la paternité est-elle l'infraction la plus flagrante des droits de l'enfant, conséquemment des droits de l'homme", Deraisme, Maria. 1887. *Les droits de l'enfant*. Paris: éd. E. Dentu, 22; cf. Société générale de protection pour l'enfance abandonnée ou coupable. 1884–86. Bonjean, Maurice.1884-86. *Congrès international de la protection de l'enfance, tenu au palais du Trocadéro les 15, 16, 18, 19, 20, 21, 22 et 23 juin 1883. Compte rendu des travaux, publié au nom de la Commission internationale permanente*, Société générale de protection pour l'enfance abandonnée ou coupable. Paris: G. Pedone-Lauriel. Cf. Mori 1890 (as n. 38) 692–69. Leoni 1892–98 (as n. 1) 282, recalls also what had emerged from the sitting of March 21, 1875 of the *Societé d'Economie sociale*.

[67]A review can be found in: Mori 1890 (as n. 38) 692 ss.; Leoni 1892–98 (as n. 1) 281 ss.; Accollas 1870 (as n. 12) 105 ss.; Dorlhac, Augée. 1891. *De la condition juridique des enfants naturels dans le passè, dans le present, dans l'avvenir*. Paris: A. Rousseau, 195, 290, 311–317. Cf. also Coulet, Paul, Vaunois, Albert. 1880. *Étude sur la recherche de la paternité* (avec une préface de Léon Renault). Paris: A. Maresq Ainé.

[68]Cf. Halpérin, Jean-Louis. 1996. *Histoire du droit privé depuis 1804*. Paris: PUF; di Renzo Villata 2001 (as n. 1) 770.

rather difficult, could be deemed reasonably certain[69] and the push to reform was shared, also in Italy, by many scholars of social issues.[70]

The realties of post-unification Italy then offered new situations which kindled considerable concern. A serious and complex problem was posed by the legal condition of children born to people united in canonical matrimony, but not married according to the law of the State.[71]

It seemed quite difficult to find an global solution—it was found only in 1929, through the Lateran Pacts between the Catholic Church and the Italian State. Legal writers were well aware of this and kept asking themselves how to limit the damage at least for the sake of the most innocent victims. Many observed that the canonical celebration, which ensured the union would be firm and stable, could be considered on the same level as *more uxorio* concubinage with regard to the effects on the issue.[72]

Another factor which persuaded the Italian civil lawyers that there was the need to amend art. 189 was the existence of relevant practical problems associated with the long transition from the law of the Restoration to Unification law.

The hardest transition in this field was experienced by the territories which had previously belonged to Austria and then joined the nascent Kingdom of Italy. Not

---

[69]For instance, the writing of the alleged father, already admitted by the Piedmontese Code, the *more uxorio* cohabitation of the parents and the behaviour of the alleged father toward the alleged child and how he treated it, were held to be sufficient evidence in many case by both the Sacra Rota and other tribunals such as those of the Grand Duchy of Tuscany. There were also long discussions about 'seduction' (see, for instance, Leonardi-Mercurio, Giovanni. 1890–91. La seduzione e l'art. 189 del cod. civ. ital. *Antologia giuridica* 4.8–12 (dic. 1890–apr 1891): 690–727; cf. Cazzetta 1999 (as n. 2) 290 ss). On these themes, even for a further bibliography, see Valsecchi, Chiara. 2014. Filiazione e ricerca della paternità, in *Avvocati protagonisti e rinnovatori del primo diritto unitario*, edd. Stefano Borsacchi and Gian Savino Pene Vidari, 167–200. Bologna: il Mulino; Valsecchi, Chiara. 2015. Padri presunti e padri invisibili. Filiazione e ricerca della paternità nel diritto italiano tra Otto e Novecento, in *Famiglia e matrimonio di fronte al Sinodo. Il punto di vista dei giuristi*, edd. Ombretta Fumagalli Carulli and Anna Sammassimo, 491–512. Milano: Vita e Pensiero.

[70]This was discussed in both the third international conference on hygiene, held at Turin in 1880, as well as the international conference on public charity held in Milan at the end of that same year. (Mori, 1890 (as n. 38) 692).

[71]The introduction in the Code of civil marriage as the only form recognised by the law of Italy brought about the statistic collapse of legitimate unions. Because old habits die hard or on account of ignorance, many continued to get 'married' only in the presence of a priest, without being concerned with the celebration of a second union in the presence of an official of the State and not realising that, for the civil law of Italy, they were merely concubines. Among the heavier consequences of this widespread situation featured the condition of the children born to such unions.

[72]See as an example: Bianchi Bianchi, Emilio. 1880. Le indagini sulla paternità naturale. *Archivio giuridico* 24: 162–183; Cuturi, Torquato. 1880. Studi sulla dichiarazione giudiziale della paternità dei figli naturali. *Archivio giuridico* 25: 385–426; Gabba, Carlo Francesco. 1881. La dichiarazione della paternità illegittima e l'articolo 189 del Codice civile italiano. *Annuario delle scienze giuridiche, sociali e politiche*: 178–240; Santangelo Spoto, Ippolito. 1889. I nati fuori matrimonio e la proibizione di ricerca della paternità. *Antologia giuridica* 3.9–12 (ago–nov. 1889): 186–211; Cimbali, Enrico. 1902. *Due riforme urgenti: il divorzio e la ricerca della paternità naturale*, Torino: UTET: 33–73. Further indications in Valsecchi 2015b (as n. 69).

only was it necessary to regulate the paternity question with specific transitory provisions, but the evident discrepancy between the legislations of Austria and Italy, even with regard to the legal effects of natural paternity, gave rise to numerous controversies and disparate judicial orientations, inducing legal writers to engage in debates which at times verged on the bitter.[73]

The theme of the search for one's father's identity ignited the passions of the entire legal world. It was analysed in depth, for instance at the third National Legal Congress, held in Florence in September 1891. An orientation emerged from this Congress, supported by a large majority, favouring the abolition of the prohibition to seek one's paternity. The proposal, approved almost unanimously by the plenary assembly on September 9, was thus that the search for paternity had to be admitted in certain precise situations.[74]

These clear-cut positions taken by the majority of lawyers and judges notwithstanding, no bill was approved by the Italian Parliament, despite being often supported by very authoritative jurists and parliamentarians.[75]

The advent of Fascism brought the discussions to a halt. The regime's propaganda described the family as "the State citadel at the service of the Nation".[76] It was therefore not at all surprising that the new Code of 1942 only partially acceded

---

[73]Leoni 1892–98 (as n. 1) 263–275. For more about this theme, see Valsecchi 2015 (as n. 53) 1–17.

[74]In addition to cases of abduction and rape, there were cases in which paternity transpired indirectly from sentences of the civil or criminal courts or depended on the declaration of nullity of a marriage, or from the explicit declaration made by the father in writing, the case of "seduction", when the parents had lived publicly together at the time corresponding to the conception, and lastly if the children had received "paternal treatment" from the father. The case of *more uxorio* cohabitation thus also included religious matrimony. *Atti del III Congresso Giuridico Nazionale tenutosi in Firenze l'anno 1891 pubblicati per incarico della Commissione esecutiva dall'Avv. Camillo de Benedetti, direttore della "Cassazione Unica"*. 1897. Torino: UTET, 24, 50, 232–233. On the contribution Italian lawyers gave to the debate, see Valsecchi 2014 (as n. 69).

[75]In 1891, the prominent jurist Emanuele Gianturco tabled a bill to introduce tutelage for "seduced women and young persons". But it was defeated in Parliament. In 1896, a Committee was created in Milan for the reform of art. 189. Academics and technical experts joined this Committee, alongside personalities such as Paolina Schiff, member of the League for the Defence of the Interests of Women. In the opening years of the twentieth century, the discussions still centred round the theme of the first National Congress of Italian Women, held in Milan in 1908 and on February 22, 1910 a new bill was tabled at the Senate by Vittorio Scialoja. Even this time, the bill did met with any success. There was the beginning of some opening in the provisions favouring orphans issued during the First World War. Cf. Azzariti 1939 (as n. 39) 530–531; Labriola, Teresa. 1910. La ricerca della paternità, in *Atti del 1. Congresso Meridionale "Pro Infantia"*, 28, 29, 30, 31 ottobre 1909. Città di Castello: Società tipografica coop.

[76]This well-known definition is by Ferrara, Francesco. 1940. Rinnovamento del diritto civile secondo i postulati fascisti, *Archivio di studi corporativi* 46. On these topics, see Di Simone, Maria Rosa. 1993. La condizione femminile dal codice del 1865 al codice del 1942: spunti per una riflessione. In *I cinquant'anni del codice civile*. Atti del Convegno di Milano 4–6 giugno 1992, 2. *Comunicazioni*. Milano: Giuffrè, 561–593; di Renzo Villata 2001 (as n. 1) 764 ss. and bibliography.

to the expectations of female emancipation or of the equality of rights between children manifested in legal writings and in civil society.

For instance, no change was done to legitimate filiation. The principle remained that the husband is the father of the child born in wedlock and very few amendments were made to the wording of the provisions.[77]

The new Code devoted more provisions than its predecessor to natural filiation and acknowledgement, and regulated every aspect in a detailed fashion in order to avoid interpretative uncertainties.[78] But the effects were substantially the same. Acknowledgement gave rise to a legal tie only with the parent who did it, and, in addition to the right to maintenance and some succession rights (always heavily inferior to those of the legitimate child), the acknowledged child acquired the surname of the parent, but could not be fully integrated into the family.

With regard to the search for paternity, the harsh provision of 1865 was overcome. Nonetheless, the opposite criterion of general admissibility was not achieved.

Article 269 rehashed almost word for word the proposals formulated some fifty years earlier by the third National Legal Congress. In fact, it provided that natural paternity might be judicially declared in 4 specific cases: when the mother and the alleged father had lived together in a publicly-known way, when the paternity resulted indirectly from a sentence of a civil or criminal court or from an unambiguous declaration written by the man to whom paternity is attributed, in the case of abduction or rape, and lastly if there was the concurrence of other facts which served as “serious evidence” of the tie of filiation.[79]

It is clear that in this case the legislative progress was a mere return to a more remote past, since these were substantially the cases which the decisions of the Sacra Rota and pre-Unification tradition had admitted as proof of paternity.

The advent of the Republican constitution, though accompanied by a profound innovation of principles, did not lead to an immediate overturning of the legislation.

Article 30, infact, enunciated the necessity to safeguard children born out of wedlock, declaring that their maintenance, training and education are a “duty and a

---

[77]Azzariti, Giuseppe. 1938. Filiazione (diritto civile). In *Nuovo Digesto Italiano* 7, 1136–1160. Torino: UTET.

[78]Thus, for instance, it specified the age the parents had to have to be allowed to acknowledge the child, or the possibility, already accepted without objection, that one of the parents could, subject to certain conditions, recognise even the child born in adultery or incest, or the acceptance of the acknowledgement of the predeceased child. A more pronounced opening could be seen also in the forms of the acknowledgement, which now also covered the last will made in whichever form. On the origins of the project cf. Azzariti 1938 (as n. 77) 1149 ss.

[79]In particular, if the person was treated like a son or daughter by whoever is identified as the natural father and if the latter, just like a father, provided maintenance and education and helped the child to find an employment or a profession, and furthermore if the child was constantly considered as such in social relations—these were all considered evidence. For a further analysis of these provisions of the Code, see Azzariti 1939 (as n. 39) 531–533 e Labriola, Teresa. 1933. Contributo agli studi sulla ricerca della paternità (A proposito dell’art. 334 del disegno di codice civile). In *La donna nella famiglia nella legislazione fascista*. Napoli: Edizioni de ‘La toga’, 59–66.

right of the parents". But at the same time, it conserved on the same conceptual level the distinction between the status of children born in wedlock and those born out of lawful wedlock. It also imposed a conspicuous limit to the declared necessity of tutelage, clarifying that it had to be "compatible with the rights of the members of the legitimate family". The last paragraph provided that "The law lays down the rules and the limits for the search for paternity", thereby confirming once again, in principle, the exceptionality, and not the full and absolute freedom, of the search.

The cautious wording of the constitutional principles justified for some decades the intangibility of certain rules found in the Code, even those which were frequently discussed. It explains, on behalf of the coexistence of individual rights and the unity of the family structure, why significant differences in treatment between natural and legitimate children were retained, and being particularly evident in matters of succession.[80]

The Constitution retained the 'automatic' granting of the ancient form of protection to those born to married women, represented in the status of legitimacy and by the presumption that the mother's husband is the father. With regard to the search for paternity, judicial decisions reiterated that *favor veritatis* cannot be considered a constitutionally relevant absolute value since it was up to the ordinary legislator to seek the fair balance between the needs of truth and the needs of certainty.

It was only after the Sixties and Seventies, in a social contest which had by now changed, and during a rekindled and politicised debate on these themes, that the Constitutional Court could blaze a trail of renewal leading to a broad revision of the legislative path.

That period witnessed upheavals in many European countries. In France, the value of equality inspired the law on filiation of January 3, 1972, which reviewed the institute from top to bottom. The same happened in the Federal Republic of Germany from the mid-Seventies, in Portugal and Switzerland in 1978, and in Spain between 1975 and 1981.[81]

In Italy, the law of May 19, 1975, no. 151, abrogated or rewrote many articles of the Code, radically changing the provisions regulating matrimony and filiation, in the name no longer of the protection *of* the family as such, but rather of the individuals *within* the family.

According to an authoritative and persuading reading, in parent-children relations the ancient value of family unity was replaced not by the principle of equality but by a third value, namely the interests of minors and their primary right to achieve their personal maturity.[82]

---

[80]Grassetti, Cesare. 1950. *I principi costituzionali relativi al diritto familiare*. In *Commentario sistematico alla Costituzione italiana* 1. Firenze: Barbera, 285 ss. For further bibliographical information on these aspects, see di Renzo Villata 2001 (as n. 1) 767 ss.

[81]di Renzo Villata 2001 (as n. 1) 773–774.

[82]Cavanna 2007b (as n. 11) 776.

The new provisions thus provided, for instance, that acknowledgement imposed on the parent all the duties and all the rights which they had *vis-à-vis* the legitimate child (thus the new art. 261 of the Civil Code). With regard to the judicial action to establish paternity and the judicial declaration, the new rules provided that natural paternity and maternity might be judicially declared in all situations in which acknowledgement is possible. The proof of the natural biological link might be given by any means (art. 269).

This reform was based on the principle of *favor veritatis*, which still was not affirmed in an absolute manner. Indeed, there was still a preventive control of the admissibility of the judicial action.

More generally, the overturning of the place occupied by rights and the fact that they were substantially rendered equal did not completely remove all conceptual distinctions between the different categories of children. The Code is still permeated by a diversity in the regulation of natural and legitimate filiation that has been definitively eliminated only very recently.

References

Accollas, É. (1870). *Le droit de l'enfant. L'enfant né hors mariage*. Paris: Germer Baillière, Libraire-Éditeur.

Ahrens, H. (1838). *Cours de droit naturel ou De philosophie du droit: complété, dans les principales matières, par des aperçus historiques et politiques*, trad.it. *Corso di diritto naturale o di filosofia del diritto completato nelle materie più importanti da alcuni schizzi storici e politici* (trans. Alberto Marghieri, Napoli: 1872). Bruxelles: Société Typographique Belge.

Aquarone, A. (1960). *L'unificazione legislativa e i codici del 1865*. Milano: Giuffrè.

(1897). *Atti del III Congresso Giuridico Nazionale tenutosi in Firenze l'anno 1891 pubblicati per incarico della Commissione esecutiva dall'Avv. Camillo de Benedetti, direttore della "Cassazione Unica"*.Torino: UTET.

Azzariti, G. (1938). Filiazione (diritto civile). *Nuovo Digesto Italiano, 7*, 1136–1160.

Azzariti, G. (1939). Paternità (ricerca della). *Nuovo Digesto Italiano, 9*, 527–533.

Baker, K. K. (2004). Bargaining or Biology. The History and Future of Paternity Law and Parental Status, *Cornell Journal of Law and Public Policy, 14*(1), art. 1. http://scholarship.law.cornell.edu/cjlpp/vol14/iss1/1.

(1980). *Bastardy and its comparative history: studies in the history of illegitimacy and marital nonconformism in Britain, France, Germany, Sweden, North America, Jamaica, and Japan*, edd. Peter Laslett, Karla Oosterveen and Richard Michael Smith. Cambridge, Mass.: Harvard University Press

Bianchi, E. (1880). Le indagini sulla paternità naturale. *Archivio giuridico, 24*, 162–183.

Blaikie, A. (1993). *Illegitimacy, sex, and society: Northeast Scotland, 1750–1900*. Oxford: Clarendonpress.

Bonjean, M. (1884–86). *Congrès international de la protection de l'enfance, tenu au palais du Trocadéro les 15, 16, 18, 19, 20, 21, 22 et 23 juin 1883. Compte rendu des travaux, publié au nom de la Commission internationale permanente*, Société générale de protection pour l'enfance abandonnée ou coupable. Paris: G. Pedone-Lauriel.

Brundage James, A. (1993). Concubinage and Marriage in Medieval Canon Law. In A. Brundage James (Ed.), *Sex, law and marriage in the middle ages* (Variorum 397). Aldershot: Variorum.

Caberlotto, E. (1893). Alimenti. *Digesto Italiano, 2*(2), 342–351 (Torino: UTET).

Cadrès, É. *Traité des enfants naturels mis en rapport avec la doctrine et la jurisprudence*. Paris: Videcoq père et fils, éditeurs (=1852. *Trattato dei figli naturali messo in rapporto colla dottrina e la giurisprudenza,* prima versione italiana dell'avvocato Giuseppe Puglisi, Palermo: stamperia di D. Maccarone).

Cavagnari, C. (1891). *Nuovi orizzonti del diritto civile in rapporto colle istituzioni pupillari. Saggio di critica e riforma legislativa*. Milano: Fratelli Dumolard.

Cavanna, A. (2005). *Storia del diritto moderno in Europa. Le fonti e il pensiero giuridico* 2. Milano: Giuffrè.

Cavanna, A. (2007a). Mito e destini del *code Napoléon* in Italia (Riflessioni in margine al *Panegirico a Napoleone legislatore* di Pietro Giordani). *Scritti (1968–2002) 2* (pp. 1079–1129). Napoli: Jovene.

Cavanna, A. (2007b). Onora il padre. Storia dell'art. 315 cod. civ. (ovvero: il ritorno del flautista di Hamenlin. In *Scritti (1968–2002)* 2 (pp. 771–832). Napoli: Jovene.

Cavina, M. (2007). *Il padre spodestato. L'autorità paterna dall'antichità ad oggi*. Bari: Laterza.

Cazzetta, G. (1999). Praesumitur seducta. *Onestà e consenso femminile nella cultura giuridica moderna*. Milano: Giuffrè.

Cimbali, E. (1902). *Due riforme urgenti: il divorzio e la ricerca della paternità naturale*. Torino: Unione Tipografica Editrice.

Code civil des français. Nouvelle Édition stereotype. 1805. Paris: Fantin, Libraire.

Codice civile della repubblica e Cantone del Ticino. 1837. Bellinzona: Tipografia e Libreria patria.

Codice civile del regno d'Italia. 1866. Torino: Stamperia reale.

Código civil del imperio mexicano. 1866. Mexico: Imprenta de Andrade y Escalante.

Codigo civilportuguez approvado por carta de lei de 1 de Julho 1867. Segunda ediçao official. 1868. Lisboa: Imprencia nacional.

Codigo civil sancionado por el Congreso de los Estados Unidos de Venezuela en 1867. Caracas: Imprenta de Josè R. Enriquez.

Conti Odorisio, G. (2005). Il divieto di ricerca della paternità nello Stato liberale. In *Ragione e tradizione. La questione femminile nel pensiero politico* (pp. 175–200). Roma: Aracne.

Coulet, P., & Vaunois, A. (1880). *Étude sur la recherche de la paternité (avec une préface de Léon Renault)*. Paris: A. Maresq Ainé.

Adair, R. (1996a). *Courtship, Illegitimacy and Marriage in early modern England*. Manchester and New York: Manchester University Press.

Cuturi, T. (1880). Studi sulla dichiarazione giudiziale della paternità dei figli naturali. *Archivio giuridico, 25*, 385–426.

Dalloz, D. (1855). *Répertoire méthodique et alphabétique de législation de doctrine et de jurisprudence en matière de droit civil, commercial, criminel, administratifde droit des gens et de droit public* 35. Paris: Au Bureau de la Jurisprudence générale du Royaume.

Deraisme, M. (1887). *Les droits de l'enfant*. Paris: éd. E. Dentu.

Desan, S. (2004). *The Family on Trial in Revolutionary France*. Berkeley, Los Angeles-London: University of California Press.

di Renzo Villata, M. G. (2001). La famiglia. *Enciclopedia Italiana. Eredità del Novecento, Roma, Istituto dell'Enciclopedia Italiana, 2*, 760–776.

Di Simone, M. R. (1993). La condizione femminile dal codice del 1865 al codice del 1942: spunti per una riflessione. In *I cinquant'anni del codice civile*. Atti del Convegno di Milano 4-6 giugno 1992, 2. *Comunicazioni* (pp. 561–593). Milano: Giuffrè.

Dorlhac, A. (1891). *De la condition juridique des enfants naturels dans le passé, dans le présent, dans l'avvenir*. Paris: A. Rousseau.

Dumas, A., fils. (1883). *La Recherche de la paternité. Lettre à M. Rivet*. Paris: Calmann Levy.

Ferrara, F. (1940). Rinnovamento del diritto civile secondo i postulati fascisti. *Archivio di studi corporativi, 46*, 42–58.

Fournel, J.-F. (1781). *Traité de la séduction considérée dans l'ordre judiciaire*. Paris: Demonville

Gabba, C. F. (1881). La dichiarazione della paternità illegittima e l'articolo 189 del Codice civile italiano. *Annuario delle scienze giuridiche, sociali e politiche, 2*, 178–240.

Galeotti, G. (2009). *In cerca del padre. Storia dell'identità paterna in età contemporanea.* Roma-Bari: Laterza.

Garaud, M., & Szramkiewicz, R. (1978). *La Révolution française et la famille.* Paris: PUF.

Gaudemet, J. (1987). *Le mariage en Occident. Les moeurs et le droit.* Paris: ed. Du Cerf.

Robert, G. (1905). *Histoire de la légitimation des enfants naturels en droit canonique.* Paris: E. Leroux.

Glück, C. F. (1790). *Ausführliche Erläuterung der Pandekten, 1, Erlagen (=1888. Commentario alle Pandette 1.* Vallardi): Milano.

Grassetti, C. (1950). *I principi costituzionali relativi al diritto familiare, in Commentario sistematico alla Costituzione italiana 1.* Firenze: Barbera.

Haanebrink, H. (1921). *Code civil néerlandais traduit en français et mis en concordance avec le code civil belge.* Bruxelles: Établissements Émile Bruylant-Paris, Librairie Générale de droit.

Harris, N. (1836). *A treatise on the Law of adulterine bastardy, with a report of the Banbury case and of all other cases bearing upon the subject.* London: William Pickering.

Huc, T. (1868). *Le code civil italien et le code Napoléon. Études de législation comparée* 1. Paris: Cotillon, Libraire du Conseil d'État.

Adair, R. (1996b). *Illegitimacy, sex, and society: Northeast Scotland, 1750–1900.* Oxford: Clarendonpress.

Koenigswarter, L.-J. (1842). *Essai sur la législation des pueples anciens et modernes relative aux enfans nés hors mariage; suivi de quelques observations d'économie social su le même sujet.* Paris: Joubert, Libraire de la Cour de Cassation.

Labriola, T. (1910). La ricerca della paternità. In *Atti del 1. Congresso Meridionale "Pro Infantia"*, 28, 29, 30, 31 ottobre 1909. Città di Castello: Società tipografica coop.

Labriola, T. (1933). Contributo agli studi sulla ricerca della paternità (A proposito dell'art. 334 del disegno di codice civile). In *La donna nella famiglia nella legislazione fascista* (pp. 59–66). Napoli: Edizioni de 'La toga'.

Lefebvre-Teillard, A. (2007). Approche historique d'un grand concept juridique: la filiation. *Sartoriana, 20,* 109–130. www.sartonchair.ugent.be/file/238.

Lefebvre-Teillard, A. (2008). De la théologie au droit: naissance médiévale du concept de filiation. In *Autour de l'enfant. Du droit canonique at romain médieval au Code Civil de 1804* (pp. 149–273). Leiden-Boston: Brill.

Lefebvre-Teillard, A. (2008a). A propose d'une lettre à Guillaume: la filiation légitime dans l'ouvre d'Ives de Chartres. In *Autour de l'enfant. Du droit canonique at romain médieval au Code Civil de 1804* (pp. 239–258). Leiden-Boston: Brill.

Lefebvre-Teillard, A. (2008b). De la rétroactivité à la fiction. Notes sur la légitimation par mariage subséquent en droit canonique. In *Autour de l'enfant. Du droit canonique at romain médieval au Code Civil de 1804* (pp. 359–373). Leiden-Boston: Brill.

Lefebvre-Teillard, A. (2008c). Histoire de la legitimation des enfants naturels en droit canonique: observations sur un ouvrage Presque centenaire. In *Autour de l'enfant. Du droit canonique at romain médieval au Code Civil de 1804* (pp. 277–286). Leiden-Boston: Brill.

Lefebvre-Teillard, A. (2008d). L'effect rétroactif de la legitimation en droit canonique medieval. *Autour de l'enfant. Du droit canonique at romain médieval au Code Civil de 1804* (pp. 329–341). Leiden-Boston: Brill.

Lefebvre-Teillard, A. (2008e). L'enfant naturel dans l'ancien droit français. In *Autour de l'enfant. Du droit canonique at romain médieval au Code Civil de 1804* (pp. 259–273). Leiden-Boston: Brill.

Lefebvre-Teillard, A. (2008f). "Pater is est quem nuptiae demostrant": jalons pour une histoire de la présomption de paternité. In *Autour de l'enfant. Du droit canonique at romain médieval au Code Civil de 1804* (pp. 185–197). Leiden-Boston: Brill.

Lefebvre-Teillard, A. (2008g). "Si mieux n'aime l'épouser": marriage et relations charnelles hors marriage (France XVIe-XVIIIe s.). In *Autour de l'enfant. Du droit canonique at romain médieval au Code Civil de 1804* (pp. 31–50). Leiden-Boston: Brill.

Lefebvre-Teillard, A. (2008h). *Tanta est vis matrimonii*: l'écho français d'une vielle controverse. In *Autour de l'enfant. Du droit canonique at romain médieval au Code Civil de 1804* (pp. 301–314). Leiden-Boston: Brill.

Lefebvre-Teillard, A. (2008i). *Tanta est vis matrimonii*: remarques sur la legitimation par marriage subsequent de l'enfant adultérin. In *Autour de l'enfant. Du droit canonique at romain médieval au Code Civil de 1804* (pp. 287–299). Leiden-Boston: Brill.

Leonardi-Mercurio, G. (1890–91). La seduzione e l'art. 189 del cod. civ. ital. *Antologia giuridica, 4*(8–12) (dic. 1890–apr 1891), 690–727.

Leoni, G. (1892–98). Filiazione. In *Digesto Italiano* 11.2. Torino: Utet: 207–301.

Levene, A., Williams, S., & Nutt, T. (2005). Introduction. In *Illegitimacy in Britain*, 1700–1920, edd. Alysa Levene, Samantha Williams and Thomas Nutt. Bansingstoke: Palgrave Macmillan.

Lévy, J. P. (1989). L'évolution du droit familial français de 1789 au Code Napoléon. In *La famille, la loi, l'État de la Rèvolution au code civil*. Paris: Centre G. Pompidou, 508 ss.

Loiseau, J. (1811). *Traité des enfans naturels, adultérine, incestueux et abandonnès*. Paris: Antoine.

Luchetti, G. (1990). *La legittimazione dei figli naturali nelle fonti tardo imperiali e giustinianee*. Milano: Giuffrè.

Marongiu, A. (1958). Adulterini e incestuosi (figli) (diritto intermedio). *Enciclopedia del diritto 1* (pp. 610–611). Giuffrè: Milano.

Mattei, J. (1852). *I paragrafi del codice civile austriaco avvicinati dalle leggi romane, francesi e sarde* 1. Venezia: co' tipi di Pietro Naratovich.

Mayali, L. (1990). Note on the legitimization by subsequent marriage from Alexander III to Innocent III. In *The two laws. Studies in medieval legal history dedicated to S. Kuttner*. Washington: CatholicUniversity of America Press, 55 ss.

Montani, P. (1995). Madri nubili e tribunali. Legislazione e sentenze in età liberale. *Italia contemporanea, 200*, 455–468.

Montesi, B. (2007). *Questo figlio a chi lo do?: minori, famiglie, istituzioni (1865–1914)*. Milano: FrancoAngeli.

Mori, V. (1890). Appunti su l'azione di paternità naturale nel diritto antico e moderno. *Il Filangieri, 15*, 569–584, 594–631, 622–708.

Pecorella, C. (1968). Filiazione (parte storica). *Enciclopedia delDiritto 17* (pp. 449–456). Giuffrè: Milano.

Petroni, G. (1877). Il diritto agli alimenti dei figliuoli semplicemente naturali studiato nel codice civile italiano. *Il Filangieri, 2*, 526–544.

Pitzorno, B. (1904). *La legittimazione nella storia delle istituzioni familiari del Medio Evo*. Sassari: Satt.

Pouzol, A. (1902). *La recherche de la paternité: étude critique de sociologie et de législation comparée*. Paris: V. Giard & E. Briere.

Quartarone, M. (1884). *Il diritto agli alimenti e le azioni alimentari secondo il codice civile e il codice di procedura civile: studio teorico-pratico*. Torino: F.lli Bocca.

Regnoli, O. (1897). Prima tesi. Relazione, Parte prima "se e quali riforme siano da introdursi nel Codice civile relativamente alla ricerca della paternità, e alla condizione giuridica dei figli illegittimi". In *Atti del III Congresso Giuridico Nazionale tenutosi in Firenze l'anno 1891 pubblicati per incarico della Commissione esecutiva dall'Avv. Camillo de Benedetti, direttore della "Cassazione Unica"* (pp. 32–51). Torino: UTET.

Reid, C. J. (2004). *Power over the Body, Equality in the Family: Rights and Domestic Relations in Medieval Canon Law*. Grand Rapids, Michigan, Cambridge U.K.: William B. Eerdmans Publishing Co.

Relazione della Commissione del Senato sul Progetto del Codice Civile presentato dal Ministro Guardasigilli (Pisanelli) nelle tornate del 15 luglio e 26 novembre 1863. In *Codice civile preceduto dalle Relazioni Ministeriale e Senatoriale, dalle Discussioni Parlamentari e dai Verbali della Commissione coordinatrice*,ed. Sebastiano Gianzana, 1, *Relazioni*. Torino: UTET, 1887.

Relazione sul Progetto del primo libro del Codice Civile presentato in iniziativa al Senato dal Ministro Guardasigilli (Pisanelli) nella tornata del 15 novembre 1862. In *Codice civile preceduto dalle Relazioni Ministeriale e Senatoriale, dalle Discussioni Parlamentari e dai Verbali della Commissione coordinatrice*, ed. Sebastiano Gianzana, 1, *Relazioni*.Torino: UTET, 1887.

Santangelo Cordani, A. (2003). L'accertamento della paternità tra dottrina e prassi all'indomani del Concilio di Trento: uno sguardo alle *decisiones* della Rota romana. In Amicitiae Pignus. *Studi in ricordo di Adriano Cavanna* 3, edd (pp. 1949–1987). Antonio Padoa Schioppa,Gigliola di Renzo Villata and Gian Paolo Massetto: Milano: Giuffrè.

Santangelo Spoto, I. (1889). I nati fuori matrimonio e la proibizione di ricerca della paternità. *Antologia giuridica, 3*(9–12) (ago–nov 1889), 186–211.

(1869). *The civil code of the State of Louisiana, revised, arranged and amended by the hon. John Ray reviser of the statutes and codes under the supervision of the joint committee of revision*. Monroe LA: Office of the "Louisiana Intelligencer".

Valsecchi, C. (2014). Filiazione e ricerca della paternità. In *Avvocati protagonisti e rinnovatori del primo diritto unitario*, edd (pp. 167–200). Stefano Borsacchi, Stefano and Gian Savino Pene Vidari, Bologna: il Mulino.

Valsecchi, C. (2015a). "The determination of paternity must be admissible". Post-unification civil law theory and practice and the family law reforms. transitory law issues. *Italian Review of Legal History, 1*(13), 1–17.

Valsecchi, C. (2015b). Padri presunti e padri invisibili. Filiazione e ricerca della paternità nel diritto italiano tra Otto e Novecento. In *Famiglia e matrimonio di fronte al Sinodo. Il punto di vista dei giuristi*, edd (pp. 491–512). Ombretta Fumagalli Carulli and Anna Sammassimo, Milano: Vita e Pensiero.

Van de Wiel, C. (1992). Les différentes formes de cohabitation hors justes noces et les dénominations diverses des enfants qui en sont nés dans le droit romain, canonique, civil et byzantin jusqu'au XIII siècle. *Revue internationale des droits de l'antiquité, 39*, 327–358.

(1887). *Verbali della Commissione di coordinamento*, verbale n. 12, Seduta del 27 aprile 1865, *Codice civile preceduto dalle Relazioni Ministeriale e Senatoriale, dalle Discussioni Parlamentari e dai Verbali della Commissione coordinatrice*, ed. Sebastiano Gianzana, 3, *Verbali*. Torino: UTET.

Verduchène, J. (1860). *Observations critiques sur le code civil neerlandais, comparé avec le code napoléon. Livre I, tit. I au VI*^{e}. Maëstricht: Van Osch-America et C.

(1886). *Verhandlungen des Geschiten Deutschen Juristentages*, Zweiter Band. Berlin:Drud und Commissions-Verlag von G. Jansen.

Volterra, E. (1961). Filiazione. Diritto romano. In *Novissimo Digesto Italiano* 7. Torino: Utet, 308–309.

Volterra, E. (1975). Matrimonio (diritto romano). *Enciclopedia del diritto 25* (pp. 726–807). Giuffrè: Milano.

Honour and Guilt. A Comparative Study on Regulations on Infanticide Between the Nineteenth and Twentieth Century

Loredana Garlati

Abstract Infanticide has been judged by people in so many different ways: such differing concepts are reflected in Italian legislation. From medieval times up to the eighteenth century infanticide represented the betrayal of the 'vocation of motherhood and of maternal instinct'. Extreme measures were adopted to sanction this offence, such as capital punishment in its most cruel and aggravated form. A new understanding of infanticide emerged with the Enlightenment principles: infanticide was considered not only to deserve a milder conviction compared to that of murder, but could also be liable to being recognized as a self-standing offence. After a cursory analysis of the legislation in force in the Italian territories during the Napoleonic, Austrian and Restoration regimes, the paper focuses on the 'Italian' codes. The 1889 Zanardelli code (art. 369) defined infanticide as a lesser form of murder. The apparent straightforwardness of the formulation did not prevent the proliferation of theories and interpretations, above all as regards to qualifying infanticide as a specific crime, or, instead, as a mitigated form of a crime, in view of an honour killing; the *Corte di Cassazione* gave the crime of infanticide a special qualification; the prevailing doctrine interpreted it as a hypothesis of murder characterised by mitigating and circumstantial evidence. The 1930 code modified the regulation on infanticide: the *causa honoris* explicitly became a constitutive element of the crime and was no longer merely a lessening circumstance of the *species homicidii*.

Dedicated to Mario Montorzi

L. Garlati (✉)
University of Milano-Bicocca, Piazza dell'Ateneo Nuovo 1, 20126 Milan, Italy
e-mail: loredana.garlati@unimib.it

M.G. di Renzo Villata (ed.), *Family Law and Society in Europe from the Middle Ages to the Contemporary Era*, Studies in the History of Law and Justice 5,
DOI 10.1007/978-3-319-42289-3_11

1 The Cultural and Legislative Dimensions of Infanticide in the Period Prior to the Unification of Italy

"L'infanticidio, inteso come soppressione dei neonati indesiderati, è un fatto che ha accompagnato come un sordo rumore di fondo la storia delle specie".[1] Moreover, "non v'è, forse, azione umana che, al pari dell'infanticidio, sia stata giudicata, presso i vari popoli, a seconda del mutare dei tempi, in modi così svariati e, fra loro, così profondamente diversi".[2] Interestingly, "questa varietà di concezioni si è riprodotta pure nei Codici italiani".[3]

It is undisputed that infanticide has been a "delitto intorno al quale le legislazioni oscillarono assai, così per stabilirne la nozione, come per misurarne la pena".[4] Should infanticide be defined as aggravated murder, or an alleged or lessened attempt at murder? Over time legislations reflected each of these interpretations.

As a form of a demographic control widely used in the most ancient, pagan communities and with the spread of the Catholic religion, this crime became one of the most ruthlessly repressed offences. From medieval times up to the eighteenth century infanticide represented the juridical equivalent of what was considered the most atrocious symbol of decline of the human being: the betrayal of the 'vocation of motherhood and of maternal instinct'. Extreme measures were adopted to sanction this offence, such as capital punishment in its most cruel and aggravated form.[5]

If men symbolized 'force and muscles' in charge of hard labour, responsible for fighting and everything that included the use of their inborn physical force, women were considered reproductive figures naturally meant for maternity alone.[6] This interpretation persisted in the nineteenth century in the Positive School in criminology's identification of motherhood with women, which nature itself had assigned to and prepared for this role. However, such glorification of the maternal figure was deceptive: on one hand a woman could assert her dignity as well as her right in society to be respected and protected in view of her capacity to give birth to a human being; yet, on the other hand, maternity was viewed as a limitation of female independence, burdening women with responsibilities, and blaming them of

[1]Prosperi, Adriano. 2015. *Dare l'anima. Storia di un infanticidio.* Torino: Einaudi, 20

[2]Sighele, Scipio. 1899. Sull'infanticidio. In *Archivio giuridico* 42: 177.

[3]Pessina, Enrico. 1883. *Elementi di diritto penale* 2. Napoli: Marghieri di Guis, 23.

[4]Ambrosoli, Filippo. 1857. *Studi sul codice penale toscano confrontato specialmente coll'austriaco*. Mantova: Negretti, 125.

[5]Carfora, Francesco. 1927. Infanticidio. In *Digesto Italiano* 13.1. Torino: UTET, 663–726; Pannain, Remo. 1965. Omicidio (diritto penale). In *Novissimo Digesto Italiano* 11. Torino: UTET, 884–891; Fiore, Carlo. 1971. Infanticidio. In *Enciclopedia del diritto* 21. Milano: Giuffrè, 391–402; Merzagora, Isabella. 1992. Infanticidio. In *Digesto delle discipline penalistiche* 6. Torino: UTET, 392–396.

[6]Mellusi, Vincenzo. 1897. *La madre delinquente (studio di psicologia morbosa).* Roma: E. Loescher, 12–13.

contributing to juvenile delinquency because of their failure in educating the children correctly.[7]

Furthermore, such violent repression of infanticide was linked to Catholicism's strict religious influence constraining sexual intercourse within the boundary of matrimony, resulting in public shaming and moral condemnation of women's extramarital affairs, especially if illegitimate children were involved. These were often the reasons that forced women to suppress infants born out of wedlock.

A new understanding of infanticide emerged with the Enlightenment principles, in the light of, on one hand, economic-social transformations, changes in sexual ethics and a new vision of women and maternity;[8] and, on the other hand, the development of auxiliary sciences and the founding of ideologically orientated criminal law schools. The interpretation of the infanticide changed from being considered 'heretical'—not complying with the orthodoxy of maternity to being attached to an undefended female, victim of society, its values, as well as of men's deceitful seduction. Thus, "la nuova sensibilità sorta col Settecento trasformò le delinquenti dei secoli precedenti in figure di tragedia".[9]

The interest towards the personality and dignity of the offender, together with the social influences and the natural factors which influenced his or her behaviour, became such to consider that infanticide not only deserved a milder conviction compared to that of murder, but could also be liable to being recognized as a self-standing offence.[10]

Without disregarding the gravity of the offence at hand, the psychic condition of the mother at the moment of giving birth was also taken into consideration when defining the punishment. Cesare Beccaria's argument represented, for the first time, a clear cut between the atrocity committed in the past centuries and a purported different future interpretation: "l'infanticidio è parimente l'effetto di una inevitabile contraddizione in cui è posta una persona che, per debolezza o per violenza, abbia ceduto. Chi trovasi tra l'infamia e la morte di un essere incapace di sentirne i mali, come non preferirà questa alla miseria infallibile, a cui sarebbero esposti ella e l'infelice frutto?"[11] Other accounts of the dramatic cases of women torn between two both equally atrocious choices (safeguarding their honour or suppressing the child), can be found in the works of the Piedmontese aristocrat Alberto Radicati di Passerano,[12] or in the theories of Pestalozzi, who modified the concept of

---

[7]Garlati, Loredana. 2012a. La fine dell'innocenza. L'infanticidio nella disciplina dell'Italia post unitaria. *Corte d'Assise* 1: 17–74.

[8]Selmini, Rossella. 1987. *Profili di uno studio storico sull'infanticidio. Esame di 31 processi per infanticidio giudicati dalla Corte d'Assise di Bologna dal 1880 al 1913*. Milano: Giuffrè, 17.

[9]Prosperi 2015 (as n. 1) 75.

[10]Amore, Alessia. 2011. *L'infanticidio. Analisi della fattispecie normativa e prospettive di riforma*. Padova: Cedam, 44.

[11]Beccaria, Cesare. 1984. *Dei delitti e delle pene*. Firpo, Luigi and Francioni, Gianni (Eds.). Milano: Mediobanca, 102.

[12]Radicati, Alberto. 2003. *Dissertazione filosofica sulla morte*. Cavallo, Tomaso (Ed. and trans.). Pisa: ed. ETS, 121–123.

infanticide qualifying the offender as a victim of a misunderstood morality and of the social context[13] she was immersed in. These interpretations were later drawn on by many jurists. Suffice is to recall Gian Domenico Romagnosi[14] or Francesco Carrara's,[15] who considered *causa honoris* a main reason for mitigation of punishment.

Such solution was adopted in the first penal code drawn up after the unification of Italy, after a lengthy and tortuous period starting from the nineteenth century legislation.

The legal codes implemented prior to the unification were linked to two different regulations,[16] namely those applied by the French and the Austrians, which offered opposing view of the crime at hand. Infanticide was addressed in the French code only in Art. 302 which equated it to patricide, poisoning and carried the death sentence. In 1824 capital punishment was substituted by penal servitude, as prescribed in the law dated 28 April 1832.

The regulations introduced by the *Franziskana* legislation of 1803 referred to the legitimate or illegitimate nature of the offspring and to the omission or commission elements of the crime committed. Section 122, in fact, punished the mother with life imprisonment (*carcere durissimo*)[17] in instances where she willfully caused the death of a legitimate child, whereas a prison sentence of ten to 20 years was inflicted for the suppression of an illegitimate child. This punishment[18] was reduced by 5–10 years in cases of deliberate breach of duty of care. Said regulations were reproduced in full in section 129 of the revised 1852 legislation. The Austrian code considered the principle of mitigation of the crime of infanticide with no reference whatsoever to the motive of honour, which instead was the basis of the Italian provision at the time.

---

[13]Pestalozzi, Johann Heinrich. 1927. Über Gesetzgebung und Kindermord. In *Pestalozzis Samtliche Werke*. Berlin-Leipzig: Walter de Gruyter, 1–181; Pestalozzi, Johann Heinrich. 1999. *Sull'infanticidio* (trans. G. di Bello). Firenze: La Nuova Italia.

[14]Romagnosi, Giandomenico. 1791. *Genesi del diritto penale*. Pavia: San Salvatore, 1524.

[15]Carrara, Francesco. 1872. *Programma del corso di diritto criminale. Parte speciale* 1. Lucca: Giusti, § 1230, 341.

[16]Cadoppi, Alberto. 2001. Il "modello" rivale del code penale. Le "forme piuttosto didattiche" del codice penale universale austriaco del 1803. In Vinciguerra, Sergio (Ed.). *Codice penale universale austriaco (1803)*. Padova: Cedam, XCV–CXLI.

[17]The *carcere durissimo* implied imprisonment in a cell, being chained, hand-cuffed and having the ankles locked in shackles. Besides being deprived of any external contacts and forced to work, the offender was given bread and water only, as well as a hot meal with no meat every other day. The convicted had to sleep on planks, had no rights to being visited or to have contacts with anyone. *Codice penale universale austriaco coll'appendice delle più recenti norme generali*. 1815. Milano: I.R. Stamperia, Sect. 14, 11.

[18]In the *carcere duro* the offender had his feet locked in shackles, was fed daily with hot meals containing no meat, could have visits in the presence of the prison officer held in a language known to the latter. *Austrian criminal code* 1815 (as n. 17): § 13, 10. Garlati, Loredana. 2002. *Nella disuguaglianza la giustizia. Pietro Mantegazza e il codice penale autriaco (1816)*. Milano: Giuffrè, 86–88.

The basis of 1800s pre-unification Italian legal codes, with the sole exception of those adhered to in Tuscany, can be found in the Napoleonic legislation. Infanticide was, in fact, considered murder in the Neapolitan legal code (Articles 349 and 352), in the code implemented in Sardinia in 1859, in Parma (Art. 308) and that of the Vatican which envisaged capital punishment (Art. 276, section 7), as well as in the Este code (Art. 351 and 358, sect. 1).

The legal code in Tuscany, however, distinguished malicious and unintentional infanticide (Articles 316–320), the former being punished with a prison sentence from 10 to 15 years if the woman had premeditated the crime prior to being in labour, and from 5 to 10 years in other instances, in which case a milder sentence was inflicted if the mother had acted without premeditation.

A similar interpretation was supported in legal medicine literature, which acknowledged on a legislative level that the woman in labour experienced a particular condition of physical weakness and psychic alteration—either mania or puerperal insanity[19]—which could degenerate into a psychiatric pathology. In such cases the punishment was reduced from 6 months to 2 years in the case of infanticide on newborns born alive but devoid of vitality (Art. 319). This articulation was the topic of heated debates both in doctrine and legislation over the subsequent years. However, unintentional infanticide carried a prison sentence from 2 months to a year for the murder of offspring born alive and well (Art. 320).

Yet, all legal regulations during that period provided for a mitigation of the punishment when the mother was forced to commit the crime for a specific reason: in defense of her honour.[20]

2 Provisions on Infanticide in the 1889 Penal Code

It took a 30-year long process and various drafts, each providing opposing solutions,[21] until, finally, a longed-for unification of the penal code was reached. The 1889 code took into consideration only part of the proposals examined in the past (above all related to the 1868 first draft) and defined infanticide as a lesser form of murder. Art. 369, for instance, provided that when the crime had been committed on an infant whose civil status had not been registered, and within the 5 days from the birth date, in order to save the honour of the husband, his wife, his mother, of his heirs, of an adopted daughter if any, or of the sister, the punishment consisted in detention from 3 to 12 years, considerably reduced compared to the prison sentence of 18 to 21 years foreseen by Art. 364 in cases of murder.

[19]Stoppato, Alessandro. 1887. *Infanticidio e procurato aborto*. Verona-Padova: Drucker e Tedeschi, 36–56.

[20]Garlati 2012b (as n. 7) 17–25.

[21]Garlati 2012b (as n. 7) 26–31.

All reference to illegitimate offspring, which had been mentioned at length in the preparatory drafts when justifying the motive of honour, had disappeared. The concept of infant was framed in terms of *tempus commissi delicti*.[22] Furthermore, each subject involved was clearly mentioned in the provision.

The apparent straightforwardness of this article did not prevent the proliferation of theories and interpretations in which legislation and doctrine were often in contrasting positions, above all as regards qualifying infanticide as a specific crime, which was contested in no mean terms during the preparatory phase of the legislation,[23] or, instead, as a mitigated form of a crime, in view of the motive of honour.

The Court of Cassation (*Corte di Cassazione*), immediately after the Zanardelli penal code came into force, with a seminal ruling held that "a differenza del soppresso Codice Penale [...] il nuovo Codice fa dell'infanticidio un titolo speciale di reato quando trattasi di renderlo scusabile in considerazione della causa di onore".[24] Such principle was further confirmed in a series of subsequent sentences,[25] in which the motive of honour was clearly not to be considered as a simple mitigating circumstance, but as a constitutive element of the crime. For instance, it was held that contrary to murder, which involved the will to kill and subsequent death, the crime of infanticide required other elements, namely the lack of registration of the birth of the victim, its taking place within the first 5 days of life of the infant and the protection of the honour of the mother. In the light of these reasons, the punishment was not referred to as a simple *deminutio* for a murder crime, but represented a self-standing, separate punishment.

The direction constantly followed by the Supreme Court, which was judged by Luigi Majno[26] as being quite absurd, did not encounter acceptance in the prevailing doctrine, in which infanticide was interpreted as a hypothesis of murder characterised by mitigating and circumstantial evidence.[27] Yet, there were conflicting opinions in which infanticide—in line with case law, constituted a separate hypothesis of crime,[28] on the basis of the lack of mediated offence, in the light of the victim's inability to perceive the danger it was subjected to and considering the lack of a general, social awareness of the risks involved; in fact, nobody had any reason to be afraid of seeing their own child being killed by other individuals for motive of honour.[29] Different consequences resulted from choosing one or the other

[22]The five days envisaged by the civil code (Art. 371) for the compulsory registration of the birth, providing it with an official civil status in the registry.

[23]Perroni-Ferranti, Giacomo. 1879. Un pensiero sul titolo di infanticidio. In Perroni-Ferranti, Giacomo. *Pagine sparse. Studi di diritto criminale e di rito civile*. Messina: Capra, 5–10.

[24]Cassazione. 7 ottobre 1891. *Il foro penale* 1 (1892): 127.

[25]Cassazione. 15 gennaio 1892. *Rivista Penale* 35 (1892): 297–298; 27 gennaio 1892. *Rivista penale* 35 (1892): 397; 24 agosto 1897. *Giustizia penale* 3 (1897): 1464; 17 ottobre 1900. *Monitore dei tribunali* 42 (1901): 458.

[26]Impallomeni, Giovan Battista. 1899. *L'omicidio nel diritto penale*. Torino: UTET, 556.

[27]Impallomeni (as n. 26) 556.

[28]Pinto, Manfredo. 1895–96. *Infanticidio (art. 369 cod. pen.)*. Campobasso: G. e N. Colitti, 18.

[29]Balestrini, Raffaello. 1888. *Aborto, infanticidio ed esposizione d'infante*. Torino: Bocca, 81.

solution, the most important of which concerned the treatment of accomplices. By considering infanticide as a self-standing crime, those who participated in the offence were allowed to claim the motive of honour, which gave them the possibility of carrying a milder sentence normally given to the mother, which would be mitigated compared to that of a sentence of murder. If this was not the case, the *causa honoris* provided for mitigating circumstances and as such was treated as strictly personal.

The Supreme Court, in line with its own parameters of interpretation, decided upon the former solution: over the years, in a series of rulings, it constantly recognized infanticide as a crime *sui generis*[30] and the accomplices liable under Article 369.

Yet, these rulings were heavily criticised in doctrine and the Supreme Court was accused of "bizantino formalismo"[31] in contrast with the 1889 code, which held that infanticide had to be considered under the category of murder crimes.[32]

Contrary to previous legislations, the Zanardelli code had used wordings such as *neonato* (newborn) or *nato di recente* (born recently) to define the passive subject of the crime, preferring to consider, rather than the word *infante* (*infant*), the time factor (5 days from the birth) and an official record (prior to the birth registration); in other words, according to the example indicated in Neapolitan code. The existence of the child therefore became juridically confirmed once the birth had been registered, or when it was presumably known by all 5 days after the birth.

According to the most accredited interpretation, once the birth of the child had been made public, the motive of honour—the only true cause which alone reduced the punishment compared to a sentence of murder—was excluded.

Although the definition of a time limit was, according to many, a significant step forward compared to the prior legislation, some considered it illogical to punish the mother in one way for murdering the child within 5 days from its birth, and in a completely different way if the crime was committed on the sixth day of the infant's life. Infanticide's characterising element was not to be found in the *tempus commissi delicti* but in the intention of the murderer, aiming at concealing the birth.

The concept of birth itself implied several epistemological doubts. Above all, it was necessary to distinguish an abortion caused purposely and an infanticide: in the former case a growing human being was brutally and prematurely aborted; in the second case "un organismo umano, in uno stato di formazione sufficiente a condurre una vita extrauterina autonoma"[33] was murdered.

[30]Cassazione. 6 marzo 1896, *Rivista Penale* 43 (1896): 518; 11 gennaio 1899. *Rivista Penale* 49 (1899): 422; 30 gennaio 1899. *Il Foro italiano* 24 (1899): 171–172.

[31]Majno, Luigi. 1894. *Commento al codice penale italiano* 2. Verona: D. Tedeschi, 130.

[32]Impallomeni, Giovan Battista. 1889. I delitti contro la persona. In *Completo trattato teorico e pratico di diritto penale secondo il codice unico del Regno d'Italia* 2.2. Milano: Vallardi, 289–290; Impallomeni, Giovan Battista. 1892. Il titolo del reato per gli effetti della competenza. *Rivista penale* 35: 1–24.

[33]Majno 1894 (as n. 31) 544.

In order to ascertain that infanticide had been committed, evidence was needed to prove that the child was alive when born. This was instrumental in ruling out the crime whenever it was possible to provide evidence of violence on a stillborn baby, in which case the anti-juridical action would be missing. To ascertain that the child was alive when born was a very sensitive matter requiring the coroner's intervention.

On the basis of the principle that "breathing is living", the floating lung test (*Docimasia pulmonum hydrostatica*) was considered, despite various reservations, the most acceptable form of evidence.[34] Once it had been ascertained that the infant was alive at birth, the next step was to verify the natural or violent cause of death. Such verification was carried out solely by experts and coroners appointed by the Court.[35] Their task was particularly complex given that the most frequent methods of suppressing infants could be often confused with accidental causes of death. A fracture of the skull could, in fact, be willingly caused or the consequence of an accidental fall in the numerous cases in which the mother declared to have given birth in a standing position or when she was unable to prevent the slimy body of the newborn child slipping out of her hands. In the case of death by strangling, this could have been caused by the twisting of the umbilical cord around the child's throat. By the same token, it could have been a deliberate action, another example of which is when the newborn child could have suffocated accidently from caul or "da muco che passi dalle fauci alle glotide"[36] or again by a deliberate action caused by the mother; all forms of bone dislocation could have been caused by a particularly difficult labour or by a willing action. With the progress of medical science uncertainty was gradually reduced and it was possible to explain why, during the period between 1890 and 1892 around 31 % of the crimes related to infanticide were considered as inexistent or not constituting a crime. This rate dropped to 24 % during the period 1891–1895 and down to 11 % between 1918 and 1930.[37]

Yet, the crime of infanticide was more frequently identified with motive of honour. The nature of infanticide as a *reato proprio* (an offence specific to a certain class of offender) which the subjects mentioned in Art. 369 could be charged with, was undeniable. Yet, it was also true, pursuant to Art. 364, that the offender would be charged with murder if the motive of the crime was not safeguarding one's honour or that of the family, but a different one, for example revenge or one related to profit-making purposes.

The legal code introduced by Zanardelli preferred not to limit to the mother the extent of the application of an exceptional reduction of the punishment, but also challenged it on a more general level: the motive of honour could, in fact, be

[34]Ziino, Giuseppe. 1872. *Compendio di medicina legale in trenta lezioni secondo le leggi dello Stato e più recenti progressi della Scienza*. Napoli: Pasquale, 281–303 and 469–498.

[35]They were increasingly present in the Courtrooms and gradually taking over competences which were once the monopoly of the magistrates only.

[36]Poma, Angelo. 1834. *Dizionario anatomico-medico-legale*. Padova: Minerva, 236–238.

[37]Spallanzani, Alfredo. 1931. *I reati di infanticidio e di procurato aborto secondo le statistiche giudiziarie italiane*. Roma: Istituto Poligrafico dello Stato, 7–9.

invoked by a few close relations only (the husband, the son/daughter, the heirs, the parents, even adopted parents, the brother/sister of the mother), holding that, although not involved in the mother's personal situation at the time of the birth of the infant, they considered the birth of said infant, in agreement with the mother, as a threat to their honour. For the persons indicated in Art. 369, the motive of honour was applicable, despite their involvement or not in the crime with the mother and even though the mother had played no role in the crime. The application of Art. 369 did not derive from any help bestowed upon the mother, but concerned their intent to save their social status.[38]

Certain perplexities arose in deciding whether the husband of the woman would be amongst those benefiting from a milder punishment for the crime ("un'ipotesi da romanzo" in the words of Majno),[39] but the prescription was in line with the choice of the lawmaker to avoid any reference to the illegitimate *status* of the infant to justify the crime. This meant that even the husband could be interested in saving the honour of his wife, besides his own honour and that of his family, especially if the woman who gave birth to a child conceived it out of wedlock.

No reference to the biological father of the child was made in the regulation, thus excluding him from the possibility of invoking a mitigation of punishment as per article 369. Some considered it an unjustified choice,[40] while others believed that such limitation would mean avoiding the improper use of the mitigating circumstance by those who, after dishonouring a woman, invoked a cause in the defense of honour to justify their own criminal actions.[41]

The motive of honour was the criminal incentive for the offender, the main reason[42] for committing the offence: such concept was strictly connected to sexual ethics and, at the same time, was considered in objective terms as an appraisal of the subjects' social reputation or 'civic virtue'. In other words, honour represented a key social value and was not only a dimension of one's sensitivity or a subjective appreciation of another person. The fear of losing credibility (the ancient *fama*) caused such a psychological pressure, sense of guilt and an abnormal state of unrest that the offender preferred to suppress a human being rather than facing his/her own ruin. Honour, thus, became almost a commodity and the criminal act a means for the subject's reinstatement in society,[43] hence a motive subject to leniency,[44]

---

[38]Carfora 1927 (as n. 5) 704.

[39]Majno 1894 (as n. 31) 129.

[40]Majno 1894 (as n. 31) 130–131; Carfora 1927 (as n. 5) 714.

[41]Puglia, Ferdinando. 1905. I delitti contro la persona. In *Trattato di diritto penale* 6. Milano: Vallardi, 200; Arena, Pasquale. 1896. *L'infanticidio per ragion d'onore: studio giuridico-sociologico*. Napoli: de Angelis & Bellisario, 58–60.

[42]Balestrini 1888 (as n. 29) 266–267.

[43]Selmini 1987 (as n. 8) 35.

[44]Puglia 1905 (as n. 41) 198.

"elemento morale diminuente"[45] or in the words of the Court of Appeal *the ratio* behind Art. 369.[46]

In the light of the above reasons, the pre-existence of the honour to be safeguarded was essential in order to invoke the application of Art. 369. A prostitute, for instance, could not be granted a milder sentence to that indicated in the provisions, since she had no honour to save.[47] The same could be said of mothers of illegitimate children and therefore no question of honour to be defended[48] or for frequent cases of infanticide by the same mother which revealed her wicked nature or inclination towards committing a crime, as held by the exponents of the Positive School.

3 Article 578 and the Penal Code Introduced in 1930: Old and New Perspectives

The 1930 code modified the regulation on infanticide, part of which derived from the proposals emerged in the doctrinal debate and jurisprudence developed over the previous years. In the *Relazione Ministeriale* (hereafter *Relazione*), which explained the ratio behind the penal code, the Minister of Justice clearly underlined that "notevoli modificazioni" had been introduced to Art. 369. However, without disregarding key changes, we cannot but accept a substantial continuity with the past, both as regards the questions subject to interpretation as well as the solutions reached therein. The new provisions of Art. 578, which included the regulation of infanticide in the 1930 penal code text, do not seem to have significantly altered the grounds for contrasting interpretations in doctrine. The debate included all the instances already investigated by the judges representing liberal Italy, many of whom continued to be active in the Courts during fascism.[49] Thus, the exegetic and systematic work after the Zanardelli code was continued, demonstrating how liberalism in Italy at the end of the eighteenth century was still "conservatore e autoritario, statalistico e patriottico e non aveva difficoltà ad incontrarsi con il fascismo senza neppure diventare fascista ma semplicemente rimanendo fedele a se medesimo".[50]

[45] Stoppato 1887 (as n. 19) 195–197.

[46] Cassazione. 9 gennaio 1895. *Annali della Giurisprudenza Italiana* 29 (1895): 66; 19 luglio 1911. *Giurisprudenza Italiana* 63 (1911): 320.

[47] Crivellari, Giulio (but Suman, Giovanni). 1896. *Il codice penale per il Regno d'Italia* 6. Torino: UTET, 829.

[48] Impallomeni 1899 (as n. 26) 553.

[49] *I giuristi e il fascino del regime (1918–1925)*. 2015. Birocchi, Italo, and Loschiavo, Luca (Eds.), Roma: Roma-Tre Press.

[50] Ferrajoli, Luigi. 1999. *La cultura giuridica nell'Italia del Novecento*. Roma-Bari: Laterza, 36.

The *Relazione* pointed out the difficulty encountered in regulating infanticide due to the diverging parameters that had evolved over time. If, on the one hand, some supported the need to provide for mitigation of punishment for infanticide, on the other hand, given the upcoming implementation of the new code, others referred to the pre-meditation theory and the victim's inability to defend itself, advocating, as in the past, harsher punishments.[51]

Alfredo Rocco recalled the theory which was the basis of the aggravation of punishment for murder, on the presumption that infanticide was premeditated, a theory supported by Impallomeni[52] and others. However, this theory was not agreed upon by everyone. Carrara and Stoppato, among others, were against the presumption *in re ipsa* regarding premeditation,[53] but their observations were fiercely criticised, in particular by Calabresi who held that "escludendo sempre la premeditazione, si viene, sotto veste di teorica generale, a dar vita a una nuova presunzione che l'infanticidio non possa mai essere premeditato".[54]

The legal code introduced by Rocco rejected the idea of premeditation, as well as that of the impossibility of the victim of defending herself/himself, as a basis for more severe punishment, whereas the motive and the time frame in which the murder was carried out were stressed. The former's purpose was to avoid "mediante l'occultamento della nascita, il disonore e la vergogna che conseguono alla pubblica conoscenza del parto".[55] Such element was subjective, distinctive and differentiating the crime from any other.[56] From an objective point of view, it was important to determine the precise moment beyond which, in defense of one's honour, it was no longer possible to invoke *honoris causa* as a motive.[57]

At long last the ambiguity on which Art. 369 was based was definitely resolved: the *causa honoris* explicitly became a constitutive element of the crime and no longer merely a lessening circumstance of the *species homicidii*. Forty years of

---

[51]"Ogni qualvolta viene ripresa in esame questa materia, risorgono e si rinnovano le discrepanze che, con alterna vicenda, presenta, dal punto di vista storico, la disciplina penale concernente la uccisione dei neonati. Ancora oggi, alcuno poté autorevolmente riproporre dubbi sulla opportunità di questa disposizione che, mitigando notevolmente le pene, sembra diminuire la efficacia intimidatrice del comando, che impone di non distruggere, nei suoi albori, una vita umana. Ma io non ho creduto si potesse, in un Progetto che attribuisce la massima importanza alla valutazione dei moventi, quale indice di pericolosità del colpevole, rimettere in onore il rigore di una teoria, che volle, in ogni caso, più gravemente punito il delitto di infanticidio, partendo dai due presupposti che in esso fosse sempre a presumere il concorso della premeditazione, e che avesse a costituirsi una più energica protezione di coloro i quali non hanno ancora, da soli, alcun mezzo di difesa" (Relazione al progetto definitivo del codice penale. 1929. In *Lavori preparatori del codice penale e del codice di procedura penale* 5.2. Roma: Tipografia delle Mantellate, 370).

[52]Impallomeni 1891 (as n. 26) 170.

[53]Carrara 1872 (as n. 15) § 1214, 310–311; Stoppato 1887 (as n. 19) 70.

[54]Calabresi, Armando. 1899. *L'infanticidio (commento teorico-pratico all'art. 369 c.p.)*. Ferrara: Taddei, 39.

[55]Relazione 1929 (as n. 51) 370.

[56]Relazione 1929 (as n. 51) 370.

[57]Relazione 1929 (as n. 51) 371.

doubt were put to an end and this solution, already adopted by the Courts when the Zanardelli code was in force, was finally implemented in the new code.

It was no longer possible to misunderstand or misinterpret the code introduced by Rocco: infanticide was to be considered a self-standing offence. "Una questione che ha affaticato giuristi e interpreti, e della quale un interessante riflesso si ebbe nella discussione seguita innanzi la Commissione Ministeriale, si riferisce alla natura del delitto d'infanticidio, sostenendo taluno che esso costituisca titolo autonomo di reato, ed altri, per contro, affermando che esso non sia se non una circostanza diminuente dell'omicidio".[58] The debate continued even during the final stages of the drafting of the penal code, as can be seen in Art. 578 as it "contiene una definizione del delitto d'infanticidio assolutamente indipendente da quella dell'omicidio; il che serve a stabilire, in modo non equivoco, l'intendimento del legislatore di creare un titolo autonomo di reato".[59]

This was unanimously confirmed in doctrine[60] and even though there was a minority who found in Giuseppe Maggiore a proud supporter of harsher punishments. While it was held that no value, not even in defense of honour, could justify an action that destroyed a life and maternity, the primary manifestation of motherhood,[61] at the same time it must be pointed out that there was an obvious contradiction between the indications of the Fascist regime directed towards an increase in the population and the incomprehensible weak punishment inflicted upon those who had killed their own children, which, in turn, prevented the development of the nation. Maggiore, in particular, obstinately refused to abandon his ideals even when faced with the Rocco's argument confirming that "quantunque elevato a un titolo autonomo, l'infanticidio resta sempre, nella sua essenza, un omicidio attenuato dalla *causa honoris.* [...]. L'autonomia del reato resta alquanto discutibile. È da augurarsi che prima o poi, si ritorni a quella, che è l'unica costruzione logica, dell'omicidio scusato dall'umanità del motivo".[62]

The wording of Art. 578, under the section *Infanticidio per causa d'onore,* showed a certain discontinuity compared to the previous legislation. More specifically, the regulation indicated that "chiunque cagiona la morte di un neonato immediatamente dopo il parto, ovvero di un feto durante il parto, per salvare l'onore proprio o di un prossimo congiunto, è punito con la reclusione da tre a dieci anni. Alla stessa pena soggiacciono coloro che concorrono nel fatto al solo scopo di favorire taluna delle persone indicate nella disposizione precedente. In ogni caso, a coloro che concorrono nel fatto si applica la reclusione non inferiore a dieci anni. Non si applicano le aggravanti stabilite nell'art. 61."

---

[58]Relazione 1929 (as n. 51) 372.

[59]Relazione 1929 (as n. 51) 372.

[60]Vannini, Ottorino. 1935. *Il delitto di omicidio.* Milano: Società Editrice Libraria, 90; Manzini, Vincenzo. 1937. Delitti contro la persona. In *Trattato di diritto penale italiano secondo il codice del 1930* 8. Torino: UTET, 51.

[61]Maggiore, Giuseppe. 1961. *Diritto penale. Parte speciale: delitti e contravvenzioni* 2.2. Bologna: Zanichelli, 747.

[62]Maggiore 1961 (as n. 61) 749.

A series of new aspects, starting from the legal person actively involved in the crime, were introduced. Contrary to the Zanardelli code, the criminal offence could have been committed not only by the mother or by close relatives, but also by "anyone else" who acted with the sole aim of safeguarding his/hers own honour or that of a close relative. Art. 307 together with Art. 540[63] treated close relatives, to all legal effects, including heirs (legitimate or illegitimate), the husband, the brothers and sisters, the aunts and uncles, the nephews and nieces all on the same level.

However, this development was, in part, deceptive. Despite the wording of Art. 307 seemed inclined towards the inclusion of infanticide amongst common criminal offences, the nature of infanticide as *reato proprio* in the light of the motive of honour, couldn't be disregarded either.

The interpretation of the article and its *incipit* seemed to question the matter generically, identifying an undetermined offender. Yet, it was necessary to consider the goal of the criminal action, given that the indefinite pronoun "chiunque" (anyone) was used and referred only to those who acted with the sole aim of protecting their own honour or that of a close relative, directing their criminal action not against an obscure subject, but exclusively against the newborn child of the woman whose honour was in danger.[64] As in the Zanardelli code, the list of subjects was to be considered as compulsory. Thus, for the same reasons mentioned above, the biological father of the child or the lover of the woman were excluded from the reduced prison sentence, even if both claimed that they had acted to save her honour.

The word "*neonato*" (newborn) was used once again in the penal code substituting "infante" (infant) used in Article 369 of the 1889 code. The use of the two terms over time revealed the difficulty in identifying one which would define the passive subject of the crime in an unequivocal manner. The use of these general terms, for different reasons, created problems of interpretation. There was no doubt whatsoever regarding the non-alignment between the juridical and semantic value of the word *infante*. In fact, by law "la parola *infante* non esprime la *infanzia* in generale, ma solo un brevissimo periodo di quella, e precisamente la prima aurora della vita estrauterina".[65] The legal codes in force prior to the unification of Italy had provided a variety of linguistic solutions in this regard. The Neapolitan legal code indicated that the offense was such if the child was recently born but not yet baptized, nor its civil status registered (Art. 349); according to the code of Parma it would concern a child just born (Art. 308); in the Piedmont code it concerned a recently born child (Art. 525) and for the Este code it referred to a newborn child (Art. 351).

[63]On the equation of legitimate and illegitimate filiation, in which the relationship between relatives constituted an important element or was considered as an aggravating or mitigating circumstance in connection with the criminal offence.

[64]Pedio, Tommaso. 1954. *La soppressione del neonato per causa di onore*. Milano: Giuffrè, 106.

[65]Carrara 1872 (as n. 15) § 1212, 304.

Both the Zanardelli and Rocco codes, using different terms (*infante and neonato*, respectively), reconnected their juridical meaning to *tempus commissi delicti*, but from diverging grounds, as explained below. The provision of Art. 578 regarding the suppression of the foetus resulting in infanticide was of great importance in this regard. Long standing debates which involved both juridical as well as forensic medicine issues were resolved with the 1930 code. For the first time the juridical concept of foeticide was introduced, for a motive of honour, committed in the final phase of labour, before the final detachment from the mother's womb. The juridical explanation emerging from the trial records supplied precise indications as to the most frequent methods of suppression of the foetus: giving birth in water with the consequent risk of drowning or hitting the newborn child's head during the expulsion phase. If the foetus was suppressed during the final phase of labour it was not considered as an abortion, which was understood as exclusively pertaining to the interruption of the physiological process of the pregnancy; neither was it considered murder or infanticide, as the foetus had still not begun living independently from the womb.

The regulatory gap existing prior to the Rocco code was overcome with different solutions. If, on one hand, some wanted to avoid the impunity implied in the lack of a specific provisions related to foeticide in the Zanardelli code, deemed unacceptable in the light of the participatory nature involved in the abortion and infanticide,[66] on the other hand Carrara pointed out the danger of getting involved in a debate exclusively focused on the physiological aspect of the crime. In fact, "sbarazzarsi da simili ambagi" was fundamental, as it was "una necessità adeguare in regola il nascente al nato, salvo le debite cautele nel giudizio pratico sulla realtà della vita".[67]

A good part of the interpretations in doctrine had forcefully resolved the question posed in the provisions of Article 369 by equating foeticide to infanticide, thus including the killing of the child[68] yet to be born. Further acceptance was found in jurisprudence, whereby "il legislatore spiega la sua protezione e difende la vita dell'uomo sino al momento della fecondazione" and it was further specified that the killing of a foetus at the termination of the pregnancy and when the expulsion of the child was spontaneous, was to be considered infanticide.[69] However, contrasting opinions held that the woman, in this way, would be punished even more severely compared to those who had eliminated the foetus only a few hours, or weeks from the birth, or after a longer than usual pregnancy, claiming that such induced

[66]Stoppato 1887 (as n. 19) 128.

[67]Carrara 1872 (as n. 15) § 1225, 325–327.

[68]Impallomeni 1899 (as n. 26) 544–550; Balestrini 1888 (as n. 29) 242; Salmonj, Giacomo. 1875. *L'infanticidio ed il Nuovo Codice Penale pel Regno d'Italia. Osservazioni*. Roma: Tipografia del Popolo romano, 17, n. 1.

[69]Cassazione. 2 giugno 1891. *Annali della Giurisprudenza Italiana* 25 (1891): 195–196.

abortion would be punished according to Art. 381 with a prison sentence from 1 to 4 years.[70]

The new vision of Art. 578 clearly emerges in the light of these further clarifications. In this regard, a Central European regulation that finally reached Italy's most recent legal Codes should be recalled, namely section 139 of the Austrian penal code of 1803 equating the suppression of the infant during labour to that of the child already born ("la madre che nel parto toglie la vita al proprio figlio [...]").

Therefore, infanticide in the Rocco code acquired a clearer independent configuration compared to other types of criminal offences against living persons.[71] Once again, the *Relazione* emphasized the changes that had been adopted. The leveling of the suppression of the child being born and that of the newly born infant aimed at putting an end to the "dispute medico-legali sul trattamento penale di questo fatto, che, in quanto compiuto durante il parto su infanti tuttora viventi di vita fetale, non potrebbe rientrare nella nozione del delitto di procurato aborto, la obbiettività del quale è costituita dalla interruzione del processo fisiologico della gravidanza, né, sulla scorta del vigente art. 369, potrebbe parimenti esser compreso nel titolo d'infanticidio, che presuppone un infante nato vivo. Da molti si dubitò della opportunità di incriminare il feticidio, attesa la grave difficoltà di stabilire, attraverso una delicata indagine non scevra da incertezze ed equivoci, la capacità del feto alla vita extra-uterina".[72]

However, it must be further confirmed that both the crimes of foeticide and infanticide received the same treatment only if the motives were identical, that is in defense of honour, leaving the question of the qualification of infanticide committed for different reasons[73] still open.

Once again, this grey area was the basis for the development of contrasting theories, since the penal code did not envisage foeticide as a self-standing offence. However, it was possible to strongly back the non-punishment of foeticide committed for reasons other than the motive of honour. According to some scholars it could not be treated as murder which assumed that the child was born and thus detached from the mother's womb, nor under the category of abortion, since it would take place spontaneously and no violation of the pregnancy had been

---

[70] Crivellari 1896 (as n. 47) 829; Puglia, Ferdinando. 1885. Del reato di infanticidio. In *Studi critici di diritto criminale*. Napoli: E. Anfossi, 178–179; Arena 1896 (as n. 41) 23.

[71] Fiore 1971 (as n. 5) 396.

[72] "Ma ho ritenuto che ciò non possa, da solo, costituire argomento valido e sufficiente per conservare una manifesta alcuna nella tutela penale, perpetuando quelle difficoltà di applicazione, che inducevano, per le incoercibili esigenze della pratica, a improprie equiparazioni". Relazione 1929 (as n. 51) 371.

[73] "Va subito osservato che, se la soluzione adottata nell'art. 578 risolve il problema della qualificazione agli effetti penali del feticidio per causa d'onore, resta nondimeno la questione se in via generale il feticidio, non commesso per salvare l'onore, realizzi la fattispecie dell'omicidio" (Ambrosetti, Enrico Maria. 1992. *L'infanticidio e la legge penale*. Padova: Cedam, 27).

committed. Very few scholars were prepared to accept this "Rigorosa interpretazione, se pur ingiusta".[74]

A similar view repelled most of the scholars who held that "anche il così detto feto, nascente vivo, è "uomo", passibile di omicidio, di guisa che, se nell'uccisione di esso non ricorrono gli altri requisiti dell'Art. 578, è applicabile il titolo comune di omicidio [...]. Il termine "feto" è quindi usato impropriamente, perché il nascente vivo non è più feto, né in senso biologico, né in senso giuridico, bensì *persona*; qualità che si acquista per il solo fatto di nascere vivo. Se anche si volesse ritenere necessaria l'espulsione dall'utero, questa è già avvenuta durante il parto, quantunque il nascente non sia ancora staccato interamente dal corpo della madre".[75] Therefore foeticide committed for a reason different from *causa honoris* would be punished according to the legal provisions indicated in Art. 575 qualifying it as murder. Furthermore, the 1930 code identified *tempus commissi delicti* not with the already confirmed terms of 5 days for the registration of the child's birth, but as from the moment of delivery, which meant returning to laws enforced in Austria and Tuscany.

Only if the crime had been committed during delivery or immediately afterwards—thus translating into foeticide and infanticide, respectively—it was possible to ascribe the offence to a state of confusion or bewilderment typical of those who finds themselves facing the tragic dilemma of being exposed to public disdain or to eliminate an innocent creature. The provisions regarded, for the most part, the legal position of the mother: the law recognized that the experience of giving birth affected the mental state of the mother, causing psychological imbalance, which determined, according to a minority, but not for this reason less important, an alteration of the soundness of her mind equivalent to a partial infirmity, as per Article 89.[76]

Yet, this latter interpretation was not considered acceptable. It was further confirmed that infanticide could, indeed, be committed by someone who was affected by partial mental infirmity; yet, the state of mind referred to in Art. 578 could not always and necessarily exclude or lessen the offender's responsibility.

In its ruling dated 31 May 1937 the Supreme Court held that "in tema d'infanticidio il turbamento psichico, che rappresenta uno degli elementi fondamentali per cui, alla madre che ha ucciso la sua creatura, possono applicarsi sanzioni più miti [..], non può confondersi, ai fini dell'applicabilità dell'art. 578, con la minorata capacità d'intendere o di volere derivante da infermità mentale".[77]

[74]Pannain, Remo. 1937a. L'uccisione del feto nascente. *Il Nuovo Diritto* 14: 514; Pannain, Remo. 1938. Feticidio. In *Nuovo Digesto Italiano* 5. Torino: UTET, 1086–1087; Pannain 1965 (as n. 5) 887–888.

[75]Manzini 1937 (as n. 60) 62–63.

[76]Cassazione. 27 maggio 1940. *Giustizia penale* 47 (1941): 138.

[77]Cassazione. 31 maggio 1937. *Giustizia penale* 44.2 (1938): 541–542.

The wording "*immediatamente dopo il parto*" (immediately after birth) led to further complications: the criteria on which to ascertain whether the time between the delivery and the murder was sufficiently brief enough to justify application of Art. 578 were left entirely to the discretion of the judge. According to the *Relazione* "Trascorso qualche tempo, si quieterà la eccitazione dolorosa, e la uccisione appare non più frutto di un violento impulso, ma di meditato e freddo calcolo [...]. Occorre determinare il momento oltre il quale, presumendosi divulgata la conoscenza della nascita, non più sia ammissibile la possibilità di una difesa dell'onore, in quanto ormai si sarebbe pubblicamente manifestata la vergogna a cui il colpevole vorrebbe sottrarsi".[78]

Rocco's words seemed like an invitation to cling to a vague regulation with an indication of a precise time limit, leaving it up to doctrine and legislative practice to define the methods with which to combine the turmoil the mother was experiencing with the fear of dishonour and the disclosure of the birth.

Doctrine and jurisprudence responded to this appeal with a flexible interpretation of the concept of immediacy. It did not necessarily coincide with the hours following the birth, in a sort of *in flagrante delicto*, or the following days when the birth of an illegitimate child could still be concealed. In fact, the more lexical rather than conceptual amendment introduced with Art. 578 was misleading, since the criteria adopted referred to the parameters established by the Zanardelli code, tying the possibility of saving one's honour to the non-disclosure of the birth. The assessment of the mother's physiological and mental condition was indeed an essential requirement, but at the same time it was connected to a time frame.

In order to establish whether infanticide had been committed, the murder had to occur whilst the guilty party was still in a state of acute anxiety deriving from the birth of an illegitimate child, but having still the possibility of concealing the illegal affair detrimental to her honour.[79] In fact "la locuzione 'immediatamente dopo il parto' usata dal legislatore nell'art. 578 c.p. [...] non comporta soltanto un accertamento di carattere cronologico, ma richiede altresì l'accertamento correlativo diretto a stabilire se detto elemento cronologico corrisponda all'insorgere o al ragionevole perdurare nel soggetto attivo, di quel particolare stato psichico (esasperazione, angoscia ecc.) derivante dal verificarsi del paventato evento".[80] Therefore, according to the judges, the requisite of immediacy existed as per art. 578 in case of suppression of a newborn child which took place 2 days after the birth but before the news of the newborn child had been made known.[81]

On the contrary, "si ha omicidio e non infanticidio nel caso in cui il neonato sia stato ucciso tre giorni dopo il parto, quando era anche stato denunciato allo stato civile"[82] or in the case in which the mother drowned her own child 8 days after the

[78]Relazione 1929 (as n. 51) 371.

[79]Cassazione. 2 gennaio 1939. *Giustizia penale* 45 (1939): 747.

[80]Cassazione. 27 gennaio 1953. *Rivista penale* 58 (1953): 450.

[81]Cassazione. 6 marzo 1946. *Rivista penale* 51 (1946): 920.

[82]Cassazione. 15 febbraio 1935. *Giustizia penale* 41 (1935): 1153.

birth, when news of the pregnancy and the birth were known within the family environment, but also by the public.[83] In this regard, Maggiore pointed out that if the murder took place immediately after the birth, the crime should be considered "non nel senso rigoroso di "senza intervallo di tempo", bensì nel senso relativo di termine breve, da valutarsi di volta in volta dal magistrato e, comunque, mai oltre il quinto giorno dalla nascita".[84]

However, if the birth was in some way or other made known, the question of saving the mother's honour was no longer necessary. In fact, the suppression of the newborn child was considered murder, as indicated by the Supreme Court in its ruling dated 17th November 1947: "la parola immediatamente esprime la necessità di una successione temporale tra il parto e la consumazione del delitto, restringendola in un periodo di tempo, in cui effettivamente esiste la necessità della difesa del proprio onore [...]. Trascorso qualche tempo dal parto, l'uccisione del neonato, anziché determinata da quel sgomento o turbamento psichico di cui si è parlato, appare come conseguenza di un calcolo freddo e premeditato".[85]

Even the wording "*per salvare l'onore proprio o di un prossimo congiunto*" (to save one's own honour or that of a close relative) raised doubts regarding the possibility of other people being involved. It appears clear that the provision was primarily aiming at protecting the honour of the mother and that the close relatives could not put forward the scope of saving their own by extension: they had to be charged with the crime of infanticide only if they had acted exclusively to save the mother's honour.[86]

A possible legal extension to the husband was less obvious. Such a dilemma had already emerged with the Zanardelli code. Pannain offered a rather narrow interpretation of the law in this regard, holding that the only applicable honor in this regard was that of the mother.[87] Part of the law scholars, however, refers to the idea of a *family honour*, which allowed the husband, in the case of *illegitimate conception* to claim this honor for himself.[88] Subsequently, under Art. 578, the offence could have been committed by *anyone* to save the honour of either one of the married couple or the honour of both of them: the persons involved besides the mother and her closest relatives, were relations or persons connected to the husband, who were not close relatives of the wife (for example, the uncle or husband's nephew).[89]

This argument resulted in the possibility of invoking *causa honoris* even if the mother had died whilst in labour, as infanticide was justified by protecting the

[83]Cassazione. 27 marzo 1942. *Giustizia penale* 49 (1943): 200.

[84]Maggiore, Giuseppe. 1938. *Principi di diritto penale. Parte speciale*. Bologna: Zanichelli, 626.

[85]*Rivista Italiana di Diritto Penale* 1 n.s. (1948): 150–152.

[86]Pannain, Remo. 1937. Infanticidio per causa d'onore. In *Nuovo Digesto Italiano* 6. Torino: UTET, 1062.

[87]"La madre, la quale, per salvare l'onore proprio, e il prossimo congiunto, che, per salvare l'onore della madre, cagiona la morte ecc. [...]. L'onore rilevante per la *causa honoris* è soltanto quello della madre" (Pannain 1965 (as n. 5) 885).

[88]Fiore 1971 (as n. 5) 399.

[89]Pedio 1954 (as n. 64) 112–113 and 115.

honour of the husband.[90] Obviously, those who considered the cause of honour applicable only to the mother were of a different opinion. According to Pannain, honour is not applicable to a deceased person, as death suppresses the moral personality besides the physical body; hence, in this particular case, the *causa sceleris* was not valid.[91] Pannain, however, later modified his argument amending his position.[92]

Compared to the previous legislation, the regulation regarding the involvement of other persons was modified: the punishment envisaged in Art. 578 was applicable when it involved the complicity of one of the persons indicated by the provisions with the aim of facilitating the crime.

The new and complex regulation introduced in 1930 put an end to the ambiguity of the Zanardelli law, which as we have seen above, derived from an ambiguous definition of the crime as self-standing or resting on circumstantial evidence. According to Art. 578, the persons involved, not directly related to the family and even with no honour to safeguard, but whose actions were aimed at the same or a different scope so as to prevent the mother's dishonor, would not be subject to the ordinary regulation for involvement in murder as per articles 110 et seq. of the penal code. Art. 578, distinguished the punishment according to motive, identifying two categories of persons and without modifying the nature of the offence. Those who were involved in the crime with the only scope of supporting any of the persons standing trial, had to be convicted for the same offence and consequently subject to the same punishment.[93] In other words, they would be considered as contributing to the crime with the same willful misconduct of the *intraneus*; thus, with the same awareness and willingness to contribute to the preparation or carrying out of infanticide for the sake of honour.[94] However, on the other hand, there were those who although aware of taking part in a murder were acting for their own reasons (namely money, revenge, etc.) and anyway not exclusively with the scope of supporting the intraneus. Said persons would be accused of the same crime offence but the punishment envisaged in this case would be imprisonment for no less than 10 years. The same punishment was applicable for the *intranei* involved in the crime with a different scope than that of honour.

The connection between the two legislations was clearly the question of honour, identified with the reputation of the woman in society and not as the woman's subjective perception of her moral dignity, as provided for in the 1930 code, The subjective and objective meaning of honour was clearly outlined in the *Relazione*: "l'onore che, in senso lato, rappresenta un bene individuale immateriale, protetto

---

[90]Pedio 1954 (as n. 64) 115–116; Fiore 1971 (as n. 5) 399.

[91]Pannain 1937 (as n. 86) 1057.

[92]Pannain 1965 (as n. 5) 889.

[93]This, thus, does not mean that "in concreto, a loro dovrà essere inflitta una quantità di pena identica a quella che viene inflitta alla madre o al prossimo congiunto" (Pannain 1965 (as n. 5) 886).

[94]Fiore 1971 (as n. 5) 399.

dalla legge per consentire all'individuo la esplicitazione della propria personalità morale, racchiude in sé una duplice nozione. Inteso in senso soggettivo, esso si identifica con il sentimento che ciascuno ha della propria dignità morale, e designa quella somma di valori che l'individuo attribuisce a sé stesso [...]. Inteso, invece, in senso oggettivo è la stima e l'opinione che gli altri hanno su di noi; rappresenta cioè il patrimonio morale che deriva dall'altrui considerazione, e che, con termine chiaramene comprensivo, si definisce reputazione".[95]

The *Relazione*, though, created some confusion, in that it led to envisage in a case of infanticide the existence of a real state of necessity as prescribed in Art. 54. More specifically, "il timore del disonore crea una specie di stato di necessità che, nella sua nozione, importa, oltreché un contenuto essenzialmente psicologico, anche limiti obbiettivi che ne circoscrivono la applicazione".[96]

Ottorino Vannini had thought about the possibility of excuse or justification for mothers guilty of infanticide,[97] as per Art. 54. However, this was excluded on the basis of a textual consideration. The state of necessity, according to the law, called for a moment of danger involuntarily caused by the offender. As regards the crime in question, if the danger was liable to create serious implications for the honour of the woman, the hypotheses of an illegitimate but consensual sexual relationship were difficult to support as involuntary. The theory of the state of necessity could, according to Vannini, be applicable if the woman had been victim of a rape or "*involontariamente fecondata*" (had been made pregnant against her wishes): an appealing assumption which was bound to remain an isolated case in the general interpretation of the law.

The question of honour is once again connected to the sphere of sexuality,[98] within the limits of a patriarchal mentality and a pedagogic concept of woman miles away from being democratic: therefore "il valore della verginità e l'immoralità della trasgressione sessuale prima del matrimonio, difendendo così la famiglia legittima ed il modello della maternità possibile solo per le coniugate"[99] was further confirmed. An *illegitimate pregnancy*, besides degrading the woman and her reputation, would have a negative effect on the child itself, who would carry the disgrace of his birth for the rest of his life. The dishonour was exclusively caused by the woman, without any possibility of attributing the responsibility whatsoever to seducers or lovers. Men, in their positions as fathers, husbands, brothers, would benefit from a lesser punishment envisaged for infanticide should they reinstate the lost family honour, even with an extreme action.

The prevailing interpretation in doctrine insisted on the fact that the disapproval of society (and therefore the loss of honour) was exclusively the consequence of an

---

[95]Relazione 1929 (as n. 51) 402.

[96]Relazione 1929 (as n. 51) 370.

[97]Vannini, Ottorino. 1958. *Delitti contro la vita e la incolumità individuale*. Milano: Giuffrè.

[98]Pannain 1937 (as n. 86) 1062.

[99]Di Bello, Giulia and Meringolo, Patrizia. 1997. *Il rifiuto della maternità. L'infanticidio in Italia dall'Ottocento ai giorni nostri*. Pisa: ETS, 91.

illegitimate sexual relationship, which created perplexity in those who considered a similar explanation as devoid of textual grounds, but was the result of a stretched interpretation rather than a critical examination of the regulation, which had clearly excluded any reference to the illegitimate *status* of the newborn child.

The references made to the Zanardelli code once again re-emerged. This *déjà vu* seemed to demonstrate a prevailing doctrinal interpretation more than pure legislative orientations. Manzini could, therefore, claim "la scusa [sott. dell'onore] è ammissibile in rapporto ad ogni donna, che non sia già conosciuta come madre illegittima o altrimenti diffamata per immoralità sessuali. Quindi essa può applicarsi tanto rispetto alla donna mantenutasi sinora onesta sotto ogni aspetto, quanto alla donna disonesta o immorale per colpe diverse dalle colpe sessuali: non quindi alla meretrice, all'adultera già condannata o notoria, a colei che notoriamente procreò altri figli illegittimi, ecc".[100] As in the past, the motive of saving the honour was not acceptable in the cases involving a woman already sexually dishonoured. "Naturalmente, se l'infanticida, pur avendo un passato disonorevole, ignora che esso sia notorio e agisce nella ragionevole opinione che, sopprimendo il neonato, potrà evitare il disonore, si deve egualmente applicare l'Art. 578".[101]

A different awareness of the issue at hand emerged in the 1950s. The Supreme Court stated that it is not always the case that "una donna la quale abbia avuto un figlio naturale, sia per questo soltanto divenuta una donna perduta; come del pari non è detto che una donna la quale abbia una volta mancato all'onore femminile, non abbia mai potuto cercare di rimediarsi e non vi sia anche riuscita, rendendosi di nuovo degna della considerazione sociale".[102] Furthermore, "una filiazione illegittima anteriore alla soppressione del nuovo nato non è di ostacolo alla sussistenza della causa d'onore, ai fini del delitto previsto dall'art. 578 c.p., quando alla prima nascita sia seguito un periodo di riabilitazione morale e purché si agisca col fine e non con il pretesto di salvare l'onore".[103]

However, a reforming provision was eventually implemented only with law no. 42 dated 5 August 1981. The amended form of Art. 578 indicated the mother as the main offender "che cagiona la morte del proprio neonato immediatamente dopo il parto, o del feto durante il parto, quando il fatto è determinato da condizioni di abbandono materiale e morale connesse al parto", thus involving society's responsibility in the offender's action. Society has, in fact, the responsibility of guaranteeing the fulfillment of individual rights, by supporting unmarried mothers in overcoming the solitude and indifference which they have always been subjected to. The concept of state of neglect is dominant in the criminal offence at hand, even though its role still gives way to diverging interpretations as regards the subjective

---

[100] Manzini 1937 (as n. 60) 48–50.

[101] Fiore 1971 (as n. 5) 398.

[102] Cassazione. 26 maggio 1951. *Giustizia penale* 57 (1952): 128.

[103] Cassazione. 9 aprile 1953. *Archivio penale* 9 (1953): 485.

or objective nature of the crime, the verification methods and its relationship with guilt.[104]

As mentioned earlier, Art. 578, in its original version, even in its attempt at improving the previous regulation, continued to point to honour as the constitutive element of infanticide, in an interpretation and with a "sensitivity", which evolved over the following years, subsequent to the implementation of the legal code and along often unsatisfactory or inadequate changes in society.

For different reasons, infanticides had enjoyed a sort of lenient treatment over a long period of time. Research demonstrates that the number of acquittals was around half of the total number of the women prosecuted and that the moral attitude which the women accused of murdering their own newborn children were subjected to, was inspired by pity. Some were acquitted regardless of the clear and convincing evidence of guilt.

Acquittals were often the result of the perception that the offenders had been incited to commit the crime by an almost irresistible force. Moreover, honour was considered "bene suscettibile di scambio e di reintegrazione":[105] if it was lost, it could be reinstated by means of a criminal act intended to remove the evidence of the dishonorable conduct.

The offence committed by the woman was seen as a sort of redemption and the result "di due cause concomitanti ciascuna delle quali—la fragilità femminile da un lato, la difesa dell'onore dall'altro—si doveva rivelare capace di suscitare non solo compassione ma anche sentimenti di ambigua solidarietà".[106]

The lawmaker thus laid the basis for a social evaluation prior to a juridical one. A newborn child, often illegitimate, and honour were both being balanced on the scales of Justice. Inevitably, the latter relentlessly continued to be of prime importance: social redemption and the attempt at recovering "moral virginity" paradoxically were worth the sacrifice of an innocent creature, whose life was despised right from its birth in consideration of the unhappy existence that was to follow. The illegitimate children were the pariah of society and represented an expense—especially if they were abandoned in public institutions—or a cancer, in consideration of the arguments put forward by the Positive School who saw them as naturally and biologically bound to an existence of idleness and crime.[107]

The crime of infanticide committed for motive of honour "per la pena edittale assai lieve e quasi mai scontata per l'incidenza di diminuenti largamente concesse e per la prassi dell'indulto aveva portato a conseguenze ormai sentite dalla coscienza sociale come incongrui e aberranti". The regulation was thus considered as "un

[104]Mantovani, Ferrando. 1995. *Diritto penale. Parte speciale. Delitti contro la persona* 1. Padova: Cedam, 168.

[105]Selmini 1987 (as n. 8) 35.

[106]Prosperi 2015 (as n. 1) 80.

[107]Garlati, Loredana. 2012. Delinquenti nati. Minori ed illegittimi criminali nell'Italia di fine Ottocento. *La Corte d'Assise* 3: 403–428.

ramo secco dell'ordinamento destinato inevitabilmente a cadere".[108] Yet, it took 50 years and a lawmaker incorporating this change of general consensus into the new regulation.

References

Sources

1815. *Codice penale universale austriaco coll'appendice delle più recenti norme generali.* Milano: I. R. Stamperia.
Cassazione. 2 giugno 1891. *Annali della Giurisprudenza Italiana* 25 (1891): 195–196.
Cassazione. 7 ottobre 1891. *Il foro penale* 1 (1892): 127.
Cassazione. 15 gennaio 1892. *Rivista Penale* 35 (1892): 297–298.
Cassazione. 27 gennaio 1892. *Rivista penale* 35 (1892): 397.
Cassazione. 9 gennaio 1895. *Annali della Giurisprudenza Italiana* 29 (1895): 66.
Cassazione. 6 marzo 1896, *Rivista Penale* 4 (1896): 518.
Cassazione. 24 agosto 1897. *Giustizia penale* 3 (1897): 1161.
Cassazione. 11 gennaio 1899. *Rivista Penale* 49 (1899): 422.
Cassazione. 30 gennaio 1899. *Il Foro italiano* 24 (1899): 171–172.
Cassazione. 17 ottobre 1900. *Monitore dei tribunali* 42 (1901): 458.
Cassazione. 19 luglio 1911. *Giurisprudenza Italiana* 6 (1911): 320.
Cassazione. 15 febbraio 1935. *Giustizia penale* 41 (1935): 1153.
Cassazione. 31 maggio 1937. *Giustizia penale* 44.2 (1938): 541–542.
Cassazione. 2 gennaio 1939. *Giustizia penale* 45 (1939): 747.
Cassazione. 27 maggio 1940. *Giustizia penale* 47 (1941): 138.
Cassazione. 27 marzo 1942. *Giustizia penale* 49 (1943): 200.
Cassazione. 6 marzo 1946. *Rivista penale* 51 (1946): 920.
Cassazione. 17 novembre 1947. *Rivista Italiana di Diritto Penale* 1 n.s. (1948): 150–152.
Cassazione. 26 maggio 1951. *Giustizia penale* 57 (1952): 128.
Cassazione. 9 aprile 1953. *Archivio penale* 9 (1953): 485.
Cassazione. 27 gennaio 1953. *Rivista penale* 58 (1953): 450.
1929. Relazione al progetto definitivo del codice penale. In *Lavori preparatori del codice penale e del codice di procedura penale* 5.2. Roma: Tipografia delle Mantellate.

Literature

Ambrosetti, E. M. (1992). *L'infanticidio e la legge penale.* Padova: Cedam.
Ambrosoli, F. (1857). *Studi sul codice penale toscano confrontato specialmente coll'austriaco.* Mantova: Negretti.
Amore, A. (2011). *L'infanticidio. Analisi della fattispecie normativa e prospettive di riforma.* Padova: Cedam.
Antolisei, F. (2008). *Manuale di diritto penale. Parte speciale*, 1. Milano: Giuffrè.

[108]Antolisei, Francesco. 2008. *Manuale di diritto penale. Parte speciale* 1. Milano: Giuffrè, 59.

Arena, P. (1896). *L'infanticidio per ragion d'onore: studio giuridico-sociologico*. Napoli: de Angelis & Bellisario.

Balestrini, R. (1888). *Aborto, infanticidio ed esposizione d'infante*. Torino: Bocca.

Beccaria, C. (1984). *Dei delitti e delle pene*. Firpo, Luigi and Francioni, Gianni (Eds.). Milano: Mediobanca.

Cadoppi, A. (2001). Il "modello" rivale del code penale. Le "forme piuttosto didattiche" del codice penale universale austriaco del 1803. In *Codice penale universale austriaco (1803)*, Vinciguerra, Sergio (Ed.). Padova: Cedam.

Calabresi, A. (1899). *L'infanticidio (commento teorico-pratico all'art. 369 c.p.)*. Ferrara: Taddei.

Carfora, F. (1927). Infanticidio. In *Digesto Italiano* 13.1 (pp. 663–726). Torino: UTET.

Carrara, F. (1872). *Programma del corso di diritto criminale. Parte speciale* 1. Lucca: Giusti.

Crivellari, G. (but Suman, Giovanni). (1896). *Il codice penale per il Regno d'Italia*, 6. Torino: UTET, 829.

Di Bello, G., & Meringolo, P. (1997). *Il rifiuto della maternità. L'infanticidio in Italia dall'Ottocento ai giorni nostri*. Pisa: ETS.

Ferrajoli, L. (1999). *La cultura giuridica nell'Italia del Novecento*. Roma-Bari: Laterza.

Fiore, C. (1971). Infanticidio. In *Enciclopedia del diritto* 21 (pp. 391–402). Milano: Giuffrè.

Garlati, L. (2002). *Nella disuguaglianza la giustizia. Pietro Mantegazza e il codice penale autriaco (1816)*. Milano: Giuffrè.

Garlati, L. (2012a). La fine dell'innocenza. L'infanticidio nella disciplina dell'Italia post unitaria. *Corte d'Assise 1*, 17–74.

Garlati, L. (2012b). Delinquenti nati. Minori ed illegittimi criminali nell'Italia di fine Ottocento. *La Corte d'Assise 3*, 403–428.

I giuristi e il fascino del regime (1918-1925). (2015). I. Birocchi & L. Loschiavo (Eds.), Roma: Roma-Tre Press.

Impallomeni, G. B. (1889). I delitti contro la persona. In *Completo trattato teorico e pratico di diritto penale secondo il codice unico del Regno d'Italia* 2.2 (pp. 289–290). Milano: Vallardi.

Impallomeni, G. B. (1892). Il titolo del reato per gli effetti della competenza. *Rivista penale 35*, 1–24.

Impallomeni, G. B. (1899). *L'omicidio nel diritto penale*. Torino: UTET.

Maggiore, G. (1938). *Principi di diritto penale. Parte speciale* . Bologna: Zanichelli.

Maggiore, G. (1961). *Diritto penale. Parte speciale: delitti e contravvenzioni* 2.2. Bologna: Zanichelli.

Majno, L. (1894). *Commento al codice penale italiano* 2. Verona: D. Tedeschi.

Mantovani, F. (1995). *Diritto penale. Parte speciale. Delitti contro la persona* 1. Padova: Cedam.

Manzini, V. (1937). Delitti contro la persona. In *Trattato di diritto penale italiano secondo il codice del 1930* 8. Torino: UTET.

Mellusi, V. (1897). *La madre delinquente (studio di psicologia morbosa)*. Roma: E. Loescher.

Merzagora, I. (1992). Infanticidio. In *Digesto delle discipline penalistiche* 6 (pp. 392–396). Torino: UTET.

Pannain, R. (1937a). L'uccisione del feto nascente. *Il Nuovo Diritto 14*, 514.

Pannain, R. (1937b). Infanticidio per causa d'onore. In *Nuovo Digesto Italiano* 6 (p. 1062). Torino: UTET.

Pannain, R. (1938). Feticidio. In *Nuovo Digesto Italiano* 5 (pp. 1086–1087). Torino: UTET.

Pannain, R. (1965). Omicidio (diritto penale). In *Novissimo Digesto Italiano* 11 (pp. 884–891). Torino: UTET.

Pedio, T. (1954). *La soppressione del neonato per causa di onore*. Milano: Giuffrè.

Perroni-Ferranti, G. (1879). *Pagine sparse. Studi di diritto criminale e di rito civile*. Messina: Capra.

Pessina, E. (1883). *Elementi di diritto penale* 2. Napoli: Marghieri di Guis.

Pestalozzi, J. H. (1927). Über Gesetzgebung und Kindermord. In *Pestalozzis Samtliche Werke* (pp. 1–181). Berlin-Leipzig: Walter de Gruyter.

Pestalozzi, J. H. (1999). *Sull'infanticidio* (trans. G. di Bello). Firenze: La Nuova Italia.

Pinto, M. (1895–96). *Infanticidio (art. 369 cod. pen.)*. Campobasso: G. e N. Colitti.

Poma, A. (1834). *Dizionario anatomico-medico-legale*. Padova: Minerva.
Prosperi, A. (2015). *Dare l'anima. Storia di un infanticidio*. Torino: Einaudi.
Puglia, F. (1885). Del reato di infanticidio. In *Studi critici di diritto criminale* (pp. 178–179). Napoli: E. Anfossi.
Puglia, F. (1905). I delitti contro la persona. In *Trattato di diritto penale* 6 (p. 200). Milano: Vallardi.
Sighele, S. (1899). Sull'infanticidio. *Archivio giuridico 42*, 177–209.
Selmini, R. (1987). *Profili di uno studio storico sull'infanticidio. Esame di 31 processi per infanticidio giudicati dalla Corte d'Assise di Bologna dal 1880 al 1913*. Milano: Giuffrè.
Radicati, A. (2003). *Dissertazione filosofica sulla morte*. Cavallo, Tomaso ed. and trans. Pisa: ed. ETS.
Romagnosi, G. (1791). *Genesi del diritto penale*. Pavia: San Salvatore.
Salmonj, G. (1875). *L'infanticidio ed il Nuovo Codice Penale pel Regno d'Italia. Osservazioni*. Roma: Tipografia del Popolo romano.
Spallanzani, A. (1931). *I reati di infanticidio e di procurato aborto secondo le statistiche giudiziarie italiane*. Roma: Istituto Poligrafico dello Stato.
Stoppato, A. (1887). *Infanticidio e procurato aborto*. Verona-Padova: Drucker e Tedeschi.
Vannini, O. (1935). *Il delitto di omicidio*. Milano: Società Editrice Libraria.
Vannini, O. (1958). *Delitti contro la vita e la incolumità individuale*. Milano: Guffrè.
Ziino, G. (1872). *Compendio di medicina legale in trenta lezioni secondo le leggi dello Stato e i più recenti progressi della Scienza*. Napoli: Pasquale.

Children of a Lesser God. The Legalized Exploitation of Child Labour as Revealed by the Liberal Era Judicial Record (Late 19th—Early 20th Century)

Filippo Rossi

Abstract In this chapter, the author explores the legal treatment of children employed in factories from the second half of the 19th century to the early 20th century (the so-called Liberal Era). To do so, he will examine the legislative record (ranging from the first bills proposed on the issue to the reforms of 1886, 1902, 1907 and 1910); the legal doctrine of the time, which essentially legitimized "the legalized exploitation" of about 10 % of the population under the age of 15 (without counting figures that were left 'off the books'); jurisprudence (both civil and penal), who made the bigger steps forward, fighting for children right's recognition, such as a limited working hours and breaks. Only an in-depth look will suggest that, still at the outbreak of World War I, the legal system as a whole suffers from the same disease of the past: insufficient resources for inspection and oversight, lack of clarity and imprecise norms. This situation, in other words, can legitimately be considered a 'legalized exploitation'. The only way to understand this problem is to accept an underlying truth: in the time period examined in the present paper, Italy—unfortunately—had no choice but to resort to young labourers. Given the economic and social hardship of the time, children work was justified as a 'necessary evil'. So, in the brutal transition from the home to the plant, the 'rule of the home' gave way to the rules of the factory, which were just as 'domestic' and brusque.

F. Rossi (✉)
University of Milan, Via Festa del Perdono 7, 20122 Milan, Italy
e-mail: filippo.rossi@unimi.it

M.G. di Renzo Villata (ed.), *Family Law and Society in Europe from the Middle Ages to the Contemporary Era*, Studies in the History of Law and Justice 5,
DOI 10.1007/978-3-319-42289-3_12

1 Introduction

In his 1865 review of *La Medicina del pauperismo* by Antonio de Petris, Karl Mittermeier expressed particular appreciation for the section dedicated to "serious issues regarding the importance of labour".[1]

In light of such praise, one might have expected a modern book that acted as a forerunner in facing up to the scourge of child labour. Yet in its over 400 pages, which went from sharply criticizing "the aberration of socialism" to hoping for reforms in compulsory education, the topic of children in factories appeared in just one passage, wherein the author notes how alongside young pupils "live those who have already started working in factories".[2] This was a clear demonstration of the indifference of an entire society, jurists included.

The year 1865 was important for Italy. Legal unification had finally been achieved after the political unification of 1861. Yet this Italy was struggling with a seemingly overwhelming modernity, and there were many issues to resolve. Economically speaking, "almost everything was still to be done",[3] and very few people were concerned with child labour, despite the fact that the phenomenon was well-documented at the time.

In fact, according to early censuses, about 320,000 children had been taken from needy families and sent to slave away on assembly lines and suffocate in mines: this amounted to 10 % of the population between the ages of 9 and 15, without counting figures that were left 'off the books'.[4]

In the face of such misery, it was of little importance that the Civil Code for the Kingdom of Italy—which had been enacted in that fateful 1865—called for both parents "to maintain, raise, and educate their children" (article 138). As it was difficult to reconcile these two essential qualities of paternal power, it would be societal reasons and family survival that crushed the capabilities and aspirations of young Italians. Hunger drove families to send their children to work, and at most,

[1]Mittermaier, Karl Joseph Anton. 1866. Sui nuovi lavori pubblicati in Italia relativamente alle scienze giuridiche (trans. Marcello Noli). *Monitore dei Tribunali* 7: 627.

[2]De Petris, Antonio. 1865. *La medicina del pauperismo. Studi economici.* Venezia: Naratovich, 224.

[3]Rossi, Alessandro. 1876. Di una proposta di legge sul lavoro dei fanciulli e delle donne nelle fabbriche. *Nuova Antologia di scienze, lettere ed arti* 31.1: 168.

[4]For example, see *Censimento della popolazione del Regno d'Italia (31 dicembre 1881).* 1882. Roma: Tipografia Fratelli Centenari; Monteleone, Giulio. 1974. La legislazione sociale al parlamento italiano. La legge del 1886 sul lavoro dei fanciulli. *Movimento operaio e socialista* 20.1: 277; Castronovo, Valerio. 2006. *Storia economica d'Italia. Dall'Ottocento ai giorni nostri. Nuova edizione accresciuta.* Torino: Einaudi, 3–105.

the courts would intervene in the more delicate issues that might have arisen from such a situation.[5]

Apart from that, there were no social norms or legal restrictions that applied to employing children in the labour force. As children were unemancipated, it was necessary for parents to grant their authorization, but such authorization "does not need to be *expressed*": indeed, it could be implicit and result from circumstances which the judge was responsible for recognizing, such as accompanying the child to the factory, collecting his or her wages, or "not saying anything about the child's contract despite knowing its terms, which would equate to approval thereof".[6]

1.1 From Unification to the First Law on Child Labour

Let us now examine how child labour was treated from a legislative and juristic point of view between the second half of the 19th century and the outbreak of World War One. It must be stated that the situation was truly depressing right from the outset, as children had no rights whatsoever[7]: in the brutal transition from the home to the plant, the 'rules of the house' gave way to the rules of the factory, which were just as 'domestic' and brusque.

Legal doctrine had made no significant contributions to the matter in the period just before Unification. Penal law experts were concerned about the social consequences of such degradation (especially in terms of how to deal with youth crime).[8] Civil law experts were consumed with the technicalities of property rights (such as the ability to undertake obligations through promissory notes, the validation of sales, or unjust enrichment).[9]

[5]On this topic, see Vita Levi, Marco. 1876. *Della locazione di opere e più specialmente degli appalti* 1. *Della locazione delle opere.* Torino: Unione Tipografico-Editrice, § 33, 27–28. See also Marracino, Alessandro. 1928. Patria potestà. In *Il Digesto Italiano* 17. Torino: Unione Tipografico-Editrice, 800.

[6]Vita Levi 1876 (as n. 5) 28.

[7]Minesso, Michela. 2007. L'Italia liberale e le politiche sociali. In Michela Minesso (ed.), *Stato e infanzia nell'Italia contemporanea. Origini, sviluppo e fine dell'Omni 1925–1975.* Bologna: il Mulino, 33.

[8]Pace Gravina, Giacomo. 2000. *Il discernimento dei fanciulli. Ricerche sull'imputabilità dei minori nella cultura giuridica moderna.* Torino: Giappichelli, 93–165. Lastly, see Garlati, Loredana. 2014. Colonia agricola e rieducazione giovanile: l'isola che non c'è. Proposte forensi nel primo decennio postunitario. In Borsacchi, Stefano, and Pene Vidari, Gian Savino (eds.), *Avvocati protagonisti e rinnovatori del primo diritto unitario*, 589–611. Bologna: il Mulino, as well as the bibliography cited therein.

[9]See Milan Court of Trade, 28 January 1864. *Monitore dei Tribunali* 5: 844; Venice Court of Appeal, 14 April 1877. *Giornale dei Tribunali* 6: 129.

The few people who strove for reforms that could impact those on the fringes of society preferred to dedicate their efforts to deaf-mutes,[10] the mentally unbalanced[11] and the illiterate.[12] No one spoke of a minimum age limit, wages or working conditions for children.

There had long been requests for legislative measures to address industrial employment, yet lawmakers paid no heed. Even during the Restoration, the suggestions of Carlo Ilarione Petitti di Roreto—the liberal jurist from Piedmont who had made social reform his vocation[13]—were ignored. So too were the proposals put forth by the Lombard economist Cesare Correnti in the *Annali di Statistica*. As early as the 1840s, both men had rightfully shed light on the "physical" and "moral" disorder that young people were exposed to in the "unseemly toil of modern industry".[14]

True to its contradictory nature, the Code of 1865 chose to look the other way in the face of such an unpleasant phenomenon: given the economic and social hardship of the time, it was justified as a 'necessary evil'. However, lawmakers did choose to take measures when they deemed it necessary, as evidenced by the law enacted on 21 December 1873, which introduced a "ban on employing children in wandering trades" (*divieto di impiego di fanciulli nelle professioni girovaghe*).[15] In other words, vagrants would not be tolerated, yet, all things considered, having little children exploited in factories would be. In a technologically underdeveloped society that was lacking in resources, where "pity was a luxury that fathers could not afford",[16] resorting to a young workforce was an ineliminable part of the continuous manufacturing cycles that characterized industrial production.[17]

---

[10]Baldassare Poli. 1866. Relazione sull'annuario per l'anno 1864–65, intitolato Studj e Rendiconti dei sordo-muti poveri di campagna della provincia di Milano, del prof. Baldassarre Poli, membro effettivo del R. Istituto Lombardo, letta nell'adunanza del 7 giugno 1866. *Annuali universali di statistica*, nuova serie, 27.60: 117–129.

[11]Castiglioni, Cesare. 1867. *Idee per una legge sugli alienati*. Milano: G. Chiusi.

[12]Gaudio, Angelo. 2006. Legislazione e organizzazione della scuola, lotta contro l'analfabetismo. In Pavone, Claudio (ed.), *Storia d'Italia nel secolo ventesimo. Strumenti e fonti* 1, *Elementi strutturali*. Roma: Ministero per i beni e le attività culturali, 355–360.

[13]Petitti di Roreto, Carlo Ilarione. 1841. *Sul lavoro de' fanciulli nelle manifatture. Dissertazione*. Torino: Stamperia Reale, especially § XIII, necessità dell'intervento governativo, 30. Lastly, see Casana Testore, Paola. 2013. Petitti di Roreto, Carlo Ilarione. In Birocchi, Italo, Cortese, Ennio, Mattone, Antonello, and Miletti, Marco Nicola (eds.), *Dizionario Biografico dei Giuristi Italiani (XII–XX secolo)* (*DBGI*) 2, 1558–1559. Bologna: il Mulino.

[14]Correnti, Cesare. 1844. Voto della Commissione nominata nel V Congresso degli Scienziati Italiani per riferire sul lavoro dei fanciulli negli opifici italiani. *Annali universali di statistica,* 81: 303, 309 and 312–316. See Soresina, Marco. 2014. *Non potendo esser fiori contentiamoci di essere radici: una biografia di Cesare Correnti*. Milano: Biblion.

[15]On law n. 1733 of 21 December 1873, see Barbieri, Maria Cristina. 2010. La riduzione in schiavitù: un passato che non vuole passare. Un'indagine storica sulla costruzione e i limiti del 'tipo'. *Quaderni fiorentini* 39: 256–258.

[16]Russell, Bertrand. 1950. *Storia delle idee del secolo XIX*. Torino: Einaudi, 96 (=Russell, Bertrand. 1934. *Freedom and organization, 1814–1914*. London: Allen and Unwin, 87).

[17]On this topic, please refer to Merli, Stefano. 1976 (second edition). *Proletariato di fabbrica e capitalismo industriale. Il caso italiano 1880–1900*. Firenze: La Nuova Italia, 212–239; Maifreda,

Not even the courts reached out to help the youngest workers. One of the first sentences handed down established the right to go to the authorities in order to obtain preventive safety measures in silk factories, but this did not actually protect workers; on the contrary, it was meant to protect "the rental value" of the buildings that were adjacent to the plant. It was 1870, in Monza.[18] All of this indifference clashed with the principle of safeguarding "public health"—a principle which, paradoxically, the very same Court appealed to, and which it believed extended "to moral and intellectual life, to safety within and outside of the national family."

With all of its contradictions, this sentence represented an effective summary of the socio-economic situation that existed around that time. Quite simply, there were widely held, deeply rooted beliefs that were difficult to dispute. It should be added that entrepreneurs, not to mention quite a few intellectuals, saw the "arrogant, envious, improvident, ill-bred"[19] working class as a source of wealth for those who were able to manage its intemperance.

It is thus clear why, even 10 years after Unification, some courts continued to regard salaried workers as "simple servants to their owners".[20] And that also explains why as late as 1910—paradoxical though it may seem at first—one of the most disenchanted jurists that history has ever known, Francesco Carnelutti, did not hesitate to compare a *caruso* (a young boy who worked in the Sicilian mines) to a beast of burden. His reason was plain: "A *caruso* is a man and a beast is a…beast: but their master needs both for their energy".[21] Whether children or adults, workers were just cogs in the assembly line: and they were not to get jammed.

As industry developed, these precious cogs in the production machine became exposed to more and more dangers. Thus, in an appeal to the principles of conscientiousness and good faith (articles 1224 and 1124 of the civil code),

(Footnote 17 continued)

Germano. 2011. Libertà e controllo. La disciplina ottocentesca dello spazio di fabbrica tra costruzioni giuridiche e regolamenti interni. In Antonielli, Livio (ed.), *La polizia del lavoro: il definirsi di un ambito di controllo* [Seminario di Studi, Messina, 30 novembre–1° dicembre 2007], 117–136. Soveria Mannelli: Rubbettino,122.; D'amico, Nicola. 2015. *Storia della formazione professionale in Italia. Dall'uomo da lavoro al lavoro per l'uomo*. Milano: FrancoAngeli, 207–229.

[18]Court of Monza, 26 June 1870. *Monitore dei Tribunali* 12: 161–163. See De Gioannis Gianquinto, Giovanni. 1864. *Nuovo diritto amministrativo d'Italia*. Pavia: Bizzoni, 21 (as well as Cianferotti, Giulio. 2013. De Gioannis Gianquinto, Giovanni. In *DBGI* (as n. 13) 1, 678–679).

[19]Rossi 1876 (as n. 3) 178.

[20]Court of Pinerolo, 6 June 1876, reversed by the Court of Cassation in Turin on 28 February 1877. *Monitore dei Tribunali* 18: 380.

[21]Carnelutti, Francesco. 1910. Il vizio redibitorio nel contratto di lavoro. *Rivista di diritto commerciale* 8: 519 (see Orlandi, Mauro. 2013. Carnelutti, Francesco. In *DBGI* (as n. 13) 1, 455–459). On the meaning of 'caruso', see Rocca, Rosario. 1891. *Dizionario siciliano-italiano. Importante, economico e utile per le famiglie e per le scuole di Sicilia*. Catania: Federico Gravina Editore, 72.

jurisprudence called for minimum safety standards; and violators would be subject to tort liability.[22]

One of the first examples of this was provided in 1875 by Turin's Court of Cassation, which required an industrialist "to take the necessary safety precautions, as should any conscientious father of a family [...] exact, attentive and provident".[23] Experts and academics (Francesco Schupfer and Gian Pietro Chironi, but also Ulisse Gobbi, who went on to become Rector of Bocconi University) came to take similar stances to those presented by courts of law.[24] In 1883, a law was enacted which introduced a mandatory insurance system.[25]

Meanwhile, France was headed in the same direction. Again in 1883, the Court of Cassation in Paris passed a sentence on the Olive printing-house, as its failure to comply with all the laws had resulted in serious injury to a certain apprentice by the name of Gamerre, who had not yet turned sixteen. The court ruled that the entrepreneur had to fit "the dangerous parts" of his equipment with "protection" in order to avoid "accidents" and offset the "recklessness" of young workers. The sentence was promptly published in one of the most prestigious legal journals in Italy, the *Monitore dei Tribunali*, which listed it in the index under a heading that was making its appearance for the first time: *Child labour*.[26]

For the first 20 years of Italian legal history, that is all we have. Anyone who might want to track down records on what the law had to say about child labourers in that period will have to go through dozens of books and leaf through countless pages, only to find nothing that could satisfy their curiosity. And that would be the case until 1888, when courtrooms began hearing the first challenges to the highly

---

[22]Massetto, Gian Paolo. 1988. Responsabilità extracontrattuale, diritto intermedio. In *Enciclopedia del diritto* 39, 1179–1185. Milano: Giuffrè, with the rich bibliography included therein, and Cazzetta, Giovanni. 1991. *Responsabilità aquiliana e frammentazione del diritto comune civilistico (1865–1914)*, Milano: Giuffrè, 166–175.

[23]In the event of a dispute, the employer would have had to rely on testimony provided by his employees, and it would not have been in the employer's best interest to have unsafe working conditions, "as they would be necessary witnesses [and] such a circumstance might damage the credibility they are due" (see *Giurisprudenza italiana* 27.1, 524–525). On this topic, please refer to Rossi, Filippo. 2015. L'emersione del licenziamento in età liberale (1865–1914) fra codice, dottrina e giurisprudenza. *Giornale del diritto del lavoro e di relazioni industriali* 146.2: 243.

[24]See Schupfer, Francesco. 1883. *La responsabilità dei padroni per gli infortuni del lavoro*. Roma: Tip. eredi Botta; Chironi, Gian Pietro. 1884. Della responsabilità dei padroni rispetto agli operai e della garanzia contro gli infortuni sul lavoro. *Studi senesi* 1.2 and 1.3: 127–155, and 231–305; Gobbi, Ulisse. 1883. *Gli infortuni del lavoro. Conferenza tenuta il 17 maggio 1883 all'Accademia Fisio-Medico-Statistica in Milano*. Milano: s.n.; Gobbi, Ulisse. 1885. *Gli infortuni del lavoro nel 1883 e 1884 e la responsabilità degli imprenditori. Relazioni della Commissione d'inchiesta*. Milano: Tip. Bellini. On this topic, see Cazzetta, Giovanni. 2007. *Scienza giuridica e trasformazioni sociali. Diritto e lavoro in Italia tra Otto e Novecento*. Milano: Giuffrè, 114–120. See also Cazzetta, Giovanni. 2013. Chironi, Gian Pietro, and Conte, Emanuele. 2013. Schupfer, Francesco, both in *DBGI* (as. n. 13) 1, 529–531 and 2, 1829–1831.

[25]Passaniti, Paolo. 2006. *Storia del diritto del lavoro* 1. *La questione del contratto di lavoro nell'Italia liberale (1865–1920)*. Milano: Giuffrè, 79–94.

[26]Court of Cassation in Paris, 22 February 1883. *Monitore dei Tribunali* 24: 476–477.

criticized child labour law passed on 11 February 1886 (*sul lavoro dei fanciulli*), as well as objections to the set of norms (*regolamento*) issued the following 17 September, which brought the law into force without actually improving on its flaws.[27]

2 The Child Labour Law of 11 February 1886

The origin of Italy's first child labour legislation is a simple story to tell. While the majority of European countries had long had child labour laws on the books (just think of Prussia in 1839[28] or France in 1841[29]), in Italy such middle-class reformism—conservative though it was—was held in check by an industrial class clinging to the rearguard. The year 1869 marked the point after which it was no longer possible to brazen it out: thus began an unrelenting legislative process that would be handled by 13 governments over the course of 6 legislatures.[30]

Finally, in 1886, a disillusioned coalition government brought an end to a battle that had dragged on for years, by passing a reform that at least kept up appearances.[31] But it was all simply smoke and mirrors.

---

[27]*Gazzetta Ufficiale del Regno d'Italia*, 1886, n. 40, 18 February 1886, 316; n. 226, 28 September 1886, 5423–5428.

[28]Regulativ über die Beschäftigung jugendlicher Arbeiter in Fabriken vom 9. März 1839. In *Gesetz-Sammlung für die Königlichen Preußischen Staaten*. 1839. Berlin: G. Decker, 156–158 (see Kanster, Dieter. 2004. *Kinderarbeit im Rheinland: Entstehung und Wirkung des ersten preußischen Gesetzes die Arbeit von Kindern in Fabriken von 1839*. Köln: SH-Verlag, 177–178).

[29]See Loi du 22–24 mars 1841 relative au travail des enfants employées dans les manufactures, usines ou ateliers. In Duvergier, Jean-Baptiste (ed.). 1841. *Collection complète des lois, décrets, ordonnances, réglements et avis du Conseil d'État* 41, 33–57. Paris: A. Guyot et Scribe. On this topic, see also Pierrard. Pierre. 1987. *Enfants et Jeunnes Ouvriers en France (XIXe–XXe siècle)*. Paris: Les Éditions ouvrières, 66–67; Vernier, Olivier. 2014. L'histoire du droit social. In Krynen, Jacques and d'Alteroche, Bernard (eds.), L'*Histoire du droit en France. Nouvelles tendances, nouveaux territoires*, 460–466. Paris: Classiques Garnier.

[30]See Monteleone 1974 (as n. 4); Castelvetri, Laura. 1994. *Il diritto del lavoro delle origini*. Milano: Giuffrè, 60–72; Fortunati, Maura. 2007. Il ministro e lo spazzacamino. Osservazioni sul progetto di legge sul lavoro dei fanciulli del 1879. *Materiali per una storia della cultura giuridica* 37.1. Bologna: il Mulino, 214.

[31]On the regulations passed in 1886, please refer to Ballestrero, Maria Vittoria. 1978. Tre proposte ottocentesche per la disciplina legale del lavoro dei fanciulli. In Tarello, Giovanni (ed), *Materiali per una storia della cultura giuridica* 8, 217–263. Bologna: il Mulino; Sala Chiri. Maurizio. 1981. Alle origini della legislazione in Italia sul lavoro dei minori (L'evoluzione storica fino al Testo unico del 1907). *Il diritto di famiglia e delle persone* 10: 1238–1240; Allio, Renata. 1994. Luigi Luzzatti e il dibattito sul lavoro minorile. In Ballini, Pier Luigi and Pecorari, Paolo (eds.), *Luigi Luzzatti e il suo tempo. Atti del Convegno Internazionale di studio (Venezia, 7–9 novembre 1991)*, 391–408.Venezia: Istituto veneto di scienze lettere ed arti, 407–408; Ashley, Susan A. 2003. *Making Liberalism Work: The Italian Experience, 1860–1914*. Westport: Praeger, 77–80; Passaniti, Paolo. 2008. *Filippo Turati giuslavorista. Il socialismo nelle origini del diritto del lavoro. Prefazione di Umberto Romagnoli*. Manduria-Bari-Roma: Piero Lacaita Editore, 58–61.

That might explain why the minister of agriculture, industry and commerce, Bernardino Grimaldi, made sure to specify that this faint attempt "to prevent wasting the immature strength of young generations, and to ensure the physical development of children" did not go against the "legitimate needs" of the "national labour system". The safeguards put in place were half-hearted at best, even more so when compared to the solutions that the rest of Europe had experimented with.[32] Even the minister himself admitted that "the new laws" were "among the least severe".[33]

First and foremost, the reform really suffered from the contradictory nature of the principles that inspired it. On the one hand, it required that all minors under the age of 15 have their physical fitness for work verified (article 1 paragraph 2)—these children were also spared from working in dangerous and/or unhealthy factories (article 2). On the other hand, in order to ease the worries of industrialists, the law permitted the hiring of children over the age of 9 (article 1, paragraph 1) in industrial factories, quarries and mines, though their shifts were limited to 8 h a day if they were under 12 (article 3).

There was also a basic problem underneath it all: the norms were deliberately ambiguous in their wording, and industrialists interpreted them as they wished. In order to prevent spurious misinterpretations, in as early as 1889 the magistrates' court (=pretura) in Milan specified that the calculation of the 8 h not only included "the time of *manual* work", but also "that of *assistance* to *work* carried out in some other way". While the far-sighted Lombard judge who penned the decision conceded that child labour tasks were "less tiring and easier", these "little workers" nevertheless had to "remain at their assigned post, keep their faculties sharp [...] and rush to assistance as soon as the need arose". Thus, he charged a certain Frattini with having violated article 3: in this case, the industrialist had engaged children of a tender age for longer than the lawful amount of time, having assigned them the task of "changing bobbins that were mechanically controlled, even though the manual operation of changing them is only done at intervals". The judge's conclusion on the matter demonstrated a level of sensitivity that was difficult to find elsewhere in those years: "machines are a tool controlled by the hands, and by the mind, however the work of a machine is nevertheless the work of man".[34]

---

[32]See Salvioli, Giuseppe. 1892. Il lavoro delle donne e dei fanciulli nelle leggi straniere più recenti. *Scuola positiva* 2: 68–94; Gallavresi, Emilio. 1900. *Il lavoro delle donne e dei fanciulli.* Bergamo: Tipografia Raffaele Gatti, 16–17, 18–19, and 21; Faraggiana, Giuseppe. 1904. *Il lavoro delle donne e dei fanciulli. Commento alla Legge 19–6–902 con richiami di giurisprudenza (Progetto Turati 19–5–904).* Genova-Torino: Renzo Streglio, 34–44. See also Nolan, Aoife. 2014. *Children's Socio-Economic Rights, Democracy and the Courts.* Hart Publishing: Oxford and Portland, Oregon.

[33]Ministry of Agriculture, Industry and Commerce Circular n. 17263, 23 September 1886. In *Annali dell'Industria e del Commercio. 1886. Legislazione sul lavoro dei fanciulli.* Roma: Tipografia Eredi Botta, 3–4.

[34]Magistrates' (=Praetor) Court of Milan, 24 April 1889. *Monitore dei Tribunali* 30: 436.

The law was then supplemented by the *regolamento* issued on 17 September, which itself was just as contradictory in reconciling industrial development with safety in factories. On the one hand, it forbade minors from handling motors and from cleaning moving parts of machines (article 10), set forth regulations concerning a child worker's work booklet (*libretto di lavoro*; articles 3, 5 and 6), and established requirements relating to notices and postings of norms and shift schedules (article 4). Yet at the same time, the *regolamento* laid out a definition of *industrial factory* (*opificio industriale*) that permitted the employment of children under the age of 9 in the case of factories that had fewer than ten workers, and if the work itself did not require the use of a "mechanical motor" (article 1).

Similarly, there were specific charts that made a distinction between those jobs that were considered unquestionably dangerous and unhealthy, and those that, while no less risky, were nonetheless subject to special exemption provided certain limits and precautions were taken (article 7). As far as night work was concerned, article 2 of the law had deemed it unhealthy and permitted a maximum shift of 6 h; article 9 of the *regolamento*, however, lowered the minimum age from 15 to 12, and even then, the minimum age limit was completely ignored "in industrial factories where round-the-clock work is necessary for technical and economic reasons".

Another problem with the *regolamento* was that it assumed compliance on the part of those to whom it applied. And clearly, it was in their best interest to ignore it altogether. Each time Minister Grimaldi placed his trust in the "good faith of the industrialists", they would invariably pay him no heed. Articles 12 and 13 required an "intermediate rest for meals" that was to be at least 1 h long for a 6-h shift, in rooms that were healthier than those where work was carried out: this rule was ignored.

Article 2 required that the presence of any workers under the age of 15 be declared when new industrial factories were opened: once again, no one complied. Article 1 did not grant any protection to child workers in manufacturing units that had fewer than ten workers: when industrialists informed the authorities of the size of their workforce, the number was invariably under this limit.[35]

That's not all. All things considered, when it comes to imposing unwelcome conditions, Hobbes summed it up best: "covenants, without the sword, are but words".[36] Indeed, the entire reform's real Achilles heel was its inefficient system of inspection and oversight. The *regolamento* assigned mining engineers and industrial inspectors the task of entering factories (articles 14–16) and reporting any violations (article 17).

First of all, the Minister invited these "officials" to carry out their task without having their presence in the factories "become an annoying intrusion or an illegitimate inspection of the industry". And obviously, he claimed, inspectors would

[35]Circular n. 17263 (as n. 33) 5, 6 and 9.

[36]Hobbes, Thomas. 1651. *Leviathan or the matter, forme, & power of a Common-Wealth Ecclesiastical and Civill*. London: Andrew Crooke, at the Green Dragon in St. Paul's Churchyard, ch. 17.2, 85.

have it that much easier if the directors of manufacturing units welcomed them "in good faith".[37]

Above all, however, the number of engineers and inspectors could literally be counted on one hand, as there were only four of them. They had just a small group of assistants at their disposal, and they could only inspect quarries and mines. The consequences became clear in no time: the percentage of children hired in accordance with these norms was just over 20 %,[38] and that was a generous approximation!

2.1 Child Labour Jurisprudence

Italy's child labour law was limited. If children were to be protected, then it would be of little use to count on the *regolamento* that brought the law into force; rather, it would require goodwill and knowledge of the principles underlying the legal system. In order to deal with the extremely small number of government employees in charge of inspections, the magistrates' court in Milan suggested granting inspection authority to the police force as well.[39] After all, the penal procedure code of 1865 explicitly assigned officers and agents of the judiciary police the task of determining violations and subsequently reporting them to the magistrate (articles 61, 62 and 68).[40]

On another occasion, the magistrates' court objected to anyone who might suggest that the agents lacked the "technical competence" of industrial inspectors, stating that, on the contrary, such tasks could be carried out by anyone because "the child labour law is of a superior and general nature, the objective of which is to avoid potential ills and damage in the public interest, and namely to protect the development of the physical strength of child workers". Moreover, the magistrates' court struck down any spurious arguments by observing that regardless of any irregularities that might plague the inspectors' reports, there was no reason why a judge could not issue a sentence "based on other legal findings in the case": according to the court, it was a "general principle of the *ius commune*". The magistrates' court concluded by saying that, in the end, if a report was somehow not in conformity, then article 339 of the penal procedure code permitted them to "draw on records or reports or testimony or other means that are not prohibited by law".[41]

[37]Circular n. 17263 (as n. 33) 9.

[38]See Monteleone 1974 (as n. 4) 276–277.

[39]Magistrates' Court of Milan, 21 January 1889. *Monitore dei Tribunali* 30: 326–327.

[40]See *Codice di procedura penale del Regno d'Italia*. 1865. Torino: Stamperia Reale, 33–34, and 38.

[41]Magistrates' Court of Milan, 29 May 1888. *Monitore dei Tribunali* 29: 699–700 (but see also *Codice di procedura penale* (as n. 40) 164).

Disputes over child labour began to come before the Court of Cassation in the 1890s, and the magistrates continually focused their attention on the procedural aspect of the cases; this sometimes turned into a defence of civil liberties. What was certain at that point was that the law of 1886 did not deviate from "the general rules on the powers and authority of the judiciary police". Thus, reports could be drawn up by all public officials, just as the court in Milan had argued.[42]

Nonetheless, more often than not it was this exaggerated adherence to formalities that led many procedures against blatant violations to nowhere; once again, the reform's already weak guarantees were crushed even further.

One such example could be found towards the end of the century, when the supreme court repudiated the traditionally Lombard approach of guaranteeing civil liberties, which had allowed the public prosecutor to officially prosecute any violators of the regulations. That meant that cases were unprosecutable if the prefect had failed to provide the provincial health board with the appropriate documents—a condition that had actually been set forth in article 5 of the law.[43] The result was that a series of spurious appeals were accepted, such as the one brought forward by Guerrino Pedrazzo, who was acquitted in 1899 of having employed several children in a night shift for well over the limit of 6 h. It was written that "the report was not given to the prefect", and that was enough for the Court of Cassation to clear the industrialist of any wrongdoing.[44]

This was a thorny issue that had already been debated in the Chamber of Deputies on 8 February 1886: Pietro Nocito, an expert on criminal procedure, objected that such an interpretation of the law would grant the prefect "the liberty of starting the criminal procedure", to which Grimaldi responded by saying that on the contrary, this preliminary step was necessary.[45]

However, in those years the Court of Cassation was capable of holding violators to their responsibilities whenever it managed to avoid all the bureaucratic red tape. Specifically, between 1893 and 1897, the court ruled that violations would not be treated as a single criminal act resulting in multiple offences, but rather as multiple criminal acts resulting in multiple offences. There was an underlying principle that the court continually reaffirmed: "there are as many violations as children

[42]Court of Cassation, criminal section, 4 July 1890. *Monitore dei Tribunali* 31: 1020. But see also Court of Cassation, criminal section, 2 April 1895. *Giurisprudenza Italiana* 47: 716, and Court of Cassation, criminal section, 19 November and 21 December 1895. *La Legge* 36.1: 243 and 605.

[43]"Prosecution and the validity of the process are dependent upon the prefect's intervention, even if the reporting officers belong to the judiciary police" (see Court of Cassation, criminal section, 1 December 1898. *Monitore dei Tribunali* 40: 517). But see also Court of Cassation, criminal section, 11 January 1899. *Il Circolo giuridico* 30: 44, and 4 April 1899. *Monitore dei Tribunali* 40: 517 (also in *La Legge* 39.1: 818).

[44]Court of Cassation, criminal section, 23 November 1899. *Monitore dei Tribunali* 41: 76. But see also Court of Cassation, criminal section, 18 November 1897. *Monitore dei Tribunali* 39, 276–277 (also in *Il Foro italiano* 23: 145–148).

[45]*Atti parlamentari*, Camera dei Deputati, session of 8 February 1886, *Discussioni*, Roma: Tipografia della Camera dei Deputati, 16611, and 16616–16617. See also Fugazza, Emanuela. 2013. Nocito, Pietro. In *DBGI* (as n. 13) 2, 1443–1444.

[employed] in breach of the law or norms".[46] As concerned the widespread practice of hiring children without a work booklet, "each omission" amounted to "a special violation". It explained that "each one remained whole in and of itself".[47] Furthermore, the magistrates enforced article 79 of the 'new' criminal code in stating that "the director of an industrial factory cannot escape a charge based on the circumstance that fifteen-year-old children working a night shift for over 6 h had been assigned to do so by the previous director, as this is considered a continuing violation, and as such, in his capacity as director, he should have ceased such activity".[48]

One example of such a strict stance is worth mentioning here. The Court issued a sentence in 1899 in which it included sewing factories in the ambiguous legal category of *industrial factory*, thereby rejecting the appeal of a certain Guizzardi, who had already been sentenced by the magistrates' court in Bologna for having hired nine young girls under the age of fifteen without the proper documentation. Indeed, in his "workshop for packaging luxury women's apparel [...] whether it was the narrowness of the place, the lack of air and light, or its proximity to unhealthy places", the general working conditions were exactly those that the reform was attempting to fight. Any other interpretation would go against "the reason of law": "protection of the weak, such as children, from the ills that might afflict their health by working in industrial factories".[49]

This goal of protecting the weak must have also been the reason behind a sentence issued in 1897, which once again reaffirmed that the legal minimum age of 9, as set forth in article 1 of the *regolamento*, could only be derogated from in manufacturing units with fewer than ten workers.[50]

As the twentieth century approached, there were legal scholars who began to inveigh against the minimum age limit of 9, because they believed minors of that age could not be held liable for their actions.[51]

It was also time to discuss the degree of intent on the part of an employer when a violation was committed. To that end, the Court of Cassation specified that a violation "could consist in merely failing [...] to ascertain whether the child was working in lawful conditions", in accordance with article 45 of the Zanardelli Code. Thus, there was no hope for Giacinto Guffanti, a resident of Bergamo, to have his

[46]Court of Cassation, criminal section, 21 December 1897. *Monitore dei Tribunali* 39: 438 (also in *La Legge* 38.1: 315). In a similar sense, see also Court of Cassation, criminal section, 7 October 1893. *Monitore dei Tribunali* 35: 58.

[47]Court of Cassation, criminal section, 6 December 1895. *Monitore dei Tribunali* 37: 136.

[48]Court of Cassation, criminal section, 18 February 1898. *La Legge* 38.1: 536.

[49]Court of Cassation, criminal section, 12 May 1899. *Monitore dei Tribunali* 40: 817 (also in *Il Circolo giuridico* 29: 29).

[50]Court of Cassation, criminal section, 17 September 1897. *La Legge* 38.1: 65.

[51]As found in Amalfi, Gaetano. 1897. Irresponsabilità del minore de' nove anni (Commento e critica dell'art. 53 c.p.). *Il Filangieri* 22: 115–122.

spurious appeal accepted. Indeed, Guffanti maintained that the action he had committed had not been unlawful. The action—or rather, actions—under discussion were the following: Guffanti had hired an apprentice by the name of Giuseppe Carrera, not yet 15 at the time, to work in a limestone and cement factory (and as such, an unhealthy and dangerous workplace); Carrera had worked a night shift that lasted for more than 8 h, without a break; and all of this had been done without a medical certificate or work booklet.[52]

In order to avoid any spurious misinterpretations, the Court of Cassation would come back to the topic of breaks at work in the ensuing years, specifying that a 1-h break was obligatory for every 6 h of work, and that a break could be repeated during the workday in the event that a shift lasted longer than the limit established by the *regolamento*.[53] The Court also specified, however, that a break could not be broken up into "short periods of rest", as these were too short "to restore one's strength".[54]

I would like to be able to say more about the corrective measures taken by the courts to make the law of 1886 more 'presentable', but up until 1901, we have to make do with about thirty sentences. All things considered, it really could not have been any other way: there was an exceedingly high level of non-compliance with the requirements of the reform, combined with an almost complete lack of resources—including human resources—to fight violations.

Members of parliament realized that it was impossible to do any better, and thus they had reluctantly approved the law: "a downright travesty" to put it in the words of the socialist Antonio Maffi. It was as if they had been the unknowing prophets of this sad state of affairs. For once, there were even exponents of the Historical Right who echoed the opinion of the Milanese socialist, such as Antonio Cardarelli, a native of Campania who thundered: "This law, as a law, is worthless".

Despite their vote in favour of the law, members of the left wing were making statements that indicated their utter rejection thereof: Medoro Savini claimed the bill "had the effect of throwing flowers in the coffin of a dead child", while Andrea Costa had a more realistic view of things, saying simply that he had "no illusions as to the practical effectiveness" of a reform that "in reality, will not be enforced".[55]

[52]Court of Cassation, criminal section, 22 September 1899. *Monitore dei Tribunali* 40: 855 (also in *La Legge* 39.2: 749). But see also *Codice penale per il Regno d'Italia*. 1889. Roma: Stamperia Reale, art. 45, 18.

[53]"Article 12 of the norms […] is to be understood in the sense that a rest of 1 h is necessary for every 6 h [of work], and not that one rest is enough even when the work exceeds more than double the 6 h" (Court of Cassation, criminal section, 18 April 1900. *Il Foro italiano* 25: 359).

[54]Court of Cassation, criminal section, 18 December 1901. *Monitore dei Tribunali* 43: 239.

[55]*Atti parlamentari* (as n. 45) 16598, 16599, 16601, and 16603.

3 Laws for Workers in the Early 1900s and Children's Rights

The political class that gave Italy its first child labour law had shown their disappointment during the parliamentary debate of 8 February 1886, but while they were sceptical about the present, they nonetheless expressed hope for "a broader and more courageous reform" in the future.

Thus, while admitting to the inconclusive nature of their discussions, members from both the left and the right offered future legislators some suggestions to help them avoid the mistakes that had just been made. For example, they recommended raising the minimum age for factory work and limiting the length of a workday (Cardarelli); a disciplinary system that handed out stiffer penalties, with more active oversight (Ercole Lualdi); and the introduction of a weekly rest day for young workers, as well as sparing them once and for all from night work (Pietro Paolo Trompeo and Luigi Indelli).[56]

These were the same points that the courts had insisted on since 1888, and they would each be addressed by the patchwork of norms that regulated child labour in the early twentieth century (the so-called 'Giolittian Era').

To be more precise, I am referring to the laws of 19 June 1902 and 7 July 1907, as well as the *testo unico* of 10 November 1907, which brought all the laws under one regulatory framework once it came into force with the implementation regulation (*regolamento attuativo del testo unico*) of 14 June 1909. As one can see, the frenetic pace at which these measures were passed matched the rate at which the governments that approved them took turns running the country. The idea was to consolidate the regulations into a single set of norms that applied to women and children: a demographic known as the "mezze forze" (weaker workforce).[57]

Overall, the new norms raised the minimum age for factory work from 9 to 12, and raised the minimum age for night work from 12 to 15. In addition, any worker under the age of 15 was guaranteed a weekly day of rest (articles 1, 5 and 9 of the *testo unico*).[58]

A factory without a mechanical motor would be considered an industry if it had 5 or more workers (art. 1 of the *regolamento* of 1903 and art. 2 of the *regolamento* of 1909), and not 10 or more as had been the case previously. The norms also beefed up regulations concerning the following issues: dangerous and unhealthy jobs (art. 1 paragraph 2 of the *testo unico*, and art. 29 of the *regolamento attuativo*

[56] *Atti parlamentari* (as n. 45) 16598–16118.

[57] Bonini, Roberto. 1996. *Il diritto privato dal nuovo secolo alla prima guerra mondiale. Linee di storia giuridica ed europea*. Bologna: Pàtron Editore, 34–36 and 256–261; Sala Chiri 1981 (as n. 31) 1241–1255. On women, please refer to Morello, Maria. 2012. La maternità al centro delle prime forme di tutela della salute e della sicurezza delle lavoratrici. *I working papers di Olympus* 15: 8–19.

[58] See articles 1, 5 and 9 from law n. 242 on 19 June 1902 (cited here from Faraggiana 1904 (as n. 32) 51, 82 and 97).

del testo unico); requirements related to work booklets and medical certificates (art. 2 of the *testo unico*, and art. 21 of the *regolamento* of 1909); means of reporting violations (art. 3 of the *testo unico*); and procedures regarding notices and postings (articles 27 and 28 of the *regolamento* of 1907).

The issues that had faced the greatest opposition and non-compliance—namely, shift lengths and daily breaks—were addressed through a tiered system that integrated previous regulations on the matter, albeit in a rather complicated fashion: first of all, shifts could not exceed 8 h for workers under the age of 10 and 11 h for those under the age of 12 (art. 2 of the 1902 law, art. 6 of the 1907 law and art. 7 of the *testo unico*), and it was now obligatory to have a break of 1 h, one and a half hours, and 2 h when the shifts exceeded 6, 8 or 11 h respectively (art. 8 of the 1902 law, art. 7 of the 1907 law and art. 8 of the *testo unico*).[59]

3.1 Jurisprudence's Approach in the Early 20th Century

Working hours and breaks were nothing new for the courts. As early as 1889, the magistrates' court in Milan had ruled that the length of a workday included any time spent in the factory, regardless of the task being carried out (manual work or assistance). And in 1900, the Court of Cassation permitted a second break from work for particularly long shifts.[60]

The law was changing, but the Court of Cassation maintained its stance with the arrival of 1902. If an industrialist was to be absolved from guilt, then he would have to demonstrate that a young worker who had remained at the workplace past the legal time had not carried out any work whatsoever: a highly unlikely scenario. This was an indication that an active and determined magistracy had finally cut through the ambiguity of the law and asserted its full authority over how workers were to be treated, which directly influenced the lives of young workers.[61]

From the socialists' point of view, the regulatory framework that was pushed through in the early twentieth century raised some real doubts.[62] Indeed, the new

[59]See *Testo unico della legge sul lavoro delle donne e dei fanciulli*, consulted here by Bonini 1996 (as n. 57) 256–261.

[60]*Supra*, footnotes 34 and 53.

[61]Court of Cassation, criminal section, 10 December 1901, cited in Faraggiana 1904 (as n. 32) 94 and Court of Cassation, 18 December 1904. La *Cassazione unica* 13: 530.

[62]As far back as the end of the nineteenth century, the socialists had made demands and proposed bills that would have established a ban on factory work for anyone under the age of 15, a ban on night work for anyone under 20, enforcement of the norms for domestic and agricultural work, a reduction in shifts, and more still. The well-known bill of 24 May 1901 had been preceded by a series of various initiatives which had disclosed almost all of the bill's content beforehand: for example, see the bill drawn up by Anna Kuliscioff (Schema di progetto di legge per la protezione del lavoro delle donne e dei fanciulli redatto dal gruppo femminile socialista di Milano (20–21 November 1897), cited here from Merli, Stefano. 1973. *Proletariato di fabbrica e capitalismo industriale. Il caso italiano: 1880–1990*. 2, *Documenti*. Firenze: La Nuova Italia, doc. 226, 669–

law of 1902 still suffered from the same major problem that had afflicted the 1886 law: oversight of its enforcement. Although it was clear right away that the oversight system was inefficient, the uselessness of inspectors and engineers was never brought to the liberal left's attention while the bill was under debate (despite the fact that over 90 % of inspections between 1900 and 1904 were carried out by judiciary police officers!).[63]

Rather, suggestions were put forward on how to co-opt others to carry out inspections (utilizing some of the workers themselves, for example, as proposed by the socialist Angiolo Cabrini and the radical Giuseppe Girardini), or precautions to take so as not to irritate industrialists (for example, the liberal Catholic Silvio Crespi advised asking permission before entering a factory).[64] Legal scholars stood by and watched: Carlo Cattaneo limited himself to examining the legal language pertaining to the issue, while Giuseppe Faraggiana placed his trust in the "general [oversight] bodies",[65] seemingly unconcerned with what could only be described as a disastrous past.

Widespread disinterest and only superficial compliance with the regulatory provisions contributed to the fact that no objections were brought before the courts regarding the *enforcement and oversight of the law* of 1902 (article 12). Rather, the Court of Cassation dealt with the issue of multiple offences, reaffirming what had already been established in the 1890s, namely that "there are as many violations as people [employed] in breach of the law or norms".[66]

Just before the bill of 7 July 1907 became law, the same court had also sought to break down the wall put up by industrialists, that is to say, their attempt to differentiate between the manual tasks of adults and the assistance carried out by children (the latter having been too often passed off as "light work, almost like a game that only required attention, and no effort").[67] In this way, work that was considered absolutely dangerous—and thus banned—came to include "that of merely *packaging*" as well, if carried out "*in the type foundry industry*".[68]

The magistrates' court in Caselle Torinese also forbade working in a furnace,[69] while the Court of Cassation finally addressed a much more important issue that had

(Footnote 62 continued)

672). On the socialist bill, see *Atti parlamentari*, Camera dei Deputati, session 1900–1901, *Documenti* n. 280, and Passaniti 2008 (as n. 31) 185–187.

[63]See Sala Chiri 1981 (as n. 31) 1249, note 24.

[64]*Atti parlamentari*, Camera dei Deputati, session of 23 March 1902, *Discussioni*, Roma: Tipografia della Camera dei Deputati, 486 and 488–489.

[65]Cattaneo, Carlo. 1902. Il progetto di legge sul lavoro delle donne e dei fanciulli. *Monitore dei Tribunali* 43: 321–322 (see Liberati, Gianfranco. 2013. Cattaneo, Carlo. In *DBGI* (as n. 13) 1, 488–490). Faraggiana 1904 (as n. 32) 106.

[66]Court of Cassation, criminal section, 21 October 1905. *Monitore dei Tribunali* 46: 998.

[67]Merli 1976 (as n. 17) 216.

[68]Court of Cassation, criminal section, 4 June 1907. *Monitore dei Tribunali* 48: 597–598.

[69]Magistrates' Court of Caselle torinese, 17 June 1907. *Bollettino dell'Ufficio del lavoro* 8: 948.

been unjustifiably ignored up until that moment: namely, the inhuman treatment of the young *carusi* in the sulfur mines.

I say 'unjustifiably ignored' because the plight of those poor young boys had already been brought to almost everybody's attention in 1876, when Leopoldo Franchetti and Sidney Sonnino published their famous study of life in Sicily. Often only 7 years old, the *carusi* were forced to carry loads of mineral weighing from 25 to 70 kg up through narrow, scorching hot tunnels for 8–10 h a day. Furthermore, they were subject to harassment and abuse (including sexual abuse) on the part of their employers.[70]

In April of 1904, the Court of Cassation finally worked up the courage to declare that "the hauling of materials on the shoulders or head from underground excavation points to the mine entrance is to be included among dangerous and unhealthy occupations, and thus forbidden for children under the age of 15".[71]

Truly remarkable was the fact that the sentence was published by a Palermo-based legal journal called *Circolo giuridico*, which had been around for 35 years and up to that point had expressed very little interest in work-related issues, let alone child labour: indeed, Sicilian mines were home not only to staggering conditions of slavery, but also to the highest rate of non-compliance with the norms in place to fight such circumstances.[72]

Things were better (but not by much) in the more industrialized North, where the driving force of the economy was not young labourers but rather machines. Nonetheless, children were required to assist these machines in their functioning. The courts fought all attempts to 'declassify' the *mechanical motor* to the category of simple equipment—which would have meant no obligation to report the employment of children to the authorities, as per article 3—by stating that anything used "to carry out a task" would be considered a machine, regardless of how it was put in motion.[73]

Meanwhile, local magistrates' courts from Naples to Asti were united in promoting a strict interpretation of the law: thus, an industrialist would be held liable for failing to notify the authorities of a child worker even in the case of temporary work, or even if the industrialist had not been able to fill in the appropriate notification forms because they were unavailable at the time.[74] This pro-civil liberties approach was also behind the effort to expand the concept of *industry* to include the broadest possible range of manufacturing units.

[70]Franchetti, Leopoldo, Sonnino, Sydney (1877). *La Sicilia nel 1876* 1, *Condizioni politiche e amministrative della Sicilia*. Firenze: G. Barbera, § 133, *Il Lavoro dei carusi* (see also Merli 1976 (as n. 17) 234–235).

[71]Court of Cassation, criminal section, 9 April 1904. *Il Circolo giuridico* 35: 63.

[72]Out of the 3,928 reports of child labour filed between 1886 and 1889, only 61 were from the 404 sulfur mines in Caltanissetta (see Monteleone 1974 (as n. 4) 276)!

[73]Court of Cassation, criminal section, 23 January 1908. *Monitore dei Tribunali* 49: 317–318.

[74]Magistrates' Court of Naples, 13 April 1907 and Magistrates' Court of Asti, 7 June 1907. *Bollettino dell'Ufficio del lavoro* 8: 947–948.

One such example was when the Court of Cassation took on a case of cocoon harvesters in the area around Imola: seasonal work yes, but work that deserved protection nonetheless, because the law and its enforcement were to be applied "regardless of the importance or length of occupations".[75]

While jurisprudence may have taken some small steps forward in those years, it was also guilty of tumbling backwards at times: such was the case in 1908, with the Court of Cassation's sudden reversal on the concept of multiple acts leading to multiple violations.

Up until then, this notion had been invoked to ensure that safeguards were in place, and it had gone undisputed. The Court's change of opinion was based in part on a far too literal interpretation of the norms, even though article 13 did in fact speak of *violation* in the singular form; but what really made the sentence aberrant was the fact that the "eminently social nature" of the law was linked with an organicist vision of the working class. Indeed, the working class was treated as a whole only when it came time to "adjust the punishment to fit the crime", in the exclusive interest of the industrialists. One Court of Cassation judge really mixed things up by declaring that any volitional act constituting a prosecutable violation was to be considered a single act, in that it predominantly harmed society as a whole, thus individualizing the victims of the crime into a single entity. And so Giovanni Rivetti, an industrialist from Biella who was guilty of having put a hundred girls to work in his factory "with excessive night-time hours", was only made to pay a very modest fine.[76]

Even the year before, a company run by the Belotti family had received a similar sentence: according to the magistrates' court in Milan, the various violations they had been charged with were to be considered a single negligent act, which itself was nothing but one of the constituent elements of a crime.[77]

It is important to bear these aspects in mind, for fear of attributing too much credit to the reform of 1902. Indeed, it did not build on the innovations of the first child labour law; on the contrary, much like the law before it, it rode an easy wave of demagoguery that resulted in a limited number of regulations coming into force. It completely ignored domestic work and work in the fields. Yet more than anything, it did not make even the slightest change to the highly inefficient compliance oversight system.

As often happens in the progression of events, more and more innovations were carried through as the years went by. A Labour Office was created in 1902. A special office dedicated to oversight was created in 1904, which relieved industrial inspectors from their duties. In 1906, these duties were assigned to labour

---

[75]Court of Cassation, criminal section, 13 February 1908. *Monitore dei Tribunali* 49: 538–539, and joint session of the Court of Cassation, 22 December 1908. *Monitore dei Tribunali* 50: 179 (*contra*, Magistrates' Court of Conegliano, 14 August 1906. *Bollettino dell'Ufficio del lavoro* 8: 319).

[76]Court of Cassation, criminal section, 11 June 1908. *Monitore dei Tribunali* 49: 737, also in *La Legge* 49: 377.

[77]Court of Cassation, criminal section, 25 November 1907. *Monitore dei Tribunali* 49: 39–40.

inspectors who worked in various inspection divisions stationed around the most important industrial hubs of northern Italy; in this case, police officers nonetheless retained the power to carry out inspections.[78] Once up and running, this new oversight system guaranteed a significantly higher number of *inspection visits*, above all thanks to the crucial contribution made by the police force (more than 6,000 police officers carried out inspections, compared to 2,000 inspectors).[79]

Nonetheless, a more in-depth look at the enforcement of laws for female workers between 1906 and 1907 leaves much to be desired. Let us start with a report delivered to the Chamber of Deputies by the minister of agriculture, industry and commerce, Francesco Cocco-Ortu, in which he gave details of the first few months of the inspectors' work.

The minister was required to do so in accordance with the 1904 agreement between France and Italy on the reciprocal protection of workers in the two countries; it was in fulfilment of that same agreement that the 1906 law had granted the ministry some 70,000 lire to boost inspections. And the inspections were not long in coming: 2,236 visits were conducted in 1,985 factories in less than 6 months! Quite a few, considering that there were no more than a dozen new officials to help the mining engineers and judiciary police, with the former described as being "completely absorbed with their main duties" and the latter as hard workers but lacking in "technical knowledge".

As usual, there was no escaping the facts: the "sad state of enforcement of the laws" persisted. There was a total disregard of the rules when issuing work booklets, if they were issued at all (the minister commented that "perhaps no other part of the law […] revealed irregularities as serious as this one").

Medical certificates were either absent or forged, the latter provided by corrupt doctors (in Brescia, the engineer Locatelli came across "booklets issued to girls who were physically underdeveloped", so much so that "some industrialists refused to accept them").

Even more worrying was the widespread practice of prolonging shift hours as long as possible and reducing the length of breaks, especially "in small factories and specifically in workshops dedicated to clothing manufacture, fashion and the like". And then there was night work, which was "completely outside the law". Finally, the posting of laws and working hours (the so-called "formal part" of the regulations) was often done in an extremely haphazard way, and violations were only very reluctantly reported: not even 23 % of the time in the sample surveyed.[80]

---

[78]Respectively, see law n. 246, 29 June 1902, *che istituisce presso il Ministero di agricoltura, industria e commercio un ufficio del lavoro* and law n. 380, 19 July 1906, *che autorizza una maggiore assegnazione per il servizio di vigilanza per l'applicazione delle leggi operaie* (in *Raccolta Ufficiale delle leggi e dei decreti del Regno d'Italia*. 1902.3. 2433–2438. Roma: Stamperia Reale, 1906.3, 2530–2531). See also Sala Chiri 1981 (as n. 31) 1250–1251.

[79]Ispettorato del lavoro e applicazione della legge sul lavoro. *Bollettino dell'ufficio del lavoro* 7: 209–210, 380–383, 828–833; 8: 304–312, 531–535, 922–927, 1236–1237, and 1525–1526.

[80]Relazione sull'impiego dei fondi nel servizio di vigilanza per l'esecuzione delle leggi operaie (articolo 2 della legge 19 luglio 1906, n. 380) presentato alla Camera dei Deputati dal Ministro

4 From the *Testo Unico* to World War One

With this scenario serving as a backdrop to child labour in the early twentieth century, it really seems that over 20 years later, the regulations still suffered from the same "servile and unjustifiable indulgences", "indecision", "uncertain terms" and "exceptions" that tarnished the 1886 law.

A famous and oft-cited case was that of the progressive Emilio Gallavresi (source of the condemnatory words cited above) and the fifty-odd reports filed for violations in factories in the Bergamo area in 1893, none of which led to any trial.[81]

A lawyer and socialist deputy, Gallavresi tried in vain to kindle a flicker of awareness of young workers' rights in the valleys he called home. He even appealed—albeit erroneously—to direct intervention on the part of the kingdom's public prosecutor. Yet at that time, the law was much different than what it would become with the *testo unico* of 1907 and the implementation regulation (*regolamento attuativo*) of 1909. For the years to come, these legislative measures would essentially put an end to what could only be described as a regulatory disaster.

Nonetheless, the 1909 *regolamento attuativo* did bring with it some innovative reforms, which, while not groundbreaking, are worthy of mention. It took previous bills and reforms into account, as well as recommendations provided by the courts and even society's pangs of conscience, which can exert a slight influence over legislators from time to time.

Thus, the law came to include the rebuttable presumption according to which children "who are found to be in places where manual labour is carried out are to be regarded, by law, as employees" (article 3). It was also now required to report even seasonal or temporary workers to the authorities (articles 22–23). Lastly, the part regarding "safety and hygiene requirements" (title VII) was much more extensive than in the past.[82] Nonetheless, while the characters may have changed, the script remained the same: insufficient resources for inspection and oversight, combined with lack of clarity and imprecise norms meant that once again, industrialists were able to circumvent the laws. The reforms ended up being nothing more than 'legal cosmetics', while society remained impervious to change.

Thus, it was up to the judges to clamp down on violations at all costs. For example, between November and December 1910, the magistrates' court in Milan reaffirmed that the set of norms that had been established for the *mezze forze* (weaker workforce composed of women and children) was also to be enforced "in

(Footnote 80 continued)

dell'Agricoltura, Industria e Commercio (Cocco-Ortu) il 6 maggio 1907. *Bollettino dell'ufficio del lavoro* 7: 1314–1325.

[81]Gallavresi 1900 (as n. 32) 10 (the case is cited in Merli 1976 (as n. 17) 225).

[82]See the decree from 14 June 1909, which approved the norms regarding the enforcement of the *testo unico* (Royal decree n. 818, 10 November) on female and child labour (Gazz. Uff., 28 July 1909). In *Raccolta Ufficiale delle leggi e dei decreti del Regno d'Italia*. 1909.3, 2732–2755. Roma: Stamperia Reale.

sewing factories, where many girls are employed", because "the law aims to protect [one's] physical and moral welfare from the hazards that communal work might cause". Meanwhile, the magistrates' court in Genoa reminded doctors in charge of filling in medical certificates to do so scrupulously, so as not to be held criminally liable.[83] Two years later, the Court of Cassation once again discouraged industrialists from trying to circumvent the law on the minimum number of employees for a manufacturing unit to be considered an industry, specifying that the calculation must also include "the owner of the workshop and his family".[84]

We can see echoes of the same biased interpretations of the law and the same conspiratorial manoeuvring that had been the root cause of all the failures associated with child labour regulation ever since it first appeared in 1886. Almost everything was the same as back then.

It would be unreasonable to say that this was only happening in Italy: there was no shortage of "episodes of odious exploitation" in France; violations of daily working hours and Sunday rest were quite frequent in Austria; and in Germany, from Prussia to Württemberg, the work booklet "[did] not seem to serve its purpose".[85]

Yet the situation in Italy was characterized by an almost complete lack of shame when it came to respecting norms. An inspector from Brescia by the name of Magrini put it quite nicely when he said that there was "great deal of laxity in observing the laws"; this was made even worse by the disciplinary system that was in place, which only hit industrialists in the wallet, and mildly at that. The great migrations of the early twentieth century had helped work cross national borders and expand across Europe, leading to the first international treaties on child labourers (such as the labour agreement between Italy and France, which I mentioned above, or the Berne Conventions of 1906); yet because of its reputation, Italy was a signatory kept under 'special surveillance'.[86]

It would mark the beginning of a lively debate on labour law. The combination of private law sources, multilateral agreements and the principles of national legal systems would give rise to new legal instruments and classifications. Barthelemy Raynaud's contribution to *droit international ouvrier* comes to mind, which made its way across the Alps to Italy, where it was subsequently inserted into an intense scientific debate that often led to excellent results (Scipione Gemma was a shining example thereof).[87]

---

[83]Magistrates' Court of Milan, 28 December 1910 and Magistrates' Court of Genoa, 25 November 1910. *Bollettino dell'Ufficio del lavoro* 16: 241 and 439.

[84]Court of Cassation, criminal section, 22 February 1912. *Monitore dei Tribunali* 53: 414–415.

[85]Applicazioni delle leggi all'estero. *Bollettino dell'Ufficio del lavoro* 11: 1119–1127.

[86]Lastly, see Amorosi, Virginia. 2013. "Un jour viendra…". Diritto internazionale del lavoro e discorso giuridico nel primo Novecento. *I-Lex. Scienze giuridiche, Scienze Cognitive e Intelligenza artificiale* 18: 102–103, 107–108, and the bibliography cited therein.

[87]Raynaud, Barthelemy. 1906. *Droit international ouvrier*. Paris: A. Rousseau; Gemma, Scipione. 1912. *Il diritto internazionale del lavoro*. Roma: Athenaeum.

It was as if these new international standards had been transplanted into a single, emerging set of norms, thereby regenerating a body of laws that would have otherwise been left in a state of atrophy.

In the meantime, however, our local rules were paying the price of a decidedly narrow-minded approach. The words of Emanuele Gianturco proved prophetic when, in 1895, he spoke of the "profound economic and social transformation [that] was slowly taking place, by means of agonizing crises", in a country where "dangers [will be] less imminent, but more serious, paving the way for our apathy towards the problems of industrial work". As a jurist and politician from Basilicata, Gianturco had much to draw on regarding "our so-called factory legislation", which consisted of but a few measures, including "a child labour law [that] unfortunately, to this day, has not been put into effect".[88]

Prophetic indeed. At the very least, Italy would languish in those 'agonizing crises' up until the outbreak of World War One: an inevitable consequence of its unwillingness to address its problems.

In those years, reforms were passed begrudgingly and no one was willing to take risks; meanwhile, there was dissension among those in power, between those who hoped to achieve legislation that truly defended civil liberties, and those many who actually feared such an outcome. It is a bit surprising, considering that reforms were thriving in Europe (from Spain to Luxembourg) and around the world (from Uruguay to Mexico), many of which achieved satisfactory results.[89]

Nonetheless, the situation would soon improve with the creation of the International Labour Organization (ILO). Two conventions were adopted on 28 November 1919 at the ILO conference in Washington, which established a minimum age of 14 years for admission to industrial employment and prohibited workers who were not yet 18 years old from performing night work between ten o'clock in the evening and five o'clock in the morning.[90]

In reality, Italy only ratified the latter convention through royal decree 1021 on 20 March 1923, but at that point a chain of events had already been set in motion, such that the country would be forced to reform its entire legislation of the matter and enact law n. 653 on 26 April 1934—well before the country's constitutional 'adventure' of 1948.[91]

---

[88]Discorso tenuto agli elettori del collegio di Acerenza il 18 maggio 1895, in Gianturco, Emanuele. 1909. *Discorsi parlamentari,* 5–6 Roma: Tipografia della Camera dei Deputati (see Treggiari, Ferdinando. 2013. Gianturco. Emanuele. In *DBGI* (as n. 13) 1, 992–994).

[89]For example, see the collection of foreign legislation 1912–1913. *Bollettino dell'Ufficio del lavoro* 20: 363–368.

[90]See ILO—Convention Fixing the Minimum Age for Admission of Children to Industrial Employment C5, art. 2, and ILO—Convention concerning the Night Work of Young Persons Employed in Industry C6, art. 3 (consulted here in the online database provided by *Olympus. Osservatorio per il monitoraggio permanente della legislazione e giurisprudenza sulla sicurezza del lavoro*).

[91]See Gaeta, Lorenzo (ed). 2014. *Prima di tutto il lavoro. La costruzione di un diritto dell'Assemblea Costituente*. Roma: Ediesse.

5 Conclusions

The 'social woes' brought on by industrial employment have led us to assess "the development of a population's moral civilization and social progress"[92] based on the level of protection afforded to the weakest members of society. The exploitation of children is a subject that strikes a deep chord with us still today, and there are so many overlapping and clashing variables (many of which are not legal in nature) that it is not possible to formulate a universally valid and unbiased opinion on the issue.

I believe that utter condemnation is justifiable only when the exploitation is found in the more prosperous production cycles of welfare economics, where the right to have a childhood is so firmly established that it cannot be disputed, let alone taken away.

But the problems of industrial development tore Italy to pieces between the nineteenth and twentieth centuries, creating a much more complex state of affairs. I think the only way to understand it is to accept an underlying truth: in the time period examined in the present paper, Italy unfortunately had no choice but to resort to young labourers.

Let us return, then, to children in the factories. As late as 1909, this situation could still legitimately be considered legalized exploitation, as even a cursory reading of the laws that dealt with the issue revealed how they betrayed their very nature.

For example, the norms on working hours—which were not the best to begin with—were subject to a number of derogations (articles 31–33). The same *regolamento* also increased the number of years a child was to attend compulsory elementary school education before receiving the necessary documentation for employment (article 10), but then allowed for several exceptions (articles 12 and 13). In addition, these norms actually degraded the value of a school education—which should be a right—by treating it as merely a procedural formality. Indeed, it was included under the title dedicated to the formal requirements needed for admission to industrial employment. Thus, the logical conclusion would be to place all the blame on the *child labour laws*.

However, that would not be entirely correct. Certainly, the fact that late nineteenth-century states were so centred around norms would seem to support such a conclusion: the state did not recognize innate or constitutionally-guaranteed rights, but only "laws that specifically deal with [such rights], and it is in these [laws] that we must seek them".[93] In sum, if there were no laws, there were no rights.

---

[92]D'Harmant François, Antonio. 1960. *La tutela del lavoro femminile e minorile nella regolamentazione dell'O.I.L.* Roma: Istituto di medicina sociale, 4.

[93]As found in Racioppi, Francesco, and Brunelli, Ignazio, 1909. *Commentario allo Statuto del Regno* 2. Torino: UTET, 34 (on this topic, please refer to Fioravanti, Maurizio. 2009. *Costituzionalismo. Percorsi della storia e tendenze attuali.* Roma-Bari: Laterza, 97, which is the source of the citation).

Yet taken to the extreme, such an interpretation ends up ignoring the grey areas (sometimes there are laws that do not grant any rights) and neglecting that inescapable moment when norms must be enforced.

Emilio Gallavresi offered a perspective that essentially returned to the root of the problem: "So that it might emerge from barbarism, every society strives to establish a Social Authority, which, on everyone's behalf, quells the abuses of individual arrogance". He understood that an additional step was necessary if the legal system was to guarantee a right that had been recognized by law.

Thus, he attempted to describe the role of this institution by making a brief yet incisive comparison, especially if we think of the conflicts that were taking place in his day. Specifically, he explained that "it would be useless now to try to create a factitious unity among the classes. They have separate and conflicting interests; there are those who have been worn down and subjugated for centuries, and who, unarmed, would not resist against the others in an open competition; the others being those who have a monopoly over the means of labour, and therefore possess that lethal weapon that is exploitation. [Thus,] a provident and peacemaking Social Authority needs to intervene, so as to moderate the conflict".[94]

Now, this 'social authority' can take on different forms. It could coincide with the power of the state to enforce the laws. Nonetheless, we cannot expect judges to have much success as mediators between conflicting class interests, at least not in those particular circumstances.[95]

First and foremost, they did not present a united front. One such example was the growing rift over the interpretation of article 11 of the *testo unico*. On the one hand, there were those who endorsed its strict interpretation; on the other hand, there were those local districts—especially in the Center and South of Italy—that took a more indulgent approach, allowing an entrepreneur "who personally attends to his trade" to disregard the rule requiring a weekly rest day. Things came to a head in 1910, when not even the Court of Cassation was able to straighten out the dissident local courts.[96]

Secondly, judges were poor mediators because a young worker was never the center of attention in their sentences: rather, the focus was on what substantive and (above all) procedural norms were violated by a non-compliant industrialist.

Upon closer examination, perhaps the term 'social authority' could take on a broader meaning, so that it corresponds to those bodies in charge of enforcing the law (the police? oversight bodies?): the greater their incisiveness, the more protection they can provide. Unfortunately, as this paper has shown, the few resources employed in overseeing compliance with the law were anything but incisive, resulting in a law that was completely ineffectual.

---

[94]Gallavresi 1900 (as n. 32) 30.

[95]On the other hand, judges were much more committed—especially ordinary judges—to the legal origins of dismissal from employment. See Rossi 2015 (as n. 23) 240–258.

[96]On this topic, see Braccianti, Enrico. 1910. L'art. 11 della legge sul riposo settimanale e la giurisprudenza. *Monitore dei Tribunali* 51: 181–183.

Were its scope to expand, Gallavresi's concept of authority would end up coinciding with the social reality of labour itself; and as the correlation between de jure and de facto existence of rights begins to fade, it would lose any connotation of the state entirely. Perhaps Gallavresi intended it to have such a broad and indistinct meaning, but at this point, the boundaries would become so blurred that this enigmatic institution would be left without the role it was meant to perform, namely as a provider of legal safeguards.

No matter how it is analysed, the roots of child labour lay in the conflict between those who wanted to break from the past and those who were afraid of progress. The result: policies nowhere to be found, faint-hearted jurisprudence and almost no legal interpretation of the issue (apart from the comments that were occasionally made on reforms).

It was a failure, and the legal system as a whole simply looked on. Only in the end did it show remorseful compassion, when it realized that it had missed out on an opportunity. Yet at that point, to borrow from Medoro Savini's striking metaphor, there was nothing left to do but throw flowers "in the coffin of a dead child"—a child that the legal system should have saved.

References

Sources

1839. Regulativ über die Beschäftigung jugendlicher Arbeiter in Fabriken vom 9. März 1839. In *Gesetz-Sammlung für die Königlichen Preußischen Staaten* (pp. 156–158). Berlin: G. Decker.

1841. Loi du 22–24 mars 1841 relative au travail des enfants employées dans les manufactures, usines ou ateliers. In J.-B. Duvergier (Ed.), *Collection complète des lois, décrets, ordonnances, réglements et avis du Conseil d'État* (Vol. 41, pp. 33–57). Paris: A. Guyot et Scribe.

1865. *Codice di procedura penale del Regno d'Italia*. Torino: Stamperia Reale.

1882. *Censimento della popolazione del Regno d'Italia (31 dicembre 1881)*. Roma: Tipografia Fratelli Centenari.

1886. Legge 11 febbraio 1886 n. 3657 sul lavoro dei fanciulli (pubblicata nella Gazzetta Ufficiale del Regno d'Italia il 18 febbraio 1886, n. 40). In *Raccolta Ufficiale delle Leggi e dei Decreti del Regno d'Italia* (pp. 144–147). Roma: Stamperia Reale.

1886. *Gazzetta Ufficiale del Regno d'Italia* (Vol. 40, pp. 5423–5428), 18 February 1886, 316; 226, 28 September 1886.

1886. Circolare del Ministero di Agricoltura, Industria e Commercio n. 17263, 23 settembre 1886. In *Annali dell'Industria e del Commercio. 1886. Legislazione sul lavoro dei fanciulli* (pp. 3–4). Roma: Tipografia Eredi Botta

1886. *Atti parlamentari*, Camera dei Deputati, session of 8 February 1886, *Discussioni* (pp. 164587–16622). Roma: Tipografia della Camera dei Deputati.

1889. *Codice penale per il Regno d'Italia*. Roma: Stamperia Reale.

1902. *Atti parlamentari*, Camera dei Deputati, session of 23 March 1902, *Discussioni* (pp. 475–516). Roma: Tipografia della Camera dei Deputati.

1902. Legge n. 246, 29 giugno 1902, che istituisce presso il Ministero di agricoltura, industria e commercio un ufficio del lavoro. In *Raccolta Ufficiale delle leggi e dei decreti del Regno d'Italia* 3 (pp. 2433–2438). Roma: Stamperia Reale.

1906. Legge n. 380, 19 luglio 1906, *che autorizza una maggiore assegnazione per il servizio di vigilanza per l'applicazione delle leggi operaie*. In *Raccolta Ufficiale delle leggi e dei decreti del Regno d'Italia* 3 (pp. 2530–2531). Roma: Stamperia Reale.

1909. Decreto n. 818, 14 giugno 1909, che approva il regolamento per l'applicazione del testo unico (Regio decreto 10 novembre, n. 818) della legge sul lavoro delle donne e dei fanciulli (Gazz. Uff., 28 luglio 1909). In *Raccolta Ufficiale delle leggi e dei decreti del Regno d'Italia* 3 (pp. 2732–2755). Roma: Stamperia Reale.

Literature

Allio, R. (1994). Luigi Luzzatti e il dibattito sul lavoro minorile. In P. L. Ballini & P. Pecorari (Eds.), *Luigi Luzzatti e il suo tempo. Atti del Convegno Internazionale di studio (Venezia, 7–9 novembre 1991)* (pp. 391–408). Venezia: Istituto veneto di scienze lettere ed arti.

Amalfi, G. (1897). Irresponsabilità del minore de' nove anni (Commento e critica dell'art. 53 c.p.). *Il Filangieri, 22*, 115–122.

Amorosi, V. (2013). "Un jour viendra…". Diritto internazionale del lavoro e discorso giuridico nel primo Novecento. *I-Lex. Scienze giuridiche, Scienze Cognitive e Intelligenza artificiale, 18*, 99–112.

Ashley, S. A. (2003). *Making liberalism work: The Italian experience, 1860–1914*. Westport: Praeger.

Ballestrero, M. V. (1978). Tre proposte ottocentesche per la disciplina legale del lavoro dei fanciulli. In G. Tarello (Ed.), *Materiali per una storia della cultura giuridica* (Vol. 8, pp. 217–263). Bologna: il Mulino.

Barbieri, M. C. (2010). La riduzione in schiavitù: un passato che non vuole passare. Un'indagine storica sulla costruzione e i limiti del 'tipo'. *Quaderni fiorentini, 39*, 229–257.

Bonini, R. (1996). *Il diritto privato dal nuovo secolo alla prima guerra mondiale. Linee di storia giuridica ed europea*. Bologna: Pàtron Editore.

Braccianti, E. (1910). L'art. 11 della legge sul riposo settimanale e la giurisprudenza. *Monitore dei Tribunali, 51*, 181–183.

Casana Testore, P., (2013). Petitti di Roreto, Carlo Ilarione. In I. Birocchi, E. Cortese, A. Mattone & M.N. Miletti (Eds.), *Dizionario Biografico dei Giuristi Italiani (XII–XX secolo)* (Vol. 2, pp. 1558–1559). Bologna: il Mulino.

Carnelutti, F. (1910). Il vizio redibitorio nel contratto di lavoro. *Rivista di diritto commerciale, 8*, 519–532.

Castelvetri, L. (1994). *Il diritto del lavoro delle origini*. Milano: Giuffrè.

Castiglioni, C. (1867). *Idee per una legge sugli alienati*. Milano: G. Chiusi.

Castronovo, V. (2006). *Storia economica d'Italia*. Dall'Ottocento ai giorni nostri. Nuova edizione accresciuta. Torino: Einaudi.

Cattaneo, C. (1902). Il progetto di legge sul lavoro delle donne e dei fanciulli. *Monitore dei Tribunali, 43*, 321–322.

Cazzetta, G. (1991). *Responsabilità aquiliana e frammentazione del diritto comune civilistico (1865–1914)*. Milano: Giuffrè.

Cazzetta, G. (2007). *Scienza giuridica e trasformazioni sociali. Diritto e lavoro in Italia tra Otto e Novecento*. Milano: Giuffrè.

Cazzetta, G. (2013). Chironi, Gian Pietro. In I. Birocchi, E. Cortese, A. Mattone & M.N. Miletti (Eds.), *Dizionario Biografico dei Giuristi Italiani (XII–XX secolo)* (Vol. 1, pp. 529–531). Bologna: il Mulino.

Chironi, G. P. (1884). Della responsabilità dei padroni rispetto agli operai e della garanzia contro gli infortuni sul lavoro. In *Studi senesi* 1.2 and 1.3: 127–155, 231–305.

Cianferotti, G. (2013). De Gioannis Gianquinto, Giovanni. In I. Birocchi, E. Cortese, A. Mattone & M. N. Miletti (Eds.), *Dizionario Biografico dei Giuristi Italiani (XII–XX secolo)* (Vol. 1, pp. 678–679). Bologna: il Mulino.

Conte, E. (2013). Schupfer, Francesco. In I. Birocchi, E. Cortese, A. Mattone & M. N. Miletti (Eds.), *Dizionario Biografico dei Giuristi Italiani (XII–XX secolo)* (Vol. 2, pp. 1829–1831). Bologna: il Mulino.

Correnti, C. (1844). Voto della Commissione nominata nel V Congresso degli Scienziati Italiani per riferire sul lavoro dei fanciulli negli opifici italiani. *Annali universali di statistica, 81*, 301–328.

D'amico, N. (2015). *Storia della formazione professionale in Italia. Dall'uomo da lavoro al lavoro per l'uomo*. Milano: FrancoAngeli.

De Gioannis Gianquinto, G. (1864). *Nuovo diritto amministrativo d'Italia*. Pavia: Eredi Bizzoni.

De Petris, A. (1865). *La medicina del pauperismo. Studi economici*. Venezia: Naratovich.

D'Harmant François, A. (1960). *La tutela del lavoro femminile e minorile nella regolamentazione dell'O.I.L.* Roma: Istituto di medicina sociale.

Duvergier, J.-B. (Ed.). (1841). *Collection complète des lois, décrets, ordonnances, réglements et avis du Conseil d'État 41*. Paris: A. Guyot et Scribe.

Faraggiana, G. (1904). *Il lavoro delle donne e dei fanciulli. Commento alla Legge 19–6–902 con richiami di giurisprudenza (Progetto Turati 19–5–904)*. Genova-Torino: Renzo Streglio.

Fioravanti, M. (2009). *Costituzionalismo. Percorsi della storia e tendenze attuali*. Roma-Bari: Laterza.

Fortunati, M. (2007). Il ministro e lo spazzacamino. Osservazioni sul progetto di legge sul lavoro dei fanciulli del 1879. *Materiali per una storia della cultura giuridica 37*(1), 213–224.

Franchetti, L., & Sonnino, S. (1877). *La Sicilia nel 1876 1, Condizioni politiche e amministrative della Sicilia*. Firenze: G. Barbera.

Fugazza, E. (2013). Nocito, Pietro. In I. Birocchi, E. Cortese, A. Mattone & M. N. Miletti (Eds.), *Dizionario Biografico dei Giuristi Italiani (XII–XX secolo)* (Vol. 2, pp. 1443–1444). Bologna: il Mulino,

Gaeta, L. (Ed.). (2014). *Prima di tutto il lavoro. La costruzione di un diritto dell'Assemblea Costituente*. Roma: Ediesse.

Gallavresi, E. (1900). *Il lavoro delle donne e dei fanciulli*. Bergamo: Tipografia Raffaele Gatti.

Garlati, L. (2014). Colonia agricola e rieducazione giovanile: l'isola che non c'è. Proposte forensi nel primo decennio postunitario. In S. Borsacchi & G. S. Pene Vidari (Eds.), *Avvocati protagonisti e rinnovatori del primo diritto unitario* (pp. 589–611). Bologna: il Mulino.

Gaudio, A. (2006). Legislazione e organizzazione della scuola, lotta contro l'analfabetismo. In C. Pavone (Ed.), *Storia d'Italia nel secolo ventesimo. Strumenti e fonti* 1, *Elementi strutturali* 355–373. Roma: Ministero per i beni e le attività culturali.

Gemma, Scipione. 1912. *Il diritto internazionale del lavoro*. Roma: Athenaeum.

Gianturco, E. (1909). *Discorsi parlamentari*. Roma: Tipografia della Camera dei Deputati.

Gobbi, U. (1883). *Gli infortuni del lavoro. Conferenza tenuta il 17 maggio 1883 all'Accademia Fisio-Medico-Statistica in Milano*. Milano: s.n.

Gobbi, U. (1885). *Gli infortuni del lavoro nel 1883 e 1884 e la responsabilità degli imprenditori. Relazioni della Commissione d'inchiesta*. Milano: Tip. Bellini.

Hobbes, T. (1651). *Leviathan or the matter, forme, & power of a Common-Wealth Ecclesiastical and Civill*. London: Andrew Crooke, at the Green Dragon in St. Paul's Churchyard.

Kanster, D. (2004). *Kinderarbeit im Rheinland: Entstehung und Wirkung des ersten preußischen Gesetzes die Arbeit von Kindern in Fabriken von 1839*. Köln: SH-verlag.

Liberati, G. (2013). Cattaneo, Carlo. In I. Birocchi, E. Cortese, A. Mattone & M. N. Miletti (Eds.), *Dizionario Biografico dei Giuristi Italiani (XII–XX secolo)* (Vol. 1, pp. 488–490). Bologna: il Mulino.

Maifreda, G. (2011). Libertà e controllo. La disciplina ottocentesca dello spazio di fabbrica tra costruzioni giuridiche e regolamenti interni. In L. Antonielli (Ed.), *La polizia del lavoro: il definirsi di un ambito di controllo* [Seminario di Studi, Messina, 30 novembre–1° dicembre 2007] (pp. 117–136). Soveria Mannelli.

Marracino, A. (1928). Patria potestà. In I. Digesto (Ed.), *Italiano 17, 800*. Torino: Unione Tipografico-Editrice.

Massetto, G. P. (1988). Responsabilità extracontrattuale, diritto intermedio. In *Enciclopedia del diritto* (Vol. 39, pp. 1099–1186). Milano: Giuffrè.

Merli, S. (1973). *Proletariato di fabbrica e capitalismo industriale. Il caso italiano: 1880–1900*. 2, *Documenti*. Firenze: La Nuova Italia.

Merli, S. (1976). *Proletariato di fabbrica e capitalismo industriale. Il caso italiano 1880–1900* (2nd ed.). Firenze: La Nuova Italia.

Minesso, M. (2007). L'Italia liberale e le politiche sociali. In M. Michela (Ed.), *Stato e infanzia nell'Italia contemporanea. Origini, sviluppo e fine dell'Omni 1925–1975* (pp. 31–48). Bologna: il Mulino.

Mittermaier, K. J. A. (1866). Sui nuovi lavori pubblicati in Italia relativamente alle scienze giuridiche (Trans. M. Noli). *Monitore dei Tribunali, 7*, 625–628.

Monteleone, G. (1974). La legislazione sociale al parlamento italiano. La legge del 1886 sul lavoro dei fanciulli. *Movimento operaio e socialista, 20*(1), 229–284.

Morello, M. (2012). La maternità al centro delle prime forme di tutela della salute e della sicurezza delle lavoratrici. *I working papers di Olympus* 15.

Nolan, A. (2014). *Children's Socio-Economic Rights, Democracy and the Courts*. Oxford and Portland, Oregon: Hart Publishing.

Orlandi, M. (2013). Carnelutti, Francesco. In I. Birocchi, E. Cortese, A. Mattone & M. N. Miletti (Eds.), *Dizionario Biografico dei Giuristi Italiani (XII–XX secolo)* (Vol. 1, pp. 455–459). Bologna: il Mulino.

Pace Gravina, G. (2000). *Il disciernimento dei fanciulli. Ricerche sull'imputabilità dei minori nella cultura giuridica moderna*. Torino: Giappichelli.

Passaniti, P. (2006). *Storia del diritto del lavoro. 1. La questione del contratto di lavoro nell'Italia liberale (1865–1920)*. Milano: Giuffrè.

Passaniti, P. (2008). *Filippo Turati giuslavorista. Il socialismo nelle origini del diritto del lavoro. Prefazione di Umberto Romagnoli*. Manduria-Bari-Roma: Piero Lacaita Editore.

Petitti di Roreto, C. I. (1841). *Sul lavoro de' fanciulli nelle manifatture. Dissertazione*. Torino: Stamperia Reale.

Pierrard. P. (1987). *Enfants et Jeunnes Ouvriers en France (XIXe–XXe siècle)*. Paris: Les Éditions ouvrières.

Poli, B. (1866). Relazione sull'annuario per l'anno 1864–65, intitolato Studj e Rendiconti dei sordo-muti poveri di campagna della provincia di Milano, del prof. Baldassarre Poli, membro effettivo del R. Istituto Lombardo, letta nell'adunanza del 7 giugno 1866. *Annuali universali di statistica*, nuova serie, *27*(60), 117–129.

Racioppi, F., & Brunelli, I. (1909). *Commentario allo Statuto del Regno 2*. Torino: Unione tipografico editrice torinese.

Raynaud, B. (1906). *Droit international ouvrier*. Paris: A. Rousseau.

Rocca, R. (1891). *Dizionario siciliano-italiano. Importante, economico e utile per le famiglie e per le scuole di Sicilia*. Catania: Federico Gravina Editore

Rossi, A. (1876). Di una proposta di legge sul lavoro dei fanciulli e delle donne nelle fabbriche. *Nuova Antologia di scienze, lettere ed arti, 31*(1), 166–196.

Rossi, F. (2015). L'emersione del licenziamento in età liberale (1865–1914) fra codice, dottrina e giurisprudenza. *Giornale del diritto del lavoro e di relazioni industriali, 146*(2), 231–272.

Russel, B. (1834). *Freedom and organization, 1814–1914*. London: Allen and Unwin.

Russel, B. (1950). *Storia delle idee del secolo XIX*. Torino: Einaudi.

Sala Chiri, M. (1981). Alle origini della legislazione in Italia sul lavoro dei minori (L'evoluzione storica fino al Testo unico del 1907). *Il diritto di famiglia e delle persone, 10*, 1238–1240.

Salvioli, G. (1892). Il lavoro delle donne e dei fanciulli nelle leggi straniere più recenti. *Scuola positiva, 2*, 68–94.

Schupfer, F. (1883). *La responsabilità dei padroni per gli infortuni del lavoro*. Roma: Tip. eredi Botta.

Soresina, M. (2014). *Non potendo esser fiori contentiamoci di essere radici: una biografia di Cesare Correnti*. Milano: Biblion.
Treggiari, F. (2013). Gianturco. Emanuele. In I. Birocchi, E. Cortese, A. Mattone & M. N. Miletti (Eds.), *Dizionario Biografico dei Giuristi Italiani (XII–XX secolo)* (Vol. 1, pp. 992–994). Bologna: il Mulino.
Vernier, O. (2014). L'histoire du droit social. In J. Krynen & B. d'Alteroche (Eds.), L*'Histoire du droit en France. Nouvelle tendances, nouveaux territoires* (pp. 455–477). Paris: Classiques Garnier.
Vita Levi, M. (1876). *Della locazione di opere e più specialmente degli appalti. 1. Della locazione delle opere*. Torino: Unione Tipografico-Editrice.

Table of cases

Decisions of the French Court of Cassation

Cassation, 22 February 1883. *Monitore dei Tribunali* 24: 476–477.

Decisions of the Italian Courts of Appeal, Court of Cassation and lower Courts

Milan Court of Trade, 28 January 1864. *Monitore dei Tribunali* 5: 844.
Court of Monza, 26 June 1870. *Monitore dei Tribunali* 12: 161–163.
Court of Pinerolo, 6 June 1876, *Monitore dei Tribunali* 18: 380.
Court of Cassation of Turin, 28 February 1877. *Monitore dei Tribunali* 18: 380.
Venice Court of Appeal, 14 April 1877. *Giornale dei Tribunali* 6: 129.
Magistrates' Court of Milan, 29 May 1888. *Monitore dei Tribunali* 29: 699–700.
Magistrates' Court of Milan, 24 April 1889. *Monitore dei Tribunali* 30: 436.
Court of Cassation, criminal section, 4 July 1890. Monitore dei Tribunali 31: 1020.
Court of Cassation, criminal section, 7 October 1893. *Monitore dei Tribunali* 35: 58.
Court of Cassation, criminal section, 2 April 1895. *Giurisprudenza Italiana* 47: 716.
Court of Cassation, criminal section, 19 November and 21 December 1895. *La Legge* 36.1: 243 and 605.
Court of Cassation, criminal section, 6 December 1895. *Monitore dei Tribunali* 37: 136.
Court of Cassation, criminal section, 17 September 1897. *La Legge* 38.1: 65.
Court of Cassation, criminal section, 18 November 1897. *Monitore dei Tribunali* 39, 276–277 (also in *Il Foro italiano* 23: 145–148).
Court of Cassation, criminal section, 21 December 1897. *Monitore dei Tribunali* 39: 438 (also in *La Legge* 38.1: 315).
Court of Cassation, criminal section, 18 February 1898. *La Legge* 38.1: 536.
Court of Cassation, criminal section, 1 December 1898. *Monitore dei Tribunali* 40: 517.
Court of Cassation, criminal section, 11 January 1899. *Il Circolo giuridico* 30: 44.
Court of Cassation, criminal section, 4 April 1899. *Monitore dei Tribunali* 40: 517 (also in *La Legge* 39.1: 818).
Court of Cassation, criminal section, 12 May 1899. *Monitore dei Tribunali* 40: 817 (also in *Il Circolo giuridico* 29: 29).
Court of Cassation, criminal section, 23 November 1899. *Monitore dei Tribunali* 41: 76.
Court of Cassation, criminal section, 22 September 1899. *Monitore dei Tribunali* 40: 855 (also in *La Legge* 39.2: 749).
Court of Cassation, criminal section, 18 April 1900. *Il Foro italiano* 25: 359.

Court of Cassation, criminal section, 10 December 1901, cited in Faraggiana, Giuseppe. 1904. *Il lavoro delle donne e dei fanciulli. Commento alla Legge 19–6–902 con richiami di giurisprudenza (Progetto Turati 19–5–904).* Genova-Torino: Renzo Streglio 1904, 94.
Court of Cassation, criminal section, 18 December 1901. *Monitore dei Tribunali* 43: 239.
Court of Cassation, criminal section, 9 April 1904. *Il Circolo giuridico* 35: 63.
Court of Cassation, 18 December 1904. La *Cassazione unica* 13: 530.
Court of Cassation, criminal section, 21 October 1905. *Monitore dei Tribunali* 46: 998.
Magistrates' Court of Conegliano, 14 August 1906. *Bollettino dell'Ufficio del lavoro* 8: 319.
Magistrates' Court of Naples, 13 April 1907. *Bollettino dell'Ufficio del lavoro* 8: 947.
Court of Cassation, criminal section, 4 June 1907. *Monitore dei Tribunali* 48: 597–598.
Magistrates' Court of Asti, 7 June 1907. *Bollettino dell'Ufficio del lavoro* 8: 948.
Magistrates' Court of Caselle torinese, 17 June 1907. *Bollettino dell'Ufficio del lavoro* 8: 948.
Court of Cassation, criminal section, 25 November 1907. *Monitore dei Tribunali* 49: 39–40.
Court of Cassation, criminal section, 23 January 1908. *Monitore dei Tribunali* 49: 317–318.
Court of Cassation, criminal section, 13 February 1908. *Monitore dei Tribunali* 49: 538–539.
Court of Cassation, criminal section, 11 June 1908. *Monitore dei Tribunali* 49: 737, also in *La Legge* 49: 377.
Court of Cassation, 22 December 1908. *Monitore dei Tribunali* 50: 179.
Magistrates' Court of Genoa, 25 November 1910. *Bollettino dell'Ufficio del lavoro* 16: 439.
Magistrates' Court of Milan, 28 December 1910. *Bollettino dell'Ufficio del lavoro* 16: 241.
Court of Cassation, criminal section, 22 February 1912. *Monitore dei Tribunali* 53: 414–415.

What Can We Learn from a Family Law Course? The Teachings of an Early 20th Century Italian Professor

Annamaria Monti

Abstract This article aims to explore the concept of the family in Italian legal thought from the end of the 19th century up to the first 15 years of the 20th century. Focus is placed on a source which has been largely untapped by historiographers, namely the lecture notes from law courses taught at Italian universities. Specifically, this article shall examine the lecture notes which recorded the teachings of Alfredo Ascoli (1863–1942), an eminent jurist who held professorships of Italian Private Law at the University of Pavia and Bocconi University in Milan during the period under examination. Ascoli was also a co-founder of the law journal *Rivista di diritto civile* (1909), as well as a future member of the Royal Commission for the Post-war period (1917). The Italian Civil Code of 1865 struggled in many ways to meet the needs of a society that had already embarked upon the path of industrialization. At the same time, many Italian jurists were seeking new solutions in order to reform the legal method. By examining the teaching of law, it is possible to evaluate not only the state of teaching methodologies at the time, but also the extent to which the era's profound social and economic changes were being dealt with in university lecture halls, where the country's future ruling class received their education.

1 Preliminary Remarks

It is a well-known fact that whenever there are momentous economic, social or political changes in the world, the basic organizational units of society are the first to feel the effects—and this especially applies to the family. There is evidence of this every day in our globalized world, even more so now with new discoveries in science and advancements in medicine. Nevertheless, those same basic units are more often than not the last parts of society to actually see legal reforms resulting from such changes.

A. Monti (✉)
Bocconi University, Department of Legal Studies, Via Röntgen 1, 20136 Milan, Italy
e-mail: annamaria.monti@unibocconi.it

M.G. di Renzo Villata (ed.), *Family Law and Society in Europe from the Middle Ages to the Contemporary Era*, Studies in the History of Law and Justice 5,
DOI 10.1007/978-3-319-42289-3_13

As far as family law is concerned, legislators normally adopt a conservative approach aimed at safeguarding the established order and legal certainty. Rarely is a law passed that is 'ahead of its time' so to speak, or that does not at least have the backing of the majority of citizens. Look no further than the current public debate going on in Italy, which ranges from civil unions and same-sex marriage to 'stepchild adoptions' for homosexual couples.

Looking back on the 19th and 20th centuries, another example that stands out is the controversial issue of divorce in Italy, which was only legalized in 1970. Napoleon had introduced it to Italy in 1806 with his civil code, but Italian society was not ready to change its customs, being deeply influenced by the teachings of the Church. Indeed, there were very few cases of divorce recorded during the 15-year period of French rule.[1]

The issue of divorce in Italy would be debated on several occasions after Italian unification. One such example was in the aftermath of World War One, when lawful wives of missing soldiers were remarrying under the presumption that they had been widowed. Problems arose when a husband who was thought to have died on the front lines had in actuality been a prisoner of war: upon his return home, he would find his place 'taken'. Once again, there were heated debates and bills proposed, but in the end the issue was dropped.[2]

While the Italian Civil Code of 1865 had introduced civil marriage, at the same time it had excluded its dissolution through divorce.[3] Furthermore, Italian society in the wake of unification was still heavily influenced by Catholicism, which was the dominant tradition in the country, and the lower social classes were mostly illiterate. Such circumstances meant that even though government legislation provided for a civil marriage, citizens still preferred a religious marriage ceremony, officiated by ministers of religion and regulated by canon law.[4]

This resulted in an almost paradoxical situation that troubled politicians and legislators in unified Italy: citizens were opting for the canonical form of marriage, even though such a marriage did not produce any civil effects in the Italian legal system. Several proposals were made to remedy the problem, and in the late 1920s a solution was adopted: the so-called "concordatory" marriage. This type of

[1]Ungari, Paolo. 2002 (first edition 1974). *Storia del diritto di famiglia in Italia 1796–1975*. Bologna: Il Mulino; Vismara, Giulio. 1978. *Il diritto di famiglia in Italia dalle riforme ai codici*. Milano: Giuffrè; di Renzo Villata, Gigliola. 2001. La famiglia. In *Enciclopedia Italiana. Eredità del Novecento*, 759–776. Roma: Istituto dell'Enciclopedia Italiana.

[2]Valsecchi, Chiara. 2004. *In difesa della famiglia? Divorzisti e antidivorzisti in Italia tra Otto e Novecento*. Milano: Giuffrè, 594–609.

[3]Solimano, Stefano. 2003. *"Il letto di Procuste". Diritto e politica nella formazione del codice civile unitario. I progetti Cassinis (1860–1861)*. Milano: Giuffrè, 280–291; Valsecchi 2004 (as n. 2) 1–69. Lastly, see di Renzo Villata, Gigliola. 2014. Il matrimonio civile. Diritto, politica e religione tra avvocati "impegnati" prima e dopo l'Unità. In Borsacchi, Stefano, and Pene Vidari, Gian Savino (eds.), *Avvocati protagonisti e rinnovatori del primo diritto unitario*, 123–166. Bologna: il Mulino.

[4]Passaniti, Paolo. 2011. *Diritto di famiglia e ordine sociale. Il percorso storico della società coniugale in Italia*. Milano: Giuffrè, 264–267.

marriage was first introduced in the Lateran Pacts of 1929 between the Catholic Church and the Italian State, and was later amended by an agreement in 1984 between the Holy See and the Italian Republic.[5] According to this agreement—which is still in force today—a concordatory marriage is valid in the eyes of both civil and canon law as long as certain conditions are met.[6]

Clearly, the legal technicalities of family law implied delicate issues that had a profound influence over the decisions of legislators, the rulings of judges and the stance taken by legal doctrine. The same is still true today: when the very structure of society is at stake, it inevitably leads to hesitancy, uncertainty and debate, revealing the ideological biases and moral qualms of all involved.

Building on the above, this article aims to explore the concept of the family in Italian legal thought from the end of the 19th century up to the first 15 years of the 20th century. Focus is placed on a source which has been largely untapped by historiographers, namely the lecture notes from law courses taught at Italian universities. The present article—which by no means claims to be comprehensive—draws on a much broader and still ongoing research project into these aforementioned lecture notes.[7]

By examining the teaching of law, it is possible to evaluate the state of teaching methodologies at the time and their relationship with the legal doctrine and practice. In addition, it provides an opportunity to assess the extent to which university lectures were coming to grips with the profound social and economic changes of the era. After all, the country's ruling class received their education in those very classrooms, as two-thirds of the Italian parliament during the Liberal Era were lawyers.

There are overlapping points of view in conducting an analysis of this sort. Firstly, at that time the Civil Code of 1865 struggled in many ways to meet the needs of a society that had already embarked upon the path of industrialization. This was compounded by the fact that the industrialization process had led to a progressive 'urbanization' of the masses, as well as the beginnings of women's emancipation. Changes in the ways people lived and worked were clearly reflected in the realm of family law.

Secondly, the historical period under examination was an age in which Europe as a whole was thoroughly rethinking how law was to be interpreted. For their part, Italian jurists too sought new solutions in order to reform the legal method.[8] The codes in force at the time were still rooted in the 19th century and could not satisfy the needs of a rapidly changing society. The more open-minded interpreters of law strove for innovative solutions, drawing on ideas from the social sciences and

[5]Pertici, Roberto. 2009. *Chiesa e Stato in Italia. Dalla grande guerra al nuovo concordato (1914–1984).* Bologna: Il Mulino, 143 ff.

[6]From a practical point of view: Di Marzio, Paolo. 2008. *Il matrimonio concordatario e gli altri matrimoni religiosi con effetti civili.* Padova: Cedam.

[7]Monti, Annamaria. 2014. Tradizione e rinnovamento nella didattica giuridica: prime riflessioni per un'indagine sull'Italia liberale. *Rivista di storia del diritto italiano* 87: 287–312.

[8]Refer to Grossi, Paolo. 2002. *Scienza giuridica italiana. Un profilo storico.* Milano: Giuffrè.

modern comparative law, but also—and no less importantly—from Germany's influential legal doctrine, which itself was going through a period of heated critical debate.[9]

Thirdly, the renewal of legal doctrine was having a direct effect on the academic world in Italy,[10] as well as in Germany,[11] France[12] or Spain[13] between the end of the 19th century and World War One—the latter event being a watershed and point of no return in the history of law as well.[14] As a result, new courses and teaching methods were introduced, which in turn gave rise to new scientific disciplines that would be further developed over the course of the 20th century.[15]

Looking specifically at the Italian peninsula, the Casati Law (1859) had begun the process of standardizing university teaching in the years immediately following unification. As far as legal studies were concerned, this meant that an education in law could only be obtained at universities, under the tutelage of tenured professors, associate professors and private lecturers. The selection of these aforementioned teachers was to be merit-based, with tenured professors selected nationally and the others selected locally.[16]

Lastly, a final preliminary remark must be made about the source being analyzed in the present article, namely the lecture notes pertaining to courses taught by professors, which were collected by the students themselves and later published as lithographs.[17] While these notes were study material that reflected what was taught

[9]Halpérin, Jean–Louis. 2015. *Histoire de l'état des juristes. Allemagne, XIXe–XXe siècles*. Paris: Classiques Garnier, 207 ff.

[10]See Cianferotti, Giulio. 1989. La prolusione di Orlando. Il paradigma pandettistico, i nuovi giuristi universitari e lo Stato liberale. *Rivista trimestrale di diritto pubblico* 4: 995–1023.

[11]Schiera, Pierangelo. 1987. *Il laboratorio borghese. Scienza e politica nella Germania dell'Ottocento*. Bologna: Il Mulino.

[12]Audren, Frédéric. 2011. Les professeurs de droit, la République et le nouvel esprit juridique. Introduction. *Mil neuf cent. La Belle Epoque des juristes. Enseigner le droit dans la République* 29: 7–33.

[13]Petit, Carlos. 2005. De la *historia* a la *memoria*. A propósito de una reciente obra de historia universitaria. *Cuadernos del Instituto Antonio de Nebrija* 8: 237–279.

[14]Lobban, Michael and Willem H. van Boom. 2014. The Great War and Private Law. *Comparative Legal History* 2:2: 163–183.

[15]See Monti, Annamaria. 2013. La concorrenza sleale e gli esordi del diritto industriale nell'Italia liberale: verso una teoria generale della concorrenza? In Sciumé, Alberto, and Fusar Poli, Elisabetta (eds.), *«Afferrare ...l'inafferrabile». I giuristi e il diritto della nuova economia industriale fra Otto e Novecento*, 130–134. Milano: Giuffrè; Monti, Annamaria. 2015. Enseigner le droit en Italie au début du XXe siècle: les cours de législation comparée de Giovanni Pacchioni (1867–1946). In *Aux confins du droit. Mélanges–Hommage amical à Xavier Martin*, 305–314. Paris: LGDJ.

[16]Porciani, Ilaria, and Moretti, Mauro. 2007. La creazione del sistema universitario nella nuova Italia. In Brizzi, Gian Paolo, Del Negro, Piero and Romano, Andrea (eds.), *Storia delle Università in Italia* I, 323–379. Messina: Sicania.

[17]Chiosso, Giorgio. 2009. Stampatori ed editori per l'Università e la scuola tra Otto e primo Novecento. In Brizzi Gian Paolo, and Tavoni, Maria Gioia (eds.), *Dalla pecia all'e-book. Libri per l'Università: stampa, editoria, circolazione e lettura*, 648–653. Bologna: CLUEB.

in lectures, they did not always bear the approval of the professor himself. Indeed, they often had a bad reputation in the academic world, especially when the professor had not re-read and approved them, and this is something to keep in mind when examining them. Nonetheless, these notes today represent a precious tool for researchers, allowing them to have in-depth access to the teaching methodology of the time so that they can appreciate its form and content.

It would be impossible to cover such a vast field of research in its entirety, not least because—as mentioned above—the project is still ongoing. As such, this article shall take the form of a case study, focusing on the lecture notes which recorded the teachings of Alfredo Ascoli (1863–1942) on the subject of family law. Ascoli was an eminent law professor who held the chair of Italian Private Law at the University of Pavia and Bocconi University in Milan in the early 20th century.

2 Alfredo Ascoli's Family Law Lectures

Alfredo Ascoli was a Tuscan jurist of Jewish origins who studied under Filippo Serafini at the University of Pisa in the 1880s.[18] He was a full professor of Italian Private Law at the University of Pavia in 1903–1904, and his lessons that academic year on natural and legal persons were diligently recorded by some of his students. In particular, two third-year students—Domenico Moretto and Guido Scotti—recorded notes on the rights of natural persons, which is of specific interest to the present article. Ascoli himself had re-read the notes before they were published as lithographs by the *Premiato Stabilimento tipo-litografico successori Marelli*—one of the city's printing houses—and then distributed among all the law students, to help them study for the exam.[19]

The course material was clearly and articulately presented, starting off with the definition of personal law and an overview of the entire course. Ascoli's goal was to range over the concepts of 'natural person' and 'legal person', and to then go more in depth on legal capacity, the capacity to act and the legal status of natural persons—in other words, "the various conditions in which a person might find himself in civil

[18]Osti, Giuseppe. 1943. Alfredo Ascoli. *Rivista di diritto civile* 35: 1–4; Abbondanza, Roberto. 1962. Ascoli, Alfredo. In *Dizionario Biografico degli Italiani* 4, 377–379. Roma: Istituto della Enciclopedia italiana; Bonini, Roberto. 1973. *Problemi di storia delle codificazioni e della politica legislativa*. Bologna: Pàtron Editore, 243–250; Grossi 2002 (as n. 8) 465–487; Femia, Pasquale. 2013. Ascoli, Alfredo. In Birocchi, Italo, Cortese, Ennio, Mattone, Antonello, and Miletti, Marco Nicola (eds.), *Dizionario Biografico dei Giuristi Italiani (XII–XX secolo)* 1, 111–114. Bologna: il Mulino. See also Chiodi, Giovanni. 2007. «Innovare senza distruggere»: il progetto italo–francese di codice delle obbligazioni e dei contratti (1927). In Alpa, Guido, and Chiodi, Giovanni, *Il progetto italo francese delle obbligazioni (1927). Un modello di armonizzazione nell'epoca della ricodificazione*, 43–146. Milano: Giuffrè.

[19]Ascoli, Alfredo. 1904. *Lezioni di diritto civile (diritto delle persone). Appunti presi da Domenico Moretto III anno—Guido Scotti III anno e riveduti dal Chiarissimo Professore. Anno 1903–1904*. Pavia: Premiato Stabilimento Tipo Litografico Successori Marelli.

society".[20] The professor would explain the concepts and then point out exactly where such concepts were provided for in the Italian legal system of the time.

Ascoli was not one to linger over methodological issues during his lectures, nor was it his wont to do so in his strictly scientific publications; thus, the transcriptions of his lessons showed no trace of the heated debates on the legal method that so engaged many of his contemporaries. Nonetheless, his lectures were not merely a gloss on the sources of law, but rather an accurate and critical explanation of the provisions contained in the Italian Civil Code of 1865, which is what the students were there to learn.

Those lessons were the result of extensive teaching experience that Ascoli had built up in the years prior, starting in Macerata, where the jurist had taught Roman Law, and continuing in Perugia and Messina. By the beginning of the new century he had secured the chair of Italian Private Law at the University of Pavia, as mentioned above. Ascoli's career as a university professor would conclude at Sapienza University in Rome, where he moved immediately after the war.[21]

Undoubtedly, the most interesting part of his private law course in Pavia was when he examined a person's *status familiae*, "the condition according to which an individual is bound to other individuals by familial ties, which [in turn] determine certain consequences [such as] the obligation of maintenance and the ways in which succession is administered, if nothing else". He illustrated the legal concepts of kinship and affinity, specifying how "family status is the position that a given person has in a household, which is composed of persons descending from a common ancestor".[22]

On the topic of natural kinship, Ascoli elaborated on that which derived from adultery or incest, illegitimate unions that were considered 'criminal' at the time. Both adulterous and incestuous unions were subject to moral condemnation, and as such, both were lacking in legal safeguards for any children that may have resulted. Only *pietatis causa* would such children have a right to maintenance. In any case, Ascoli refrained from making any comment that did not focus on the law as it stood at the time.

Ascoli also cautioned against confusing status with legal capacity, which some French writers frequently seemed to do. Rather, the two concepts were to be kept distinct: a person's 'status' did not change his or her legal capacity, though it could still have an effect on his actions. On the other hand, a person's legal capacity could be changed by other aspects, such as gender, age, health, and kinship—conditions that had a direct influence on one's legal capacity to act.[23]

The professor used a similar theoretical premise to tackle the key issue of the legal status of women, which he considered very interesting "both from a historical

[20]Ascoli 1904 (as n. 19) 11–13.

[21]See Ascoli, Alfredo. 1922. *Istituzioni di diritto civile: corso dettato nella Regia Università di Roma*. Napoli: Perrella.

[22]Ascoli 1904 (as n. 19) 160–167.

[23]Ascoli 1904 (as n. 19) 12.

point of view and a practical point of view." Nevertheless, he was of the opinion that the issue lost much of its relevance when seen under Italian positive law: as a general rule, women were granted the same legal status as men for what concerned all family and property rights.[24]

In reality, Ascoli acknowledged that there was no explicit provision in Italian law that affirmed this supposed equal status; on the contrary, the Civil Code never spoke of men and women together, but always used masculine articles and adjectives. And to tell the truth, if today we re-examine the legal status of women in Italy between the late 19th and early 20th centuries, it certainly seems far-fetched to speak of 'equal status': look no further than the fact that married women were required to obtain the authorization of their husbands for acts of extraordinary administration.[25]

In that light, how could the professor support his thesis with such conviction? First of all, he cited an ancient Roman maxim to justify the linguistic choices of Italian legislators in 1865, which held that the feminine is contained within the masculine: thus, there could be no doubt that the provisions of the Civil Code referred to women as much as it did to men, save certain special cases. And seeing as how he could not deny that the Code had set out a series of restrictions on women's capacity to act, he preferred to view it as "a special condition" for women themselves; one might have objected that it depends on the point of view!

Ascoli insisted: a woman could marry at the age of fifteen if she had her parents' consent (a man had to wait until he was eighteen), and she could contract a marriage without her parents' consent at the age of twenty-one (a man had to wait until he was twenty-five). But were these really special conditions? Or rather, was it the legacy of a society in which women were essentially destined to become wives and mothers?

Whatever it was, Ascoli was forced to admit to his (mostly male) students that when it came to guardianship, there were indeed some serious restrictions: the Italian Civil Code did not grant women the right to become legal guardians, except under special circumstances. The professor deemed it "a relic of the age-old disparity between the two sexes, and of the ancient principle that was adhered to in drawing up our Code, that guardianship is a *virile munus* and as such is not conferrable upon a woman"; he then proceeded to briefly compare the situation to other countries' legislation.[26]

The professor's intellectual honesty was not at issue when he declared that men and women enjoyed equal status in the eyes of the civil legislation in force in Italy

---

[24]Ascoli 1904 (as n. 19) 214–229, 214–323.

[25]See Guerra Medici, Maria Teresa. 1990. Due secoli di storia dell'emancipazione femminile: dalle leggi giacobine alla costituzione repubblicana. *Studi Senesi* 102: 149–168; Passaniti 2011 (as n. 4) 269–328; Di Simone, Maria Rosa. 2014. Le discussioni sui diritti delle donne per il codice civile unitario. In Borsacchi and Pene Vidari (as n. 3) 95–121.

[26]Ascoli 1904 (as n. 19) 226–229.

at the time—nonetheless, perhaps his assessments were too optimistic. Ascoli possessed a generally open-minded way of thinking, but it was certainly not yet 'modern'. His interpretation of the norms in force confirmed as much.

On the one hand, and in spite of himself, he was forced to admit that the husband's authorization as required by article 134 of the Civil Code amounted to a gender-based restriction: said article stated that a married woman could not carry out certain legal acts regarding the family estate without her husband's authorization, or in some cases without court authorization. And it was of no consolation that French legislators had been even more inflexible on the matter; it would have been more appropriate to follow in the footsteps of German law, which did not have such restrictions, and 'very rightfully so' in his opinion.

On the other hand, he did not cease in defending his thesis that fundamentally speaking, the Civil Code was based on the principle of recognizing women's full legal capacity, except for the few cases described in the code itself. The way he saw it, the fact that a married woman was dependent upon her husband was not because women were seen as weaker- minded, but simply because of a need for a dominant authority in the family, "and this authority was given to the man".[27]

A separate though closely-related issue was that of a woman's legal capacity when it came to public or not exclusively public activities. These cases were not regulated by the Civil Code but rather by other legislation, and concerned such matters as the right to vote, access to certain positions in public office such as the magistracy, or the possibility to be chosen as a juror.

According to the Albertine Statute of 1848, which was the constitution in force during Italy's Liberal Era, all subjects were equal before the law. They all enjoyed the same civil and political rights, and they were all permitted to hold civil or military positions, "except for the exceptions established by law" (article 24).

Now, given what Ascoli deemed "the state of the social conscience" at the time these laws were enacted, it was commonly understood that women were excluded from rights such as the right to vote or from official positions such as the magistracy—this despite the fact that such exclusion had never actually been explicitly stated. No one had dared take up an opposing view, as it would have been in direct opposition "to the general conscience"; thus, any laws that made no mention of women's legal capacity were to be interpreted in a restrictive sense: it was understood that women were excluded.[28]

However, there were some cases in which a woman working in certain professions would not have been considered an 'affront' to the public conscience, even if—once again—the rules governing the admission requirements for such positions did not specify whether they could be held by a woman or not. Such professions included that of a lawyer or solicitor. There was much debate at the time over the best interpretation of these laws, and even though he was on record as generally

[27]Ascoli 1904 (as n. 19) 280–286.

[28]Ascoli 1904 (as n. 19) 231 ff.

being in favor of not excluding women from such official positions, Ascoli was against allowing women to practice the legal profession.

Ascoli would return to this issue on different occasions in the years to come, though he would refrain from expressing any opinion on the matter. One such example was in 1912, when the Teresa Labriola case broke out.[29] As editor of the *Rivista di diritto civile* (Civil Law Journal),[30] Ascoli took the opportunity to publish an account of the debate over whether a woman could practice the legal profession. Almost 30 years had passed since two rulings issued by the Turin Court of Appeal in 1883 and 1884 had sparked a heated debate in Italy, and now it was worthy of discussion once again.[31] With his usual articulateness and conciseness, the professor explained the state of the issue from a doctrinal and jurisprudential point of view, while at the same time drawing attention to the most recent legislation on the matter.[32]

Lastly, to return to Ascoli's lessons on the legal capacity of women, the professor included another category of laws—such as the law on labor disputes of 1893—which explicitly permitted women to vote and run for positions in workers' arbitration boards.[33] The state of industrialization by the end of the century had opened up new possibilities for women: a woman could now act as a judge or arbitrator for work-related issues. *Nulla quaestio* as to a woman's legal capacity in this case.[34]

In addition to this lengthy digression on the legal status of women, Ascoli also placed much focus on the laws governing absence in the technical sense. As he himself explained, he was interested in those cases in which an individual was away from a certain place and no information was available on said individual, thus making it "uncertain whether he is alive or dead". In such circumstances, a number of interests had to be taken into account for several parties, above all for what concerned the absentee himself.[35]

It is worth taking a closer look at the lessons Ascoli gave on absence during his course at the University of Pavia in 1903–1904, as the topic was directly related to the absentee's familial relations.[36] Indeed, it almost acted as a catalyst for debate

[29]Taricone, Fiorenza. 1994. *Teresa Labriola. Biografia politica di un'intellettuale tra Ottocento e Novecento*. Milano: Angeli, 13–19.

[30]Furgiuele, Giovanni. 1987. La «Rivista di diritto civile» dal 1909 al 1931. *Quaderni Fiorentini* 16: 519–630.

[31]Refer to Tacchi, Francesca. 2009. *Eva togata. Donne e professioni giuridiche in Italia dall'Unità a oggi.* Torino: Utet, 3–35.

[32]Ascoli, Alfredo. 1912. Le donne e l'avvocatura. *Rivista di diritto civile* 4: 704–705.

[33]Passaniti 2011 (as n. 4) 309–311.

[34]Ascoli 1904 (as n. 19) 232–233.

[35]See Di Renzo Villata, Gigliola. 2011. L'absence dans la jurisprudence après l'unification italienne le modèle français et quelques nouveautés. In Hoareau Jacqueline, Métairie Guillaume (eds.), *L'absence. Du cas de l'absent à la théorie de l'absence*, 339–361. Limoges: Pulim, and the bibliography cited therein.

[36]Ascoli 1904 (as n. 19) 31–106.

over a series of thorny questions in Italian family law, such as marriage, separation and filiation.

In particular, paternal authority would be transferred to the mother. Additionally, an absent husband could no longer exercise his authority over his wife, and thus a woman no longer needed her husband's authorization, as mentioned above. Nonetheless, the marriage remained indissoluble even in cases of prolonged absence: as stated above, Italian legislation did not provide for divorce at the time.[37]

In that regard, Ascoli noted that the law in force did not provide for the presumption of death, which meant that the absentee's wife was legally bound to him until it was possible to prove his death. In this case, any second marriage that was contracted would be considered invalid. Nevertheless, the law established that the nullity of such a marriage could not be enforced unless the absentee had returned or had been proved to be alive.

In his explanation of how the Italian Civil Code governed the legal status of absent persons, Ascoli made detailed reference to Roman law and medieval law, as well as to the different concept of "presumption of death" that was present in German custom. Furthermore, he referenced the work of the French jurist Pothier and the choices made under Napoleon, with a focus on the key concept of "uncertainty" that dominated legal institutions in the French and Italian codes. According to this concept, a declaration of absence was never a presumption of death. Ascoli did not hesitate to declare his preference for the German system, as he believed that a presumption of death was more practical than the system adopted by the Italian and French codes.[38]

Though he could not have known it at the time, the professor's lectures were actually a preview of the issues that he would have to deal with as a legislator several years later (examined below).

Regardless of the topics presented in his lectures, Ascoli demonstrated extraordinary lucidity and originality of thought, which he combined with his extensive cultural knowledge of legal history and a receptiveness to comparative law in the broadest sense of the term.

Ascoli never failed to go in depth on the crucial issues, so as to illustrate the historical evolution of laws: after all, he had carried out serious studies on Roman law, especially at the beginning of his career, and his expertise extended to medieval and modern law as well. His friend Angelo Sraffa[39] described him as "an expert in civil law as well as Roman law".[40] Moreover, his lessons always made sure to compare legislation, and it was not simply an academic exercise; in particular, he focused on the choices made by French, Austrian and German legislators. The professor showed a preference for French legislation, doctrine and

---

[37]Ascoli 1904 (as n. 19) 95–97.

[38]Ascoli 1904 (as n. 19) 38–40.

[39]Monti, Annamaria. 2011. *Angelo Sraffa. Un 'antiteorico' del diritto*. Milano: Egea.

[40]"Civilista *doublé* di romanista": Sraffa, Angelo. 1898. Alfredo Ascoli. Trattato delle donazioni secondo il diritto civile italiano. Firenze, Cammelli, 1898. *Giurisprudenza italiana* 1898: IV/220.

jurisprudence when explaining the various topics to his students, which was understandable given that a good part of the Italian Civil Code of 1865 was influenced by France.

Ascoli brought a similar approach to the lectures he taught at another university in the early twentieth century: the recently established Bocconi University in Milan. This university did not provide an education for jurists, however, but rather for future entrepreneurs and economic scholars.[41] Ascoli started at Bocconi immediately in 1902–1903: it is likely that the abovementioned Angelo Sraffa, his long-time friend and colleague, had asked him to do so.[42] Indeed, Sraffa himself was very close with the one man who had done more than anyone else in organizing the curriculum offered by the new university: Leopoldo Sabbatini.[43]

Studies in law were of fundamental importance to the economic education provided by Bocconi at the time,[44] especially private law, public law and commercial law—Alfredo Ascoli was put in charge of the private law courses.

The notes from his lectures at Bocconi were recorded regularly by his students between 1902 and 1918, and even though they were lessons for students who would not go on to become jurists, they still featured the same rigor and exactitude that were hallmarks of his time in Pavia, as seen above.

Ascoli's treatment of family law varied from year to year, but in any case the most interesting issues that he tackled were marriage and divorce.[45]

---

[41] Cattini, Marco, Decleva, Enrico, De Maddalena, Aldo, Romani, Marzio A. 1992. *Storia di una libera università*, I, *L'Università Commerciale Luigi Bocconi dalle origini al 1914*. Milano: Giuffrè.

[42] Bagiotti, Tullio. 1952. *Storia della Università Bocconi 1902–1952*. Milano: Università Bocconi, 12.

[43] Romani, Marzio A. 1997. *Costruire le istituzioni. Leopoldo Sabbatini (1860–1914)*. Soveria Mannelli: Rubbettino.

[44] Porta, Pier Luigi. [1998]. Istituzioni e centri di elaborazione della cultura economica. In Porta, Pier Luigi (ed.), *Milano e la cultura economica nel XX secolo*, I, *Gli anni 1890–1920*, 172–175. Milano: Angeli.

[45] See Ascoli, Alfredo. 1905. *Diritto privato: 1. corso UCLB*. [S.l.: s.n.]; Ascoli, Alfredo. 1908. *Università commerciale Luigi Bocconi. Istituzioni di diritto privato: anno accademico 1907–1908*. Pavia: Premiato stabilimento tipo–litografico succ. Bruni; Ascoli, Alfredo. [1909]. *Università commerciale Luigi Bocconi. Istituzioni di diritto privato 1908–1909 del chiarissimo prof. Alfredo Ascoli*. Pavia: Premiato stabilimento tipo–litografico succ. Bruni; Ascoli, Alfredo. [1910]. *Università commerciale Luigi Bocconi. Diritto privato: anno accademico 1909–1910. Lezioni del chiarissimo prof. Alfredo Ascoli*. [S.l.: s.n.]; Ascoli, Alfredo. 1911. *Università commerciale Luigi Bocconi. Diritto privato anno accademico 1910–1911. Lezioni del chiarissimo prof. Ascoli [raccolte da Pietro Tramalloni]*. Pavia: Tacchinardi e Ferrari; Ascoli, Alfredo. 1912. *Università commerciale Luigi Bocconi. Istituzioni di diritto privato. 1. corso: anno 1911–1912 [prof. A. Ascoli.] Appunti raccolti da Lanfranco Di Brenzone*. Pavia: Tacchinardi e Ferrari; Ascoli, Alfredo. [1913]. *Università commerciale Luigi Bocconi. Lezioni di diritto privato tenute dal chiarissimo prof. Ascoli*. Pavia: Premiato stabilimento tipo– litografico succ. Bruni; Ascoli, Alfredo. [1914]. *Università commerciale Luigi Bocconi. Lezioni di istituzioni di diritto privato tenute dal chiarissimo prof. A. Ascoli*. [S.l.: s.n.]; Ascoli, Alfredo. [1918]. *Università commerciale Luigi Bocconi. Lezioni di istituzioni di diritto privato tenute dal chiarissimo prof. Ascoli. Anno accademico 1917–1918*. Milano: Tipo–litogr. Tenconi.

Regarding the former, Ascoli provided a good account of the age-old problem that still remained unresolved at the time, namely the relationship between a civil marriage and a religious marriage. Specifically, he examined religious marriage ceremonies that were neither preceded nor followed by civil ceremonies, as well as several bills that were debated—and rejected—by the Italian parliament in the Liberal Era regarding the obligation to perform a civil ceremony before the canonical form of marriage.[46]

The professor offered an objective and matter-of-fact perspective on the real issues and political debates of the era, which centered around the relationship between the Church and State in Italy as well as the prevailing customs in many regions of the country.[47] There would be other opportunities for Ascoli's clear thought to be exhibited even further in the years to come, for example through publications in the *Rivista di diritto civile* during World War One, which saw him criticize those who were "excessively respectful of the *freedom of conscience*" just as he was critical of those "most jealous defenders of the State's civil authority".[48]

As far as divorce was concerned, the professor's digressions once again ranged from classical Roman law to Justinian's law. He also compared the Italian legal system—which did not allow divorce—with other legislation that indeed provided for it.

During his lessons, Ascoli made a distinction between a stricter, 'Latin' form of legislation and 'looser' legislation: an example of the former could be found in France, where divorce was allowed in cases in which Italian legislation would have permitted the legal separation of the spouses; an example of the latter was in Switzerland, where no specific grounds for a divorce were necessary in the event that the bond of marriage was irreparably damaged. Moreover, Swiss legislation allowed a marriage to be dissolved "not only by mutual consent, but also upon the request of one of the spouses": Ascoli equated this to an outright legalization of repudiation. Evidently he did not understand the importance of the Swiss law in terms of what it meant for freedom and modernity.

As far as the situation in Italy was concerned, the professor provided an account of the debates on the subject up to that point, explaining that the arguments for or against legalizing divorce had been more sociological and political in nature than anything else, and that they had concerned "the customs of a people and the state of their culture". Thus, there were no arguments rooted in the law itself, and indeed it could not have been any other way: as long as marriage was considered a religious sacrament, the problem would not present itself. But now that the civil marriage had been introduced, the issue could be debated;[49] though there would be no rule

---

[46]Valsecchi 2004 (as n. 2) 69–131.

[47]See King, Bolton, Okey, Thomas. 1904. *L'Italia oggi*. Bari: Laterza, 399–401.

[48]Ascoli, Alfredo. 1909. La circolare del ministro guardasigilli sui matrimoni religiosi non preceduti o seguiti dal matrimonio civile. *Rivista di diritto civile* 1: 671–676. See also Ascoli, Alfredo. 1916. La precedenza obbligatoria del matrimonio civile sul religioso e le pensioni di guerra. *Rivista di diritto civile* 8: 371–375.

[49]On these debates refer to Valsecchi 2004 (as n. 2).

forbidding Catholics from considering marriage indissoluble, if their conscience so compelled them.

Ascoli went on to say that while indissolubility was a “very beautiful” ideal, it was nonetheless impossible to deny that achieving it on a case by case basis often conflicted with the more pressing need of peace of mind in the individual and in the family. This was especially true in a society like Italy’s at the time, in which the ties of family “were becoming weaker and weaker”, while more and more importance was being placed on “the individual freedom of each [family] member”.[50] The professor had no doubt that this “spirit of individualism” would eventually come to dominate the bond of marriage as well, and that Italy too would ultimately legalize divorce.

Ascoli offered the following concluding remarks during his course: “We do not know whether this will be for good or for ill, and it is beyond the scope of our discussion to find out: what is sure is that when our people’s conscience has matured, divorce will be introduced here as well”.[51] Years later, at the conclusion of World War One, Ascoli would become a legislator and align himself with supporters of the introduction of divorce in Italy. He felt that the time was ripe, but they would fail in their efforts, and Ascoli would be labeled as a *divorzista*, or pro-divorce activist.

On the other hand, another Jewish professor of Italian private law would go on to be considered a clear-thinking champion of the anti-divorce movement for years to come: Vittorio Polacco, who was actually Ascoli’s friend and colleague at Sapienza University in Rome immediately after the war, and who had delivered his famous lecture entitled *Contro in divorzio* at the University of Padua in 1892.[52]

3 Conclusions

What can be learned from Ascoli’s lectures, and in particular from his treatment of specific areas of family law?

A historiographical reconstruction based on lecture notes cannot reproduce the moment a lesson was given, nor can it capture the learning experience of a student in the classroom. By their very nature, these notes can offer but a limited idea of the

[50]Ascoli 1905 (as n. 45) 87–90.

[51]As n. 50.

[52]Polacco, Vittorio. 1893. *Contro il divorzio. Lezione tenuta il 2 maggio 1892 nella Regia Università di Padova*. Padova: Fratelli Drucker. Refer to Grossi, Paolo. 1989. “Il coraggio della moderazione” (Specularità dell’itinerario riflessivo di Vittorio Polacco). *Quaderni fiorentini* 18: 197–251; Valsecchi 2004 (as n. 2) 475–488.

liveliness of the professor's teaching.[53] Nevertheless, it is undeniable that these sources have great value as material for individual study, a written record of the topics, ideas and issues that were discussed during the course.

The professor's task was to teach his students the laws in force in Italy, and from that point of view Alfredo Ascoli's lessons revealed his solid background and articulateness in the field. In some specific areas of family law, Ascoli dared to take a fresh stance that went beyond the purely legal aspects of the matter and came to include moral and social issues. At times it was possible to discern a certain degree of modernity in his thought, which often went against the mainstream legal doctrine of his era.

At the same time, he always respected the strict canons governing the interpretation of laws: as seen above, he would propose an extensive or restrictive interpretation on a case by case basis. Ascoli was a jurist and reasoned as such, and he made an effort to teach his students a type of reasoning that was rigorous and exact. He provided them with an example of a legal mindset that paid close attention to the individuality of those to whom the laws applied. He was not at all inclined to dwell on theoretical or methodological issues.

Once again, in reconstructing the thought of a jurist and professor such as Ascoli, it becomes clear just how extensive his background was in various fields of law—not only regarding Italian law, but also Roman law, legal history and comparative law. Indeed, this was a common trait among other private law professors of the time, who were at the height of their profession in those first 15 years of the twentieth century. Such a vast background would become progressively less common as the years went on, until it essentially became unheard of after the middle of the century.

Furthermore, reading through the pages of lecture notes reaffirms how professors would often speak at length on the topics that were dearest to them during their lessons—just as they do today. Often they would express their opinions on legislative choices and the interpretation of current laws right there in the classroom with the students, and sometimes they would even try out new theories.

Specifically, it was shown how Alfredo Ascoli cultivated a keen interest in the issue of absent persons. Indeed, by the time he was teaching at the University of Pavia (1903–1904), the laws on absence in the Italian Civil Code had been put to the test with the Battle of Adwa, fought in 1896 during Italy's colonial campaign in Abyssinia (East Africa). The Italian army had suffered a terrible defeat on that occasion, and many dead and injured had been left on the battlefield, in addition to a high number of prisoners and missing persons.

Italian law faced what must have been an even more arduous challenge on two other occasions: first in 1908, when Messina was struck by a terrible earthquake and subsequent tsunami, and then World War One, which resulted in an extremely high number of missing soldiers on the front lines. There were countless dead in both

---

[53]On Ascoli's teaching see Valsecchi, Emilio. 1942. Alfredo Ascoli. *Rivista di diritto privato* 12.1: 195–196.

disasters, but above all there was no way to ascertain whether a missing person was alive or dead, as it was impossible to recover any mortal remains. The laws on absence proved useless, as they had been based on the idea that sooner or later an absent person would return. As a result, various special laws were passed to introduce a new mechanism to be applied in specific cases of "presumptive death": a missing person was presumed dead and his or her estate would be administered accordingly.[54]

When the *Commissione Reale per il Dopoguerra* (Royal Commission for the Post-war period) was established in Italy at the end of 1917, its task was to manage the transition to peace by specifically dealing with the vast amount of wartime legislation that had affected both private law and family law:[55] none other than Alfredo Ascoli himself was put in charge of reforming the laws governing absence.[56]

Fifteen years had passed since his course in Pavia, but the world had changed forever. Moreover, thanks to the work carried out by the Royal Commission for the Post-war period, the requirement of a husband's authorization was finally abolished in 1919.[57] Ascoli's role on the commission was not that of a professor asked to convey his knowledge as a jurist to his students; now, he was in charge of writing new laws for an Italian society that had just survived World War One. In that regard, his contribution was nothing short of original, lively and even 'courageous'.

He decided to propose the inclusion of 'presumptive death' in the Italian legal system's treatment of absence. In terms of personal and familial relationships, Ascoli was clearly in favor of allowing spouses of anyone presumed dead to have the freedom to dissolve the marriage. His words were unambiguous: "If we do not have the courage to admit this exceptional and sporadic hypothesis of divorce, then it is better to limit the effects of presumptive death to property rights alone and condemn the surviving spouse to perpetual widowhood".[58]

---

[54]Monti, Annamaria. 2011. Repenser l'absence: la doctrine italienne après la Première Guerre mondiale. In Hoareau, Métairie (as n. *) 363–380.

[55]See Braccia, Roberta. 2012. La legislazione della Grande Guerra e il diritto privato. In Sciumé, Alberto (ed.), *Il diritto come forza. La forza del diritto. Le fonti in azione nel diritto europeo tra medioevo ed età contemporanea*, 187–215. Torino: Giappichelli; Latini, Carlotta. 2014. The Great War and the Reorientation of Italian Private Law. *Comparative Legal History* 2.2: 242–263, and the bibliography cited therein.

[56]Ascoli, Alfredo. 1917. Questioni relative alla guerra. I provvedimenti per dopo la guerra. *Rivista di diritto civile* 9.2: 579–580. See Bonini 1973 (as n. 18) 147–164, 250–256.

[57]Ascoli, Alfredo. 1917. Disegni e proposte di legge. I. Disposizioni relative alla capacità giuridica della donna. *Rivista di diritto civile* 9.2: 208–211.

[58]Commissione reale per il dopoguerra. 1920. *Studi e proposte della Prima sottocommissione presieduta dal sen. Vittorio Scialoja. Questioni giuridiche, amministrative e sociali (giugno 1918–giugno 1919)*. Roma: Tip. Artigianelli, 202.

References

Abbondanza, R. (1962). Ascoli, Alfredo. In *Dizionario Biografico degli Italiani* (Vol. 4, pp. 377–379). Roma: Istituto della Enciclopedia italiana.

Ascoli, A. (1904). *Lezioni di diritto civile (diritto delle persone). Appunti presi da Domenico Moretto III anno – Guido Scotti III anno e riveduti dal Chiarissimo Professore. Anno 1903–1904*. Pavia: Premiato Stabilimento Tipo Litografico Successori Marelli.

Ascoli, A. (1905). *Diritto privato: 1. corso UCLB*. [S.l.: s.n.].

Ascoli, A. (1908). *Università commerciale Luigi Bocconi. Istituzioni di diritto privato: anno accademico 1907–1908*. Pavia: Premiato stabilimento tipo-litografico succ. Bruni.

Ascoli, A. (1909a). La circolare del ministro guardasigilli sui matrimoni religiosi non preceduti o seguiti dal matrimonio civile. *Rivista di diritto civile, 1*, 671–676.

Ascoli, A. (1909b). *Università commerciale Luigi Bocconi. Istituzioni di diritto privato 1908–1909 del chiarissimo prof. Alfredo Ascoli*. Pavia: Premiato stabilimento tipo-litografico succ. Bruni.

Ascoli, A. (1910). *Università commerciale Luigi Bocconi. Diritto privato: anno accademico 1909–1910. Lezioni del chiarissimo prof. Alfredo Ascoli*. [S.l.: s.n.].

Ascoli, A. (1911). *Università commerciale Luigi Bocconi. Diritto privato anno accademico 1910–1911. Lezioni del chiarissimo prof. Ascoli [raccolte da Pietro Tramalloni]*. Pavia: Tacchinardi e Ferrari.

Ascoli, A. (1912a). Le donne e l'avvocatura. *Rivista di diritto civile, 4*, 704–705.

Ascoli, A. (1912b). *Università commerciale Luigi Bocconi. Istituzioni di diritto privato. 1. corso: anno 1911–1912 [prof. A. Ascoli.] Appunti raccolti da Lanfranco Di Brenzone*. Pavia: Tacchinardi e Ferrari.

Ascoli, A. (1913). *Università commerciale Luigi Bocconi. Lezioni di diritto privato tenute dal chiarissimo prof. Ascoli*. Pavia: Premiato stabilimento tipo-litografico succ. Bruni.

Ascoli, A. (1914). *Università commerciale Luigi Bocconi. Lezioni di istituzioni di diritto privato tenute dal chiarissimo prof. A. Ascoli*. [S.l.: s.n.].

Ascoli, A. (1916). La precedenza obbligatoria del matrimonio civile sul religioso e le pensioni di guerra. *Rivista di diritto civile, 8*, 371–375.

Ascoli, A. (1917a). Questioni relative alla guerra. I provvedimenti per dopo la guerra. *Rivista di diritto civile 9.2*, 579–580.

Ascoli, A. (1917b). Disegni e proposte di legge. I. Disposizioni relative alla capacità giuridica della donna. *Rivista di diritto civile*, *9*(2), 208–211.

Ascoli, A. (1917c). Disegni e proposte di legge. I. Disposizioni relative alla capacità giuridica della donna. *Rivista di diritto civile*, *9*(2), 208–211.

Ascoli, A. (1917d). Questioni relative alla guerra. I provvedimenti per dopo la guerra. *Rivista di diritto civile*, *9*(2), 579–580.

Ascoli, A. (1918). *Università commerciale Luigi Bocconi. Lezioni di istituzioni di diritto privato tenute dal chiarissimo prof. Ascoli. Anno accademico 1917–1918*. Milano: Tipo–litogr. Tenconi.

Ascoli, A. (1922). *Istituzioni di diritto civile: Corso dettato nella Regia Università di Roma*. Napoli: Perrella.

Audren, F. (2011). Les professeurs de droit, la République et le nouvel esprit juridique. Introduction. *Mil neuf cent. La Belle Epoque des juristes. Enseigner le droit dans la République, 29*, 7–33.

Bagiotti, T. (1952). *Storia della Università Bocconi 1902–1952*. Milano: Università Bocconi.

Bonini, R. (1973). *Problemi di storia delle codificazioni e della politica legislativa*. Bologna: Pàtron Editore.

Braccia, R. (2012). La legislazione della Grande Guerra e il diritto privato. In A. Sciumé (Ed.), *Il diritto come forza. La forza del diritto. Le fonti in azione nel diritto europeo tra medioevo ed età contemporanea* (pp. 187–215). Torino: Giappichelli.

Cattini, M., Decleva, E., De Maddalena, A., Romani, M.A. (1992). *Storia di una libera università, I, L'Università Commerciale Luigi Bocconi dalle origini al 1914*. Milano: Giuffrè.

Chiodi, G. (2007). Innovare senza distruggere: il progetto italo–francese di codice delle obbligazioni e dei contratti (1927). In *Alpa G. & Chiodi G., Il progetto italo francese delle obbligazioni (1927). Un modello di armonizzazione nell'epoca della ricodificazione* (pp. 43–146). Milano: Giuffrè.

Chiosso, G. (2009). Stampatori ed editori per l'Università e la scuola tra Otto e primo Novecento. In G.P. Brizzi & M. G. Tavoni (Eds.), *Dalla pecia all'e–book. Libri per l'Università: stampa, editoria, circolazione e lettura* (pp. 648–653). Bologna: CLUEB.

Cianferotti, G. (1989). La prolusione di Orlando. Il paradigma pandettistico, i nuovi giuristi universitari e lo Stato liberale. *Rivista trimestrale di diritto pubblico, 4*, 995–1023.

Commissione reale per il dopoguerra. (1920a). *Studi e proposte della Prima sottocommissione presieduta dal sen. Vittorio Scialoja. Questioni giuridiche, amministrative e sociali (giugno 1918–giugno 1919)*. Roma: Tip. Artigianelli.

Commissione reale per il dopoguerra. (1920b). *Studi e proposte della Prima sottocommissione presieduta dal sen. Vittorio Scialoja. Questioni giuridiche, amministrative e sociali (giugno 1918–giugno 1919)* (p. 202). Roma: Tip. Artigianelli.

Di Marzio, P. (2008). *Il matrimonio concordatario e gli altri matrimoni religiosi con effetti civili*. Padova: Cedam.

di Renzo Villata, G. (2001). La famiglia. In *Enciclopedia Italiana. Eredità del Novecento* (pp. 759–776). Roma: Istituto dell'Enciclopedia Italiana.

di Renzo Villata, G. (2011). L'absence dans la jurisprudence après l'unification italienne le modèle français et quelques nouveautés. In J. Hoareau & G. Métairie (Eds.), *L'absence. Du cas de l'absent à la théorie de l'absence* (pp. 339–361). Limoges: Pulim.

di Renzo Villata, G. (2014). Il matrimonio civile. Diritto, politica e religione tra avvocati "impegnati" prima e dopo l'Unità. In S. Borsacchi & G. S. Pene Vidari (Eds.), *Avvocati protagonisti e rinnovatori del primo diritto unitario* (pp. 123–166). Bologna: il Mulino.

Di Simone, M. R. (2014). Le discussioni sui diritti delle donne per il codice civile unitario. In S. Borsacchi & G. S Pene Vidari (Eds.), *Avvocati protagonisti e rinnovatori del primo diritto unitario* (pp. 95–121). Bologna: il Mulino.

Femia, P. (2013). Ascoli, Alfredo. In I. Birocchi, E. Cortese, A. Mattone & M. N. Miletti (Eds.), *Dizionario Biografico dei Giuristi Italiani (XII–XX secolo)* (Vol. 1, pp. 111–114). Bologna: il Mulino.

Furgiuele, G. (1987). La «Rivista di diritto civile» dal 1909 al 1931. *Quaderni Fiorentini, 16*, 519–630.

Grossi, P. (1989). "Il coraggio della moderazione" (Specularità dell'itinerario riflessivo di Vittorio Polacco). *Quaderni fiorentini, 18*, 197–251.

Grossi, P. (2002). *Scienza giuridica italiana, Un profilo storico*. Giuffrè: Milano.

Medici, G., & Teresa, M. (1990). Due secoli di storia dell'emancipazione femminile: dalle leggi giacobine alla costituzione repubblicana. *Studi Senesi, 102*, 149–168.

Halpérin, J.–L. (2015). *Histoire de l'état des juristes. Allemagne, XIXe–XXe siècles*. Paris: Classiques Garnier.

King, B., & Okey, T. (1904). *L'Italia oggi*. Bari: Laterza.

Latini, C. (2014). The Great War and the Reorientation of Italian Private Law. *Comparative Legal History*, 2(2), 242–263.

Lobban, M., & van Boom, W. H. (2014). The great war and private law. *Comparative Legal History*, 2(2), 163–183.

Monti, A. (2011a). *Angelo Sraffa. Un 'antiteorico' del diritto*. Milano: Egea.

Monti, A. (2011b). Repenser l'absence: la doctrine italienne après la Première Guerre mondiale. In J. Hoareau, G. Métairie (Eds.), *L'absence. Du cas de l'absent à la théorie de l'absence* (pp. 363–380). Limoges: Pulim.

Monti, A. (2013). La concorrenza sleale e gli esordi del diritto industriale nell'Italia liberale: verso una teoria generale della concorrenza? In A. Sciumé & E. Fusar Poli (Eds.), *«Afferrare ...*

l'inafferrabile». I giuristi e il diritto della nuova economia industriale fra Otto e Novecento (pp. 109–141). Milano: Giuffrè.
Monti, A. (2014). Tradizione e rinnovamento nella didattica giuridica: prime riflessioni per un'indagine sull'Italia liberale. *Rivista di storia del diritto italiano, 87*, 287–312.
Monti, A. (2015). Enseigner le droit en Italie au début du XXe siècle: les cours de législation comparée de Giovanni Pacchioni (1867–1946). In *Aux confins du droit. Mélanges–Hommage amical à Xavier Martin* (pp. 305–314). Paris: LGDJ.
Osti, G. (1943). Alfredo Ascoli. *Rivista di diritto civile, 35*, 1–4.
Passaniti, P. (2011). *Diritto di famiglia e ordine sociale*. Giuffrè: Il percorso storico della società coniugale in Italia. Milano.
Pertici, R. (2009). *Chiesa e Stato in Italia. Dalla grande guerra al nuovo concordato (1914–1984)*. Bologna: Il Mulino.
Petit, C. (2005). De la *historia* a la *memoria*. A propósito de una reciente obra de historia universitaria. *Cuadernos del Instituto Antonio de Nebrija, 8*, 237–279.
Polacco, V. (1893). *Contro il divorzio. Lezione tenuta il 2 maggio 1892 nella Regia Università di Padova*. Padova: Fratelli Drucker.
Porciani, I, & Moretti, M. (2007). La creazione del sistema universitario nella nuova Italia. In G. P. Brizzi, P. Del Negro & A. Romano (Eds.), *Storia delle Università in Italia* (Vol. I, pp. 323–379). Messina: Sicania.
Porta, P. L. (1998). Istituzioni e centri di elaborazione della cultura economica. In P. L. Porta (Ed.), *Milano e la cultura economica nel XX secolo*, I, *Gli anni 1890–1920* (pp. 163–192). Milano: Angeli.
Romani, M. A. (1997). *Costruire le istituzioni. Leopoldo Sabbatini (1860–1914)*. Soveria Mannelli: Rubbettino.
Schiera, P. (1987). *Il laboratorio borghese. Scienza e politica nella Germania dell'Ottocento*. Bologna: Il Mulino.
Solimano, S. (2003). *"Il letto di Procuste". Diritto e politica nella formazione del codice civile unitario. I progetti Cassinis (1860–1861)*. Milano: Giuffrè.
Sraffa, A. (1898). Alfredo Ascoli. Trattato delle donazioni secondo il diritto civile italiano. Firenze, Cammelli, 1898. *Giurisprudenza italiana, 1898*, IV/220.
Tacchi, F. (2009). *Eva togata. Donne e professioni giuridiche in Italia dall'Unità a oggi*. Utet: Torino.
Taricone, F. (1994). *Teresa Labriola. Biografia politica di un'intellettuale tra Ottocento e Novecento*. Angeli: Milano.
Ungari, P. (2002). *Storia del diritto di famiglia in Italia 1796–1975* (1st ed. 1974). Bologna: Il Mulino.
Valsecchi, C. (2004). *In difesa della famiglia? Divorzisti e antidivorzisti in Italia tra Otto e Novecento*. Milano: Giuffrè.
Valsecchi, E. (1942). Alfredo Ascoli. *Rivista di diritto privato, 12*(1), 195–199.
Vismara, G. (1978). *Il diritto di famiglia in Italia dalle riforme ai codici*. Milano: Giuffrè.

Torts of Minor Children and Parental Civil Liability: Cases in Nineteenth and Early Twentieth Century Italy

Giovanni Chiodi

Abstract According to the Italian 1865 civil code, the father (or the mother) were liable for the torts of minor children living with them, unless they proved that they could not prevent the wrongful act. Like in France, in this system, liability was based on a presumption of fault, which could be rebutted by evidence to the contrary. This paper analyses the way in which exculpatory proof was interpreted by the Italian courts during the time the 1865 civil code was in force. Starting in the period following the Unification of Italy, the tradition laid the foundations of longstanding arguments thanks to some interpretative choices whose repercussions lasted well beyond the first Italian civil code. However, to this day there is still no historical analysis of the decisions taken by the courts. The most typical situations of parental civil liability are examined, together with the lines of defence allowed by the judges. Following a widespread line of orientation in case law, the courts considered the parents liable for negligence both in supervising and in educating the child. From the analysis of the cases it emerges that the courts judged the parents according to a series of parameters, such as the nature of the tort, the child's character and temperament, the existence of specific reasons for suspicion, and age. The cases show that the post-Unification experience in Italy was more varied and better developed than is commonly thought. Tendencies denoting extreme strictness in claiming the parents were negligent, for instance, when children committed intentional crimes and were generally ill-natured, or when they rode bicycles or motor vehicles, co-existed with more liberal perspectives, which allowed for the parents' exemption from liabilities by concretely assessing negligence in a more flexible and balanced way, especially when the children were close to the age of majority.

G. Chiodi (✉)
University of Milano-Bicocca, Piazza dell'Ateneo Nuovo 1, 20126 Milan, Italy
e-mail: giovanni.chiodi@unimib.it

M.G. di Renzo Villata (ed.), *Family Law and Society in Europe from the Middle Ages to the Contemporary Era*, Studies in the History of Law and Justice 5,
DOI 10.1007/978-3-319-42289-3_14

1 Introduction

Parental civil liability for the torts of minor children was an important chapter of nineteenth century Italian private law, as it was also in other European countries. It was a category of liability that generated numerous problems in application and abundant litigation which has only in part been documented by law journals since Italy's unification.

In the Italian 1865 civil code, parental civil liability for the torts of minor children living with their parents was regulated by art. 1153. It was modelled on the French *code civil*, and according to the general view it introduced a presumption of fault from which the father, and subordinately the mother, could be exempted if they proved they were unable to prevent the tort from occurring. The same provision can be found for both parents in art. 2048 of the 1942 civil code. Contemporary civil lawyers share the opinion that the exonerating proof laid down in the code is interpreted more strictly than the law requires, as the parents not only have to demonstrate that they have watched over their children adequately, but also that they have educated them properly.

In the first decades of application of the new civil code of 1942 some jurists considered the traditional orientation of the courts with criticism.[1]

The critical review of the problems of civil liability begun by Italian scholars of private law in the 1960s regarded also parental liability, albeit marginally, and contributed to increase the interest for the arguments used by the courts and to stress the crisis of the fault paradigm.[2]

Elsewhere, such as in France, there were fundamental studies reconsidering the subject that were based on a thorough and original analysis of cases and judges' strategies.[3]

---

[1]See Capaccioli, Enzo. 1946. Responsabilità del genitore per il fatto illecito del figlio minore. *Rivista del diritto commerciale e del diritto generale delle obbligazioni* 44.2: 257–279; Trabucchi, Alberto. 1947. Note to Cass. 22 febbraio 1946, n. 187. *Giurisprudenza italiana* 99.1: 181–184; Contursi Lisi, Lycia. 1949. Responsabilità civile dei genitori e violazione dell'obbligo di educare la prole. *Rivista trimestrale di diritto e procedura civile* 3: 977–981; Pasetti, Giulio. 1949. In tema di responsabilità del genitore per mancata educazione del figlio. *Giurisprudenza italiana* 101.1: 291–298; Trabucchi, Alberto. 1953. Sulla prova liberatoria della presunzione di colpa esimente dalla responsabilità indiretta del genitore. *Giurisprudenza italiana* 105.1: 283–286; Venditti, Arnaldo. 1955. Il dovere dei genitori di educare e vigilare la prole in relazione alla prova liberatoria dalla responsabilità per i fatti illeciti commessi dai figli minori. *Giustizia civile* 5.2: 1620–1626. The height of this line is the note of Majello, Ugo. 1960. Responsabilità dei genitori per il fatto illecito del figlio minore e valutazione del comportamento del danneggiato ai fini della determinazione del contenuto della prova liberatoria. *Diritto e giurisprudenza*: 44–50.

[2]See the important remarks of Rodotà, Stefano. 1964. *Il problema della responsabilità civile*. Milano: Giuffrè, 153–160. See also Trimarchi, Pietro. 1961. *Rischio e responsabilità oggettiva*. Milano: Giuffrè, 21–23, and the critical survey of cases of Visintini, Giovanna. 1967. *La responsabilità civile nella giurisprudenza*. Padova: Cedam, 334–358 (§§ 45–46).

[3]A new approach began with the pivotal study of Ollier, Pierre-Dominique. 1961. *La responsabilité civile des père et mère. Étude critique de son régime légal (art. 1384 al. 4 et 7 c.*

Studies like these have subsequently been conducted in Italy, above all since the 1980s, but they have inevitably considered interpretations of art. 2048 of the 1942 civil code.[4]

(Footnote 3 continued)

civ.). Préface de Jean Carbonnier. Paris: Librairie Générale de Droit et Jurisprudence. R. Pichon et R. Durand-Auzias (with large bibliography). Amongst the previous books on the subject see Blanc, Emmanuel. 1953. La responsabilité des parents. *Préface de M. André Besson. Paris: Librairie du Journal des notaires et des avocats.*

For the transformations of parental liability in France after the 1990s see the authoritative book of Viney, Geneviève, and Jourdain, Patrice. 1998 (2nd edition). *Les conditions de la responsabilité.* Ouvrage couronné par l'Académie des sciences morales et politiques (Prix Demolombe, 1989). *Traité de droit civil.* Sous la direction de Jacques Ghestin. Paris: Librairie Générale de Droit et de Jurisprudence, E.J.A., 974–1011, especially 978–982, 1000–1006; Viney, Geneviève. 2004. Les difficultés de la recodification du droit de la responsabilité civile. In *Le Code civil. 1804–2004. Livre du Bicentenaire*, 255–281. Paris: Dalloz-LexisNexis Litec, 270, 278–281. For a comparison between common law and models of civil law in this field see Giliker, Paula. 2010. *Vicarious Liability in Tort: A Comparative Perspective.* New York: Cambridge University Press, Chap. 7, 197–226, in particular 210–217 for French law.

[4]See especially Patti, Salvatore. 1984. *Famiglia e responsabilità civile.* Milano: Giuffrè, in particular 232–285, 292–297, 300–303 (with further bibliography of the previous discussion); and Visintini, Giovanna. 1987. *I fatti illeciti. 1. L'ingiustizia del danno.* Padova: Cedam, 509–529. See also the survey of cases of Mantovani, Manuela. 1987. Responsabilità dei genitori, dei tutori, dei precettori e dei maestri d'arte. In *La responsabilità civile. Una rassegna di dottrina e giurisprudenza*, diretta da Guido Alpa e Mario Bessone. II. Tomo primo, 1–51. Torino: Utet. In these works the fault paradigm is no longer considered valid to justify parental liability as applied by the courts. Critical opinions were already expressed, *inter alia*, by Trimarchi, Pietro. 1975 (2nd edition). *Istituzioni di diritto privato.* Milano: Giuffrè, 112–113; Busnelli, Francesco Donato. 1976. Nuove frontiere della responsabilità civile. *Jus* 23: 41–79; Rossi Carleo, Liliana. 1979. La responsabilità dei genitori ex art. 2048 c. c. *Rivista di diritto civile* 25.2: 125–151; Bessone, Mario. 1982. Fatto illecito del minore e regime della responsabilità per mancata sorveglianza. *Il diritto di famiglia e delle persone* 11: 1011–1015; Alpa, Guido, and Bessone, Mario. 1984. I fatti illeciti. In *Trattato di diritto privato.* Diretto da Pietro Rescigno. 14. *Obbligazioni e contratti.* Tomo sesto. Torino: Utet, 322–325.

The debate amongst legal scholars considerably expanded from the 1990s, as a fundamental part of treatises on Italian tort law. See, for example, Franzoni, Massimo. 1993. Dei fatti illeciti. Art. 2043–2059, In Galgano, Francesco (ed.), *Commentario del codice civile Scialoja-Branca, Libro quarto – Delle obbligazioni*, 347–398. Bologna-Roma: Zanichelli Editore, Soc. ed. del Foro italiano; Visintini, Giovanna. 1996. *Trattato breve della responsabilità civile. Fatti illeciti. Inadempimento. Danno risarcibile.* Padova: Cedam, 597–606; Monateri, Pier Giuseppe. 1998. Le fonti delle obbligazioni. 3. La responsabilità civile. In *Trattato di diritto civile* diretto da Rodolfo Sacco. Torino: Utet, 929–976; Comporti, Marco. 2012 (2nd edition). Fatti illeciti: le responsabilità presunte. In *Il Codice Civile.* Commentario fondato e già diretto da Piero Schlesinger, continuato da Francesco Donato Busnelli. *Artt. 2044–2048.* Milano: Giuffrè, 205–278. Scholars argued that in many cases the high standard of the exculpatory proof required by the courts imposed a real strict liability upon the parents instead of a liability based on the fault: see Franzoni 1993, 377–380; Monateri 1998, 945–946, 970–974; Pardolesi, Roberto. 1997. Danni cagionati dai minori: pagano sempre i genitori?. *Famiglia e diritto* 3: 221–225. All the commentaries of the civil code put a great emphasis on the cases about parental liability, displaying a critical approach towards the case law and making proposals of reform. See, amongst others, Venchiarutti, Angelo. 2008. Responsabilità dei genitori, dei tutori, dei precettori e dei maestri d'arte. In Diurni, Amalia, Negro, Antonello, Sella, Mauro, and Venchiarutti, Angelo. Artt. 2043–2053. Fatti illeciti. Generalità, responsabilità per fatto altrui, attività pericolose, danni da cose, da animali, da rovina di edificio. In Cendon, Paolo (ed.), *Commentario al codice civile*, 693–734. Milano: Giuffrè Editore.

In reality, as observed by the most attentive civil lawyers, in the application of art. 2048 much has been carried over from the doctrinal schools of thought and case law of the previous age.[5] In legal practice this previous trend has not so much re-emerged as been perpetuated, without closure, despite some evident signs of discontinuity signalled and exploited by interpretations that aspire to move on from settings that no longer correspond to the nature of today's families.

Despite the importance of the subject between the nineteenth and twentieth centuries, little is known about its early stages.

This essay therefore seeks to fill in the gaps by reconstructing the way in which the courts interpreted the exculpatory proof granted to the father by the 1865 civil code and by analysing the particularly numerous decisions.

The aim of the essay is to outline an initial frame of reference of the Italian experience under the 1865 civil code by examining a large sample of cases. In the field of civil liability, which has been profoundly shaped and developed by judges, the analysis must necessarily investigate the case law.

Indeed it is not possible to understand the mechanism of exculpatory proof without analysing the typical situations of parental liability and the defences admitted by the judges. No commentary or treatise of the time considered here is able to substitute this work: although books by Italian scholars of private law cite the cases, they have never conducted a complete analysis.[6]

As Italian judges, like scholars, obtain examples and doctrines also from other courts outside Italy, this study includes some of these judgments. For historical

[5]See n. 1 and Patti 1984 (as n. 4) 268–272; Visintini 1987 (as n. 4) 515; Monateri 1998 (as n. 4) 971; Carbone, Enrico. 2008. La responsabilità aquiliana del genitore tra rischio tipico e colpa fittizia. *Rivista di diritto civile* 54.2: 1–16, 1; Comporti 2012 (as n. 4) 207–212, 237–248.

[6]Amongst the first commentators of the civil code, the most interesting discussions of parental liability can be found in Borsari, Luigi. 1877. *Commentario del codice civile italiano* 3.2. Torino: Unione Tipografico-Editrice Torinese, 342–352 (§§ 3052–3056); Ricci, Francesco. 1886 (2nd edition). *Corso teorico-pratico di diritto civile. 6. Delle obbligazioni e dei contratti in genere*. Torino: Unione Tipografico-Editrice, 128–133 (§§ 91–94); Pacifici-Mazzoni, Emidio. 1886 (3rd edition). *Istituzioni di diritto civile italiano. 4. Parte speciale. Delle obbligazioni in generale. Donazioni – Contratto di matrimonio*. Firenze: Eugenio e Filippo Cammelli, 144–147, 155–157 (§§ 82 and 86).

Parental liability was also discussed by Giorgi, Giorgio. 1886 (2nd edition). *Teoria delle obbligazioni nel diritto moderno italiano esposta con la scorta della dottrina e della giurisprudenza. 5. Fonti delle obbligazioni. Quasi contratti – Fatti illeciti – Legge*. Firenze: Eugenio e Filippo Cammelli, 376–383 (§§ 259–266).

A turning point was marked by the huge book of Chironi, Gian Pietro. 1903 (2nd edition). *La colpa nel diritto civile odierno. Colpa extra-contrattuale* 1. Torino: Fratelli Bocca Editori, 122–123 (§ 39); and mainly Chironi, Gian Pietro. 1906 (2nd edition). *La colpa nel diritto civile odierno. Colpa extra-contrattuale* 2. Torino: Fratelli Bocca Editori, Chap. XI, especially 131–159, 183–203. Chironi's work (1st ed. 1886 and 1887) was the leading monograph on the subject: see Cazzetta, Giovanni. 1991. *Responsabilità aquiliana e frammentazione del diritto comune civilistico (1865–1914)*. Milano: Giuffrè, 221–263.

The most detailed discussion of the jurisprudence can be found in Cesareo Consolo, Giovanni. 1908. *Trattato sul risarcimento del danno in materia di delitti e quasi delitti*. Torino-Milano-Roma-Napoli: Unione Tipografico-Editrice Torinese, 325–362 (Chap. IX).

reasons there is a particularly active channel of communication between Italy and France which is borne out by the translation of some decisions by French courts of appeal and the Court of Cassation in Italian law journals. Moreover, it is interesting to note how Italian jurisprudence also keeps an eye on the rich jurisprudence of the Swiss courts, which is understandable in view of the quantity and quality of their judgements.

A further aspect is the physiognomy of parental responsibility and relations between parents and children in the Italian family between the nineteenth and twentieth centuries. Here too the material seems particularly interesting as it captures what persisted and what changed in the educational and pedagogical standards of minors during this period. Over time, parental authority altered its role as social and family relations developed, together with different concepts on bringing up children, the relationship between authority and liberty in the family microcosm, and the role assigned to the figure of the father and mother in the domestic and social context. Also from this point of view, an examination of the jurisprudence provides particular insights into the bourgeois, proletarian and rural families of Italy after unification.

2 The Two Faults of the Father

In Italy the 1865 civil code was inspired by the archetype of the French *code civil.* Article 1153 of the Italian civil code provided for parental liability for the torts of minor children together with other forms of liability for others.[7] The content of the text was virtually identical to that of art. 1384 of the French *code civil.*[8] For the purposes of this essay, only some of the conditions of parental liability emerging from the doctrinal debate of the period will be discussed here.[9]

---

[7]Article 1153[1]. A person is liable not only for the damages he causes by his own act, but also for that which is caused by the act of persons for whom he is responsible, or by things which are in his custody.

[2]The father and if he is unavailable the mother are liable for the damages caused by their minor children who live with them.

[6]The above liability exists, unless the parents, the tutors, the teacher and the craftsman prove that they could not prevent the act which gives rise to that liability.

[8]Article 1384[1] On est responsable non seulement du dommage que l'on cause par son propre fait, mais encore de celui qui est causé par le fait des personnes dont on doit répondre, ou des choses que l'on a sous sa garde.

[2]Le père, et la mère après le décès du mari, sont responsable du dommage causé par leurs enfants mineurs habitant avec eux.

[5]La responsabilité ci-dessus a lieu, à moins que les père et mère, instituteurs et artisans, ne prouvent qu'ils n'ont pu empêcher le fait qui donne lieu à cette responsabilité.

[9]See n. 6 for a biographical survey of the Italian sources. For nineteenth century French scholars, amongst the first commentators of the Code civil the broadest exposition can be found in Toullier, Charles Bonaventure. 1824. *Droit civil français, suivant l'ordre du code*, ouvrage dans lequel on a taché de réunir la théorie a la pratique. Tome onzième. A Paris: chez Warée, oncle, Libraire de la

The first point to highlight is that the subject who was liable was first of all the father, and only when he was unavailable (in his absence, or for other reasons) was the mother considered so.[10] The judges therefore focused their attention above all on the behaviour of the father, the head of the family.

(Footnote 9 continued)

Cour Royale, Cour de la Sainte-Chapelle, n° 13. Parée, fils ainé, Libraire au Palais de Justice, 359–385 (§§ 259–281). See also Delvincourt, Claude-Étienne. 1813. *Cours de Code Napoléon. Ouvrage divisé en deux Parties, dont la première contient la Troisième Édition des Institutes de Droit Civil Français, du même Auteur, revue et corrigée par lui; et la seconde, les Notes et Explications sur lesdites Institutes*. Tome second. Paris: chez P. Gueffier, Imprimeur-Libraire, 288–289, 749–750; Duranton, Alexandre. 1841 (4th edition). *Cours de droit français, suivant le code civil*. Tome septième. Bruxelles: Société Belge de Librairie Hauman et Ce, 508–510 (§§ 708–719).

A special place deserves the reference book of Sourdat, Auguste-Jean-Baptiste. 1852. *Traité général de la responsabilité ou de l'action en dommages-intérêts en dehors de contrats* [...]. Tome second. Paris: Imprimerie et Librairie générale de jurisprudence De Cosse, succ[r] de Cosse et N. Delamotte, 131–155.

For the debate in the second half of the century, the following sources will be considered: Zachariae, Karl-Salomo. 1858. *Le droit civil français*. Traduit de l'allemand sur la cinquième édition. Annoté et rétabli suivant l'ordre du Code Napoléon par MM. G. Massé—Ch. Vergé. Tome quatrième. Paris: Auguste Durand, Libraire-Éditeur, 22–23 (§ 628); Demante, Antoine-Marie, and Colmet de Santerre, Edmond-Louis-Armand. 1865. *Cours analytique de Code Napoléon*. 5. Art. 1101–1386. Paris: Henri Plon, Imprimeur-Éditeur, 682–684 (§§ 365–365 bis); Marcadé, Victor. 1866 (5th edition). *Explication théorique et pratique du Code Napoléon contenant l'analyse critique des auteurs et de la jurisprudence et un traité résumé après le commentaire de chaque titre*. Tome cinquième. Paris: Delamotte, administrateur du répertoire de l'enregistrement par. M. Garnier, 279–281 (art. 1384); Aubry, Charles, and Rau, Charles-Frédéric. 1871 (4th edition). *Cours de droit civil français d'après la méthode de Zachariae*. Tome quatrième. Paris: Imprimerie et Librairie générale de jurisprudence. Marchal, Billard et Cie, Imprimeurs-Éditeurs. Libraires de la Cour de Cassation et de l'ordre des avocats a la même Cour et au Conseil d'État, 756–759 (§ 447); Laurent, François. 1876. *Principes de droit civil français*. Tome vingtième. Paris-Bruxelles: A. Durand & Pedone Lauriel, Bruylant-Christophe & Comp., 591–603 (§§ 553–565); Demolombe, Charles. 1882. *Cours de code civil*. Édition augmentée de la législation et de la jurisprudence belges et d'une table chronologique des arrêts des cours françaises et belges. Tome quinzième. *Traité des engagements qui se forment sans convention*. Bruxelles: J. Steinon, Éditeur, 181–193 (§§ 561–602); 187–188 (§ 586); Larombière, Léobon-Valéry-Léon-Jupile. 1885. *Théorie et pratique des obligations ou commentaire des titres III et IV, livre III du code civil*. Articles 1101 à 1386. Nouvelle édition tenue au courant de la jurisprudence. 7. Articles 1349 à 1386. Paris: A. Durand et Pedone-Lauriel, Editeurs. Libraires de la Cours de la Cour d'appel et de l'Ordre des Avocats. G. Pedone-Lauriel, successeur, 592–628 (art. 1384, nn. 1–24); Huc, Théophile. 1895. *Commentaire théorique et pratique du Code civil*. Tome huitième. *Contrats et obligations (suite); Modes d'extinction; Paiement; Subrogation; Compensation, etc.; Modes de preuve; Chose jugés, etc.; Quasi-contrats; Quasi-délits*. Art. 1234 à 1386. Paris: Librairie Cotillon. F. Pichon, Successeur, Éditeur, 582–589 (§§ 440–443).

[10]A typical situation was the emigration of the father. See App. Palermo, 14 Feb 1913. Puccio v. Mannino. *Monitore* 54 (1913): 474–475; Cass. Firenze, 18 Feb 1918. Sandri v. Sandri. *Monitore* 60 (1919): 49–50; App. Palermo, 10 Feb 1922. Moscato v. Martorana. *Monitore* 63 (1922): 500–502; Cass., 12 May 1924. Gregoraci v. Marano. *Monitore* 65 (1924): 848–849; Cass., 17 Jan 1931. Lendaro v. Lendaro. *Il foro italiano* 56.1 (1931): 440–442; App. Milano, 8 Nov 1932. Gnemmi v. De Mattia. *Monitore* 74 (1933): 347–348. See Messa, Gian Carlo. 1913. La responsabilità civile dei genitori nel caso di lontananza dal domicilio. *Monitore dei Tribunali* 54: 681–682.

The code, according to the large majority of jurists, established a presumption of parental fault for the torts committed by minor children cohabiting with them.[11] However, this presumption of fault could be proven otherwise, contrary to what was established with regard to masters for the damage inflicted by servants in the exercise of their duties.[12] The father or mother were therefore allowed to prove that they could not have prevented the fact, and most of the controversy centres on the father's exculpatory proof.

---

[11]Borsari 1877 (as n. 6) 342, 351; Ricci 1886 (as n. 6) 129–130; Pacifici-Mazzoni 1886 (as n. 6) 144; Giorgi 1886 (as n. 6) 376; Chironi, Gian Pietro. 1889. *Istituzioni di diritto civile italiano.* Volume II. Torino: Fratelli Bocca Editori, 190–191; Chironi, Gian Pietro, and Abello, Luigi. 1904. *Trattato di diritto civile italiano.* Volume I. Parte generale. Torino: Fratelli Bocca Editori, 519; Chironi 1906 (as n. 6) 112–127; Cesareo Consolo 1908 (as n. 6) 327–329; Messa 1913 (as n. 11) 681. See also Simoncelli, Vincenzo. 1914. *Istituzioni di diritto privato. Lezioni.* Roma: Athenaeum, 308–309; Ferrini, Contardo. 1926. Delitti e quasi-delitti. In *Il Digesto italiano. Enciclopedia metodica e alfabetica di legislazione, dottrina e giurisprudenza* [...] diretta da Luigi Lucchini. Volume IX, parte prima, 727–820. Torino: Unione tipografico-editrice torinese, 806 (1st edition 1887–1898); Brugi, Biagio. 1914 (3rd edition). *Istituzioni di diritto civile italiano con speciale riguardo a tutto il diritto privato.* Milano: Società editrice libraria, 497–498; Barassi, Lodovico. 1921. *Istituzioni di diritto civile.* Milano. Casa Editrice Dottor Francesco Vallardi, 358; De Ruggiero, Roberto. 1926 (4th edition). *Istituzioni di diritto civile. 2. Diritti di obbligazione. Diritti di famiglia. Diritto ereditario.* Messina: Casa editrice Giuseppe Principato, 461; Pacchioni, Giovanni. 1940. *Diritto civile italiano. 2. Diritto delle obbligazioni. 4. Dei delitti e quasi delitti.* Padova: Cedam, 224–225; Cicu, Antonio. 1941. Responsabilità indiretta dei genitori. *Rivista di diritto civile* 33: 183–184, 183; and, under the new code, De Cupis, Adriano. 1946. *Il danno. Teoria generale della responsabilità civile.* Milano: Giuffrè, 305–309. But see the original remarks of Barassi, Lodovico. 1948 (2nd edition). *Teoria generale delle obbligazioni.* Milano: Giuffrè, 572–576, who devised an evocative metaphor to describe parental liability as "intermediate system between subjective and objective liability": "attacking battalion towards objective liability" (575).

In the French doctrine see especially Toullier 1824 (as n. 9) 363–364; Demante, and Colmet de Santerre 1865 (as n. 9) 682; Laurent 1876 (as n. 9) 591. Subsequently see Baudry-Lacantinerie, Gabriel, and Barde, Louis. 1908. *Traité thèorique et pratique de droit civil. Des obligations.* Tome quatrième. Paris: Librairie de la Sociètè du Recueil J.-B. Sirey et du Journal du Palais. Ancienne Maison L. Larose & Forcel, 594; Planiol, Marcel, Ripert, Georges, and Esmein, Paul. 1930. *Traité pratique de droit civil français. Obligations.* Première partie. Paris: Librairie générale de droit et de jurisprudence, 855 (but see the doubts expressed at p. 859); Mazeaud, Henri, and Mazeaud Léon. 1931. *Traité théorique et pratique de la responsabilité civile délictuelle et contractuelle.* Préface de M. Henri Capitant. Tome premier. Paris: Librairie du Recueil Sirey (Société Anonyme), 566–568. The traditional idea was rejected by Josserand, Louis. 1939. *Cours de droit civil positif français conforme aux programmes officiels des facultés de droit.* Ouvrage couronné par l'Institut (Prix Chevallier, 1931). 2. *Théorie générale des obligations. Les principaux contrats du droit civil. Les suretés.* Paris: Librairie du Recueil Sirey Société anonyme, 313 ("cette conception est tout de surface", "la fiction est trasformée en realité"); and Ollier 1961 (as n. 3) 15, 193–223; Mazeaud, Henri et Léon, and Tunc, André. 1965 (6th edition). *Traité théorique et pratique de la responsabilité civile délictuelle et contractuelle.* Préface par Henri Capitant. Tome premier. Ouvrage couronné par l'Académie des Sciences Morales et Politiques (Prix Dupin Aîné, 1932). Paris: Éditions Montchrestien, 893–896.

[12]Presumption of fault could be contradicted by evidence to the contrary: Aubry, and Rau 1871 (as n. 9) 750; Laurent 1876 (as n. 9) 601; Demolombe 1882 (as n. 9) 187; Larombière 1885 (as n. 9) 625; Mazeaud 1931 (as n. 11) 562–563.

In specifying its content, in other words defences against liability, the interpretations of the legal experts and of the courts were conspicuous for their creative character ever since the nineteenth century. The main elements outlined here will be analysed in greater depth later on in the essay.

The father, first of all, could not avoid the presumption of fault simply by proving that he was not present at the event, in the place and at the time it took place: otherwise, it was said, civil liability would be illusory. This objection, longstanding and already raised by the French doctrine,[13] was replicated in the Italian.[14] Instead the father had to provide positive proof that he had properly supervised his child. It was the general opinion therefore that the code had introduced a presumption of fault whose foundations rested above all (but not exclusively) in the obligation to supervise that was incumbent upon the person who had authority over the children.

Besides a positive connotation, exculpatory proof therefore assumed a broader, more complex and well-structured dimension, as although the father was absent at the event, he had to demonstrate that his child had been properly supervised. Over time a legal rule developed according to which the father was not obliged to supervise his child constantly every moment of the day, on account of his work and of margins for the specific activities of the child (school, play, other recreational activities, work). There developed an awareness that the impossibility of preventing the damage cited in law was relative and not absolute, and it varied according to variations in some parameters.

At least in theory, it was considered that the measure of supervision depended on the age and decreased step by step as the minor approached majority, a period in which he was conceded greater room for autonomy and independence. In reality, for the purposes of judging liability the judges took into account a plurality of circumstances. Factors deemed of the greatest importance were the character and temperament of the child, and his behaviour before the offence. A minor of good character, good behaviour, with a good record could be allowed more freedom than a child with a difficult character, rebellious, dangerous or of dissolute temperament, unless some special circumstance should give the father reason to suspect the imminent commission of an offence.

A considerable number of cases concerned the importance of paternal consent to the exercise of legal but dangerous activities, such as the use of a firearm, bicycle or automobile. One wonders whether the father's permission automatically rendered him responsible for the damage done due to deficient supervision or negligence.

The father's obligation to supervise his child ceased the moment the child's guardianship had been transferred to others: to the mother or to another suitable

---

[13]Delvincourt 1813 (as n. 9) 749; Toullier 1824 (as n. 9) 366; Duranton 1841 (as n. 9) 510 (responsibility would be illusory); Aubry, and Rau 1871 (as n. 9) 759; Laurent 1876 (as n. 9) 602; Demolombe 1882 (as n. 9) 188; Larombière 1885 (as n. 9) 626; Baudry-Lacantinerie, and Bard 1908 (as n. 11) 601; Planiol, Ripert, and Esmein 1930 (as n. 11) 858; Blanc 1953 (as n. 3) 128; Ollier 1961(as n. 3) 155.

[14]Ricci 1886 (as n. 6) 132; Giorgi 1886 (as n. 6) 380; Messa 1913 (as n. 10) 682.

person, in the case of justified absence, such as to an institution or a teacher. But there too the father could be considered liable if he had neglected his child's education.

Surveillance was therefore not the father's only obligation towards minor children. The father was expected to be not only a good guardian, but also a good educator of his children. All this was reflected with regard to the father's civil liability. Legal experts and judges interpreted this as a form of civil sanction for having failed in the fundamental moral and legal duty of the parent, namely that of bringing up and educating minor children.[15]

On the basis of this interpretation the father was liable in civil law for offences committed by his child due to defective upbringing: for bringing up his child badly, or for neglect in exercising his parental responsibility, according the most commonly used expressions. This was so even if it could be demonstrated that the father could not materially or physically supervise his son due to illness, justified absence, and so on, or even though he could prove he had properly supervised his child's upbringing.

For a long time this interpretation of the code did not give rise to any objections or criticism in the doctrine. From the outset, the father's negligence was represented in the doctrine in two ways: in the supervision and in the education (or upbringing) of the minor.

The historical origins of this perspective, which made exculpatory proof more difficult, can be found in the French scholars of private law in whose footsteps the Italian lawyers followed. The final outcome of this construction can be described in the following way. To be held responsible, the father had to be at fault firstly as supervisor or secondly as educator. In reality, in the courts the relationship between the two faults varied, depending on the situations considered.

3 Crime and Punishment: Corrupted Children

In this study the cases are organized along the lines that seem most closely to correspond to the judges' actual strategies. From this point of view, the elements of exculpatory proof varied according to the situations. The judges' attitudes changed, depending on whether they were confronted with damage caused by an intentional crime by a minor or with facts arising from negligence. In each of these two situations it was fundamental to investigate a series of circumstances which included the character, temperament, and good conduct of the child, and the age and environment in which he lived, in order to reach a decision. Assessment of these elements was left to the judge's discretion.

[15]Demogue 1925 (as n. 11) 7; Planiol, Ripert, and Esmein 1930 (as n. 11) 855; Mazeaud 1931 (as n. 11) 544; Ollier 1961 (as n. 3) 37; Viney 1998 (as n. 3) 979.

In cases regarding the recovery of damages deriving from intentional crimes, which were very numerous between the nineteenth and twentieth centuries, what was important above all was the examination of the former elements. A child whose character was rebellious, violent or deviant, if not already delinquent, required greater and very active supervision by his father[16]: given the premises, the offence did not arise from unforeseen causes and could not be considered something that inevitably happened. In such a case, it was unlikely for the father to be exonerated from his responsibility. Exoneration could only come about if the father could demonstrate that he had undertaken all the necessary supervisory measures to prevent his son from committing a crime (for instance, by preventing his son from leaving the house armed with a knife, from frequenting taverns and so on).

3.1 Proof of Proper Supervision

In practice, in post-unification Italy it is possible to identify numerous cases in which the father was sentenced to pay damages deriving from an intentional crime committed by a minor because he had not exercised sufficient supervision over his son, taking into account decisive elements such as bad character, previous crimes, the tendency to offend, and the presence of good reasons for suspicion.

Proof of good supervision, however, was particularly difficult to demonstrate. Most of the time the father was not able to demonstrate what the judges required, as they expected proof of positive acts of surveillance of delinquent or 'difficult' children. Some examples can illustrate this point.

In 1878 the Turin Court of Appeal judged a father to be at fault because, after learning of his son's first theft at his workplace, he had not done everything he could to prevent the second theft from being committed.[17]

In Genoa in 1881 the court convicted a father because it turned out that his son had already committed acts of violence and the father was therefore obliged to intervene.[18]

In 1895 the Turin Court of Appeal convicted the father of a son who was nearly of age and whose character was provocative for allowing him to go out on a public holiday with a sharp and pointed knife.[19]

The Cagliari court, in 1909, stated that the rebellious character of a son increased his father's obligation of surveillance.[20]

[16]See Laurent 1876 (as n. 9) 603. Subsequently see Savatier 1951 (as n. 11) 322.

[17]App. Torino, 8 Feb 1878. R. v. F. *La Legge* 18.1 (1878): 698–699. On this case see the remarks of Giorgi 1886 (as n. 6) 382.

[18]App. Genova, 12 Apr 1881. Gaggero v. Deluchi. *Giurisprudenza italiana* 33.2 (1881): 326–328.

[19]App. Torino, 31 May 1895. Capello v. Enrico. *La Legge* 35.2 (1895):166–168.

[20]App. Cagliari, 19 Apr 1909. Lazio v. Pinna. *Monitore* 50 (1909): 951–952.

A more intense duty of supervision, in general, was required for any child, even one without a difficult character, if there were reasonable motives for suspecting the likelihood of his committing a crime: for instance, if there existed a situation of risk, which the father knew or could have known, liable to give rise to a crime.

A prime example of this was a sentence of 24 October 1902 by the Casale Court of Appeal. The father proved he had brought up his son well (he had sent him to school until 14 years old, then he had put him to work in the fields); his good conduct was a good example to his son who was of a docile and obedient character. But the crime (murder) had not been unpredictable: the cause (jealousy) was known and the father could therefore have prevented it.[21]

Nevertheless, the courts considered that the father was not responsible if it turned out that he did not know about the crime the son was about to commit or about the situation that gave rise to the crime.

This rule can be deduced first of all from a French case, which was also known in Italy, which was decided by the Toulouse court on 7 December 1832. The case regarded a father who was considered not liable for a duel because he did not know about the duel and its cause, and because his son's conduct until that moment had been irreprehensible.[22]

A classic example of this was an Italian case decided by the Genoa Court of Appeal on 3 March 1905 regarding a serious sexual offence (indecent assault). The father was exonerated, because it was considered that he could not be blamed for not having supervised his son properly. The Court decided that this had a limit, obtained from the teachings of the Belgian civil lawyer Laurent (an authority also in Italy[23]), and an author who was "not very inclined to exculpate". This was because a different interpretation would "require constant surveillance, every moment, to prevent; this is morally impossible". Therefore the father could be considered liable if he allowed his quarrelsome son to wear a sword (this was one of Pothier's examples[24]). or if he put his son, who had already stolen in the past, at the service of a lawyer (as decided by the Venice Court of Appeal on 16 May 1876). In the Genoa indecent assault case, there was no proof that the father could suspect the "foul contact" of which his youngest son was responsible. Other circumstances revealed that the father was not to blame. Indeed there were no "examples of sleaze, albeit

[21]App. Casale, 24 Oct 1902. Giacobbe v. Manara. *Monitore* 44 (1903): 331–332.

[22]Toulouse, 7 Dec 1832. Décamps v. Rivière. S. 1833.2: 620.

[23]Cesareo Consolo 1908 (as n. 6) 349–351.

[24]Pothier, Robert-Joseph. 1831. Traité des obligations. In *Oeuvres*, contenant les traités du droit français. Nouvelle édition mise en meilleur ordre et conforme a celle publiée par M. Dupin ainé. Tome premier. A Bruxelles: chez H. Tarlier, Libraire-Editeur, rue de la Montagne, n° 51, 143 (§ 454). See Lemonnier-Lesage, Virginie. 2013. La responsabilité des père et mère du fait de l'enfant dans l'ancien droit: Le devoir d'éducation des pères de famille. In Putnam, Emmanuel, Agresti, Jean-Philippe, and Siffrein-Blanc, Caroline (eds.). *Lien familial, lien obligationnel, lien social.* 1. *Lien familial et lien obligationnel*, 149–165. Marseille: Presse Universitaires d'Aix-Marseille, 155–156. Pothier's opinion was well known by Italian scholars: see Giorgi 1886 (as n. 6) 380.

frivolous" at home. There was not even "a fact that could arouse suspicion and the need for special prevention in the father".[25] Likewise, in another lawsuit, decided by the Milan Court of Appeal on 18 February 1913, the father was not sentenced to pay damages for the offence of seduction because there was insufficient proof that he knew of his 17-year-old son's amorous relationship in time to intervene.[26]

This argument, used to defend a father, was however rejected by the Turin Court of Appeal in 1930. When the father put forward the argument that the seduction had taken place without his knowledge, the Court rebutted by claiming that if he had exercised proper supervision he would have forbidden his son to go to work for the family of the girl the latter seduced.[27]

When there were reasonable motives for suspicion, the father was exonerated from liability only if he had taken steps to prevent a potential situation of conflict of which he had become aware from worsening and thus providing the opportunity for the commission of a crime.

This means of defence of the father was applied by the Court of Agen in a case decided on 21 February 1866. The Court excluded paternal liability for a murder committed by his 20-year-old daughter by means of a rifle found in his house as the father had tried to prevent the victim from molesting his daughter, with repeated prohibitions and complaints to the local authorities. The father had therefore done everything he could to inspire good feelings in his daughter and to keep her safe from persecution by the victim.[28]

The same reasoning was applied by the Italian Court of Cassation in a case decided on 5 August 1940 regarding once again a crime of seduction. The case regarded a young student of the Mathematics Faculty of Rome University who had received a normal upbringing and education. As soon as the father heard of his son's romantic relationship he went to Rome and warned the family where his son was living to intensify their surveillance, and he told the girl's family to get her to leave his son alone. Moreover, the crime that followed arose in an unexpected and unforeseen manner, as a reaction to illegitimate provocations by the girl and by members of her family. As a result, the lack of a valid reason to suspect that the minor could commit a serious crime entailed the father's exoneration from liability.[29]

The following case is a significant one. In 1925 a 15-year-old boy, apprentice at a workshop, injured another worker with a pair of compasses after being attacked with a hammer. The fact had taken place outside the workshop and therefore outside the artisan's sphere of supervision. The Bari Court of Appeal considered that "the impossibility of the father's preventing his son's act was not absolute but

---

[25]App. Genova, 3 Mar 1905. Verda v. Sasso. *Monitore* 46 (1905): 495–496.

[26]App. Milano, 18 Feb 1913. Massa v. Pizzocaro. *Monitore* 54 (1913): 354–356.

[27]App. Torino, 17 Jan 1930. Robasto v. Chialva. *Monitore* 71 (1930): 553.

[28]Agen, 21 Feb 1866. Sarrade v. Lasserre. S. 1866.2: 272–278.

[29]Cass., 5 Aug 1940. Raimondo v. Campanella. *Il foro italiano* 66.1 (1941): 318–320. See Cicu 1941 (as n. 11).

relative in relation to the legal concept of the diligence of a bonus paterfamilias. In this case the father was a small tradesman, he had seven children, and he had removed the son in question from technical school and started him on the path to a career as a mechanic. The father could not and did not have to accompany his son to the workshop every day, nor did he have to be more diligent in his supervision, as there were no special circumstances that made it necessary. Moreover, the crime was motivated by the previous violence he had suffered from his workmate".[30]

In 1929 also the Naples Court of Appeal stated the principle according to which the duty of the parents to supervise minor children was in relation to the legal capacity of the children themselves: "supervision cannot but follow by degrees the conditions of capacity of the minor, starting from the maximum supervision of the first years of the child's life and attributed also for a very slight fault, up until minimum supervision, and attributed only for gross negligence until the child is to reach the age of majority […] especially when the good upbringing given and the previous behaviour of the children have not given any reason for suspicion".[31] The son was 18 years old and he was judged liable for sexual assault at the expense of a female worker.

3.2 Proper Education

The father could be considered liable also for negligent education of his child.

There was some debate as to whether the presumption of paternal fault established by art. 1153 regarded also *culpa in educando*. The solution played a significant role for the burden of proof. If the fault was presumed, the father was liable, unless he could prove that he had given his son a proper education.[32] The practical significance of the controversy was scaled down in practice, as in most cases it was up to the father to prove he had given his child a proper education.

There were various concepts of a 'proper education'. First, a proper education was to educate the children or set them up in a trade: this was the general or common proper education. However, some courts considered it irrelevant for the father to demonstrate that he had given his child a proper education and given him a good example through his own life, according to this acception. A proper education, in this further meaning, required further positive deeds, such as constant advice or incitement by the father: paternal *lógos,* good advice, which reinforced his good examples.

---

[30]App. Bari, 16 Jan 1925. Piazzola v. Cardinale. *Monitore* 66 (1925): 786–787.

[31]App. Napoli, 15 July 1929. Turino v. Persico. *Monitore* 71 (1930): 18–19.

[32]Against this interpretation: Chironi 1906 (as n. 6) 183–185; Cesareo Consolo 1908 (as n. 6) 353; Ferrini 1926 (as n. 11) 808. For the opposite view see De Cupis 1946 (as n. 11) 312. In France argued against the extension of the presumption: Demogue 1925 (as n. 11) 16, criticised by Mazeaud 1931 (as n. 11) 560; Josserand 1939 (as n. 11) 306; Blanc 1953 (as n. 3) 35–38, 119–121; Mazeaud, and Tunc 1965 (as n. 11) 878–879.

At the extremes, a proper education meant the use of means of correction: it was a proper education to discipline. Relaxation of domestic discipline, omitting to use the means of correction provided for in art. 222 of the civil code was a fault that the father could not be exempt from, above all if he had children of difficult character. It was a strict and inflexible method of education, which marked the passage from the father's house to the house of correction. The father was obliged to use this extreme method, according to the judges, if he did not wish to risk civil liability for offences otherwise committed by his son.[33]

However, not all courts went so far as to assess in concrete terms the existence of a proper education for two main reasons. The first was that many judges considered it a priority to investigate the father's good and thorough supervision. If the father was found wanting, proof of a proper education was rendered superfluous. The second reason was that for many courts proof of a bad education was presumed from the commission itself of the crime: the *culpa* was *in re ipsa,* according to a method of reasoning that was itself rather debatable and established even in today's practice. The consequence was that attention was focused on the father's concrete supervision of the child and he was found liable if he did not demonstrate that he had most assiduously supervised.

The concept of fault for 'negligent education' had first appeared in the works of French scholars[34] and in the decisions. These influenced post-unification Italian legal practice through various distribution channels.

In the French courts the debate was sparked off by a series of decisions made in the 1820s which were considered very authoritative by French and Italian lawyers.

---

[33]For 'deviant children' and practices of parental correction see the huge research of Quincy-Lefebvre, Pascale. 1997. *Familles, institutions et déviances. Une histoire de l'enfance difficile. 1880-fin des années trente.* Paris: Economica. For further and detailed information about the category of the 'bad children' in post-Unification Italy see Gramigna, Anita. 1998. *Storia della maleducazione. I bambini cattivi nel secolo XIX.* Bologna: Clueb, 59–61, 64–68, 70–71, 87–88, 130–131. See also Montesi, Barbara. 2007. *Questo figlio a chi lo do? Minori, famiglie, istituzioni (1865–1914).* Prefazione di Marcello Flores. Milano: Franco Angeli, 21–29. For an account of the houses of correction in Italy see Raimondo, Rossella. 2015. *Discoli incorreggibili. Indagine storico-educativa sulle origini delle case di correzione in Italia e in Inghilterra.* Milano: Franco Angeli.

[34]The first important sources are Delvincourt 1813 (as n. 9) 749–750 and Toullier 1824 (as n. 9) 363–367 (§§ 262–264), especially 364: "l'excuse ne devrait pas être reçue, si l'impossibilité d'empêcher l'action a été précédée d'une faute du père, sans laquelle l'événement qui a causé le dommage ne serait pas arrivé". Subsequently see Duranton 1841 (as n. 9) 509–510 (§§ 715 and 718); Sourdat 1852 (as n. 9) 148–150 (§§ 832–834), with reference to Toullier (149); Zachariae 1858 (as n. 9) 22–23 (§ 628); Demante, and Colmet de Santerre 1865 (as n. 9) 684; Marcadé 1866 (as n. 9) 279–281; Aubry, and Rau 1871 (as n. 9) 756–759 (§ 447); Laurent 1876 (as n. 9) 591–603 (§§ 562–565), in particular 601–603 (§§ 564–565); Demolombe 1882 (as n. 9) 188; Larombière 1885 (as n. 9), 625–627 (art. 1384, nn. 23–24); Huc 1895 (as n. 9) 587–588 (§§ 442–443). Subsequently see Baudry-Lacantinerie, and Bard 1908 (as n. 11) 595, 601; Demogue 1925 (as n. 11) 6–7, 15–17; Mazeaud 1931 (as n. 11) 543–568, in particular 560 and 563. On the other hand, contemporary scholars emphasise the ambiguity of the code: see Carbonnier, Jean. 1993 (17th edition). *Droit civil.* 4. *Les Obligations.* Paris: Presses universitaires de France, 440–441; Viney 1998 (as n. 3) 979–980.

They contributed towards strengthening the thesis that the father was not exonerated from liability by the sole fact of not being present at the crime. Moreover, these decisions considered as examples of 'negligent education' the failure to use means of correction or a bad example in the family. At the beginning of the nineteenth century, these were the two typical elements that indicated a fault in the education of the child. This reasoning was acquired from a trilogy of *arrêt*: Bourges 1821, Cass. 1827 and Bordeaux 1829.[35]

The most fully motivated sentence was the 9 March 1821 one of the Bourges Court of Appeal. The judges approved the civil code for having produced a 'wise restriction' to the principle according to which fathers were liable for the damage caused by minor children living with them. Indeed fathers could be cleared every time they were able to demonstrate that had been unable, physically and morally, to prevent the offence.

At that point the Court listed a series of typical cases in which fathers could be considered to be at fault. In the list were examples of *culpa in vigilando*: entrusting work to their children, not supervising their conduct, leaving them to themselves at too young an age, allowing them more freedom than was suited to their age. There were also examples of *culpa in educando*: allowing children to give way to idleness and libertinage, and not giving them a proper education.

These were the criteria according to which exculpatory proof could be accorded as introduced by the authors of the code, according to the Court, following the Pothier model. Taking inspiration from a directive issued by the tribune Tarrible during the drafting of the *code civil*, the judges stated that fathers had to be exempt from all reproach. On the other hand, exculpatory proof was opportune: the opposite system was unjust and would render illusory the restriction provided by the law.

Nevertheless, in practice the judges sentenced a father to pay damages for the harm caused by his 20-year-old son, considering the former guilty of *relâchement de discipline domestique* (this was the term already used by Tarrible),[36] in other words the father had not corrected his son's bad tendencies.[37]

In 1827 the Court of Cassation, in the Pestel homicide case, sentenced that the physical impossibility of supervision due to illness was not sufficient to exculpate a father from his civil liability, as the previous bad conduct of his son should have

[35]Zachariae 1858 (as n. 9) 23 n. 5; Sourdat 1852 (as n. 9) 150; Aubry, and Rau 1871 (as n. 9) 759; Larombière 1885 (as n. 9) 627; Baudry-Lacantinerie, and Bard 1908 (as n. 11) 601; Blanc 1953 (as n. 3) 121 n. 5.

[36]Fenet, Pierre-Antoine. 1968. *Recueil complet des travaux préparatoires du code civil.* Tome treizième. Réimpression de l'édition 1827. Osnabrück: Otto Zeller, 488. See Lemonnier-Lesage 2013 (as n. 24) 156. Tarrible's speech was often quoted by the French scholars: see for example Laurent 1876 (as n. 9) 591–592; Mazeaud 1931 (as n. 11) 544, 552, 560, 562–563; 566–567. See also Blanc 1953 (as n. 3) 25–27, 121. Tarrible was often mentioned also in Italy: see Cesareo Consolo 1908 (as n. 6) 328; Messa 1913 (as n. 10) 681.

[37]Bourges, 9 Mar 1821. Guillier v. Saignol. S. 22 1822.2: 238–239. See Toullier 1824 (as n. 9) 363–364.

induced the parent to use the legal means of correction to repress his deviant behaviour. As a result, he had failed in the duties provided by the law for parents to educate their children to virtue and to make them good citizens.[38]

In 1829 the Court of Bordeaux, referring to the Bourges *arrêt,* in a case of serious violence during a brawl, decided that the father's absence at the crime scene did not integrate proof of the father's being unable to prevent it from happening. The father was considered liable for slackened domestic discipline, resulting in the bad example provided by the mother and tolerated by the father's weakness.[39]

Thirty years later, a fundamental decision on the subject was issued by the Court of Aix on 11 June 1859. The much reasoned sentence stated that a father's first duty was the education of his children (art. 203), which was sanctioned in the means of correction (art. 375). The case regarded a 17-year-old son who was at the service of others as a carter. The father defended himself by putting forward the argument that it was the master's responsibility to supervise his son. But the Court observed that it was not a question of imprudence or *maladresse*, it was an issue of acts of violence and *debauche*, so of facts that were far from regarding the work carried out in service, being instead the result of the minor's depraved habits and therefore of a bad education. The father, therefore, had failed in his duty to 'moralize' his children.

The words of the Aix judges were particularly indicative of a widespread mentality, so it is opportune to report them here. The magistrates considered that parental liability was established above all for the purposes of domestic interest and of social interest. It was set up for the purposes of domestic interest so that a father knew that his first duty was to 'moralize' his children, because of the 'solidarity of honour' that united all the members of the family. For the purposes of social interest, it existed because nobody should be exposed to suffering damage resulting from an offence or crime consequent to the bad education of a child, who was almost always insolvent, without there being serious recourse against the father who was financially solvent and who had failed in his obligation to properly raise his child, as it was important to society that the father should prepare his son to be a man and citizen. In this case, the father had not fulfilled his duty to provide his youngest son with the religious and moral education required (the son had not had his first communion and he had a dishonourable disease).[40] Such evaluations were shared also by the Italian lawyers of the time.[41]

---

[38]Ch. crim. Cass. 29 Mar 1827. Pestel v. Gogin. S. 28 1828.1: 373.

[39]Bordeaux, 1 Apr 1829. Boisrousseau v. Audouin. S. 29 1829.2: 259.

[40]Aix, 11 June 1859. M. v. Jourdan. S. 1860.2: 193–195.

[41]See Borsari 1877 (as n. 6) 342–344, 351–352, quoting Larombière and admitting that it was an extensive interpretation of the code; Ricci 1886 (as n. 6) 133; Giorgi 1886 (as n. 6) 380–382; Chironi 1906 (as n. 6) 183–185; Ferrini 1926 (as n. 11) 808; Cesareo Consolo 1908 (as n. 6) 328, 353–354; Messa 1913 (as n. 10) 681. After 1942 see Brasiello, Teucro. 1949. Dei fatti illeciti. In D'Amelio, Mariano, La Lumia, Isidoro, De Bernardinis, Angelo, Anichini, Ugolino, and Brasiello, Teucro (eds.), *Codice civile. Libro delle Obbligazioni*. Volume III. *Delle promesse unilaterali. Dei titoli di credito. Della gestione di affari. Del pagamento dell'indebito. Dell'arricchimento senza*

Also in the Italian law courts cases were presented in which the father was considered at fault not only because he had failed in his duties of supervision, but also because he had not provided a proper education to his son, because for example he had omitted to resort to the means of correction and therefore to the proper 'disciplinary' education. Also in these cases, this regarded children whose character was difficult and dangerous.

Thus in 1881 the Casale Court of Appeal, in relation to damages from intentional injury, decided that "it would not be enough for the father to prove […] that he had his children brought up by educating them to the feelings of work, tranquillity and respect […]. It would instead be necessary for him to prove that he had exercised over his son an assiduous supervision, adopting also the means of strictness required by the latter's wicked nature, and preventing him with all his powers from going to the inn and picking fights and from wandering about armed at night".[42]

Even more severe was the Catania Court in 1902, in representing the father of the author of the damage: he "was not a good family father, nor excellent citizen, because instead of using the means of correction and discipline necessary for the education of children, he reveals himself to be not only excessively indulgent and negligent, but what is worse he gives a bad example with his conduct held after the crimes in question" (rural crimes repeatedly committed by his son).[43]

For the Turin Court of Appeal, in 1904, the means of correction were the most suitable response to the acts of bravado of unruly children.[44]

This orientation was to last a long time. It was confirmed by the Court of Cassation in 1931. The Court declared that it was not sufficient for a father to send a son to school and make him work in his free time to deduce that he had given his child a proper education. With a 13-year-old troublemaker son, the father should have resorted to "stricter and more energetic means of education", and exercised "stricter surveillance, with the aim of being able to say that his education had been seriously taken care of".[45]

However, judges did not always ask for proof of the use of means of correction. Sometimes proof of precise and concrete acts of proper education, such as giving good advice, was sufficient: if this failed, the father was convicted.

An elaborate sentence by the magistrate of Saronno, issued on 26 May 1905, may be considered paradigmatic of the strictness of the jurisprudence in interpreting the father's educational duties.

After establishing that school had to be completed and integrated at home, and the master's work had to be completed and integrated by the parents, the magistrate

(Footnote 41 continued)

causa. Commentario, *diretto da Mariano D'Amelio ed Enrico Finzi, 249–252. Firenze: G. Barbèra Editore, 251; De Cupis 1946 (as n. 11) 310.*

[42]App. Casale, 7 May 1881. Conti v. Perfino. *La Legge* 22.1 (1881): 271.

[43]App. Catania, 10 Dec 1902. Cristaldi v. Catalano. *Monitore* 44 (1903): 236–237.

[44]App. Torino, 27 Oct 1904. Bendino v. Roggero. *Monitore* 46 (1905): 194–196.

[45]Cass., 6 July 1931. Spadaro v. Ruggeri. *Monitore* 73 (1932): 90–91.

observed bitingly that "a father has not exhausted his task and obligation as an educator, when he started his son off at school; moreover, if a father conducts an honest and laborious life thus giving a good example to his children, but on the other hand does not take care of them, and allows them to live abandoned to themselves, they acquire bad habits and they grow useless and morally undisciplined. Without reprimanding them to mastering and imitating his conduct, that father certainly cannot be said to have well fulfilled his task as educator".

In this case, the children of a street cleaner had committed a theft. The father defended himself by saying that he had given his children the compulsory and religious education and that he could not supervise them on a permanent basis as he was away from home for work. The magistrate objected, cynically, that it was not necessary to shadow one's children: "it is enough that, when he comes home from his laborious day, instead of drowning in sleep and wine the sorrows of it and the tiredness of the hard labour (as many in the condition of Arnaboldi and perhaps the majority, unfortunately, do) he takes care of what his child has done during his day, he admonishes him and reprimands him if he has erred, and with words and with his example he encourages him and he educates him to improve himself and to do good". The father instead did not bring his children back to the straight and narrow "as soon as he had realised that they were deviating from it or gave reason to suspect that they had strayed from it".

The sentence further warned that the father's duty was "the double duty of education and supervision, which is imposed on him by the law of nature and by the law that is written". The sentence admitted that "there are rebellious temperaments, and every attempt to educate them and lead them to conform with the rules of righteous living turns out to be useless and fruitless." For this reason the father could be exculpated of his liability, because it would be unjust to consider him liable if "he had done everything that the law and nature imposed". The proof, however, was strictly interpreted.[46]

More elastic, in comparison, was the yardstick adopted by the Genoa Court of Appeal in a case of 1905 for indecent behaviour, examined above. The Court made it clear that art. 1153 only contemplated a presumption of failure to supervise and not of bad education, expressly accommodating the thesis maintained in the doctrine by Chironi.[47] Secondly, the judges established that "diligence could not be expected beyond the obligation to educate according to the possibilities, place, profession and social conditions of the person obliged". A good education should be taken to mean the 'common education': "otherwise fathers would have to answer for everything that their children did, even psychic idiosyncrasies, that in the physical body have atavistic recurrence, where often one sees degenerate in the sons the glories of the fathers". In this case, the Court considered that proof of a bad education was not satisfactory, as the family were "very simple, ignorant farmers". The crime had been committed between peers, "who have the greatest freedom in

[46]Pretura Saronno, 26 May 1905. Fumetti v. Arnaboldi. *Monitore* 48 (1907): 383–384.

[47]See n. 32.

the country, and perhaps, everywhere". The father had a recalcitrant son and had behaved with him as other fathers did: he rebuked his son for working too little and playing too much, he followed his son's attendance at school, he gave him good advice. The father had therefore attempted to 'moralize' his son. Here the proof of a good education ascertained by specific acts was considered sufficient, at least for children who were not particularly problematic.[48]

Instead the Court considered the bad examples in the family (the father had been convicted of theft and his two brothers for theft and injury) to be irrelevant for the purposes of proof of a bad education, also because they did not regard offences against public decency. The Genoa judges declared that they did not wish to create "new presumptions of fault, absolute and unlimited", and that they did not intend to attribute at all costs the faults of children to their parents: "the records of the children, who not infrequently, and often due to their deficient nature, are deaf to the most shining paternal examples, would be an eternal punishment for the parents themselves".[49]

Another rule that clearly emerged from the cases of this period regarded when the father entrusted his children to third parties. In doing so, the father ceased to be liable for failure to supervise or for insufficient supervision of his child, but this did not mean that he was exonerated from all fault in educating the minor.[50] So if the child caused harm to others, whether or not this was a crime of negligence or of intent, the father could not be exempted from the proof of proper education. This emerges from a series of important French and Italian precedents.

It would therefore appear that for malicious crime the judges' decision was severe, as already seen in the 1859 Aix Court judgement.[51] For *negligent torts,* however, judges were more indulgent.

For example, in 1908 the Montpellier Court established that when a child was under the teacher's supervision, his father was no longer liable for failure to supervise. Nevertheless, in that case the Court did not admit parental liability for negligent education, as it was a sudden, inevitable act, not preceded by a quarrel (harm inflicted with a pen on another schoolchild).[52]

Also the Paris Court, on 9 July 1914, exonerated a mother from liability for her 15-year-old son's negligent wounding of another person with a toy pistol. Her son was employed as a telegraph operator on the premises of the stock exchange. The mother was cleared because she could not supervise him, and because she was not at fault in allowing her son to buy a toy pistol.[53]

---

[48]But the proof was necessary: Trib. Caltanissetta, 20 Dec 1898. Corrado v. Sciandra. *Monitore* 40 (1899): 799.

[49]App. 1905 3 Mar 1905 (as n. 25).

[50]Aubry, and Rau 1871 (as n. 9) 757; Huc 1895 (as n. 9) 587 ("d'après une jurisprudence assez severe"); Demogue 1925 (as n. 9) 16.

[51]See n. 40.

[52]Montpellier, 31 Oct 1908. Bartès v. Constans and the State. *Monitore* 51 1910: 296.

[53]Paris, 9 July 1914. Dame Potier Rousseaux v. Sauton. S. 1915.2.56. *Monitore* 57 1916: 59.

In Italian jurisprudence two cases were particularly important with regard to malicious crimes. The first was decided by the Milan Court of Appeal in 1913. In a case regarding a son who had committed an act of misappropriation to the detriment of the company he worked for, the judges required "the proof of conclusive and decisive facts that exclude any fault of neglected supervision, bad education and improvidence, or neglected exercise of parental responsibility" in order for the father to be cleared of liability.[54]

Even more important was the case decided by the Milan Court of Appeal on 27 May 1925, after indictment by the Court of Cassation, for the remarks expressed on the content of the exculpatory proof. The trial regarded a father's liability for the brutal blows inflicted by his 14-year-old son on a classmate at school. The father's defence was that he was not required to supervise his son as the son had been entrusted to the teachers. Like the Tribunal, in the appellate proceeding the Appeal Court had accepted the defence, specifying that the teacher had replaced the father as supervisor, "unless this regards a minor who is abnormal or dangerous or in any case very badly behaved and the parent had not taken care to warn the school management, or when the son had, on account of defective supervision by his parents, taken a weapon from home and used it in the school against other persons", excluding the fact that the dangerousness of the minor could be exclusively deduced from the violence of the offence. The father, therefore, had a double duty: to inform and to supervise.

The school appealed, and the Court of Cassation instead decided that the "liability of the parent exists also when the father has neglected his son's education", thus rendering it always necessary to conduct an investigation on the education the parents had given the child to make sure that "if the harmful act, committed by the minor, were not for an escapade depending on the failure to provide a proper education, that had caused the formation of a corrupted character, prone to bad deeds".

The Court of Appeal was once more assigned the case. The Court considered that the adequacy of the proof could also result from the fact that the child had been entrusted to institutes "in which he could be not only instructed in the various branches of knowledge, but also in life, receiving a useful educational development". There appears to have been an important evolution in the proof of a proper education, as the father fulfilled his duty also by entrusting his son to suitable educators.[55]

From the case law it is possible to discover a further legal rule which could be formulated thus: if the father heard of the offence after it had been committed, and he tolerated it, this determined his liability for violation of the obligation to educate.

The doctrine, albeit previous in date, was expressed in a precise form by the Court of Cassation in a sentence of 14 November 1924 which considered a father to

[54]App. Milano, 18 Apr 1913. Ditta M. Baer & C. v. Maderna Leopoldo and Pilade. *Monitore* 54 (1913): 616.

[55]App. Milano, 27 May 1925. Cavalli v. Ronconi and Mambretti. *Monitore* 66 (1925): 629–631.

be liable for not using the right of correction on his child of rebellious character, and guilty of a passive form of indulgence and excessive weakness for tolerating the seduction committed by his son on military service. Parental responsibility, the judges officially declared, was founded "on the principle of defence of social relations, of public morality and of order in the family".[56]

In the application of these criteria, it was rare for a father to be freed of liability when he had a difficult or delinquent son.[57]

For these reasons, the case that in 1910 induced the judges of the Catanzaro Court to exonerate the father of all civil liability regarding a delinquent son was particularly significant. A 16-year-old shepherd had injured another shepherd with the back of an axe because the latter had insulted him on the previous day. The crime was therefore premeditated and the minor was considered "not a bad person, not a profligate, not a negligent person, but truly a criminal". The court also took into account the fact that the father had ten children, that he had always given good advice, that it could not "expect from the father uninterrupted supervision of the conduct of his son [...], because the juvenile criminal always manages to elude even the shrewdest supervision."[58] The judges limited their examination only to the aspect of supervision.

On the other hand there were some cases in which a father's fault for the crimes committed by his children was particularly evident. For example, in 1914 the Trani Court of Appeal had to judge damages deriving from a premeditated murder perpetrated by a simpleton son who had been set by his father to guard his land: the father had armed his son with a carbine without giving him a licence and had left him alone in the countryside also at night.[59] Even more striking was a crime that took place in a very degraded family context which was submitted to the Naples Court of Appeal in 1927. It took place in Fuorigrotta: a boy killed a 14-year-old with a shot from a revolver which was fired during a brawl among different family groups. It was the last of a series of rows between the two families, and the father of the minor had taken part in some of them.[60]

All in all, it appeared to be easier to find proof of good supervision and proper education when a crime was committed by a child who was not *per se* rebellious or violent.[61]

---

[56] Cass., 14 Nov 1924. Cecere v. Donzelli. *Monitore* 66 (1925): 251.

[57] See Mazeaud 1931 (as n. 11) 564; Mazeaud, and Tunc 1965 (as n. 11) 887, 890, 893–894; Viney 1998 (as n. 3) 1001.

[58] App. Catanzaro, 9 July 1910. Novello. *Monitore* 52 (1911): 295.

[59] App. Trani, 7 Feb 1914. Frascella v. Marzia. *Monitore* 55 (1914): 813–814.

[60] App. Napoli, 28 Nov 1927. Grillo v. Arata. *Monitore* 69 (1928): 336–337.

[61] See App. Torino, 8 May 1903. Ferraglia v. Micheletto. *Monitore* 44 (1903): 613–614; App. Milano, 9 Dec 1903. Ditta Balconi v. Mariani and Valli. *Monitore* 45 (1904): 411–412.

4 Negligent Torts of Minor Children

In Italy the jurisprudence acted in a different way, depending on whether the minor had committed real malicious crimes or negligent torts, which could have emerged in the activities of the minors from infancy through to their majority.

The gradual or relative conception of the duty of supervision, according to the nature, age and occupations of the minor had already been considered in a clear cut way by some of the sentences examined here above. This same conception was used also to decide on a father's liability for his minors' imprudence or omissions. The son's social environment was also considered: in the country the supervision required was lesser than in the town.

An important point to stress is that if the son had a good character and had always behaved irreprehensibly, the duty of supervision was interpreted by the jurisprudence in a less absorbing and strict manner in consideration of the minor's age. As was often pointed out, the father was not required to shadow his son and he could allow him appropriate room for autonomy.

The courts also spoke of the *moral* impossibility of preventing the crime when the father had no reasonable motive for stopping the son from doing the activity from which the harm arose. Fathers were exonerated from liability when there were no special reasons for tighter and more attentive supervision: the proof of proper education and the demonstration of the child's previous good conduct were therefore enough to justify a relaxing of the duty of supervision, which could become less continuous, less systematic and assiduous.

In Italian practice between the nineteenth century and the first decades of the twentieth, however, it is possible to identify at least three distinct legal trends.

4.1 Children at Play and Proof of Proper Supervision

The most liberal line was that followed by the courts in the presence of damage caused unintentionally by children at play. Here they interpreted the exculpatory proof of the father's proper supervision in a more flexible way and, after considering a series of elements such as the children's good character, the proper education they had received, and how the fact had taken place, they would reject the claim for damages against the father. The web of protection of the child that the parent was required to guarantee was conceived in broader terms.

Once more, the origins of this tradition were the French styles of justice. For example, in the Leclercq case, decided by the Douai Court on 7 November 1893, the judges considered the case of a fire started imprudently by a child with some matches. The father was absent for work, he had a numerous family, he had obliged his children to attend school assiduously, and he had them supervised by the mother outside school hours. Both parents were an example of irreprehensible honesty, the children were models of good behaviour, scrupulousness and application at school.

The fact took place on the way home, in the company of several fellow students; the matches had not been supplied by the parents; no previous deed by the child could have predicted what happened. The Court exonerated the father.[62] Also the Court of Cassation, with a sentence of 30 June 1896, considered that the parents had not committed any imprudence in allowing their son to go out of the house with another, on the latter's invitation: the child did not take with him any dangerous object, nor any weapon; nor was he naughty or quarrelsome (*ni méchant ni querelleur*) and he had been properly brought up.[63]

In Italy, in 1897, the Milan Court of Appeal was called upon to assess the liability of a father for an injury caused by his 8-year-old child who was intent on playing with a sharp knife that his father did not know he possessed. The Court cleared the father of all liability. They were "country people, Olgiati an innkeeper, Castelli a carter, and it is not possible to expect those who also have their occupations to constantly keep their children locked up at home, or shadow their every step".[64]

In 1933 the Milan Court of Appeal followed suit. The harm was done while two children were playing, one (12 years old) was throwing stones and the other was spinning a hoop: the latter was hit by mistake in the eye with a stone. The Court stated that the impossibility of preventing the fact "is to be interpreted in the relative and appreciated sense with criteria of reasonable moderation, as it is inconceivable, as this is *culpa aquiliana*, that the necessary supervision that the father has to exercise over his child, should not be interrupted, and that the child should be constantly within view". In this case the 12-year-old boy had been properly educated, his character was good-natured, at school he had always behaved well, in the absence of his father he was supervised by his mother. The expectation of damages was rejected as it was excessive, "not being possible to prevent even with the best education that a 12-year-old child, in a village street, should not amuse himself by throwing some stones close to the ground".[65]

The Court referred to a sentence of the Court of Cassation of 25 July 1932, from which the rule cited above was taken, in confirmation of a sentence by the Milan court that had acquitted the father of a child who had hit a play mate of his in the eye with a snowball.[66]

---

[62]Douai, 7 Nov 1893. Leclercq v. Min. publ. et Dutronquoy. D. 1894.2: 159. For a positive evaluation of this decision: Baudry-Lacantinerie, and Bard 1908 (as n. 11) 600; Demogue 1925 (as n. 11) 11; Ollier 1961 (as n. 3) 156, 189 n. 25.

[63]Req., 30 June 1896. Courtine v. Vergnes. D. 1897.1: 198.

[64]App. Milano, 16 June 1897. Oliati Francesco v. Castelli Giovanni. *Monitore* 38 (1897): 709–712.

[65]App. Milano, 11 July 1933. Cetti v. Braga. *Monitore* 74 (1933): 788–789.

[66]See instead, taking into account other circumstances, App. Cagliari, 30 Dec 1926. Perra v. Paulis. *Monitore* 68 (1927): 951–952.

4.2 Negligence of Minors Under 15 Years Old

Instead, according to another, more rigorous doctrine, proof of a proper education was not required, and in any case was not useful, when there was negligence committed by minors under 15 years old, as it was presumed that their father could prevent this through more careful supervision. Proof of such supervision was, however, very hard to provide.

There were two very significant cases that followed this line of reasoning. The first was decided by the Casale Court of Appeal on 18 November 1908. The judges adopted an inflexible maxim: "the supervision that a parent must exercise over a child of his who is a minor has to be serious and constant, in such a way as to prevent as far as possible that thoughtlessness, imprudence, and carelessness that are typical of youth may cause harm to others; this supervision can be greater or lesser, depending on the age of the child, according to his character, and the occupations he attends to". The father proved that his 15-year-old son had been properly educated, besides being very good-natured and of good morality, but he was in any case convicted of not having properly supervised the boy. The sentence underlined the fact that the son was 15 years old, "and so he had not yet reached that age in which the child is absolutely abandoned to his own devices, and it is hard if not impossible for the parents to exercise constant and effective supervision".[67]

The second episode to signal was one solved by the Milan Court of Appeal on 3 November 1916. There was an accident involving the loss of an eye caused by a stick hurled with violence during a quarrel between two boys. According to the judges, the father could not exculpate himself from liability by proving circumstances such as "proper education, the good-natured character of the minor, the instruction given to this boy and his not being quarrelsome". This could be helpful in a crime committed by a minor. But in this case, it was imprudence, which the father could have prevented by teaching his son not to use a piece of wood that was in itself a dangerous object.[68]

4.3 Presumption of Negligent Education

Another severe tendency, already seen at the beginning of the twentieth century, was that of courts which deduced proof of a negligent education by the father from the way in which the offence had been committed and then convicted the father. The sole fact that the minor had behaved in an incorrect or badly behaved manner was indicative of a negligent education.

[67]App. Casale, 18 Nov 1908. Sambuelli v. Cellerino. *Monitore* 50 (1909): 252–253.

[68]App. Milano, 3 Nov 1916. Quadri v. Zacchetti Bossolo. *Monitore* 57 (1916): 950–952.

These were the reasons why on 22 January 1901 a father was sentenced by the Trani Court of Appeal to pay compensation for the harm caused by his son, who had brusquely pushed another youth for a joke that was defined as ‘rather boorish’. From the sentence it emerged that the father must have tried to defend himself by simply reporting his absence and the rebellious character of his son. The Court therefore reminded him that, while the first defence was not only insufficient, but even placed him at fault for having abandoned his son to his idleness, the second made him even more guilty as “it is education that has to fight defects” and when a son was ‘defective’, moreover, the father had to supervise him even more carefully.[69]

Likewise, in 1902 the Milan Court of Appeal sentenced the father of a 17-year-old boy for having let him play by running wildly along a narrow and dimly lit pavement. The judges also observed the lack of supervision, but they insisted above all on his negligent education. In this case, the father had put forward the defence that he had not been present at the scene of the crime, and this attitude had a negative effect on the judges. They observed that “the father has proved nothing, nor has he attempted to prove anything” and they reminded him that this type of ‘passive’ defence had long been considered insufficient.[70] At this point they clearly deduced from the events the proof that “in relation to his social position” the youth had not had the “right and proper” education.[71]

In conclusion, the two decisions were important and enabled both courts to confirm that the technique of ascertaining the fault *in re ipsa* was by no means unknown to Italian courts.

5 Damage Caused by Dangerous Objects

Another recurring situation which constituted a definite source of civil liability for the father was that of injury caused by dangerous objects which the father might have imprudently left unattended around the house in a place where the underage child may easily come into contact with them. This behaviour indicated a carelessness for which the parent was answerable. More specifically, we are dealing with accidents caused by guns or hunting weapons.

This *ratio decidendi* emerges already from a decision of 1898 of the Milan Court of Appeal, in a case where the versions of the two parties were at variance. The victim was intent on proving that the father was aware that his son used to go hunting unlawfully with his father’s gun and that, despite this, the father used to leave the gun, loaded, hanging in the shop at his son’s disposal. The father was intent on demonstrating that, far from leaving the gun lying around, he kept it

[69]Trani, 22 Jan 1901. Lefèvre v. Lefèvre. *Monitore* 42 (1901): 656–657.

[70]See also App. Napoli, 31 Dec 1906. Sibilia v. Conte. *Monitore* 48 (1907): 648–649.

[71]App. Milano, 11 Feb 1902. Calcaterra v. Panceri. *Monitore* 43 (1902): 456–457.

hidden, and that he was unaware that his son had found it and used it to go hunting.[72]

Confirming this case law are two examples dating from the beginning of the twentieth century.

In 1901, the Trani Court of Appeal ruled that "common and basic prudence suggests that a father possessing firearms in the house should keep them hidden in a place where underage children cannot have access to them".[73]

In 1917 the Genoa Court of Appeal reaffirmed that "excluding the requirement that the father should never to leave his child and be by the child's side at all times, as such a requirement does not constitute one of the necessities of life, the father is held responsible for keeping the gun in a place which was easily accessible to the underage son".[74]

5.1 Authorisation of the Father

The question was much more complex in cases relating to the father's liability for injury caused during activities he has expressly authorised.

From the case law on the subject it is possible to identify a first operative rule, which can be articulated thus: if the child was good-natured, reliable, and close to the age of majority, the father was exonerated from liability even if he had let his child engage in an activity during which the injurious episode took place. This rule could be applied, for instance, when the father gave consent to his child to go to a dance: in the absence of any special circumstances, the Courts considered the father's authorisation to be prudent and reasonable. There are three examples of this kind of decision.

In a judgment of 1892, the Turin Court of Appeal made a distinction between the physical impossibility and the moral impossibility of preventing a criminal act. There was moral impossibility when the parent had no reason or motive to prevent the child from going to a place where harm would be caused to others. In this specific case, the son was 19 years old and well-behaved, and the judges deemed the father as not responsible for the injury the son caused at the dance.[75]

The Casale Court of Appeal, on 31 October 1904, used the same argument in a case dealing with a wound caused during a fight: given the son's temperament, his closeness to the age of majority, and his educational background, the father's authorisation was considered reasonable.[76]

[72]App. Milano, 2 Mar 1898. Annoni Carlo v. Fumagalli Giuseppe. *Monitore* 39 (1898): 768.

[73]App. Trani, 4 Feb 1901. Vaccina v. Pellegrino. *Monitore* 42 (1901):451.

[74]App. Genova, 31 Oct 1917. Piombo v. Brignole. *Monitore* 59 (1918): 181.

[75]App. Torino, 27 Feb 1892. Garbato v. Penna. *Monitore* 33 (1892): 340.

[76]App. Casale, 31 Oct 1904. Ferrara v. Armano. *Monitore* 46 (1905): 237.

Finally, a Court of Cassation sentence of 30 November 1926 established that "surveillance cannot be conceived as being so totally absorbing as to keep the parent from other activities necessary for procuring subsistence for the family; it must be understood instead in the normal sense which combines individual and social necessities with keeping a careful distance, which is necessary to instil in youths an enterprising spirit and sense of responsibility." In this specific case, the father had given consent to the son to take part in a religious procession, and it was established that the injurious episode was due to the carelessness of the organisers.[77]

Case law was less consistent in the case of the father authorising dangerous activities, such as handling firearms or guns, hunting, riding a bicycle or driving a motor vehicle. The outcomes and arguments were different for each of these situations, but there were essentially two possible paths.

On the one hand the father, having given his consent to a dangerous activity such as hunting, accepted the risks of injuries that his son might cause while performing that activity. Such was the argument applied to the Barbel case by the Caen Court, during an important *arrêt* on 2 June 1840, much cited in French legal theory and therefore also in Italian civil law. A father was held responsible for injuries caused allowing his child to go hunting at the age of 19. The incident was due to the *maladresse* of Eugène Barbel. The father's liability was certain, because the law did not require the father's personal imprudence for him to be held responsible. Simply by authorising the activity, or by not preventing it, the father exposed himself to the risk of being accountable for the harm his son's imprudence might cause on that occasion.[78]

In spite of the authoritativeness of this precedent, Italian courts did not follow it strictly. It was in fact overturned by a ruling of 1872 of the Bologna Court of Appeal. The ruling of first instance was reformulated because the episode was deemed to have been an 'unfortunate accident': the son was 20 years old and had a hunting licence, and the father had no reason to stop him from going hunting. The judges in this case applied a line of defence for the father which we have also seen employed on another occasion to exonerate him from liability.[79]

The opposite situation to the one outlined above, i.e. that of the presence of reasonable grounds for suspicion, can be found in a decision of the Court of the Cassation on 6 April 1909; the ruling in this case was the exact opposite to the one just discussed. In this case, the son's "excessively capricious, overbearing, and violent" nature meant that the father's authorisation was deemed ill-advised: "strict

[77]Cass., 30 Nov 1926. Pennacchi and others v. Gregori. *Monitore* 68 (1927): 48.

[78]Caen, 2 June 1840. Barbel v. Dupin. S. 40 1840.2: 538. These scholars agreed upon the strict solution: Sourdat 1852 (as n. 9) 150; Aubry, and Rau 1871(as n. 11) 759; Demolombe 1882 (as n. 9) 188; Larombière 1885 (as n. 9) 626. On the other hand, for a critical view: Demogue 1925 (as n. 11) 9 ("une intérpretation qui évidemment sort des idées traditionelles"); Mazeaud 1931 (as n. 11) 565 n. 79, 568 ("excessive"); Blanc 1953 (as n. 3) 134–135.

[79]App. Bologna, 18 Nov 1872. Parmigiani v. Bianchi. *Annali della giurisprudenza italiana* 7 (1873): 125–126. Ricci 1886 (as n. 6) 113 mentioned this case in his commentary.

repressive action … in the interest of the health and safety of the community" should have been the appropriate response.[80]

Italian case law also provides an interesting example of juxtaposition between the two arguments illustrated above in a case where, in the first instance, the tribunal embraced the theory of risk, while in the second instance the court applied the theory of culpability, which led to the exoneration of the prudent father from liability for damages.

The Genoa Court of Appeal declared liability on grounds of risk in a major ruling of 17 January 1913, which condemned a father for merely having handed a firearm to his underage son, in spite of the son's previous behaviour and his ability to handle guns.[81]

The Turin Court of Cassation, on the other hand, declared liability on grounds of negligence, and thus on 31 October 1913 overturned the previous ruling, rejecting the argument according to which the father's consent for his son to handle guns made him automatically liable under civil law for the offence, even when the parent had no reason or motive for preventing his son from handling a gun. According to the Court,[82] why should the judge not consider as having ceased the possibility of the father supervising his son's conduct when close to the age of majority? In the absence of any valid reason for forbidding hunting activities for the son close to the age of majority, why should the father be held liable for the injury caused by the son's carelessness?

The Parma Court of Appeal adopted a harder line against the father in a judgment of 15 January 1915. The Court held the father liable, affirming that he was in fact obliged to supervise his 20-year-old son even after obtaining his licence to carry arms.[83]

There might be cases when injury occurred while the minor was playing with a weapon which was not lethal but was nevertheless dangerous: this indeed was the outcome of a dangerous game with an airgun where the Swiss Federal Tribunal, in a ruling of 7 June 1917, reported also in the *Monitore dei Tribunali*, condemned the father for his imprudence for not having advised his 15-year-old son about the weapon.[84]

Judges were more willing to exempt the father from liability when the weapon was handed to the son by a third party.

In this regard it is possible to quote a judgment of 29 October 1898 by the Geneva Court, translated by the *Monitore dei Tribunali*, in which the Swiss judges

---

[80]Cass. pen., 6 Apr 1909. Ric. Carrozza. *Monitore* 50 (1909): 556–557.

[81]App. Genova, 17 Jan 1913. Fossa v. Benvenuto. *Monitore* 54 (1913): 353–354.

[82]Cass. Torino, 31 Oct 1913. Benvenuto v. Fossa. *Monitore* 55 (1914): 24.

[83]App. Parma, 15 Jan 1915. Magnani v. Gonzaga. *Monitore* 56 (1915): 352–354.

[84]Trib. fédéral suisse, 7 Jun 1917. Zufferey v. Raspizio. *Monitore* 59 (1918): 61–62.

established that the father is not liable if the weapon was handed to the son (aged thirteen and a half) by a third party.[85]

There is also an authoritative Court of Cassation judgment of 5 January 1915. A son obeyed his father by going to church, but without parental supervision. He met other youths and followed them to the abode of a third party to pick up hunting guns. Jokingly, he pointed a gun, which he thought was unloaded, at another youth, and wounded him. The Court of Cassation overturned a previous ruling on the case, claiming that, beyond the limits of human possibility, the norm would be arbitrary and unjustifiable, as it is impossible for the father to be able to predict the future, and he could not be expected to supervise his son night and day to stop him from committing an offence.[86]

5.2 Modern Times: Harm Caused by Accidents with Bicycles and Motor Vehicles

The fluctuation between rigorous and more liberal judgments can be seen again when examining case law regarding paternal liability for injuries deriving from riding bicycles and motor vehicles. In this historical period, both cases constitute dangerous activities with a high risk of accidents. This is therefore the field which lends itself the most to rigorous judgments in case law: behind the formal affirmation of liability for negligence, the law essentially sees the father as objectively liable. This is what seems to emerge from the analysis of a few cases between the late 19th century and the early 20th century.

For Italy an important precedent is that of the decision of the Milan Court of Appeal of 9 September 1896. It saw the father of a cyclist as responsible for simply having consented to the son's use of the bicycle. The judgment is clearly stated, and offers a realistic glimpse of daily life in a metropolis at the end of the century, when accidents of the kind were frequent: "it is well-known that a bicycle is capable of high speed, compared with other means of transport; it is hard to stop, silent, small and short, and therefore not easily discernible amongst pedestrians, horses, carts, carriages, omnibuses, trams, and all the coaches of which our populous city is full".[87]

A few years after we find the same technique applied in France. It is, once more, the case of an *arrêt* which explicitly applies the theory of risk. The Rouen Court, in fact, on 30 December 1913, made a distinction between injuries caused without the presence of the parents or tutor when they are the outcome of an act they have

---

[85]Cour de justice civile de Genève, 22 Oct. 1898. Borcard v. Schälpfer and Orcellet. S. 1899.4: 28–29. *Monitore* 40 (1899): 433, approved by Baudry-Lacantinerie, and Bard 1908 (as n. 11) 601.

[86]Cass. pen. 5 Jan 1915: Ric. Vignola. *Monitore* 56 (1915): 455.

[87]App. Milano, 9 Sep 1896. Piccioni Luigia ved. Clerici v. Brambilla cav. Camillo ed Ettore. *Monitore* 37 (1896): 879–882.

forbidden or of which they were at least unaware, and when they are the outcome of an authorised deed, even if it is lawful such as hunting with a gun, driving a car, or riding a bicycle. Accepting the risks deriving from these activities is the necessary consequence of the authorisation or of mere tolerance.[88]

It was possible to reach similar results also when applying a very strict version of liability for negligence, which corresponded in essence to objective liability through risk. This was the outcome of a judgment of 11 May 1900 at the Bologna Court of Appeal; it is an interesting case as it highlights the phenomenon described above.

Specifically, the incident was caused by a 19-year-old youth. In the first instance the father had asked the court to allow for a demonstration of proof that his son was an expert in handling a bicycle, but the Bologna Court rejected the request, saying that such proof would be unhelpful.

The Court of Appeal also affirmed that the circumstances the father wished to prove would be insufficient to justify the freedom granted to the son. The father should, rather, prove the "other concurring circumstances", "as nothing suggests that the son's ability to handle a bicycle corresponded to his good sense and docility in moderating his liveliness or youthful carelessness, the susceptibility of his temperament without the inhibiting influence of vigilant paternal authority".[89] The proof, in this case, is not impossibile, but it is certainly more difficult. The judges, in spite of the age of the son, demand a higher standard of evidence, based on a plurality of elements.

Incidents which had occurred using bicycles which did not technically comply with legal standards, or where there was a breach of the highway code, painted a different picture. In these cases, liability for negligence was attributed without hesitation. This was deemed dangerous behaviour which was symptomatic of a poor education. In the 1920s there are two significant precedents which confirm this line of reasoning.

The first is a sentence of the Swiss Federal Tribunal of 22 November 1923: a boy of 13 was sent by his father to run a few errands on a bicycle which was bigger than normal, and ridden carelessly, and a number of offences were committed. The father defended himself claiming that the youth was an able, alert cyclist, but the Court judged him to be fully liable for the accident.[90]

The second case comes from the Venice Court of Appeal, and it deals with a judgment of 25 June 1927. A father was deemed responsible for granting his son the use of the bicycle, even if his son was good-natured, prudent, and an able cyclist: the important detail to be noted is that the bicycle did not have a light.[91]

[88]Rouen, 30 Dec 1913. Ve Daunout v. Larchevèque. S. 1914.2: 223–224. This solution was still approved by Colin, and Capitant 1931 (as n. 11) 390, but criticised by Mazeaud 1931 (as n. 11) 565 (excessive opinion, as in the Rouen *arrêt*) and 568 (against the risk theory). Josserand 1939 (as n. 11) 314 noted that the basis of this decision was the risk. Negative opinions: Blanc 1953 (as n. 3) 134–135; Ollier 1961 (as n. 3) 140 n. 1, 151 n. 43.

[89]App. Bologna, 11 May 1900. Pellicciardi v. Caroli. *Monitore* 42 (1901): 574–575.

[90]Trib. fédéral suisse, 22 Nov 1923. Gabathuler v. Peter. *Monitore* 65 (1924): 595–597.

[91]App. Venezia, 25 June 1927. De Nardi v. Passoni. *Monitore* 69 (1928): 264.

The first decades of the 20th century provide a varied and interesting set of case law judgments. One orientation was to receive greater consensus in the future, namely the affirmation of the father's lack of responsibility concerning the granting of freedom to children close to the age of majority. This orientation emerges from the ruling of the Swiss Federal Tribunal of 13 October 1926, which is also well-known in France.

The Court clearly stated that the father's degree of supervision needed to be examined on its merits, though it might not constitute unequivocal exonerating proof. The judgment had to be based on the customs, necessities of life, age, and character of the individual who depends on the parental authority. In this case, the author of the injurious act was 19 and had been riding on the motorcycle of a friend who possessed a lawful licence. The youth had never breached the highway code and his physical and mental development was normal. There was nothing to suggest that the father should have forbidden him to use the motorcycle. It was not reasonable to expect the father to supervise the son constantly, as he was very often beyond parental surveillance. The son had reached an age which, in the social environment in which he lived, was essentially that of an adult: it was therefore not feasible to expect the father to guard his son to such an extent as to stop him from using a friend's motorcycle. The Court asserted that it was not possible to impose such a strict duty on the holder of the domestic authority and interpret art. 333 of the civil code in such a rigid way that it did not correspond to real life.[92]

The note accompanying the judgment, reported in a well-known French law journal, pointed out that Swiss law was different from French law: it was more flexible, probably due to the different formulae used to define the details of exonerating proof.[93]

We can conclude this overview on the cases of paternal liability for harm caused by their offspring by examining a few episodes concerning motor vehicles, where we clearly observe how the case law of the first decades of the twentieth century was rather strict.

This can be seen particularly clearly in the ruling of the Florence Court of Appeal of 22 April 1913. A father was condemned "for consenting his underage son to drive a car for which the highest level of calm, prudence, and foresight is required, qualities not normally attributable to persons of a young age. There have already been innumerable victims of this admirable yet terrible means of transport, and it is right that the courts should also defend human life, which is too often threatened by the folly which easily takes hold of drivers of motor vehicles wishing to emulate the speed of the wind."

[92]Trib. fédéral suisse, 13 Oct 1926. Mme Girardin v. Auguste and César Rubin. S. 1927.4: 14. Solution approved by Mazeaud 1931 (as n. 11) 565–566.

[93]Art. 333 [1] If damage is caused by a member of the household who is a minor, suffers from a mental disability, is subject to a general deputyship, or is mentally ill, the head of the family is liable unless he can show that his supervision of the household was as diligent as would normally be expected in the circumstances prevailing.

The Court claimed the activity in question was "notoriously dangerous". The son moreover had already had an accident with the family car; he was also driving too fast, at a speed defined as "ruthless and impudent", with insolence and without respect of private rights.[94]

In the 1930s, this orientation in case law was supported and endorsed by the Milan Court of Appeal.

A judgment of 19 June 1930 stated that it was the circumstances of the accidents which revealed the culpability of the father who had given his consent for a driving licence to be issued. He should instead have taken it away from him, or even better denied his consent. His son, in fact, had breached the highway code and had behaved "like a madman", driving at high speed at night, using the car not "as a gentleman", but "to commit criminal offences".[95]

The ruling of 25 November 1932 was founded on the same *ratio decidendi*. The father, the Court pointed out, was exonerated of liability only if he showed that, on the basis of the education imparted to his son, and of the demonstrations of prudence the son had shown in difficult circumstances, he had reason to think that his son would have behaved wisely to avoid any offence. The father's responsibility also lied in the fact that the son breached the highway code.[96]

The mere fact that a son should drive an unlawful vehicle, or should breach the highway code, exposed the father to civil liability for not having supervised or educated his son properly.

6 Conclusions

After having analysed the cases in question it is possible to draw a few conclusions. In the case-studies taken into consideration I have firstly attempted to point out some of the most frequent situations of harm caused by underage persons in Italian daily life. Secondly, I have studied the lines of reasoning most frequently used by the courts in reaching a judgment, and the possible lines of defence used by parents so as to be exempted from liability. It may be noticed that both judges and jurists have often supported the idea that the father, or subordinately the mother, could be liable for negligence both in supervising and in educating the children. The ways of ascertaining negligence, however, have differed according to the situation: strict rulings are juxtaposed with more liberal ones.

The duty of supervision was not measured univocally: on the contrary, it was interpreted according to the presence of given determining factors, such as the character and temperament of the child, the existence of motives for suspicion, and age. From the analysis of the cases one fact appears to be particularly significant:

---

[94]App. Firenze, 22 Apr 1913. Rimbotti v. Mori. *Monitore* 54 (1913): 774–776.

[95]App. Milano 19 June 1930. Gilardi v. Società noleggio automobili. *Monitore* 72 (1931): 102.

[96]App. Milano, 25 Nov 1932. Raffa v. Bernasconi. *Monitore* 74 (1933): 550–551.

the first three elements emerge particularly when the child had committed an intentional crime.

If the child had a difficult nature, or had already shown a tendency to commit offences, then the bearer of domestic authority—principally, the father—had to exercise a strict form of control. Furthermore, in these hypotheses the father was not only liable for not having kept an eye on the child adequately (by forbidding, for instance, the child from carrying dangerous objects or frequenting certain places), but also for not providing the child with a proper education. This extension of the exculpatory proof was widely accepted: the father's home was, in fact, the child's "main instrument of socialization".[97]

The concept of a good/negligent education, however, was not straightforward. In a restrictive sense, it extended from setting a good example to punishment and adopting adequate measures to correct the child's bad tendencies. The "school of the family" was considered to play an absolutely fundamental part in bringing up good citizens. According to the Italian 1865 civil code, it was the father who played the main role within the family: he had the basic task of teaching his children shared values, which were also moral and religious.

The father's moral role emerges clearly if we examine specific cases. The obligation to educate was taken very seriously, especially if the child had intentionally committed a crime. Indifference towards the child, as might happen in large families or in situations of deprivation among people of a poor social background, or tolerance of bad behaviour, made the father liable. It was the father's duty to take measures. The consequence of this mentality is that the courts only rarely exempted fathers on grounds of exculpatory proof. Although on occasion the judges did exempt fathers from liability when dealing with underage delinquents, in the majority of cases it really seems as though the father, in spite of the civil law's predisposition to allow him to win as regards the presumption of negligence, assumed the role of warrantor of the offences committed by difficult or problematic children. The duty to educate, as stated above, turned into a verification of the result of the child's education, more than the concrete analysis of parental conduct.[98]

It was easier for judges to exempt the father from liability when the tort was committed by the child in extraordinary circumstances, and when the father actively attempted to prevent it. A typical example is that of the harm arising from seduction, which judges saw as a situation which the father had the duty to prevent with the utmost vigilance, by keeping a close eye on the child's sentimental

[97]Pollock, Linda A. 2001. Parent-Child Relations. In *Family Life in Early Modern Times. 1500–1789*. Kertzer, David I., and Barbagli, Marzio (eds.). *The History of the European Family*. Volume One, 191–220. New Haven and London: Yale University Press, 197. Italian translation: Pollock, Linda. 2002. Il rapporto genitori-figli. In Barbagli, Marzio, and Kertzer, David I. (eds.) *Storia della famiglia in Europa. Dal Cinquecento alla Rivoluzione francese*, 263–306. Roma-Bari: Laterza, 272.

[98]Franzoni 1993 (as n. 4) 379. See also Monateri 1998 (as n. 4) 945, 949; Comporti 2012 (as n. 4) 248–252.

relationships even when nearing the age of majority, and by doing everything in his power to keep the child away from relationships outside wedlock.

The proof of good education was valid also when the father had entrusted his child to the custody of a third party: in this case there could be no liability for the duty of supervision, but the father could be held responsible for not having given his child a solid education.

Another important feature which emerges from this research is that when dealing with unintentional or negligent crimes, the judges' attitude tended to be less consistent: discussions were more open, and judgments were less univocal. In practice there were two lines of reasoning: one liberal, the other stricter. The former leaded to the rule according to which the duty of supervision should not be interpreted unconditionally but relatively, according to parameters such as age, character, conduct, education, and social environment. In applying this principle the father was often exempted from liability.

A stricter line of reasoning, on the other hand, considered the duty of supervision very rigidly for minors under the age of 15, so as to consider the father liable for the child's negligence. To complete the picture, it is necessary to point out that if the offence, even if committed unintentionally, derived from the child's bad or rude behaviour, the judges considered the father automatically responsible on the grounds of *culpa in educando*. In both cases, the presumption of negligence was transformed from relative into absolute.

Viceversa, Italian judgments on matters of activities authorised by the father followed a liberal line of reasoning right from the start. In fact, Italian courts, unlike the French courts, and in accordance with criticism from Italian civil lawyers, refused to consider the father as automatically liable merely for allowing the child to carry out activities which would harm third parties, if the circumstances showed that the parent had no reason to forbid the child from carrying out such activities. In other words, the courts did not accept the idea of risk-based liability, i.e. hypotheses according to which, already at that time, it was possible to verify the relevance of an educational model which gave greater responsibility to underage children in relation to their development and age. This kind of decision could be applied, for example, when the parent granted his/her child permission to take part in leisure activities such as dancing, but also when s/he let him go hunting, or ride a bicycle, or drive a car.

Nevertheless, in the last three cases the problem became more delicate, as they dealt with activities which, though lawful, involved the use of dangerous objects. It is possible therefore that the judges might not be content merely with the father's permission for his child to use weapons or drive a vehicle (the proof of "knowing how to", as Giovanni Cesareo Consolo eloquently defined it as he considered it valid and more than sufficient to exonerate the parents from negligence),[99] but they might ask the father to provide more elements. Moreover, there were even more liberal rulings, with an inclination to value the independence and responsibility of

[99]Cesareo Consolo 1908 (as n. 6) 353.

underage adults: such is the case of the decisions of the Swiss Federal Tribunal, translated in Italy in the *Monitore dei Tribunali*—the law journal with the biggest number of Italian Court judgments on parental civil liability.

By analysing these cases we have arrived at a greater awareness of the fact that a number of criteria to establish parental liability originated during the application of the 1865 civil code. It is nevertheless important to point out that amongst these we find not only some strict criteria, such as the one according to which, to be exempted from negligence, it is not sufficient to claim the parent was not present at the time of the offence, or that the parent was not physically able to monitor the child, or the criterion which gives importance to negligence in educating the child. But there are also more liberal, flexible judgments, such as the rule according to which the father's liability should be established concretely and not abstractly, bearing in mind a plurality of circumstances, since the parents' duty to monitor the child cannot be conceived as being totally absorbing but must be commensurate to the age, character, temperament, education, and abilities of the child, and the surrounding environment. The picture which emerges from the long experience of post-Unity Italy is therefore not monolithic, but multifaceted: objective tendencies, which rigidly denote parental liability, co-exist with other lines of action which favour individual elements in the judgment of negligence, and tend not to make the fathers pay for the entirety of their children's torts, especially when the latter are close to the age of majority.

References

Alpa, G., & Bessone, M. (1984). I fatti illeciti. In *Trattato di diritto privato*, diretto da Pietro Rescigno, 14, *Obbligazioni e contratti*. Tomo sesto. Torino: Utet.

Aubry, C., & Rau, C.-F. (1871). *Cours de droit civil français d'après la méthode de Zachariae* (4th edn). Tome quatrième. Paris: Imprimerie et Librairie générale de jurisprudence. Marchal, Billard et Cie, Imprimeurs-Éditeurs. Libraires de la Cour de Cassation et de l'ordre des avocats a la même Cour et au Conseil d'État.

Barassi, L. (1921). *Istituzioni di diritto civile*. Milano: Casa Editrice Dottor Francesco Vallardi.

Barassi, L. (1948). *La teoria generale delle obbligazioni. Le fonti* (2nd edn, Vol. II). Milano: Giuffrè.

Baudry-Lacantinerie, G., & Barde, L. (1908). *Traité thèorique et pratique de droit civil. Des obligations*. Tome quatrièeme. Paris: Librairie de la Sociètè du Recueil J.-B. Sirey et du Journal du Palais. Ancienne Maison L. Larose & Forcel.

Bessone, M. (1982). Fatto illecito del minore e regime della responsabilità per mancata sorveglianza. *Il diritto di famiglia e delle persone*, *11*, 1011–1015.

Blanc, E. (1953). *La responsabilité des parents*. Préface de M. André Besson. Paris: Librairie du Journal des notaires et des avocats.

Borsari, L. (1877). *Commentario del codice civile italiano* 3.2. Torino: Unione Tipografico-Editrice Torinese.

Brasiello, T. (1949). Dei fatti illeciti. In D'Amelio, Mariano, La Lumia, Isidoro, De Bernardinis, Angelo, Anichini, Ugolino, and Brasiello, Teucro (Eds.), *Codice civile. Libro delle Obbligazioni*. Volume III. *Delle promesse unilaterali. Dei titoli di credito. Della gestione di affari. Del pagamento dell'indebito. Dell'arricchimento senza causa. Commentario*, diretto da Mariano D'Amelio ed Enrico Finzi, 249–252. Firenze: G. Barbèra Editore.

Brugi, B. (1914). *Istituzioni di diritto civile italiano con speciale riguardo a tutto il diritto privato* (3rd edn). Milano: Società editrice libraria.

Busnelli, F. D. (1976). Nuove frontiere della responsabilità civile. *Jus, 23*, 41–79.

Capaccioli, E. (1946). Responsabilità del genitore per il fatto illecito del figlio minore. *Rivista del diritto commerciale e del diritto generale delle obbligazioni, 44*(2), 257–279.

Carbone, E. (2008). La responsabilità aquiliana del genitore tra rischio tipico e colpa fittizia. *Rivista di diritto civile, 54*(2), 1–16.

Carbonnier, J. (1993). *Droit civil.* 4. *Les Obligations* (17th edn). Paris: Presses universitaires de France.

Cazzetta, G. (1991). *Responsabilità aquiliana e frammentazione del diritto comune civilistico (1865–1914)*. Milano: Giuffrè.

Cesareo Consolo, G. (1908). *Trattato sul risarcimento del danno in materia di delitti e quasi delitti*. Torino-Milano-Roma-Napoli: Unione Tipografico-Editrice Torinese.

Chironi, G. P. (1889). *Istituzioni di diritto civile italiano* (Vol. II). Torino: Fratelli Bocca Editori.

Chironi, G. P. (1903). *La colpa nel diritto civile odierno* (2nd edn). *Colpa extra-contrattuale* 1. Torino: Fratelli Bocca Editori.

Chironi, G. P. (1906). *La colpa nel diritto civile odierno. Colpa extra-contrattuale* (2nd edn). Torino: Fratelli Bocca Editori.

Chironi, G. P., & Abello, L. (1904). *Trattato di diritto civile italiano* (Vol. I). Parte generale. Torino: Fratelli Bocca Editori.

Cicu, A. (1941). Responsabilità indiretta dei genitori. *Rivista di diritto civile, 33*, 183–184.

Colin, A., & Capitant, H. (1931). *Cours élémentaire de droit civil français* (6th edn). Ouvrage couronné par l'Académie des Sciences Morales et Politiques (Prix Chevallier). Tome deuxième conforme au programme de deuxième année. Paris: Librairie Dalloz.

Comporti, M. (2012). Fatti illeciti: le responsabilità presunte. In *Il Codice Civile*. Commentario fondato e già diretto da Piero Schlesinger, continuato da Francesco Donato Busnelli (2nd edn). *Artt. 2044–2048*. Milano: Giuffrè.

Contursi Lisi, L. (1949). Responsabilità civile dei genitori e violazione dell'obbligo di educare la prole. *Rivista trimestrale di diritto e procedura civile, 3*, 977–981.

De Cupis, A. (1946). *Il danno. Teoria generale della responsabilità civile*. Milano: Giuffrè.

De Ruggiero, R. (1926). *Istituzioni di diritto civile. 2. Diritti di obbligazione. Diritti di famiglia. Diritto ereditario* (4th edn). Messina: Casa editrice Giuseppe Principato.

Delvincourt, C.-É. (1813). *Cours de Code Napoléon. Ouvrage divisé en deux Parties, dont la première contient la Troisième Édition des Institutes de Droit Civil Français, du même Auteur, revue et corrigée par lui; et la seconde, les Notes et Explications sur lesdites Institutes*. Tome second. Paris: chez P. Gueffier, Imprimeur-Libraire.

Demante, A.-M., & Colmet de Santerre, E.-L.-A. (1865). *Cours analytique de Code Napoléon*. 5. *Art. 1101–1386*. Paris: Henri Plon, Imprimeur-Éditeur.

Demogue, R. (1925). *Traité des obligations en général*. 1. *Sources des Obligations (Suite et fin)*. Tome V. Paris: Librairie Arthur Rousseau. Rousseau et Cie.

Demolombe, C. (1882). *Cours de code civil*. Édition augmentée de la législation et de la jurisprudence belges et d'une table chronologique des arrêts des cours françaises et belges. Tome quinzième. *Traité des engagements qui se forment sans convention*. Bruxelles: J. Steinon, Éditeur.

Duranton, A. (1841). *Cours de droit français, suivant le code civil* (4th edn). Tome septième. Bruxelles: Société Belge de Librairie Hauman et Ce.

Fenet, P.-A. (1968). *Recueil complet des travaux préparatoires du code civil*. Tome treizième. Réimpression de l'édition 1827. Osnabrück: Otto Zeller.

Ferrini, C. (1926). Delitti e quasi-delitti. In *Il Digesto italiano. Enciclopedia metodica e alfabetica di legislazione, dottrina e giurisprudenza* […] diretta da Luigi Lucchini. Volume IX, parte prima (pp. 727–820). Torino: Unione tipografico-editrice torinese.

Franzoni, M. (1993). Dei fatti illeciti. Art. 2043–2059, In F. Galgano (Ed.), *Commentario del codice civile Scialoja-Branca, Libro quarto – Delle obbligazioni*. Bologna-Roma: Zanichelli Editore, Soc. ed. del Foro italiano.

Giliker, P. (2010). *Vicarious Liability in Tort: A Comparative Perspective*. New York: Cambridge University Press.

Giorgi, G. (1886). *Teoria delle obbligazioni nel diritto moderno italiano esposta con la scorta della dottrina e della giurisprudenza. 5. Fonti delle obbligazioni. Quasi contratti – Fatti illeciti – Legge* (2nd edn). Firenze: Eugenio e Filippo Cammelli.

Gramigna, A. (1998). *Storia della maleducazione. I bambini cattivi nel secolo XIX*. Bologna: Clueb.

Huc, T. (1895). *Commentaire théorique et pratique du Code civil*. Tome huitième. *Contrats et obligations (suite); Modes d'extinction; Paiement; Subrogation; Compensation, etc.; Modes de preuve; Chose jugés, etc.; Quasi-contrats; Quasi-délits. Art. 1234 à 1386*. Paris: Librairie Cotillon. F. Pichon, Successeur, Éditeur.

Josserand, L. (1939). *Cours de droit civil positif français conforme aux programmes officiels des facultés de droit*. Ouvrage couronné par l'Institut (Prix Chevallier, 1931). 2. *Théorie générale des obligations. Les principaux contrats du droit civil. Les suretés*. Paris: Librairie du Recueil Sirey Société anonyme.

Larombière, L.-V.-L.-J. (1885). *Théorie et pratique des obligations ou commentaire des titres III et IV, livre III du code civil articles 11010 a 1386*. Nouvelle édition tenue au courant de la jurisprudence. 7. *Articles 1349 à 1386*. Paris: A. Durand et Pedone-Lauriel, Editeurs. Libraires de la Cours de la Cour d'appel et de l'Ordre des Avocats. G. Pedone-Lauriel, successeur.

Laurent, F. (1876). *Principes de droit civil français*. Tome vingtième. Paris-Bruxelles: A. Durand & Pedone Lauriel, Bruylant-Christophe & Comp.

Lemonnier-Lesage, V. (2013). La responsabilité des père et mère du fait de l'enfant dans l'ancien droit: Le devoir d'éducation des pères de famille. In E. Putnam, J.-P. Agresti, & C. Siffrein-Blanc (Eds.), *Lien familial, lien obligationnel, lien social*. 1. *Lien familial et lien obligationnel* (pp. 149–165). Marseille: Presse Universitaires d'Aix-Marseille.

Majello, U. (1960). Responsabilità dei genitori per il fatto illecito del figlio minore e valutazione del comportamento del danneggiato ai fini della determinazione del contenuto della prova liberatoria. *Diritto e giurisprudenza*, 44–50.

Mantovani, M. (1987). Responsabilità dei genitori, dei tutori, dei precettori e dei maestri d'arte. In *La responsabilità civile. Una rassegna di dottrina e giurisprudenza*, diretta da Guido Alpa e Mario Bessone. II. Tomo primo (pp. 1–51). Torino: Utet.

Marcadé, V. (1866). *Explication théorique et pratique du Code Napoléon contenant l'analyse critique des auteurs et de la jurisprudence et un traité résumé après le commentaire de chaque titre* (5th edn). Tome cinquième. Paris: Delamotte, administrateur du répertoire de l'enregistrement par M. Garnier.

Mazeaud, H., & Léon, M. (1931). *Traité théorique et pratique de la responsabilité civile délictuelle et contractuelle*. Préface de M. Henri Capitant. Tome premier. Paris: Librairie du Recueil Sirey (Société Anonyme).

Mazeaud, H. L., & Tunc, A. 1965. *Traité théorique et pratique de la responsabilité civile délictuelle et contractuelle* (6th edn). Préface par Henri Capitant. Tome premier. Ouvrage couronné par l'Académie des Sciences Morales et Politiques (Prix Dupin Aîné, 1932). Paris: Éditions Montchrestien.

Messa, G. C. (1913). La responsabilità civile dei genitori nel caso di lontananza dal domicilio. *Monitore dei Tribunali, 54*, 681–682.

Monateri, P. G. (1998). Le fonti delle obbligazioni. 3. La responsabilità civile. In *Trattato di diritto civile* diretto da Rodolfo Sacco. Torino: Utet.

Montesi, B. (2007). *Questo figlio a chi lo do? Minori, famiglie, istituzioni (1865–1914)*. Prefazione di Marcello Flores. Milano: Franco Angeli.

Ollier, P.-D. (1961). *La responsabilité civile des père et mère. Étude critique de son régime légal (art. 1384 al. 4 et 7 c. civ.)*. Préface de Jean Carbonnier. Paris: Librairie Générale de Droit et Jurisprudence. R. Pichon et R. Durand-Auzias.

Pacchioni, G. (1940). *Diritto civile italiano. 2. Diritto delle obbligazioni. 4. Dei delitti e quasi delitti*. Padova: Cedam.

Pacifici-Mazzoni, E. (1886). *Istituzioni di diritto civile italiano. 4. Parte speciale. Delle obbligazioni in generale. Donazioni – Contratto di matrimonio* (3rd edn). Firenze: Eugenio e Filippo Cammelli.

Pardolesi, R. (1997). Danni cagionati dai minori: pagano sempre i genitori? *Famiglia e diritto, 3*, 221–225.

Pasetti, G. (1949). In tema di responsabilità del genitore per mancata educazione del figlio. *Giurisprudenza italiana, 101*(1), 291–298.

Patti, S. (1984). *Famiglia e responsabilità civile*. Milano: Giuffrè.

Planiol, M., Ripert, G., Esmein, P. (1930). *Traité pratique de droit civil français. Obligations*. Première partie. Paris: Librairie générale de droit et de jurisprudence.

Pollock, L. A. (2001). Parent-Child Relations. In D. I. Kertzer, & M. Barbagli (Eds.), *Family Life in Early Modern Times. 1500–1789. The History of the European Family* (Vol. 1, pp. 191–220). New Haven and London: Yale University Press. Italian translation: Pollock, L. A. (2002). Il rapporto genitori-figli. In M. Barbagli & D. I. Kertzer (Eds.) *Storia della famiglia in Europa. Dal Cinquecento alla Rivoluzione francese* (pp. 263–306). Roma-Bari: Laterza.

Pothier, R.-J. (1831). Traité des obligations. In *Oeuvres*, contenant les traités du droit français. Nouvelle édition mise en meilleur ordre et conforme a celle publiée par M. Dupin ainé. Tome premier. A Bruxelles: chez H. Tarlier, Libraire-Editeur, rue de la Montagne, n° 51.

Quincy-Lefebvre, P. (1997). *Familles, institutions et déviances. Une histoire de l'enfance difficile. 1880-fin des années trente*. Paris: Economica.

Raimondo, R. (2015). *Discoli incorreggibili. Indagine storico-educativa sulle origini delle case di correzione in Italia e in Inghilterra*. Milano: Franco Angeli.

Ricci, F. (1886). *Corso teorico-pratico di diritto civile. 6. Delle obbligazioni e dei contratti in genere* (2nd edn). Torino: Unione Tipografico-Editrice.

Rodotà, S. (1964). *Il problema della responsabilità civile*. Milano: Giuffrè.

Rossi Carleo, L. (1979). La responsabilità dei genitori ex art. 2048 c. c. *Rivista di diritto civile, 25* (2), 125–151.

Savatier, R. (1951). *Traité de la responsabilité civile en droit français civil, administratif, professionnel, procédural*. Préface de Georges Ripert. 1. *Les sources de la responsabilité civile* (2nd edn). Ouvrage couronné par l'Institut (Prix Chevailler 1940). Paris: Librairie générale de droit et de jurisprudence. R. Pichon et R. Durand-Auzias.

Simoncelli, V. (1914). *Istituzioni di diritto privato. Lezioni*. Roma: Athenaeum.

Sourdat, A.-J.-B. (1852). *Traité général de la responsabilité ou de l'action en dommages-intérêts en dehors de contrats* [...] Tome second. Paris: Imprimerie et Librairie générale de jurisprudence De Cosse, succ[r] de Cosse et N. Delamotte.

Toullier, C. B. (1824). *Droit civil français, suivant l'ordre du code, ouvrage dans lequel on a taché de réunir la théorie a la pratique*. Tome onzième. A Paris: chez Warée, oncle, Libraire de la Cour Royale, Cour de la Sainte-Chapelle, n° 13. Parée, fils ainé, Libraire au Palais de Justice.

Trabucchi, A. (1947). Note to Cass. 22 febbraio 1946, n. 187. *Giurisprudenza italiana, 99*(1), 181–184.

Trabucchi, A. (1953). Sulla prova liberatoria della presunzione di colpa esimente dalla responsabilità indiretta del genitore. *Giurisprudenza italiana, 105*(1), 283–286.

Trimarchi, P. (1961). *Rischio e responsabilità oggettiva*. Milano: Giuffrè.

Trimarchi, P. (1975). *Istituzioni di diritto privato* (2nd edn). Milano: Giuffrè.

Venchiarutti, A. (2008). Responsabilità dei genitori, dei tutori, dei precettori e dei maestri d'arte. In Diurni, Amalia, Negro, Antonello, Sella, Mauro, and Venchiarutti, Angelo. Artt. 2043–2053. Fatti illeciti. Generalità, responsabilità per fatto altrui, attività pericolose, danni da cose, da animali, da rovina di edificio. In P. Cendon (Ed.), *Commentario al codice civile* (pp. 693–734). Milano: Giuffrè Editore.

Venditti, A. (1955). Il dovere dei genitori di educare e vigilare la prole in relazione alla prova liberatoria dalla responsabilità per i fatti illeciti commessi dai figli minori. *Giustizia civile, 5*(2), 1620–1626.
Viney, G., & Jourdain, P. (1998). *Les conditions de la responsabilité* (2nd edn). Ouvrage couronné par l'Académie des sciences morales et politiques (Prix Demolombe, 1989). *Traité de droit civil*. Sous la direction de Jacques Ghestin. Paris: Librairie Générale de Droit et de Jurisprudence, E.J.A.
Viney, G. (2004). Les difficultés de la recodification du droit de la responsabilité civile. In *Le Code civil. 1804–2004. Livre du Bicentenaire* (pp. 255–281). Paris: Dalloz-LexisNexis Litec.
Visintini, G. (1967). *La responsabilità civile nella giurisprudenza*. Padova: Cedam.
Visintini, G. (1987). *I fatti illeciti. 1. L'ingiustizia del danno*. Padova: Cedam.
Visintini, G. (1996). *Trattato breve della responsabilità civile. Fatti illeciti. Inadempimento. Danno risarcibile*. Padova: Cedam.
Zachariae, K.-S. (1858). *Le droit civil français*. Traduit de l'allemand sur la cinquième édition. Annoté et rétabli suivant l'ordre du Code Napoléon par MM. G. Massé – Ch. Vergé. Tome quatrième. Paris: Auguste Durand, Libraire-Éditeur.

Table of Cases

Decisions of the French Courts of Appeal and Court of Cassation

Bourges, 9 Mar 1821. Guillier v. Saignol. S. 22 1822.2: 238–239.
Ch. crim. Cass. 29 Mar 1827. Pestel v. Gogin. S. 28 1828.1: 373.
Bordeaux, 1 Apr 1829. Boisrousseau v. Audouin. S. 29 1829.2: 259.
Toulouse, 7 Dec 1832. Décamps v. Rivière. S. 1833.2: 620.
Caen, 2 June 1840. Barbel v. Dupin. S. 40 1840.2: 538.
Aix, 11 June 1859. M. v. Jourdan. S. 1860.2: 193–195.
Agen, 21 Feb 1866. Sarrade v. Lasserre. S. 1866.2: 272–78.
Douai, 7 Nov 1893. Leclercq v. Min. publ. et Dutronquoy. D. 1894.2: 159.
Req., 30 June 1896. Courtine v. Vergnes. D. 1897.1: 198.
Montpellier, 31 Oct 1908. Bartès v. Constans and the State. *Monitore* 51 1910: 296.
Rouen, 30 Dec 1913. Vve Daunout v. Larchevèque. S. 1914.2: 223–224.
Paris, 9 July 1914. Dame Potier Rousseaux v. Sauton. S. 1915.2.56. *Monitore* 57 1916: 59.

Decisions of the Italian Courts of Appeal, Court of Cassation and Lower Courts

App. Bologna, 18 Nov 1872. Parmigiani v. Bianchi. *Annali della giurisprudenza italiana* 7 (1873): 125–126.
App. Torino, 8 Feb 1878. R. v. F. *La Legge* 18.1 (1878): 698–699.
App. Genova, 12 Apr 1881. Gaggero v. Deluchi. *Giurisprudenza italiana* 33.2 (1881): 326–328.
App. Casale, 7 May 1881. Conti v. Perfino. *La Legge* 22.1 (1881): 271.
App. Torino, 27 Feb 1892. Garbato v. Penna. *Monitore* 33 (1892): 340.
App. Torino, 31 May 1895. Capello v. Enrico. *La Legge* 35.2 (1895):166–168.
App. Milano, 9 Sep 1896. Piccioni Luigia ved. Clerici v. Brambilla cav. Camillo ed Ettore. *Monitore* 37 (1896): 879–882.
App. Milano, 16 June 1897. Oliati Francesco v. Castelli Giovanni. *Monitore* 38 (1897): 709–712.
App. Milano, 2 Mar 1898. Annoni Carlo v. Fumagalli Giuseppe. *Monitore* 39 (1898): 768.
Trib. Caltanissetta, 20 Dec 1898. Corrado v. Sciandra. *Monitore* 40 (1899): 799.
App. Bologna, 11 May 1900. Pellicciardi v. Caroli. *Monitore* 42 (1901): 574–575.
Trani, 22 Jan 1901. Lefèvre v. Lefèvre. *Monitore* 42 (1901): 656–657.

Trani, 4 Feb 1901. Vaccina v. Pellegrino. *Monitore* 42 (1901):451.
App. Milano, 11 Feb 1902. Calcaterra v. Panceri. *Monitore* 43 (1902): 456–457.
App. Catania, 10 Dec 1902. Cristaldi v. Catalano. *Monitore* 44 (1903): 236–237.
App. Casale, 24 Oct 1902. Giacobbe v. Manara. *Monitore* 44 (1903): 331–332.
App. Torino, 8 May 1903. Ferraglia v. Micheletto. *Monitore* 44 (1903): 613–614.
App. Milano, 9 Dec 1903. Ditta Balconi v. Mariani and Valli. *Monitore* 45 (1904): 411–412.
App. Torino, 27 Oct 1904. Bendino v. Roggero. *Monitore* 46 (1905): 194–196.
App. Casale, 31 Oct 1904. Ferrara v. Armano. *Monitore* 46 (1905): 237.
App. Genova, 3 Mar 1905. Verda v. Sasso. *Monitore* 46 (1905): 495–496.
Pretura Saronno, 26 May 1905. Fumetti v. Arnaboldi. *Monitore* 48 (1907): 383–384.
App. Napoli, 31 Dec 1906. Sibilia v. Conte. *Monitore* 48 (1907): 648–649.
App. Casale, 18 Nov 1908. Sambuelli v. Cellerino. *Monitore* 50 (1909): 252–253.
Cass. pen., 6 Apr 1909. Ric. Carrozza. *Monitore* 50 (1909): 556–557.
App. Cagliari, 19 Apr 1909. Lazio v. Pinna. *Monitore* 50 (1909): 951–952.
App. Catanzaro, 9 July 1910. Novello. *Monitore* 52 (1911): 295.
App. Genova, 17 Jan 1913. Fossa v. Benvenuto. *Monitore* 54 (1913): 353–354.
App. Palermo, 14 Feb 1913. Puccio v. Mannino. *Monitore* 54 (1913): 474–475.
App. Milano, 18 Feb 1913. Massa v. Pizzocaro. *Monitore* 54 (1913): 354–356.
App. Milano, 18 Apr 1913. Ditta M. Baer & C. v. Maderna Leopoldo and Pilade. *Monitore* 54 (1913): 616.
App. Firenze, 22 Apr 1913. Rimbotti v. Mori. *Monitore* 54 (1913): 774–776.
Cass. Torino, 31 Oct 1913. Benvenuto v. Fossa. *Monitore* 55 (1914): 24.
App. Trani, 7 Feb 1914. Frascella v. Marzia. *Monitore* 55 (1914): 813–814.
Cass. pen. 5 Jan 1915: Ric. Vignola. *Monitore* 56 (1915): 455.
App. Parma, 15 Jan 1915. Magnani v. Gonzaga. *Monitore* 56 (1915): 352–354.
App. Milano, 3 Nov 1916. Quadri v. Zacchetti Bossolo. *Monitore* 57 (1916): 950–952.
App. Genova, 31 Oct 1917. Piombo v. Brignole. *Monitore* 59 (1918): 181.
Cass. Firenze, 18 Feb 1918. Sandri v. Sandri. *Monitore* 60 (1919): 49–50.
App. Palermo, 10 Feb 1922. Moscato v. Martorana. *Monitore* 63 (1922): 500–502.
Cass., 12 May 1924. Gregoraci v. Marano. *Monitore* 65 (1924): 848–849.
Cass., 14 Nov 1924. Cecere v. Donzelli. *Monitore* 66 (1925): 251.
App. Bari, 16 Jan 1925. Piazzola v. Cardinale. *Monitore* 66 (1925): 786–787.
App. Milano, 27 May 1925. Cavalli v. Ronconi and Mambretti. *Monitore* 66 (1925): 629–631.
Cass., 30 Nov 1926. Pennacchi and others v. Gregori. *Monitore* 68 (1927): 48.
App. Cagliari, 30 Dec 1926. Perra v. Paulis. *Monitore* 68 (1927): 951–952.
App. Venezia, 25 June 1927. De Nardi v. Passoni. *Monitore* 69 (1928): 264.
App. Napoli, 28 Nov 1927. Grillo v. Arata. *Monitore* 69 (1928): 336–337.
App. Napoli, 15 July 1929. Turino v. Persico. *Monitore* 71 (1930): 18–19.
App. Torino, 17 Jan 1930. Robasto v. Chialva. *Monitore* 71 (1930): 553.
App. Milano 19 June 1930. Gilardi v. Società noleggio automobili. *Monitore* 72 (1931): 102.
Cass., 17 Jan 1931. Lendaro v. Lendaro. *Il foro italiano* 56.1 (1931): 440–442.
Cass., 6 July 1931. Spadaro v. Ruggeri. *Monitore* 73 (1932): 90–91.
App. Milano, 8 Nov 1932. Gnemmi v. De Mattia. *Monitore* 74 (1933): 347–348.
App. Milano, 25 Nov 1932. Raffa v. Bernasconi. *Monitore* 74 (1933): 550–551.
App. Milano, 11 July 1933. Cetti v. Braga. *Monitore* 74 (1933): 788–789.
Cass., 5 Aug 1940. Raimondo v. Campanella. *Il foro italiano* 66.1 (1941): 318–320.

Decisions of Swiss Courts and Federal Tribunal

Cour de justice civile de Genève, 22 Oct. 1898. Borcard v. Schälpfer and Orcellet. S. 1899.4: 28–29. *Monitore* 40 (1899): 433.
Trib. fédéral suisse, 7 June 1917. Zufferey v. Raspizio. *Monitore* 59 (1918): 61–62.

Trib. fédéral suisse, 22 Nov 1923. Gabathuler v. Peter. *Monitore* 65 (1924): 595–597.
Trib. fédéral suisse, 13 Oct 1926. Mme Girardin v. Auguste and César Rubin. S. 1927.4: 14.

Abbreviations

D.: *Jurisprudence générale. Recueil périodique et critique de jurisprudence, de législation et de doctrine en matière civile, commerciale, criminelle, administrative et de droit public.* Recueil fondé par M. Dalloz ainé, et par M. Armand Dalloz, son frère, continué sous la direction de MM. Edouard Dalloz fils, Charles Vergé, Gaston Griolet, Ch. Vergé fils. A Paris: Au Bureau de la Jurisprudence générale.

Monitore: *Monitore dei tribunali. Giornale di legislazione e giurisprudenza civile e penale.* Milano: Società editrice libraria.

S.: *Recueil général des lois et des arrêts, en matière civile, criminelle, commerciale et de droit public.* Fondé par. J.-B. Sirey, redigé, depuis 1831, par L.-M. Devilleneueve (jusqu'en1859), A.-A. Carette et P. Gilbert, avec le concours de MM. Nachet, Paul Pont, G. Massè. Paris: Bureaux de l'administration du recueil.

Springer List of Contributors

Giovanni Chiodi is Full Professor of Medieval and Modern Legal History, University of Milano-Bicocca, Piazza dell'Ateneo Nuovo 1, 20126 Milano, Italy (giovanni.chiodi@unimib.it).

Tomàs de Montagut is Full Professor of Legal History, University Pompeu Fabra of Barcelona, Plaça de la Mercè 10–12, 08002 Barcelona, Spain (tomas.montagut@upf.edu).

Gigliola di Renzo Villata is Full Professor of Medieval and Modern Legal History, University of Milan, Via Festa del Perdono 7, 20122 Milano, Italy (gigliola.direnzovillata@unimi.it).

Loredana Garlati is Full Professor of Medieval and Modern Legal History, University of Milano-Bicocca, Piazza dell'Ateneo Nuovo 1, 20126 Milano, Italy (loredana.garlati@unimib.it).

Richard Helmholz is Ruth Wyatt Rosenson Distinguished Service Professor of Law, University of Chicago, 1111 E. 60th St., Chicago IL 60637, USA (dick_helmholz@law.uchicago.edu).

Julius Kirshner is Professor Emeritus of Medieval and Renaissance History, University of Chicago, 227–237 East Delaware Place, Chicago IL 60611, USA (jkir@uchicago.edu).

Thomas Kuehn is Professor of History, Clemson University, Clemson SC 29634, USA (tjkuehn@clemson.edu).

Andrea Massironi is Researcher of Medieval and Modern Legal History, University of Milano-Bicocca, Piazza dell'Ateneo Nuovo 1, 20126 Milano, Italy (andrea.massironi1@unimib.it).

Yves Mausen is Full Professor of Legal History and Religious Law, University of Fribourg, Av. de l'Europe 20, 1700 Fribourg, Switzerland (yves.mausen@unifr.ch).

Tünde Mikes is Associate Professor of Legal History, University of Girona, Campus Montilivi, 17003 Girona, Spain (tunde.mikes@udg.edu).

Annamaria Monti is Associate Professor of Medieval and Modern Legal History, Bocconi University, Via Röntgen 1, 20136 Milano, Italy (annamaria.monti@unibocconi.it).

Filippo Rossi is Researcher with Grant, University of Milan, Via Festa del Perdono 7, 20122 Milano, Italy (filippo.rossi@unimi.it).

M.G. di Renzo Villata (ed.), *Family Law and Society in Europe from the Middle Ages to the Contemporary Era*, Studies in the History of Law and Justice 5,
DOI 10.1007/978-3-319-42289-3

Stefania Salvi is Tenured Researcher, University of Milan, Via Festa del Perdono 7, 20122 Milano, Italy (stefania.salvi@unimi.it).

Mathias Schmoeckel is Full Professor of Legal History and Civil Law, Universität Bonn, Institut für Deutsche und Rheinische Rechtsgeschichte, Adenauerallee 24–42, 53113 Bonn (rgesch@uni-bonn.de).

Chiara Valsecchi is Full Professor of Medieval and Modern Legal History, University of Padua, Via 8 Febbraio 2, 35122 Padova, Italy (valsecchi@giuri.unipd.it).

MIX
Papier aus verantwortungsvollen Quellen
Paper from responsible sources
FSC® C105338

If you have any concerns about our products,
you can contact us on
ProductSafety@springernature.com

In case Publisher is established outside the EU,
the EU authorized representative is:
Springer Nature Customer Service Center GmbH
Europaplatz 3, 69115 Heidelberg, Germany

Printed by Libri Plureos GmbH
in Hamburg, Germany